Computers!

Computers!

SECOND EDITION

TIMOTHY N. TRAINOR
DIANE KRASNEWICH

Mitchell Publishing, Inc.
Innovators in Computer Education
A Random House Company

We dedicate this book to our siblings
Donna, Michele, Nancy, Sally, Terri, Todd, and Tom
"If a child lives with approval, he learns to like himself."

Dorothy Law Nolte

Art Coordinator: Richard S. Mason
Composition: Cecelia Morales (Arizona Publication Service)
Copyeditor: Carol Dondrea
Cover Photo: Gary Gay
Illustrator: Mary Burkhardt
Interior and Cover Designer: Juan Vargas (Vargas/Williams Design)
Photo Researcher: Monica Suder
Printer: R. R. Donnelley and Sons
Product Development: Raleigh Wilson
Production Manager: Richard S. Mason (Bookman Productions)
Sponsoring Editor: Erika Berg

All inquiries should be addressed to Mitchell Publishing, Inc., 915 River Street, Santa Cruz, CA 95060, (408) 425-3851 or (800) 435-2665. Published in the United States by Mitchell Publishing, Inc., a subsidiary of Random House, Inc., New York and simultaneously in Canada by Random House of Canada Limited, Toronto. Distributed by Random House, Inc.

Printed in the United States of America
10 9 8 7 6 5 4 3 2 1

Library of Congress No. 88-061892

ISBN: 0-394-39420-8

BRIEF TABLE OF CONTENTS

DETAILED TABLE OF CONTENTS

UNIT I

OVERVIEW

CHAPTER 1

COMPUTERS: HELPING PEOPLE TO SOLVE PROBLEMS 2

CHAPTER 2

HISTORY OF COMPUTING: SOLVING INFORMATION PROBLEMS 22

CHAPTER 3

WHAT IS A COMPUTER SYSTEM? 54

UNIT II

COMPUTER TECHNOLOGY

CHAPTER 4

PROCESSING HARDWARE: MICROCOMPUTERS TO MAINFRAMES 76

CHAPTER 5

STORAGE DEVICES AND FILE ORGANIZATION 102

CHAPTER 6

INPUT/OUTPUT OPERATIONS 128

CHAPTER 7

DATA COMMUNICATIONS: DISTRIBUTING PROCESSING POWER 152

UNIT III

SOFTWARE: CONCEPTS AND APPLICATIONS

CHAPTER 8

CHAPTER 9

CHAPTER 10

ELECTRONIC SPREADSHEETS: WORKING WITH NUMBERS 226

CHAPTER 11

GRAPHICS: WORKING WITH COMPUTER IMAGES 250

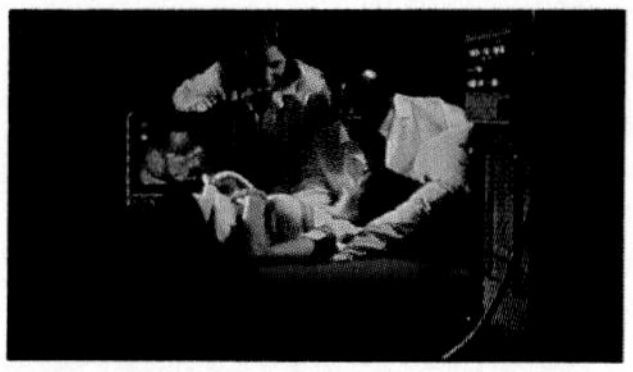

CHAPTER 12

DATABASES AND INTEGRATED SOFTWARE: PULLING IT ALL TOGETHER 272

UNIT IV

INFORMATION SYSTEMS

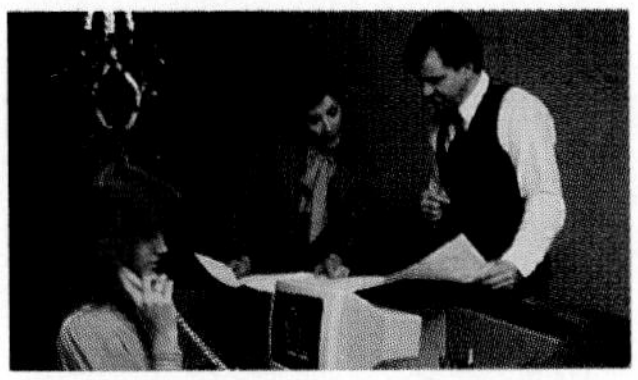

CHAPTER 13

MANAGEMENT AND DECISION MAKING SYSTEMS 300

CHAPTER 14

PRIVACY, COMPUTER CRIME, AND SECURITY 322

CHAPTER 15

SYSTEMS DEVELOPMENT 344

CHAPTER 16

SOFTWARE DEVELOPMENT 376

UNIT V

LOOKING AHEAD

CHAPTER 17

TRENDS *410*

CHAPTER 18

KEEPING UP WITH CHANGE *440*

APPENDIX A

APPENDIX B

PREFACE

In writing *Computers!*, we have tried to focus on the needs of students in computer courses. Our objective is to create a flexible set of course materials that can help you teach your students who:

- have never used a computer and want to learn how;
- have used turnkey systems and now want to understand how computers work;
- would like to find out more about computers and about how computers can help them become more effective in their careers; or
- must take a computer class as part of a graduation requirement.

The result is a full-color textbook written in an easy-to-read style, supported by a variety of instructional photographs and drawings. A comprehensive instructor's manual and student study guide clearly identify chapter objectives and important concepts. Furthermore, if you have access to a computer lab, *Computers!* can be packaged with software and tutorials for popular word processing, electronic spreadsheet, and database packages. Thirteen thirty-minute video tapes are also available to coordinate with the text.

Changes From the First Edition

We are excited about this second edition of *Computers!* because it reflects the invaluable comments and suggestions we have received from first edition users. As you read through the second edition, you will find these new features:

From the User's Point of View. Each chapter now opens with a special section written in response to the perennial student question "Why do I have to learn this?" These sections explain why we think the material in the chapter will be important and useful to the reader.

Increased Microcomputer Emphasis. The microcomputer orientation parallels hands-on activities that students increasingly experience in the introductory course. For example, DOS and booting procedures are introduced early in the second edition, and a microcomputer perspective has been added to the discussion of systems development.

Expanded Coverage of Artificial Intelligence and Expert Systems. The applications of artificial intelligence, especially expert systems, have expanded into many fields. Since these systems will be an integral part of tomorrow's workplace, we have increased their coverage in the second edition.

Do-It-Yourself Approach to Insights. New two-page Insights, found in selected chapters, have taken on a "you can do it" emphasis. Subjects range from building your own microcomputer to dialing an information utility or using a desktop publishing system.

Key Features

Computers! integrates fundamental concepts with proven aids to learning. This increases the ways you can organize your class and deliver quality instruction. The text provides a range of features including the following.

Pedagogy

This textbook is carefully designed to provide complete definitions of key terms. However, learning about computers is not just a question of memorizing terms and concepts. Students must be able to use this knowledge in order to work with changing technology. The following pedagogical materials have been placed throughout the text to support these goals:

- From the User's Point of View
- Key Ideas
- Integrated Study Questions
- Boxed "Clips" With Questions
- Graphic Two-Page "Insights"
- Chapter Conclusions
- Chapter Facts
- Key Terms
- Review Questions
- Exercises and Projects
- Glossary and Index

Additional assignments and accompanying worksheets are provided in the student study guide. As a result, students have a foundation on which to build future learning.

Emphasis on Personal Productivity

Designing a book that will give you an opportunity to integrate hands-on applications with fundamental concepts is a difficult task. It is impossible to anticipate all the situations under which this text could be used—the hardware available, the computer lab arrangement (if any), the background and experience of the instructor, and so on.

Our goal is versatility. For example, Unit III presents a general overview of personal productivity software features and their practical applications:

Chapter 9	Word Processing: Working With Words
Chapter 10	Electronic Spreadsheets: Working With Numbers
Chapter 11	Graphics: Working With Computer Images
Chapter 12	Databases and Integrated Software: Pulling It All Together

Those classes with access to hardware can enhance this overview by taking advantage of the applications software and manuals that are available with this book. Packaging software with the text eliminates the need for you to obtain on-site licenses or to maintain legal copies of software for each student.

An introduction to booting microcomputers using MS/PC-DOS appears in Appendix A. It includes an overview of the DOS format, directory, and copy commands. Additional opportunities for hands-on applications are presented through the BASIC programming tutorial found in Appendix B. If little or no hardware exists for student use, instructors can show hands-on computer applications through the Insight sections in the text and the supplementary videotapes.

Real-World Examples and Application Scenarios

Teaching students about computer technology is exciting because of the very nature of this high-tech, ever-changing subject. Students reading about computers in *Computers!* will find many examples that relate to their own real-life experiences. By describing situations familiar to the reader, we are able to explore the behind-the-scene role computers play as a part of everyday life. Clips and Insights popular in the first edition are once again employed to emphasize this point.

Several Clips from newspapers and popular magazines are found in each chapter. Each Clip links subjects in the text to "real world" activities reported by the media. In addition, the following two-page Insights provide graphic introductions to hot topics in the computer industry:

Chapter 1	End-User Computing: The Power Is in Your Hands
Chapter 2	The Microprocessor: From Chips of Quartz to Silicon Chips
Chapter 4	Building Your Own Microcomputer
Chapter 5	Lasers: Lighting the Way
Chapter 7	A World of Information—Just One Call Away
Chapter 9	Desktop Publishing: Integrating Graphics With Words
Chapter 10	Graphics: A Picture Is Worth a Thousand Words
Chapter 11	Is it Art . . . or Output?
Chapter 12	RX: Medical Expertise With a Touch of Computer Technology
Chapter 13	Developing an Expert System
Chapter 14	Privacy: Is it Still Possible?
Chapter 15	How to Select a Microcomputer System
Chapter 16	Programming Languages: No Matter How You Say It
Chapter 18	Emerging Career Opportunities

The result, *Computers!*, is a comprehensive, flexible, multimedia package designed to help you introduce computer concepts and promote computer awareness to students with various backgrounds and needs.

Supplementary Materials

Various classroom settings and instructional philosophies are supported by the following supplementary materials:

Application Software and Manuals. A variety of step-by-step, hands-on tutorials, available with and without software, supplement *Computers!*, including:

- *Using Application Software: WordPerfect, dBASE III PLUS, and VP-Planner*, by Pitter (with software)
- *Application Software for the IBM PC: PC-Type+, PC-Calc+, and PC-File III+*, by Shuman (with software)
- *Spreadsheet Software Using VP-Planner*, by Pitter (with or without software)
- *Spreadsheet Software Using Quattro*, by Shuman (with software)
- *Word Processing: Using WordPerfect 5.0*, by Larsen and Leeburg
- *Word Processing Software Using WordStar*, by Topham (with or without software)
- *Relational Database! Using dBASE III PLUS*, by Price (with or without software)
- *Integrated Software! Using Enable*, by Barnes and Feiler
- *Using AppleWorks*, by Pitter

Comprehensive Instructor's Manual. The instructor's manual includes definitions, detailed lecture outlines, answers to all study questions in the text, worksheet and project answers, additional class exercises, teaching tips, and references.

Lecture Notes/Study Objectives on Diskette. Detailed lecture notes are available on diskette to allow easy modification. In addition, study questions (without answers) for each chapter are arranged on disk. Instructors can provide these files to students who wish to complete the study questions using word processing software.

Student Study Guide. The student study guide includes terms, space for answering in-text study questions, projects with related worksheets, mix-and-match exercises, and references.

Computerized Testbank. Over 2000 testbank test questions are coded to correspond to the text's study questions. A new test generator allows the instructor to add, delete, and modify questions in the testbank. Also, tests with answer keys can easily be generated.

Transparency Masters. The text is supported by two sets of transparencies. Some are based on figures in *Computers!*. Others focus on state-of-the-art topics and expand on the text.

Broadcast Quality Videotapes. "Computers at Work," the popular documentary-style videocourse broadcast extensively by PBS and numerous state-wide consortia, has been enhanced to complement this new edition of *Computers!*. The revised series can be supplemented by the Student Videocourse manuals, which key reading assignments in *Computers!* to each of the following thirteen video lessons:

1. The Information Age
2. A Computer System
3. Computer Hardware
4. Computer Software
5. Business Systems Development
6. Computer Communications
7. Database Systems
8. Microcomputers
9. Computers in Society
10. Artificial Intelligence and the Future

APPENDICES:

A. The Automated Office
B. Computer Crime and Security
C. Computer Careers and Your Future

Special Acknowledgements

The development of an instructional package such as *Computers!* takes the dedicated effort of many people. We have identified the people to whom we owe a great deal of thanks in the following acknowledgments. However, there are always a few whose effort and professionalism go beyond the call of duty.

First and foremost, Erika Berg of Mitchell Publishing supplied us with inspiration and energy when we needed them the most. Her tireless work in bringing all the pieces of this project together is greatly appreciated.

The development of this book was a team effort that could not have been done without the help of the production experts: Raleigh Wilson, Richard Mason, Juan Vargas and Edie Williams, Cecelia Morales, Carol Dondrea, Mary Burkhardt, and Monica Suder.

C. Brian Honess, University of South Carolina, gave us hard-hitting reviews of the book's content and wrote the original BASIC tutorial found in Appendix B. Steve Watson, Washington State University, also provided us with insightful feedback and innovative ideas for the supplementary materials. Both Brian and Steve deserve a very special thank you.

In addition, we owe a great deal to the following people, who helped bring the many facets of *Computers!* together: Julius Archibald, Plattsburgh State University; Jack Breglio, Rancho Santiago College; Harry Brown, Muskegon Community College; William Cornette, Southwest Missouri State University; Pat Fenton, West Valley College; Terry Hamberger, York College of Pennsylvania; Frank Hannum, Eight-Bit Corner; Linda Lantz, Community College of Aurora; Paula McClurg-Ziemelis, Muskegon Community College; Herb Rebhun, University of Houston–Downtown; Fred Scott, Broward Community College; Rosemary Skeele, Seton Hall University; Jesse Sprayberry, Muskegon Area Skills Training Center; Jeff Stipes, Muskegon Community College; Roger Stoel, Muskegon Community College; Kenneth Walker, Weber State University; and Louis Wolff, Moorpark College.

Thanks are still in order for those who helped on the first edition: Geoff Alexander, Cabrillo College; Steve Deam, Milwaukee Area Technical College; Enid Irwin, Santa Monica College; Peter Irwin, Richland College; Thom Luce, Ohio University; Michael Michaelson, Palomar College; and David Wen, Diablo Valley College.

Timothy N. Trainor
Diane Krasnewich
Muskegon, Michigan

UNIT ONE

OVERVIEW

Throughout history people have turned to technology to help them solve problems. Chapter 1 discusses reasons for studying about computers and overviews how these problem-solving machines are used in society. It also examines the four-step cycle that computers and other tools employ when working. In addition, the chapter explores situations where the computer cannot or should not be used. ▸ Chapter 2 examines the development of computer technology from an historical perspective by looking back at the roots from which computerized data processing grew. Changes in technology are seen from early adding machines to an emerging generation of computers that simulate human reactions and intelligence. This growth results from the need to provide timely and accurate information to decision makers. ▸ Computers are just one component of a unified system. Besides the actual machines, a computer system also requires people, procedures, data, and programs. Chapter 3 examines how these components fit together to solve a variety of problems. The five-component model is a common thread tying together the diverse applications for computer systems presented throughout the book.

CHAPTER ONE

COMPUTERS: HELPING PEOPLE TO SOLVE PROBLEMS

KEY IDEAS

- **From the user's point of view**
  Computers are now an integral part of modern society. What can this technology do for people and what are the limitations?
- **Why learn about computers?**
  Computers help people to solve problems and improve their productivity.

  Impact on critical thinking
  Every day, in many ways, computers help you solve problems and make wise decisions.

  Promoting the competitive edge
  Computers are agents for change. People need knowledge to facilitate the process of change and to adapt to changes around them.
- **Turning data into information**
  Computers process data and deliver information required by people.

  The IPOS cycle
  All computer results are delivered using a fixed pattern: input, processing, output, and storage.

  The processing breakthrough
  Computers store sets of instructions (programs) and complete complex tasks without assistance or intervention.
- **People and computers**
  Computers extend the physical and intellectual capabilities of people.

  Expanding your capabilities
  Computers can perform billions of computational or logical operations each second, tirelessly.

  What computers can and cannot do
  Computers can operate in places that are unsafe for people. Computers cannot think; they carry out instructions from people.

  Dealing with change
  For people who qualify themselves through education, computers present exciting opportunities.

FROM THE USER'S POINT OF VIEW

There is hardly a person alive who is not aware that computers are now an integral part of society. You can treat an emerging technology two ways: with fear or by embracing it. In this chapter (and book) we would like to show you the advantages of welcoming computer technology into your life. Some of the scenarios we present will be familiar to you. Review them, keeping in mind there is a computer in the background. Other situations may be new. In either case, we hope to show you the influence of computers in new ways, as a tool for critical thinking and a means of making yourself more competitive in whatever you do.

WHY LEARN ABOUT COMPUTERS?

As John Morse and Sally Anderson stared in disappointment, the building began to vibrate. The shaking was slight at first, then increased. Finally, the building swayed and the main entrance crumpled and collapsed. After a few seconds, the vibrations stopped, leaving a partially standing, unbalanced building. Silence had dominated the room from the first shocks.

"Let's see if we can pinpoint the problem," Sally said. She made a few entries on the keyboard beneath the screen where they had viewed the simulated effects of an earthquake. A computer printer located nearby in the small architectural office clattered for several seconds. John tore off a sheet of paper and shared its contents with Sally.

"There it is," John said. "We have to beef up the strength of that cross beam over the entrance."

Sally was all enthusiasm. "This is great," she said. "With hand calculations, it would have taken us weeks to do this analysis. With the computer, we have our answers in less than half an hour."

"And we have more assurance that our building will be safe," John concluded. "It's hard to remember how we did things before we got the computer."

John stopped to think about how the computer had changed his professional life—and had increased his own, personal productivity.

- Architects have had formulas for measuring structural strength for more than 100 years. Computers have taken accepted techniques and improved them. A computer can complete computations in minutes that used to take days for people.
- People who use computers can concentrate on solving major problems. Previously, people were mainly involved in solving mathematical equations, or "crunching numbers." Computers allow people to become more creative and productive by doing the calculations for them.
- Computers perform multiple jobs. In John's office, secretaries and architect's assistants use computers with word-processing programs for correspondence, for structural specifications, for proposals to clients, and for other jobs.

FIGURE 1.1

Computer-aided design capabilities help to solve problems and increase productivity for architects and engineers.

Photo by L.A. Schwaber-Barzilay

Impact on Critical Thinking

Since the 1950s, people have turned to the computer for help in solving problems. A ***computer*** is a machine that processes facts and figures to produce useful information. Through the years, computers have become smaller and less expensive. As more computers are sold, people become more skilled in their use. As a result, computers influence the way people think about and approach a problem. The average person depends on, is served by, or actually operates some type of computer several times each day.

It follows, then, that computers will be a part of everyone's future. Your future success will require a basic level of computer-related knowledge and skill. This book is designed to help you gain these experiences. As you read and complete assignments in this text, you will learn to involve computers in your critical thinking. You should understand how computers affect your life and how they are used to solve everyday problems. You should be able to talk intelligently about computers. Equally important, you should be prepared for the changes computers will bring into your life.

FIGURE 1.2

Computers assist people in all professions and occupations, including health care, as in this computerized medical laboratory.

Computers are installed in cars, toys, and appliances. They are used by musicians, waitresses, bank tellers, and teachers. Computers forecast the weather, track the migration of reindeer across the arctic tundra, and identify stolen cars. People research, write, and edit books with the aid of computers. Then, with assistance from computers, they print out the words many miles away in the blink of an eye. Doctors, lawyers, pilots, auto mechanics, and sales clerks all depend on computers. Computers help people to organize and save their thoughts. Thought itself can be stimulated by computers that serve as storehouses of facts and figures. These facts and figures about people, things, ideas, and events are called ***data***.

Promoting the Competitive Edge

With each passing year, computers become more powerful and less expensive. As more people use computers, new technological advances are introduced. Many of these improvements are intended to make computers easy to use, or more ***user friendly***. Thus, computers will allow you to become more competitive in the workplace and more efficient at home.

FIGURE 1.3

Buying and selling of stocks and other investment securities are supported by computer networks that include links in offices of individual brokers.

Courtesy of IBM Corporation

FIGURE 1.4

The clothes you wear are designed with the aid of computers. Specialists in this photo are designing patterns for textile manufacture.

Courtesy of IBM Corporation

- At home, computers are responsible for many comforts and conveniences. Microwave ovens, using computers and meat probes, turn themselves off when the proper internal temperature is reached. Computerized clothes dryers continually monitor the moisture level of clothes and shut off when a preset level of dryness has been reached. These situations are examples of ***process control***, where computers constantly monitor and adjust an activity without direct human intervention. ***Process control*** is just one of several labor-saving tasks computers perform.
- Many forms of recreation also depend on computers. Some people spend their leisure time at video arcades filled with computer-driven games. Computer ***simulations*** generate images that imitate real life or imaginary situations such as high-speed race tracks, jungle obstacle courses, or intergalactic battlefields. Other people make use of computerized ticket agencies to reserve seats at a sports stadium, rock concert, or theater. At sporting events, people keep track of what is happening with the help of computerized scoreboards.
- With the aid of computers, scientists perform ***data storage and retrieval***. They store data from current research and search data libraries to find relevant reference materials. The data often are organized and cross-referenced in large collections called ***databases***. With computers, this kind of data retrieval takes a fraction of the time required to find the same information by hand. Computers also can simulate scientific experiments, monitor instruments used in lab tests, and analyze collected data.
- In health care, computers assist physicians in diagnosing illnesses by relating symptoms to information in a medical database. Computers monitor vital signs, such as heart rate, of critically ill patients. Other computers record a patient's medical history for attending health professionals. Computer technology has generated many new medical techniques.
- The competitive business world requires successful people to use a computer's speed and accuracy for ***data processing***. By utilizing computers to convert

facts and figures into useful information, businesspeople can keep track of their inventory, have immediate access to sales information, and can quickly identify potential customers.

- Computers can meet the individual needs of a classroom full of students. Computers can be tutors by presenting materials to students and quizzing them later. These machines also are a tool for students; they help retrieve information for papers, type and edit the papers, produce graphs and drawings, compute answers to problems, and simulate dangerous lab experiments or historical battles. Behind the scenes, teachers are using computers to grade tests and keep student records.

Computers, then, touch every aspect of your life. Understanding computers and learning how to use them is a necessary skill now and will be in the future.

STUDY QUESTIONS

1. Define computer, data, user friendly, and database.
2. Briefly describe the following tasks computers perform every day: process control, simulations, data storage and retrieval, and data processing.

TURNING DATA INTO INFORMATION

Computers help people save time and solve problems. As a problem-solving tool, the computer has much in common with other tools you use regularly. To illustrate, you have just enjoyed a delicious dinner and now have a problem: dirty dishes.

The IPOS Cycle

You have some options in deciding how to solve this problem. You can use a tool—a dishwasher—or do the dishes by hand. Prospective computer users often face the same kind of decision. They can use a computer to do a job or can do it by hand. Using the dishwasher and other tools involves four basic steps:

1. INPUT. You put something into the device.
2. PROCESSING. The device changes the input in some way.
3. OUTPUT. You take results out.
4. STORAGE. You may save any results that have future value.

Assume you decide to use the dishwasher. You know the result you want. You also know the pattern of events that has to take place. Your solution is easy:

1. INPUT. You put dirty dishes and soap into a dishwasher.
2. PROCESSING. The dishwasher washes and rinses the dishes, changing them from dirty to clean.
3. OUTPUT. You have the result you wanted, clean dishes.
4. STORAGE. You realize your final result by stacking the dishes in the cupboard.

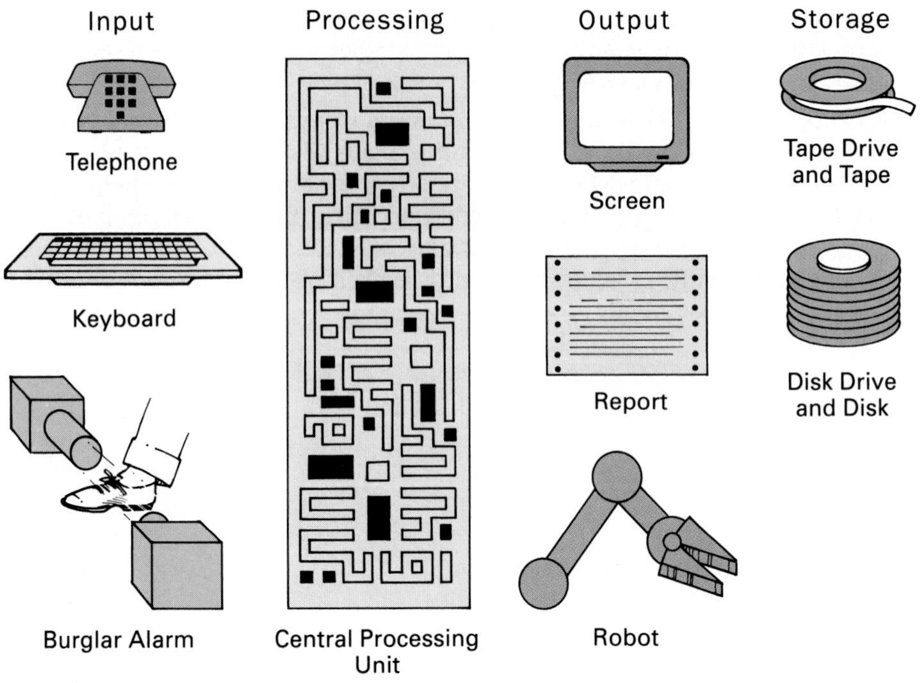

FIGURE 1.5

The IPOS cycle defines the steps common to all information processing systems: input, processing, output, and storage.

This four-step process, diagrammed in Figure 1.5, often is identified by its initials: IPOS. All uses for a computer, ***computer applications***, conform to the first three steps (IPO) of the cycle. The last step, storage, is included in many applications.

An activity as simple as ordering a cheeseburger at a fast-food outlet follows the IPOS cycle. As you place the order, the data are entered into a keyboard. The keyboard is an example of input equipment. In fast-food outlets, keyboards often have pictures of items on the menu. Pictures that represent data are known as ***icons***. When an icon on the keyboard is pressed, the computer retrieves the stored description and pricing information for the corresponding menu item. After all items have been ordered, the processing step begins.

The computer uses information input previously to calculate and print out a receipt. The receipt includes descriptions and prices for all entered items. At the same time, the item descriptions and quantities are output in the kitchen, where cooks prepare the food. The computer also stores information on the order for later use. This completes the IPOS cycle.

By exchanging your money for the food, you have participated in a ***transaction***, or exchange of value. At the end of the day, the computer processes all sales transactions to produce a sales report the manager can use. The report helps the manager to order more supplies and schedule employees to match customer buying patterns.

The IPOS cycle for this system is:

1. INPUT. The counterperson presses keys to identify ordered items and quantities.
2. PROCESSING. The computer multiplies quantities by prices, calculates tax amounts, and determines a total.
3. OUTPUT. Items and totals are printed in the kitchen and at the counter. This information is used by cooks and customers.
4. STORAGE. Data on sales, by product and time of day, are stored for later use.

Keyboards commonly are used to type data directly into the computer. However, dialing a telephone or activating a monitor with light or sound are also ways to input data. Processing may involve sorting names into alphabetical order or applying mathematical functions to sets of numbers. When processing is complete, information is output in the form of a screen display or a printed report. Output also takes several other forms. The action of a mechanical arm as it swings into place to tighten a bolt on a new motorcycle is another example of output. The processed data then are stored on special computer-operated devices if needed. Stored information may be used as input in other applications, putting the IPOS cycle into motion again.

FIGURE 1.6

The food you buy is sold with the aid of computers that sense identification information from package labels.

Courtesy of National Semiconductor

The Processing Breakthrough

A computer is similar to another problem-solving tool with which you are familiar—a calculator. Computers and many calculators are ***programmable***, or capable of following a sequence of stored instructions for processing inputs. However, computer capabilities go far beyond those of calculators. Most calculators can work only with ***numeric data*** such as numbers, decimal points, and signs. A computer, on the other hand, also can work with ***textual data***, or ***text*** (letters, numbers, and punctuation marks), and ***physical data*** (data from the environment, such as sound, light, and temperature).

Both computers and calculators perform ***arithmetic operations***, computations with numbers, such as addition and subtraction. The computer also can compare two values to determine if one is larger, smaller, or equal to the other. This is called a ***logical operation***. The processing step in the IPOS cycle is built around the computer's ability to perform logical and arithmetic operations.

For example, suppose a chemistry student needs to convert a series of temperatures from Fahrenheit to Celsius. With a nonprogrammable calculator, the following formula would have to be entered repeatedly and new values keyed each time:

$$\text{Celsius} = (\text{Fahrenheit} - 32) * (5/9)$$

With this amount of repetition, the risk of error is high. With a computer, the equation, along with input and output steps, can be captured in a ***computer program***. This program provides a series of instructions followed in sequence to control the input, processing, output, and storage performed by the computer. Figure 1.7 shows

```
10      REM: PROGRAM TO CONVERT FAHRENHEIT TEMPERATURES
20      REM: TO CELSIUS
30      REM ***** INPUT ROUTINE *****
40      INPUT "ENTER FAHRENHEIT TEMPERATURE: "; F
50      REM ***** PROCESSING ROUTINE *****
60      C = (F - 32) * (5/9)
70      REM ***** OUTPUT ROUTINE *****
80      PRINT "CELSIUS: "; C
90      INPUT "ANOTHER CONVERSION (Y/N) "; ANSWER$
100     IF ANSWER$ = "Y" THEN GO TO 40
110     END
```

FIGURE 1.7

Computer programs make it possible for people to communicate with computers in terms understandable both to humans and machines.

FIGURE 1.8

A user enters a Fahrenheit temperature into the computer, which uses the program in Figure 1.7 to convert data into their Celsius equivalent.

a program that a chemistry student could use to complete the computation.

When the program is in place, the student enters only the Fahrenheit temperature for each conversion. The resulting information is displayed on a screen (see Figure 1.8). It also could be printed on paper or stored for later use.

The ability to follow a program sets computers apart from most tools. However, a new generation of tools ranging from typewriters to electronic ovens will have ***embedded computers***, or built-in computers. These tools will be flexible because they are programmable and have many uses.

STUDY QUESTIONS

3. Define computer application, icon, transaction, programmable, text, computer program, and embedded computer.
4. What is the four-step cycle used by computers and other tools?
5. What are three types of data computers can use as input?
6. What are two ways in which calculators and computers are similar and two ways in which they are different?
7. Describe two processing operations that computers perform.
8. Why do embedded computers make tools more flexible?

PEOPLE AND COMPUTERS

Computers are limited chiefly by the imaginations of the people who program and operate them. Computer applications already cover a wide range of human needs and wants. These uses range from optimizing cattle feed to navigating aircraft and predicting the weather. Computers, then, are a powerful tool for solving problems and meeting needs in today's world. With support from human intelligence, computers can expand human capabilities.

How Can a Computer Help People?

- Computers permit easy access to large volumes of data
- Computers perform lengthy computations quickly and accurately
- Computers identify relationships among large amounts of data
- Computer-controlled devices go where people cannot
- Computers can simulate human performance

FIGURE 1.9

Computers increase our capacity to control the environment in many ways.

Expanding Your Capabilities

Computers generally are equipped with vast storage capacities that permit easy access to great volumes of knowledge. Suppose a doctor receives a call from an anguished mother about a child who has swallowed a poisonous substance. The physician can be connected immediately to a computer database that provides exact information on antidotes, their dosages, and other treatment information. No matter how experienced a physician might be, it would be impossible for him or her to store and remember such volumes of information.

Fast processing speeds enable computers to perform lengthy computations or establish relationships among large amounts of data within seconds. Such speeds reduce the time people spend in routine tasks. The ability of a computer to process data quickly and accurately is invaluable for monitoring physical activity. Changes in a patient's pulse rate or in the radiation level at a nuclear power plant can be detected and reported immediately by a computer. If the correct instructions have been entered, the computer also can react automatically. For example, the computer can sound an alarm if a patient's health is endangered. If a nuclear reactor shows danger symptoms, the computer can initiate a shutdown sequence.

Computers also go where people cannot. In space, under the sea, and inside volcanoes, nuclear reactors, and oil refineries, computers monitor conditions and warn people when dangerous situations arise. Inside people, computers monitor body functions; inside machines, such as car ignitions or microwave ovens, computers control operations.

Further, some computers can simulate, or imitate, human performance: Voice synthesizers, computer-operated limbs, and Braille printers increase the ability of physically handicapped people to move about or to communicate. Computers increase the capacity of people to control their environment.

What Computers Can and Cannot Do

Since computers are products of high technology, they tend to be regarded as mysterious. People have attributed human, even superhuman, qualities to computers. This simply is not so. Computers are merely tools, designed by people, programmed by people, and used by people. A computer's most basic limitation is that it cannot think. Neither can a computer solve problems or make decisions by itself.

Computers are, however, useful in organizing information to expedite problem solving and decision making by people. By following well-written programs, computers can do amazing things. But people must do the thinking to formulate the detailed instructions.

Computers exist to benefit and assist people, not to replace them. Computers cannot, for example, make emotional judgments, disobey instructions entered by

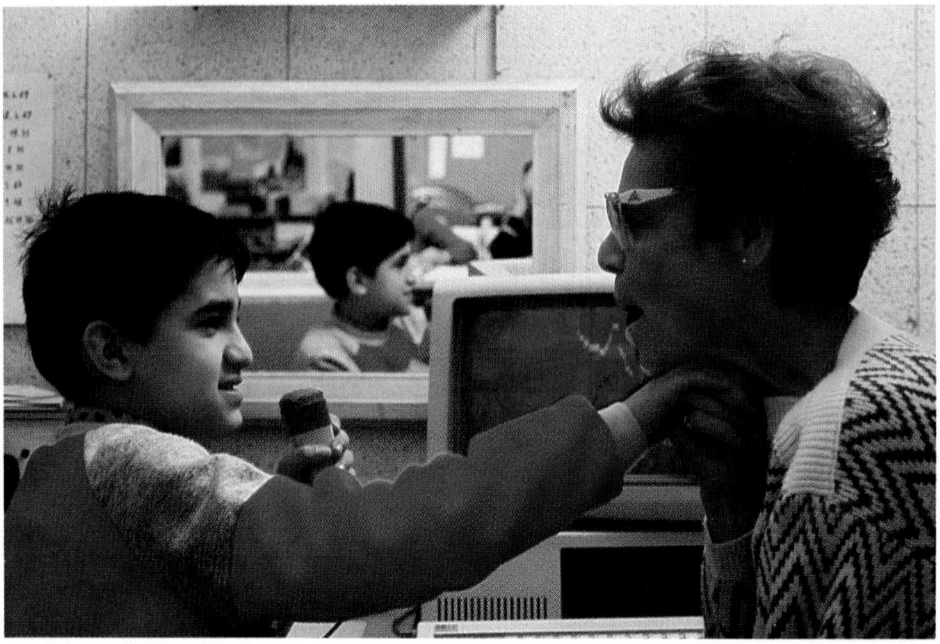

FIGURE 1.10

Computers can help hearing-impaired people to speak. However, computers cannot replace the relationship between a teacher's smile and a child's look of joy.

Courtesy of IBM Corporation

humans, read people's minds or replace interpersonal relationships. On the contrary, people must be extremely explicit in instructing a computer to perform even the simplest commands. What computers can do, however, is:

- Store data in vast amounts
- Process data quickly and accurately
- Simulate possible outcomes based on a given set of conditions
- Recommend or take action based on output

Computers cannot be effective unless the people using them are able to identify what results they need and how to achieve those results. Ultimately, computers are dependent on people.

Accordingly, people should not relinquish their decision-making responsibilities to computers. Humans need to be on hand to interpret conditions reported by computers, particularly if medical treatment, national defense, air traffic control, or even loan processing are involved. Nonprogrammable, human factors must complement computer readouts for a complete and fair analysis.

At times, computers may appear to make decisions. In monitoring a refinery, for example, a computer might trigger a fire extinguishing system. Another computer, used for monitoring vital signs, might regulate the flow of oxygen to a patient. In both cases, however, although the computer initiates action, it does not make a decision. Rather, the decisions of these process control systems were made by the human beings who programmed the machines to respond to a particular set of conditions. Therefore, people must take complete responsibility for a computer's actions. They must anticipate all potential problems and direct computers to avoid them.

While computers may be able to enhance a person's capabilities, they can never adequately replace interpersonal relationships. Even the most sophisticated computing machinery cannot supplant parent-to-child and teacher-to-student relationships. Similarly, the rapport between physician and patient is essential for successful treatment.

EARTHQUAKES ON VIDEODISC

Architects can see how their building designs will hold up against earthquakes with the help of a new interactive video program. "Earthquake-aware" architects can save money and lives, says W. Davis van Bakergem, an assistant professor of architecture at Washington University in St. Louis. Van Bakergem has designed an interactive videodisc program with computer animation to help educate building professionals about the need to consider earthquake resistance from the earliest stages of building design.

Using van Bakergem's interactive videodisc program, architects "design" a building by making a series of decisions that simulate the process. The videodisc then uses computer animation to show how the design will withstand shaking ground and offers possible remedies to problems.

A high first-floor ceiling makes a multistory building more vulnerable to earthquake damage. Another dangerous design is a combination of weak columns and strong beams—often occurring in schools and office buildings with long, uninterrupted bands of glass.

Frame houses, on the other hand, are very stable and illustrate the life-saving potential of proper building design, says Erie Jones, executive director of the Central United States Earthquake Consortium in Marion, Illinois. Frame houses aren't designed with earthquakes in mind, says Jones, but they happen to have many of the elements needed to withstand shaking.

Jones believes conscientious architects are even more important than "seismically considerate" building codes. "By nature, codes reflect the barest minimum," he says. But properly educated architects can integrate safety and building design to increase earthquake-survival odds.

Source: Washington University, Box 1070, St. Louis, Missouri 63130.

Key Question: How can architects become earthquake-aware when creating building designs for active areas?

FIGURE 1.11

Expanded capabilities for learning and research have been opened through the availability of computers to college students.

Courtesy of Apple Computer, Inc.

People, then, are an integral part of any computer system that accepts input, processes it, and delivers output. People control computer systems through program design, by monitoring operations, and through making final decisions based on computer output. They should not give up decision-making responsibilities because interpreting computer-delivered results requires the human qualities of analysis, reasoning, and compassion. Computers, then, cannot operate independently. Humans are the driving force behind computer processing.

Dealing with Change: Your Challenge

Change is a way of life for people in today's society. The average adult, according to some estimates, will change jobs four to seven times. To cope successfully with a changing world, the individual must recognize that change can be constructive. People who resist change because they fear new technology undermine their own potential to become more effective. Still, people fear computers for many reasons:

- Some people don't understand how computers work. The "magic box" that performs seemingly amazing operations is viewed as mysterious and terrifying. However, the qualities of the computer are not mystical. Computers should be regarded as tools to be manipulated by people.
- People think computers will take away their jobs. The computer is more predictable and more efficient than humans. Often it is responsible for employee displacement. Actually, the introduction of computers and automation can increase the number of jobs within a company. But, the new jobs often require computer knowledge. Since this trend is likely to continue, people should learn to make computers work for them. Few benefits can be gained by rejecting computers out of fear or resentment.
- People think computers will replace free will and decision making. Fears that a machine can assume control of human thinking are unfounded. At all times, people instruct computers. When computers provide information and advise decision makers, they do so according to criteria specified by people. How-

ever, computers do identify and assemble decision-related information quickly and efficiently. By using computers, decision makers can be more efficient.

- Humans are reluctant to give up old habits. Some people think change is bad. Often using new computer technology requires learning new procedures. This requirement can disrupt the "comfort level" in a job. Once people are willing to discard outdated procedures, they can promote progress. They increase their productivity, and may be able to make their lives easier, by allowing computers to take up some of their work load.

By overcoming the urge to cling to the status quo, people can accept computers as an integral part of their lives. There are many opportunities gained by such acceptance. Computers provide people with more information in less time. Records can be changed immediately, allowing people to act on the most current information. With fast feedback, problems can be identified and dealt with promptly. The efficiency of any operation can be enhanced with increased access to information—the primary output of computers.

In addition, computers provide access to hundreds of information sources. Tapping these resources can provide new insights, or even prevent the waste of time and effort involved in duplicating work. For example, during the early days of the U.S. space exploration program, $250,000 was spent on a metallurgic study. It was then discovered that the same research already had been conducted by Soviet scientists and reported in a Soviet journal. Had the U.S. scientists been aware of Soviet contributions in the field, they might have built upon the available knowledge. Instead, they duplicated it—an action that resulted in wasted money, effort, and time. In cases such as this, access to several sources of information is extremely valuable.

STUDY QUESTIONS

9. What are five ways in which computers increase the capacity of people to control their environment?
10. What is the chief limitation of computer technology?
11. List four activities that computers cannot perform.
12. List four general activities that computers can do well.
13. Why should people avoid giving up decision-making responsibilities to computers?
14. What are four misunderstandings that people have about computer technology?

CONCLUSION

Computers are powerful machines that can be used to solve complex problems quickly and accurately. They store vast amounts of information that people can access as needed. The more that we know about computers and how they work, the better able we are to apply their capabilities to everyday life. Computers are just one tool in our modern grab bag of problem-solving machines.

Now that computers have become an integral part of society, there can be no turning back. To accept change requires the acceptance of computers. New technologies open industries and new opportunities within existing industries. The challenge lies in discovering and capitalizing on these trends.

I N S I G H T

END USER COMPUTING: THE POWER IS IN YOUR HANDS

Until recently, users had to depend upon computer professionals to help them with all aspects of the Input-Processing-Output-Storage cycle. Now, with the advent of user-friendly computer hardware and software, you can control your own computing.

Input

Although a computer professional will typically input large amounts of data, any user can easily enter data in many forms, as shown in these figures.

Traditional letters and numbers...

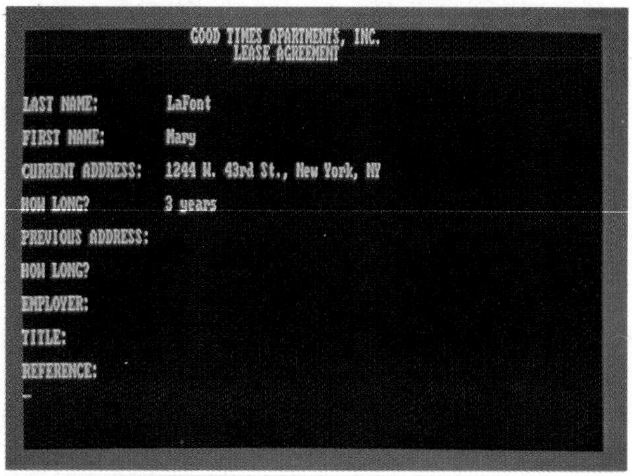

...to colors and shapes.

Processing

Writing instructions for a computer (programming) is no longer limited to engineers and mathematicians. Any person with some knowledge about what they want the computer to do can control the processing.

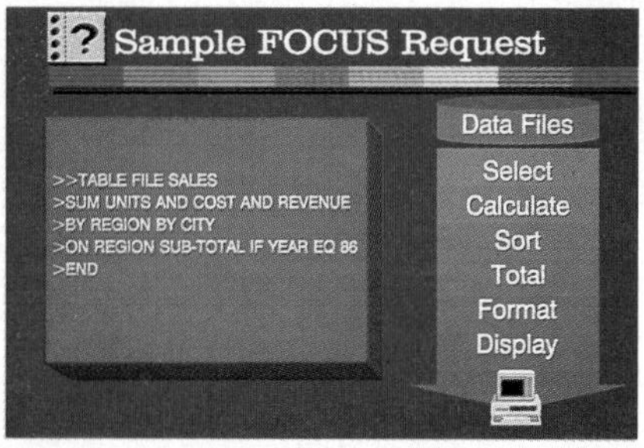

In English commands...

...or instructions a child can understand.

Output

In addition to traditional reports and screen displays, users can dictate the form of output most useful to them.

From aid to the sightless...

...to filling the room with sound.

Storage

With the freedom to make your own computing choices comes the responsibility to maintain and manage your own data or ethically use the data of others.

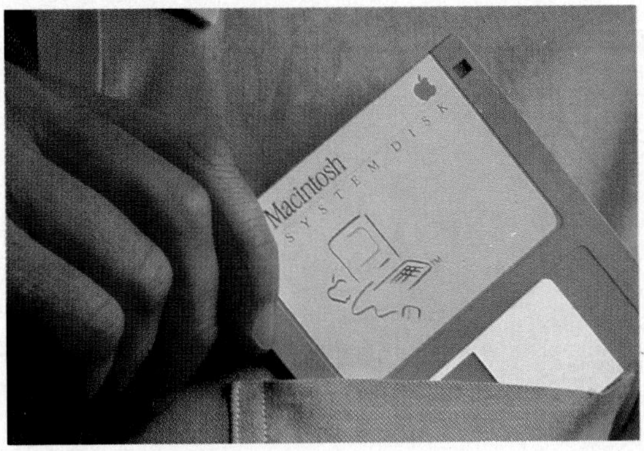

Data kept on pocket-sized disks are used in later processing...

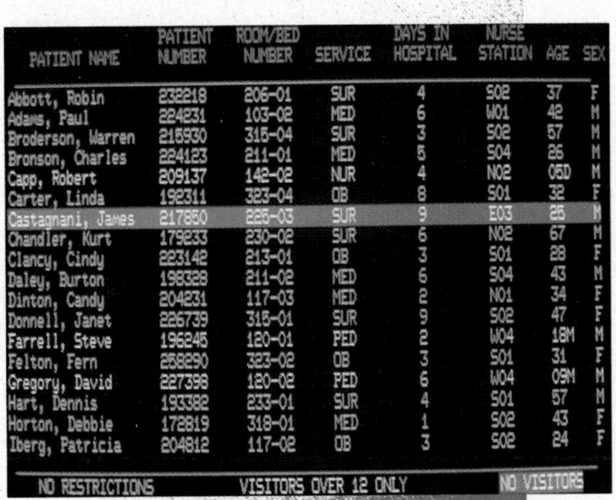

PATIENT NAME	PATIENT NUMBER	ROOM/BED NUMBER	SERVICE	DAYS IN HOSPITAL	NURSE STATION	AGE	SEX
Abbott, Robin	232218	206-01	SUR	4	S02	37	F
Adams, Paul	224231	103-02	MED	6	W01	42	M
Broderson, Warren	216930	315-04	SUR	3	S02	57	M
Bronson, Charles	224123	211-01	MED	5	S04	26	M
Capp, Robert	209137	142-02	NUR	4	N02	05D	M
Carter, Linda	192311	323-04	OB	8	S01	32	F
Castagnani, James	217850	226-03	SUR	9	E03	25	M
Chandler, Kurt	179233	230-02	SUR	6	N02	67	M
Clancy, Cindy	223142	213-01	OB	3	S01	28	F
Daley, Burton	198328	211-02	MED	6	S04	43	M
Dinton, Candy	204231	117-03	MED	2	N01	34	F
Donnell, Janet	226739	316-01	SUR	9	S02	47	F
Farrell, Steve	196245	120-01	PED	2	W04	18M	M
Felton, Fern	258290	323-02	OB	3	S01	31	F
Gregory, David	227398	120-02	PED	6	W04	09M	M
Hart, Dennis	193382	233-01	SUR	4	S01	57	M
Horton, Debbie	172819	318-01	MED	1	S02	43	F
Iberg, Patricia	204812	117-02	OB	3	S02	24	F

NO RESTRICTIONS VISITORS OVER 12 ONLY NO VISITORS

...data stored by others can be retrieved for your use.

Your involvement in computing is limited only by your knowledge and desire. Take the power in your own hands...

C L I P

TEN WAYS TO GET AHEAD WITH INFORMATION TECHNOLOGY

Telemarketing

Testing cold leads by telephone first—using computer runs to ferret out the best prospects—helps slash sales-force expenses and boost productivity.

Customer Service

By letting customers tap into your data base to track their orders and shipments, you build loyalty and smooth relations.

Training

Training or retraining workers lets them learn at their own speed—and lets you cut training costs.

Sales

Giving salespeople portable computers so they can get messages faster and enter orders directly adds up to quicker deliveries, better cash flow and less paperwork.

Better Financial Management

By setting up computer links between the treasurer's office and your banks, you can obtain financial information faster.

Product Development

By providing a toll-free number for consumer questions and complaints, you get ideas for product improvements and new products. In-house electronic publishing can help turn out product manuals faster.

Market Intelligence

By assembling and manipulating data on demographics and competitors, you can spot untapped niches, develop new products, and avoid inventory crunches.

New Businesses

Information technologies make whole new operations possible. Federal Express, for one, could not work without computer-equipped trucks and facilities.

Locking In Customers

By creating exclusive computer communications with customers for order entry and exchange of product and service data, you can help thwart competitors.

Selling Extra Processing Power

You can use off-peak processing power to develop completely new services for outsiders. That way, you can transfer some of the high costs of building your information network.

Source: Courtesy of *Business Week*, October 14, 1985.

Key Question: In what ways can these ten information technologies be used in your school to give it a competitive edge?

CHAPTER FACTS

- Computers process facts and figures. They have been used as problem-solving tools since the 1950s. As computers have become more user friendly, they have been adapted for a variety of applications by many levels of users.
- The facts and figures a computer uses to solve problems are called data.
- Many computer applications take the form of: process control, simulations, data storage and retrieval, and data processing.
- Computers and other tools operate under the four-step IPOS cycle: Input, Processing, Output, and Storage. Once it is completed, the cycle can be repeated with different inputs.
- Data can be input into a computer through use of a keyboard, by dialing a telephone, or by activating a video screen with light, sound, or touch.
- Computer output can be a screen display, a printer report, action of a mechanical arm, sound, and others.
- Data can be numeric, textual, or physical. All three types of data may be input to or output from a computer.
- Computers and calculators both perform arithmetic operations upon numeric data. Only computers can do logical operations and work with textual and physical data. All computers and some calculators are programmable, or capable of storing a series of instructions.
- A program is a set of instructions that is followed to produce a desired result.
- The chief limitation of computers is that they cannot think. They also cannot replace the decision-making power of people, make emotional judgments, disobey their programming, or read people's minds.
- Computers effectively store large amounts of data, perform processing quickly and accurately, simulate outcomes on the basis of given conditions, and recommend actions.
- Computers depend on people to provide correct data and instructions. Computer output must be interpreted by people as a basis for making decisions.
- Some misunderstandings arise when people don't realize how computers work. People may feel computers will replace them on the job or make decisions previously made by humans. Also, people are reluctant to change to new technology, even if the new methods will increase their productivity.

TERMS TO REMEMBER

arithmetic operation
computer
computer application
computer program
data
database
data processing
data storage and retrieval
embedded computer
icon
logical operation
numeric data
physical data
process control
programmable
simulation
text
textual data
transaction
user friendly

CHECK YOUR UNDERSTANDING

1. An organized collection of data that can be retrieved and cross-referenced by a computer is called a(n) ___________.
2. One thing all computers and calculators have in common is the ability to work with numeric and textual data. (True/False)
3. Two types of operations that computers perform are arithmetic and ___________.
4. Computers are not the only machines that perform an IPOS cycle. (True/False)
5. The second step in a computer's IPOS cycle always involves mathematical calculations. (True/False)
6. The third step in a computer's IPOS cycle could involve producing a printed report. (True/False)
7. The set of instructions a computer uses is called a(n) ___________.
8. What are the facts and figures that are input into a computer?
   a. computer program
   b. data
   c. arithmetic operations
   d. output information
   e. none of the above
9. A computer built inside of another type of tool is called a(n) ___________ computer.
10. Which of the following can a computer not do?
    a. store large amounts of data
    b. simulate possible outcomes from inputs about given conditions
    c. recommend action on the basis of input
    d. make decisions on emotional issues
    e. none of the above

APPLYING WHAT YOU'VE LEARNED

1. Computers are being used as tools in many jobs. In fact, few areas of work are untouched by computer technology. Can you see a place for computers in your chosen career? How would computers be used? If you don't think computers can be involved, why not?
2. Identify the input, processing, output and storage (if relevant) steps in each of these situations:
   a. making a chocolate milk shake
   b. a car being driven
   c. studying for an exam
   d. a solar-powered generator
   e. a building security system
3. The IPOS cycle is applied in the use of many tools. Pick a tool not mentioned in the text and identify the four steps in its cycle. What types of data are used? How are data input? What form does the output take?
4. Two common forms of output are reports and screen displays. Describe three situations in which a printed report is more useful than a display. Describe three situations in which a display is more useful.

5. Identify which type(s) of data (numeric, textual, or physical) would be used in these situations:
   a. taking an exam on a computer
   b. monitoring a baby for continuous breathing
   c. playing a video game
   d. sensing earthquake tremors
   e. computerized telephone directory assistance
   f. writing a term paper on a computer
   g. calculating income tax through use of a computer
6. Embedded computers are found in many devices you use each day. Name a tool you use that could be improved by embedding a computer. What type of data would the computer use? What kind of processing would it do?
7. Despite the many applications for computers, they are not the solution to all problems. Name three situations in which use of a computer would be unethical, impractical, or pointless. What could be done to prevent computer use in these situations?

CHECK YOUR UNDERSTANDING ANSWERS

1. database
2. false
3. logical
4. true
5. false
6. true
7. computer program
8. b
9. embedded
10. d

CHAPTER TWO

HISTORY OF COMPUTING: SOLVING INFORMATION PROBLEMS

KEY IDEAS

- **From the user's point of view**
  The history of computing is characterized by a series of increasingly complex information processing problems. How has technology helped people to overcome these problems?

- **Information needs before computers**
  People use technology to meet transportation, communication, and information needs.

  Calculating tools
  Expanding commerce led to the need for calculating tools.

  Impact of the Industrial Revolution
  People looked for new technology to solve the information and distribution requirements of a quickly expanding society.

  A processing challenge: The 1890 census
  A growing population needed more efficient technology to complete the census. Punched-card processing was born.

- **Early computers**
  World War II demands expanded expertise in punched card use and stimulated development of computers.

  First-generation computers
  Early computers used vacuum tubes as electronic components.

  Second-generation computers
  The transistor replaced the vacuum tube in the 1950s.

  Third-generation computers
  Integrated circuits made processing faster and more efficient.

- **Computers today and tomorrow**
  Computers became smaller, faster, and less costly with the microprocessor.

  Fourth-generation computers
  More advanced computers use microprocessors and other sophisticated circuitry.

  Fifth-generation computers
  The next era of computers will simulate human expertise and actions.

FROM THE USER'S POINT OF VIEW

You will find that an historical perspective often lets you put new terms and concepts into a logical framework. Do not view this chapter as a series of unrelated names and dates. Instead, approach it as the natural evolution of technology. The problems with data handling and needs for information solicited technological responses from the people involved. Furthermore, this is history that you or people you know have witnessed from the beginning—the first electronic computer was made just a little over 40 years ago. However, the need to solve problems and control information began centuries ago.

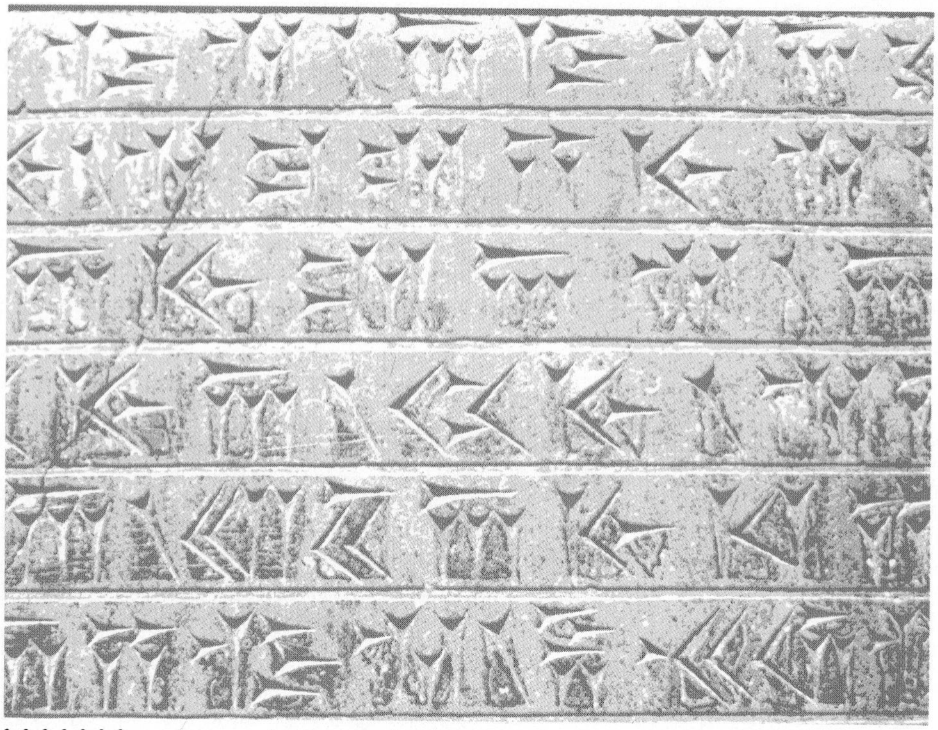

FIGURE 2.1

Information recording dates back to the earliest days when people began to form communitites. This is an example of some of the earliest known communication, using picture-like symbols to represent information.

INFORMATION NEEDS BEFORE COMPUTERS

History has shown that people use technology to solve problems. In other words, needs exist, people develop and apply new technology, and changes occur. Primitive people had problems transporting loads of heavy materials. The wheel was developed in response to this problem. From animal-drawn carts to cars and trains, the technology of the wheel has increased people's range of movement as their needs have grown more sophisticated.

To deal with information needs, technology developed as interactions among people became more complex. The earliest humans required only spoken communication. As communities grew, so did information requirements.

The need for numbers emerged when people began trading goods. As the volume of trade increased and spread across national boundaries, a system for conducting trade—the monetary system—appeared. Transactions were recorded first on clay tablets, then on papyrus. People eventually developed the double-entry bookkeeping techniques that are the basis for today's accounting methods.

FIGURE 2.2

The abacus has enjoyed popularity as a calculating device for many centuries.

Calculating Tools

Expanding commerce and the need for accurate record keeping led to the evolution of tools for calculation. One of the first calculating tools to emerge was the abacus. It was invented in China more than 4000 years ago and is still in use today.

Even before the Industrial Revolution, people attempted to mechanize the computations needed for business. In the 1640s, the first mechanical adding machine was created by Blaise Pascal. The 18-year-old inventor called it the numerical wheel calculator.

In the 1800s, Charles Babbage sought to use the mechanical technology available at that time to develop problem-solving tools. He was a man far ahead of

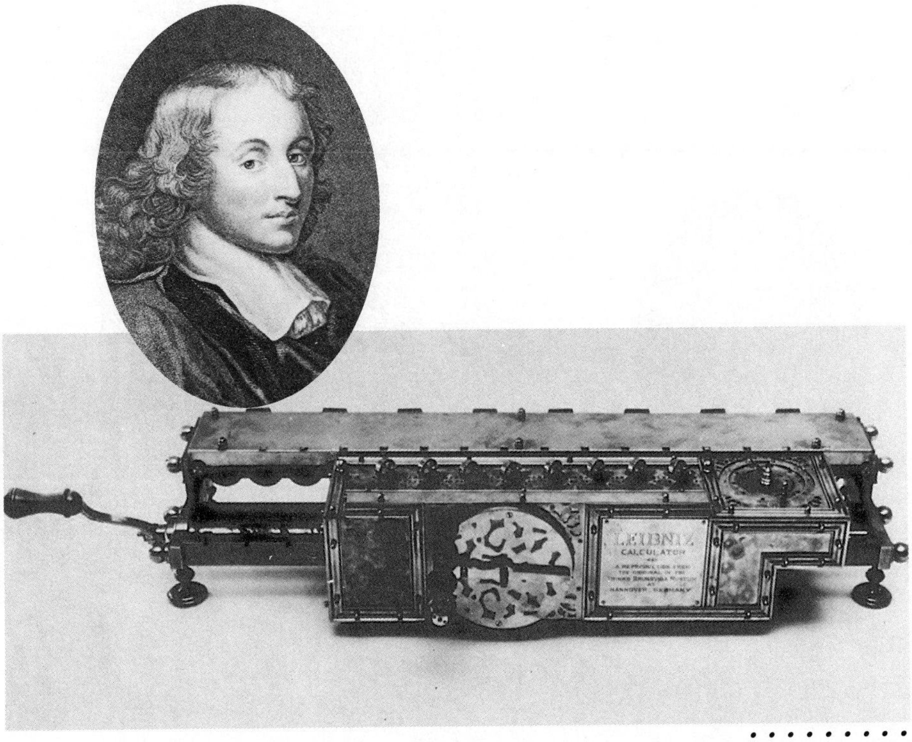

FIGURES 2.3 AND 2.4

Blaise Pascal invented one of the first mechanical calculators. Leibnitz's mechanical calculator was also well-known at this time.

Pascal portrait from the Bettmann Archive

his time. Babbage's achievements reflected the basic ideas underlying computers long before computers ever materialized. Some time prior to 1822, Babbage and his friend, John Herschel, ran into a problem. While they were checking data calculated manually for the Astronomical Society, the pair found many errors. In frustration, Babbage remarked to Herschel, "I wish to God these calculations had been executed by steam!" Steam engines were a common source of power in Babbage's day.

Babbage defined his problem: Find a way to perform calculations quickly and without error. He then began work on a solution. The outcome of the scientist's efforts was a blueprint for the "difference engine." Composed of gears and wheels, the difference engine would compute functions in the form:

$$y = a + bx + cx^2 + \ldots + gx^6$$

Although his work was funded by grants from the British government, Babbage was never able to complete the difference engine. While he was working on the project, he developed the concept for a new device, the "analytical engine." This machine was designed to compute any mathematical function, in any form.

Babbage's design for the analytical engine used many ideas later found in modern computers. The "engine" contained a "store" for numeric data that had room for 1000 variables of 50 digits each. Arithmetic operations were done in the "mill." Programs for the mill were to be written on punched cards. The "engine" would perform logical operations by ringing a bell when a variable went below zero or above capacity. The machine also was intended to drive a typesetter for output. All operations were to work mechanically.

A scientific paper written in Italian by L. F. Menabrea disseminated Babbage's theories. This paper was translated from Italian to English by Ada Augusta, Countess of Lovelace and daughter of the poet Lord Byron. The countess was an excellent mathematician who understood Babbage's concepts perhaps better than

FIGURES 2.5 AND 2.6

Charles Babbage invented the Difference Engine, which used many of the computational principles found in modern computers.

anyone. She added 50 pages of notes to Menabrea's 20-page paper. Ada, a major programming language adopted recently by the U.S. Department of Defense, is named in her honor.

The foundation for computer logic was set by a nineteenth-century mathematician, George Boole. The basis of Boole's theory of logic was that any mathematical representation was in one of two states: true or false. This theory led to Boolean algebra—the foundation of computer circuitry and logic. All computer circuits function in one of two states: on or off. The on condition is represented by the value 1, and the off condition by the value 0. These two values are binary digits, or ***bits***. They are the building blocks for the ***binary code*** used to program instructions for computers. Binary means consisting of two parts. Different patterns of the bits in a binary code can be used to represent characters or operations. For example, the bit pattern 1000001 might represent the letter A, while 1111110 might represent an add instruction.

FIGURE 2.7

Ada Augusta, Countess of Lovelace, annotated texts describing Babbage's work with mechanical calculators.

Impact of the Industrial Revolution

The dawn of the Industrial Revolution in the late 1700s brought more than the mechanization of labor and myriads of new inventions. The Industrial Revolution increased the information needs of a quickly expanding society, and also increased demands for ways of distributing that information. These problems led people to look at new technologies for solutions.

- As industries grew, so did the need for accurate information and record keeping. Manual calculating was enhanced by improvements in adding machines to support commercial transactions.
- Volumes of correspondence grew with the expansion of commerce. The need to produce documents quickly and legibly led to the development of the typewriter.
- Greater need for textiles resulted in the mechanization of looms. In 1801, Frenchman Joseph Marie Jacquard developed a loom that used punched cards

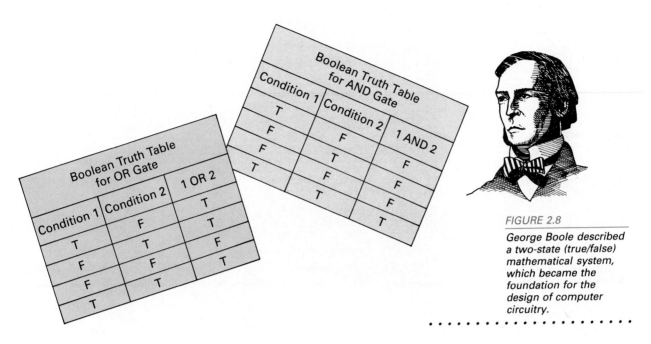

Boolean Truth Table for OR Gate

Condition 1	Condition 2	1 OR 2
T	F	T
F	T	T
F	F	F
T	T	T

Boolean Truth Table for AND Gate

Condition 1	Condition 2	1 AND 2
T	F	F
F	T	F
F	F	F
T	T	T

FIGURE 2.8

George Boole described a two-state (true/false) mathematical system, which became the foundation for the design of computer circuitry.

FIGURES 2.9 AND 2.10

Joseph Marie Jacquard invented an automatic textile loom that established weaving patterns through the use of punched cards.

Jacquard portrait from the Bettmann Archive

to control its operation. Needles fell through holes in the cards; different combinations of punched holes created different designs and patterns in the woven material. Punched cards were to reemerge in information processing more than 80 years later in the United States.

Mechanization assisted people in performing arithmetic, creating documents, and producing textiles. In each case, an identified need led to the development of an invention designed to go beyond manual operations to solve problems.

FIGURES 2.11 AND 2.12

Dr. Herman Hollerith invented punched-card machines that greatly increased productivity in the compilation of results from the U.S. Census of 1890.

A Processing Challenge: The 1890 Census

Information processing jobs kept getting bigger. From 1880 to 1890, the United States population grew from 50 million to more than 60 million. This explosive rate of growth led to an unprecedented processing challenge: counting and classifying each resident to generate overall census statistics.

The U.S. Bureau of the Census is legally bound to complete a census count every 10 years. Using methods available, Census Bureau employees took more than 7 years to complete the 1880 count. With the burgeoning population, it was estimated the 1890 census would require more than 10 years to finish. Thus, work on the 1900 census would begin before the 1890 census was completed. To solve this problem, Dr. Herman Hollerith developed a series of machines that compiled the 1890 census information mechanically. With the help of the Hollerith inventions, the 1890 census count took only six weeks. However, census results were not announced until December of 1890 in order to double-check the results.

Hollerith's machines operated on a principle similar to that of the Jacquard loom. Numeric data were punched into cards. Each number was represented by hole in a specially designated area of the card. Each card could store 80 digits. As the Hollerith machine processed cards, a pin would fall through each hole into a pan of mercury. This action closed an electrical circuit and registered the count on a meter. The Hollerith device translated punched holes into meaningful information. Also, use of punched cards made it possible to record census data only once and retain the data for future use. This eliminated the need to duplicate work and increased the productivity of the census employees.

Hollerith decided he had a marketable idea and formed his own company. He adapted his machines for commercial use. Organizations would store data on punched cards by using keyboard-operated devices called ***keypunches***. Eventually, early computers were built around punched cards. An input device known as a ***card reader*** read the cards and translated the holes into input data for processing. Processed data were punched into new cards by ***card punches*** and stored for later use. In 1924, Hollerith's company merged into an organization that eventually became International Business Machines (IBM), the world's largest computer company.

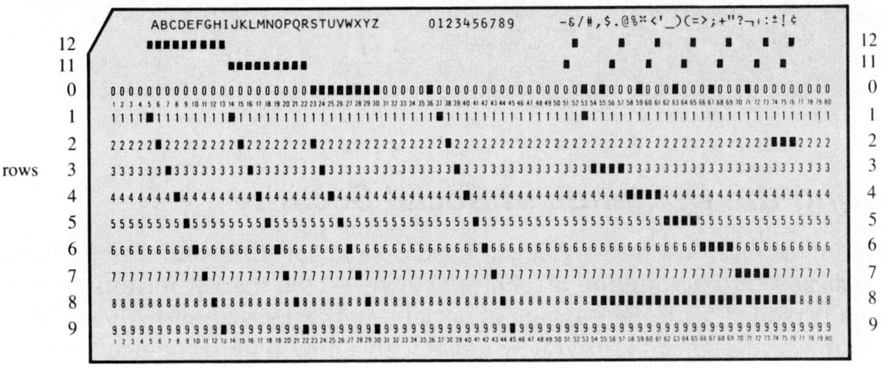

LETTER	ZONE PUNCH ROW	DIGIT PUNCH ROW
A	12	1
B	12	2
C	12	3
D	12	4
E	12	5
F	12	6
G	12	7
H	12	8
I	12	9
J	11	1
K	11	2
L	11	3
M	11	4
N	11	5
O	11	6
P	11	7
Q	11	8
R	11	9
S	0	2
T	0	3
U	0	4
V	0	5
W	0	6
X	0	7
Y	0	8
Z	0	9

NUMBER	DIGIT PUNCH ROW
0	0
1	1
2	2
3	3
4	4
5	5
6	6
7	7
8	8
9	9

SPECIAL CHARACTERS	ROWS
&	12
.	12,3,8
+	12,6,8
–	11
!	11,2,8
$	11,3,8
*	11,4,8
/	0,1
#	3,8
,	0,3,8
?	0,7,8

FIGURE 2.13

Punched-card methods dominated the information processing field for many years. Here we see machine sorting of cards to sequence data for a report.

FIGURE 2.14

Social security legislation in the 1930s placed additional data processing demands on business. Storing and processing data from punched cards helped to solve this record-keeping problem.

Courtesy of the National Archives

Meeting the Demands of Social Security

Until the mid-1930s, only the very largest business and governmental organizations used punched card accounting machines. However, the market for this type of machine exploded with the passage of social security legislation in 1935. This legislation was designed to provide workers with a minimum income in their old age. Though humane in intent, the social security program caused huge data processing problems. Employers were required to withhold a percentage of their employees' earnings and to supplement that amount. The Social Security Administration was put in charge of this program.

Prior to 1936, employers merely multiplied the hours worked by an employee's pay rate. With the new social security requirements, payroll computation became much more complicated. Employers figured the proper deduction for each worker, withheld it from his or her check, and added a matching contribution. The funds then were sent to the federal government. Also, records of all transactions had to be accumulated and reported.

The problem was obvious: Employers needed a system to compute and record payroll deductions quickly and accurately. Technology provided the solution through punched card systems adapted for payroll processing.

STUDY QUESTIONS

1. What is the relationship between problems and technical solutions?
2. Define bit and binary code.

FIGURES 2.15 AND 2.16

The MARK I mechanical computer is shown here. The team that developed the MARK I was headed by Howard G. Aiken. Aiken is seated in the front row, third from left, next to Grace Hopper, who went on to lead the team that developed the COBOL programming language and to become the highest ranking female naval officer.

Courtesy of Harvard University, Cruft Laboratory

3. What contributions did Blaise Pascal, Charles Babbage, Ada Lovelace, George Boole, Joseph Marie Jacquard, and Herman Hollerith make to the development of problem-solving machines?
4. Why did early computer systems use punched cards for storage?
5. What are the functions of a keypunch, card reader, and card punch?
6. How did the passage of social security legislation affect demand for computing equipment?

EARLY COMPUTERS

World War II brought new demands and needs to the nation in the 1940s. Financing the war meant additional taxes and changes to payroll processing. An armed force with millions of people created new challenges in administration and record keeping. New weapons required countless calculations and tests. As a result, the U.S. government supported the development of large-scale computing devices.

First-Generation Computers

The war effort provided a catalyst for the development of the first computers. As a prelude, Howard G. Aiken, working in conjunction with IBM, unveiled an electro-mechanical calculator in 1944. Called the MARK I, Aiken's machine used mechanical counters stimulated by electrical devices to perform basic arithmetic.

FIGURES 2.17 AND 2.18

The first electronic computer was the ENIAC, shown here with its developmental team, headed by J. Presper Eckert (far left) and John W. Mauchley (fourth from right).

Courtesy of University of Pennsylvania

At the same time, the U. S. government signed a contract with the University of Pennsylvania to develop an electronic computer. In 1946, the Electronic Numerical Integrator and Calculator (ENIAC) was designed by J. Presper Eckert and John W. Mauchley. ENIAC contained 19,000 vacuum tubes, 70,000 resistors, and 5 million soldered joints. Computers and associated equipment became known as ***hardware***, a term still used today. ENIAC was able to perform 5000 additions per second and used so much power it caused the lights to dim in one section of Philadelphia.

The MARK I and ENIAC were considered general-purpose computers because they were able to perform a wide variety of jobs. However, they were not programmable by today's definition. To change ENIAC's program, it was necessary to rewire the master program circuits, a task requiring much expertise and time. The first programmers for the MARK I and ENIAC were women. Grace Hopper of the U. S. Navy programmed the MARK I, and Adele Goldstein programmed ENIAC. Both were talented mathematicians.

Although Mauchley and Eckert often are given credit for building the first electronic computer, ENIAC actually was based in part on the work of John V. Atanasoff. Atanasoff was a professor at Iowa State University. By 1939, he had developed many ideas for an all-electronic computer. In 1942, he and a graduate student, Clifford Berry, completed an electronic computer that could solve linear equations. Unfortunately, Atanasoff lost funding for further research. His work went unrecognized for many years.

The next breakthrough involved building a general-purpose computer that could be reprogrammed easily. This goal was realized through the efforts of John

FIGURES 2.19 AND 2.20

Prominent computer pioneers John V. Atanasoff (left) and Clifford Berry (right) who developed the ABC computer that solved linear equations.

Courtesy of Iowa State University

FIGURE 2.21

John von Neumann's idea of storing programs and data in an internal memory unit became the foundation of modern computer design.

Courtesy of the Institute for Advanced Study

von Neumann, who joined the Eckert–Mauchley team in the mid-1940s. Von Neumann's design included a memory unit that temporarily stored a program and data. His stored program principles became the foundation of computer design for the next 30 years.

Fittingly, the first computer offered for commercial purposes tabulated the census of 1950. The UNIVAC I, or UNIVersal Automatic Computer, was delivered to the Bureau of the Census in 1951 and used continuously until 1963. The original machine now resides in the Smithsonian Institution.

In 1952, a UNIVAC was put to work processing payroll for the General Electric company. This launched the use of computers in business. Computers manufactured in the 1950s were known as first-generation computers. The programs, or sets of instructions that operate a computer, are known as ***software***. First-generation software was written in ***machine language***. Each computer had a unique machine language that conformed to its own electronic components.

Programmers who used machine languages had to write in binary code to express operating instructions. Binary code also was used to assign memory locations for each data value. Coding in machine language required extensive technical knowledge. Programmers found its use difficult and prone to error.

FIGURE 2.22

The first commercially successful computer was the UNIVAC I. The first system was delivered to the U.S. Bureau of Census in 1951, the second to General Electric in 1952.

Courtesy of Sperry Univac

Early computers could run only one program at a time. After each run, the computer had to be stopped and set up again for the next operation. Most first-generation computers used magnetic drums for data storage. Data were recorded on a series of tracks on the surface of a polished metal cylinder. In addition, computers relied on vacuum tubes as their primary processing components. Because of the number and size of vacuum tubes, these early machines were huge. A large first-generation computer contained row upon row of racks fitted with vacuum tubes. Typically, it would occupy a room the size of a large auditorium. Since the vacuum tubes frequently burned out, a staff of a half-dozen people had to run around replacing them. These enormous machines generated tremendous amounts of heat, were expensive to run, and often failed. Their shortcomings would be addressed and overcome by the next generation of computer systems.

Second-Generation Computers

The invention of the transistor won Bell Lab researchers William Shockley, John Bardeen, and Walter Brattain the 1956 Nobel Prize in physics. Transistors ushered in the second generation of computers, as unwieldy vacuum tubes became obsolete. Computers built with transistors decreased in size, increased in dependability, operated more quickly, and involved lower costs. During this developmental era, every computer system had built into it a memory unit based on von Neumann's idea.

Second-generation computers were programmed with ***assembly languages***, which used abbreviations to represent machine language operating instructions. Programmers no longer needed to wade through long lists of binary code. Although most were highly detailed, assembly languages were much easier to master and use

Machine Language Instruction	Description
0111 0110 1101 0001	Clear accumulator A
0111 0110 1101 0010	Clear accumulator B
1101 0001 1001 1100	Move value from memory location 12 to accumulator A
0010 0001 1011 1000	Move 8 to accumulator B
1101 0111 0110 1110	Multiply accumulator A by accumulator B
0001 0111 1011 1010	Move answer in accumulator B to memory location 10

FIGURE 2.23

The machine language used by computers represents the computer's operating instructions as a series of binary codes.

```
;******************** RSTR:  READ STRING SUBROUTINE ********************
RSTR:      CLR           R2      ; CLEAR UPPER HALF OF ACCUMULATOR
           CLR           R3      ; CLEAR LOWER HALF OF ACCUMULATOR
LOOP:      JSR       P,  READIN  ; READ A CHARACTER VIA "READIN"
           CMPB     R0,  #15     ; IS THIS CHARACTER A CARRIAGE RETURN?
           BEQ    DONE           ; YES - BRANCH TO "DONE"
           MOVB     R0,  (R4)    ; MOVE THIS CHARACTER TO OUTPUT AREA
           INC           R4      ; MOVE BUFFER POINTER TO NEXT POSITION
           BIC #177760,  R0      ; CONVERT FROM ASCII TO BINARY
           MUL     #12,  R3      ; MULTIPLY ACCUMULATOR BY 10 (12 OCTAL)
           ADD      R0,  R3      ; ADD THIS CHARACTER TO ACCUMULATOR
           BR     LOOP           ; BRANCH TO "LOOP" TO READ NEXT DIGIT
DONE:      MOV     #12,  R0      ; SET UP A LINE FEED
           JSR       P,  PRNT    ; "PRNT" EXECUTES THE LINE FEED
FILL:      CMP      R4,  R5      ; IS THE OUTPUT BUFFER FULL YET?
           BGT  ENDSTR           ; YES - BRANCH TO "ENDSTR"
           MOV     #40,  (R4)    ; NO - MOVE A SPACE TO OUTPUT BUFFER
           INC           R4      ; MOVE BUFFER POINTER TO NEXT CHARACTER
           BR     FILL           ; LOOP TO "FILL" & CONTINUE SPACE FILLING
ENDSTR:    RTS       P           ; RETURN TO CALLING ROUTINE
```

FIGURE 2.24

Assembler languages bridged a gap from binary coding to instructions that people could read.

than machine languages. For example, an assembly language might represent the addition operation with ADD and the operation for storing a variable with memory with STO. Memory locations are labeled with names instead of binary numbers. For example, TAX might signify the location in memory of a tax percentage. Assembly language names served as memory aids and expedited computer programming.

Despite these breakthroughs, assembly languages still required a separate instruction for each program step. Computers still could process only one assembly program at a time. To speed things up, certain input and output operations were done ***offline***, or away from the computer. For example, punched cards could be read, translated, and sorted into processing sequence without a computer. In addition, a printer could generate output from cards while the computer processed other data. With these offline methods, the computer didn't stand idle during input and output operations. A team of computer operators would process data in large batches to keep the machine as busy as possible. This procedure, which was repeated throughout the day, was known as ***batch processing***.

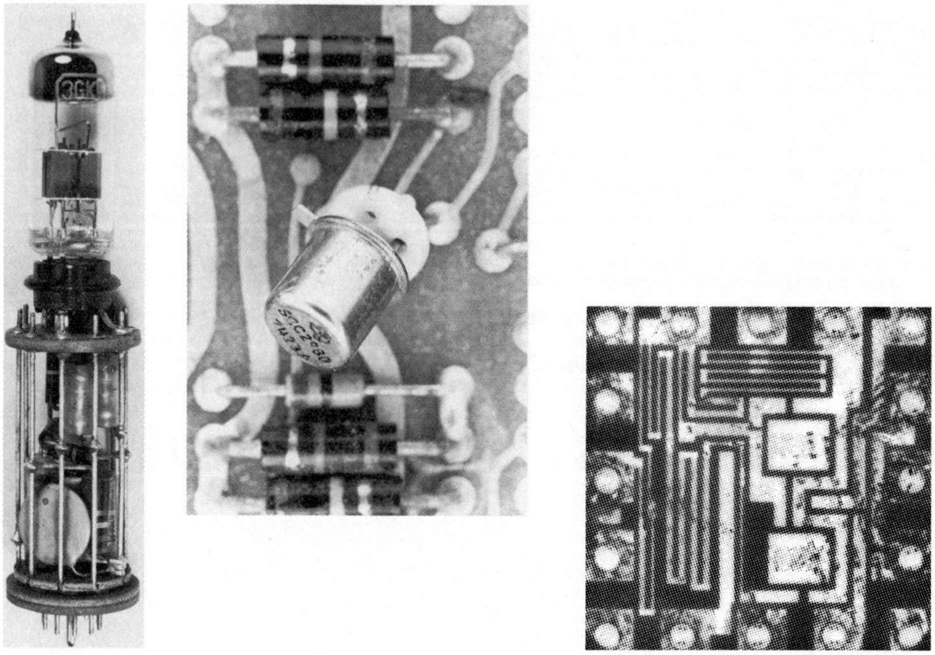

FIGURE 2.25

The first three computer generations are best represented by the vacuum tube, transistor, and integrated circuit.

Third-Generation Computers

By the late 1950s, the continued demand for fast and accurate computing devices came from many sectors of society. More businesses wanted access to affordable, easy-to-use computer technology. By 1961, President Kennedy's commitment to send men to the moon focused attention on the need for smaller, more dependable computer components. Transistors were too heavy and generated too much heat for use in space exploration. Once again, technology rose to the challenge.

Computers from the third generation used integrated circuits instead of transistors. ***Integrated circuits*** are tiny silicon wafers that hold the equivalent of hundreds of transistors and other electronic components. Use of these wafers, or ***chips***, made computers smaller, faster, and lighter than their predecessors.

Computers now could be programmed with ***high-level languages***, which resemble human languages. These new high-level languages thus eliminated the need for programmers to memorize unique abbreviations (assembly language instructions) for different types of computers. IBM's FORTRAN, or FORmula TRANslator, language uses words such as READ, WRITE, and STOP as programming statements. FORTRAN also is capable of dealing with complex mathematical equations. This language was introduced in 1957 and came into widespread use during the 1960s. Because FORTRAN eases the transition from mathematical notation to computer programming, its popularity has persisted through today.

Data processing needs in business were met with the development of COBOL (COmmon Business-Oriented Language) in 1960. COBOL provides businesspeople with extensive capabilities for creating and maintaining large data files. The language also can be used on several different models of computers. COBOL helped bring computers into business as a widely accepted, even indispensable, tool.

The third generation witnessed development of sophisticated ***operating systems***, or programs that control and monitor computer hardware. With operating systems overseeing memory, computers can run several programs concurrently. This capability is known as ***multiprogramming***. Instead of grouping data into

FORTRAN

```
   INTEGER NUM1, NUM2, SUM
   READ (5,10) NUM1, NUM2
10 FORMAT (I4,I4)
   SUM = NUM1 + NUM2
   WRITE (6,20) NUM1, NUM2, SUM
20 FORMAT (10X,'THE SUM OF', I4, '+', I4, 'IS', I5)
   STOP
   END
```

COBOL

```
IDENTIFICATION DIVISION.
 PROGRAM-ID. ADDITION.

ENVIRONMENT DIVISION.
 INPUT-OUTPUT SECTION.
    .
    .
    .
DATA DIVISION.
 FILE SECTION.
 FD DATA-IN
    LABEL RECORDS ARE STANDARD.
 01 NUMBERS-TO-BE-PROCESSED.
    05 NUMBER-1-IN      PIC 999.
    05 NUMBER-2-IN      PIC 999.

 FD ANSWER-OUT
    LABEL RECORDS ARE OMITTED.
 01 SUM-TO-BE-PRINTED    PIC X(27).

 WORKING-STORAGE SECTION.
 01 TEMPORARY-WORK-AREA.
    05 FILLER           PIC X(10)    VALUE "THE SUM OF".
    05 NUMBER-1-OUT     PIC 999.
    05 FILLER           PIC XXX      VALUE " + ".
    05 NUMBER-2-OUT     PIC 999.
    05 FILLER           PIC X(4)     VALUE " IS ".
    05 SUM-OUT          PIC 9(4).

PROCEDURE DIVISION.
 PROCESSING-ROUTING.
    OPEN INPUT DATA-IN
         OUTPUT ANSWER-OUT.
    READ DATA-IN.
    ADD NUMBER-1-IN, NUMBER-2-IN GIVING SUM-OUT.
    MOVE NUMBER-1-IN TO NUMBER-1-OUT.
    MOVE NUMBER-2-IN TO NUMBER-2-OUT.
    WRITE SUM-TO-BE-PRINTED
        FROM TEMPORARY-WORK-AREA.
    CLOSE DATA-IN
          ANSWER-OUT.
    STOP RUN.
```

FIGURE 2.26

High-level programming languages such as FORTRAN and COBOL let programmers write instructions by using English phrases and terms.

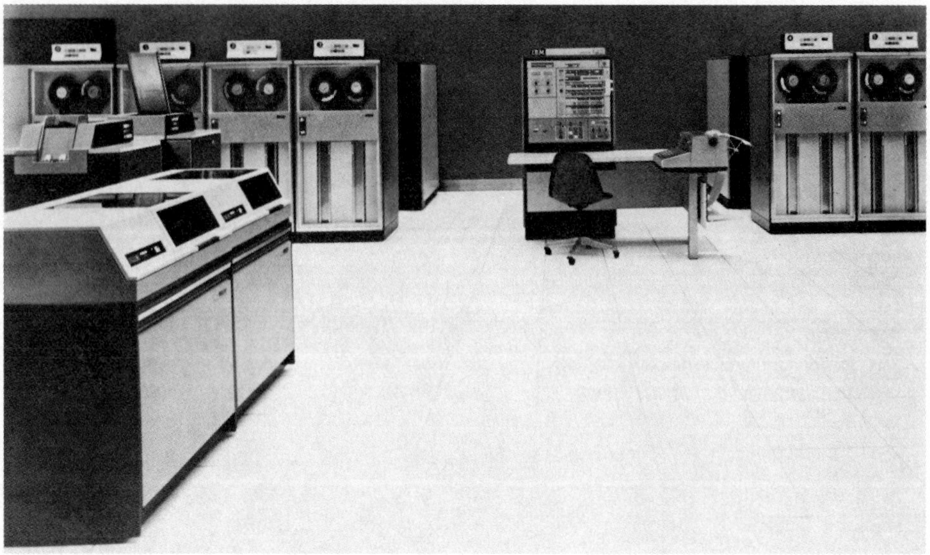

FIGURE 2.27

One of the best-selling third-generation computers was this IBM 360.

Courtesy of IBM

batches, third-generation computers could have data input directly for processing. Known as ***online*** processing, this technique enabled users to input data immediately into the computer for processing. Thus, third-generation computers eliminated the need for offline activities to increase productivity.

As online systems proliferated, new applications surfaced. In warehouses, online order entry systems recorded transactions immediately. With up-to-the-minute information on sales and supplies, salespeople can respond immediately to customer inquiries or orders. Airlines developed online seat reservation systems that give travel agents immediate access to current flight information.

As computers provided greater power and more versatility, larger businesses often housed these powerful devices—known as ***mainframes***—in huge computer centers. As a result, computer power was centralized. One of the first general-purpose mainframes using integrated circuit technology, was IBM's System/360. Several other manufacturers modeled their own computers after the System/360.

At the same time, ***minicomputers*** emerged as an affordable alternative to larger systems. The minicomputer offers capabilities similar to those of a mainframe computer, but is physically smaller and less powerful. Small- and medium-sized businesses find minicomputers to be well suited for their modest needs. This acceptance helped to spread computing power to a large number of organizations.

STUDY QUESTIONS

7. Define hardware, software, machine language, assembly language, offline, batch processing, integrated circuit, chip, high-level language, operating system, multiprogramming, online, mainframe, and minicomputer.
8. What contributions did Howard G. Aiken, John W. Mauchley, J. Presper Eckert, Grace Hopper, Adele Goldstein, John V. Atanasoff, Clifford Berry, and John von Neumann make to developing problem-solving machines?
9. What were the main characteristics of first-generation computers and software?
10. What features of second-generation computers and software distinguished them from the first generation?

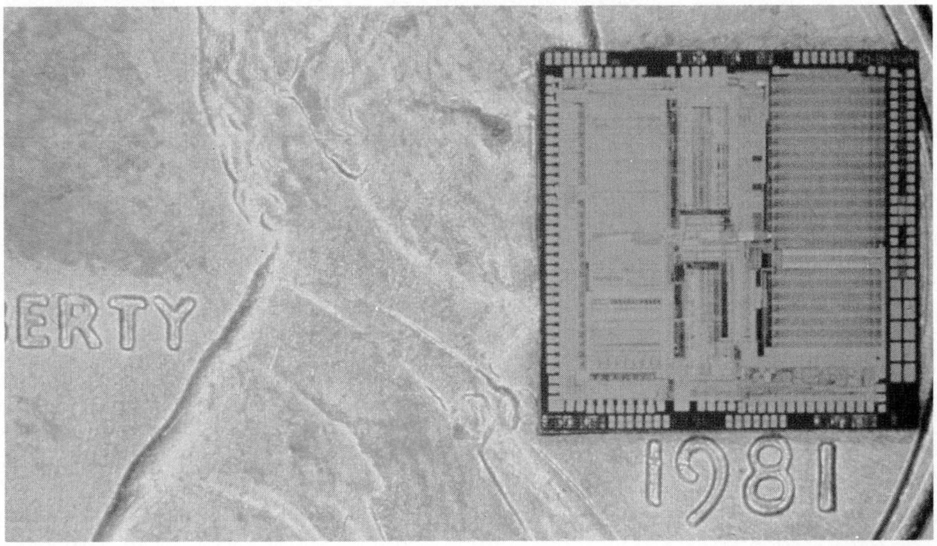

FIGURE 2.28

Microchip technology has made possible computing equipment that has become increasingly smaller and, at the same time, more powerful.

Courtesy of Intel Corporation

11. What is one advantage of working offline?
12. What are the characteristic features of third-generation computers and software?
13. What is one advantage of multiprogramming?

COMPUTERS TODAY AND TOMORROW

The continued demand for smaller, faster, and easy-to-use computers persisted. The miniaturization of computers continued into the 1970s with the development of the ***microprocessor***. Previously, computer capabilities were distributed among several integrated circuits. Microprocessors combined many processing circuits on a single chip. Computers built around microprocessors were called ***microcomputers***. The computing power that occupied an entire room during the 1950s today can reside on a slice of silicon smaller than a dime.

Fourth-Generation Computers

Fourth-generation computers are characterized by their use of microprocessors and other sophisticated integrated circuits. Because of the power of each tiny chip, some computers have been reduced to desk-top size. At the other extreme, the latest generation of integrated circuits has made it possible to pack even more power into large mainframes. The result has been a special family of high-capacity machines known as ***supercomputers***. These computers were specifically developed to handle large volumes of scientific computations. Much of the early work in designing supercomputers was done by Control Data Corporation's Seymour Cray. Cray later went on to form his own company, Cray Research, which is still the largest manufacturer of supercomputer technology (see Figure 2.33).

The first commercially developed microprocessor—the Intel 4004—was developed in 1971. A few years later, the Intel 8008 expanded the capacity of the original version by providing multiuse arithmetic and control circuitry. By 1974, two companies, Intel and Motorola, were manufacturing microprocessors for build-it-yourself computer kits. Computer hobbyists purchased the kits, which came

FIGURES 2.29, 2.30, AND 2.31

This Apple I computer was built in a garage by two teenagers, Steve Wozniak and Steve Jobs. They went on to form the Apple Computer Corporation, which is now one of the top 500 companies in the U.S.

complete with assembly instructions and all the necessary parts—including a microprocessor.

Like other hobbyists in 1976, one teenager purchased a $20 microprocessor and built his own computer from scratch. By today's standards, the computer was somewhat primitive. It had a little keyboard and no case. Yet, at the time, people were impressed. The teenager, Steve Wozniak, formed a partnership with Steve Jobs to sell these computers at a local store. Jobs sold his Volkswagen Beetle and Wozniak sold several expensive calculators to raise money to buy parts. Over the next several months, they built and sold hundreds of their Apple I computers. By the end of 1977, the Apple II was announced, and the partnership went on to become the Apple Computer Corporation. Meanwhile, other companies began to follow suit. As a result, the Commodore PET and the Tandy Radio Shack Model I were built and ready for sale in 1977.

Through the 1970s, small computers were used primarily by hobbyists and a few schools. The popularity of microcomputers exploded with the increasing availability of ***personal productivity software***. This software helped people to harness the power of computers for their own use. Personal productivity software is characterized by programs that help people write and edit reports (word processors), manipulate rows and columns of numbers (electronic spreadsheets), create charts and diagrams (graphics packages), pass data between distant computers using telephones (telecommunications software), and manage large databases (database programs).

The array of personal productivity software on the market kept expanding. Organizations and individuals started to view the microcomputer as a necessary business and personal tool. In response to growing market demand, IBM announced the IBM Personal Computer (PC) in August of 1981. Small computers had taken their place in businesses, as well as in schools and homes.

Competition led to dramatic price reductions. Consequently, more and more people interested in increasing their productivity became computer literate.

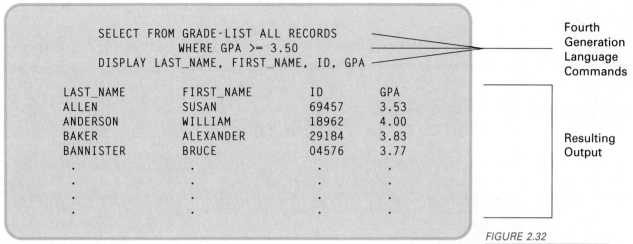

```
     SELECT FROM GRADE-LIST ALL RECORDS
                WHERE GPA >= 3.50
     DISPLAY LAST_NAME, FIRST_NAME, ID, GPA

LAST_NAME        FIRST_NAME       ID        GPA
ALLEN            SUSAN            69457     3.53
ANDERSON         WILLIAM          18962     4.00
BAKER            ALEXANDER        29184     3.83
BANNISTER        BRUCE            04576     3.77
   .                .               .         .
   .                .               .         .
   .                .               .         .
   .                .               .         .
```

Fourth Generation Language Commands

Resulting Output

FIGURE 2.32

Fourth-generation languages (4GLs) help non-programmers access data. In this example, a few 4GL commands create an honor roll from a list of semester grades.

Computer literacy, or the basic comprehension of computers and their functions, became a necessary job qualification, as well as a personal skill.

In the future, the ability to mass-produce microprocessors will make computers even less expensive. Since microprocessors can be programmed to handle a wide range of applications, their usefulness will extend even further beyond the computer industry. Today, stereos, microwave ovens, automotive ignition systems, games, and appliances can be controlled by embedded computers. Fourth-generation technology thus provides price reductions, size reductions, and greater flexibility in programming.

Fourth-generation languages (4GLs) have supported these developments. Characterized by easy-to-use commands and diverse application capabilities, 4GLs have given programming power to users who have minimal training. Unlike earlier high-level languages, the user-friendly 4GLs help the user to specify program requirements. The 4GLs, as shown in Figure 2.32, are nonprocedural since they can build complex programs on the basis of a few commands supplied by the user. Users only need to indicate input, processing, output, and storage requirements. These nonprocedural languages then use built-in logic to specify program sequence. Since 4GLs help users create their own software for specific personal needs, 4GLs are often referred to as ***application generators***.

Fourth-generation languages serve as a buffer between the user and the complex technical aspects of programming. Guided by such languages, users define their processing problems; then, a special program translates the problem definition into solution software. Fourth-generation languages have led to increased user participation in designing computer applications. Ultimately, 4GLs enable users to gain control over how they use their computing resources.

Fifth-Generation Computers

The next computer generation will be able to simulate human thought and judgment. One type of software application is known as ***artificial intelligence (AI)***. This growing area of development synthesizes computer science, psychology, linguistics, and other specialized fields in order to perform tasks with humanlike logic. However, the key element in the term *artificial intelligence* is "artificial." Computer capabilities cannot rival the abilities of humans to apply intuition in decision

THE COMPUTER AGE
A Time Line, 1946 A.D. to 2000 A.D.

1946
J. Presper Eckert, John Mauchley and a team of 50 complete the Electronic Numerical Integrator and Computer (Eniac), the first large-scale electronic digital computer, at the University of Pennsylvania's Moore School. Weighing 30 tons, standing two stories and covering 15,000 square feet, Eniac operates at 357 multiplications per second. Sponsored by the Army, the $500,000 project is aimed at designing a computer for the rapid calculation of military ballistics tables.

1947
Grace Hopper documents the first computer bug, a dead moth found in a cabinet of the Mark II. She immortalizes the insect by pasting it in her logbook beside a note about the incident.

1948
Jealous of Eniac's success and miffed at Howard Aiken, who snubbed IBM at the Mark I dedication, Thomas J. Watson, Sr., orders built an Eniac-like computer, the Selective Sequence Electronic Calculator (SSEC). With more than 12,000 vacuum tubes, SSEC becomes the target of cartoonists and motion picture makers, who use its huge size and flashing lights to illustrate the outlandishness of computers of the period.

1949
Maurice Wilkes of England's Cambridge University builds the first stored-program computer, the Electronic Delay Storage Automatic computer (EDSAC). A student at Eckert's and Mauchley's Moore School lectures, Wilkes works with a copy of John von Neumann's draft on the Electronic Discrete Variable Automatic Computer (EDVAC) to beat out the Americans.

1950
Von Neumann's EDVAC is finally complete. Having lost the distinction as the first stored-program computer, it is still the first to use binary or digital mathematics.

1951
The Universal Automatic Computer, Univac I, made by Remington Rand and operating at a rate of 2,000 computations a second, is delivered to the U.S. Bureau of the Census as the first American commercially produced computer.

1953
IBM introduces the first magnetic tape device, the Model 726. It can pack 100 characters per inch and move at 75 inches per second.

1954
Fortran, or Formula Translation programming language, is developed by John Bakus at IBM.

1956
The term "artificial intelligence" is coined by Dartmouth College Assistant Professor John McCarthy, who organizes the Dartmouth Conference in Hanover, N.H., with the help of Marvin Minsky of MIT.

1958
Seymour Cray builds the first fully transistorized supercomputer for control Data Corp., the CDC 1604.

1959
Jack Kilby of Texas Instruments and Robert Noyce of Fairchild Semiconductor develop "the monolithic idea," creating the integrated circuit, a breakthrough that will allow the dream of smaller and more affordable computers to become a reality.

Cobol, for Commercial and Business-Oriented Language, based on Grace Hopper's FlowMatic, is created by Codasyl, the Committee on Data Systems Languages. Hopper invents a compiler that makes Cobol run on many types of computers.

1960
The first modern computer generation ends as vacuum tubes, punched cards and machine codes give way to second-generation transistors, magnetic tape and procedural languages in computer design and operation.

1963
CDC ships the first supercomputer using silicon transistors to Lawrence Livermore National Labs in California.

1964
In the first computer crime involving criminal prosecution, *Texas v. Hancock*, a programmer who stole $5 million worth of his employer's software is convicted and sentenced to five years.

1965
Beginner's All-Purpose Symbolic Instruction Code (Basic) language is created by Tom Kurtz and John Kemeny of Dartmouth.

1966
Texas Instruments offers the first solid-state hand-held calculator.

Operation Match computer dating service opens in Cambridge, Mass.

1967
The third generation is under way, with integrated circuits, floppy disks and nonprocedural languages becoming prominent in computer construction and usage.

1968
Gordon Moore and Robert Noyce found Integrated Electronics (Intel) Corp.

1969
The Intel 4004 becomes the first microprocessor.

1970
The first robot supermarket, Telemart, opens in San Diego. The idea was that shoppers would use their Touch-Tone phones to call into a computer that would help them select their groceries and have them delivered. The supermarket closes because so many shoppers call that the computer can't handle the orders.

1971
Intel markets the 4004 microprocessor, which paves the way for the micro revolution.

The floppy disk is introduced to feed instructions to the IBM 370.

Pascal, named after the famous mathematician, is developed by Niklaus Wirth of Switzerland as a programming language for systems development.

1975
The Cray-1 supercomputer is introduced as the fastest computer on Earth, performing a million more calculations per second than Eniac in a space a thousand times smaller.

Microsoft Corp. is founded by Bill Gates and Paul Allen after they adapt Basic to the Altair microcomputer.

1977
Apple Computer, founded by Steve Wozniak and Steve Jobs, introduces the Apple II personal computer.

Originally developed for computerized astrology by Gary Kildall, CP/M is marketed by Digital Research as a standard control program for personal computers.

1978
Dan Bricklin and Bob Frankston create Visicalc, electronic spreadsheet software.

1979
Micropro International releases Wordstar, one of the best-selling word processing programs.

1980
Shugart Associates introduces the Winchester disk drive, which stores 30 times more data than a small floppy.

1981
The IBM Personal Computer debuts, and Microsoft's MS-DOS becomes its standard operating software.

"Factory Robot Kills Worker" reads the headline about the first reported death caused by a robot: Kenji Urada, 37, is killed when a self-propelled robot cart in a Japanese factory runs him over as he tries to repair it.

Osborne Computer introduces the Osborne I, the first portable computer.

1983
Lotus' 1-2-3 takes Visicalc's place as the popular spreadsheet program marketed by company founder Mitch Kapor.

Hewlett-Packard offers the first touch-screen personal computer, the HP-150.

1985
Technological trends and innovations include the use of IBM PC-DOS and Unix operating systems as standards, the start-up of fault-tolerant computer firms and the invention of the one-million-bit random-access memory chip.

1988
Computers containing a million processors are set to work solving complex problems.

1990
The advent of parallel processing and greatly increased processing power is expected to make this truly the year of artificial intelligence.

2000
Experts predict that computers containing a billion processors will be technologically feasible, exceeding the power of the human brain.

Reprinted by permission, *Computerworld*

Key Question: Which one of these computer-oriented innovators has had the most impact on your life? Why?

I N S I G H T

THE MICROPROCESSOR: FROM CHIPS OF QUARTZ ROCK TO SILICON CHIPS

Computers process and store data. The first computers were huge, requiring rooms of vacuum tubes. Today's computers use electronic circuitry embedded on tiny silicon chips to do the same thing—at much greater speeds and far less cost.

The brains of computers, as well as the growing number of smart appliances, are microprocessors. Today's microprocessor can fit through the eye of a needle.

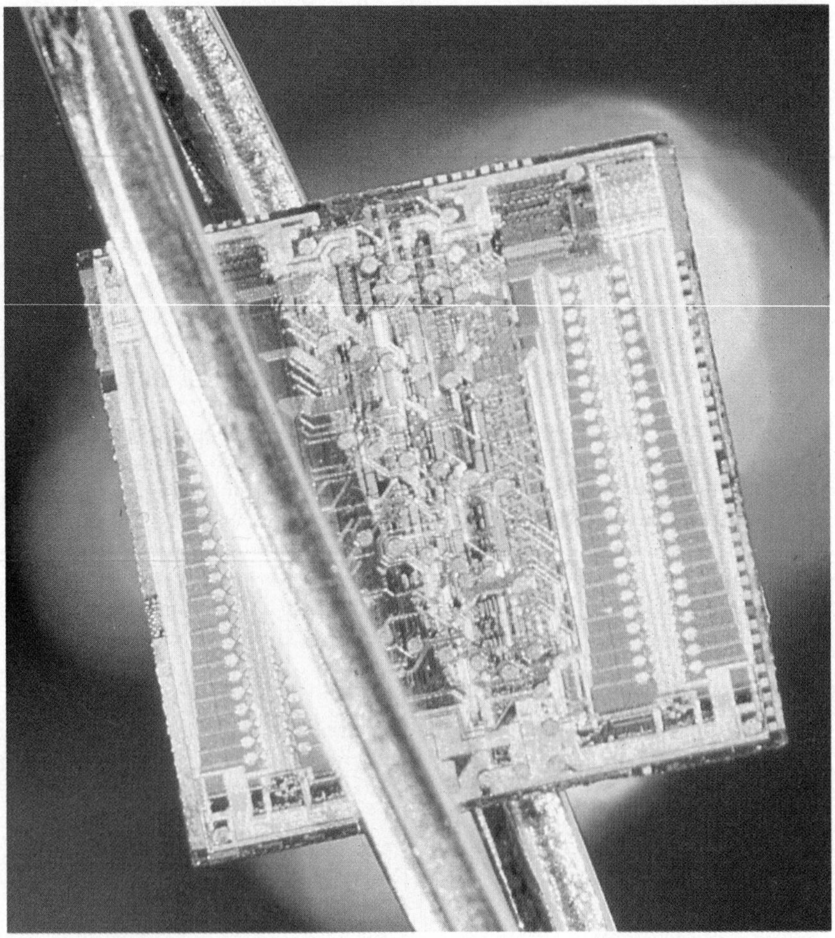

A microprocessor and other integrated circuits are often called silicon chips because they are made from silicon (quartz) rocks.

These rocks are melted into nearly pure silicon and formed into ingots or silicon crystals 2 to 6 inches in diameter.

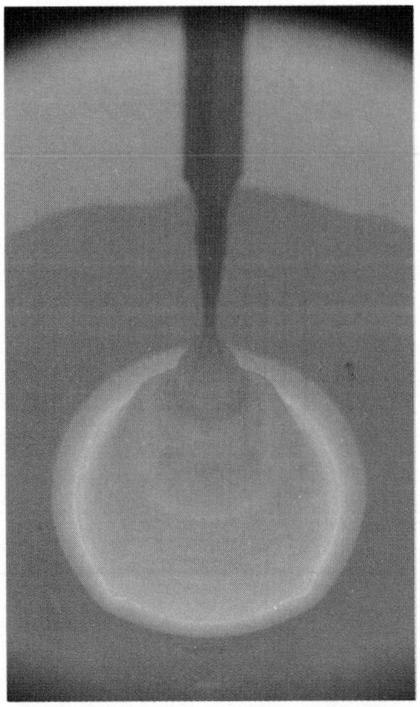

Wafers are sliced from the ingot and polished. These wafers are then sent to clean rooms to avoid contamination from dirt and dust, which would disrupt the circuitry being transferred onto their surface.

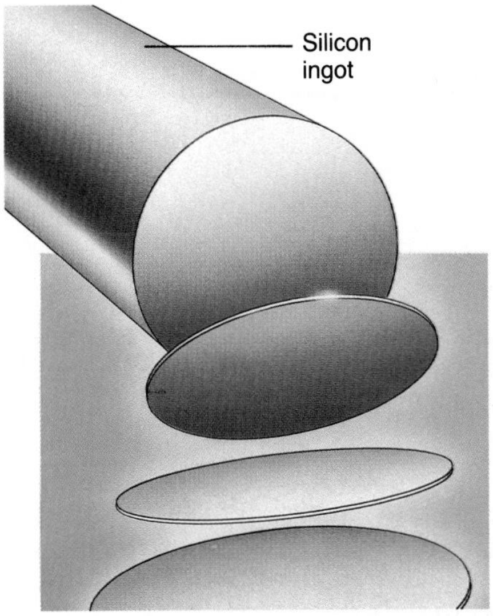

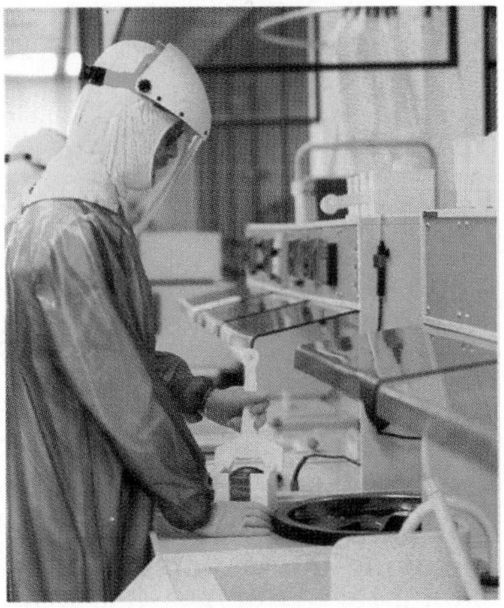

Enlarged circuit designs are carefully examined for accuracy before reduction to microscopic size for transfer onto wafers.

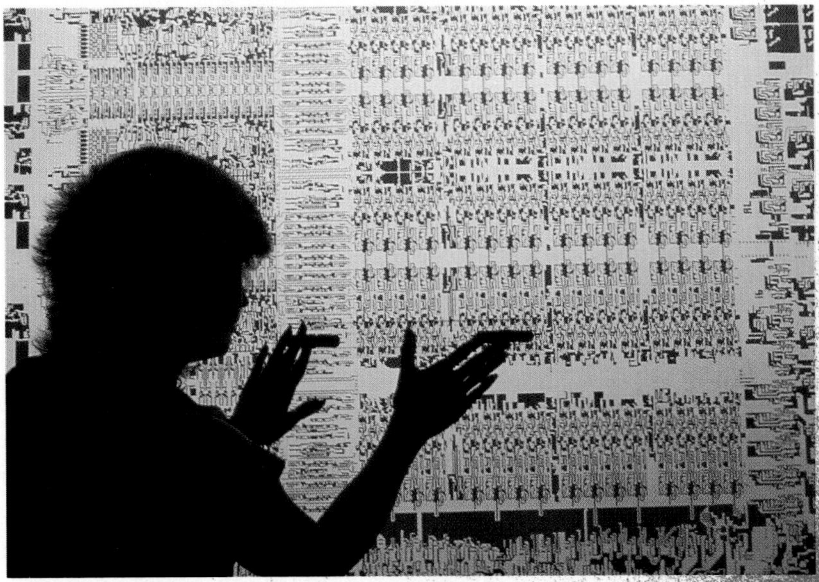

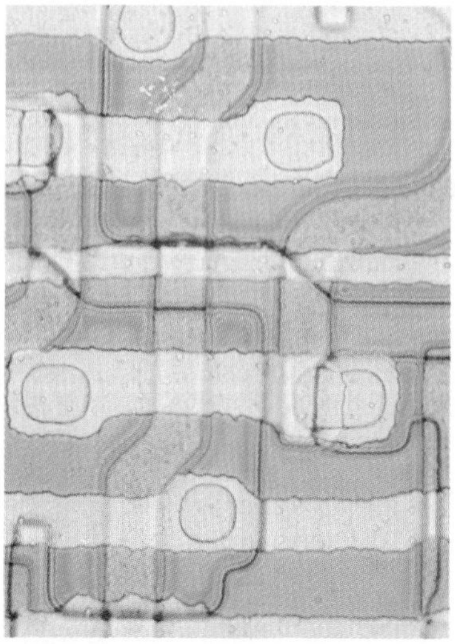

In the clean room, a light-sensitive plastic, a photoresist, is applied to the wafer. The circuit design is etched into the photoresist with ultraviolet light shined through a masking plate containing the design.

The wafer is then dipped into an acid bath to remove the photoresist from the exposed areas. This process of masking the wafer and removing the photoresist is repeated several times until the intricate, multilevel circuit design is etched onto the wafer.

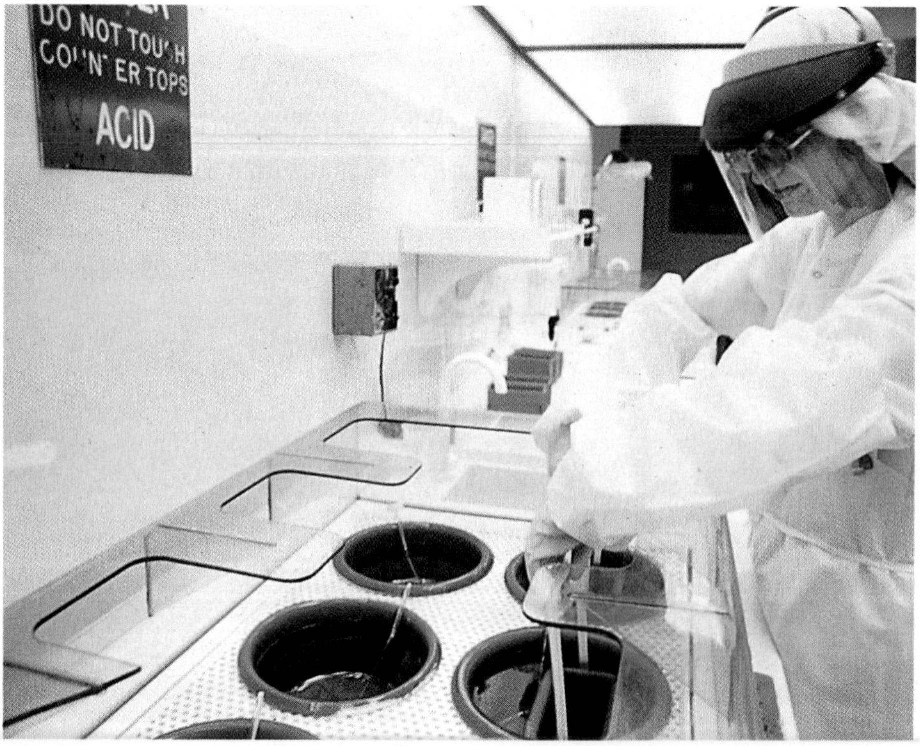

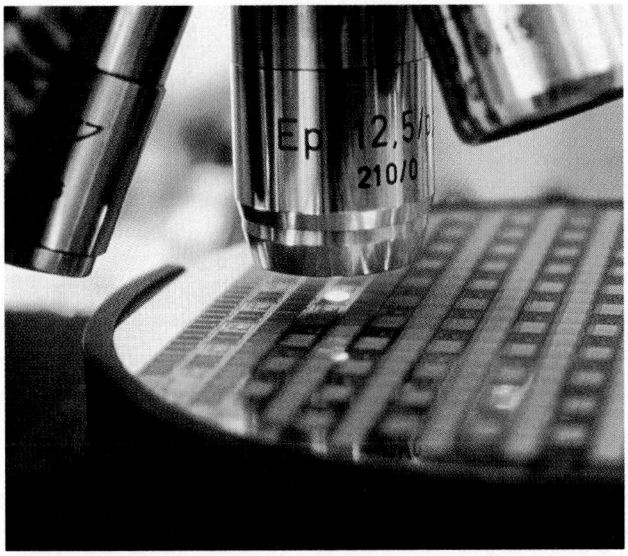

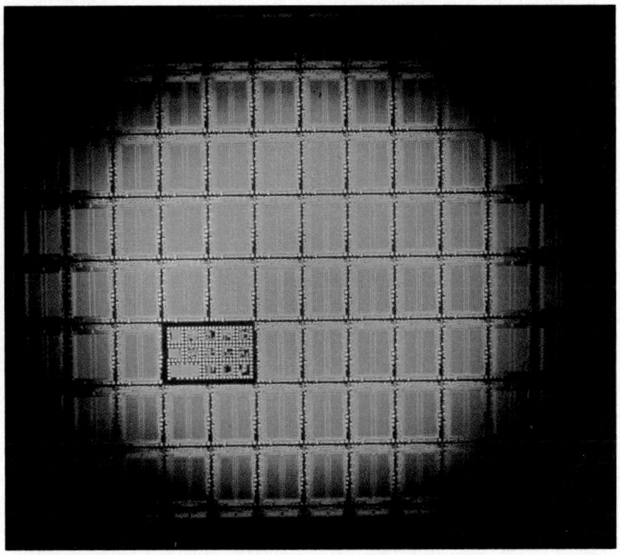

The wafer is baked at temperatures of 1,400° Celsius and inspected after every acid bath.

The result is a single wafer that contains several hundred silicon chips. The wafer is cut into individual chips by a diamond saw.

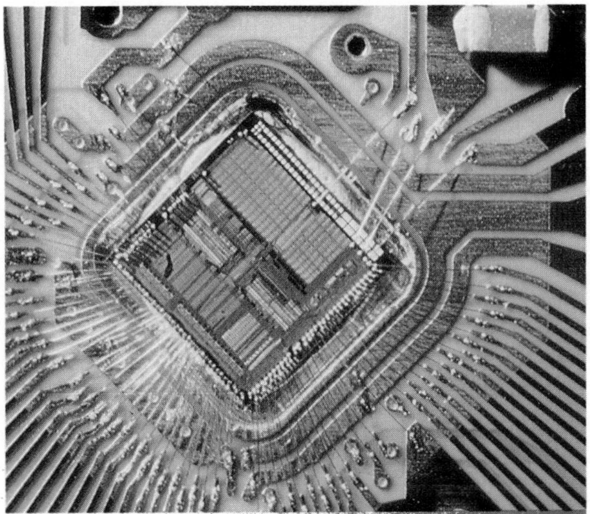

These chips are then embedded into computers and other "smart" appliances.

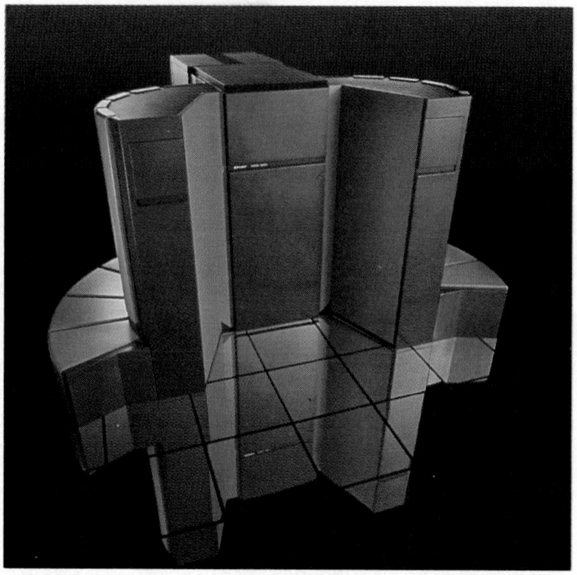

FIGURES 2.33 AND 2.34

Seymour Cray and a Cray Y-MP supercomputer.

making. The computer will be able to enhance human intelligence, but cannot replace human imagination and judgment.

Among the AI developments expected in fifth-generation computers are heuristic problem-solving techniques. The term ***heuristic*** describes a method by which problems are solved through application of general rules and information based on experience. Instead of following precise sequences of instructions to devise solutions, heuristic software applies rules proven to be effective in the past. As an example, heuristic techniques are used to develop programs that play chess. A vast number of moves is possible in a game of chess. With heuristic capabilities, the computer is able to evaluate different moves to build a game strategy. Thus, the chess-playing computer is able respond to a variable situation in several different ways.

Fifth-generation technology also may produce computer systems that accept spoken instructions, translate foreign languages, and program themselves. However, a new hardware generation must keep pace with faster processing speeds and provide easy access to large databases. The first four computer generations processed one instruction at a time, sequentially. All processing was done through a central processor. This will not fit the needs of fifth-generation software.

Computer scientists are currently working on fifth-generation hardware that does ***parallel processing***. These machines have rows of microprocessors, just as early computers had rows of vacuum tubes. Programs will be broken into modules and processed simultaneously by the parallel processors. The results will be faster, more efficient computers.

STUDY QUESTIONS

14. Define microprocessor, microcomputer, supercomputer, personal productivity software, fourth-generation languages (4GLs), artificial intelligence (AI), heuristic, and parallel processing.

15. What contributions did Steve Wozniak and Steve Jobs make to the development of problem-solving machines?
16. Identify five types of personal productivity software.
17. Why are fourth-generation languages called application generators?
18. What are the characteristic features of fourth- and fifth-generation computers and software?
19. What are two human attributes that would be difficult to duplicate with artificial intelligence?
20. How do computer scientists see fifth-generation hardware being fundamentally different from earlier hardware?

CONCLUSION

Throughout the generations of computers, new technology has arisen to meet society's challenges. The problems have varied: the need for increased communications, record keeping, defense systems, space exploration, and processing capabilities for individuals and businesses. The solutions have been to decrease the size and cost of computers while increasing their speed, reliability, and capacity. New developments have taken computers out of the hands of experts and provided easy-to-use solutions for everyone.

CHAPTER FACTS

- Blaise Pascal built the first mechanical adding machine, called the numerical calculator, in the 1640s.
- In the 1800s, Charles Babbage designed a difference engine and an analytical engine to solve certain mathematical functions. They were never completed. Babbage's ideas were disseminated through a paper in Italian by L. F. Menabrea. The paper was translated later by Ada Lovelace.
- George Boole formulated an algebra based on two-state (true/false) conditions. Later, Boolean algebra became the basis for binary logic, which is used by computers.
- In a computer, the electronic circuitry can be on or off. These conditions are represented by the bits (binary digits) 1 and 0, respectively. Bits are arranged in patterns called binary code. Binary code is used to represent data as well as instructions in the computer.
- Joseph Marie Jacquard invented a loom in 1801 that used punched cards to control its operation. Needles went through the patterned holes to create weaving patterns.
- In the 1880s, Herman Hollerith invented a computing machine that used punched cards to analyze the 1890 U. S. Census.
- John V. Atanasoff and his student, Clifford Berry, completed the first electronic computer in 1942. Lack of funding curbed further research, and these achievements went unrecognized for a long time.
- In 1944, Howard G. Aiken developed an electromechanical calculator. At the same time, J. Presper Eckert and John W. Mauchley were credited with building the first electronic computer, the ENIAC.
- John von Neumann's ideas on storing programs and data in a memory unit became a foundation for computer design.

- The first commercial use of computers was to analyze the 1950 census.
- A computer was first used in private industry by General Electric in 1952.
- First-generation computers used vacuum tubes for processing, magnetic drums for data storage, and punched cards for input. Software was written in machine language, a binary code unique to each computer.
- Second-generation computers used transistors for processing. These decreased the cost and size of this equipment and also increased speed and dependability. However, only one job could be done at a time. Software was written in assembly language. Data were first processed offline, away from computers. Batch processing also was started at this time.
- Third-generation computers used integrated circuits for processing. High-level languages were introduced. Operating systems were developed to control the computer's resources. This allowed online data activity. The need for computing power in smaller businesses led to the development of minicomputers.
- Computers became even smaller and more powerful during the fourth generation. Many integrated circuits were combined on a microprocessor, the basis for microcomputer processing power.
- Personal productivity software developed during the fourth generation. This allowed people to use computers for personal applications. Fourth-generation languages (4GLs or application generators) allowed nonprofessionals to program computers.
- Fifth generation computers will use artificial intelligence (AI) software to simulate human thought. Computer systems may be able to accept spoken input, do language translations, and be self-programming. Hardware will run under parallel processing systems.

TERMS TO REMEMBER

application generator
artificial intelligence (AI)
assembly language
batch processing
binary code
bit
card punch
card reader
chip
fourth-generation language (4GL)
hardware
heuristic
high-level language
integrated circuits
keypunch
machine language
mainframe
microcomputer
microprocessor
minicomputer
multiprogramming
offline
online
operating systems
parallel processing
personal productivity software
software
supercomputer

INFORMATION TECHNOLOGY PIONEERS

Blaise Pascal
Charles Babbage
L.F. Menabrea
Ada Lovelace
George Boole
Joseph Marie Jacquard
Herman Hollerith
Howard G. Aiken
John W. Mauchley
J. Presper Eckert
Grace Hopper
Adele Goldstein
John V. Atanasoff
Clifford Berry
John von Neumann
William Shockley
John Bardeen
Walter Brattain
Seymour Cray
Steve Jobs
Steve Wozniak

CHECK YOUR UNDERSTANDING

1. Next to each type of processing equipment, put a number (1, 2, 3, or 4) to show the generation of computers to which it belongs.
   ___ integrated circuit
   ___ microprocessor
   ___ transistor
   ___ vacuum tube
2. __________ invented accounting machines that used punched cards to analyze the 1890 U.S. Census.
3. Input and output operations performed away from the computer are called __________.
4. Which programming language first used abbreviations to represent binary code?
   a. machine language
   b. FORTRAN
   c. nonprocedural language
   d. assembly language
   e. 4GL
5. Processing data in groups to keep the computer busy is called __________.
6. Microcomputer is another name for an integrated circuit wafer. (True/False)
7. Number these computers in order (1 to 4) from the smallest (1) to largest (4).
   ___ mainframe
   ___ microcomputer
   ___ supercomputer
   ___ minicomputer
8. Which of the following is not a type of personal productivity software?
   a. database program
   b. electronic spreadsheet
   c. graphics package
   d. operating system
   e. word processor

9. __________ is the ability of a computer to run several programs concurrently.
10. An application generator allows users to specify program requirements with easy-to-use commands. (True/False)

APPLYING WHAT YOU'VE LEARNED

1. Pick one of the historical figures mentioned in the text or another person important to the development of computer technology. Research his or her life and contributions to computer technology. Write a short paper on your findings. (*Note*: Some of the people mentioned in this chapter are still alive and involved with computers.)
2. Many companies besides IBM and Apple got into the computer business. Some have expanded their involvement. Others have dropped out of the computer business. Still others develop only specialized computer-related equipment. Investigate one of these companies and write a report on that company's involvement with computers and what the organization is doing presently. Some companies to consider are: IBM, Apple, RCA, General Electric, Radio Shack, AT&T, Commodore, UNISYS, Honeywell, and many of the typewriter/business/copying machine companies.
3. Although women were some of the first computer programmers, there are, today, far fewer women than men in high technology development. In fact, there are more boys than girls in elective grade school computer classes. In some areas the proportions are slowly improving. What do you think contributes to this lack of female interest in computers? What could be done about it at the grade school level? High school? College? Workplace?
4. One of the factors influencing computer power and reliability throughout history has been processing hardware: vacuum tubes, transistors, integrated circuits, and microprocessors. Talk to a technician who has worked with early components in television sets, radios, or computers. Or research these components in literature. Find out the advantages and disadvantages of each component type. How difficult was troubleshooting? How easy was repair and/or replacement? What kind of training was required?
5. Many innovations in computer technology were developed at universities under federal funding and at businesses with government defense contracts. Do you feel that government should keep a financial hand in technology development? Why or why not? Should financial support like this be increased? Who should own the patents and rights to these inventions—the universities and businesses, the government, or the inventors themselves?
6. It is said that if people don't learn from history they are doomed to repeat it. Babbage's failure to complete his designs and Atanasoff's lack of public recognition may have deterred the pace of computer development. Are there problems you see with the computer industry today that may be slowing down the development of computer technology?
7. Throughout history, the trend in computer technology has been toward smaller, faster, more powerful, and more reliable equipment. Imagine yourself in the year 2010. How can you see computers affecting your life then?

CHECK YOUR UNDERSTANDING ANSWERS

1. 3 (integrated circuit), 4 (microprocessor), 2 (transistor), 1 (vacuum tube)
2. Herman Hollerith
3. offline
4. d
5. batch
6. false
7. 3 (mainframe), 1 (microcomputer), 4 (supercomputer), 2 (minicomputer)
8. d
9. multiprogramming
10. true

C H A P T E R

T H R E E

WHAT IS A COMPUTER SYSTEM?

KEY IDEAS

- **From the user's point of view**
  Every solution to a computer–related problem consists of five components. What are these five components and why is each one important?
- **People**
  People build and control computers to solve problems and to support decision making.

  Computer users
  For users, computers provide information to solve problems.

  Computer professionals
  These specialists operate computer equipment or develop new computer systems.
- **Hardware**
  Hardware comes in many sizes and with a wide range of capabilities.
- **Software**
  Computer hardware follows instructions provided by a computer program when processing or retrieving data.

  System software
  Operating systems and other system software oversee the computer's memory and the transfer of data.

  Application software
  Informed users utilize application software to improve their personal productivity.
- **Data**
  Data represent facts about people, things, ideas, and events.

  Types of data
  Computers work with numeric data, text, and even physical data from the environment.

  The value of data
  Data must be accurate and input correctly in order to produce desired results.
- **Procedures**
  Procedures guide people in learning to use a computer system.

  Operating procedures
  People use procedures to show them how to use equipment and programs.

FROM THE USER'S POINT OF VIEW

You will find computers come in many makes, models, and sizes—from processors the size of your fingernail, to desk–top microcomputers, to mainframes that occupy entire rooms. It may be surprising to discover that computer equipment is only part of a ***computer system***. A system is a collection of elements that work together to solve a specific problem. Regardless of size, every computer needs other components to produce results. The components of a computer system are:

- People
- Hardware
- Software
- Data
- Procedures

These components are integral to every computer system. Every time you use a computer to generate information, you become one of the five system components.

FIGURE 3.1

Convenience from computers in services such as this computer-controlled gasoline pump results from integrated systems that involve people, data, hardware, software, and procedures.

Courtesy of Figgie International, Inc.

PEOPLE

Computer systems are developed for people. People build and control computer systems to help them make decisions and solve problems. The components of a computer system are brought together by people. These people fall into two categories:

- Users
- Computer professionals

Both groups are necessary for a computer system to function.

Computer Users

Users are the driving force behind the development of computer systems. The user must identify problems, then direct the computer system to produce information that supports a solution. People's demands for answers and assistance pull technological development forward.

A computer user applies information produced by a computer. Users include anyone who receives a bill from the telephone company, withdraws money through an automatic teller machine, or listens to synthesized music. At times, you may become a computer user by circumstance rather than by choice. For example, choosing an outside activity according to the weather report is an action that depends on a computer. Weather forecasts result from computer analysis of weather data. Indirectly, the computer influences your decision. In many situations like this, you are a user, but not by direct choice. However, you can choose whether or not you will be an ***informed user***.

Informed users understand how the components of a computer system work together to perform a task. They know what a computer can and cannot do. Most important, informed users can apply computer output to their benefit, and to the benefit of others.

FIGURE 3.2
People are the key to the development and use of computer systems.

Users working in large organizations typically rely on computer professionals to deliver the results of computer processing. The users' responsibilities in these situations are to communicate their needs clearly to the professionals. Increasingly, however, users in all types of jobs are satisfying their computer needs on their own through ***end-user computing***. This implies that the user is responsible for data entry, computer operations, and utilization of the resulting output. Many of these people go on to become ***user-developers***, who design and write their own computer programs. As a result, they have been able to meet their own processing needs with minimal aid from computer professionals.

Computer Professionals

People who work directly with the development and operation of computer technology are called ***computer professionals***. Some examine user needs to help design computer-assisted solutions. Others operate the computer equipment. Still other computer professionals manage all computer acquisition and activity in an organization. The career opportunities for computer professionals are in systems development, operations, and management.

FIGURE 3.3
Systems analysts observe existing systems and determine user needs as a basis for improving methods or creating new procedures.

Systems Development

Systems analysts work with users to develop computer systems that satisfy specific requirements. They are the link between users in everyday situations and the technical world of computers.

Systems analysts must have excellent communication skills. They need these skills to convey the capabilities of computer systems to users. In addition, good communication helps a systems analyst determine what users really need and want from systems. Users, too, must have good communication skills in order to express their needs as clearly and completely as possible. Users describe what they need to an analyst, who coordinates the development of a new system. In this way, users and systems analysts work together to build effective computer systems.

FIGURE 3.4

Programmers create and review massive system documentation as a basis for their work in modifying existing programs or developing new systems.

Photo courtesy of Liane Enkelis

Programmers work less with people and more with machines. Their duties include writing and testing instructions for the computer. To accomplish this, they first determine which processing functions must be performed. Then, they construct a sequence of computer operations that fulfill those functions and code the operations in a programming language. Finally, they run tests to check the program for errors in logic or coding.

Sometimes, instead of generating new programs, programmers adapt existing programs to meet new needs. Program revisions are often made to bring applications into compliance with changing laws or company policies. People just entering the computer profession often start out as maintenance programmers. The responsibilities of the position familiarize them with a company's standard procedures and policies "on the job," as they modify working programs. In fact, 50 to 75 percent of the life-long cost of a program is for its maintenance.

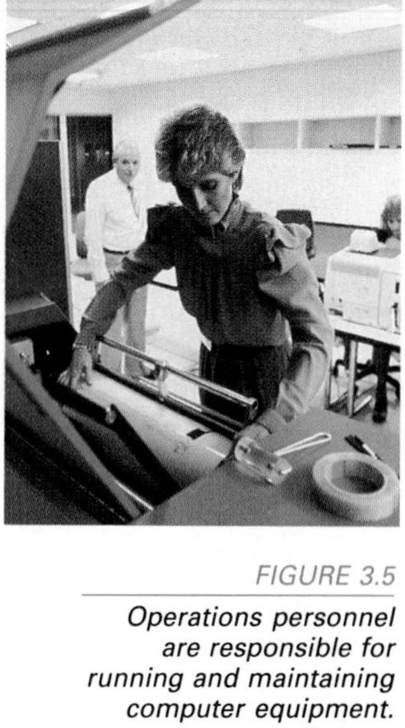

FIGURE 3.5

Operations personnel are responsible for running and maintaining computer equipment.

Operations

Operations personnel are responsible for the daily IPOS cycles within a computer center. In addition, they must know how to respond to emergencies that may stop the cycle. Operations personnel work at several different levels of responsibility: data entry, computer operations, and control of computer center equipment and output.

The work performed by operations personnel follows the IPOS cycle common to all computer systems. Clerks supply data to data entry operators, who input the data into the computer. Computer operators ensure that all equipment is functioning properly and set up storage devices and printers. Final output is given back to the clerk, who delivers the information to the appropriate users. Thus, the IPOS cycle is reflected in the tasks of operations personnel.

Management

In any organization that uses a computer system, the ***computer center manager*** is ultimately responsible for ensuring that the computer resources are used effectively.

FIGURE 3.6

The computer center manager is ultimately responsible for the timely and correct completion of every data processing job.

This means coordinating employees so that computing jobs are completed on schedule and within budget. Managers also analyze computer operations to detect inefficiencies or opportunities for improvement. In some organizations, computer center managers work closely with top-level management on plans and decisions concerning computer resources and company operations.

Managers often are promoted from related jobs within the company. In addition to job experience, managers usually need an advanced education in the computer field. Good communication skills are vital. Managers must be able to instruct and oversee employees working under them, and also to explain computer operations to company executives.

People—whether they are users, analysts, programmers, operators, or managers—all work together to make a computer system function properly. At times, one person may perform several jobs. With a home computer system, one person does everything. Usually several people are involved with a computer system. For the successful operation of that system, coordination of effort is imperative.

STUDY QUESTIONS

1. Define informed user, end-user computing, and user-developer.
2. What are the five components of a computer system?
3. What career options are available to computer professionals?
4. Identify the responsibilities of the following jobs: systems analyst, programmer, and computer center manager.

HARDWARE

The second computer system component, hardware, comes in several varieties, depending on what the computer system is designed to do. Hardware can fill

FIGURE 3.7

Portable terminals bring computer hardware capabilities to any location where people work.

several floors of a large office building or can fit on top of your desk. Different types of hardware are used for each step of the IPOS cycle:

- Input hardware. Input hardware is used to enter data into the computer. A keyboard at the ticket outlet where you reserve seats for a basketball game is a type of input hardware. The checker who slides your groceries over a scanner to record a sale uses another type of input hardware. Even restaurants are beginning to use input devices. A waiter or waitress can enter your order directly into a hand-held device. The device sends the data into a computer that coordinates cooking time, prints the bill, checks food inventories, and reorders stock.
- Processing hardware. The computer itself is processing hardware. A computer is composed primarily of a memory unit and a processing unit. A memory unit, or ***memory***, provides temporary storage for input data, programs, and results of processing. The processing unit, or ***processor***, interprets the program instructions in memory, controls the flow of data into and out of memory, and performs arithmetic and logic operations. The processor fetches the program instructions one at a time, along with any needed data. When that instruction is complete, results are sent to the memory and the next instruction is brought in. This cycle continues until the program is completed. Processing hardware can be as small as an embedded computer or as large as a supercomputer.

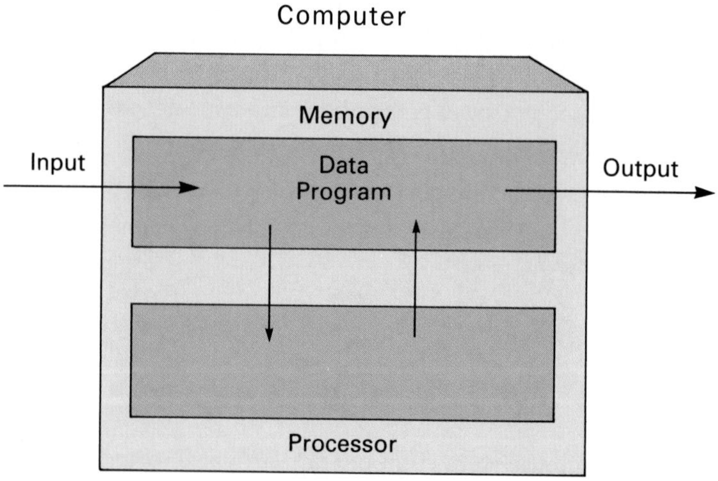

FIGURE 3.8

A computer is a piece of processing hardware. Using the program and data in memory, the processor performs calculations and comparisons that result in the final output.

Common Computer Hardware

Input Hardware
- Keyboard
- Scanner

Processing Hardware (contains memory and processor)
- Embedded Computer
- Microcomputer
- Minicomputer
- Mainframe Computer
- Supercomputer

Output Hardware
- VDT (video display terminal)
- Printer

Storage Hardware
- Tape Drives
- Disk Drives

FIGURE 3.9

A computer configuration includes input, processing, output, and storage hardware.

- Output hardware. Output hardware provides processed information to the user. The two primary forms of output hardware are ***video display terminals (VDTs)*** and ***printers***. VDTs hold information on a screen for temporary use. Directory assistance operators, for instance, enter a name into a computer, which displays the telephone number on a VDT. On the other hand, printers deliver copies of output on paper for long-term use. Printed outputs include report cards and bills.
- Storage hardware. Since the computer's memory has only a limited capacity for holding data, storage hardware is needed. Storage hardware is made up primarily of ***tape drives*** and ***disk drives***. These devices are used to retain large amounts of data on tape or disk for later use. Computer systems are much like stereo systems in this regard. In both systems, when the machinery is not in use, the music or the data must be stored on tapes or disks. There also are similarities in the storage media. Both music and data can be stored magnetically on reel-to-reel tapes or cassette tapes. However, the analogy stops here. Floppy disks (diskettes) or hard disks are not at all like record albums that store music. Floppy disks are flexible plastic platters with a special metal-oxide recording surface stored inside a protective cover. Hard disks are just that, metal platters coated with the same type of recording surface as diskettes. Hard disks usually hold more data and are more expensive than floppy disks. In addition, hard disk drives have faster access to the data on disk than do diskettes.

FIGURE 3.10

Hard disk drives store data permanently and allow users direct access to a wide variety of information.

Photo courtesy of L.A. Schwaber-Barzilay

Thus, each step of the cycle—input, processing, output, and storage—has an accompanying set of hardware. Traditionally, the equipment used for processing is called the computer. Online equipment used for storing, entering, and outputting data are generally referred to as ***peripherals***.

STUDY QUESTIONS

5. Describe the function of: memory, processor, video display terminal (VDT), printer, tape drive, disk drive, and peripheral.
6. Name one type each of input hardware, processing hardware, output hardware, and storage hardware.

SOFTWARE

Software is the third computer system component. Software instructs the hardware how to conduct processing. The computer is merely a general-purpose machine that requires specific programs to perform a given task. Computers can input, calculate, compare, and output data as information. Software determines the order in which these operations are performed. Like data, programs are stored on tape or disk. Storage hardware reads the instructions into the computer's memory. The programs then direct processing. Programs usually fall into one of two categories:

- System software
- Application software

System Software

An operating system controls computer activity with ***system software***. This collection of programs aids in the operation of a computer regardless of the application that is being used. When a computer is first turned on, one of the system programs is ***booted***, or loaded, into the computer's memory. This software contains information about memory capacity, the model of the processor, the disk drives to be used, and the model of the printer.

System programs are designed to work with specific pieces of hardware. These programs coordinate peripheral hardware and computer activities. For example, microcomputers primarily use disks for storing data and programs. Therefore, microcomputer users initially use a disk with the ***disk operating system (DOS)*** to boot their equipment. When the computer is turned on, one system program from the DOS disk is loaded into memory. As the user works with the

FIGURE 3.11

Before turning on a computer, the DOS disk with system software must first be in a disk drive. Loading the system software first allows it to control internal operations and support application software.

FIGURE 3.12

Users today can select from a variety of application software available at local stores.

Photo courtesy of Liane Enkelis

computer, whether it is a micro or mainframe, DOS will transfer input from keyboard to memory, then from memory to storage, and allocate storage space on disks for data files. Many of the services provided by DOS are transparent to users; that is, the services are performed without users being aware of this support.

Application Software

Application programs are sets of instructions used to solve specific processing problems. Common applications for programs found in many organizations include payroll, accounting, inventory, budgeting, and personnel management.

Personal productivity programs are another type of application software. Often, personal productivity software is sold in packages that contain the program itself, operating instructions, and a user's manual. The most popular packages available include:

- ***Word-processing programs*** expedite report and letter writing. Typically, word-processing programs enable the user to insert, move, copy, and erase words on screen. Upon request, the programs will center headings and number pages, among other capabilities.
- ***Electronic spreadsheet*** software creates documents that organize financial data into columns and rows for processing and analysis. The software formats data and also performs arithmetic operations or complicated formulas. Thus, electronic spreadsheets are valuable as a time-saving tool.
- ***Graphics packages*** generate pictures, drawings, charts, and diagrams on a screen or paper. Some graphics software is guided by information produced from electronic spreadsheets. Numbers from the spreadsheet can be used to

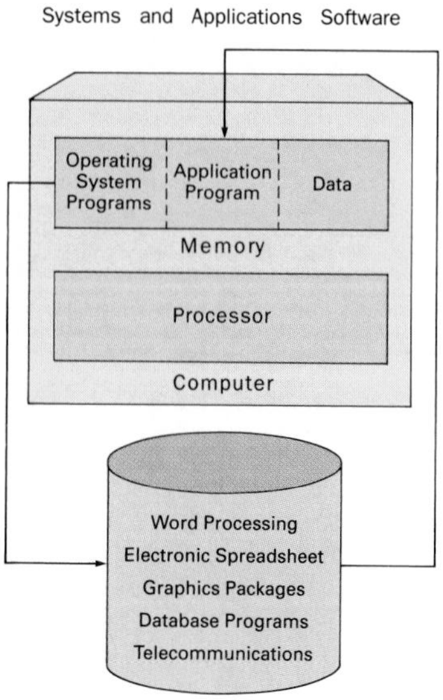

FIGURE 3.13

Systems software controls the flow of applications software and data in and out of the computer's memory.

draw bars on a graph, points on a diagram, or slices of a pie. Other graphics software enable users to draw pictures. The screen becomes an empty canvas and the keyboard becomes a paintbrush. Most packages even let the user select the size of paintbrush to be used. Graphics software often enables users to select shades and colors for the drawings. Specially equipped printers can "paint" the computer-created drawings on paper.

- ***Telecommunications software*** links computers together through telephone networks. As a result, computer literate librarians in Kalamazoo can be linked to computers at the Library of Congress in Washington, D.C. By entering the Library of Congress computer's telephone number, the telecommunications software can call Washington, D.C., connect the two computers, and pass data back and forth.
- One type of software that sets up data for computer processing is called a ***database program***. Database programs assist users in assembling data to answer questions and solve problems. Database software provides capabilities for loading and modifying databases. These packages enable users to extract, format, and report pertinent data with ease. A school's registrar, for example, could request information from a database instead of sifting through piles of student records. The registrar might ask such questions as: How many sophomores are enrolled in Calculus II? How many science majors have a GPA exceeding 3.5? Which classes still have empty seats? Within minutes, a database program could provide lists of students or classes meeting the specified conditions. Building or using a database requires an understanding of the many ways in which data interrelate and how the data can be used.

STUDY QUESTIONS

7. Define boot and disk operating system (DOS).
8. What are three functions of system software?
9. Describe the difference between system software and application software.
10. Describe the functions of these application programs: word processing, electronic spreadsheet, graphics, telecommunication, and database.

DATA

FIGURE 3.14

Driver's license testing and vehicle registration are supported by large computer systems in most states.

The fourth component of a computer system, data, represents facts about people, things, ideas, and events. For example, contact lenses, glue, indigestion, brown hair, motor oil, and six feet tall all are items of data. Taken individually, they have little significance. However, when data are combined and processed to form information, these items have meaning for people. From the above list, contact lenses, brown hair, and six feet tall can be extracted. Combined on a driver's license, these data items could form a partial description of your brother.

The most basic unit of data is the ***character***, represented by a letter, number, or symbol. A related group of characters is referred to as a data item, or ***field***. A related group of fields is known as a ***record***. Records that have a commonality of meaning are grouped together to form a ***file***. To understand these relationships, consider your brother's driver's license application. The license application number, V8051337, is a field made up of numeric and alphabetic characters. Sometimes

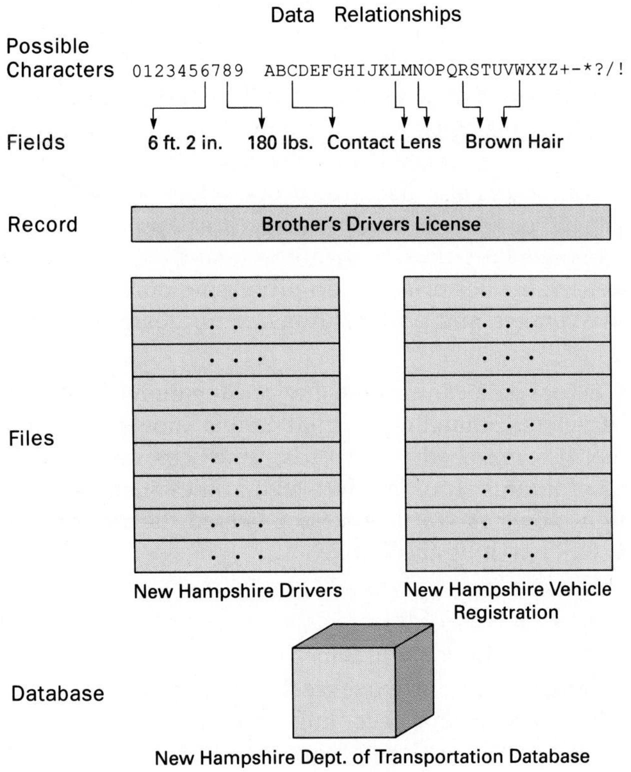

FIGURE 3.15

Relationships among data items are recorded and implemented through the use of computer database designs.

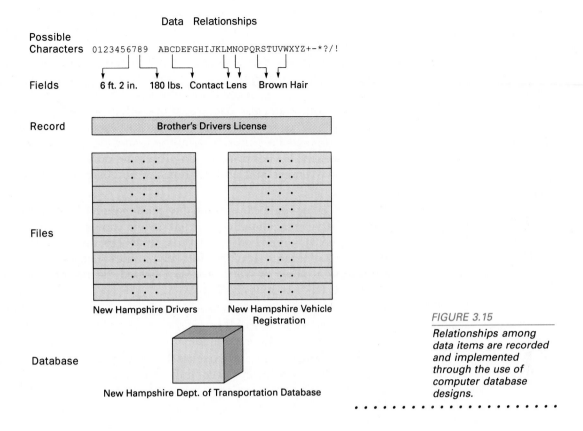

a single character, such as "M" or "F"—indicating the sex of the driver—can be used as a field. Additional fields hold data about physical descriptions, including need for corrective lenses, hair color, height, and weight. Taken separately, each field conveys little information. When the fields are combined into a record, a driver's license, their relationships become apparent. In this case, the record provides information about the driver's identity and appearance.

When several driver's licenses are brought together, they can be analyzed to produce even more information. For example, examination of all licenses in New Hampshire can show how many drivers in the state are over 21 years old. This collection of licenses—or records—constitutes a file. A file groups similar records that can be associated to increase knowledge. Additional information can be obtained by processing the related records as a file. At times, people must use several files to meet their information needs.

Information contained in one file often pertains to information in several other files. Computer systems permit access to a wide range of files. Systems allow people to share, modify, and manipulate files to increase knowledge. Cross-referencing files is made easier with the aid of a database program. Users of databases are able to access information selectively, on the basis of their specific needs.

Types of Data

A computer can process data only if they are in a machine-readable form. In other words, computers must be able to interpret the data that are input. An example of machine-readable data is the bar code found on many grocery store items. A computer scanner at the check-out stand reads the widths and spacing of the bars to

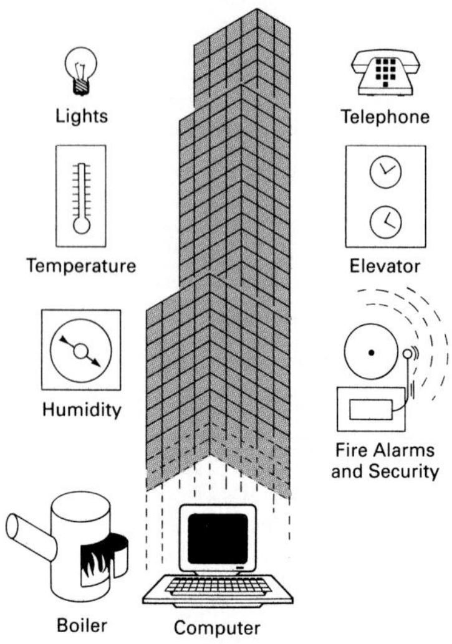

FIGURE 3.16

Data representing physical events or environmental conditions are integrated to provide vital services in large buildings or major real estate complexes.

identify the product. Various input devices are used to convert the following types of data into machine-readable form:

- Numeric. Numeric data consist of numbers and decimal points, as well as symbols such as the plus (+) and minus (-) signs. Arithmetic operations performed on numeric data include addition, subtraction, multiplication, and division. Computers also use logical operations to compare two numbers, determining if they are equal, or if one is greater than or less than the other. An electronic spreadsheet uses both numeric and textual data. However, a spreadsheet's value lies primarily in processing numeric data. Spreadsheets can figure averages and add columns of numbers with great speed and accuracy.
- Textual. Textual data can contain any combination of letters, numbers, and special characters. Sometimes textual data is known as ***alphanumeric data***. Usually, text is organized into words, sentences, and paragraphs. Word-processing programs accommodate textual files such as the words you are reading right now. A word processor helped the authors add, move, and delete text while writing this book.
- Physical. Physical data are captured from the environment. For example, light, sound, voice, temperature, and pressure all are types of physical data. The temperature of the room in which you are sitting may be controlled by a computer. A thermostat is set to sense the air temperature. When the temperature exceeds a specified level, a cooling system is turned on. The warmth of the air is used as physical data input into a thermostat to regulate room temperature. In many large buildings, computer systems process several kinds of physical data to regulate operations. Computers can set off security alarms, control temperature and humidity, or turn lights on and off, all in response to physical data. These applications increase people's safety and save them time and money.

Stored data are organized according to their use. Some files are very rigidly organized, while others are largely unstructured. Numeric data can be arranged into uniform fields and records to expedite processing. Thus, numeric files tend to be highly structured. Text files, on the other hand, are not suited to predetermined structures. Word, sentence, and paragraph lengths cannot be known before the text is actually written. A key feature of word processing is the ability to be flexible in adding and editing text.

The Value of Data

Complete and correct data are essential to the successful completion of the IPOS cycle. Computers have impressive capabilities, but they do not have intuition or judgment. Data-entry personnel must check the correctness and completeness of input data. Accurate results depend on accurate input. This notion is the basis for what computer professionals refer to as ***GIGO***: "Garbage in, garbage out."

As data are accumulated and transformed into information, they become a valuable product in their own right. People use computers to obtain information, and the foundation of information is data. Without data, many human and organizational functions would be stymied. If your school lost all its student records, you would have a difficult time proving you completed required courses. If your bank's data files were destroyed, there would be no record of your money holdings. All your savings could be lost. As you can see, collections of data are major assets in large organizations and for individuals.

FIGURE 3.17

Data are such important assets to this organization that they are stored in a fire-proof tape library.

STUDY QUESTIONS

11. Define character, field, record, file, alphanumeric data, and GIGO.
12. Describe the three types of data.
13. What two characteristics must data have for successful completion of the IPOS cycle?

PROCEDURES

Procedures are the final component of a computer system. They are systematic courses of action that help people use software, data, and equipment. Procedures identify what needs to be done and how to do it. They also help new users to understand how to work with computer systems.

A typical set of procedures for a processing session might include:

- Flipping the computer switch to the on position
- Booting a microcomputer by loading systems software into the computer's memory
- Using the disk operating system (DOS) to format a new disk
- Verifying the correctness of data
- Inputting data or text material completely and correctly
- Saving the input on the formatted disk
- Copying disk files onto a second disk
- Loading and running application programs
- Preparing the printer for output
- Distributing outputs to authorized parties
- Turning off the computer

FIGURE 3.18

Procedures direct the activities of people who operate computers and use systems.

CLIP

THE WELL-TRAVELED COMPUTER

Do you know the three things you should never do when traveling with a computer? Could you get help with a software or hardware problem on a vacation a thousand miles from home? Will moving your hard disk destroy the valuable data on it?

Whether you're carrying a featherweight laptop on your vacation or you're moving a big-iron desktop system across the country, learning the answers to these questions, together with a few simple tips, can save you from disaster and make traveling with your micro or moving it a pleasant experience.

Get It Ready

Before you pack your computer, you need to get it ready for its move. The first order of business is to back up all your data. If the computer has a hard disk, make sure all the important information is copied to floppies. If you have a laptop with volatile RAM storage, save the contents to a safer medium.

If you have a desktop with an old hard disk, it's a good idea to run a program to park the heads before you move the computer. If you have a newer hard disk or a portable with a hard disk, the chances are that it automatically parks its heads when the power is turned off.

Floppy disk drives need some attention, too. When you received your computer, each floppy disk drive probably came with a cardboard head protector inserted in the disk's place. If you saved these, insert one into each drive and close the door.

One last prepacking chore: It may be worth your while to check your insurance policy. Is your computer covered if it's stolen or damaged during your trip? Does your policy have any special restrictions?

Pack It Up

Packing is next, with the emphasis on protection. If you're moving a desktop system, pack it in its original cartons, filling any open spaces with wadded newspaper or packing popcorn.

If you're carrying a laptop with you, the theme should be to dress it down, making it as inconspicuous as possible. An expensive-looking case may tempt a thief.

In addition to your computer, you'll need to carry some extras. If you're a laptop user, you have the biggest packing list. First and foremost, you'll need batteries, an AC adapter, and a recharger—if your computer uses one. If you're traveling abroad, a transformer is a necessity. If your computer is going to be a working partner on your sojourn, you'll want to make sure you have all the software you'll need, and backups of your important programs. Extra disks—more than you think you'll need—are also a must.

Perhaps the most important item on the packing list of desktop movers and laptop luggers should be documentation for hardware and software. No matter how familiar you are with your tools, don't deny yourself the comfort of having manuals close at hand.

Laptop users should consider the peripherals they'll need on their trip. It's frustrating to be a thousand miles from home and discover that you need a printer or a second disk drive. If you'll be transferring files from your machine to another computer, you'll need a null modem and cable, and you may need some translation or transfer software. Take time to think through your requirements. Try to be prepared. For example, if you're taking a printer, carry extra paper and ribbons. Whatever you decide to take, *don't forget to pack the cables.*

Arrange It

Next, a few arrangements are in order. An important consideration for laptop travelers is communications. Don't forget your modem, if it's external, and, for a long trip, consider a subscription to a nationwide information service like Compu-Serve, The Source, or GEnie. And don't forget to carry any necessary phone numbers or access codes with you.

With the arrangements made, your computer packed or bagged, you're ready to hit the road. For those moving a desktop system, most of the work has been done. You can sit back, enjoy the trip, and look forward to unpacking your system at its destination. For lap-top users, things are just beginning. These three important *don'ts* cover most of the bases:

- Don't leave your laptop where it will be exposed to extreme temperatures—LCDs are sensitive to wide thermometer swings.
- Don't leave you laptop lying unguarded on a table somewhere—the screen might as well be blinking *Take me, I'm yours!*
- And finally, don't let strangers play with your computer—a few keystrokes in the wrong places can zap hours of work.

Source: Courtesy of *Compute*, Clifton Karnes

Key Question: What should you never do when travelling with a computer?

Operating Procedures

Anyone owning or operating a small computer must follow procedures. Before a computer can be put to work, ***operating procedures*** are used to turn on the machine. Locating, copying, and erasing files on a diskette all require operating procedures for proper execution.

Whatever size computers are used, procedures exist. First of all, users need ***data entry procedures***, which describe the preparation and input of data. Included in data entry procedures would be a manual check of data before entry to ensure they are accurate and complete. The term ***verification*** is used when the data entry operator takes responsibility for checking data for errors. The data should be verified after they are entered. Computer programs are also written that check for errors as part of data entry procedures; this is called ***editing***. For example, the data entry operator verifies that every address has a corresponding zip code, while a computer program edits the telephone number field by checking for nonnumeric characters.

Error recovery procedures are adopted for confronting and eliminating processing errors. Technicians follow ***preventive maintenance procedures*** for cleaning equipment and running checks on computer circuitry. Preventive maintenance procedures help keep the computer in good operating condition. A task as simple as cleaning a computer keyboard should be regarded as an important procedure. Another maintenance procedure is cleaning the disk drive's read/write heads, which input and output disk-stored data. Printers, too, must be cleaned regularly.

In addition, informed users and operators should follow ***backup procedures*** to protect their computer files. By backing up, or copying, data and information onto an auxiliary disk, users minimize the possibility of losing data.

FIGURE 3.19

Data entry is a fast-paced job that requires established procedures to achieve high volume coupled with accuracy.

Photo courtesy of Liane Enkelis

Emergency Procedures

Emergency procedures prepare users to handle a computer ***crash***, or failure. These procedures may enable people to recover important data and start the system working again. Often, standardized emergency procedures are included in com-

FIGURE 3.20

Extensive monitoring capabilities are built into large computer installations to keep track of equipment status and to avoid or deal with emergency situations.

Photo courtesy of Liane Enkelis

puter manuals. Many computer manufacturers have established hotlines at which experts staff phones to answer users' questions in the event of a crash.

To find the cause of a crash, people use ***troubleshooting procedures***. One of the most important troubleshooting procedures involves using ***diagnostic software*** to track down malfunctioning components in a computer. With diagnostic software, a user can detect and eliminate a problem in computer circuitry before more damage is done.

Procedures are essential to the upkeep of any computer system. The cost of implementing these procedures is dwarfed by the potential costs of repairing neglected systems.

STUDY QUESTIONS

14. Define verification, editing, crash, and diagnostic software.
15. What is included in each of these procedures: operating, data entry, error recovery, preventive maintenance, backup, emergency, troubleshooting?

CONCLUSION

Every computer system must contain five components in order to be complete. The people component encompasses anyone who ever uses computer-generated information, as well as those who make computers the focus of their profession. Hardware is needed to process the data, and software is needed to instruct the hardware. Computer systems are, of course, dependent on data, one of the most important assets an organization or individual can have. Finally, procedures must be established to deal with day-to-day processing, as well as emergency situations. People, hardware, software, data, and procedures thus work together to create an effective and efficient computer system.

CHAPTER FACTS

- A computer system is made up of five components: people, hardware, software, data, and procedures.
- People can be users or computer professionals. A user applies information produced by a computer. Informed users participating in end-user computing understand a computer's uses and limitations. User-developers can set up and program their own computers.
- Computer professionals work directly with computer technology. They can be involved with systems development, operations, or management.

FIGURE 3.21

Operation and use of computers centers around maintaining and following stored instructions and established procedures. All five components of a computer system are closely interrelated.

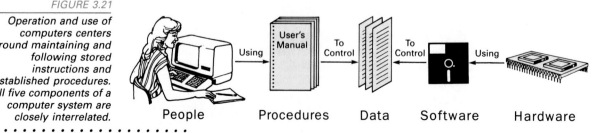

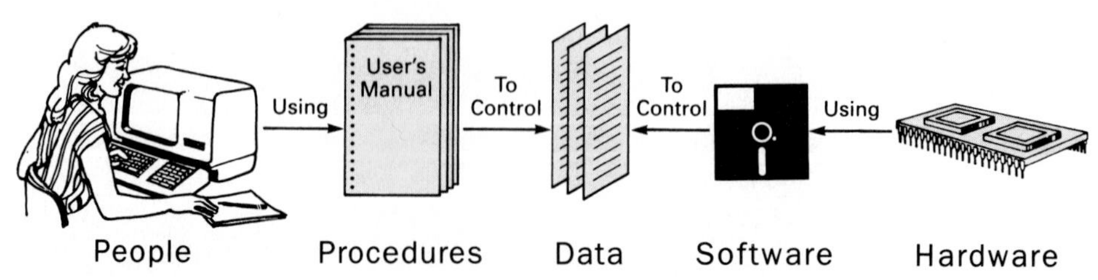

- Professionals who are a part of the systems development process include systems analysts, who relate users' problems to computer system solutions, and programmers, who write the instructions computers follow.
- Operations-oriented professionals enter data, operate peripheral equipment, oversee computer activities, or control the flow of data into and out of the computer center.
- Computer center managers supervise work and personnel in a computer center.
- Hardware is classified by the IPOS cycle. Input hardware may be a keyboard or scanner. Processing hardware consists of the memory unit and processing unit within all sizes of computers. Output hardware may be a VDT or printer. Storage hardware may be disk or tape drives.
- Software is divided into two categories: system software and application software. System software is the series of general programs that control the computer's resources. Application software solves specific user processing problems.
- Five common types of application software are: word processing, electronic spreadsheets, graphics packages, telecommunication software, and database programs.
- Data are organized into fields, which make up records. Records are combined into files. Related files may be organized into databases.
- There are three types of data: numeric, textual, and physical.
- Procedures are instructions to help people use data, software, and hardware. Procedures can concern data entry, error recovery, preventive maintenance, operating, backup, emergency, and troubleshooting.

TERMS TO REMEMBER

alphanumeric data
backup procedure
boot
character
computer center manager
computer professional
computer system
crash
database program
data entry procedures
diagnostic software
disk drive
disk operating system (DOS)
editing
electronic spreadsheet
emergency procedures
end-user computing
error recovery procedures
field
file
GIGO
graphics package
informed user
memory
operating procedures
operations personnel
peripheral
preventive maintenance procedures
printer
procedure
processor
programmer
record
system software
systems analyst
tape drive
telecommunications software
troubleshooting procedures
user-developer
verification
video display terminal (VDT)
word processing program

CHECK YOUR UNDERSTANDING

1. Which of the following is *not* a component of a computer system?
   a. hardware
   b. software
   c. data
   d. processing
   e. procedures
2. __________ links computers together through telephone networks.
3. A computer center manager is responsible for writing programs to run on new hardware. (True/False)
4. Which of the following is a general term for the online equipment used to input, output, and store data?
   a. console
   b. peripheral
   c. backup
   d. file
   e. procedure
5. A(n) __________ puts together the computer system components by helping to identify the needs of users.
6. Which of the following makes up a single record?
   a. a group of files
   b. a group of software
   c. a group of fields
   d. a group of databases
   e. a group of operations
7. The three types of data are number, textual, and __________.
8. The processor stores programs and data temporarily in the computer. (True/False)
9. A(n) __________ is a group of systems programs that controls the use of a computer's resources that depend on disk storage.
10. Which of the following is *not* a type of procedure used for work with computer systems?
    a. error recovery procedures
    b. operating system procedures
    c. backup procedures
    d. preventive maintenance procedures
    e. data entry procedures

APPLYING WHAT YOU'VE LEARNED

1. Pick three examples of computer systems you have seen in action. Identify what is involved in each of the five components of every system. If you are unsure of a component or the correct term to be used, describe what is included in that component.
2. Of the five components of a computer system, which do you feel is the most important? Why? Are there any situations in which one or more of the components could be omitted without affecting the system?
3. Find several ads for one of the computer professional positions mentioned in the text. Remember that the actual name of the position may be different. Summarize requirements for experience and education, as well as pay and benefits offered.

4. When incorrect output appears, or a computer system does not work properly, you'll often hear the excuse "The computer did it!" In light of GIGO, and the need for good procedures and well-trained people, what could be some possible causes of the following situations:
   a. You get a home telephone bill for $42,450.00.
   b. Your mother's plane reservation back from Bermuda is not on the airline computer; but she has a ticket.
   c. A five-item grocery bill on the store's computer does not agree with the amount you have on your calculator (and you're right!).
   d. When he applies for a loan, your brother is told he has a bad credit rating (but he's never applied for credit before).
5. Identify the content of the fields, records, and files for these applications:
   a. information about patients entering a hospital
   b. a university's collection of data about presently enrolled students
   c. the customer ordering system for a fast-food restaurant
6. Trouble comes when procedures are not written down or when they are ignored by people. Some people say, "If at first it doesn't work, then read the instructions." Make a list of essential procedures for one of these situations or one of your own choosing.
   a. using and maintaining a new car
   b. operating a special tool or piece of equipment you know how to use
   c. installing an electrical outlet or replacing a fuse
   d. cooking an involved or delicate dish like baked alaska or a soufflé

CHECK YOUR UNDERSTANDING ANSWERS

1. d
2. telecommunications software
3. false
4. b
5. systems analyst
6. c
7. physical
8. false
9. disk operating system (DOS)
10. b

UNIT TWO

COMPUTER TECHNOLOGY

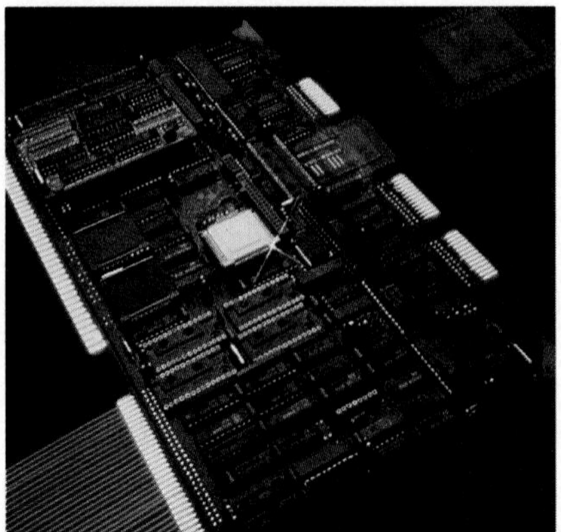

Unit II explores the internal workings of computer technology. Different types of processing hardware are presented in Chapter 4. Processing hardware ranges in power from single-purpose microcomputers to high-capacity mainframes and supercomputers. Characteristics of each type of processing hardware are discussed along with the problems they solve best. In addition, the chapter examines, from a user's point of view, the basic principles of electronic data processing common to every computer. ▸ Storing information for later retrieval is an important feature common to every computer system. Chapter 5 looks at how data are organized and stored on tape and disk. The related hardware and their basic operations for examining computers as problem-solving tools are discussed. Ways are presented in which data storage and retrieval are used to integrate information with technological solutions. ▸ The usefulness of computer-generated information is only as good as the input data and output formats. Since everyone's need for information varies, Chapter 6 examines different techniques for entering data into a computer system and the hardware involved. Output hardware also comes in diverse forms to support temporary and permanent information requirements. Together, input and output hardware represent a direct link between people and computer technology. ▸ Chapter 7 concludes this unit with an in-depth look at data communication applications and equipment. A mobile society requires that information travel with its members. For this reason, the chapter examines how processing power and information are distributed to users, no matter where they are.

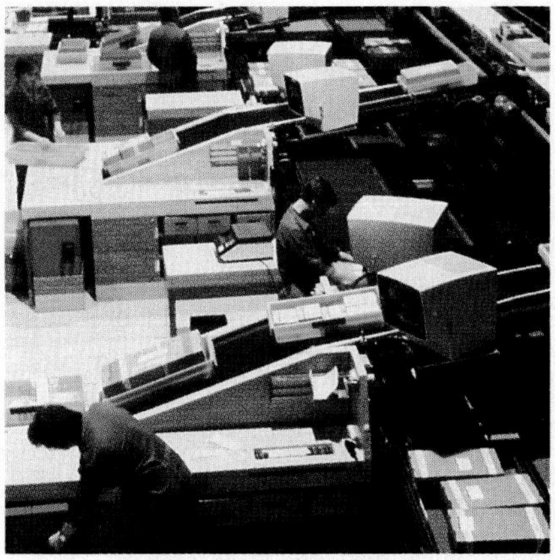

CHAPTER FOUR

PROCESSING HARDWARE: MICROCOMPUTERS TO MAINFRAMES

KEY IDEAS

- **From the user's point of view**
  Why do we need so many different kinds of computers? When and why would you use a mainframe? A minicomputer? A microcomputer? And other specialized processing hardware?

- **Expanding processing power**
  Computer processing power has grown continuously while costs have dropped.

  Real-time processing
  Users at remote sites enter data and receive results within time frames of routine transactions.

  Teleprocessing
  Communication lines connect remote terminals to a single computer.

  Distributed processing
  Processing power is delivered to users at remote sites through computers that communicate with each other.

  Multiprogramming and time-sharing
  These techniques permit multiple users and programs to share computer facilities.

  Multiprocessing
  Applications are executed concurrently among several computers.

- **Hardware to solve different problems**
  Hardware is classified by size, cost, storage, number of users, and processing power.

- **Binary codes for data and instructions**
  Computers use only data and instructions that are represented in binary coding by 1 or 0 bits.

- **The central processing unit**
  The CPU includes control, computation, and memory capabilities.

  The processor
  The processor performs arithmetic and control functions.

  Memory
  Data and programs are held in memory before and after processing.

FROM THE USER'S POINT OF VIEW

You are aware by now of the many kinds of processing hardware available. By connecting computers with each other and with specialized peripherals, a user can tailor a system to fit individual needs. Even if you never design a computer system, it is important that you be aware of the options available and of how the computer itself works. Like an automobile driver, it is not essential that you understand the internal workings of an engine, but this knowledge helps you know the limits of the vehicle and explain performance problems to technicians. Likewise, understanding the processing components of a computer helps you troubleshoot problems or, at least, adequately explain difficulties to a computer professional.

EXPANDING PROCESSING POWERS

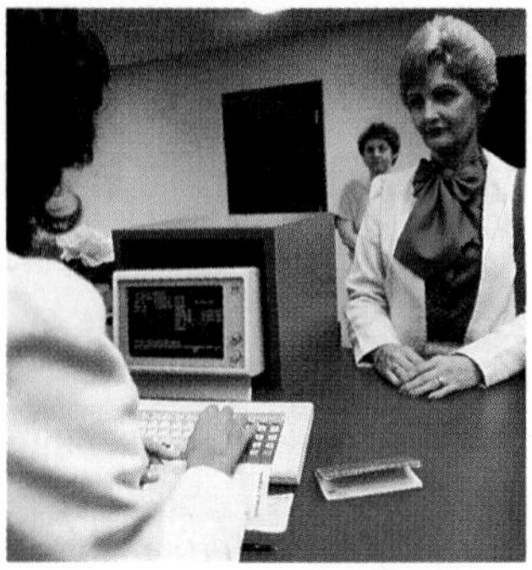

FIGURE 4.1
Real-time processing delivers results within the time frame of a normal transaction. Banking services demand real-time processing.

Photo courtesy of L.A. Schwaber-Barzilay

Present-day computers have fast processing speeds and a variety of capabilities. These powerful machines are solving an expanding array of problems as people customize computer systems for their own organizational needs. Users want computers to provide immediate information on demand. They need to distribute data across large geographic areas. Also, computers have to be able to handle several tasks concurrently. Online capabilities, which allow users to be in direct communication with the computer, have been expanded to provide solutions to these problems.

Real-Time Processing

One of the most significant computer advancements has been the availability of real-time processing. ***Real-time processing*** is a type of online application in which results are returned to users as soon as processing is complete. For example, suppose you open a new bank account with $2000 the morning you register and pay for classes. If the bank processes the deposit as part of a batch, your money may not be immediately available. Real-time processing allows the bank teller to update your record at the time you deposit the money. As a result, deposits made in the morning are immediately available to you through another real-time system, an automatic teller.

Real-time processing has allowed computers to monitor industrial processes. A paper mill uses real-time processing to control the mix of chemicals in paper production. The real-time processing system receives data from sensors that detect the acidity of the incoming wood pulp. This data influences how the wood pulp will be processed. Decisions affecting the chemical breakdown of the wood pulp are continuously being made as the input changes.

Teleprocessing

An important problem for many organizations is where processing power should lie when data are shared over a large geographic area. One popular solution is ***teleprocessing***. In a teleprocessing system, communication lines connect remote components to a single computer. Often, a computer disseminates information to terminals at several locations. A ***terminal*** is any device at the end of a communication line where data originates and information terminates. Usually, a terminal has a keyboard and a screen. Other remote hardware, such as disk drives, tape drives, sensors, or printers, may also be attached.

Consider the problems the airline companies would have without teleprocessing. Millions of people at thousands of locations need to reserve seats. Coordination of reservations needs to be centralized. Terminals at many travel agencies are linked, as part of a teleprocessing system, to one large computer. The computer keeps track of each ticket request and updates flight information on disk files. With real-time processing, travel agents can provide up-to-the-minute information on flight schedules. When they book seats on particular flights, that information is sent through communication lines and recorded immediately, in real time, to prevent overbooking.

Distributed Processing

Sometimes processing is more efficient if it takes place where the data are actually collected. Local processing reduces communication costs and gives users more

FIGURE 4.2

Teleprocessing capabilities allow users to communicate across large geographical areas.

Photo courtesy of Robert Koch

control over processing. For instance, individual auto parts stores in a franchise cannot keep parts for every make of car in stock at one time. To order more inventory, the store's computer can communicate with another computer located at the franchise's centralized warehouse. In addition, since stores are individually owned, each must keep its own financial records. In this case, the store can use its computer to track its own inventory and compute bills.

The auto parts store uses ***distributed processing***. A distributed processing system differs from a teleprocessing system in that it contains more than one computer, while a teleprocessing system depends on only one computer. Each computer in a distributed processing system is capable of processing local data and communicating with other remote computers in the system. This kind of system helps a chain of stores coordinate inventory while maintaining the autonomy of individual stores.

Multiprogramming and Time-Sharing

Large computers are often asked to perform several processing jobs at one time. Since modern computers perform operations with time to spare for most applications, the operating system can divide the computer's processing power among different applications and users. As a result, multiprogramming and time-sharing are two features that allow more than one user to take advantage of the computer's power.

As you may recall, multiprogramming is the ability of a computer system to handle several programs concurrently. Actually, each program is given a priority. The program with top priority is processed until the computer has to wait for input or output. Instead of standing idle, operating systems with multiprogramming capabilities shift to the program with the next highest priority. When the input/output for the first program is ready, the computer resumes processing the instructions from the top priority program.

For example, a business with a single computer may find that the computer is not utilized to its full capacity when order clerks use it to enter phone orders. However, with multiprogramming capabilities, the computer can work on weekly sales reports when no orders are coming in. Since the order-entry program has top

FIGURE 4.3

Large computers with timesharing capabilities allow students to share software and eliminate the need for personal disks to store data.

priority, the operating system will interrupt the report program and return to order entry when an operator begins to enter a new order.

Time-sharing is a special type of multiprogramming. Instead of one program getting special priority over others, time-sharing assigns each program a slice of time. The programs are then processed in a round-robin pattern. However, each user is served individually and is unaware that others are being served at the same time. Students using a university's main computer system find themselves in a room time-sharing the computer with dozens of other students. Since each student is given a time slice, it seems as if each has the computer to himself or herself.

Multiprocessing

Unlike time-sharing, ***multiprocessing*** enables complex applications to be executed simultaneously by linking two or more computers. Time-sharing uses only one computer, which alternates between programs. Multiprocessing is useful when processing needs fluctuate, sometimes requiring more resources than a single computer has available. This is common in intricate scientific applications.

During the launching of a space vehicle, a great deal of processing must occur at the same time. The computational power of many computer systems is needed and linked together through multiprocessing. Once the vehicle is safely in orbit, a single computer system can handle the routine operations. Multiprocessing is again necessary during special missions, such as space walks or scientific experiments. Teaming computers boosts the processing power of the entire system.

STUDY QUESTIONS

1. Define real-time processing, teleprocessing, terminal, distributed processing, time-sharing, and multiprocessing.

FIGURE 4.4

Space missions often use multiprocessing capabilities together with several computers working on the same complex application.

2. What are practical applications of real-time processing, teleprocessing, distributed processing, time-sharing, and multiprocessing?

HARDWARE TO SOLVE DIFFERENT PROBLEMS

Computers come in various sizes to solve all kinds of problems. Just as operating systems have capabilities that meet different problems, processing hardware also is diversified. In general, processing hardware is characterized by cost, size, storage capacity, number of users, and processing speed. In many cases, there is a considerable amount of overlap among groups. Three of the most commonly used sizes of computer hardware are:

- Mainframes
- Minicomputers
- Microcomputers

Mainframes

Mainframes are large, relatively expensive machines that offer extensive problem-solving capabilities. Mainframes can have memory capacities measured in billions of characters and more. The largest mainframes can process several million instructions per second, or ***MIPS***. Their operating systems usually handle time-sharing. Data storage is primarily on hard disks, with tapes used as backup. Mainframes serve as the heart of an entire system of computers. Minicomputers and microcomputers can be linked to mainframe computers as part of a distributed processing system, or the mainframe may act alone as a teleprocessing system. When a microcomputer is connected to a mainframe, it is often referred to as a ***workstation***. This distinction is made to differentiate between the processing hardware (microcomputer) connected to a mainframe and the mainframe itself.

FIGURE 4.5

Large mainframe systems are like information-processing factories that can handle the needs of hundreds of users.

Courtesy of Burroughs

Few individuals and medium-sized businesses require the massive processing capabilities offered by mainframes. These machines are used primarily by government organizations and big businesses. Such organizations have extensive processing needs, as well as the financial means, to purchase or lease costly mainframes. People use mainframes for very complex problems or large-volume jobs. Major banks can process bills for credit card holders all over the world with the aid of a mainframe. Insurance companies use mainframes to process millions of policies. Large research projects, such as the Strategic Defense Initiative (SDI), use the vast mainframe memory, storage capacities, and superfast processing speeds to conduct tests and coordinate operations. Thus, mainframes have met the hefty processing demands of larger organizations.

Minicomputers

The minicomputer is a scaled-down version of the mainframe. Both the processing power and cost of minicomputers are reduced. Yet minicomputers have larger memory sizes and faster processing speeds than microcomputers. They are well suited to the needs of small- and medium-sized organizations. Since minicomputer prices range from about $10,000 to several hundred thousand dollars, many smaller companies prefer to lease them.

FIGURE 4.6

A minicomputer can fill a large closet and serve up to one hundred users simultaneously.

Memory capacities in today's minicomputers are measured in millions of characters. Minis have fast processing speeds and operating systems with multiprogramming capabilities. They can be equipped with drives for floppy disks and tape, as well as for hard disks. Tapes and floppy disks are inexpensive media for backing up important data files and programs.

With minicomputers, more than just large organizations have access to computer problem-solving power. Data and information held in minicomputers are invaluable to researchers who need to locate pertinent facts quickly and easily. People who run small businesses use minicomputers for payroll processing and other business needs. The real-time monitoring of scientific equipment often is assigned to a minicomputer. Many organizations will use several minicomputers as a part of a distributed processing system instead of one mainframe. The advantage to this design is that all processing power is not dependent on a single machine.

Comparison of Microcomputer, Minicomputer, and Mainframe Computer Capabilities

	Cost	Size	Storage Capacity	Number of Users	Processing Speeds
Microcomputer	$100 to $10,000	Fit on desktop	64,000 to 16 million characters	1	60 to 1 million instructions per second
Minicomputer	$10,000 to $250,000	Fill a closet	4 million to 64 million characters	1 to 100	1 million to 5 million instructions per second
Mainframe Computer	$250,000 and more	Fill a room	32 million characters or more	1 to 1500	5 million or more instructions per second

FIGURE 4.7

A comparison of processing features from small microcomputers to large mainframes.

Microcomputers

Advancing computer technology has brought computers into the home, the schoolroom, and the workplace. Called home computers, personal computers, microcomputers, or micros, these machines are powerful, yet easy to operate. They are capable of performing many jobs once handled by only the largest computers. Purchase prices for micros range from $100 for home units to $5000 or more for professional models. A typical microcomputer memory unit stores from 64,000 to 16 million characters of data.

Microcomputers usually are equipped with keyboards for data entry and a VDT to display output. Cassette tape recorders or disk drives are used to store data. Some microcomputers, such as cash registers, are dedicated to one job. Others perform a variety of jobs directed by application programs. For instance, people use micros to play games, write letters, and keep accounts for a small business. Most micros have the capacity to perform only one job at a time, but do handle real-time processing.

Millions of people have used microcomputers to solve a wide range of problems and to increase their personal productivity. Software packages for micros work as personal assistants to users. Typically, they provide clocks, calendars, calculators, daily schedule reminders, and notepads, all brought to the screen by pressing a few keys.

As users have become more experienced with microcomputers, demands have grown. These demands have promoted the development of even more powerful microcomputers and the software to support them.

FIGURE 4.8

Microcomputers can handle the processing needs of a single user.

Computers for Special Problems

Sometimes microcomputers, minicomputers, and mainframes are not sufficient to handle special processing requirements for some users. As a result, newer and more specialized processing hardware has been developed. This includes:

- Embedded computers
- Supercomputers
- Fault-tolerant computers

Thinking of buying a computer through the mail? Here's a checklist of things to watch for.

• Compare Apples with Apples—or clones with clones. Make sure the price cited in the ad includes a monitor and keyboard in addition to the CPU (central processing unit). Does the price include one disk drive or two (or a hard disk)? A DOS (disk operating system) disk? How much RAM (random-access memory)—256K or the more desirable 640K? Some ads "sucker" buyers by quoting "box only" prices that will leave you with an incomplete system.

• How long has the outlet been around? It's best to go with an established firm, keeping in mind that in the PC business, two years is an eternity. Ask around among friends and associates for a reputable house, or go to the library and check out the ads in an old issue of BYTE or PC magazine.

• Be clear on return policies. Most outlets honor manufacturers' warranties, usually at least 90 days. But the better houses offer a no-risk, no-questions-asked return policy ranging from 10 days to a month or more. Ask who pays for return shipping. Make sure the return policy provides for a full refund (not just exchange) in case you want to back out entirely.

• Read the ad's fine print. Compare shipping and handling costs. Find out what those little asterisks next to quoted prices mean. You don't want any surprises when the bill comes.

• If you're buying a computer, find out whether it has been checked out for glitches. Have they done a 48-hour "burn-in" to test chips and circuitry (not a do-or-die requirement, but nice to have)? If you're buying a hard disk, is it formatted and ready to roll? Are appropriate cords and cables included with the system?

• What kind of support is offered? The better firms supply a toll-free hot line to answer technical questions. Give the hot line a call and see how often it's busy. If you can't get through, try someone else. Some houses also are offering on-site service through Xerox and other nationwide firms.

• How long will it take you to get your "new baby"? Some houses are offering overnight express delivery free of charge. Most others use UPS. When you order, ask whether they have the equipment in stock. If they don't, give them a cutoff date if you don't mind waiting. Otherwise, you could be in for a long siege.

• Where do you find these discount houses? The major computer magazines have dozens of ads. Computer Shopper, a fat tabloid sold primarily through newsstands, is another good source. On Sundays and Tuesdays, the New York Times runs most of the Big Apple's mail-order house ads.

• When you call to order, have your credit card ready to read off. Time is money to mail-order houses, and they don't want to wait while you fumble with your wallet. Once they've taken your card number and address and order, ask them to repeat the information back to you—especially the bottom line, final cost. If anything sounds wrong, back out! You can always go to the next house and order again tomorrow.

Source: Reprinted by permission, *San Jose Mercury News*

Key Question: Are there advantages, other than price, to ordering computer equipment by mail?

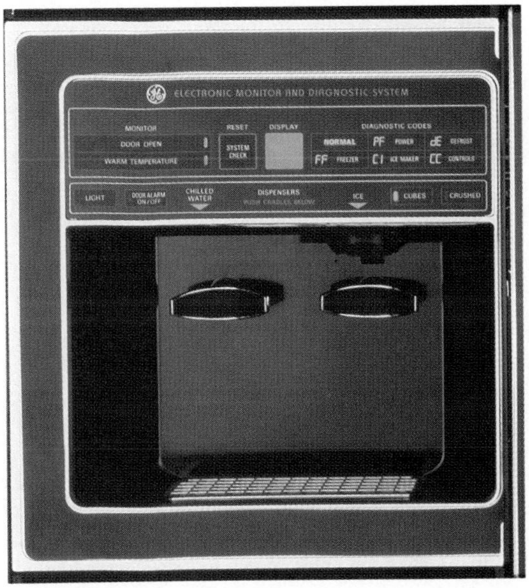

FIGURE 4.9

Appliances with embedded processors allow users to program their operations in advance.

Courtesy of General Electric

Embedded Microprocessors

Your new refrigerator, microwave oven, or stereo system may be equipped with its own microprocessor. These appliances, like many other products, are now being manufactured with embedded computers. An embedded computer is a microprocessor designed to operate within a noncomputer device. Embedded computers are, of course, not as flexible as general-purpose computers. They use microprocessors but are not microcomputers. The microprocessors used by embedded computers run only one preset program. In addition, they do not use standard input, output, and storage hardware. The microprocessor in your refrigerator will not do your math homework or help you write a letter. It will, however, regulate the refrigerator's temperature to keep your food fresh. The purpose of embedded computers is to expand the capacities of the tools you use.

In microwave ovens, embedded computers permit people to program complex cooking sequences. By entering specific times and temperatures into the oven, you can instruct it to prepare your meal to be ready at dinnertime. The oven's processor acts as a timing and control device, cooking your food according to your specifications.

Other embedded computers check for internal problems in a product. This ability to perform ***self-diagnosis*** is a safety feature. The computer identifies and reports problems to the user before serious damage is done. In a malfunctioning copy machine, an embedded computer can determine the source of the problem. If paper is jammed in the machine, the computer indicates where the problem is located. If mechanical parts have been damaged, the computer recommends that a repairperson be notified. Computers also point out problems with simple remedies, such as restocking the paper supply. These self-diagnostic features help people to eliminate small problems before they become serious, expensive ones.

Supercomputers

The most advanced and expensive type of computer is the ***supercomputer***. Processing speeds in supercomputers are extremely fast. The Cray Y-MP supercomputer can process about 500 million mathematical calculations every second. With a price tag that is equally tremendous, from $5 to $20 million, supercomputer use is limited to such organizations as the U.S. Department of Defense and the National Aeronautics and Space Administration (NASA).

FIGURE 4.10

Fault-tolerant computers are designed with duplicate hardware so that an organization is never without processing power.

Courtesy of Hewlett Packard

The U.S. Weather Bureau also uses the fast processing speeds of a Cray supercomputer to forecast the weather. To analyze data from satellites and from hundreds of weather stations, forecasters need a supercomputer's speed.

Oil companies use supercomputers for petroleum exploration. Military strategists use them to simulate defense scenarios. Genetic researchers put supercomputers to work to analyze DNA structures. Cinematic specialists use them to produce sophisticated cartoon movies. Supercomputers are flexible as well as powerful.

Fault-Tolerant Computers

Many organizations cannot afford to be without their computers, even for an hour. As a result, a few computer manufacturers specialize in building ***fault-tolerant computers***. These machines are designed so that they never crash. To achieve this end, the manufacturer duplicates all important components within the processing hardware. Fault-tolerant computers have at least two memories, processors, and disk drives, and duplicate wiring to all these parts.

The operating system is designed so that hardware is never used at more than half its capacity. Therefore, when hardware problems occur, the operating system automatically switches processing to the remaining hardware without interruption. Fault-tolerant computers are especially useful in hazardous environments or in situations where an organization cannot afford to be without processing power. Although more expensive than standard computers, hospitals, scientific laboratories, and nuclear power plants need the hardware duplication provided by fault-tolerant computers.

STUDY QUESTIONS

3. Define MIPS, workstation, self-diagnosis, and fault-tolerant computer.
4. What are five characteristics for grouping processing hardware? Use these characteristics to differentiate among microcomputers, minicomputers, and mainframes.
5. What are three applications for embedded computers and supercomputers?
6. Describe how fault-tolerant computers are different from other computers.

WHAT IS UPGRADING?

What do you do when your computer becomes "too slow?" When you desire to add more memory? When you wish to have graphics capabilities?

These are typical questions asked by individual users. These types of questions have a single, rather simple answer: You take out the old and bring in the new. Computer manufacturers, from the beginning, have developed techniques to "upgrade" user systems. No matter what computer you may be using, design features are built in so that you can replace old components with new parts that will increase computer system capabilities and, in turn, your personal and professional productivity.

Years ago, upgrading hardware was quite expensive. However, with the advent of microcomputers built from standard components, a new breed of manufacturers, known as "third-party vendors," have entered the marketplace. These companies specialize in providing components designed to add new features and to upgrade capabilities of existing systems. The presence of third-party vendors assures you that there is a group of companies trying to think up ways to enhance the value of your computer. A few examples of how to upgrade your computer:

Need more memory? Purchase an expansion board.

Want to add graphics capabilities? Add a graphics card and a high-resolution monitor, either color or monochrome.

Looking for increased processing speed? You need a co-processor, or accelerator card.

The more knowledgeable you become as a user, the more conscious you will be of potential benefits from added hardware features, and of the need to shop with caution. Ask some critical questions, such as the following:

Is the upgrade you are considering fully compatible with your existing computer system? You may find that you have to buy special connecting devices to use a given component with the system you have. You also may find that the manufacturer has neglected to state that an upgrade device is not compatible with your system.

Will service be available both for your computer and for the attachment? If your system has a mix of parts from different vendors, who will be responsible for service? Will any of the parties refuse service because you have attached "foreign" devices?

Look out for yourself! You are the customer. Know what you are buying.

Key Question: What capabilities can you add to a personal computer at a later time?

BINARY CODES FOR DATA AND INSTRUCTIONS

No matter what size the processing hardware, every computer follows George Boole's theory of two-state mathematics. Boole held that all conditions could be described as either true or false. Computers are an application of this theory. When electricity is present, circuits or paths in the computer's configuration may be either open or closed to the electrical flow. An electronic switch is set to either on or off, controlling the flow of electricity through a circuit. These bi-state features, based on Boolean algebra, are present in all computers.

Machine Code

As a result of the computer's bi-state configuration, assembly, high-level, and fourth-generation languages using English words or abbreviations must be translated into binary codes. Processors manufactured by different companies each have their own binary machine language, or ***machine code***. These codes represent the processor's internal switches with a 0, usually designating an open switch, and a 1, designating a closed switch. Different switch settings perform different operations.

Figure 4.11 shows how one line from a high-level BASIC program must be translated into four lines of machine code. The first two binary codes identify the location in memory of the number of TICKETS sold and the COST of each ticket. The next line of machine code tells the processor to multiply TICKETS by COST. The last binary instruction indicates where the results, called TOTAL, are stored in memory.

Standard Codes for Data

Electronic pulses are also expressed as binary codes. These pulses can represent alphanumeric data or ***control characters***, special instructions for cursor movement, tabulation, carriage return, and so on. The electrical pulses are expressed as digits, with 1 indicating the presence of electricity and 0, its absence. Recall that the 1 and 0 notations are known as binary digits, or bits. Different combinations of bits represent numeric, textual, and physical data. Computers that process data as binary digits are called ***digital computers***.

Bits are numeric representations of the electronic pulses that represent data. As an example, a light can be described as 1 when it is on and 0 when it is off. A panel of light switches can display a collection of 1 and 0 notations. Although computers are not composed of panels of light switches, they do contain switchlike devices that are either on or off.

A group of bits forms a bit pattern, known as a ***byte***, which represents a single character of data. Several standard codes exist to represent data. As a result, no

```
                              Machine Code

      One High-Level              Several Machine
    Program Instruction   =    Language Instructions


TOTAL = TICKETS * COSTS   1011 0011 1001 0100
                          (Location of TICKETS in memory)
                          1111 0101 1101 1100
                          (Location of COST in memory)
                          0001 1000 0010 1001
                          (Initiates multiplication)
                          1110 1010 0110 0100
                          (Memory location for answer = TOTAL)
```

FIGURE 4.11

One instruction in the high-level programming language of BASIC translates into several lines of machine code.

	ASCII			ASCII			ASCII	
CHARACTER	BINARY	DECIMAL	CHARACTER	BINARY	DECIMAL	CHARACTER	BINARY	DECIMAL
a	1100001	97	A	1000001	65	0	0110000	48
b	1100010	98	B	1000010	66	1	0110001	49
c	1100011	99	C	1000011	67	2	0110010	50
d	1100100	100	D	1000100	68	3	0110011	51
e	1100101	101	E	1000101	69	4	0110100	52
f	1100110	102	F	1000110	70	5	0110101	53
g	1100111	103	G	1000111	71	6	0110110	54
h	1101000	104	H	1001000	72	7	0110111	55
i	1101001	105	I	1001001	73	8	0111000	56
j	1101010	106	J	1001010	74	9	0111001	57
k	1101011	107	K	1001011	75	(space)	0100000	32
l	1101100	108	L	1001100	76	.	0100001	33
m	1101101	109	M	1001101	77	"	0100010	34
n	1101110	110	N	1001110	78	#	0100011	35
o	1101111	111	O	1001111	79	$	0100100	36
p	1110000	112	P	1010000	80	%	0100101	37
q	1110001	113	Q	1010001	81	&	0100110	38
r	1110010	114	R	1010010	82	(	0101000	40
s	1110011	115	S	1010011	83	)	0101001	41
t	1110100	116	T	1010100	84	*	0101010	42
u	1110101	117	U	1010101	85	+	0101011	43
v	1110110	118	V	1010110	86	.	0101110	46
w	1110111	119	W	1010111	87	/	0101111	47
x	1111000	120	X	1011000	88	<	0111100	60
y	1111001	121	Y	1011001	89	>	0111110	62
z	1111010	122	Z	1011010	90	?	0111111	63

FIGURE 4.12

The ASCII code format is used by computers to represent data.

single standard has been established for all computers. Typically, computers use codes that assign either seven or eight bits per byte. Codes vary according to the type of computer system used.

Many smaller computers use a seven-bit code called the American Standard Code of Information Interchange, or ASCII (pronounced as' kee). ASCII was used originally by the communication industry for data transmission over telegraph lines. This code has been adopted as the standard for many computers, particularly microcomputers. With ASCII, users can transmit data from one computer to another, even if the machines have different internal coding systems. Noncompatible data from one computer are converted to the widely compatible ASCII code for transmission. The second computer receives the ASCII data and converts them to its own internal code. As a result, the use of ASCII increases opportunities to share data. A recently developed version of ASCII uses eight-bit bytes. This expansion increases the number of bit combinations possible and the number of characters that can be represented. For example, the bit pattern for the letter A in ASCII is 1000001, a comma is represented by 0101100, and a control character like the TAB is 0001001. (See Figure 4.12.)

Larger computers typically use an eight-bit code called the Extended Binary Coded Decimal Interchange Code, or EBCDIC, (pronounced eb' sih dik). The letter A in EBCDIC is 1100 0001 and a comma is encoded 0111 1101. While ASCII is used most commonly for data communication, EBCDIC is used primarily for internal data handling by larger computers. Developed by IBM, a leader in the computer market, EBCDIC has come into wide acceptance.

STUDY QUESTIONS

7. Define machine code, control character, digital computer, and byte.
8. Describe how Boole's two-state mathematics is applied to computer-based instructions and data.
9. How are ASCII and EBCDIC used?

THE CENTRAL PROCESSING UNIT

Once data have been converted into byte form, they are ready to be processed. Processing transforms data into information. Computer-executed transformations occur within the ***central processing unit***, or ***CPU***. Central processing units condense all the computational functions of a computer into just two parts:

- The processor combines arithmetic, logic, and control/communications operations on one or more chips, depending on the size of the computer.
- Memory requires several chips to store data and programs during a specific IPOS cycle.

Operations executed (performed) within the processor and memory are synchronized by an electronic clock built into the CPU. The clock emits electrical pulses at a fixed rate. These pulses are used to coordinate program executions.

The Processor

Data transformation, though seemingly sophisticated, is actually based on a simple premise. Computers can add and compare values. These operations take place at tremendous speeds within the processor. The speeds are measured in fractions of a second as ***milliseconds*** (thousandths), ***microseconds*** (millionths), ***nanoseconds*** (billionths), and ***picoseconds*** (trillionths). Instead of executing highly complex operations, it conducts many simple operations very quickly. This is the essence of computer processing power.

To make use of this power, the processor relies on the three operations:

- Arithmetic
- Logic
- Control/communication

Arithmetic

Computer arithmetic is, essentially, addition. The computer can add two numbers to obtain a sum. Subtraction is actually negative addition, multiplication is repeated

```
BASIC PAYROLL PROGRAM

100  REM *** PROCESSING SECTION OF PAYROLL PROGRAM ***
110  REM PROGRAM CODE TO COMPUTE REGULAR AND OVERTIME PAY
120  OVERTIME = 0
130  IF HOURS > 40
        THEN REGPAY = RATE * 40
             OVERTIME = (HOURS - 40) * (RATE * 1.5)
        ELSE REGPAY = RATE * HOURS
140  GROSSPAY = REGPAY + OVERTIME
```

Example A

Rate = $5.00 and Hours = 40

OVERTIME = 0
SINCE 40 IS NOT > 40
REGPAY = 200 (5.00 * 40)
GROSSPAY = 200 (200 + 0)

Example B:

Rate = $5.00 and Hours = 45

OVERTIME = 5
SINCE 45 IS > 40
REGPAY = 200 (5.00 * 40)
OVERTIME = 37.50 ((45-50) * (5.00 * 1.5))
5 * 7.50
GROSSPAY = 237.50 (200 + 37.50)

FIGURE 4.13

This BASIC program can make logical comparisons to compute overtime pay when an employee works over forty hours per week.

addition, and division is repeated negative addition. That is, a computer will use addition to find solutions to the following problems:

$6 - 3 = n$	$6 * 3 = n$	$6 / 3 = n$ [Here, the computer determines the answer (2) by counting the number of –3s that must be added before 0 is reached.]
$6 + (-3) = 3$	$6 + 6 + 6 = 18$	$6 + (-3) + (-3) = 0$

Simple addition, then, enables the computer to solve complex mathematical problems. Repetitions of arithmetic functions take very little time, since millions of instructions can be processed every second.

Logic

Computer logic is, simply, the comparison of two values. Computers can determine whether a value is equal to, greater than, or less than another value. While this idea is simple, it holds the potential for great processing power. For example, computer logic can determine whether the number of seats in a theater is "equal to" the number of tickets sold. If so, the show is sold out.

Payroll processing also makes use of computer logic. If the number of hours an employee has worked in a week is "greater than" 40, the computer can adjust the pay scale to reflect overtime. The program in Figure 4.13 shows how this logic is coded in the BASIC programming language to compute overtime. The resulting figure would be your gross earnings.

Computer logic also can be used to sort data into alphabetical or numeric order. As with arithmetic, the computer executes logical functions at ultra-high speeds, performing millions of comparisons per second.

Control/Communication

The processor, under control of a computer program, uses its control/communication operations to direct the flow of data into and out of memory and to coordinate

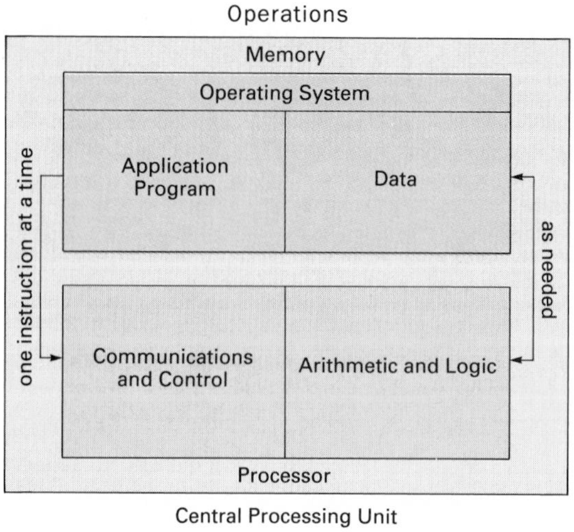

FIGURE 4.14

The interactions between the memory and processing components of a CPU drive the IPOS cycle.

arithmetic and logic operations. This control/communication operation enables the processor to place data and processing instructions into memory. It engages the arithmetic and logic operations of the processor as needed. Results are then sent back to memory by the processor.

The processor communicates with other hardware by sending out electrical pulses. Disk drives accept input data while VDTs and printers produce output by following instructions sent to them by the processor. The processor uses its control/communication operations to coordinate all aspects of processing.

Memory

In memory, data and programs are held temporarily, before and after processing is completed. Application programs instruct the computer to execute specific tasks. These instructions, along with the data, are loaded into memory, where they stay until the processor needs them. After the processor conducts arithmetic and logic operations, it returns the results to memory for temporary storage. Memory also is referred to as ***primary storage***.

The relationship between memory and the processor is analogous to you sitting at your desk next to a filing cabinet. You (the processor) are processing information found on your desk (temporary storage). Your in and out baskets are the means by which you receive (input) and send (output) data. Once you have processed information it is either thrown away (erased) or filed in the cabinet (permanent storage).

The content of memory, in most cases, is temporary and constantly undergoing change. This type of memory is known as ***volatile memory***. The content of volatile memory is subject to loss when the power is turned off. Thus, a constant electrical power supply is needed to retain data and instructions in volatile memory. Of course, data, program instructions, and the results of processing can be retained on magnetic media such as tapes and disks. These devices are known as ***secondary storage***.

Advances in memory technology have produced ***bubble memory***. Bubble memory units are special silicon chips coated with a magnetic film. When a magnetic field is applied to the chip, microscopic bubbles appear. The presence of

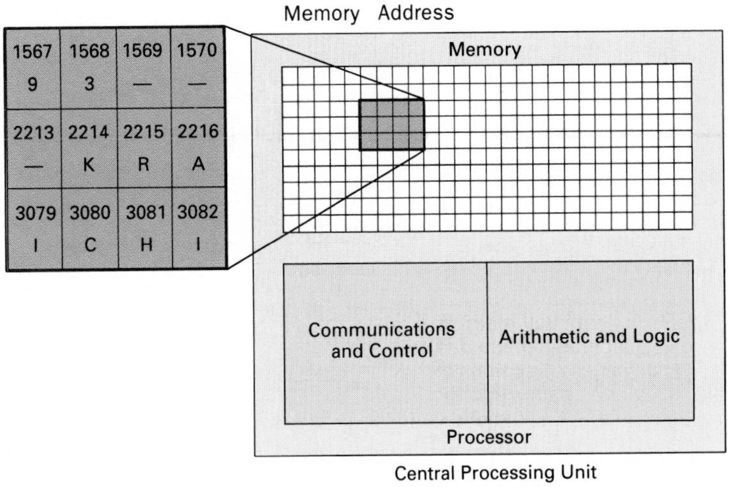

FIGURE 4.15

The RAM chips temporarily store data only while the power to the computer is on.

FIGURE 4.16

Each byte (character) is assigned a unique location in memory and is identified by its address.

a bubble indicates a 1 bit; the absence, a 0 bit. Since bubbles are produced by a magnetic field, electrical current is not needed to retain data. Data will remain in bubble memory even when the computer is turned off. This means that, unlike most forms of memory, bubble memory is ***nonvolatile***. Despite this advantage, the high cost of manufacturing has discouraged use of this technology.

In general, memory chips fall under one of two categories: ***read-only memory (ROM)*** or ***random access memory (RAM)***. Special-purpose programs are built into ROM chips during manufacturing. Since programs stored in ROM are burned into memory circuits, programs do not have to be loaded into memory. ROM is a form of nonvolatile memory, so it is typically used to hold systems programs and language translators.

In contrast, RAM is a form of ***volatile memory*** used for temporary general-purpose storage. When we think of computer memory, we usually have RAM in mind. Programs and data must be loaded into RAM from outside sources. If the power to the computer fails, RAM is completely erased. Programs and data must then be loaded again.

To locate needed data or programs for processing, the computer assigns a number, or ***address***, to each byte position in memory. Programmers working with assembly and high-level languages use words or symbols to assign labels to data needed from memory. The computer then associates these labels with its own internal address. Once the assigned address is located, the computer retrieves the specified data.

The storage capacity of memory is measured by the number of characters, or bytes, it can hold. Typically, memory is measured in thousands of bytes. A ***kilobyte (K)*** represents 1024 bytes, which is often rounded to a thousand bytes. A 512K memory, then, provides storage for roughly 512,000 characters or exactly 524,288 bytes. Memory capacities in large computers often are measured in ***megabytes (MB)***, or millions of bytes. Memories in future computers will reach ***gigabyte*** (billion byte) and ***terabyte*** (trillion byte) capacities.

One drawback of main memory is its inability to handle lengthy jobs because of the limited amount of space available for holding large, complex programs. Since only a small portion of a program can be processed at any given moment, most of the program and memory are unused. Yet the entire program takes up space in memory during processing.

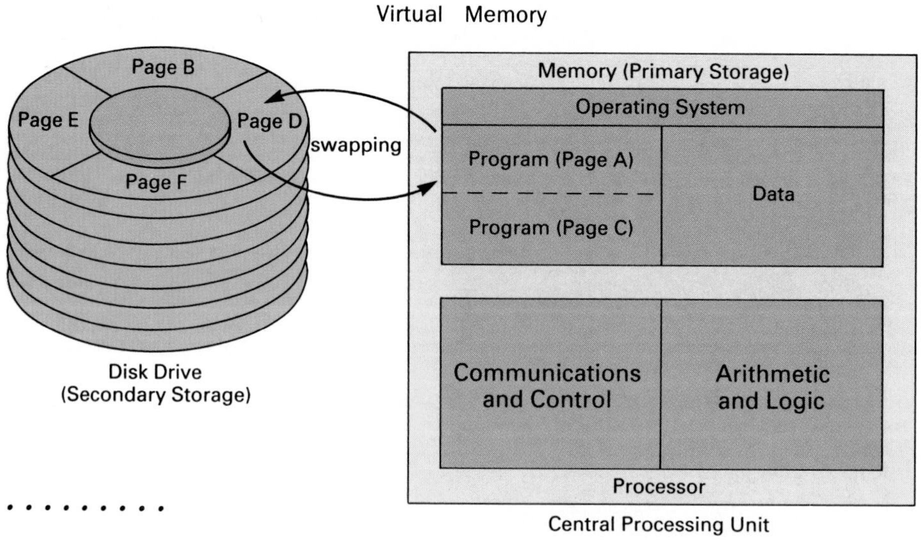

FIGURE 4.17

Virtual memory operations use disk drives as extensions of main memory.

To reduce this demand for main memory space, ***virtual memory*** evolved. Virtual memory uses secondary storage to expand primary storage. The processor treats storage on a disk drive as part of memory and detects virtually no difference between them. Large programs are broken down into sections, called pages. Pages that are not currently being used by the processor are transferred to disk. When a page is needed, the operating system swaps it into memory by replacing a completed page. Virtual memory increases the efficiency of the processor by letting it handle programs that exceed its memory capacity.

CPU Operations

The question now arises, how does the processor orchestrate all the actions involved in running a program? Processing is broken into two phases:

- Fetch phase
- Execution phase

During the ***fetch phase*** the processor's control/communication operation identifies the next program instruction and its location (address) in memory. The instruction is then loaded (fetched) into the processor. For example, in Figure 4.18 , four instructions compute ticket sales. The first instruction, locating the number of tickets sold, is recalled. This completes the first fetch phase in the figure.

The ***execution phase*** starts at this point, with the processor interpreting the instruction, transferring related data from memory, and performing the appropriate arithmetic or logic operation on the data. In Figure 4.18 the first instruction locates the value 4 (tickets sold) in memory. During the execution phase, 4 is transferred from memory into the processor. With the completion of this execution phase, the next fetch phase begins.

The fetch/execution cycle are repeated for the ticket cost—nine dollars. Once the cost and number of tickets are in the processor, the next fetch/execution cycle results in multiplying these values. When the result, called TOTAL, is returned to memory, the last execution phase in this example is finished.

The processor uses the internal clock to regulate electronic pulses so the phases do not overlap. The repetition of the fetch/execution cycle continues until all program instructions have been processed. This is IPOS in its most basic form.

Processing Phases: Fetch and Execution

When the computer processes the machine language instructions for TOTAL = TICKETS * COST, four fetch/execution cycles are performed.

1. FETCH 1011 0011 1001 0100 (Instruction locating TICKETS in memory)

   EXECUTION Move to processor

2. FETCH 111 0101 1101 1100 (Instruction locating COST in memory)

   EXECUTION Move to memory

3. FETCH 0001 1000 0010 1001 (Instruction to multiply TICKETS by COST)

   EXECUTION Multiply 4 by 9 giving 36

4. FETCH 1110 1010 0110 0100 (Instruction locating a memory location for ANSWER,TOTAL)

   EXECUTION Move to memory

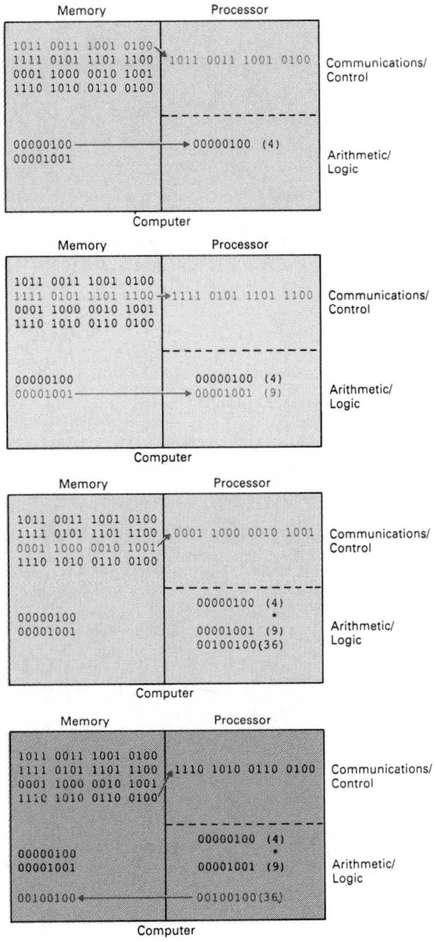

FIGURE 4.18

Four fetch/execution cycles go into computing the purchase price for concert tickets.

The Anatomy of a Microcomputer

The CPU circuitry that once required a room full of vacuum tubes connected by miles of wire now resides on several small silicon chips. That is, a microcomputer's microprocessor, RAM and ROM chips, clock, and other supporting circuitry are interconnected on a single circuit board called the ***motherboard.***

Microcomputer users who need to add to their computer's capacity can add memory, color graphics, and even modems for telecommunications through expansion slots on the motherboard. ***Expansion slots*** are designed to link the processor and existing memory to circuit boards or ***expansion cards,*** which support these new capabilities. Microcomputers will have from three to eight expansion slots on the motherboard.

Installation of new expansion cards is quite easy. For example, users wishing to add enhanced graphics need only purchase an enhanced graphics adapter (EGA) board and slip it into an expansion slot. The new graphics capabilities are immediately available, although related software packages sometimes need to be installed again.

FIGURE 4.19

A microcomputer's microprocessor, memory chips, and expansion slots are found on the motherboard.

I N S I G H T

BUILDING YOUR OWN MICROCOMPUTER

Assembling a microcomputer from its component parts may sound intimidating. However, even a novice can complete the tasks necessary in a few hours.

Getting Started

Purchase components through a reputable catalog or from a retailer. They often offer "computer kits" that contain all the necessary parts, and manuals that detail the installation steps summarized below.

Determine whether the memory chips and microprocessor work at the same clock speed. Furthermore, the power supply should be adequate for the number of disk drives you plan on installing.

Work Area

Assemble your computer in a clean, dust-free work area. Eliminate static electricity that could damage the chips, by grounding your hand to a metal pipe.

STEP 1: Add memory chips to open slots in motherboard.

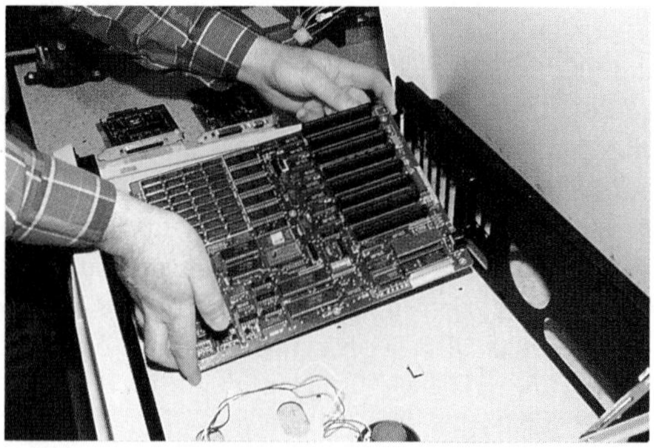

STEP 2: Screw motherboard into cabinet with screws.

STEP 3: Install power supply with screws.

STEP 4: Insert VDT and disk drive controller into respective expansion slots.

STEP 5: Install disk drive mounting bracket with screws.

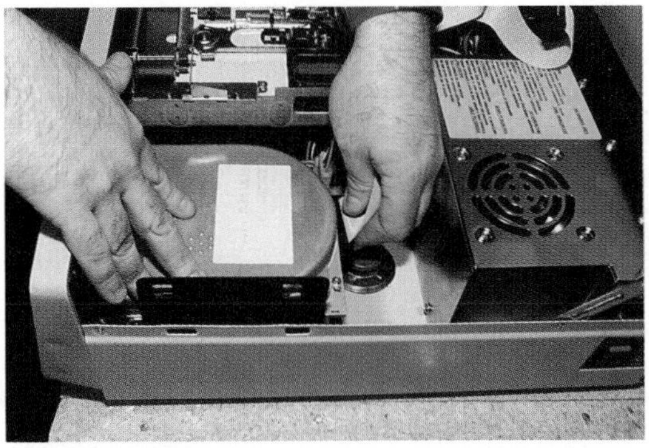

STEP 6: Insert disk drive(s) into mounting bracket with screws.

STEP 7: Connect disk drive(s) to controller card and power supply.

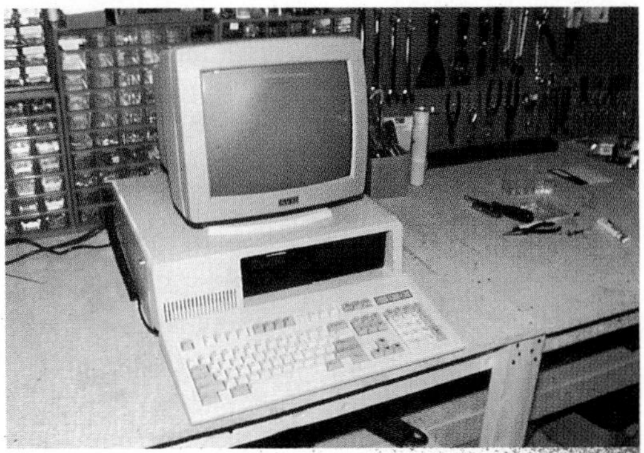

STEP 8: Close cabinet, plug in keyboard and VDT to computer and computer wall socket.

STEP 9: Insert DOS disk in floppy disk drive and turn on computer.

If problems occur, unplug computer and double check all connections and inserted chips. A DOS manual and assembly instructions will also provide troubleshooting tips.

STUDY QUESTIONS

10. Define central processing unit (CPU), millisecond, microsecond, nanosecond, picosecond, primary storage, secondary storage, bubble memory, kilobyte (K), megabyte (MB), gigabyte, terabyte, fetch phase, execution phase, motherboard, and expansion slot.
11. What are the two main parts of the central processing unit?
12. Under what simple premise does the processor work?
13. Describe the operations performed by the processor.
14. What is stored in memory?
15. Describe the difference between volatile and nonvolatile memory.
16. How are read-only memory and random access memory used?
17. Explain how the processor uses memory addresses to locate data and instructions.
18. How does virtual memory help to overcome the limits of memory?
19. How do the fetch and execution phases relate to IPOS?
20. What role does the computer's clock play in the CPU's processing cycles?
21. How are expansion cards used to add to a microcomputer's capabilities?

CONCLUSION

The power of present-day computers has expanded to solve a variety of processing problems. Computers from micros to supercomputers can now process data and return answers while users wait. These machines can distribute processing power over large areas or collect data from remote sources. The more powerful computers can share their processing resources among many applications and users. Some can even link their processing power together to meet special needs.

While these machines perform a diverse array of problem-solving tasks, their internal functions are quite simple. Data and instructions are represented by a pattern of 1s and 0s. Complex arithmetic and logic operations are actually series of simple additions and comparisons. A computer's IPOS cycle involves repetition of the fetch and execution phases at high speeds.

Regardless of the complexity of the application, computers can solve the problem. However, computers still depend on people. People must identify the problem and formulate the instructions to solve it. Only then can computers be put to practical use.

CHAPTER FACTS

- Real-time processing is an online application in which results are returned as soon as the processing is complete.
- The sharing of a single computer's processing power by several terminals over communication lines is teleprocessing. Distributed processing involves several computers linked together to share processing over long distances.

- Multiprogramming and time-sharing both allow many users to share a computer's processor. In multiprogramming, programs are prioritized and only the highest priority program is processed. In time-sharing, each program has equal priority and is given a slice of the computer's time.
- Multiprocessing is linking several processors so that more than one program can be processed at the same time.
- Mainframes are large, high-speed computers with billions of characters of memory.
- Minicomputers are smaller than mainframes, but still have large memory size and high processing speeds.
- Microcomputers are small but powerful machines. They usually perform only one job at a time, but have memories up to 16 million characters.
- Embedded computers are microprocessors built into noncomputer appliances and tools. They are permanently programmed to expand the device's capabilities.
- Supercomputers are very powerful and fast machines with large storage capacities. They are expensive and used only in applications requiring fast processing of large amounts of data.
- Fault-tolerant computers contain duplicates of all important components—processors, memories, wiring, and others. Each component is used only to half capacity. When a component fails, the duplicate takes over.
- All processing hardware works on Boole's two-state mathematics. In digital computers, data and programs are put into a series of electronic pulses called machine code, represented by 1 (presence) and 0 (absence of electricity) values.
- Standard bit codes enable computers to communicate. ASCII originally used seven bits to represent a byte. Extended ASCII uses eight bits per byte to include graphics characters. ASCII is used by most microcomputers. EBCDIC uses eight-bit patterns and is common in larger computers.
- The central processing unit (CPU), or processing hardware, is made up of the processor and memory.
- The processor performs three types of operations: arithmetic operations, logic operations, and control/communication operations.
- Memory, called primary storage, holds data and programs. It can be volatile or nonvolatile.
- Random access memory (RAM) is temporary storage. Read-only memory (ROM) is permanently programmed during manufacturing.
- Data are retrieved in the processing hardware according to memory location, or address.
- Memory capacity is measured by number of bytes. A kilobyte (K) is approximately 1000 characters. A megabyte (MB) is 1 million characters. Future memories will contain capabilities in billions (gigabytes) and trillions (terabytes) of characters.
- Virtual memory is the expansion of main memory. The computer views a secondary storage device, usually a disk drive, as extra memory.
- Processing consists of two phases: the fetch phase and the execution phase. These are coordinated by an internal clock.
- Microcomputers connect the processor, memory, clock, and other integrated circuits together on a motherboard. Expansion slots on the motherboard allow additional capacity to be added to the computer's circuitry.

TERMS TO REMEMBER

address
bubble memory
byte
central processing unit (CPU)
control character
digital computer
distributed processing
execution phase
expansion card
expansion slot
fault-tolerant computer
fetch phase
gigabyte
kilobyte (K)
megabyte (MB)
machine code
microsecond
millisecond
MIPS
motherboard
multiprocessing
nanosecond
nonvolatile memory
picosecond
primary storage
random access memory (RAM)
read-only memory (ROM)
real-time processing
secondary storage
self-diagnosis
supercomputer
teleprocessing
terabyte
terminal
time-sharing
virtual memory
volatile memory
workstation

CHECK YOUR UNDERSTANDING

1. Sharing of data and processing power between a single computer and terminals over communication lines is called ___________.
   a. real-time processing
   b. multiprocessing
   c. time-sharing
   d. teleprocessing
   e. distributed processing
2. In ___________, several processors are linked together so that jobs may be executed simultaneously.
3. A fault-tolerant computer is designed with a continuous power supply so as never to break down. (True/False)
4. ___________ computers are microprocessors used to expand the capabilities of noncomputer tools.
5. A single character is represented in memory by one ___________.
   a. bit
   b. byte
   c. digit
   d. RAM
   e. none of the above
6. The processing hardware of a computer is the CPU or central processing unit. (True/False)

7. The processor does three operations: arithmetic, logic, and ___________.
8. Disks and tapes are types of ___________.
   a. bubble memory
   b. primary storage
   c. random access memory
   d. read-only memory
   e. secondary storage
9. ROM memory is considered volatile memory. (True/False)
10. Processing consists of repeating two phases, the fetch phase and the ___________ phase.

APPLYING WHAT YOU'VE LEARNED

1. What could be practical applications (not mentioned in the text) for these processing arrangements: real-time processing, teleprocessing, distributed processing, time-sharing, multiprogramming, and multiprocessing? Include either applications you have seen or ideas about how to use computers to improve the quality of some service.
2. Besides those mentioned in the text, what five other organizations could use the continuous availability of a fault-tolerant computer?
3. Use the ASCII table in the text to encode your full name, including spaces. How many bits does it take? How many bytes? How many characters?
4. Look at the instructions that come with the school or home computer you use. How much main memory does it have? How much memory is contained in RAM? In ROM? What type of secondary storage is available?
5. Bubble memory was once announced as the memory of the future. Research on it has slowed down. Read a recent article on bubble memory. Why is it not more popular? What are its advantages? Is another type of nonvolatile memory being developed instead?
6. Classify each processing job by the type of operation it would require: arithmetic, logic, or control/communication. Some may need more than one processing operation.
   a. finding a square root of a number in memory
   b. checking if the breathing rate of a patient has stopped
   c. loading in data from a scanner into memory
   d. calculating how many males and how many females are in an employee file
   e. sending to a distant terminal the names of only those customers with unpaid bills

CHECK YOUR UNDERSTANDING ANSWERS

1. d
2. multiprocessing
3. false
4. embedded
5. b
6. true
7. control/communication
8. e
9. false
10. execution

CHAPTER FIVE

STORAGE DEVICES AND FILE ORGANIZATION

KEY IDEAS

- **From the user's point of view**
  Why do we have so many different kinds of storage hardware? How is this hardware used to organize and store data?
- **Organizing data**
  Data must be structured and organized to support intended applications.

  Different ways to access data
  Data organizations and storage media permit either sequential or direct access to data.

  Sequential files
  Data organized according to a common field.

  Relative files
  Disk files that support direct access to records.

  Indexed files
  Direct access to data through the use of indexes.

  Databases
  Sets of related files that support multiple applications.
- **Storage media and hardware**
  A wide variety of media is used by specialized equipment to store and retrieve data.

  Magnetic tape storage
  Tapes provide low-cost, high-capacity, sequential data storage.

  Magnetic disk storage
  Hard and floppy disks allow direct access to data.

  Laser disk storage
  Low-power laser light reads data from highly polished disk surfaces.

FROM THE USER'S POINT OF VIEW

As an informed user, you are not expected to know the intricacies of hardware operations, but you must be aware of their capabilities and limitations. Part of this knowledge is how data are organized, stored, and accessed in a computer system. Computers become a powerful processing tool when you not only know what data are available but also how they are best organized for quick and easy access.

When you use a computer as part of the problem-solving process, other decisions come into play. Should you use floppy disks or compact disks? Reels of tape or disk packs? A thorough understanding of storage media and hardware can help you choose the best alternatives for the problem at hand.

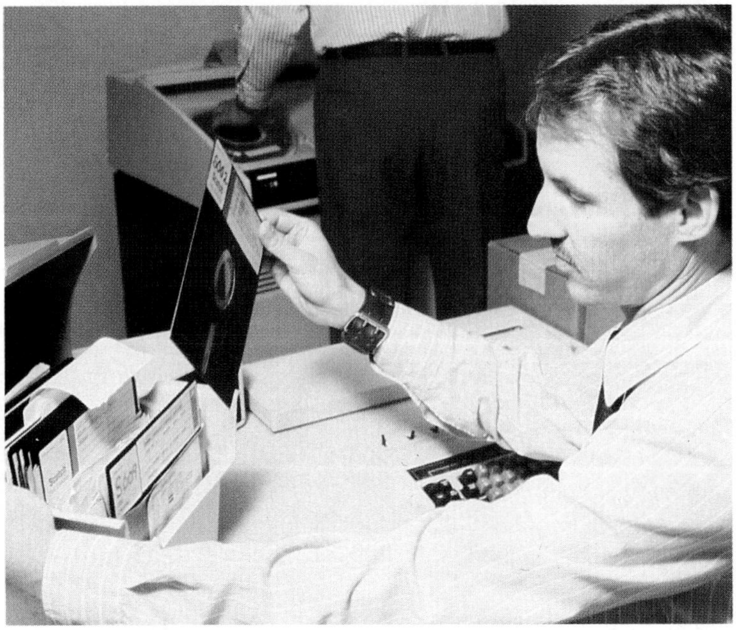

FIGURE 5.1

When organized properly, data are extremely valuable assets.

Photo courtesy of L.A. Schwaber-Barzilay

ORGANIZING DATA

Stored data are extremely valuable assets for any person or organization that uses a computer system. Individuals, schools, businesses, and other users rely on data to conduct their daily activities. Even without computers, people organize data for storage and use. In a computer, data are organized at several levels. Take, for instance, the levels of data structures used by a college's computer for registration:

- Letters, numbers, and special symbols are the simplest form of data that people use. These characters form a student's name or address.
- When characters are combined together they form data fields. Fields are the facts that can be transformed into information through processing. For each student the computer would contain the following fields: name, address, GPA, major, and so on.
- Collections of related fields form records. Each record has a specific meaning. A record describes a person, place, object, or event. In the college registration system, the data about each student would make up a student record. There also would be a record for each faculty member and each class offered.
- Files contain groups of records related by a common theme. For example, separate files would contain records for students, courses, and faculty members. The file that contains all student records might be called the student master file.
- While files typically are built for use in a single data processing application, databases store data for use in multiple applications. By relating files within a database, it is possible to allow easy access to a variety of data items. A college's computer system can integrate student, faculty, and class files into a database. This allows people to cross-reference the data, making questions like, "Which teachers of English 101 have student athletes in their class?" or "How many seniors are taking Introduction to Statistics?" easier to answer.

DID YOU KNOW?

The careless use and storage of your floppy disks can damage them. If this happens, data on the damaged disk is lost forever. You'll have to retype that term paper or ask friends for their telephone numbers again. By following a few simple procedures, you can minimize the chances of accidentally damaging your disks.

1. Always keep your disks in their paper jackets.
2. Always hold a disk by its label. Don't touch the oval access opening used by the disk drive.
3. Always use a felt-tip pen when writing on a disk label.
4. Always insert a disk into the disk drive gently and carefully.
5. Don't bend or fold disks.
6. Don't take a disk out of the disk drive when the red light is on.
7. Don't leave disks out in the sun, in a hot car, or in the cold.
8. Don't put disks on top of a working television, telephone, stereo, or any appliance which generates a magnetic field.

Key Question: What price would you be willing to pay for disks that are resistant to user-caused damage (i.e., spills, bending, or temperature)?

Protect

Never touch!

Insert carefully

No

10°-51.6°C.
50°-125°F.

Never

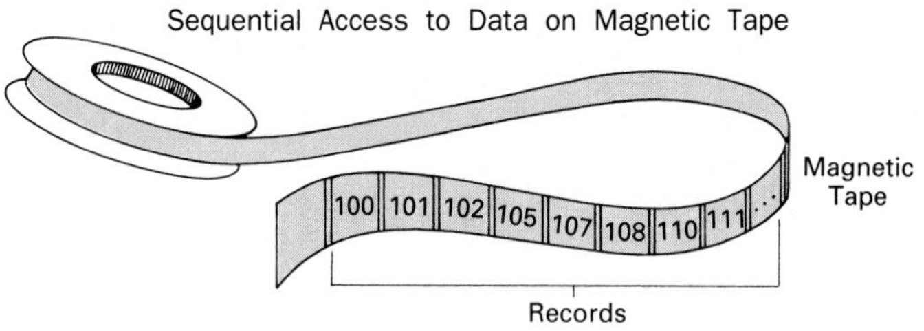

FIGURE 5.2

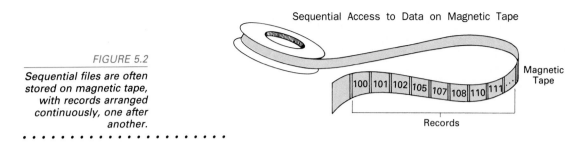

Sequential files are often stored on magnetic tape, with records arranged continuously, one after another.

Different Ways to Access Data

Stored data must be organized according to its intended use. Different file and database organizations exist for different applications. Computer systems then retrieve, or access, data files from storage in a variety of ways. Different access methods fit varying file processing requirements. In turn, these access methods determine the physical arrangement of data on storage media.

In general, two basic types of file access are available: ***sequential access*** and ***direct access***. The first method requires data to be retrieved record by record. This is done by the sequence in which the records were entered into the computer system. As an example, songs on a commercially produced music tape are organized for sequential access. When you play a tape, you hear the songs in a predetermined order. Once the songs are stored on the tape, they cannot easily be rearranged.

If you wish to hear the sixth song on a prerecorded tape, you must listen to the first five, or fast forward past them. In either case, the first five songs must be run through the tape player in sequence. Similarly, a computer that uses sequential access methods reads one record at a time to locate the desired record. To retrieve the fifty-fifth record in a data file, the first 54 must be run through the tape drive.

Direct access, also called ***random access***, is used for fast access to individual records, especially where the order of the records cannot be predicted. In a bank, for example, tellers must be able to process customer requests one at a time, in any order. Since requests are not organized by account number, the sequence of records that must be accessed cannot be anticipated. If the bank accessed account records sequentially, each transaction would require a long wait. The computer would have to search the file record by record to locate each account. At a bank with thousands of customers, each customer might have to wait a long time for service. Since this level of service is unacceptable, sequential access methods are not used for bank transactions. Instead, these transactions use direct access techniques that allow records to be processed quickly and in any order.

The method of access dictates the type of storage media. Once again, we can use listening to music as an analogy. You have two options when listening to recorded music: a record album (disk) or a tape. If you want to hear only one song,

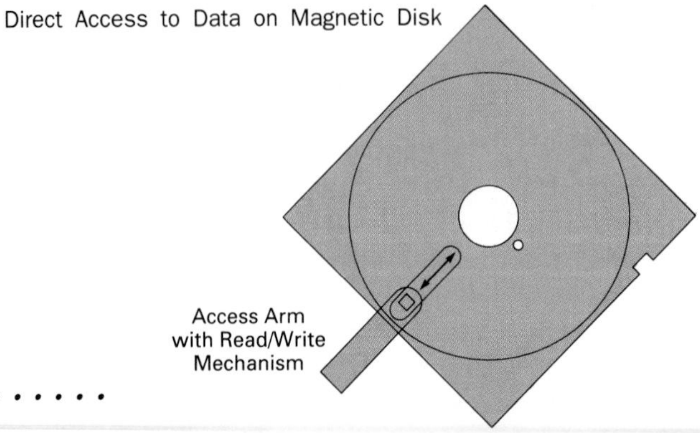

FIGURE 5.3

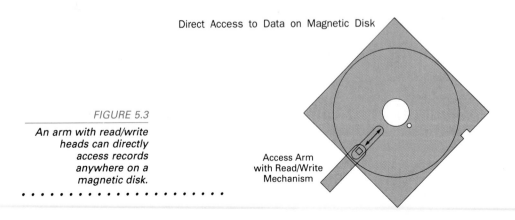

An arm with read/write heads can directly access records anywhere on a magnetic disk.

the easiest way to do so is to play an album. The record player allows you to access one song directly by placing the needle at its beginning. Data stored on disk can be accessed in a similar way. The disk drive can directly access and retrieve one data record as needed.

On the other hand, if you want to hear a series of songs, either an album or a tape can be played from beginning to end. Computer professionals would say that the music was accessed sequentially. As you can see, direct access is limited to disks, while sequential access can take place on both disks and tapes.

To prepare the computer for sequential or direct access, different ways to organize records into a file are available. Data files typically fall under one of three organizations:

- Sequential files
- Relative files
- Indexed files.

Sequential Files

The physical order in which data are recorded on tape or disk determines the organization of data in ***sequential files***. Each record held in a sequential file has a ***key field***, or key that makes the record unique. Keys serve to identify and organize records in a file. For example, in a personnel file, the key may be the social security number, which identifies an employee. Before the file is stored, the records could be placed in order by social security number. This arrangement establishes a logical organization of the data in a sequential file. Thus, in a sequential file, records are arranged in order by a key field prior to being recorded on tape or disk.

Organizing records by key fields expedites file ***updating***. Updating entails adding or deleting records within a file or changing existing records. In a data file containing a clinic's patient records, new patient records can be added. Inactive records are transferred to a history file containing records rarely used. If patients move to new addresses, or if their medical conditions change, their corresponding records must be updated to reflect those changes.

When several alterations must be made to a sequential file, the changes are stored in a separate file for updates (see Figure 5.5). Records in this file are organized by key field. When updating the original file, each record is examined. If it does not need changing, it is written to the new updated file as is. When a record requiring modification is read from the original file, the updates are included and the newly modified record is written to the updated file. New records are added to the updated file in the proper key field sequence. Records to be deleted are simply not copied to the updated file. In this manner, all records are kept in sequential order, and a new updated file is created. Since updates are ordered in the same sequence as the original file, this process can be completed with one pass.

During a processing job, each record in a sequential file must be read, whether it is used or not. Therefore, sequential files are best suited to jobs where a majority of the records must be referenced each time the file is accessed. In a bank file used to print monthly checking account statements, for example, most records will be used because most customers have checking accounts. An electric company that sends out monthly bills can also benefit from sequential processing. Since every customer will probably use electricity during the month, almost all records in a customer file will be accessed for billing.

Backup files usually consist of records stored on tape for sequential access. If data files are destroyed, these backup copies can be processed sequentially to reconstruct the original file.

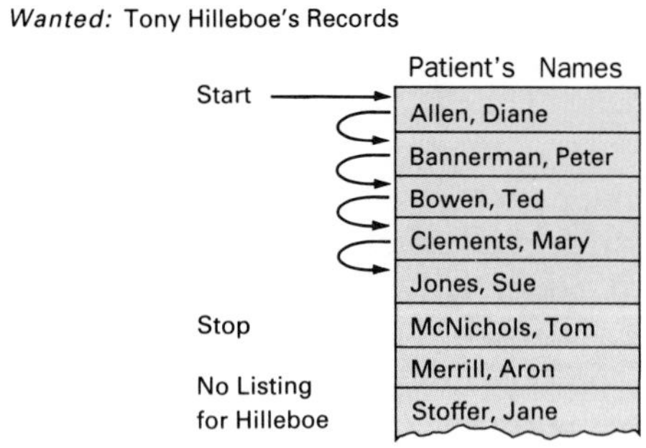

FIGURE 5.4

A sequential file search requires the user to read one record at a time in the prescribed order, from the first record to the one being sought.

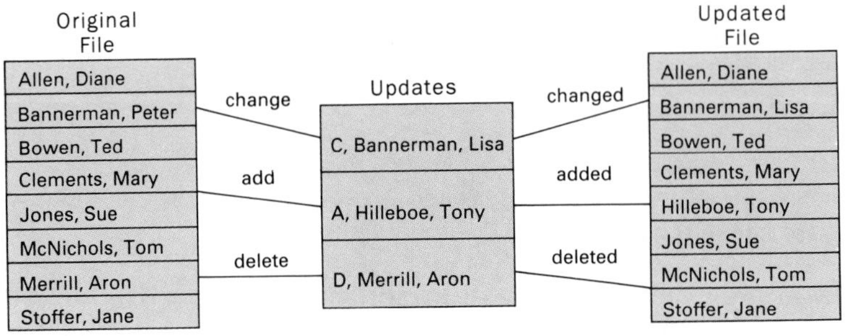

FIGURE 5.5

Sequential file updating requires the processing of all records in a file, as well as the creation of a new file containing updated records.

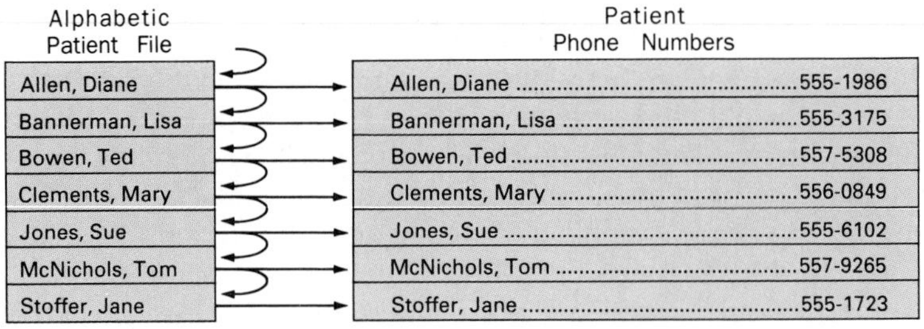

FIGURE 5.6

Data retrieval from a sequential file can be slow when the file contains a large number of records.

Relative Files

In a ***relative file,*** individual records on disk are located so they facilitate random access. The computer must be able to go directly to a specified record without first reading each record in order.

To access records from a relative file, the user provides a key field for the desired record. Given this key value, the computer has the information to go directly to that record location. If a key value of 41 is requested, the computer could look for the information in disk location 41.

Often, a file's key field consists of names or codes. Yet disk locations must be numeric to indicate the relative position on the disk. To overcome this obstacle, hashing routines were developed. ***Hashing routines*** are formulas for converting a record's key to its disk location. Programs apply hashing routines to alphabetic characters to convert them to numeric values. For example, a record's key value in a customer file might be the customer's name. If the GRANT record is requested, the hashing routine would convert each letter in the name GRANT to a number. The hashing formula would then use the numbers to determine the disk location for that record.

Other types of hashing formulas can be applied to numeric record keys. Consider, for example, a customer file using customer number as the key field. If disk addresses 000 to 999 are used to hold the file, each disk location would have to

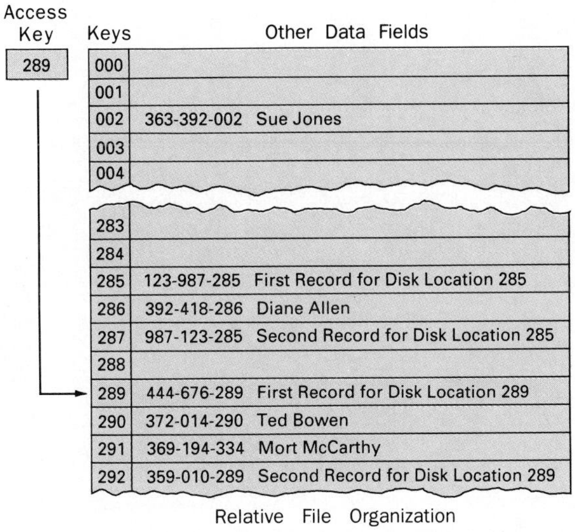

FIGURE 5.7

Relative files use hashing routines to convert a record's key to its disk location.

be a three-digit number. Similarly, the key fields that determine the disk locations would have to be expressed in no more than three digits. If customers are assigned the three-digit customer numbers 000 to 999, no hashing routine would be required. The record for customer 125 would be stored in location 125 on disk.

However, access to relative files is not always so simple. The customer file in Figure 5.7 shows nine-digit customer numbers for the key field. In this case, a hashing formula is used to isolate the final three digits of the key value. These digits indicate the record location. Sometimes, duplications occur in using hashing routines to convert key fields to record locations. For example, as seen in Figure 5.7, two customer numbers might have the same last three digits, such as 444-676-289 and 359-010-289. To solve this problem, the computer program would place one of the records in location 289. The other would be placed in the next available location, going in sequential order. The computer would begin to look for either record at location 289. If the record was not found there, the search would continue sequentially through the entire file until the desired record was found. In the figure, customer record 444-676-289 is put in location 289, matching the last digits of its key field. Customer record 359-010-289 is held in disk location 292, the next empty location at the time the record was stored.

This method of handling duplicate key values can slow down access time considerably in files containing only a few vacant locations. For instance, suppose the file shown in Figure 5.7 had only one empty available storage location, in location 990. The computer would have to store customer record 359-010-289 there. Accessing the record would require sequential checking of each location from 289 to 990.

When programmers create a relative file, they allocate a predetermined amount of disk space for the information, based on the number and type of records expected. Relative files are usually designed with at least 30 percent of their disk locations vacant, so records with duplicate keys can be stored close together.

Direct access to records in a relative file requires that mathematics or logic be applied to determine storage locations. As a result, relative file organizations allow for the fastest possible access to records on disk. However, they do have their disadvantages: First, records may be stored at seemingly random locations on disk based on the hashing routine, especially if there are few vacant locations. If the physical locations of records do not follow a logical order, sequential access is not efficient. A second disadvantage is the difficulty of file expansion. Since hashing routines are devised for a specific file size, expanding the size of a file requires

FIGURE 5.8

Direct or relative files must be stored on disks.

a complete file overhaul and a new hashing routine. Third, relative files should never be full. Since a maximum of 70 percent of disk space should be used, a good portion of the storage medium goes to waste. Despite these drawbacks, relative files are efficient in many applications that require fast access to data.

Indexed Files

Another way of controlling random access to stored records is through use of a computer-maintained index. An ***indexed file*** contains a separate directory, or table, set up to support direct access. Key fields are linked with disk locations by the index. To find any record, the computer consults the index, looks up the disk location, then performs a direct access operation.

Many computer users choose an indexed-sequential organization for their files. ***Indexed-sequential files*** maintain records in key field sequence, but also use indexes to support direct access to records. A file containing a telephone directory illustrates indexed-sequential organization. Telephone records are listed in alphabetical order. To find the number for Harold Johnson, the computer could conduct a sequential search of the file, starting with the A entries and proceeding to "Johnson." However, a sequential search is not a very efficient way to access a single record.

Indexed-sequential methods cut down on the number of records to be searched. The index directs the computer to a specific portion of the file. In the phone number index, 26 entries—one for each letter of the alphabet—would be included. Since the user requested the telephone number for Harold Johnson, the computer would go directly to the disk location associated with J after consulting the index. The need to search through all the records from A to I is eliminated. Only the names starting with J are sequentially searched until Johnson is found.

Indexed-sequential files store records in key order, permitting both sequential access and direct access. This versatility is the primary advantage of indexed-sequential file organization. The method of accessing and processing data can be altered according to users' needs. For example, files that support an automated teller machine would be prime candidates for indexed-sequential organization. Direct access would expedite individual customer transactions as they occur. But sequential access would be preferred in preparing monthly statements for each customer. Thus, indexed-sequential files provide the flexibility to meet a wide range of accessing and processing needs.

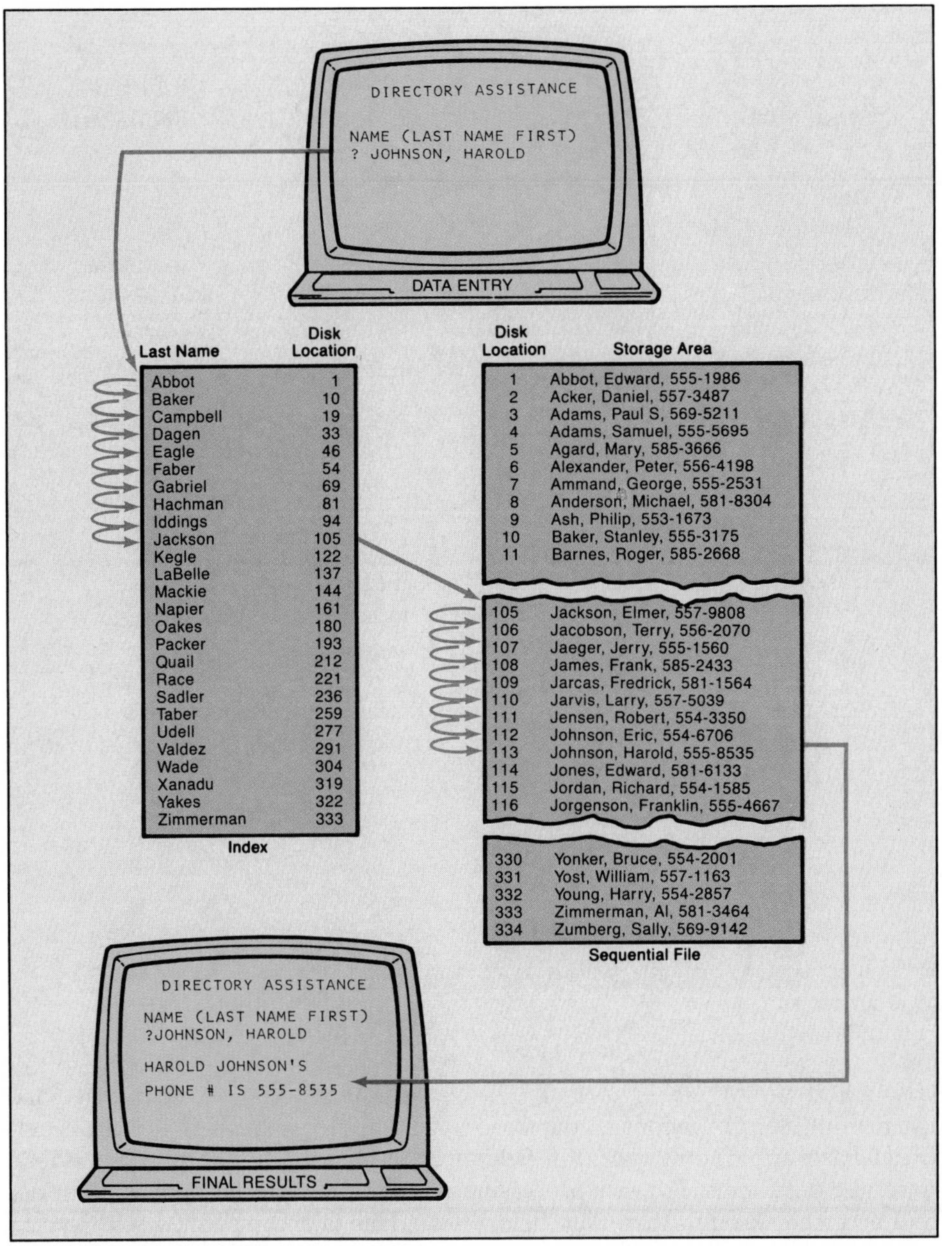

FIGURE 5.9

Indexed-sequential files can be used to access records by using an index or by searching the file one record at a time.

Databases

A traditional data file—whether sequential, relative, or indexed-sequential—contains all the information needed to support one particular application. Organizations and individuals usually maintain a separate file for each application. A hardware store might keep several files to support everyday transactions. These files provide data on customer names and addresses, credit information, billing status, and product descriptions. The same items of data might be duplicated in several different files. For example, the name of a customer could appear in the customer file, the credit file, and the billing file. In traditional file processing systems, data are retained in multiple files, and applications are executed independently.

Most processing activities in an organization are integrated. Data processed in one application might well affect several other applications. Instead of building files to meet the requirements of specific applications, databases are organized for

	Sequential	Relative	Indexed	Indexed-Sequential
Advantages	• Most practical when large percentage of records need to be accessed • Easy to use as backup	• Allows fastest possible access to individual records	• Allows direct access to individual records	• Allows both direct and sequential access to records
Disadvantages	• Very time consuming • Access individual records or key field sequence	• To maintain fast access to records, no more than 70%of the file spaces should be used • New hashing routine needed when file is expanded	• Need to use indexes makes direct access slower than relative file organizations	• Need to use indexes makes direct access slower than with relative file organizations

FIGURE 5.10

Each file organization method has its strengths and weaknesses.

use in multiple applications. A database consists of several related files. Data held in databases appear only once. Key fields are repeated in multiple locations as links to related data items. For each processing job, the data fields needed are identified and accessed through these key field links. This is accomplished with special software packages called ***database management systems (DBMSs).*** Users define data they need for a processing job, and the database program manipulates and controls access to the needed data. The database software also maintains an extensive set of indexes and cross-indexes that reflect the interrelationships among data fields. On large systems, these indexes typically are so extensive that they take up more than half of the storage used by the database.

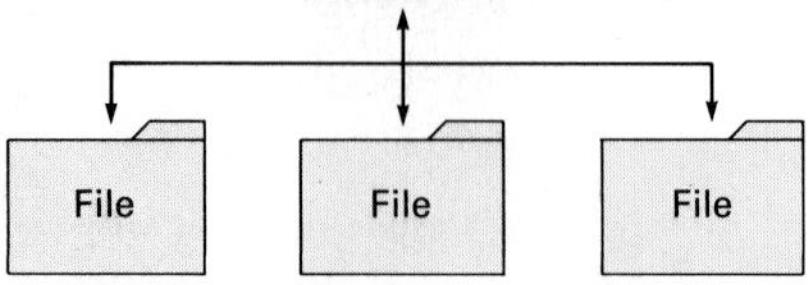

FIGURE 5.11

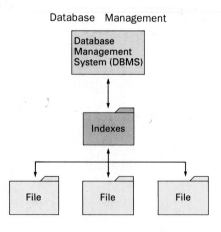

Database management systems use indexes to cross-reference data located in multiple files.

Duplication of data is avoided in databases, except for keys that tie data fields together. A customer name, for example, would not be repeated for each application in which it is used. For a mailing list, it would be combined with address information; for a bill, with credit data. The data field itself remains separate, yet combinable. By eliminating duplicate data, databases save the time and effort of users.

In a file system, a change of address would require updating records in every file in which the address appears. This repetition increases the risk of making an error. In a database only one record change should be needed. That change is good for all processing applications. Databases organize data for processing that is both versatile and efficient.

STUDY QUESTIONS

1. What are the five levels of data organization?
2. Define random access, key field, updating, hashing routine, and database management system (DBMS).
3. What is the difference between sequential and direct access? List the types of storage media used with each method.
4. Explain how a key field is used to access records from a sequential file, relative file, and indexed- sequential file.
5. What are the advantages and disadvantages to using sequential, relative, and indexed-sequential files?
6. How is file processing different from database processing?
7. What are the advantages and disadvantages of using databases?

STORAGE MEDIA AND HARDWARE

An important part of solving an application problem is choosing the correct file organization and access method. In turn, these choices determine the type of storage media and hardware that will be used. ***Storage media*** hold data before processing and store the results of processing. The term ***storage media*** refers to the materials on which data are recorded. Tapes and disks are the most common media.

Programs and data needed to complete a processing job often are accessed from storage media. Storage devices record the results of processing onto storage media. The surfaces of most storage media are coated with magnetic material on which data are retained for long periods of time. The common hardware for storing data are tape drives and disk drives.

Magnetic Tape Storage

Tape drives, which operate like tape recorder/players, provide a low-cost, high-capacity means of sequentially storing data. These drives are often used in backing up important data. Large computers use tape drives to store and read data on ***reels of tape***. Tape drives attached to early microcomputers used ***cassette tapes*** similar to those found in home or car stereo systems. Cassettes and reels are now being replaced by ***tape cartridges***. These cartridges are self-contained in a hard plastic shell and are easy to mount in a tape drive and to store when not in use.

Tape drives record data as magnetized bit patterns. The presence or absence of a magnetized spot on the tape's recording surface represents a binary 1 or 0. Running down the length of reel tape are eight or nine ***tape tracks***, or channels in which bits are held. Combinations of bit positions that cross the tracks represent individual bytes. Figure 5.13 illustrates how nine track tapes typically store data.

Any recording done on storage media requires error checking. Error checking is performed by the computer and storage hardware to ensure the accuracy of the data stored on and read from the storage media. One of the most common error checking procedures uses a special ***parity bit***.

A coding scheme such as EBCDIC requires eight bits to make up each byte. On a nine-track magnetic tape, then, eight bits are used to represent a byte of data, and one track is left over. The extra track holds the parity bit, which is used to verify that data are encoded correctly. To do this, the computer instructs the tape drive to maintain either an even or an odd number of 1 bits in each byte. The bit recorded

FIGURE 5.12

Reels and cartridges are two forms of magnetic tape storage that organize data sequentially.

LASER DISC TECHNOLOGY: ALL THE WORLD ON A DISC

What's hotter than the compact disc? It makes old songs crystal clear, and it lets current musicians make the purest-sounding music ever recorded. Even if you don't have a CD player yet, your favorite radio station probably uses one to make radio sound better than it ever has before. The sparkling star of the audio world is the compact disc.

But compact discs (CDs) aren't just for music. Even now, CD technology is beginning a successful crossover act that is taking it into the world of computers. You may already have heard about some of the varieties of Laser Disc storage—CD ROMs, WORM drives, and CD-I.

Why the sudden flurry of success for CDs? Mass production capability is the answer. The tremendous size of the worldwide consumer market prompted the industry to quickly boost both CD player and disc production into the millions. At volumes like these, just about anything can be produced at a reasonable price. Now that the technology has been perfected by the consumer industry, the smaller home and business computer industries can take advantage of it.

CD ROM

The first computer application for compact disc technology is CD ROM (Compact Disc-Read Only Memory). The term refers to the permanence of the data. Like computer ROM chips, CD ROMs come to the consumer with information already recorded on them. However, CD ROMs contain much more information than common silicon ROM chips. A single CD ROM can hold 550 megabytes—more than enough room for an entire encyclopedia of information. And you can change CD ROMs just like you change floppy disks. Imagine having an entire library of information that fits on a bookshelf.

With so much information available, how can you possibly sort through it? CD ROMs are often cross-indexed so thoroughly that the indexing takes up more of the available space on the disc than the information itself. Designers are working on new techniques to make data retrieval faster and more natural. Hypertext may play a part in solving this problem.

A CD ROM player is a modified Compact Disc player. Already, IBM PC users can take advantage of CD ROMs. Atari showed a CD ROM device for their ST line of computers at the November COMDEX computer show. It shouldn't be long before interfaces for other computers become available.

What kind of software can you expect to find on CD ROMs? Mostly information that has already been translated into electronic form. Hundreds of titles are available, covering everything from agriculture to black fiction to the *Wall Street Journal.* We recently received a single CD ROM disc that contained the entire public domain library (605 floppies worth) of a large users' group. As CD ROMs become more commonplace, more and different kinds of information will become available.

WORMs

The next step in laser disc technology is the WORM (Write Once Read Many) drive. This is a CD drive that can record data as well as play it back. Although being able to write only once sounds restrictive, the great amount of storage available on the CD makes this limitation acceptable.

For example, suppose you write a BASIC program that's 10K long. that translates to about 1/36 the storage capacity of a floppy. But that same program would use only 1/55,000 of the space of a CD ROM. You could change and resave your program as many times as you like with no noticeable loss of capacity.

Some WORM discs can be erased. So far, erasing a disk means erasing the whole disk. Many companies are working on drives that could be called CD RAM drives, which would allow you to actually delete old copies of your programs and data.

CD-I

There's a new standard that could change entertainment and education: Compact Disc Interactive (CD-I). A CD-I player is a combination audio CD player, home computer, and videodisc player. The three parts blend together to create a machine that's vastly more capable than the sum of its parts. Several well-known software publishers—including Electronic Arts, Spinnaker Software, and Aegis Development—are working to find out just what can be done on a CD-I machine.

Let's take a closer look at the elements that make up a CD-I machine. Foremost is a CD player that can play all current and future CD audio disks. The CD player also handles broadcast TV-quality video that can be displayed on your TV or monitor. The computer built into the CD-I player is based on the powerful 68000 microprocessor, the same one found in the Macintosh, Atari ST, and Amiga computers. It will have its own powerful graphics system which can be integrated with the CD video.

Imagine a possible CD-I application. you place a disc titled *Biology Class* in the CD-I player. A high-school classroom appears on your television screen. You use the CD-I player's controls to become an active participant in the simulated classroom. Walk down the aisle and stop at a desk. the student here might be dissecting a frog. Help him or her find various organs in the frog. After you've finished, take a look at the other experiments. You might want to help conduct Mendelian genetics experiments with mice or see how sunlight affects a sunflower.

CD-I is far more ambitious than CD ROM, and it is stirring up a great deal of controversy. Some industry observers doubt that consumers want to interact with their televisions. Others feel that limitations—for example, the format is not capable of full-motion video—in the standard will kill its chance for consumer acceptance. To further complicate matters, a competing standard known as DVI (Digital Video Interactive) has appeared.

Regardless of how CD-I evolves or the CD-I/DVI battle works out, laser discs are already beginning to play an increasingly varied and important role in our lives. They're changing the way we see, hear, and think.

Source: Courtesy of Rhett Anderson, *Compute*

Key Question: How could you use CD-ROM, WORM, and CD-I technology with your personal computer system?

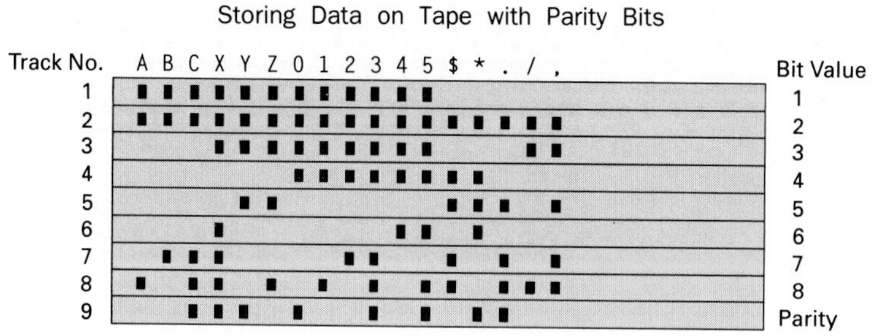

FIGURE 5.13

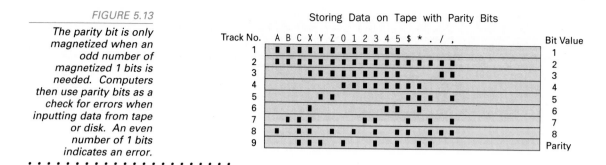

The parity bit is only magnetized when an odd number of magnetized 1 bits is needed. Computers then use parity bits as a check for errors when inputting data from tape or disk. An even number of 1 bits indicates an error.

in the parity track is used to meet that condition. This type of error checking procedure is known as ***parity checking***.

As an example of parity checking, the letter X in EBCDIC is encoded with an even number of 1 bits: 1110 0111. The computer uses the tape drive to sense the six 1 bits for the letter X. In an odd parity-checking scheme, the parity bit is recorded as a 1, bringing the total of 1 bits to seven, an odd number. The letter Z, coded 1110 1001, would require a 0 parity bit to retain the odd number of 1 bits already in the bit pattern. The computer would use this odd-parity checking scheme to check that each byte contained an odd number of 1 bits before continued processing. If a byte contained an even number of 1 bits, the computer would attempt to reread the byte. If the error showed up again, the record containing the faulty byte would be skipped, and the error reported. For most applications, the computer would then continue to process the remaining records; in other cases, all processing would stop. Figure 5.13 shows the byte structure of the EBCDIC code format with odd parity-bit-checking.

Tape drives are equipped with read/write heads. To read tape-recorded data, the read/write head senses magnetic spots, then transfers the data to memory. The read/write head also records magnetic spots in track locations to write data on tape.

Typically, tapes are driven past the read/write head in a series of start-stop actions. The head reads or writes one record at a time. Then, the tape stops momentarily before proceeding to the next record. Consequently, the tape being processed moves forward in quick jerks. To prepare the mechanism for these stops, ***interrecord gaps*** are inserted between records on tape (see Figure 5.14). Interrecord gaps are similar to the blank sections of tape between songs on a music tape. They identify a record to be read during a single read/write operation. In addition, they provide physical space for the stopping and starting of the tape drives.

The tape drive stops at each interrecord gap. Thus, the more gaps on a tape, the less efficient input or output is. To increase computer efficiency, records can be grouped in ***blocks***. By using blocking methods, several records can be read into memory or written to tape in a single processing operation. Allowances still must be made for starting and stopping the tape, however. For this purpose, ***interblock gaps*** are inserted between blocks of records. Under blocking techniques, the computer pauses less frequently than if records are processed one at a time. Also, more records can be stored within the same area.

While it may seem logical that eliminating all gaps on a tape would maximize computer efficiency, this method is not feasible. Blocks of data to be read or written are held in ***buffers***, or portions of computer memory set aside for temporary data storage. Most buffers are not large enough to accommodate an entire data file. For example, a file with 200,000 records, each with 120 characters, would require a buffer for 24 million bytes. Even the largest computers do not have that much buffer capacity. Thus, large files must be broken into smaller, more manageable sections of data. Typically, files are separated into blocks of records from 1000 to 2000 bytes long.

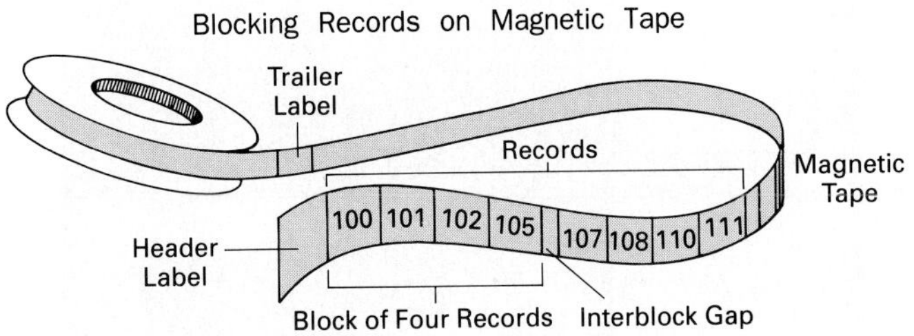

FIGURE 5.14

Records are blocked together on storage media to increase the efficiency of input and output operations.

To locate a requested file for processing, the computer refers to a ***header label***, a special-purpose record written at the beginning of a file. A user specifies a file name, then the computer sequentially searches the header labels of files on the tape to find a match. ***Trailer labels*** mark the end of each tape file and indicate when all data in a file have been processed. Checks for trailer labels are included in programs. When the trailer label is reached during data processing, the program instructs the computer to cease processing.

Magnetic Disk Storage

An alternative to tape storage is magnetic disk storage. Disks are round platters coated with a thin layer of material that can be magnetized. Disk drives record data on disks in the form of magnetized spots. The two primary types of disk in use are ***hard disks*** and ***floppy disks***. Hard disks store large amounts of data at high speeds. The read/write head does not actually touch the hard disk surface, but flies over it. A ***head crash*** occurs when the read/write head touches the surface of the disk, causing damage to both the disk and disk drive. Furthermore, dirt and dust can damage both the read/write head and the disk surface, if caught between the two (see Figure 5.15). Typically measuring 10 inches or more in diameter, hard disks can hold more than 10 million bytes of data. A collection of hard disks stacked on top of each other creates a high-capacity storage unit called a ***disk pack***.

Floppy disks, or ***diskettes***, are round, flexible pieces of plastic used primarily for data storage in microcomputer systems. However, larger systems often use diskettes as the medium for data entry, while relying on hard disks for data storage. Typical diskette sizes are 8 inches, 5.25 inches, and 3.5 inches. Windows in the diskette cover permit the read/write heads to access the surface in order to read or write data. Diskettes may wear out, since the read/write heads physically touch the diskette's surface. Because of this, it is very important for users to back up data and programs on diskettes.

Disk drives store data on disks in concentric circles called ***disk tracks***. In turn, tracks are subdivided into storage locations called ***sectors***. Individual sectors hold one record or one block of records. The computer accesses a data record by identifying its sector.

The process of establishing sectors on disk varies according to the type of disk used. On hard disks, a special magnetized code marks the beginning of each track. Diskette sectors are established according to a sensing hole or several holes. On

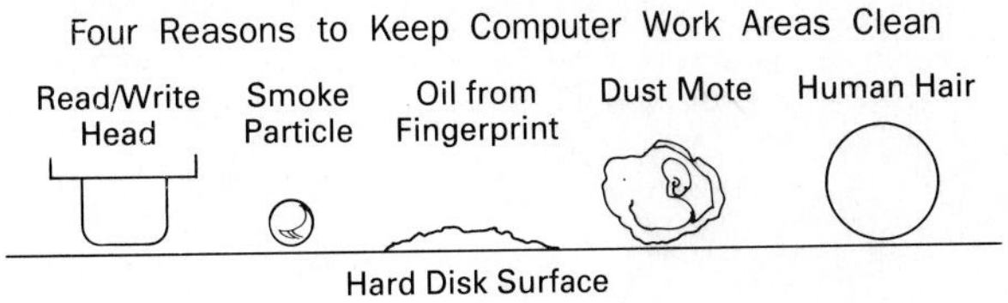

FIGURE 5.15

A hard disk's read/write head is extremely vulnerable to common contaminants that can damage the mechanism and destroy stored data.

FIGURE 5.16

Diskettes are typically either 8 inches, 5 1/4 inches, or 3 1/2 inches in diameter.

Courtesy of Radio Shack, a Division of Tandy Corp.

hard-sectored diskettes, sectors are defined by a series of sensing holes located close to the diskette's center. ***Soft-sectored diskettes*** have one sensing hole. The sectors of soft-sectored diskettes are identified by the disk drive through formatting.

Diskettes are not only distinguished by size and sectoring, but also by their storage capacity and by whether both sides are usable. Storage capacity is measured by the density in which data are packed on the disk: single, double, and quad density. Diskettes manufactured with only one usable side are considered single-sided while double-sided disks use both sides.

During the ***formatting*** process, the disk drive follows a computer program to set identification markings for each track and sector. ***Disk directories*** also are created during formatting. Directories catalog disk contents by file name and create a header label for each data file. As in tape files, header labels in disk files identify the beginning of the program or data file. The directory also keeps track of the sector locations of header labels. When a user requests access to a file on a certain disk, the disk operating system (DOS) uses the disk drive to look for the location of the header labels in the disk directory. When a match is found, the DOS locates the file by accessing the sector number provided by the directory.

For example, a user might request the "HOMEWORK" file on a diskette. DOS will search the directory to find "HOMEWORK." It will then use the sector num-

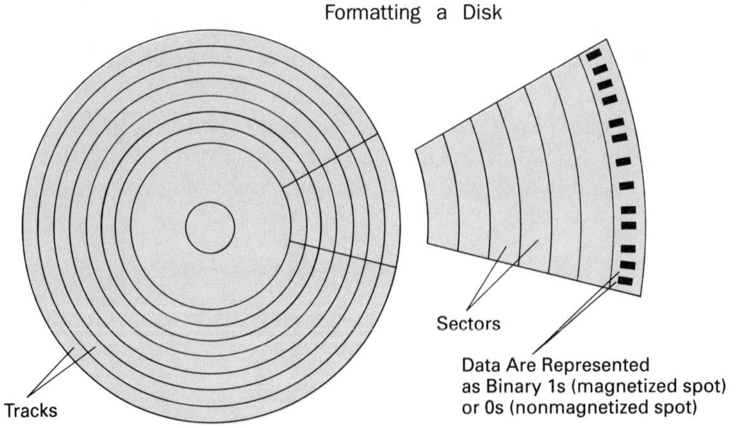

FIGURE 5.17

Formatting a disk organizes it into a series of concentric tracks that are subdivided into sectors.

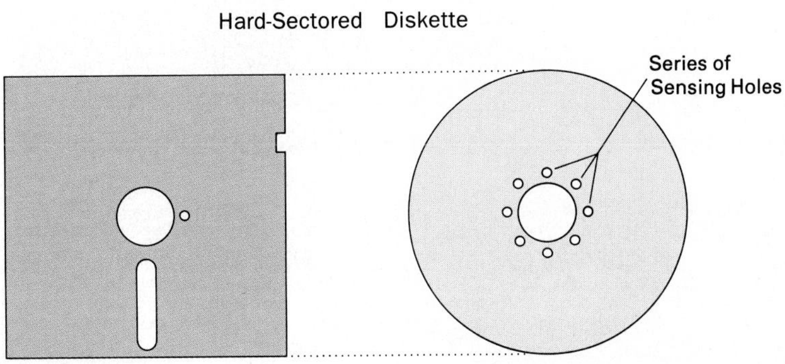

FIGURE 5.18

Sectors on a hard-sectored disk are defined by a series of sensing holes.

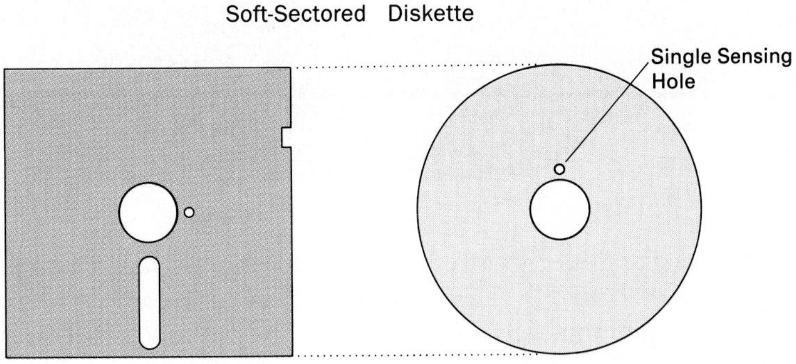

FIGURE 5.19

Soft-sectored diskettes have a single sensing hole that identifies the beginning of a track. Individual sector locations are determined when the diskette is formatted.

ber found in the directory to locate the start of the file. DOS will relocate the disk drive's read/write heads and check that sector to see if the header label of the file indeed reads "HOMEWORK." If the match is found, DOS copies the file into memory one sector at a time.

Like tape drives, disk drives are equipped with read/write heads. As the disk spins inside the drive, the read/write head passes over the surface of the disk. The head writes data on disk by magnetizing spots on the disk's tracks or retrieves data from disk by reading magnetized data already there. A system that uses hard disk packs may have several read/write heads to retrieve data from or output data to a disk surface. Figure 5.20 shows the access mechanism with read/write heads used in a removable disk drive. The disk pack illustrated provides seven recording surfaces. The bottom surface is not used. When the access arms are in a fixed position, seven tracks can be read—one on each surface. Repositioning of the arm enables seven more tracks to be read.

The collection of tracks that can be read at one position of the access arm is called a ***cylinder***. To locate a specified file on a disk pack, DOS searches the directory

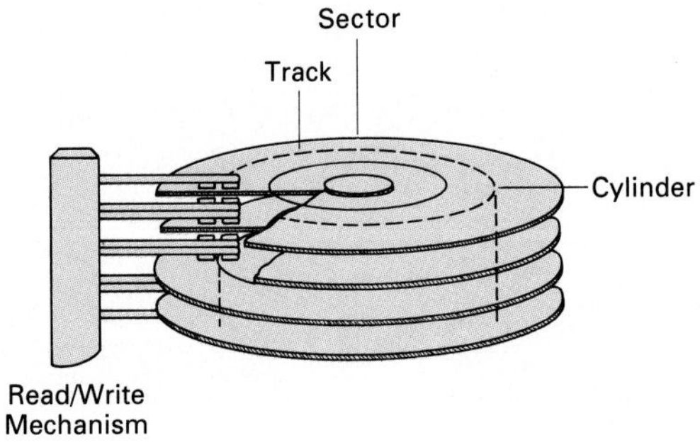

FIGURE 5.20

Direct access to data on a disk pack is accomplished through a moveable read/write mechanism that can access data on one cylinder at a time.

FIGURE 5.21

Removable disks allow peripheral operators to maximize the use of a disk drive.

for a matching name and its corresponding disk location. The access mechanism moves to the specified cylinder. Then, the read/write head for the correct track is activated, and the beginning of the file is located. The desired data then are copied into memory.

Disk packs can be mounted on drives for temporary use, or installed permanently within the drive. Such disk packs are called ***removable disks*** or ***fixed disks***, respectively. In both cases, the disk pack moves at a high speed, typically between 50 and 75 revolutions per second. After it is mounted inside a disk drive, the disk pack is protected from dirt and destructive elements in the environment. Some fixed disks have a read/write head available for each track, allowing for high-speed access, but this is much more expensive. Since fixed disk packs can never be removed, only one pack can be used for each drive.

FIGURE 5.22

Storage media are available in a wide variety of configurations, speeds, and capacities.

	Access Time	Transfer Rate	Storage Capacity
Removable Disk	30 to 100 milliseconds*	150,000 to 2 million characters per second	65 to 600 million characters
Fixed Disk	5 to 30 milliseconds*	200,000 to 2 million characters per second	10 to 120 million characters
Floppy Disk	70 to 500 milliseconds*	30,000 to 100,000 characters per second	160,000 to 1.2 million characters
Tape	10 milliseconds* to several seconds	18,000 characters per second	10 million to 60 million characters

*millisecond = 1/1000 of a second

Removable disk packs lend versatility to disk use. Since disks can be mounted and removed, the number of disk packs available for use with a drive is countless. Storage hardware varies in the time is takes to locate data on storage media, the ***access time***. It also varies in the speed at which data can be input or output, the ***transfer rate***. Figure 5.22 shows the access times and transfer rates for disk and tape drives. Compared to access times for fixed disks, those for removable disks are somewhat slower because read/write heads must position and reposition themselves for each access operation.

A variety of developments in magnetic disk technology have produced alternative storage media for large and small computers. One development is the ***Winchester disk***. Built into each Winchester disk drive is a single, high-capacity hard disk. This disk is hermetically sealed into the unit to keep out dust and other contaminants. Winchester disks are not removable. Microcomputers also can be equipped with ***disk cartridges***. Cartridges can be mounted and removed from disk drives. These storage media are compact, often measuring only 3.5 inches in diameter. Cartridges often can store as much as 10 megabytes (MB) of data. They provide portable, interchangeable, high-capacity hard disk storage for the microcomputer user.

FIGURE 5.23

Laser disk devices promise new breakthroughs in cost and capacity for secondary data storage.

Laser Disk Storage

Laser disks are high-speed storage media used primarily for storing files containing both text and physical data. Given names like video disks, compact disks (CDs), or CD-ROM, laser disks represent a new trend in small, high-capacity storage media. A single laser disk stores from 500MB to 1 gigabyte of data on each side. To put this storage capacity into perspective, a 600M laser disk holds the equivalent of 250,000 pages of text. In other words, it has enough storage capacity to save the name, address, and telephone number of everyone living in the United States, with room to spare.

To record data on a laser disk, small pinpoint holes are burned into the disk's surface to represent bit patterns (see Figure 5.24). Therefore, these disks are currently written on only once—hence the names CD-ROM (compact disk with read-only memory) and WORM (write once read many). A lower-power laser scans the disk's surface in order to read the bit patterns.

Since laser disks can hold pictures, structural drawings used by architects and engineers are well suited for this type of storage. Music lovers are drawn to the clear, crisp sound quality available from laser disks, which reproduce music that is free of the tape hiss found with magnetic tape recordings. Video sequences and library references are also recorded for educational applications. However, since laser disk drives can only read disks, on-line recording and editing are not possible. Once data are recorded on laser disks, they cannot be changed.

WORM laser disks represent the first step toward flexible laser disk technology, but magnetic tapes and disks are still the storage workhorses for most computer systems. Under development are laser disks that can be overwritten with new data. Once this research is completed, laser disks may provide the versatility needed to become a popular storage medium.

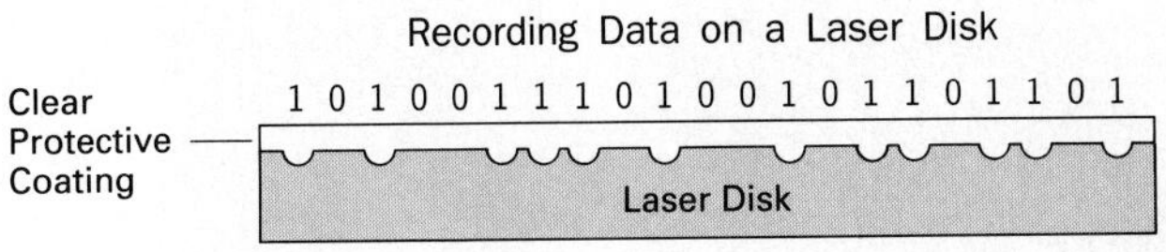

FIGURE 5.24

A laser's disk surface is pitted to represent binary 1s and left smooth for 0s. A clear plastic coating is then applied to protect the surface from damage.

I N S I G H T

LASERS: LIGHTING THE WAY

Lasers—they were called modern-day "death rays" when first developed in 1960. Now these high-intensity light beams are found in everything from tools to toys.

What Are They?

Lasers (Light Amplification by Stimulated Emission of Radiation) are produced when a crystal, liquid, or gas in a chamber is exposed to light, electricity, or radiation. The medium is "excited" or energized, producing photons. As the energy level rises, photons bounce within a chamber until they gain enough momentum to exit as a thin stream of single wavelength light.

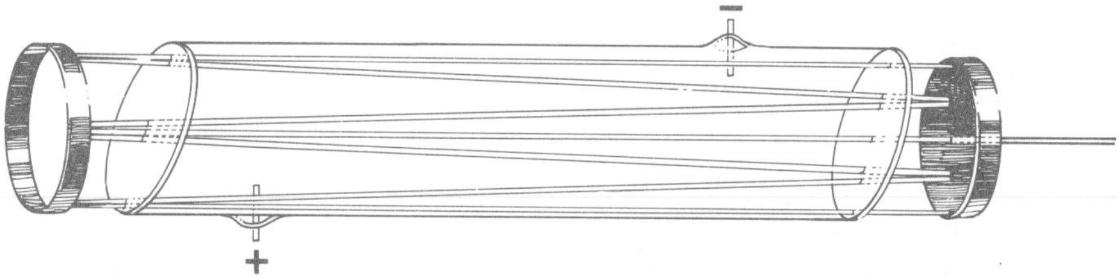

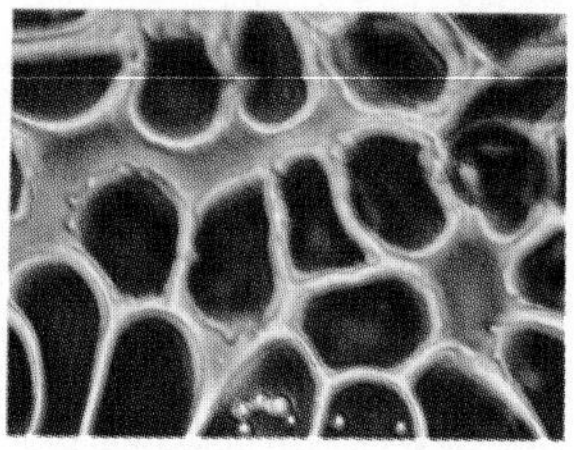

Are They Safe?

The power of a laser is determined by the amount of light or electricity used and the specific material through which it is passed. Lasers can slice thick metal or read UPC labels without harming people. The strength of the laser lies in its versatility and precision. This picture shows the hole made by a laser in a single red blood cell.

How Are They Used?

surgery without incisions
grocery store scanners
holographs—for art and credit cards
satellite communications
consumer product dating
erasing tattoos without scarring
printers
missile guidance
cornea shaping and retina repair
video and audio disks
cutting and welding
laser light shows
monitoring chemical reactions
detecting decades-old fingerprints

Here a laser scanner is used for determining precise measurements in testing aerodynamics of an aircraft design.

Lasers and Computers

Without computers, practical use of lasers would be impossible. Exact placement and duration of a laser, whether used in surgery or cutting metal parts, is computer-monitored but ultimately within human control. Here, an optical fiber transmits a laser beam to destroy an eye tumor.

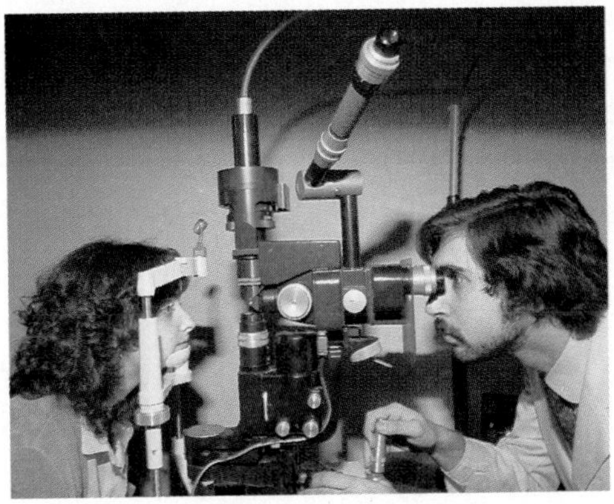

Laser printers contain a laser that scans across electronically charged drums, creating output rivalling that which is typeset or hand-drawn.

Optical disks store data encoded by a laser. Originally nonerasable and containing text, new erasable optical disks can store anything that can be digitized, such as text, music, photographs, and so on. Video disks use lasers to store sound, video, and animation.

STUDY QUESTIONS

8. Define storage media, tape track, parity bit, buffer, head crash, diskette, disk track, sector, cylinder, access time, transfer rate, and Winchester disk.
9. What are the three types of tape storage?
10. Explain how parity checking works when reading a nine-track tape.
11. What is the purpose of interrecord and interblock gaps?
12. Why are records often grouped into blocks when recorded on tape?
13. How are header and trailer labels used in file processing?
14. What are the two most common types of disk storage?
15. How are data stored in disks?
16. What are four distinguishing features of a floppy disk?
17. Describe what happens when a disk is formatted.
18. How is the disk directory used to locate files or programs on disk?
19. Give an advantage and disadvantage to using disk drives with removable and fixed disks.
20. Describe the difference between a disk pack and a disk cartridge.
21. Explain how laser disks work and identify one advantage and disadvantage to using this technology.

CONCLUSION

The ability to store data on disk and tape allows data to be organized once in machine-readable form and used many times. The application determines the type of file organization and access method used, and these, in turn, specify the storage media and hardware. Applications where a large percentage of the data need to be updated can use sequentially stored data on tape to solve the problem. If faster access is needed, disks instead of tape can be used to store data sequentially. When users need access to individual records, relative or indexed files on disk can be a solution. If both sequential and direct access to records are required, an indexed-sequential file is appropriate. To avoid duplication of data and to get the most flexible access to data, a database program is used. Without this versatility in data organization and access, the computer's IPOS cycle would be severely limited.

CHAPTER FACTS

- Data are organized for potential use into characters, fields, records, files, and databases.
- Data are retrieved from disks and tapes by sequential access, or from disks by direct access (random access). Data can be organized into sequential, relative, or indexed-sequential files.
- Sequential files are in key field order. Updates also must be ordered.
- Relative files use a hashing routine to convert key fields into disk location. The record then is accessed directly.
- Indexed-sequential files (indexed files) contain an index to general disk locations based on the key field. The computer consults the index, and goes directly to the specified disk location.

- In databases, files are linked by common key fields. This eliminates duplication of data and allows access by multiple application programs. A database program (DBMS) manages the database with extensive indexes.
- Data are captured on storage media for further processing. Tapes and disks are the most common storage media.
- Tape storage media are reels of tape, cassettes, or cartridges. Data are stored on tracks as a series of magnetized or blank spots. Parity checking ensures that data are correctly written and read by the disk drive.
- Tape records are separated by interrecord gaps to allow the drive to stop and start. Records can be blocked together for faster access.
- Files on tape begin with a header label that identifies the file name and end with a trailer label.
- Disk storage is either on hard disks or diskettes. Data are coded as magnetized spots by the disk drive on the disk's tracks. Tracks are divided into sectors.
- Disk directories list disk contents and the starting locations of files and programs. Sector numbers or cylinders are used to locate the files and programs.
- Disk packs are either removable or fixed. Winchester disks are fixed disks. Disk cartridges are small, removable hard disks used by microcomputers.
- Laser disks store pictures and text. Data are stored permanently as holes on the disk's surface.

TERMS TO REMEMBER

access time
block
buffer
cassette tape
cylinder
database management system (DBMS)
direct access
disk cartridge
disk directory
disk pack
disk track
diskette
fixed disk
floppy disk
formatting
hard disk
hard-sectored diskette
hashing routine
head crash
header label
indexed file
indexed-sequential file
interblock gap
interrecord gap
key field
laser disk
parity bit
parity checking
random access
reel tape
relative file
removable disk
sector
sequential access
sequential file
soft-sectored diskette
storage media
tape cartridge
tape track
trailer label
tracks
transfer rate
updating
Winchester disk

CHECK YOUR UNDERSTANDING

1. Data on tapes are written as bits in tape channels called:
   a. cylinders
   b. sectors
   c. tracks
   d. heads
   e. labels
2. To increase computer efficiency, records on tape and disk are grouped together into ___________.
3. Storage area on diskettes is divided into sectors. (True/False)
4. A ___________ is a section of the disk that lists all files and their locations on the disk.
5. Disks that store both pictures and text are called video disks or ___________ disks.
6. Which of the following is ***not*** included when updating a file?
   a. adding records
   b. sorting records
   c. deleting records
   d. changing records
   e. none of the above
7. Processing a file sequentially is most efficient if both the file and the changes are in key field order. (True/False)
8. Direct access can be used only when the data are stored on tape or disk. (True/False)
9. What kind of file can be accessed both directly and sequentially?
   a. relative file
   b. sequential file
   c. indexed-sequential file
   d. random file
   e. indirect file
10. Duplicate keys will result in unique disk locations when run through the hashing routine. (True/False)

APPLYING WHAT YOU'VE LEARNED

1. Look at the storage hardware available to you in school or at home. What kind is it? Are the storage media fixed or removable? How many data (in bytes) can the media hold? Is access of the data sequential or random? How fast can the data be accessed? You may need to check manuals for this information.
2. Look up the procedure for formatting a diskette on home or school equipment. Write a user's guide explaining the procedure to new students. Include any necessary pictures and warnings. Ask a fellow student to read and use the guide to see if it is clearly written.
3. If you use diskettes, obtain a copy of a diskette directory. What kinds of information are included in it?
4. Use the Extended ASCII chart from Chapter 4 to determine the bit patterns for several of the characters in Figure 5.13. List what the parity bit would be for each character if parity were odd.

5. Explore how laser disks are being presently used in education, training packages, advertising, music, or another field. Write a short report on your findings.
6. Describe two applications (not in the text) for each type of file organization: sequential, relative, and indexed-sequential. Include the fields in a typical record and identify an appropriate key field.

CHECK YOUR UNDERSTANDING ANSWERS

1. c
2. blocks
3. true
4. directory
5. laser
6. b
7. true
8. false
9. c
10. false

C H A P T E R S I X

INPUT/OUTPUT OPERATIONS

KEY IDEAS

- **From the user's point of view**
  What is the most effective way to put data into a computer? How can output be put to its most practical use?

- **The link between people and hardware**
  Innovative hardware and software designs working with well-written procedures make computer systems easier to use and access.

  Loading software and data
  Software and data must be loaded into the computer's memory before processing can begin.

  Batch operations
  Many data processing problems are solved by processing large batches of related data.

  Interactive operations
  Users often demand that computer systems supply results as soon as they are available.

- **Input options**
  Types of input hardware are as diverse as the problems they solve.

  Terminals
  Several types of terminals provide a keyboard for input and either a screen or printed output.

  Scanners
  Many input devices sense character or bar patterns and convert them into machine-readable code.

  Other input devices
  A variety of equipment—such as the mouse, light pens, and sensitive screens—input data for processing.

- **Output solutions**
  Output hardware is as varied as the applications it supports.

  Permanent output
  Processed information can be output as printed documents on paper or film.

  Temporary output
  Visual displays and audio responses are used with applications that do not need paper copy.

FROM THE USER'S POINT OF VIEW

Advances in computer technology have followed two general routes: expanding what the computer can do and making those capabilities more accessible to you. To achieve accessibility, hardware/software designs and well-written procedures have aimed to make computer systems user friendly, or easy for people to operate. User friendly qualities underscore the notion that computers are tools to benefit people. With user friendly computer systems, you can execute complex operations with a single keystroke. You can use menus to select processing options or consult help screens for explanations of operations. In short, user friendly computer systems enable you to take control.

When you call on a computer for processing help, the operating system and applications program, as shown in Figure 6.1, minimizes the need to reconfigure the machine every time a different software package is used. You need not concern yourself with the mechanics of computer processing. Rather, you can devote your energy to obtaining the specific processing results desired.

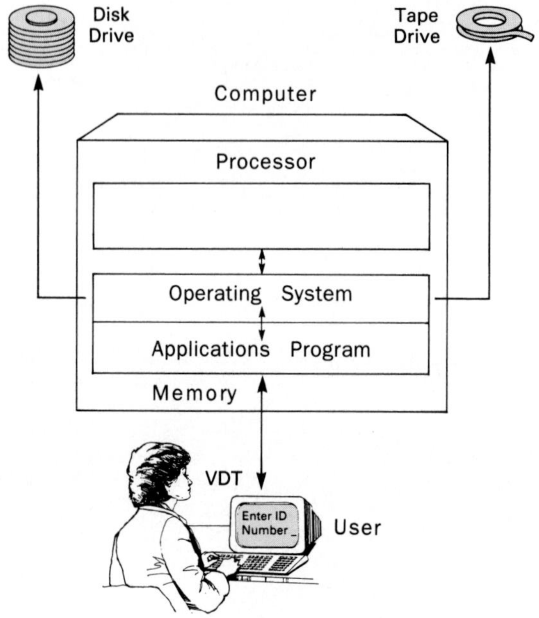

FIGURE 6.1

Layers of software are positioned between the user and the computing equipment to implement ease of access to applications and processing, or "user friendliness."

THE LINK BETWEEN PEOPLE AND HARDWARE

A mix of both software and hardware ultimately establishes a computer system's level of user friendliness. Keys to the user friendliness of any system are ***input/ output (I/O)*** operations. I/O operations are where computers and people meet. People enter data into the computer through input hardware. They then receive the results of processing from output hardware. Where user–computer interaction is most frequent, computer system friendliness is most important.

To accommodate different types of input and output hardware, a computer has several I/O ports, where the input/output—as well as storage—hardware is connected to the processing unit. Two types of I/O ports are available: serial and parallel. With a ***serial port***, as shown in Figure 6.2, data are sent between the computer and the attached hardware one bit at a time. When a ***parallel port*** is used, the entire bit pattern for a single character is sent at the same time. Different peripheral devices will have different I/O port requirements. The advantage to using a parallel port is that it is faster. However, the equipment must be relatively close to the computer. While serial ports do not provide as high a transmission speed, peripheral devices can be much further away. Part of the decision in buying a computer is to be sure sufficient ports are available to handle current and future hardware needs.

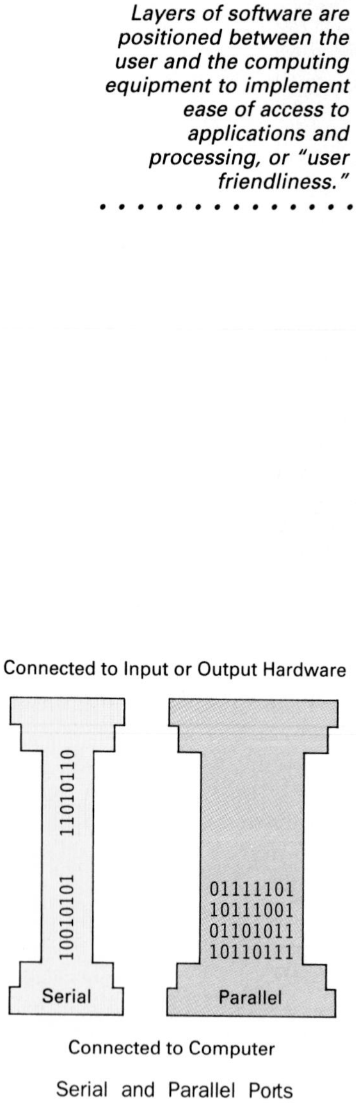

FIGURE 6.2

Serial and parallel ports allow a variety of hardware to be connected to the computer.

Loading Software and Data

Input operations supply the computer with data and directions for processing. No processing can take place until input is entered into main memory. Primarily, two types of input exist: instructions and data. Application programs are the instructions given to a computer to execute a specific processing job. The computer uses the application program to process data, which also are input by the user. Other instructions include system programs and related commands that computer operators or users enter through the keyboard.

FIGURE 6.3
Data processing at banks today would be impossible without computer terminals.

People must do more than supply the computer with programs and data. Effective use of the computer requires that users follow correct procedures to make sure their input is complete and correct. Computer-delivered results are only as good as the input provided. Our challenge lies in ensuring that the computer has fault-free input. In other words, both the content and the format of input must be appropriate for the required processing.

A computer can support input operations at several levels. At one level, the computer receives input and stores it in machine-readable form for processing at a later time. Real-time processing is another level of support. In this case, the user inputs data and the results are available as soon as processing is complete.

Batch Operations

The nature of a processing problem often dictates the type of input operation that must be used. In an organization with weekly payroll, hundreds or thousands of employee time sheets must be input each week as data for paychecks. Since employees may work overtime, it would be impractical to enter payroll data until the end of the week. The most efficient solution is a weekly batch input of all time sheets. The data are input, verified, and stored until needed. After processing, the operator can mount paychecks on the printer producing all paychecks at one time. This also allows a data control clerk to check that the output is complete and correct.

One way to check data for accuracy is to use ***control totals***. Control totals are typically used as part of batch input, where the transactions to be processed are counted manually, and the total recorded. A control total is determined by making calculations independent of the computer system to double-check input operations. For example, in financial applications, the control total is the dollar amount of all transactions to be processed. Before processing a batch of payroll time sheets, the hour amounts on all time sheets would be added and recorded as the control total. In nonfinancial processing, fields without monetary significance—such as zip codes or identification numbers—are totaled. A batch control is established by summing these nonfinancial data fields. Once processing is completed, computer-generated totals are compared with the control total. Any discrepancies indicate a possible error in data entry.

CLIP

HOT-WIRING THE HIT PARADE

Computers are music's new mothers of invention.

Processors, chips and programs are so ingrained in musical research that experts predict no new acoustic instrument will ever be developed without use of electronics, either in the design or the instrument itself.

"That's a true statement as far as I'm concerned," says Jack Taylor, director of the Center for Music Research at Florida State University. "Why should anybody hack out an instrument of metal or iron or brass or whatever when he can do it with his fingertips?"

Professional performers and composers were the first to tune in to "the whole world of possible sounds" from a single electronic instrument, says John Chowning, director of Stanford University's Center for Computer Research in Music and Acoustics. Such new-age maestros as Jean-Claude Risset of France have composed at Stanford, while USA jazz musician Stan Getz produced work written there.

Musicians use computers either to invent sounds or recreate the performance of traditional instruments. Electronically produced music is used often as background in movies or TV shows, and on commercials.

The electronic music market is much more than the rock musician who goes on tour with a synthesizer. A few years ago, Casio Inc. and Yamaha International Corp. introduced electronics to the USA home music market with inexpensive, portable electronic keyboards.

"It's the biggest boom to hit the music industry ever," says Glen Depue, marketing manager for Yamaha's portable keyboards.

Source: Reprinted by permission, *USA Today*

Key Question: Do you feel that music is any less professional or interesting when a traditional instrument is replaced by electronic equipment?

Transactions often are grouped into batches at the close of a working period. Consider, as an example, a supplier of tractor parts who fills three dozen orders in a day. Each order is recorded by a microcomputer system located in the warehouse. Linked to the microcomputer is a printer that generates an invoice for each order filled. At the end of the day, the microcomputer-recorded data are transmitted in a batch to a central mainframe to update master records. This method of input, referred to as ***remote job entry***, involves sending data to the computer through communication lines.

FIGURE 6.4

Automatic teller machines employed by banks use interactive input as a way of identifying customer needs.

Interactive Operations

In other situations, people cannot wait for batch input and processing. Bank customers must have instant access to the money in their accounts. If the customer uses an automatic teller machine (ATM), batch processing is eliminated. The customer now directly uses the computer system in real time by entering a personal identification number (PIN), the transaction desired, and the amount to be withdrawn. The money and a computer-printed receipt are taken directly from the machine by the customer/user. Although the computer system carefully edits data from the users, it is still the users who are responsible for verifying the correctness of the data. The system may be able to catch an invalid account number but cannot detect an error between a $5 and $50 withdrawal.

As these examples illustrate, input techniques can be either interactive or batch. ***Interactive*** input involves real-time processing of data and instructions. ***Batch*** input requires two stages. First data are captured, verified, and stored. Later, data are input and processed. Regardless of the technique, data must be complete and correct.

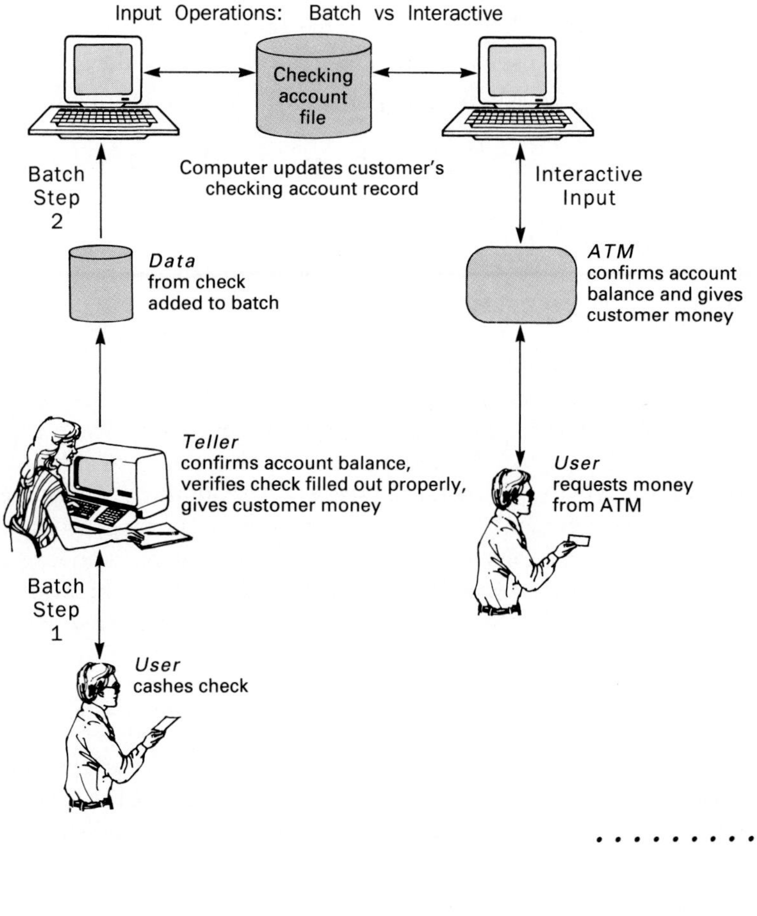

FIGURE 6.5

Input operations at a bank can take advantage of both batch and interactive data entry.

FIGURE 6.6

Hard copy terminals let users take output with them.

STUDY QUESTIONS

1. Define I/O, serial port, parallel port, control total, remote job entry, and interactive.
2. How does a computer system's user friendliness benefit people?
3. Identify two levels of software that help people to use computer technology.
4. What are two types of input that must be in the computer's memory before processing can take place?
5. What are the prerequisites for effective use of the computer?
6. Describe the difference between interactive and batch input.

INPUT OPTIONS

Implementation of input techniques—whether interactive or batch—relies on hardware. The types of input hardware available are as diverse as the processing problems they help solve.

Interactive processing accommodates a dialogue between the user and the computer. The user requests service from the computer. The computer responds, often by producing a menu or other screen display. The user enters data in response to the prompts displayed by the computer. A ***prompt*** is a request by the computer for data or instructions. The computer continues processing, prompting the user for more data or instructions as necessary. This series of exchanges is characteristic of interactive input and processing. Different types of input hardware are available to support interactive processing. The following are the most widely used devices.

Terminals

Perhaps the most popular interactive input hardware is the terminal. A terminal is the point at which input is entered or output received by the user. Terminals have built-in keyboards that enable users to interact with the computer. If the terminal

FIGURE 6.7

Dumb terminals lack processing capacity.

has a display screen, input data is reproduced, or echoed, on screen as the users type. This device is also known as a video display terminal (VDT). Since the data displayed on a VDT is not permanent, it is referred to as ***soft copy***.

Some terminals have a printing mechanism instead of a screen. A popular version of this type of terminal was produced by the Teletype Corporation. As a result, people often refer to these as teletypes. Since these machines produce a paper, or ***hard copy*** of the output, they also are known as ***hard copy terminals***. With either type of terminal, the actual input occurs when data are entered into the computer. The generation of the screen display or hard copy, is not considered part of the input operation.

Many terminals have no built-in processing power. These devices, known as ***dumb terminals***, rely on communications with a central computer. The user inputs data through the dumb terminal while the computer provides the programs, computer logic, and memory capacity to support processing. The central computer also returns output to the terminal. Since the performance capabilities of dumb terminals are limited, their cost is quite low. However, dumb terminals place a sizable processing burden on the main computer.

More expensive ***intelligent terminals*** also may be connected to powerful central computers. However, intelligent terminals, often microcomputers, are equipped with built-in processing and memory capabilities that supplement the main computer's processing power. These terminals often support their own disk or tape storage. Intelligent terminals relieve some of the processing load placed on central computers. Some processing and memory operations, such as editing input and formatting output, are executed entirely within the intelligent terminal. This reduces the need for constant communication between the terminal and the computer. Reduced demand on the main computer is the primary advantage of intelligent terminals over dumb terminals. The primary disadvantage of these input devices is their high cost.

On most terminals, keyboards are quite similar. They have typewriterlike keys for inputting letters, numbers, and other symbols. Cursor control keys manipulate the ***cursor***, a highlighted block or underline that appears on screen to indicate typing location. The four basic cursor control keys generally are marked with arrows pointing up, down, left, and right. Some keyboards have numeric keypads for easy

FIGURE 6.8
Keyboard layouts will vary in their placement of function keys, cursor control keys, special symbols, and the numeric keypad.

input of numeric data. In addition, ***function keys*** can activate special software features. With word processing software, pressing a function key might activate a page break, center a line, or search for a specified word. Many software packages allow users to define the activities associated with function keys. Function keys often let users control several operations with the mere press of a key. As shown in Figure 6.8 the placement of cursor control keys, function keys, and the presence of numeric keypads varies among keyboards. Also, special keyboards are available for foreign languages or that include keys with scientific characters.

Scanners

Input devices that collect data from products and sales tags as they are purchased are part of point-of-sales ***(POS)*** systems. Perhaps the most familiar POS system uses the universal product code (UPC) to help update inventory, track daily sales, and print sales receipts. UPC markings on all grocery items consist of a collection of bars of varying widths. For this reason, UPC often is referred to as ***bar codes***. In the UPC system, the pattern of bars on the bar code label represents the manufacturer's product code. Bar codes have been put to many other uses. For example, library books and library cards are marked with bar codes to expedite check-out.

Bar code markings are input into a computer with ***scanners***, which sense the patterns in the bars and convert them into machine-readable characters. Some scanners resemble wands; they send out a beam of light that picks up bar patterns. Other scanners are built into sales check-out counters. In each case, the scanner converts the code into machine-readable input. The computer responds by providing information associated with the given code.

The UPC markings identify a stock number. This number is the key field for records in the inventory file. By using the bar code, the computer locates the record associated with that number. The record contains information about the name and price of the product. These items are used to generate a customer receipt. This method allows stores to offer special sale prices without having to change each price tag. Instead, a single change is made to the price field in select records of the inventory file. The accompanying table seen in Figure 6.9 shows the steps used to print a receipt in the UPC system. As sales transactions are processed, the computer retains a log of all transactions. The computer uses this log to produce reports that help balance cash in the registers and reorder merchandise for the store.

Other types of scanners are used to read handwritten marks and typewritten characters. Special scanners used in ***optical mark recognition (OMR)*** methods sense the presence of a pencil mark. Popular uses for optical mark recognition are standardized tests, surveys, and questionnaires.

FIGURE 6.9
Bar code scanners initiate a six-step IPOS cycle that updates inventory records and prints grocery bills.

Six Steps to Printing Bill in UPC System

1. Bar code scanned, identifying key field.
2. Computer searches inventory file using key field.
3. Match found—disk drive transfers price & description back to computer.
4. Computer sends data to terminal at check-out counter.
5. Terminal figures sales price and tax.
6. Terminal prints price, tax, product descriptions on receipt.

SURGICAL ROBOT PERFORMS BIOPSIES

Ole has performed 18 biopsies of brain tumors, and he's less than 3 years old. Eventually, when he has gained a little more sophistication and learned to interact better with strangers, his inventor expects even greater things of the surgical robot.

Inventor and electrical engineer Yik San Kwoh directs CAT scan research at Memorial Medical Center in Long Beach, Calif. "I don't really know the end potential, but I think we've just barely scratched the surface," Kwoh says. "There are any number of situations that demand the kind of precision and stability that a robot like this offers." The hospital is planning to expand Ole's sphere of responsibility to include assists in brain stimulations, Kwoh says. A few other possibilities include eye surgery, spinal surgery and knee joint replacements.

Kwoh wrote Ole's software, which works in conjunction with a CAT scanner, during a period of three years in consultation with eight other researchers. Ole was named after a benefactor of the hospital, Sven Olsen, who underwrote the robot's purchase and much of the development expense.

The robot wields its 29-lb., six-jointed aluminum hand with accuracy that even a brain surgeon could envy. In fact, Kwoh says, the robot is so exact that it has reduced the necessary size of a biopsy incision from one-half or five-eighths of an inch down to one-eighth of an inch.

Other advantages the robot brings to this kind of work include memory precision, mobility and relative immunity. Ole is able to return to the same spot with accuracy within two-thousandths of an inch, can be moved easily from one location to another and does not suffer ill effects from X-ray exposure.

That last characteristic could be particularly valuable in reducing time spent in operations where surgeons could benefit from having continuous CAT scan readings. According to Kwoh, Ole might someday be used to perform actual surgical procedures while the human surgeons direct its hands from another room, outside the X-ray's reach.

Source: Reprinted by permission, *Computerworld*

Key Question: In what ways can a scalpel-wielding robot assist a surgeon?

ABCDEFGHIJKLM
NOPQRSTUVWXYZ
1234567890

FIGURE 6.10

Optical characters on sales tags can be read by both people and scanners.

Optical character recognition (OCR) permits users to input printed or typewritten documents with a scanner. Entire pages of text are read rapidly by scanners for direct input. Many publishers use OCR scanners. For example, news stories written on typewriters may be scanned into typesetting computers. Type for newer editions of books can be set by scanning pages from previous editions.

Magnetic ink character recognition (MICR) is similar to OCR methods because MICR employs computer-readable symbols. However, MICR requires special magnetic ink to record the symbols. MICR coding is used primarily in banking operations to enter data from checks and deposit slips. These banking documents are imprinted with MICR symbols that indicate customer account numbers, bank identification, and dollar amounts. A special MICR scanner reads the MICR character data and stores them on tape or disk for subsequent processing.

A telephone with tone dialing is used widely as an interactive input device. An example can be found in many banks. A teller dials a number that establishes a connection to a computer. Then, an account number is entered. The computer generates a voicelike response that verifies the account number and balance.

Another input device is the credit card readers used by merchants, restaurants, hotels, gas stations, and airlines. The credit card is passed through a slot, where the

FIGURE 6.11

MICR scanners input from checks the bank's and customer's account numbers along with the amount drawn on the check.

credit card number is entered. The amount of the sale is entered through a keypad. The computer responds with an approval or disapproval of the sale based on the customer's current credit level. Another type of card reader dates back to those used with Hollerith's original punched card. It is still used with punched cards, which many organizations continue to use for billing. These cards are punched with billing data and sent to customers. Customers return the punched card with payments and the billing data are read into the computer from the cards by a card reader.

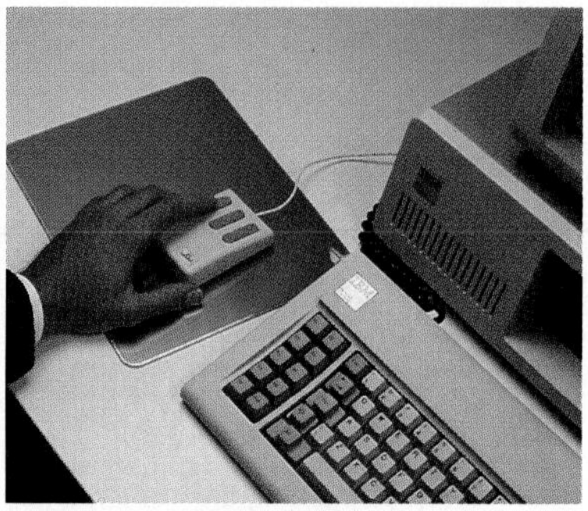

FIGURE 6.12

The mouse helps users control the cursor's location on the screen and the selection of program options.

Other Input Devices

While the keyboard and scanners are the most familiar device for input, the popularity of other input hardware is on the rise. For example, keys are not always needed for cursor control. Instead, a ***mouse*** or ***joystick*** can move the cursor. The mouse is a hand-held box with a ball on its underside. As the mouse is moved across a flat surface, such as a desk top, the motion is signaled to the computer, which moves the cursor. Used primarily for menu selection or for graphics applications, the mouse often is used in conjunction with a keyboard and increases user friendliness. People use joysticks when playing computer games. The joystick looks like a stick shift found in cars with manual transmissions. By moving the joystick's arm, players can control the movement and action of characters on the screen.

A hand-held, light-sensitive stylus attached to terminals can accept the cursor position on the screen as input. People move this ***light pen*** across a screen to make menu selections or draw shapes. A similar input device is the ***touch-sensitive screen,*** which enables users to input instructions by merely touching prompts displayed on a screen. These screens are sensitized so that the application of pressure—usually by a finger, pencil, or stylus—is read as input or is read by detecting the interruptions of a light beam.

Drafting, or drawing, ***tablets*** work on a similar principle. A stylus is applied to the surface of a flat, pressure-sensitive tablet. The pattern of pressure is sensed by wires under the surface of the tablet, then ***digitized***. That is, the location of the stylus is expressed in mathematical terms and transmitted to the computer. The image "drawn" on the drafting tablet is echoed on a screen.

By using drafting tablets or touch-sensitive screens, people can input structural drawings into the computer. The drawings then can be viewed and manipu-

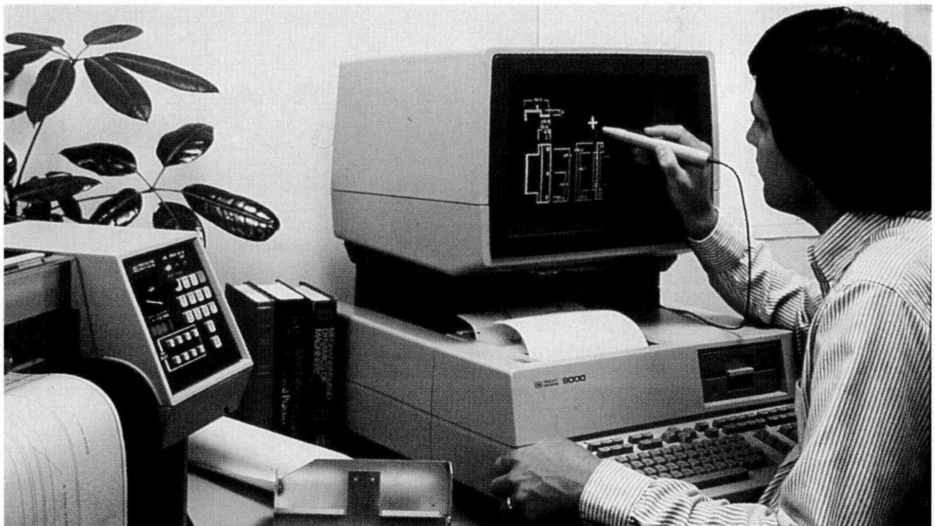

FIGURE 6.13

Light pens and touch-sensitive screens input menu selections. Furthermore, the pens can draw shapes directly on the screen.

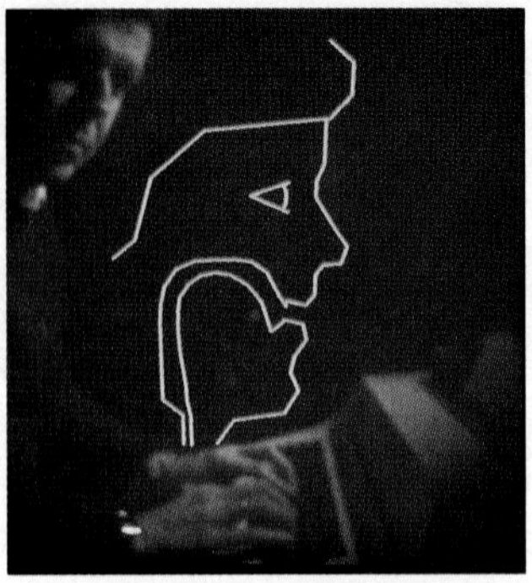

FIGURE 6.14

Researchers continue to analyze human speech patterns in order to improve the reliability and speed of voice recognition devices.

lated as if the objects they represent actually exist. An aircraft engineer can design a plane and input the specifications to the computer. The three-dimensional computer drawing can be tested as a model of the aircraft. Test flights can be simulated and design features evaluated, all under control of the computer. This enables users to detect problems in product designs and draft new designs before the product is made.

Voice recognition devices accept spoken commands as input. In one typical application, a computer using voice recognition devices accepts spoken lists of inventory as input. A worker on a loading dock need only announce the names and amounts of goods being unloaded. The computer recognizes the spoken words and converts them to input.

Today's voice recognition devices still have many drawbacks. The devices understand only a limited number of commands, and users often need to talk very slowly. In addition, computers must be programmed to recognize the speech of those people who will be using the equipment. Currently, users need to read a list of key terms into the computer to establish a working vocabulary. Still, as hardware specialists continue to refine voice technologies, voice input has the potential to come into wider use. Eventually, computers are expected to transcribe dictation into reports.

STUDY QUESTIONS

7. Define prompt, soft copy, hard copy, dumb terminal, intelligent terminal, cursor, digitize, voice recognition device, POS, and scanner.
8. Describe the difference between a VDT and a hard copy terminal.
9. What are the advantages and disadvantages to using dumb and intelligent terminals?
10. How are function keys used?
11. Explain how users interactively input data using a mouse, joystick, light pen, touch-sensitive screen, and tablet.
12. Describe an application for voice recognition devices and identify three limitations to using this equipment.
13. What is the difference among reading bar codes, optical mark recognition (OMR), optical character recognition (OCR), and magnetic ink character recognition (MICR)? Describe an application for each.
14. How can a telephone and card reader be used as part of input operations?

OUTPUT SOLUTIONS

The role of computers as problem-solving tools is most visible when users receive the actual results of computer processing. Types of computer output are as diverse as the applications they support. Generally output falls into three categories:

- Permanent output
- Temporary output
- Action output

Hardware	Characteristics
VDT (video display terminal)	Produces quick, possibly colorful, *temporary* results
Teletype	Produces permanent results
Dumb Terminal	Low cost I/O hardware which relies on computer for processing power
Intelligent Terminal	High cost I/O hardware which reduces processing demands on computer by performing some functions itself
Keyboard	Most popular data entry device. Some come with optional numeric keypads, function keys, and cursor control keys
Mouse	Used with graphic displays to control cursor
Light Pen	Hand-held hardware used to control cursor for graphic input
Touch Sensitive Screen	User touches prompts on screen to control input. No additional hardware
Tablet	Supports graphic input through free-hand drawing or tracing
Voice Recognition	Activated by user's voice after voice has been preprogrammed into computer; currently accepts limited number of vocal commands
Scanner	Accepts a wide variety of machine readable characters which include optical marks, optical characters, magnetic ink characters, and bar codes
Telephone	Used to input numeric data from long distances; some voice recognition hardware is used with telephone input
Credit Card Reader	Used for credit checks during retail purchases
Punched Card Reader	One of the oldest types of input devices, reads data from punched cards

FIGURE 6.15

Input hardware is designed to work with a variety of data as a part of either batch or interactive data entry.

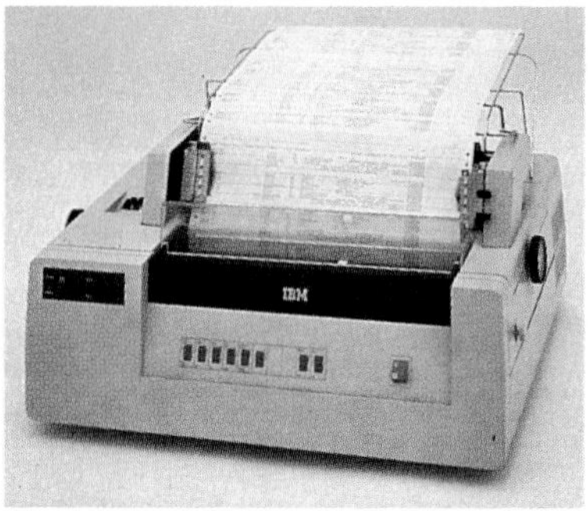

FIGURE 6.16

Draft-quality printers utilizing dot-matrix characters are found in many offices, schools, and homes.

Permanent Output

Computer-processed information in the form of printed documents, drawings, and microfilm are examples of permanent output. A vast selection of hardware is available for producing output. Different types of permanent output used together give broad support for professional or personal applications. An architect's office, for example, might use reports, graphics, and microfilm for daily support of its operations. The following sections introduce the most common types of output hardware.

Printers

Many organizations use computer applications for business correspondence, payroll processing, billing, and accounting. For example, architects deliver cost estimates and formal bids to clients as professional documents. Each application requires permanent output, produced on a printer.

Depending on the intended application of the printed document, a variety of printers is used. In-house memos may be printed with lower quality printers, while letters to clients demand a higher quality print style. The speed of printing may be an important consideration, along with the cost of producing the document.

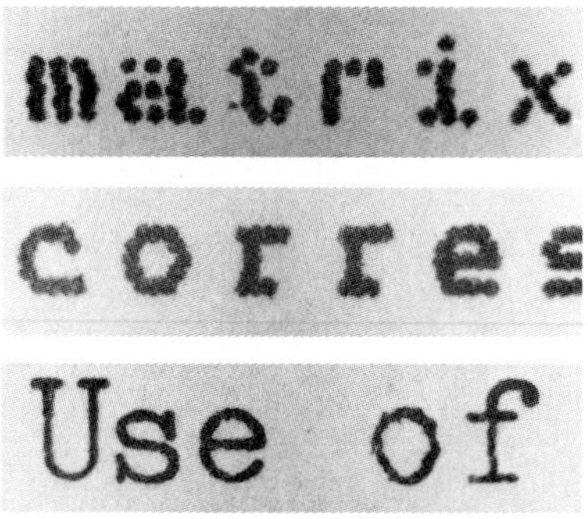

FIGURE 6.17

Printers use either dot-matrix, correspondence quality, or letter quality characters.

A popular type of printer uses ***dot-matrix characters***. These output devices form characters as a pattern of dots within a matrix. The dots are transferred to paper by a printing element that contains several wires. Different combinations of wires create designated characters. By striking an inked ribbon, each character is printed on paper.

The quality of printed characters depends on the number of dots used per character and how the character is printed. The print of a dot-matrix printer generally is not considered to be of professional quality. That is, it does not look as if it has been typed by hand on a high-quality typewriter. A printer using dot-matrix characters is also called a ***draft quality printer*** since it may be suitable for a draft, but not a final copy. However, many draft quality printers can create ***correspondence quality characters*** by typing each line twice. The dots are printed a little higher in the second pass, which fills in the character. As you might expect, printing is much slower with correspondence quality characters.

Printers that use ***full characters*** produce a top-quality output suitable for any business application. Such printers are called ***letter quality printers***. Each number, letter, and symbol available in a full-character printer is preformed, similar to a typewriter.

Print speeds are determined by the amount of text a printer can output at one time. ***Serial printers***, which print one character at a time, generally can produce from 15 to 200 characters per second. ***Line printers*** output a complete line of text at a time, at a rate of between 100 to 2000 lines per minute. Using xerographic techniques, ***page printers*** output a page at a time, reproducing up to 20,000 lines per minute.

Printers use either impact or nonimpact methods to transfer text to paper. Most draft quality and letter quality printers are impact printers. Both contain print elements that strike a ribbon for character formation. This physical contact is characteristic of impact printers. Line printers represent the fastest form of impact printing. By using either a rotating drum or chain containing every possible letter, number, and special character, a line of print can be quickly formatted. A printed line is created by striking an inked ribbon and paper against the drum or chain with small hammers. Line printers are frequently used with minicomputers and mainframes that need reliable and continuous operation from a printer.

Nonimpact printers form characters without using an inked ribbon. ***Ink-jet printers***, for example, spray tiny drops of ink to form character shapes on paper. Since characters are formed as a pattern of dots, ink-jet printers are technically dot-matrix printers. However, the quality of ink-jet output generally is much higher than that of most dot-matrix printers.

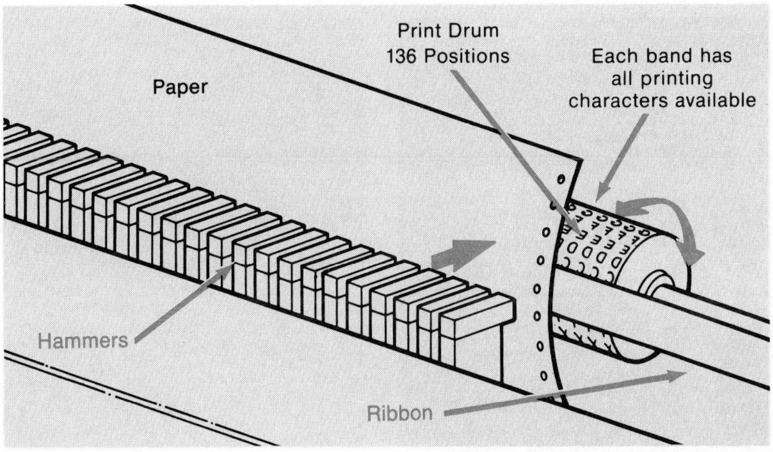

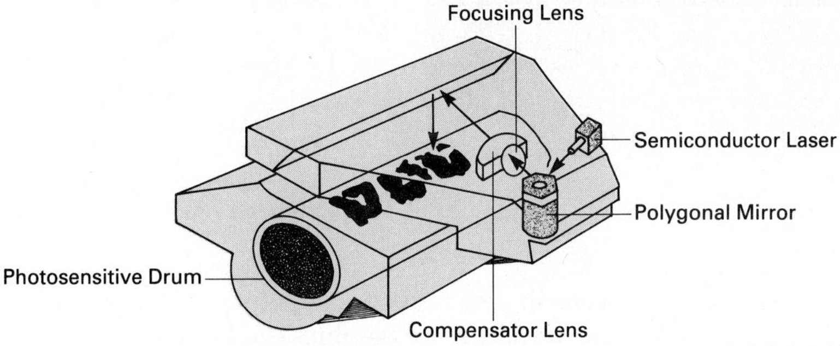

FIGURE 6.18

Line printers represent the fastest form of impact printing.

FIGURE 6.19

Draft-quality printers utilizing dot-matrix characters are found in many offices, schools, and homes.

Photo courtesy of Liane Enkelis

Other nonimpact printers form characters with such elements as heat and electricity. A ***thermal printer*** uses heated dot-matrix wires to print output on specially treated paper. ***Electrostatic printers*** emit electrical impulses that are reproduced as characters on electrostatic paper.

A nonimpact printer that produces high–quality output at very high speeds is the ***laser printer***. Laser printers operate much like copy machines. A controlled beam of intense laser light forms images on an electrically charged drum. After a developing process, the images are transferred to paper. Laser-created documents feature a high-quality print. This allows users to print their own letterheads, logos, and special forms along with the text, instead of using preprinted forms. Laser printers output a full page at a time. With new developments in laser print technologies, costs have declined steadily. As laser printers become more affordable, they will be in demand by users who need high-quality printing at superfast speeds.

Plotters

Within an architectural firm many computer applications will require graphic output in the form of graphs, maps, charts, and drawings. An architect's designs, for example, will require sketches instead of text. One kind of device that produces graphic output in permanent form is the ***plotter***. Directed by signals from the computer, the plotter moves a pen across a piece of paper. A plotter equipped with more than one pen can produce multicolor graphic output.

Two types of plotters are available. The ***flat-bed plotter*** holds a sheet of paper on a flat surface, then moves a pen across the sheet to form images. With a ***drum plotter***, the paper is wound around a drum; then the paper's rotation and pen

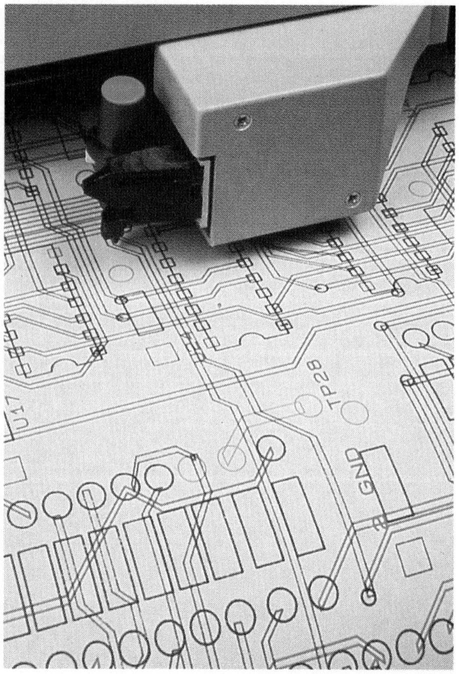

FIGURE 6.20

Plotters use one or more color pens to produce line drawings.

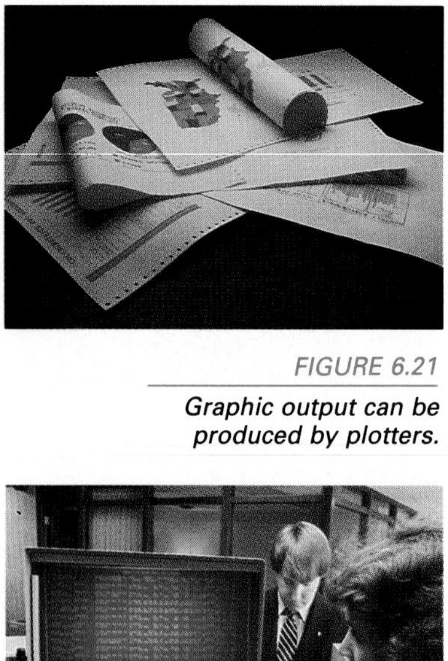

FIGURE 6.21

Graphic output can be produced by plotters.

FIGURE 6.22

Computer output on microfilm (COM) provides users with large volumes of information in relatively little space.

movement are computer-coordinated to produce an image. With both flat-bed and drum plotters, two- or three-dimensional graphics can be created.

Plotters are high-quality, low-volume devices. In other words, they produce high-quality output, but the process is time-consuming. They are unable to mass-produce graphic outputs efficiently. For high-volume graphic output, laser printers and special cameras are used.

Microfilm and Microfiche

Large volumes of information can be held on rolls (***microfilm***) or sheets (***microfiche***) of film on which miniature images are recorded. High-capacity microfilm enables users to access large numbers of full-page images quickly and conveniently. In addition, microfilm is used to preserve data permanently since film is far more durable than paper.

With ***computer output microfilm (COM)*** techniques, the results of computer processing are transferred—in miniature form—directly onto microfilm or microfiche. On microfilm, pages of data are imaged sequentially on a reel of film. Microfiche is a sheet of film measuring 4 inches by 6 inches and carries information equivalent to a 200-page report.

Microfilm output is used for distribution of airline schedules, automotive parts catalogs, medical X rays, and lists of books in print. An architectural firm can use microfilm resources to access information on building codes and zoning laws.

Temporary Output

In applications that do not require permanent output, video displays and audio responses serve as effective, yet temporary, output. Computer technology brought with it an onslaught of permanent documents. The "paper avalanche" that resulted actually became a hindrance to information retrieval. Locating pertinent pieces of information in the mountain of available documents became a time-consuming

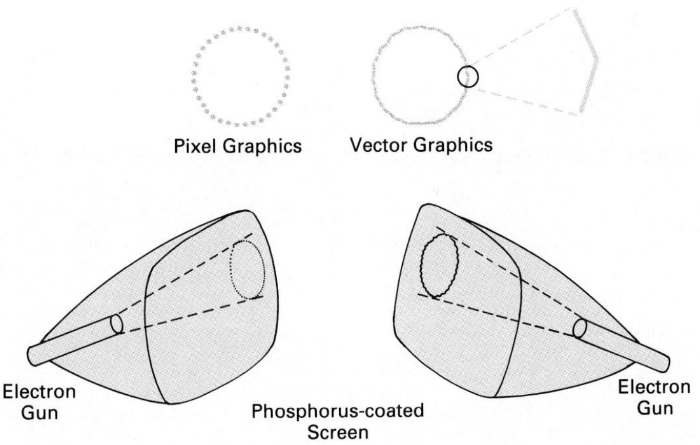

FIGURE 6.23

Displays using pixel graphics employ patterns of tiny dots to create images while those using vector graphics draw lines.

chore. Computer technology now enables users to locate needed files directly and to receive real-time service. Output used for reference does not have to be printed on paper. Video displays for temporary output have reduced this paper avalanche.

Temporary output also is useful when the information changes rapidly. In airports, screens display up-to-the-minute flight information. At a football field, scoreboards provide temporary output reflecting current score and statistics. In addition to temporary output displayed on screen, audio response and interactive devices provide output for immediate, temporary use.

Video Display Output

Video displays provide the same information as a printed report, without actually imprinting information. Video displays are sufficient for many applications where temporary use of information is desired. VDTs are either flat screens or ***cathode ray tubes (CRTs)***. CRTs operate much like television picture tubes. The computer generates signals that translate into electron beams focused on the phosphorus-coated face of the cathode ray tube.

CRTs and flat screens form images by creating patterns of dots, or picture elements, known as ***pixels***. Pixels form characters or graphic designs that appear on the screen of the VDT. Images might be displayed on ***monochrome***, or single-color, screens. Typically, monochrome screens display outputs in green or amber colors. Multicolored outputs can be produced by ***RGB monitors***, which use red, green, and blue pixels to form full-color images.

Two types of graphic displays can be produced on VDTs: ***pixel graphics*** and ***vector graphics***. With pixel graphics, characters are formed by turning different pixels on or off. Pixel graphics work well with images easily represented by rows and columns of dots. However, clear, round images are difficult to draw using pixel graphics. Vector graphics are used when more complex images are required. Images drawn on a screen are not limited to rows and columns when vector graphics are used. Lines are drawn between any points on the screen. Like pen lines drawn by a plotter, the vector graphics are crisp and continuous.

Sound and Speech Output

Sound synthesizers create messages—temporary output—that computer users can hear. Perhaps the most familiar form of audio output is heard on the telephone—weather, time, or common operator messages. In this type of temporary output, voice messages may be tape recordings of human voices or be artificially created by a ***speech synthesizer***.

FIGURE 6.24

Computers help make music by using a sound synthesizer for output.

Uses for sound and speech synthesizers are becoming more wide-ranging. Often delivered through telephones, speech output has been used to provide information about stock market prices and flight departure times. In late-model cars, a voice output reminds the driver to turn off headlights or to add fuel to an almost-empty tank. Since audio outputs require only the ability to hear, they can be of great value to people with visual handicaps and reading disabilities.

Action Output

As we have seen, computer processing can result in printed documents, printed drawings, screen displays, voice recordings, and more. These outputs depend on the sight or hearing of people for interpretation and use. Action output, on the other hand, is processing results that initiate some form of movement or process control activity. The extension of a computer-driven arm to spot-weld cars on an assembly line is action output. Computer programs identify welding specifications: where on the car welding is needed, the rate at which autos move down the line, and so on. Processing results in action. The welding arm is positioned according to program specifications. Often, designs produced using graphic displays are turned into actual products through action output hardware.

Many examples of action output are seen through robots, or computer-driven machines programmed to perform work. Robot output can be determined solely by computer programs. In other cases, output is a result of the input of physical data. Some robots are attached to cameras that allow them to "see" their surroundings and adapt their action output according to what they view.

The first robots were used to handle dangerous tasks. Robots can perform high-risk jobs such as working among toxic fumes or handling radioactive materials with no ill effects. The earliest robots thus spared people from health-threatening duties. In recent years, people have put robots to many labor-saving uses. The welding machines in Figure 6.25 are multijointed robots. The cars on the line might be completed by robots that attach doors and paint exteriors. In other industries, robots are used for shearing sheep, delivering mail, and mining coal.

Another type of action output is produced by ***numerical control (NC)*** devices. NC machines accept numeric specifications as input. They produce as output

FIGURE 6.25

Robots perform dangerous or repetitive jobs, and their actions represent one type of computer-controlled output.

machine parts that meet those specifications precisely. Programmable drill presses and lathes are NC machines that output a cutting action. People who once operated manual tools now program NC machines to produce desired results.

The field of medicine has found several uses for action output. In hospital emergency rooms, computers monitor a patient's vital signs and, as action output, regulate the flow of oxygen or medication to the patient. Microprocessors can send small electrical shocks to muscles to stimulate movement in paralyzed limbs. In this case, muscle movement is the action output.

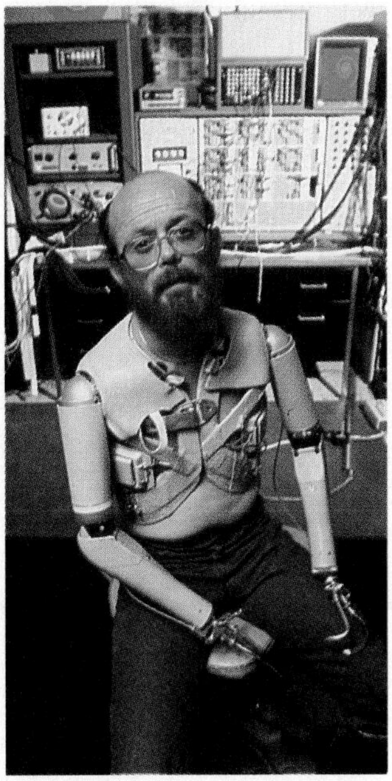

FIGURE 6.26

A victim of a power line accident tries out his new microprocessor-assisted electronic arms.

STUDY QUESTIONS

15. Define dot-matrix character, correspondence quality character, full character, flat-bed plotter, drum plotter, CRT, pixel, sound synthesizer, and speech synthesizer.
16. Describe three general categories of computer output.
17. What are the different speeds of serial, line, and page printers?
18. How do draft quality, letter quality, ink-jet, thermal, electrostatic, and laser printers work?
19. How is a plotter different from a printer? What are the advantages and disadvantages to using a plotter for output?
20. Describe two ways of storing reduced images on film.
21. Why would an organization use computer output microfilm (COM)?
22. What is the difference between monochrome and RGB monitors?
23. Explain how pictures are drawn using pixel and vector graphics.
24. Describe an application for sound and speech synthesizers.
25. How do numerical control (NC) machines work?
26. What determines the movement (output) of a robot?
27. How is action hardware used in medical applications?

CONCLUSION

Input and output operations are the critical links between people and computers. Users interact with the computer to enter data and receive the resulting information. At other times, they group data in batches before processing. A variety of input and output hardware supports these activities. Terminals, dumb or intelligent, perform both input and output operations. Specialized input hardware includes scanners, touch-sensitive screens, joysticks, tablets, and voice recognition devices.

The choice of an output device depends on how long the output is needed. Temporary output appears on VDTs and through speech synthesizers. Permanent output is obtained from printers, plotters, microfilm, and microfiche. Action output is produced by robots, NC machines, and embedded microprocessors. The application of computer technology would be highly specialized without this variety of input and output hardware.

CHAPTER FACTS

- User-friendly computer systems let people take more control of computers. I/O is the link between computers and people.
- Operating systems and application software help people use sophisticated computer technology.
- Input can take the form of system software, application programs, or data.
- Computer output is only useful when the data are complete and correct.
- Data can be entered interactively (real-time processing) or in batches. Batch processing requires two steps: First the data is collected, verified, and stored; later, it is input and processed.
- Control totals are used to ensure that the batch data are input correctly.
- A terminal is where input is entered or output received. Terminals can be dumb or intelligent. Input is via a keyboard, while output is on a screen or typewriter-like printer.
- Scanners are used to transfer user-recognizable characters into machine-readable characters. They can scan bar codes on grocery items, optical marks (OMR) on tests and surveys, optical characters (OCR) on price tags, and magnetic ink characters (MICR) on checks.
- Input hardware involves more than just a keyboard or scanner. A mouse, light pen, pointing to a touch–sensitive screen, or drawing on a tablet will let users input data interactively.
- Voice recognition systems allow vocal input based on a preprogrammed limited vocabulary.
- Input also can be sent through telephone touch–tone dialing or a credit card reader. Both can be connected to a distant computer.
- Output hardware can be permanent, temporary, or result in action.
- Permanent output usually takes the form of a hard copy from a printer. Print characters can be dot-matrix, correspondence, or full. Printer speeds depend on whether the machine is a serial, line, or page printer. Print method is either impact or nonimpact.
- Plotters can produce drawings, maps, and pictures as another form of permanent output.

- Photographically reduced images can be stored on microfiche (pages of film) or microfilm (reels of film). COM is high–volume, durable, permanent output.
- VDTs, also called flat screens or CRTs (cathode ray tubes), provide temporary output on monochrome or RGB monitors. Graphics are presented through patterns of pixels or through vector graphics techniques.
- Sound synthesizers create sounds as output, while speech synthesizers output spoken words.
- Action output is produced through the programming of robots or by numerical control (NC) machines.
- Action output is used in the health sciences for patient monitoring and for stimulating muscles connected to artificial or paralyzed limbs.

TERMS TO REMEMBER

bar codes
cathode ray tube (CRT)
computer output microfilm (COM)
control total
correspondence quality character
cursor
digitize
dot-matrix character
draft quality printer
drum plotter
dumb terminal
electrostatic printer
flat-bed plotter
full character
function key
hard copy
hard copy terminal
input/output (I/O)
ink-jet printer
intelligent terminal
interactive
joystick
laser printer
letter quality printer
light pen
line printer
magnetic ink character recognition (MICR)
microfiche
microfilm
monochrome
mouse
numerical control (NC)
optical character recognition (OCR)
optical mark recognition (OMR)
page printer
parallel port
pixel
pixel graphics
plotter
POS
prompt
remote job entry
RGB (red, green, blue) monitor
scanner
serial port
serial printer
soft copy
sound synthesizer
speech synthesizer
tablet
thermal printer
touch-sensitive screen
vector graphics
voice recognition device

CHECK YOUR UNDERSTANDING

1. A(n) ___________ is hardware containing a keyboard and VDT (or printer) that is connected to a computer.
2. A calculation made independently of the computer to check input operations is called:
   a. batch total
   b. control total
   c. control count
   d. process control
   e. none of these
3. A prompt is a user's request for a computer to send data or instructions. (True/False)
4. Grocery stores use ___________ on merchandise as machine-readable input.
5. As a mouse is rolled across a surface, its action moves a cursor on a screen. (True/False)
6. ___________ characters are small dots, printed over several times for a clearer image.
7. Complex drawings are best displayed on a screen with pixel graphics. (True/False)
8. Which of the following features of a robot makes it such a flexible tool?
   a. inexpensive
   b. easy to repair
   c. programmable
   d. all the above
   e. b and c

APPLYING WHAT YOU'VE LEARNED

1. How could voice recognition devices and sound/speech synthesizers aid in these situations?
   a. a wheel chair for a paraplegic
   b. a computer used by a child who cannot read
   c. danger and fire alarms for a blind person
   d. ordering from a catalog over a telephone
   e. a computer used by a person learning English
   f. safety features in a building during a power blackout
2. What are five applications for a robot other than those mentioned in the text?
3. What input and output hardware would be most suitable for these examples of data processing?
   a. updating fast-food restaurant inventories
   b. grading a college entrance exam and reporting the results to the students
   c. spray painting motorcycles on an assembly line
   d. checking driving records for a driver's license renewal
   e. designing and stress testing an earthquake-proof computer center
4. Some hardware buyers believe in getting the biggest and fastest hardware they can afford.
   a. What are the disadvantages to this approach?
   b. What are the disadvantages to buying the least expensive hardware?

c. Would it be better to delay purchasing necessary hardware equipment until the price comes down or to buy the newest equipment now?

5. In which environments would a voice recognition system be inappropriate? What about speech and sound synthesizers?

CHECK YOUR UNDERSTANDING ANSWERS

1. terminal
2. b
3. false
4. bar codes (UPC)
5. true
6. correspondence quality
7. false
8. c

CHAPTER SEVEN

DATA COMMUNICATIONS: DISTRIBUTING PROCESSING POWER

KEY IDEAS

- **From the user's point of view**
  How can you gain immediate access to information that is spread across large geographic areas? Once you have this information, how can it be shared with others?

- **Communication of data**
  Computer systems help meet demands for increased and improved communications.

  Digital and analog transmissions
  For computers and communication hardware to work properly, data must be encoded in a form compatible to both technologies.

  Communication hardware and software
  Special hardware and software encode and decode data for transmission over long distances.

  Communication channels
  Data can be transferred from place to place at varying speeds through many media.

  Managing data transmissions
  Procedures for sending and receiving data range from transmitting bursts of data to transmitting one character at a time.

- **Network topologies**
  Computer systems are interconnected along bus lines or in patterns resembling stars and rings.

- **Network applications**
  Networks allow people and computers to communicate in many ways.

  Local area networks
  LANs link several computers within a confined service area.

  Distributed processing
  Powerful computers connected to communication networks have brought processing power directly to the user.

  Bulletin boards
  Message systems open to the general public let users communicate with one another.

FROM THE USER'S POINT OF VIEW

You will find as you become comfortable working with a personal computer that you will need to share data and ideas with other users. The simplest way to exchange data is by using your telephone to connect the computers. Many organizations are faced with the same need. Employees with desk-top computers are finding they can use their telephones to access data available on a large central computer but still maintain their autonomy. As you might expect, a whole new vocabulary is necessary to explain the communication options available. Therefore, in this chapter we will discuss the necessary hardware, software, and new applications for sharing data over long distances.

FIGURE 7.1

Local telephone services are integrated through a vast network of computers that help callers make their connections.

COMMUNICATION OF DATA

The computer helps to meet demands for increased and improved communication. However, these demands did not emerge with the Computer Age. In the 1800s, the invention of telegraphy by Samuel Morse linked people thousands of miles away from each other. Morse's telegraph code consisted of dots and dashes that could be combined to represent letters, numbers, and punctuation. Dots and dashes were expressed as short and long sounds.

Millions of words and numbers moved over telegraph lines—long before the telephone was invented. Stockbrokers handled trading via telegraphy. Reports of newsworthy events were delivered to news services and papers over telegraph wires. Morse's contributions to communication technology were extended by Guglielmo Marconi. His invention of wireless telegraphy made Morse code a medium for international communication.

Once computers made their debut they were soon recognized as a tool for further improving communication. Computers addressed communication needs in a number of ways. Telephone companies, whose business it is to enhance communication between people, installed electronic switchboards. By pressing a few keys, you use these switchboards to call a friend across town or in another country.

To provide this service, telephone networks set up links between multiple computers. Each computer has a memory that contains locations for all interconnected phones in a certain area. When you dial a number, the number is sent to a computer switch in the central office in your area. The switch determines the destination of your call. If the call is local, the switch searches its own memory for the matching telephone link. For calls outside the area, the switch routes the number to the appropriate switch controlled by another computer in the network. This computer then places your call.

By matching the dialed number with a telephone location, the switch sets up a telephone connection. A computer switch in Valdosta, Georgia, can address a switch in Boulder, Colorado, to permit cross-state communication. Just as easily, a Los Angeles caller can dial access to a Londoner in moments.

Telephone systems are just one way in which computing and communications technologies have been joined. People have called on computers to help solve many

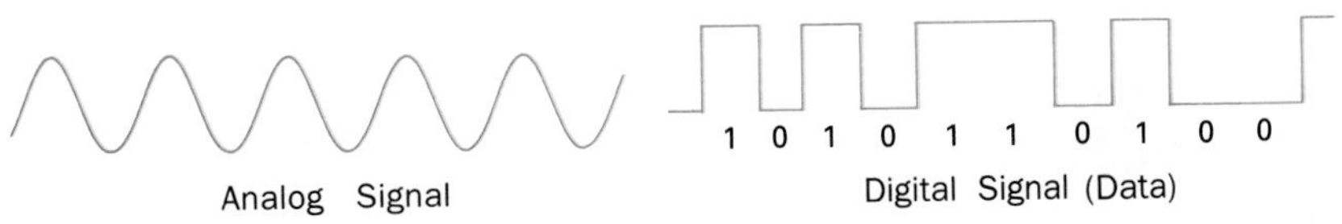

FIGURE 7.2

Data can be sent over communication channels as analog sound frequencies or as digital bit patterns.

communication problems. As people move around the country and world, they demand convenient access to data. For example, a vacationer from the West Coast may wish to make credit purchases at a Washington, D.C., department store. Although the customer is 3000 miles from home and the local bank, credit can be checked instantly. The salesperson merely runs the credit card through a card reader that transmits the card number to the bank's computer and keys in the purchase amount. Credit is verified, and the sale is approved. No words are spoken, yet a complex form of communication has taken place.

Voice communication involved in making a telephone call or the credit card transaction involve telecommunications. ***Telecommunications*** is any long–distance communications. The field of telecommunications includes the transmission of voice and the transmission of messages such as telegrams, facsimile (pictures), and data. The last is called data telecommunications, or ***data communications***. It is concerned with sending data electronically from one point to another. Another popular form of telecommunications occurs when a ***facsimile machine*** scans a document containing text or pictures, digitizes the images, and transmits them over telephone lines. Another facsimile machine then assembles the digitized images and prints them on paper.

Digital and Analog Transmissions

For the successful marriage of computers and communication devices, data must be coded in a form compatible to both technologies. Computers record data as ***digital signals***, expressed in bit patterns. Most communication devices, on the other hand, use ***analog signals***, which express data as patterns of continuous sound frequencies.

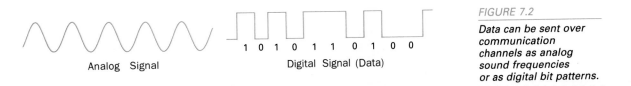

People who want to establish data communication links, therefore, have to make a choice. They can set up digital lines between computer components to carry bit patterns directly from one machine to the next. Or, they can use standard communication lines to carry data that have been converted into analog signals. Digital lines must be specially installed, and digital signals can be transmitted only over short distances. Standard telephone lines, however, are available almost everywhere. Since regular telephone lines operate on analog signals, they cannot be used to send data coded in digital form. For these reasons, most data communication links convert digital data into an analog format and then back again. As a result, communications hardware and software have been developed to resolve digital/analog incompatibilities.

Communication Hardware and Software

Computer signals and communication signals are made compatible by special devices for encoding and decoding data. These devices are known as ***modems***, a term coined from the functions they perform: ***mo***dulation and ***dem***odulation. Modems permit two computers linked by regular telephone lines to exchange data. A sending modem modulates digital data into analog form for transmission over standard phone lines. A modem at the receiving end demodulates the analog signals back into digital form for input to the receiving computer.

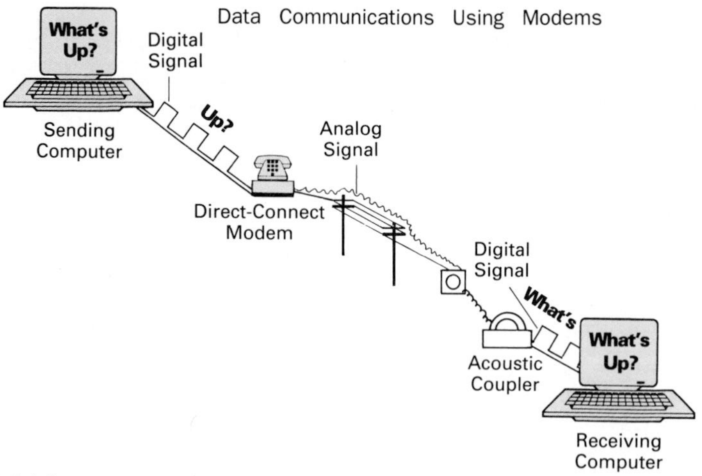

FIGURE 7.3

Modems modulate bit patterns into an analog signal for transmission over standard telephone lines, and then demodulate the signal back into its original digital form.

Two standard types of modems are available for establishing connections between computers and communication channels: acoustic couplers and direct-connect modems. Users attach ***acoustic couplers*** to their computer for each transmission of data. Rubber cups on the acoustic coupler fit over the earpiece and mouthpiece of a regular telephone handset. The cups are designed to hold the telephone handset securely for sending and receiving sounds. Once the telephone number of the receiving computer is dialed and the handset is in place, transmission can begin. Signals from the sending computer are modulated, then transmitted through the mouthpiece. At the receiving end, a modem receives the signals through the earpiece, demodulates them, and routes them to the receiving computer.

With ***direct-connect modems***, no attachments need to be made on the telephone handset because the modem is connected directly to the telephone jack in the wall. Some direct connect modems are built into expansion boards and housed inside the body of the computer. Figure 7.4 shows a stand-alone direct-connect modem as well as one on an expansion board. A person wishing to transmit data need only dial a number to establish the connection. Modulation and demodu-

FIGURE 7.4

Direct–connect modems bypass the telephone receiver and link the computer into a telephone jack to minimize unwanted sound interference during data communication.

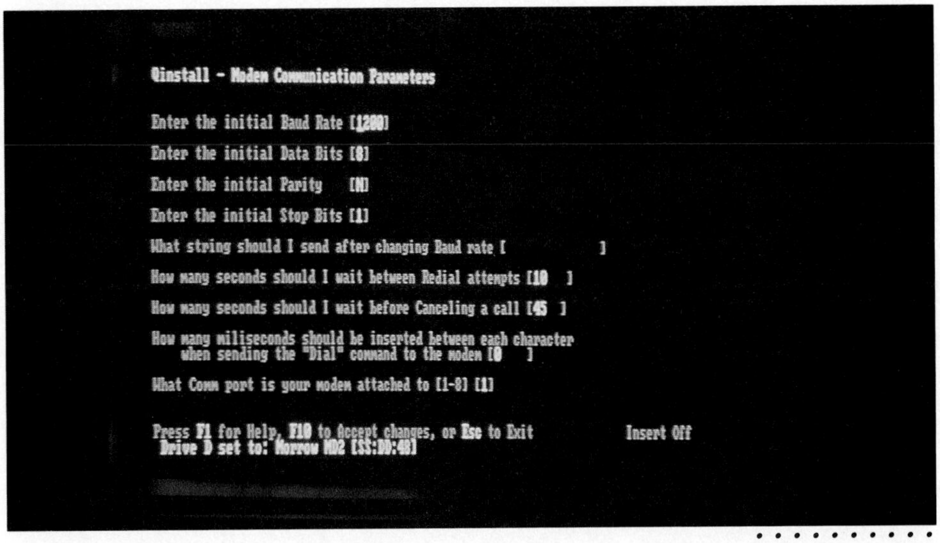

FIGURE 7.5

Communication software helps users with data communications by providing user-friendly menus.

lation take place within the body of the modem. Direct-connect modems provide data communication that is unhindered by sound interference from the surrounding area.

Modems work with ***communications software*** to coordinate data communications between computers and to check for transmission errors. One method for detecting transmission errors involves the use of either an odd or even parity-checking scheme, just like those schemes utilized by disk and tape storage hardware (see Chapter 5). The receiving computer expects either an odd or even parity standard. The sending computer will add a parity bit and turn it on or off for each transmission. If an odd-parity checking scheme is used, the parity bit is always turned on to make the number of "on" or 1 bits odd.

To minimize set up time, ***smart modems*** have their own microprocessors and draw from the computer's memory capabilities. This enables them to dial telephone numbers automatically. Communications software helps smart modems store directories of frequently used numbers, answer incoming calls from sending computers, transmit passwords to initiate data communication and generally coordinate the speed and flow of data between computers.

However, modems are designed to perform one data transmission job at a time. At large organizations or computer centers, a computer might need to accept multiple transmissions at once. To handle such large-scale demands, devices known as multiplexers and concentrators were developed. A ***multiplexer*** merges signals from several incoming transmissions or sends data to several destinations at once. In effect, the multiplexer is a switching station. The device accepts signals from several sources, switching very quickly from one source to the next. In this manner, all transmissions can be accepted concurrently and sent immediately (see Figure 7.6). ***Concentrators*** perform the same functions but in a different way. These devices save transmissions in order to send them to the computer in a group. They also are able to retain data in storage areas for transmission at a later time.

Both multiplexers and concentrators allow several users to send and receive data through a single communication line. For example, a large office building with the computer center in the basement and many users on each floor might require a separate cable between each user and the computer. To reduce the number of cables, a multiplexer or concentrator allows all users on one floor to share a single communication line. The users can even be operating a variety of input or output hardware simultaneously.

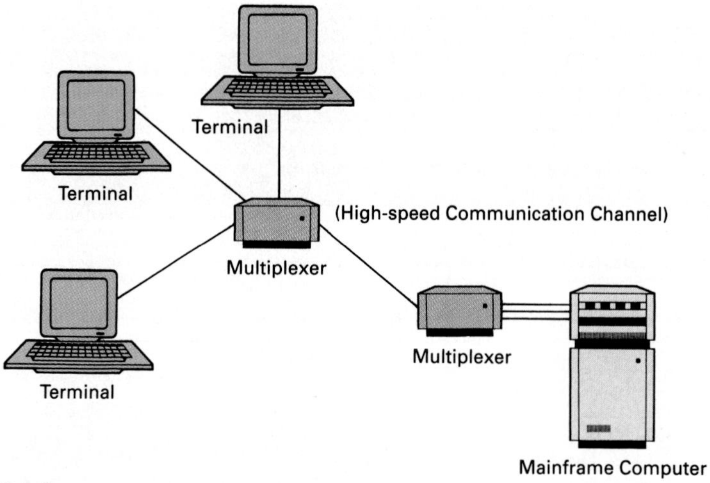

FIGURE 7.6

Multiplexers send data from several terminals through a single communication channel.

Communication Channels

The rate of data transmission is often measured by the number of ***bits per second (BPS)*** sent through a modem. However, modems are rated by their ***baud rate***, or the maximum speed in which they can change the status of a signal. The term ***baud*** is derived from Baudot, the Frenchman who developed a coding scheme for telegraph communications. Often baud rates and BPS are incorrectly interchanged. The speed at which a signal changes is not necessarily equal to the number of bits being sent. Baud rate is best used to compare modems, while BPS is a better measurement of data transmission speeds.

Data transmission speeds are determined largely by the grade of the ***communication channel*** used. The communication channel is the medium by which data communications take place. As a rule, high-grade channels have wide bandwidths that can transmit high-volume signals. For example, coaxial cables, similar to those used in cable television networks, are broadband transmission lines that accommodate transmission speeds of 2 million BPS. Since the cables are insulated, fewer transmission errors are encountered.

Faster transmission speeds are possible through satellite and microwave systems, which send data signals at speeds up to 3 million BPS through open space. Developments in optical fibers using laser technologies have led to ultra high-speed data transmission, with speeds reaching 200 million BPS.

Standard, voice-grade telephone lines using a twisted pair of copper wires have relatively tighter bandwidths. They usually permit transmission rates of 300 to 9600 BPS. In comparison, Morse's telegraph communication channels have a narrow bandwidth and transmit between 45 and 150 BPS.

Managing Data Transmissions

Before data is transmitted, both the sending and the receiving computers must be ready to accept data according to predetermined bit patterns and parity–checking schemes. Most commonly, data transmission patterns are ***asynchronous***. That is, data are transmitted byte by byte. A start bit and at least one stop bit are included in every byte transmitted (see Figure 7.8). This enables the receiving computer to register when each byte (character) has been transmitted. Asynchronous transmission generally is used for microcomputer communication and dial-up service connections.

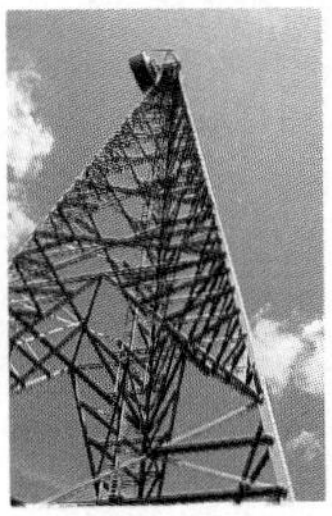

Communication Channels	Transmission Speeds (BPS—bits per second)
Telegraph	45–150 BPS
Telephone (Twisted Pair)	300–9600 BPS
Coaxial Cable	1,000,000–2,000,000 BPS
Microwave	1,000,000–3,000,000 BPS
Satellite	1,000,000–3,000,000 BPS
Optical Fibers	Up to 200,000,000 BPS

FIGURE 7.7

Data communications use a wide variety of media (channels) to transmit data, pictures, and voices.

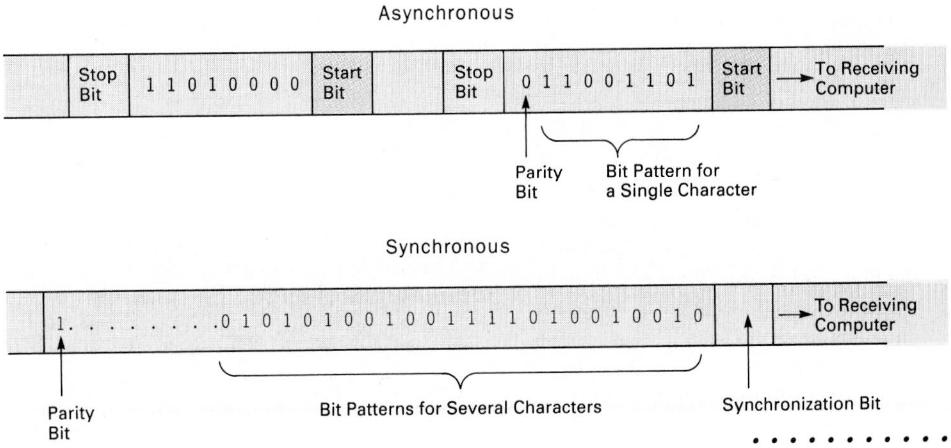

FIGURE 7.8

Asynchronous data transmission sends a single character at a time while synchronous transmission sends several characters at a time.

Providing speedier data communication is ***synchronous*** transmission, which groups bytes into blocks for transmission. Each block is preceded by a synchronization bit, which serves as a timing mechanism. When the receiving computer encounters a synchronization bit, it is prepared for the arrival of a new block of data. Thus, separate bytes need not be identified by start and stop bits. Synchronous transmission requires special buffers for holding blocks of incoming data. Fast, efficient synchronous communication is used when high-speed data transmission is required.

Data transmission between computers operates in one of three modes. The simplest type of data transmission is ***simplex transmission,*** which allows communications over a channel in only one direction. A public address system is an example of one-way communication. ***Half-duplex transmission*** permits two-way communication over a channel, but data are transmitted in only one direction at a time. A CB radio, for example, provides half-duplex service. If one party is speaking, the other cannot respond until the message is completed. Half-duplex data communication often is used for batch transmission of data.

CLIP

HOW FIBER OPTICS WORK

Fiber optics replaces electricity with light, and copper wires with hair-thin strands of glass.

A fiber-optic transmitter encodes information—computer data, human voices, text, or pictures—into modulated light waves. A tiny laser or light-emitting diode squirts the light (actually infrared energy, at a wavelength invisible to the eye) into a strand of ultrapure glass called an optical fiber. The glass confines the light waves to a narrow core region. The beam shoots down this optical tunnel by repeatedly bouncing off the glassy walls.

Optical fibers are phenomenally transparent. If seawater were as clear, the ocean bottom would be as easy to see as the floor of a swimming pool.

At the other end of the fiber, a photodetector picks up the light and transforms the optical information back into electronic energy. Ideally, the electronic signal that comes out of the photodetector exactly matches the electronic signal fed into the transmitting laser.

Fiber's biggest advantage lies in its ability to carry far more information in a given time than can the twisted pair of copper wires traditionally used by telephone companies. Several signals at once can be fed into the fiber, and light pulses sent in extremely rapid succession will remain separate and distinct even after traveling through many miles of fiber. Electrical signals, by contrast, tend to smear into each other after a comparatively short journey through copper wire.

A single optical fiber can carry hundreds of simultaneous telephone conversations or their equivalent in computer data or television pictures. Telecommunications researchers have been jumping through hoops to make copper wire carry even two simultaneous conversations.

Fiber also improves transmission quality, because light waves zip through fiber unaffected by the electrical interference that can muddy signals passing through copper. Fiber also helps ensure privacy; light waves streaming through fiber stay entirely inside the fiber, whereas copper wires leak radio waves that snoopers can detect.

Source: High Technology Business, February 1988. Reprinted with permission.

Key Question: What improvements in your life can you anticipate from advances in fiber optics?

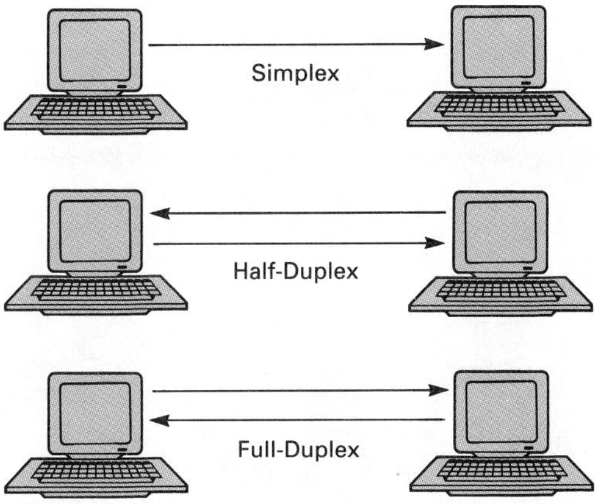

FIGURE 7.9

Data can be sent in one of three ways: simplex means that data are only sent in one direction; half–duplex means that data are sent in both directions but not at the same time; full–duplex allows both computers to send and receive data simultaneously in both directions.

Simultaneous two-way transmission is accommodated by ***full-duplex transmission***. This mode provides each computer with two communication channels, so that it can send and receive data concurrently. A telephone conversation is a familiar example of full-duplex transmission. Parties at both ends of the connection can speak or listen at any time during the conversation. Full-duplex communication is used primarily for interactive input and real-time processing.

As a result of this variety, there is a great deal of flexibility in the ways data communication systems can be tailored to special needs. The following cases demonstrate the ranges of service available for data communication:

- Harrington Hospital has modest data communication requirements. The medical staff uses remote terminals to access and modify patient files. Terminals are separate from the computer, yet all terminals are located in one building. Harrington chose a system of terminals that use multiplexers or are physically connected by wires ***(hardwired)*** to the central computer.
- Data communication in Northern Bank is considerably more complex. Northern has three branches and a credit card authorization center, located in two adjacent towns. Teller terminals and ATMs are linked to a computer in each branch by direct-connect modems or concentrators. Data compiled in the branch computers are transmitted by a microwave communication channel to a central computer in Northern's main office.
- The National Weather Bureau operates a highly complex data communication system that receives transmissions from all over the globe. Telephone lines,

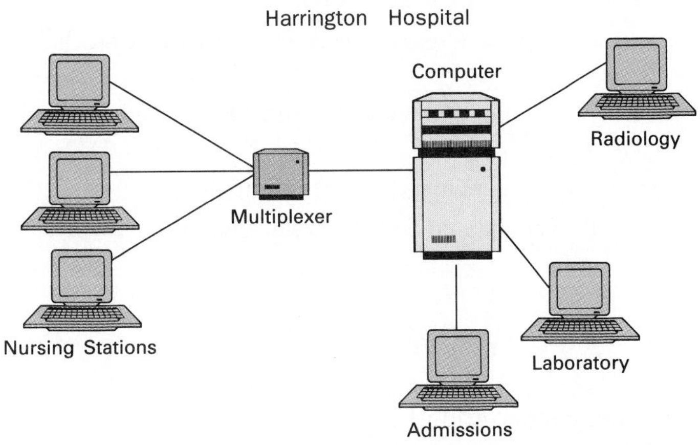

FIGURE 7.10

Hospitals might use data communication systems in a configuration similar to this one.

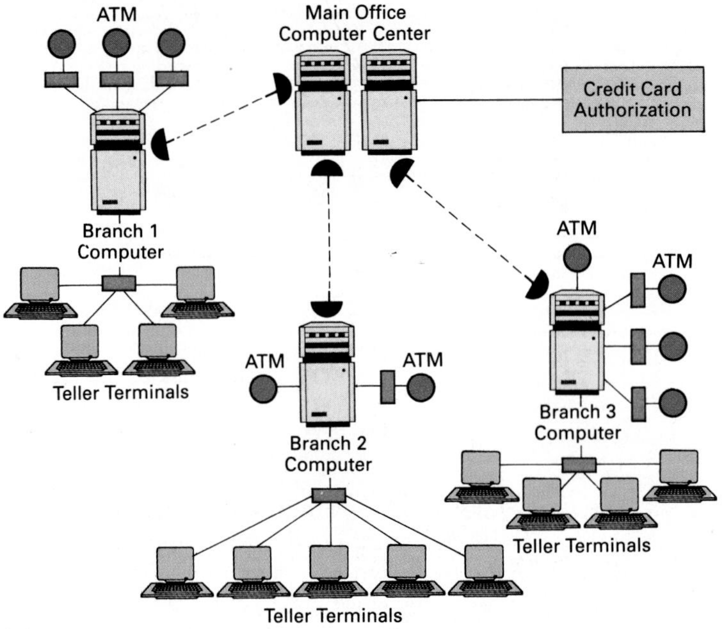

FIGURE 7.11

Bank operations spread over a large geographical area may use several types of communication channels and hardware.

coaxial cables, satellites, and microwave networks relay these worldwide signals to the NWB's central computer. Thus, different pieces of equipment that provide different levels of service must all work in concert. The required communications configuration at the bureau involves many computers and computer specialists for smooth operation.

STUDY QUESTIONS

1. Define telecommunications, data communications, facsimile machine, digital signal, analog signal, modem, communications software, baud rate, communication channel, and hardwired.
2. Explain how computer systems help people make telephone calls.
3. How do salespeople use data communications to verify a customer's credit?
4. What is difference between an acoustic coupler, direct–connect modem, and smart modem?
5. How are multiplexers and concentrators used to transmit data?
6. What units of measurement are used to compare modems and data transmission speeds?
7. Name six types of communication channels and identify the transmission speeds associated with each.
8. Explain asynchronous and synchronous data transmission.
9. How do simplex, half-duplex, and full-duplex transmissions work?

NETWORK TOPOLOGIES

Communication ***networks*** support data transmission among multiple, remote devices through the use of shared transmission facilities. A network can include

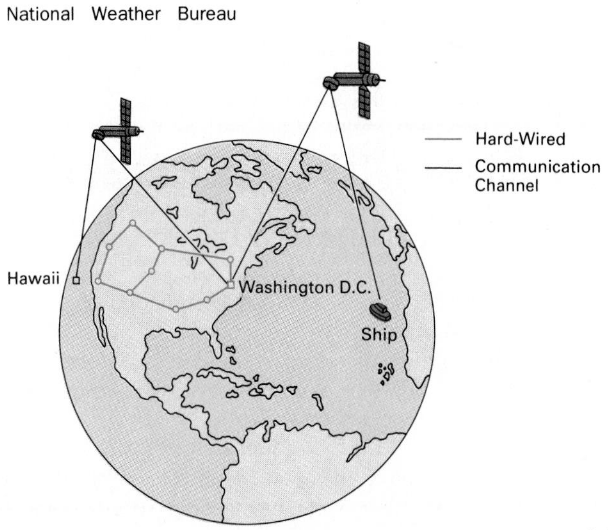

FIGURE 7.12

The National Weather Service uses a variety of satellite and surface communication links to gather data for weather forecasting.

multiple computers, terminals, multiplexers, concentrators, storage devices, and communication software. A dozen office workstations hardwired to a central computer is a small-scale network. On a larger scale, multicontinent satellite links enable users to exchange data across hemispheres. A network arrangement can be as simple or as complex as user requirements dictate. Three fundamental models, known as ***network topologies***, are used for establishing communication networks:

- ***Bus topology*** connects several ***nodes*** or communication stations, with a single cable. A node is one computer system within a communications network. All messages move over a single communication line to which all nodes are connected. Each node is capable of establishing direct communication with every other node in the network. No intermediary switching device is needed for internodal communication. This relationship is called peer-to-peer or point-to-point communication. Scientists working within the same research facility could use a bus network topology. Since each researcher needs to communicate with others, a bus topology would promote this efficient person-to-person communication and the sharing of data.

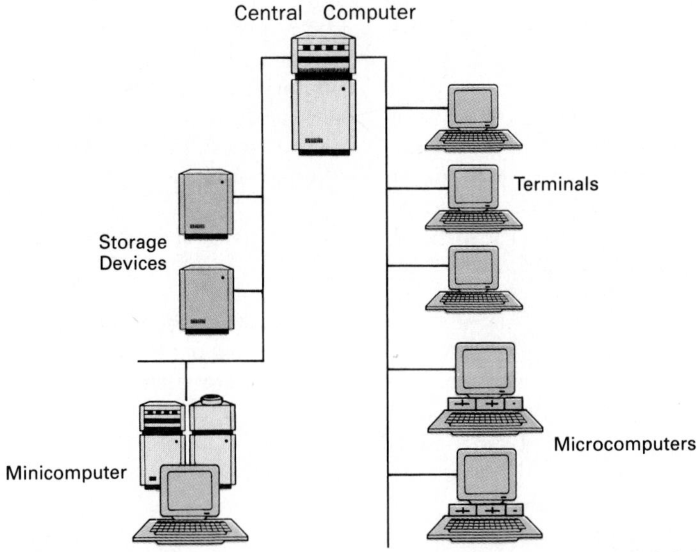

FIGURE 7.13

Bus networks connect computers along a common communication channel.

CLIP

WHY IS PROTOCOL NEEDED?

Simply hooking computers up is only half the battle in data communications. The machines must also agree on how to address each other. It is easy for a computer to convert the 0s and 1s in its memory into pulses to send down a telephone line. But the receiving machine has to know how fast the pulses are coming and how many pulses make up each "word" of data. that is where protocols come in

Communications protocols are rules to avoid computer misunderstandings. They apply to a variety of different operations, including:

- Speed of transmission. Pulses are decoded into zeros and ones according to how long they last. Both receiver and transmitter must be coding at the same speed if one 1 is not to be confused with two or three.
- Establishing connections. The machines must agree on how they are to tell each other that they are on the line and ready to communicate.
- Framing. The protocol must specify where the data begins and the administrative chit-chat ends.
- Error detection. Static on the line sometimes makes a nonsense of the pulses. A simple way of checking for errors is through a so-called parity bit. The idea is to add an extra pulse to each character which is 0 if there is an even number of 1s sent in the character or 1 if the number is odd. If the parity bit does not agree with the received character, an error has occurred. More sophisticated error-checking techniques also exist. The key thing is for both machines to know what the other is doing so that error-checking bits are not confused with real data.
- Error correction. A computer receiving nonsense often requests the sender to send the data again. The sender, obviously, must recognize that request.

Such protocols are easy to devise, but difficult to enforce. Probably the most widely used protocol today is IBM's Systems Network Architecture (SNA). But rival computer-makers and software houses are gathering behind the so-called Open Systems Interconnection (OSI). Several companies, DEC among them, offer "gateways" to link OSI systems to SNA ones.

Long-distance telecommunicators can often also take advantage of packet-switching to gain both protocol conversion and cost savings. Packet-switching systems gather messages from a variety of computers at a central point, build them into large packets and send the whole thing down a single phone line. At the other end, the packets are broken up and distributed to the individual recipients.

Because the data is reorganized anyway, the protocol between the sender and its centralized collector need not be the same as that between the recipient and its centralized distributor—so long as each of the two pairs understand each other. And sharing the central line between many computers reduces costs.

Source: The Economist, July 1986.
Reprinted with permission.

Key Question: What are the potential problems in setting one universal protocol for all data communications?

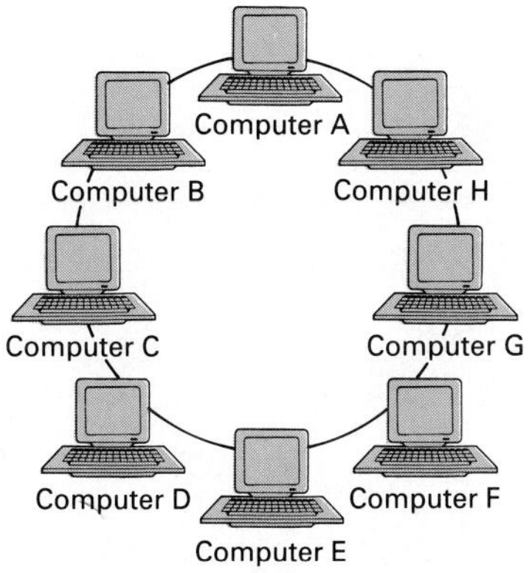

FIGURE 7.14
Ring networks connect one computer to two others as part of a peer–to–peer communication strategy.

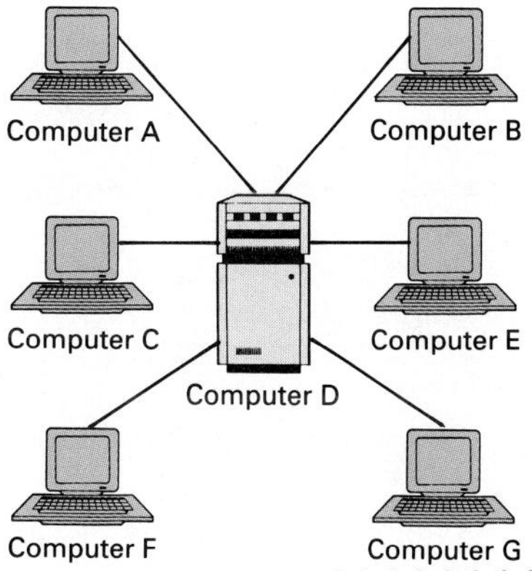

FIGURE 7.15
Star networks form around a central computer system, which coordinates communication between the various computers.

- Peer-to-peer communication also is used in a ***ring topology***. Each node in a ring network is connected to two others, ultimately forming a large circle. Transmission of data and messages in a ring network is indirect. A transmission must travel from one node to the next, around the ring, until it reaches the appropriate destination. One disadvantage of the ring topology is its risk of becoming inoperative. Failure of just one link in the network chain may shut down the entire network until that node is repaired. Often a ring topology is used to connect the computers at several large universities. Ideas and research can be passed around the network as needed. A ring network is ideal since each institution does not need to be directly connected to all others in order for information to be effectively passed around.
- At the hub of a ***star topology*** is a central controlling computer that routes all communication requests. Each node is linked solely to the central computer called the ***host***. Since no internodal connections exist, direct peer-to-peer communication is impossible. Instead, the controlling computer intervenes to deliver messages to specified destinations. A manufacturing plant with computers coordinating different phases of production could use a star network. The host would coordinate activities and maximize production schedules by acting as the intermediary between the other computers.

Two types of topologies can be linked to form a ***hybrid topology***. For example, a central computer might link several bus networks, creating a hybrid of bus and star topologies.

Communications software has additional duties in a network. It must be able to receive messages from any computer connected to its node, translate them, and send them to the correct applications program. In addition, the communications software must be able to transfer requests from local applications programs to other computers in the system. These requests could involve data kept on the other nodes.

STUDY QUESTIONS

10. Define network, network topologies, node, and host.
11. Describe bus, ring, star, and hybrid topologies.
12. What additional duties does communications software have when used in a network?

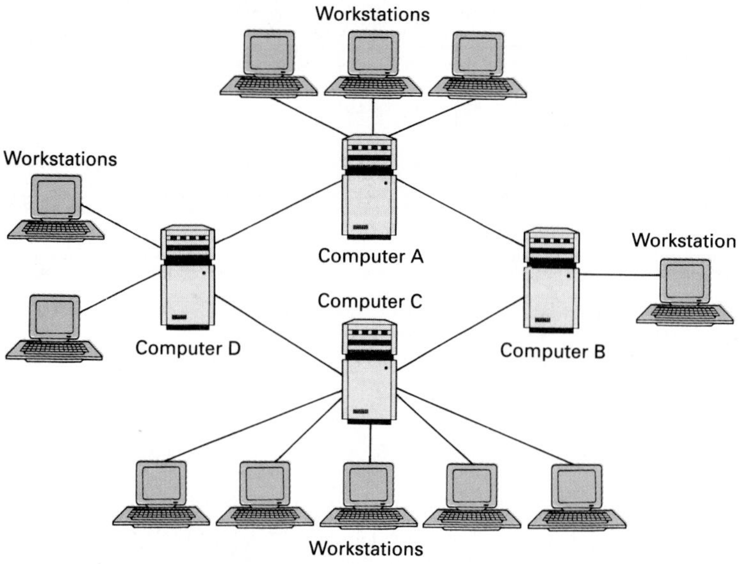

FIGURE 7.16

Hybrid networks link together computer systems on other bus, ring, or star networks.

NETWORK APPLICATIONS

Networks—whether large scale or local—expand our ability to use computers as problem-solving tools. Numerous commercial and noncommercial networks now bring a variety of services into the corporate office and the private home. In fact, it is relatively common for organizations to enhance interoffice data communication by linking people together through user-friendly computer networks. Here is a review of some of the most prominent types of network applications.

Local Area Networks

Local area networks (LANs) are privately owned networks that link several computers within a confined service area. Any of the four network topologies—bus, ring, star, and hybrid—can be used to create a LAN. LAN users share access to hardware, software, and data. They also share the cost of maintaining these resources, making the LAN a cost-effective data communication alternative to one large computer system. LANs are most efficient when they service a large number of

FIGURE 7.17

Local-area-networks link together computer systems in this office building so that users can share data and access common equipment, such as a high-speed laser printer.

users in a confined, limited area. Large office buildings, college campuses, and industrial complexes often use LANs to fulfill their data communication needs.

Distributed Processing

Large business organizations can use communication networks to decentralize computer processing power. This technique, known as ***distributed processing***, disperses processing power to several computer systems within a network. Instead of relying on one central computer to meet all processing needs, different areas within an organization conduct their own processing activities. Decentralization of computing power lightens the processing burden on the host computer. A single device is no longer responsible for processing every application program. Instead, several computers operate independently, concentrating on a small number of related applications.

Distributed processing permits each group to operate with a degree of independence. Information generated by each area then is consolidated to form a comprehensive data processing network. The diverse computer needs found within every organization are met with dedicated processing tools, and the results of processing are coordinated for use by individuals or the organization as a whole.

Consider, as an example of distributed processing, a company that manufactures bicycles. Separate functions within the company can be stated simply. The production division makes the products, the marketing division sells the products, and the accounting division sends and pays the bills. Meanwhile, the personnel division supplies the labor to support these functions. Each of these areas has its own goals and responsibilities. Consequently, each has different processing demands.

The company has adopted distributed processing. Computer systems—hardware, software, data, procedures, and people—tailored to specific needs, reside in each department. The output generated in each division is tied together by a central computer that makes the information available to all areas. Marketing, for example, writes orders for new bicycles on a small computer. Copies of the orders are used by accounting, which collects payment through billing applications. Production also uses the orders to computer-generate production schedules. If sales are increasing, production demands may require additional employees. Thus, personnel uses information from production to assess staffing needs. The bicycle company operates several independent computers that produce information shared by the network.

FIGURE 7.18

Distributed data processing allows an organization's accounting department and salespeople to exchange data with shipping clerks.

CLIP

HOW TO SELECT A DATA COMMUNICATIONS PACKAGE

In considering your needs and in selecting a data communications package, remember that you are dealing with two separate, related technologies. The special needs of each of the technologies—communications and computing—must be considered. You need a coordinated system that deals with both requirements.

When you buy a data communications package, you must install both hardware and software components. Further, these components must be compatible in terms of both the computer system and the communications link to be used. Factors to consider in package evaluation include speed, transmission mode, data format, protocol, and operating characteristics.

Transmission speed, the rate at which data are sent and received, usually is measured in baud, roughly equivalent to bits per second (bps). For microcomputers, available packages have transmission rates ranging from 300 to 9,600 baud. In general, costs of packages increase with baud rates. Also, the prospect and potential loss of data through electrical interference on lines increases at higher baud rates. Often, a decision to transmit at higher speeds leads to extra line costs to assure needed signal quality. The most common rates selected by microcomputer users are 1,200 and 2,400 baud. Some modems have fixed rates for transmission and receiving. On others, baud rates can be varied, either through use of switches or through software entries. One factor in selection of transmission speed lies in the volume of data that you want to transmit. Another factor is the rate established for the stations to which you want to transmit. The sending and receiving stations must operate at the same speeds.

Transmission modes are synchronous or asynchronous. Both sender and receiver must be set for the same mode. Most microcomputers operate in asynchronous serial mode. Formats and protocols have settled into a *de facto* standard, established by Hayes Microcomputer Products. Hayes introduced the first successful and widely accepted modem for microcomputer use. The great majority of manufacturers in this field have elected to build products compatible with Hayes standards. For microcomputer users, it is a safe practice to insist that any package proposed for data communications be Hayes compatible.

Most microcomputer users communicate over telephone lines. Therefore, important considerations in package selection lie in ease of connection between the computer and the telephone network. Also, most software packages now available provide capabilities to dial numbers from a directory maintained on a stored file. A communications package also should be able to answer and prepare itself to receive transmissions automatically, without user intervention. These features make for convenience of use.

As with any other tool for computer use, you should start your procedure for selecting a data communications package by determining what you want to do, then check packages to find the one that meets your needs best—at the most reasonable price.

Key Question: What factors should you consider when purchasing a data communications package for your personal computer system?

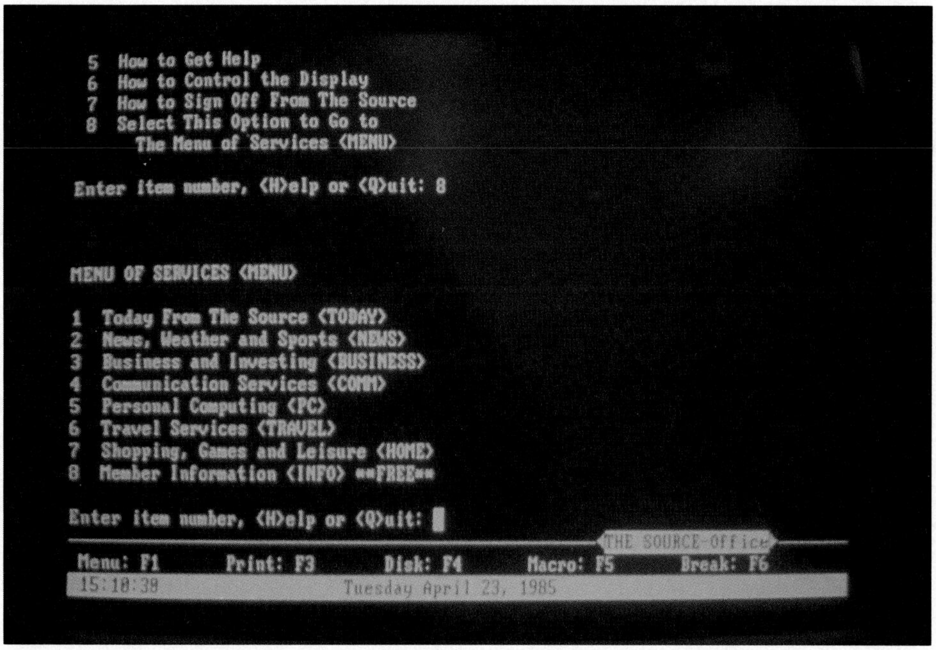

FIGURE 7.19

Information utilities offer users a wide range of services they pay for through monthly fees and/or by rates for the actual computer time used.

Bulletin Boards

Public access message systems, known as ***electronic bulletin boards***, allow users to communicate with one another, often without charge. By signing on to a bulletin board service, users can share programs, data, and messages with other bulletin board members. Participants in a bulletin board network use modems to gain access to the service. They can scan bulletins left by other users or compose their own messages.

Initially, bulletin boards were used by computer hobbyists, who exchanged information about new technologies and applications for computers. Bulletin boards have since grown to accommodate all types of callers. DNA researchers swap information via bulletin boards, as do engineers, physicians, and marine biologists.

Members of a bulletin board network also have access to noncommercial software. This ***public domain software*** is designed by fellow users and offered free of charge or for a small fee. The programs can be ***uploaded*** into the central bulletin board computer. To upload is to transfer data or programs from one computer to a host computer. Once the bulletin board receives the public domain software, it can be copied by any user in the network. This process, the transfer of a program or data from the host computer to another computer, is called ***downloading***.

Information Utilities

The growth in popularity of personal computers has spawned the development of a wide assortment of networks that provide users with access to expansive databases. These commercial services are known as ***information utilities*** and are accessible to anyone with a computer, a modem, and a phone. Information utilities offer convenient access to a huge store of information.

Users access information utilities through telephone lines, cable TV, or communications satellites. Services require payment of a minimum monthly fee or a one-time subscription fee, plus charges for time spent online with the service. The time of day and duration of access determine these charges. Access is most costly during business hours. Less expensive access times include late night, early morning, and weekends. Some of the most popular information utilities are the following:

- CompuServe Information Service offers news and business bulletins, banking services, and an online encyclopedia. Reviews of films, plays, books, and restaurants can also be accessed, as can airline schedules and video games. CompuServe provides customer access to software packages, text editors, and programming languages. As an added service, the utility runs a software exchange/distribution program.
- The Dow Jones News/Retrieval Service is geared to the needs of businesspeople. The service offers stock market quotations, reports on business and economic news, and profiles of companies. Nonbusiness information provided by the Dow Jones service includes general news stories, weather reports, and online encyclopedias.
- The Source, which targets a broad audience of computer users, provides information on many subjects. In addition to news bulletins and stock market indexes, the Source also provides games, reviews, and travel services.

In addition to these information utilities, a number of specialized dial-up services have emerged. Career opportunity networks help people who want new jobs, and even provide career counseling to network users. Utilities such as dating services target the social interests of users. Other special–interest information utilities provide news in such fields as medicine, law, education, and entertainment.

Data communication services also have enabled computer users to obtain psychological counseling online instead of in person. Clients key in their problems, worries, and thoughts. The psychologist receives the messages and sends back responses. Thus, in the middle of a working day, a computer user can dial a number and receive professional counseling. This type of dial-up service provides personal attention, rather than information.

Electronic Mail

Electronic mail services reduce the time and expense of sending documents or messages through conventional delivery services. For example, an executive might wish to send a letter to a colleague's office across town. Preparation and delivery of the letter through regular mail might take several days. With the spread of microcomputers throughout the business community, people reasoned that these machines could be used to expedite message delivery. What evolved was electronic mail networks, which enable users to exchange data and messages via computer.

Electronic mail operates on the same principles as do bulletin boards. Users can send or receive messages to any other user or everyone in the mail network. The difference lies in accessibility of the message. Users restrict access to mail by specifying one or several addresses. The recipients use special passwords to open their electronic mailboxes. Then they can erase, print, or answer the messages, as they deem appropriate.

Some commercial companies have established electronic mail networks. For a fee, users can become members of the network. The commercial service maintains a large central computer that stores all messages. Message senders deposit mail into the central computer. Recipients call the service to check for messages. Electronic mail services have the potential to increase substantially the efficiency of interoffice message delivery. However, commercial services have not met with overwhelming success, perhaps due to equipment requirements. Many offices are not equipped with the microcomputer and modem resources to participate in mail networks. Mail services have been most successful on a smaller scale. Within office buildings and on college campuses, for example, electronic mail services have met with considerable success. Students can exchange messages among themselves, and school officials can deliver online memos. As an educational tool, professors can receive and respond to student questions via electronic message services.

STUDY QUESTIONS

13. Define LAN, public domain software, upload, and download.
14. Describe and explain how people would use local area networks, distributed processing, electronic bulletin boards, information utilities, and electronic mail.

CONCLUSION

Computers are an integral part of the communications industry. They provide the resources that allow people to transmit both voices and data worldwide. A variety of equipment is used to interconnect computers into networks. These networks help people leave messages for one another and access information utilities. Networks also allow large organizations such as the U.S. Weather Bureau to coordinate and process data from geographically dispersed areas. Data communication equipment has made information a global resource.

CHAPTER FACTS

- Data communication is the sending and receiving of data electronically.
- Data coming to and from computers are in digital form. They must be converted to analog signals to be sent over communication devices.
- Digital/analog conversion is done by modems. Modems can take the form of acoustic couplers, direct-connect modems, or smart modems.
- Multiplexers merge several signals coming to a host computer and separate outgoing signals. Multiplexers accept and send concurrent transmissions immediately. Concentrators serve the same purpose but group the transmissions, which are sent at a later time.
- The communication channels available for data communication differ in their transmission speeds. Slowest are telegraph and telephone lines, followed by coaxial cables, satellites, microwave systems, and fiber optics.
- Transmission modes are half-duplex, used in batch data entry, and full-duplex, used with real-time processing.
- Data communication equipment is configured in networks, where each participating computer system is a node. Network topologies include bus, ring, star, and hybrid configurations.
- Local area networks (LANs) serve a confined area such as an office complex.
- With distributed processing, several departments can have separate computer systems yet still share information.
- Electronic bulletin boards serve as centers for leaving public messages and sharing public domain software.
- By accessing an information utility, a user can tap into a variety of online services such as reservation systems, reviews, market quotes, and encyclopedias.
- Electronic mail facilities private messages to be sent and received within organizations.

A WORLD OF INFORMATION—JUST ONE CALL AWAY

On the way home from work you realize you forgot to confirm an important out-of-town meeting with a client. Instead of waiting until tomorrow, you boot your laptop computer, connect the modem, and load compatible communications software when you get home.

The communications software is already set up to dial the information utility both you and your client use.

Courtesy of CompuServe Incorporated, an H&R Block Company

Your communications software dials the information utility's telephone number and puts you in direct contact with the utility's main computer. The computer asks you for an account number and password. Next, you select the Communications/Electronic bulletin board option from the main menu.

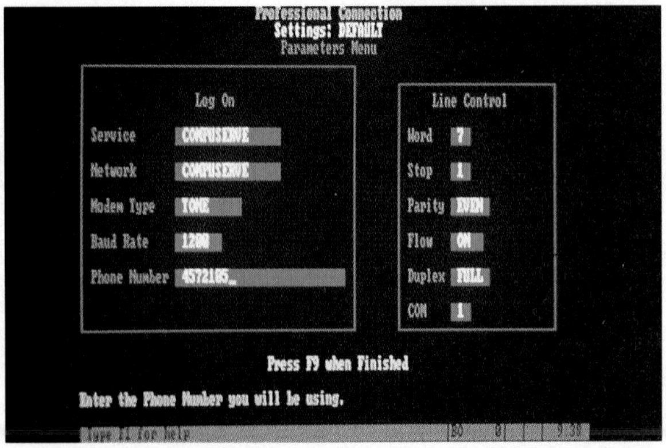

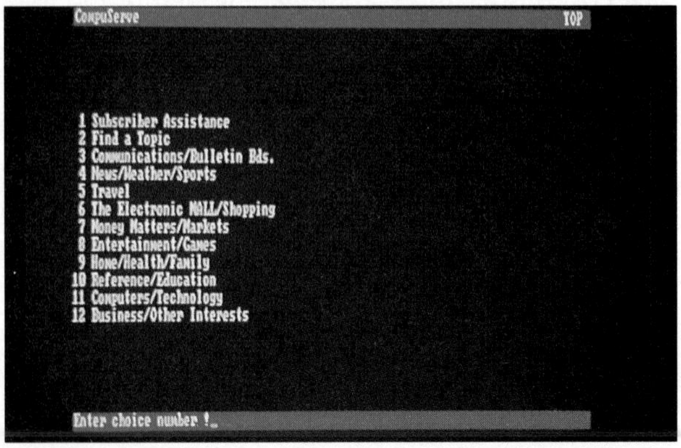

A user-friendly electronic mail system allows you to confirm your attendance at the meeting.

Since the meeting is out of town, a quick check of the weather forecast helps you decide to pack an umbrella for the trip.

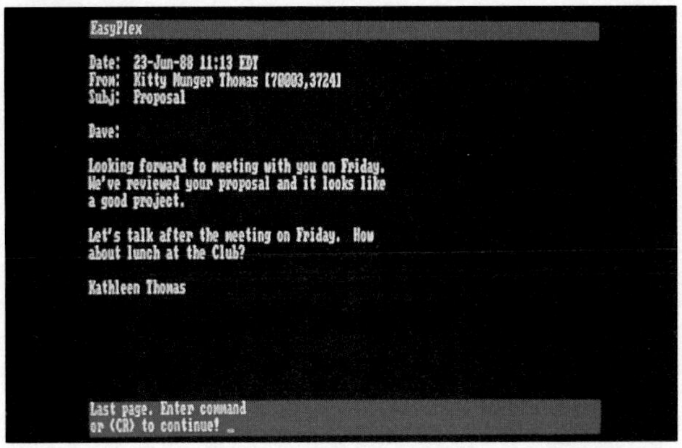

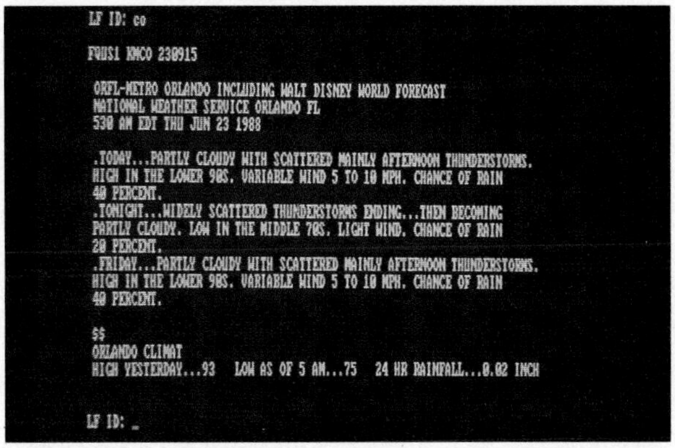

While you are at it, you decide to check the airline schedules. Finding a flight that fits into your agenda, you make round-trip seat reservations.

After signing off from the information utility, you can now relax. The whole process took no more than a half an hour and used less than a minute of computer time. Furthermore, for the computer time and airline reservation, the information utility will automatically bill the credit card you designated.

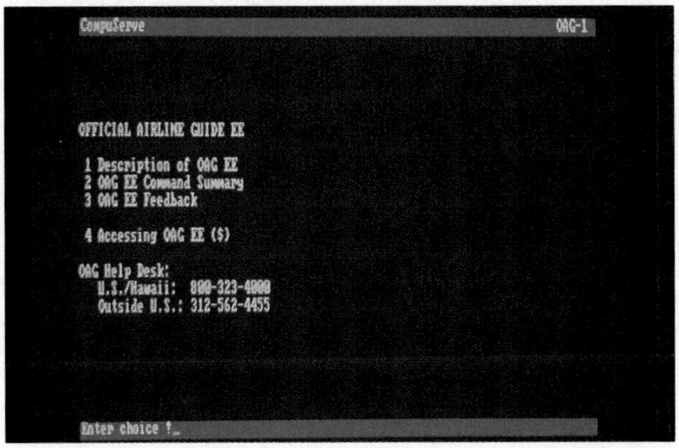

TERMS TO REMEMBER

acoustic coupler
analog signal
asynchronous
baud rate
bits per second (BPS)
bus topology
communications channel
communications software
concentrator
data communication
digital signal
direct-connect modem
distributed processing
download
electronic bulletin board
electronic mail
facsimile machine
full-duplex transmission
half-duplex transmission
hardwired
host
hybrid topology
information utility
local area network (LAN)
modem
multiplexer
network
network topology
node
public domain software
ring topology
simplex transmission
smart modem
star topology
synchronous
telecommunications
upload

CHECK YOUR UNDERSTANDING

1. ___________ is sending data electronically over distances.
2. Computers send and receive data as:
   a. baud rate
   b. analog signals
   c. half-duplex signals
   d. digital signals
   e. full-duplex signals
3. A(n) ___________ translates digital signals to analog signals and vice versa.
4. Telephone lines, microwaves, and satellites are examples of communication channels. (True/False)
5. Which of the following combine several transmission signals before sending them to a host computer?
   a. acoustic coupler
   b. concentrator
   c. multiplexer
   d. a and b
   e. b and c
6. With ___________ transmission, data are sent one byte at a time, surrounded by stop and start bits.
7. A node is a computer system that sends and receives data in only one direction at a time. (True/False)
8. Bus, ring, and star are different types of ___________.

9. Transferring data or programs from one computer to a host computer is called:
   a. LAN
   b. full-duplex
   c. downloading
   d. half-duplex
   e. uploading
10. With electronic mail, users can leave private messages for anyone else connected to the network. (True/False)

APPLYING WHAT YOU'VE LEARNED

1. Communications channels are a major part of a data communications network. Contact the telephone company to find out what types of communication channels are available through them, their baud rates, and the rates for using these channels.
2. If you wanted to join all the computers in your school into a network, which of the topologies would you use? Make a simple drawing of the network and label each node and its location.
3. Investigate one of the general information utilities mentioned in the text or another, more specialized, one. Find their out access fees and rates by contacting them directly or inquiring at a computer store. Also find out the type of equipment needed to connect to the utility and what type of information is available.
4. Aside from the examples mentioned in the text, what are two other possible sites for local area networks?
5. An electronic mail system uses a computer to store correspondence. Potentially, this could make it available to anyone with access to the system.
   a. What could be done to protect the privacy of a person's business or academic correspondence?
   b. What other losses of privacy could occur if electronic mail is used in all departments of a large organization?
6. Public domain software varies in applications and quality. Check your local schools, school district office, users group, libraries, and computer stores to see what types of public domain software are available, how it can be copied, and if anyone has evaluated the software quality.

CHECK YOUR UNDERSTANDING ANSWERS

1. data communication
2. d
3. modem
4. true
5. e
6. asynchronous
7. false
8. network topologies, or networks
9. e
10. true

U N I T
T H R E E

SOFTWARE: CONCEPTS AND APPLICATIONS

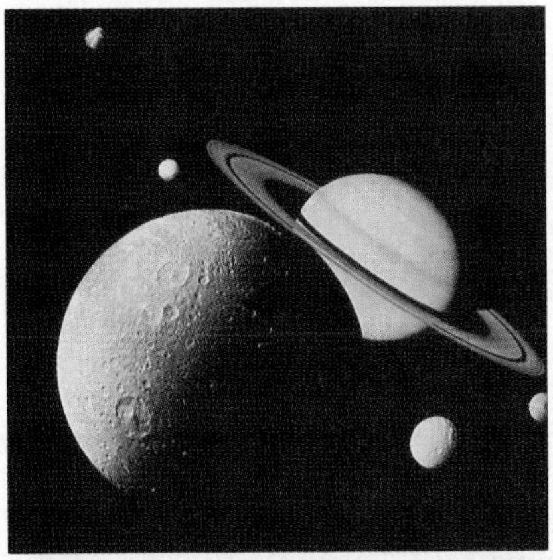

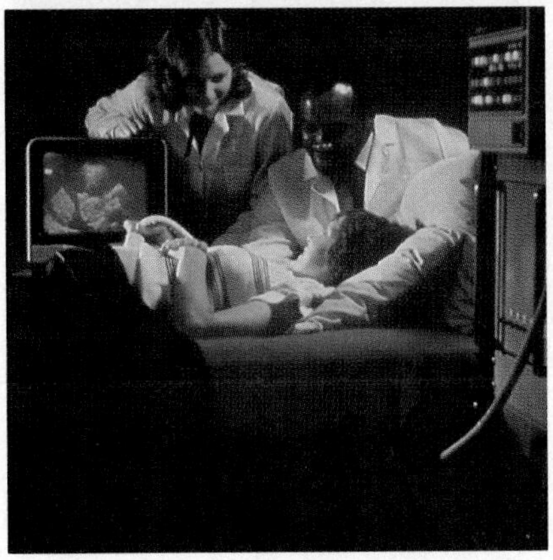

Computer programs turn a general-purpose computer system into a specialized problem-solving tool. Chapter 8 overviews the common properties of application and system software. It also emphasizes the importance of choosing software based on the user's identified needs and level of understanding. Distinguishing features of computer programs are reviewed along with sources for popular software. ▸ Chapter 9 provides an in-depth look at word processing programs. Applications for this popular personal productivity software are highlighted throughout the chapter. In addition, the features users need to create and edit documents are explained in detail. The chapter concludes with a discussion of questions to ask when purchasing a word processing package. ▸ The manipulation of numeric data through electronic spreadsheets is the focus of Chapter 10. The standard procedures for entering and organizing data in a spreadsheet's row-and-column format are discussed at length. Common applications are presented throughout the chapter to illustrate the versatility of this personal productivity software. A review of the important software features is included for those wishing to purchase such a package. ▸ Computers can help users create spectacular drawings and graphics. Chapter 11 overviews graphics packages that support free-hand drawing and the development of graphs, charts, and diagrams. A four-step process for designing presentation graphics is explained. Free-drawing graphics software turns the computer screen into an electronic canvas. The tools and techniques a graphic artist uses to produce original designs and art are shown through interrelated examples. Also included are features to look for when purchasing a graphics package. ▸ The database programs discussed in Chapter 12 represent some of the most powerful applications of computers. This chapter shows how data are organized and cross-referenced to provide useful information to database users. Database features and applications are identified through examples. In addition, the conclusion of this chapter discusses the power of integrated personal productivity software to expand the opportunities for users in applying computer technology at work and home.

CHAPTER EIGHT

USING SOFTWARE

KEY IDEAS

- **From the user's point of view**
  How does system and application software make computer systems easier for people to use? What features help you to make decisions and solve problems?

- **The software solution**
  Computers use software to oversee internal operations and to provide solutions for specific applications.

  System software
  Under the control of system software, a computer manages many of its own operations and resources.

  Application software
  People use programs that follow an input, processing, output, and storage cycle to solve a particular problem.

- **Software features and sources**
  Software is obtained from many sources and contains a variety of user-friendly features.

  What makes software user friendly?
  User-friendly software shares data with other application packages while being easy to learn and use.

  Finding the right software
  Informed users can obtain new software from a variety of resources, including stores, magazines, and user groups.

FROM THE USER'S POINT OF VIEW

Software is an interface between you and computer machinery. Ultimately, software enhances your competitive edge. Personal productivity will be greatly increased as you learn to manipulate words and numbers to maximum advantage. Since personal goals and responsibilities vary, so do software applications. Our objective is to make you aware of the many software features currently available. Your challenge is to identify those applications and features that are best suited for your areas of interest.

THE SOFTWARE SOLUTION

In general, two categories of software exist. System software oversees the internal operations of the computer, while application software directs the computer to execute specific jobs. As a computer processes data, several types of software interplay to produce results for the user. The different types of software are depicted in Figure 8.1.

Users first deal with an operating system, a type of system software that oversees the coordination and control of a computer system's resources. Another form of system software, called ***utility software***, performs standard processing tasks, such as sorting, copying, and file handling. Utility software may not be used as part of every processing job. ***Language translators*** are system software that are needed to convert application software, written in high-level programming languages, into a specific machine language.

Application programs provide directions for processing. There are two general types: ***application packages*** and ***customized programs***. Application packages include personal productivity software and a wide variety of programs designed for general applications. These applications might include computing the average monthly payment on a loan or this year's income tax payment. When purchased, these packages include software, operating instructions, a user's manual, and legal contracts to protect software copyrights.

Customized programs are designed by computer programmers for specific organizational needs such as payroll processing, monitoring hospital patients, or detecting radioactivity leaks in a power plant. The sections that follow discuss the functions and characteristics of system and application software.

System Software

System software makes a computer system user friendly by freeing users from constant involvement with computer operations. Under control of system software, a computer manages many of its own operations and resources. Given directions by an application program or user-operator, system software assumes responsibility for overseeing processing. System software consists of programs designed to run other programs. Three types of system software can be identified:

- Operating systems
- Language translators
- Utilities

Operating Systems

As its name implies, the operating system is a collection of programs that oversees all computer operations. Before any processing can occur, the operating

FIGURE 8.1

Computer software is subdivided into system software, which controls internal/peripheral operations, and application software, which provides solutions to particular user needs.

Computer Software

Systems Software
1. Operating Systems
2. Language Translators
3. Utilities

Application Software
1. Application Packages
2. Customized Programs

Two Methods for Booting an Operating System

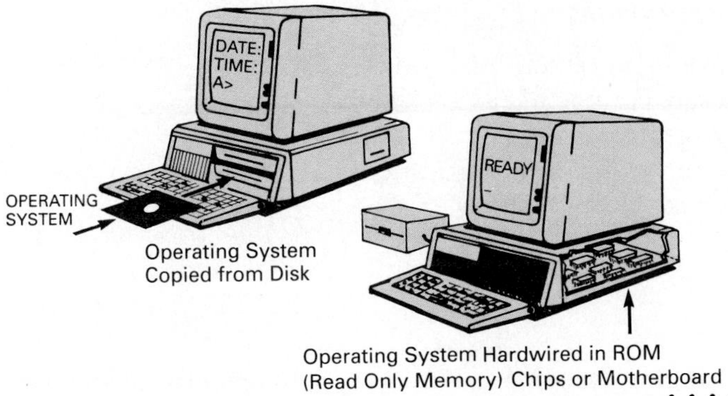

FIGURE 8.2

While most computer systems boot an operating system from disk or tape, some microcomputers have operating systems prepackaged into ROM chips on the motherboard.

system must be activated. Two methods are available for booting the operating system into memory, as shown in Figure 8.2. Some computers load the operating system automatically. The user-operator places the operating system disk in a drive and turns on the computer. Without further instructions from the operator, the computer transfers the operating system into memory, preparing the machine to begin processing. In larger computer systems the booting process may require several steps in order to identify each peripheral. Mainframe operators often refer to the booting process as the initial program load (IPL).

The second method of booting the operating system requires even less user intervention. The operator need only switch on the computer, and a built-in operating system is activated. Such systems are hard-wired into ROM (read-only memory). Hard-wired operating systems need not be loaded physically into the computer because they are permanently within it.

The operating system establishes the method of interaction between the user and the computer. That is, the operating system prepares the computer to accept specific commands through the selection of a word or icon.

The user might, for example, want to delete a file. The user would type DELETE in a ***command-driven operating system***, or point to an icon that looks like a trash can in an ***icon-driven operating system***. Figure 8.3 shows how command-driven systems use key words, such as DELETE, COPY, and FORMAT, to initiate action. In an icon-driven system, a mouse or other method is used to point to a picture representing the required action.

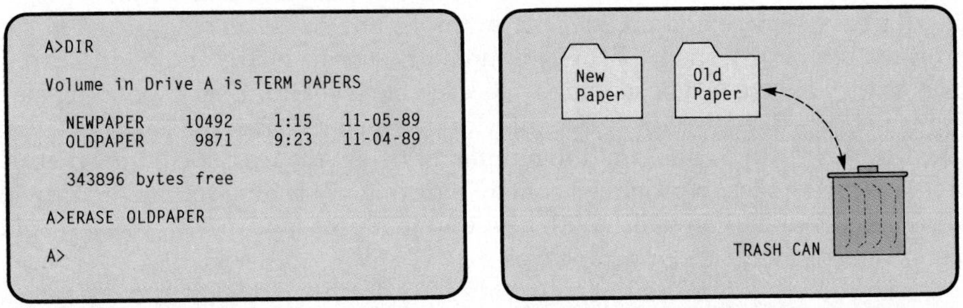

A Command-Driven Operating System in this Example Uses the Key-Word ERASE to Remove a File from Disk.

An Icon-Driven Operating System Working with a Mouse Allows Users to Point to a File Folder and then the TRASH CAN When Removing a File from Disk.

FIGURE 8.3

Erasing a file from disk using a command and icon-driven operating system.

Responsibilities of an Operating System

1. Schedule processing jobs
2. Allocate peripheral devices to jobs
3. Manage data in memory
4. Error checking of I/O operations
5. Housekeeping functions

FIGURE 8.4

Operating systems control internal computer operations and the activities of peripheral equipment.

The operating system also sets up system ***defaults***, or standard instructions and formats that the computer follows unless otherwise instructed. Default values save the user's time by preparing the computer to operate in a predetermined fashion. They are set up to handle the processing jobs most commonly run on that computer. Default values can easily be overridden by the user if nonstandard values or formats are desired. As an example, the default output device for a computer might be a specific printer. Without instructions to the contrary, the computer will assume that output will be generated on that printer. If a user wants output on a plotter, the default output values for the printer must be overridden. To override the default, the user must use a DOS command to specifically request that the computer produce plotter output. Without defaults, the user would have to repeat detailed instructions to the computer for every processing job.

Coordinating processing is another function of the operating system. These programs schedule the processing jobs to be run within a certain period of time. They then allocate input and output devices to the specific jobs, as needed. Managing files in memory and in storage is another task of the operating system. One specific program from the operating system works to coordinate all processing activities; it is sometimes called the ***supervisor***.

The supervisor activates other programs from the operating system to allocate hardware resources and to schedule processing jobs according to a scheme of priorities. A top priority job would be assigned the necessary devices for loading, processing, outputting, and terminating the job.

Once hardware resources are allocated, they are overseen by another operating system program that monitors the accuracy of input and output by using parity checking. In addition to detecting errors in data, the operating system checks for equipment malfunction and program errors. This software also detects such "error" conditions as an open disk drive door or a printer that has run out of paper.

The operating system manages computer files by performing ***housekeeping*** functions. These programs establish the order of data and files on disk, providing for easy storage and access. For example, one housekeeping program controls the use of disk space. That is, it monitors storage media and allots space to files as they are created or modified. As each file is set up, a corresponding entry is made in the disk directory. The directories list stored files, the dates they were created, their byte counts, and the number of bytes still available on the disk. In addition, some system programs contain indexing or hashing routines to provide direct access to files on disk. With a system that uses tape drives, housekeeping entails establishing labels for tape files.

The different functions of an operating system work together to ensure that a job is processed efficiently. Take, for example, the problem of producing report cards using a college's mainframe computer. When the operator first turns on the computer system, the supervisor is loaded into memory. At this point, the

```
A>dir

 Volume in drive A has no label
 Directory of A:\

COMMAND  COM    17792  10-20-83  12:00p
ANSI     SYS     1664  10-20-83  12:00p
FORMAT   COM     6912  10-20-83  12:00p
CHKDSK   COM     6400  10-20-83  12:00p
SYS      COM     1680  10-20-83  12:00p
DISKCOPY COM     2576  10-20-83  12:00p
DISKCOMP COM     2188  10-20-83  12:00p
COMP     COM     2534  10-20-83  12:00p
EDLIN    COM     4608  10-20-83  12:00p
MODE     COM     3139  10-20-83  12:00p
FDISK    COM     6369  10-20-83  12:00p
BACKUP   COM     3687  10-20-83  12:00p
RESTORE  COM     4003  10-20-83  12:00p
PRINT    COM     4608  10-20-83  12:00p
RECOVER  COM     2304  10-20-83  12:00p
ASSIGN   COM      896  10-20-83  12:00p
TREE     COM     1513  10-20-83  12:00p
GRAPHICS COM      789  10-20-83  12:00p
```

FIGURE 8.5

The PC-DOS disk directory shows the wide variety of systems programs that make up a microcomputer's operating system.

default values for the system assume operator commands will be input. At the operator's instructions, the mainframe schedules the execution of the grade reporting (application) program to begin at midnight when other demands on the computer are minimal. These instructions form the mainframe's job control language (JCL).

When execution begins at midnight, the operating system uses the JCL to allocate the line printer and one disk drive for the grade reporting program. In addition, a portion of memory is reserved for this application program and associated data. The supervisor uses other programs in the operating system for searching the disk directory to find and load the application program into memory. During processing, error checks are done on data as they are read from the disk.

If the operating system supports multiprogramming or time-sharing, it schedules work on the grade reporting program along with other programs in memory. Any data files produced or updated by this application are logged into the disk directory by the operating system housekeeping programs. Another program in the operating system monitors the printer's operation.

A microcomputer's operating system works in a similar fashion. A teacher using a microcomputer to compute final grades for a class boots the operating system when the computer is first turned on. The operating system defaults to keyboard input, screen output, and disk storage in one of the two disk drives. When loading the electronic spreadsheet used to keep grades, the housekeeping function of the operating system searches the disk directory to find the program. It then allocates space in memory for the program and incoming data. The spreadsheet uses the operating system to retrieve data from disk and to check incoming data for parity errors. The spreadsheet computes grades and automatically changes the output default to print the grades on the printer. As you can see, executing an application program on a mainframe or microcomputer requires the use of several systems programs from the operating system. The number and type of programs within the operating system vary depending on the size and sophistication of the computer being used.

FIGURE 8.6

Users and computer professionals have benefited from the development of sophisticated operating systems that help monitor and maintain computer operations.

C L I P

WHICH IS THE BEST SOFTWARE PACKAGE?

Thumbing through a microcomputer magazine can be a treat. Many people who adopt the microcomputer as an everyday tool become "gadget hounds." Enthusiasm takes over. They are ready, at any time, to browse the marketplace for new or improved additions to their systems. A microcomputer magazine meets this craving. Infinite varieties of exciting new gadgets are offered in an endless stream of ads. It seems as though every page offers some new package that promises to solve your problems or enhance the effectiveness of your computing tool.

In particular, microcomputer users seem to be interested continually in new and/or improved software packages. Which package can help you? Which should you buy? These have turned out, literally, to be billion-dollar questions, since computer owners are spending billions of dollars to satisfy their curiosities or to search for solutions.

Software selection can follow several patterns:

One approach can be called the *buddy routine.* You ask a local computer guru which software you should select. The answer generally is a description and name of the package the guru uses or has seen demonstrated. This approach tells you what the guru knows and recommends, an answer that may not correspond with your own best interests.

A second approach is similar. This is the *purchasing department choice.* A decision has been made that uniformity is necessary within the organization. An in-house guru has made a selection and everyone else has to live with it. You have no alternative. Your best bet is to find features within the pre-selected package that can be useful to you.

The next selection process exposes you to a different element of chance. This method is known as the *fire sale.* A need is identified. The cheapest solution, which may or may not deliver the best tool for the job, is selected.

If you are free to reach your own decisions, your best bet is to follow the decision-making process described in Chapter 15 of this book. Start by defining your needs. Be aware that price can be a factor, but need not be the main factor. You are out to satisfy yourself, not to conform to someone else's selections or to implement an answer that has met someone else's needs. Describe the use to which you will put any given package. Compare a number of packages. Rate these packages on how well they do your specific job. Select those which qualify according to your requirements. Then, buy the package that gives you the greatest "bang per buck," the one that provides the best combination of services and costs.

Key Question: Name one disadvantage to using each of the three software selection approaches mentioned.

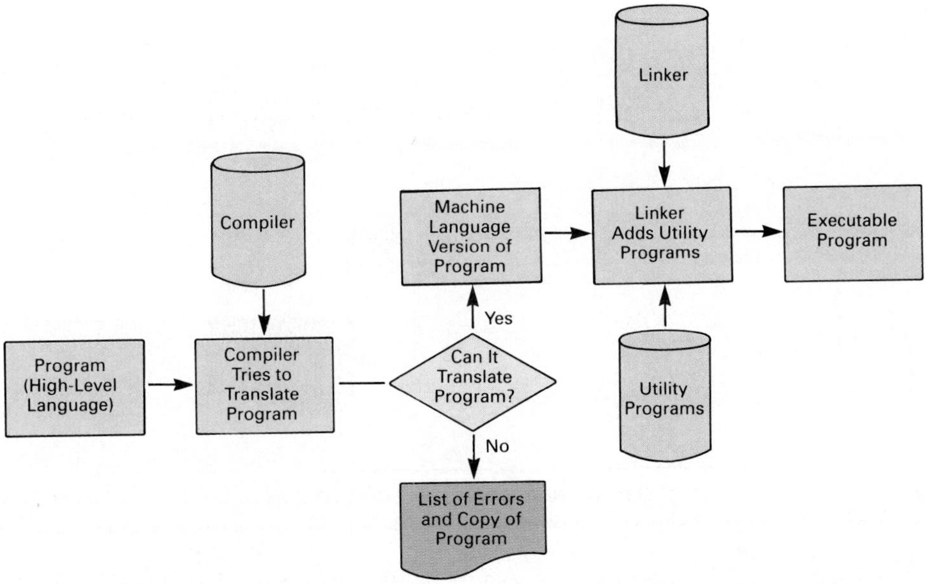

FIGURE 8.7

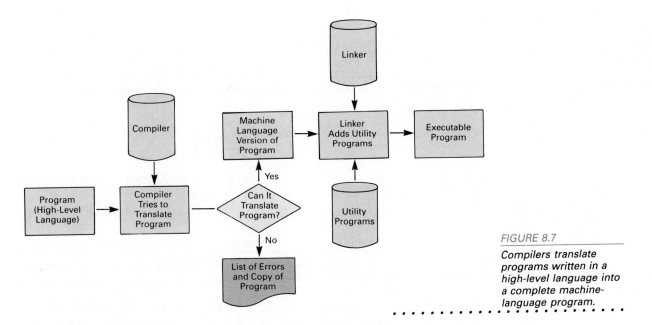

Compilers translate programs written in a high-level language into a complete machine-language program.

Language Translators

Before the advent of high-level programming languages, computers were complicated to program. Instructions had to be written in the computer's own machine language, which represents internal switch settings as 0s and ls.

You might remember from Chapter 2 that the complexity of writing machine-language programs was addressed in the 1950s when assembly languages made their debut. Programmers using assembly languages relied on translating programs, called ***assemblers***, to relieve the burden of coding computer programs in highly detailed machine language. Programs were written in symbolic assembly languages instead of bit patterns. Then, assembler software translated the programs into code that the computer could understand. Assemblers generally required one line of assembly code for each machine-language instruction to be generated. By today's standards, this method of program translation is simple but inefficient, since higher level languages do not maintain this one-to-one relationship. Nonetheless, assemblers were great time savers in their day.

Although assembler languages are still used for some types of system programming, they have been replaced by more sophisticated, user-friendly, high-level programming languages and fourth-generation languages (4GLs). These programming languages rely on sophisticated language translators. The translators are called either compilers or interpreters. Like assemblers, they convert program statements written by people into machine instructions. However, for each program statement translated, a compiler or interpreter generates several machine language statements. Compared with assemblers, these language translators allow programmers to write larger, more complex, error-free programs in less time. Chapter 16 describes many of the popular programming languages.

Still in wide use today, ***compilers*** are available for most high-level languages. Figure 8.7 shows the process of translating a COBOL program into machine code. First, the application program is loaded into memory along with a translator program. Since the program is written in COBOL, a business-oriented programming language, a COBOL compiler is used. The compiler checks the program for errors while it is translating the code into machine language.

Syntax errors may prevent the translation from being completed. A ***syntax error*** is a spelling error or misuse of the high-level language that the computer

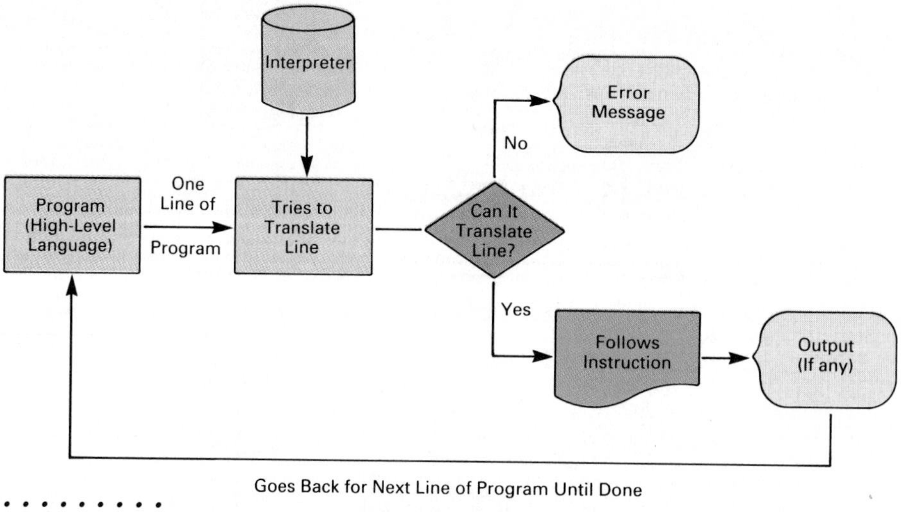

FIGURE 8.8

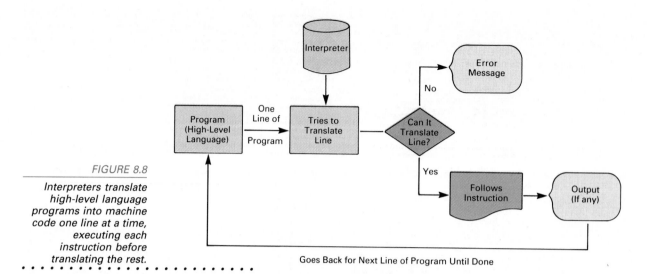

Interpreters translate high-level language programs into machine code one line at a time, executing each instruction before translating the rest.

cannot translate. For example, the COBOL instruction MULTIPLE PAY-RATE BY HOURS GIVING REGULAR-PAY cannot be translated. The COBOL compiler identifies this line as untranslatable because it does not recognize the instruction MULTIPLE. When the programmer corrects the syntax error by replacing MULTIPLE with MULTIPLY, this COBOL instruction can be translated.

A word of warning here. A language translator is not going to find ***logic errors***. This type of error is translatable but produces the wrong results. In the example above, if the programmer accidentally wrote MULTIPLY PAY-RATE BY EMPLOYEE-NUMBER GIVING REGULAR-PAY the instruction would be translated. However, the results would be incorrect since employee number is not used in pay calculations. Another example of a logic error would be using a plus sign when a minus sign is needed.

When an error-free translation results, the operating system activates a ***linker*** program. The linker embeds utility programs needed for input, output, or processing within the translated program. Now the program is complete and ready for use.

At this point, the original COBOL program is saved for future updates or modifications. The complete translation, including utilities, is either stored for future use or followed one step at a time, ***executed***, by the processing unit. To use a compiler, the computer must have enough memory to store the compiler and the application program in both its high-level and machine-language forms.

Many microcomputers translate programs written in the BASIC language in a different way. This other type of language translator is called an ***interpreter***. Interpreters translate and execute one high-level instruction at a time. Each instruction is acted upon after it is translated. Then the translation is discarded. If the program's logic dictates that instructions are repeated, each instruction must be translated again. As seen in Figure 8.8, this process is repeated until the program comes to its logical conclusion or the interpreter finds a syntax error. The advantage to using an interpreter is that it requires a minimum amount of memory. The interpreter needs only enough memory to store the instruction with which it is currently working. This can be a disadvantage because the translated version of the program is not saved. That means the original program must be translated each time it is used, which slows down processing.

Utilities

Utility software performs a variety of jobs. Utilities usually are written for preestablished routines often required by users of application programs. They include

Jobs Performed by Utility Programs

1. Erasing programs and data from storage media
2. Copy programs or data from one peripheral to another
3. Sorting data
4. Merging two data files into one file
5. Printing
6. Mathematical calculations
7. Data conversions

FIGURE 8.9

Utility programs work closely with operating systems to help users perform common tasks.

formatting new disks, erasing programs and data from disk, and copying programs from one disk to another.

Some utility programs are embedded within a compiled application program by a linker. For example, sorting, merging, copying, and printing requirements are almost universal among application programs. In addition, some utilities provide instructions for routine mathematical calculations or for converting data from one coding scheme to another, such as from a microcomputer-based ASCII to a mainframe-based EBCDIC. Since utility software is ready to use, it does not need to be specially prepared each time it is needed.

Another common utility program is used to save time when large documents are printed. A *spooler* (*s*imultaneous *p*eripheral *o*peration *onl*ine) utility coordinates the transfer of data between the computer and other peripherals, in this case the disk drive and printer. Instead of doing nothing while waiting for the document to be printed, the user can work with other programs and files. The spooler transfers the document from the computer to the disk drive and handles printing the document.

Application Software

The earliest forms of application software were executed without the assistance of system software. Computer operators and programmers had to schedule jobs, control devices, allocate memory, and direct processing for each application. In effect, these people were responsible for system control.

The advent of operating systems minimized this problem and helped people communicate more easily with computers. At first, organizations employed programmers who customized programs to their particular needs. This software development took place within the company, or ***in-house***. Computer programs to handle an organization's specific accounting, financial, statistical, inventory control, payroll, budget, and other data processing needs quickly evolved. Later, common processing needs emerged among computer users. Software applications such as word-processing, spreadsheets, and graphics, which were standard among most organizations, were identified. As computers became household tools, packaged software began to target common personal computer uses. As a result of these developments, creation and marketing of complete application packages launched a software industry that generates annual multibillion-dollar sales.

FIGURE 8.10

A wide variety of application packages can be purchased off-the-shelf at local computer stores.

Packaged application software greatly improves personal productivity with small computers. A microcomputer user can purchase a package off the shelf, take it home, and put it to work after only a few hours of preparation. Application packages quickly became a popular and inexpensive way to acquire powerful software.

CLIP

HOW COMPUTERS CAN HELP YOU SOLVE PROBLEMS

As general-purpose tools suited to a variety of tasks, word processors, spreadsheets and data bases are fundamental. In simplest terms, word processors are for writing, spreadsheets are for manipulating numbers and data bases combine qualities of the two, arranging information made up of both words and numbers. Sometimes these tools are used as stand-alone programs; other times you'll find them as part of an integrated package.

For many businesses, accounting software can be just as basic. And then there are two common business tasks—personalizing form letters and tracking appointments—with two specialized software solutions: mailmerge programs and desk-top accessories.

Word Processors

Beyond its use for writing itself (letters, reports, etc.), a business-class word processor should have a "macro" feature, sometimes called a "glossary." With this function, you make one or two keystrokes represent a large number of keystrokes (i.e., a paragraph or a complicated set of commands). Then, by pressing the key(s) you've coded for your macro, the program will automatically insert all the words or perform all the commands, assigned to it.

For example, you could set up the letter "C" on a macro to insert a standard closing of a letter. Not only does this make it easy to insert pieces of standard text (often called "boilerplate") into your documents, it also allows you to automate many of the word processor's other functions (such as mailmerge or cataloging disks), a bit time- and memory-saver. Mailmerge capacities usually are built into sophisticated business word processors.

Data Bases

One key feature to look for in a database manager is the ability to sort by date as well as by alphabetical order. The data-base manager should have a complete, built-in report function, which allows you to extract only the information you need from a mass of data. And "complete" means the ability to perform arithmetic calculations on your numeric data, such as totals or averages. That's useful in tracking inventories, printing invoices, and more.

Spreadsheets

Spreadsheet software can be the single most versatile tool for many businesses. It will take you from making appointments to bookkeeping and from tracking small inventories to financial projections. The ability to link various spreadsheets to exchange data makes accounting, for one, easier, because the "books" can then be constructed in modular form.

Source: Reprinted by permission, *San Jose Mercury News*

Key Question: Which personal productivity software would be most useful to you in your present school work?

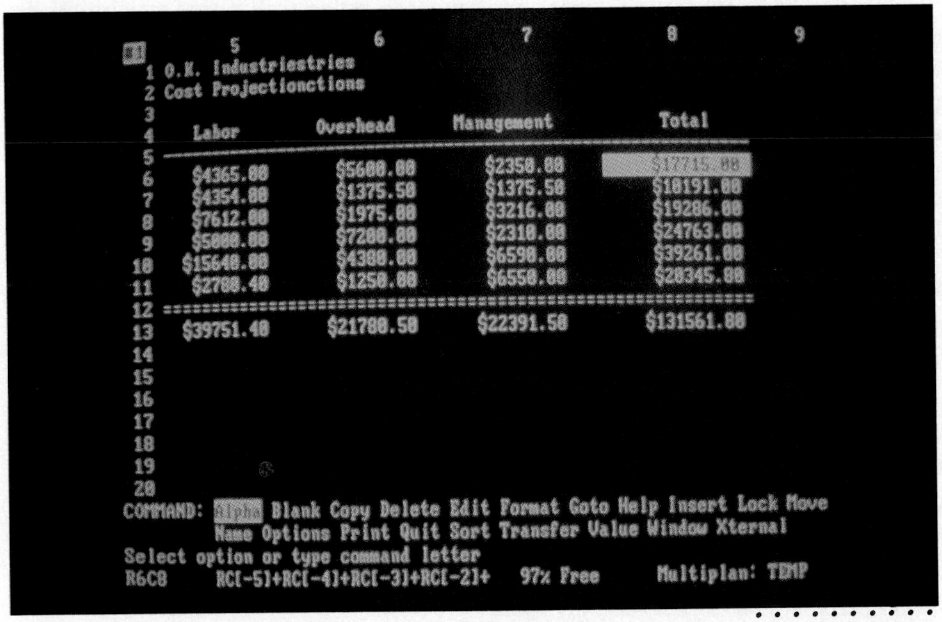

FIGURE 8.11
Electronic spreadsheets structure data in rows and columns.

Application software can be classified according to the type of data being processed: text, graphics, numbers, and so on. Processing requirements vary according to the demands of the users and structures of the data.

Data Files, Databases, and Spreadsheets

Data files are structured. They usually hold records of fixed lengths and in predetermined relationships to one another. The format of a data file, then, is predictable. This is the nature of business data. For example, a salesperson master file contains standard records for every employee. The employee's name, address, department, commission rate, deductions, and other items are fields included in the record.

A database, in turn, is a collection of related data files. Data items can be assembled in any number of ways to meet particular processing needs. Since files must be cross-referenced, their structure is crucial to the efficient operation of a database. The salesperson master file just mentioned might be cross-referenced with the customer order file in order to compute commissions and generate sales reports. By maintaining an established structure, a database program can access needed data, format them, and generate reports to meet user needs. Chapter 12 covers database features in more detail.

Another application that requires structured data is the electronic spreadsheet. As shown in Figure 8.11, spreadsheets organize data into rows and columns. As a result, a spreadsheet resembles a table of data. However, the spreadsheet does more than just organize data. It also performs calculations on specified data items and creates new rows and columns with the results. Spreadsheets also rely on structured data formats. Other spreadsheet options and applications are discussed in Chapter 10.

Text

Unlike data files and databases, text has no rigid structure. Text involves words, sentences, and paragraphs of unpredictable lengths. Capabilities for processing and storing text lagged behind those for data files because of the unstructured nature of textual documents. Once technicians met and overcame text processing challenges, however, the application began to thrive.

FIGURE 8.12

Graphics packages use vast matrices of dots or line coordinates to create drawings and graphs.

Today, text processing is the single most popular application run on microcomputers. Literally hundreds of versions of word processing packages are available. Word processing software enabled the authors to create documents, proofread them on a screen, move paragraphs around, and delete blocks of text to write this book. They repeated these tasks through four edits (original, rewrite, technical review, copy editing) until a satisfactory document was produced. The typesetters then produced—from the author's four 360K, 5 1/4-inch floppy disks—the words you are now reading.

Most word processing packages provide special capabilities, such as automatic pagination, print format options, spelling checkers, and search and replace commands. All of these functions assist in writing and editing text documents. Chapter 9 examines these operations and others in detail.

Graphics

Graphics applications convert numeric data into lines and curves that express the data pictorially. Masses of numbers and percentages—often difficult to understand on their own—can become clearer in a simple chart or diagram. Yet, graphics software poses special challenges. Transforming data into a meaningful picture requires special translation hardware and software.

As noted in Chapter 6, graphic displays will use either pixel or vector graphics. With pixel graphics each data element corresponds to a dot that is independent of all others. However, the dots can be combined to form shapes and sketches. Pixel graphics, ordered neatly into rows and columns, is well suited to business charts and diagrams. Vector graphics produces smooth, flowing, continuous lines and is useful for designs and drawings. Various options offered by graphics packages are featured in Chapter 11.

Process Controls

Process control applications use physical data to monitor and control activities. The software used in process control often instructs the computer to operate production equipment. That is, special equipment continually senses and translates physical data, then adjusts operations accordingly. Some devices that re-

FIGURE 8.13

Process control systems take advantage of a computer's ability to work for a long time without human intervention.

spond to computer-generated signals are called robots. A special set of process control applications that use robots are referred to as ***robotics***.

Many process control systems are interactive: They operate according to ***feedback***, or data resulting from operating conditions that are used to adjust processing. That is, physical data reflecting environmental and production conditions are monitored and converted into digital signals that are fed into a computer. The computer reacts to the signals according to instructions supplied by process control software. For example, in an automated air conditioning system, process control software might be used to maintain air temperature at 70 degrees Fahrenheit. The software would compare actual temperature with desired temperature. Temperature differences trigger feedback signals to activate or deactivate the air conditioner. This process control application accepts and evaluates physical data. The computer then responds to those conditions. Many of these process control applications are described in detail as part of Chapter 17.

STUDY QUESTIONS

1. Define default, supervisor, housekeeping, assembler, syntax error, logic error, execute, in–house, robotics, and feedback.
2. What are the functions of system and application software?
3. Identify and describe three types of system software and two types of application software.
4. What four items are included as part of an application package?
5. What are the two methods for booting an operating system into memory?
6. How are command-driven and icon-driven operating systems different?
7. Describe five responsibilities of an operating system.
8. How are assemblers different from high-level language translators?
9. Explain the differences between an interpreter and a compiler. Give an advantage and disadvantage to using each.
10. What is the function of a linker program?
11. Identify seven jobs performed by utility software.
12. Describe the general characteristics of software that handles data files/databases, text, graphics, and process control.

SOFTWARE FEATURES AND SOURCES

Software provides a set of instructions that allows general-purpose hardware to solve specific problems. One computer can calculate your monthly car payment in the morning and play a mean game of chess in the afternoon. Only the computer program (and data) changes. People often make this point by saying "Software drives hardware."

Software also drives hardware when purchasing a new computer system. By first looking for user-friendly software that solves a specific problem, the hardware decisions become quite simple because your software choices determine what hardware you purchase.

Computer programs differ with the individual job performed and results desired. Some features available in application packages help meet user needs

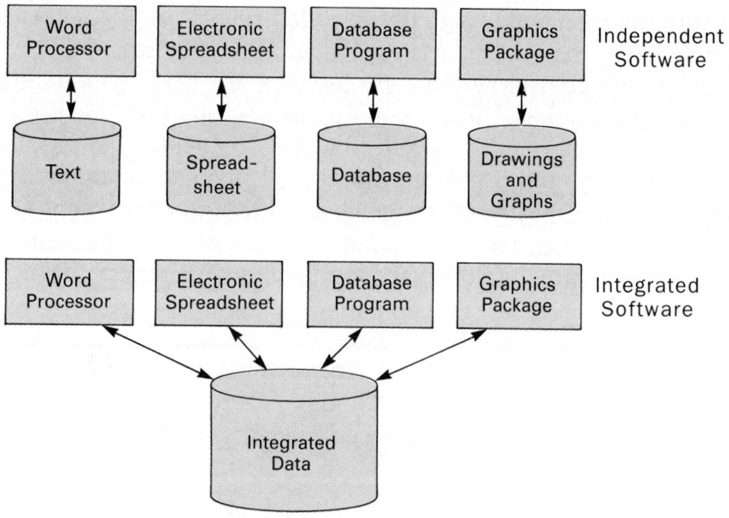

FIGURE 8.14

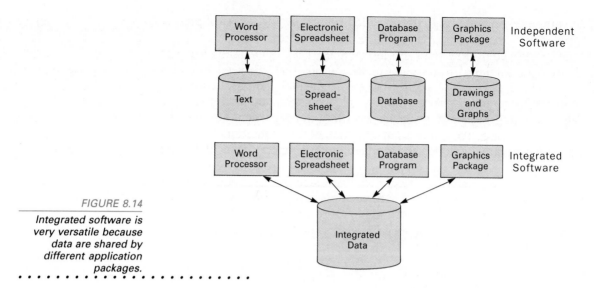

Integrated software is very versatile because data are shared by different application packages.

while other features make the software easier to use. When evaluating different application packages, users should answer these questions:

- Are the program and associated procedures easy to use?
- Does the software come with manuals and other forms of easy-to-read documentation?
- Does the software work the way the user wants it to, or will changes be necessary?
- How flexible is the program, and can people use it for more than one application?
- Can the new software access data stored by other programs and vice versa?
- On which computers does the software work?
- Does the software require special hardware?

What Makes Software User Friendly?

While problems and computer applications may differ among people, common user-friendly features are easy to identify. These features help us learn how to use the software effectively, minimize frustrations, and provide insights into future applications for the package.

Integrated vs. Independent Software

Many application packages are stand-alone. That is, they operate as single entities, and they are unable to share data with other programs. These programs are known as ***independent software*** (see Figure 8.14).

Over time, demand has grown for sharing data among multiple applications. People discovered that spreadsheets could lend support to information presented in a textual document. Also, a bar chart can clarify figures laid out in a spreadsheet. In short, people needed the capability to combine formerly independent applications. Word processing, database, spreadsheet, graphics, and data communication applications had to become compatible. This need led to the development of ***integrated software***, which permits users to share data between applications (see Figure 8.14).

Programs made compatible by integrated software can be combined for multiple uses. A company manager might use a database to track business activity. To analyze business conditions more thoroughly, the manager might use the database to create a spreadsheet. He or she could then draft written financial reports using a word processor and integrate graphics to illustrate the words. In a large company, data might need to be shared with other departments through a data communication network. With an integrated software package, each department would have easy access to all available data, without having to juggle software programs.

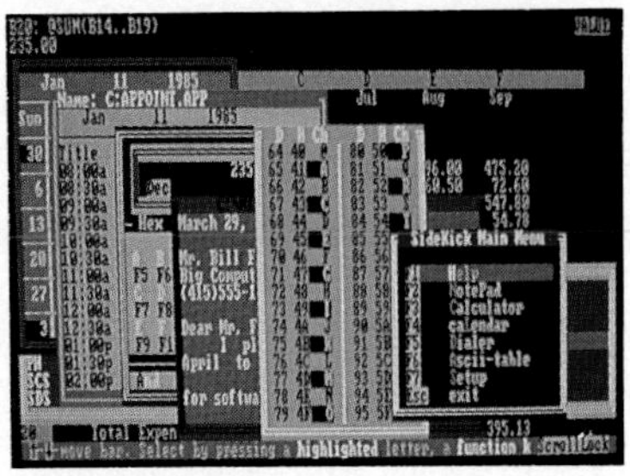

FIGURE 8.15

Desktop utility software lets users make notes, keep calendars, and use a calculator—all without leaving the computer.

Windows

Application programs, particularly integrated software, often are powerful enough to allow users to switch between two or more programs. To track this activity, a VDT screen can be divided into sections, or ***windows***. Each window displays a menu or status report on a separate program or activity. Programs used to create a financial status report, for example, might use three windows. One would display the text of the report, generated through word processing software. The second might hold a spreadsheet. Graphics tying together the words and the numbers might occupy the third window.

Windows are used widely with ***desk–top utility software***. These are integrated software packages that replace, with special assistance programs, resources commonly found on people's desks. Desk–top utilities reside in memory while other application programs are in use. When the user needs a special program, the desk–top utility can be accessed without exiting the application program. On the screen, a window appears to accommodate a variety of activities. These activities might include a calendar, a calculator, telephone directory, appointment schedule, and a notepad. Notepads often contain text editing capabilities. Teachers could use a word processor to create a test and the notepad for the answer key. They then can use the notepad's special editing capabilities to make independent changes to the answer key. All these activities take place within windows on the screen.

Menus and Icons

Some application programs provide a series of ***menus*** to inform the user of available functions. A menu is a list of program options available to the user; each option is assigned a letter or number. Using a keyboard, mouse, or other input device, people select the menu item needed. Often, one menu selection leads to a submenu that presents another list of options to the user.

Some application programs use icons instead of menus to identify functions. Operators move the cursor to the icon representing the desired function. For example, a user working with an icon-driven application might access a file by pointing to an icon that looks like a file folder.

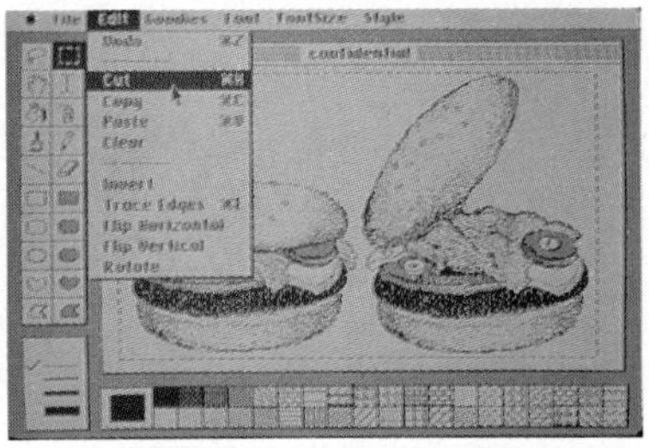

FIGURE 8.16

User-friendly features of a software package can enhance the productivity of a computer user.

Palettes and Toolboxes

To support graphics applications, a ***palette*** and ***toolbox*** display options for drawing and coloring an image (see Figure 8.16). A palette usually contains icons that correspond with different screen colors. The toolbox provides icons for brush size, shape, and width, along with other editing features. The user selects desired options by moving the cursor or pointing to the corresponding icons. As the user creates a screen drawing, the graphics package responds with the specified options. The final product reflects the combination of images and colors selected by the user.

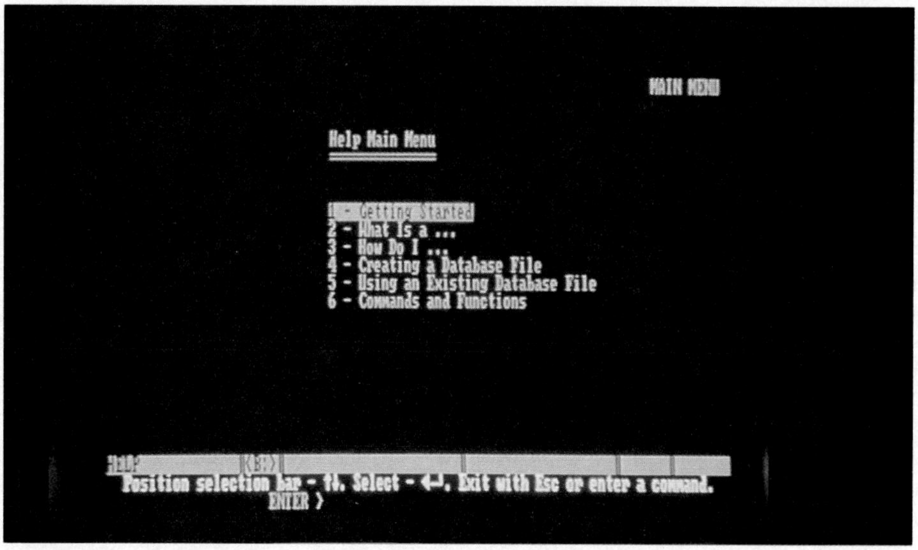

FIGURE 8.17

A help screen gives assistance to the user by involving the options available in the program.

Manuals and Help Screens

Learning to use new application programs puts the user between the computer and unknown software. When users of newly acquired software face problems or uncertainty, they must look to the ***user's manual*** for answers. The user's manual provides information on how to operate the program, descriptions of program features, a list of error messages, and company identification. This collection of information often is an accessible part of a program feature called a ***help screen***.

Help screens, such as the one illustrated in Figure 8.17, put answers at users' fingertips. The user can key in a request for information about a certain function, and a screen displaying that information will appear. This saves the user the trouble of leafing through a user's manual in search of guidance.

Different software packages provide different ways of accessing help screens. Some programs list a help directory on the menu, while others require use of a special function key. Still others require that users ask for assistance by typing in HELP.

Finding the Right Software

Software can be developed internally, leased, bought, or shared. With the abundance of prepackaged software on the market, in–house development usually is reserved for customized programs. For general applications, leased or purchased software provides needed capabilities at minimum cost. Shared software is distributed through networks and among users with similar computer needs and interests. The most popular software sources are described below.

Retail Computer Stores

Most users purchase off-the-shelf software packages at retail computer stores. These outlets provide hardware, supplies, magazines, and manuals—in addition to vast selections of software. Purchasing software through retail stores has a distinct advantage. Most retailers will allow you to test application programs before you purchase them. Also, salespeople usually are on hand to describe software features and review user's manuals. Before you buy a software package, you should use it. This gives you a chance to see if the package meets your needs.

FIGURE 8.18

Many computer magazines are being published, some specializing in a single machine or application package.

Computer Manufacturers

Manufacturers of computer hardware usually provide compatible system software. In addition, some hardware manufacturers make application programs available to customers. Since many users base their hardware decisions on availability of a specific software package, computer manufacturers often package personal productivity software with their hardware as a sales incentive. For example, a new user might be purchasing a microcomputer specifically for its word processing ability. If he or she is working with a limited budget, hardware packaged with a compatible operating system and word processing program could be highly desirable.

Magazines

Computer trade magazines are an inexpensive source of information on programs. Hundreds of magazines and newsletters publish articles and programs geared toward personal computer use. Many magazines specialize in software compatible with one or two brands of computers. Users with a certain brand of computer usually can find a magazine written for it.

Magazines sometimes run articles that list the actual program instructions line by line. Copying programs from magazines has its risks. Users who enter the programs on their own must take extreme care to ensure that the program is typed accurately. One entry error can lead to many hours spent searching for the mistake. Occasionally, the version of the program printed in the magazine will contain a typographical error. If this happens, users will surely find out about it. An article identifying the error and containing a corrected version probably will appear in a later issue. In order to avoid this transcription problem, some magazines now provide readers with a disk that contains an error-free version of the program.

Magazines also contain advertisements for software. Computer programs available through mail order may seem like a convenient way to acquire software. However, ordering anything sight unseen has its risks. Mail-order customers should try to get permission to review the software before buying it. Promotional copies sometimes are available. ***Promotional software*** allows people to try out programs with limited amounts of data. For example, a promotional database program might limit the user to 30 records. Thus, promotional copies are not useful for regular workloads. They do, however, allow the user to become familiar with the program's features before buying it.

FIGURE 8.19

User groups provide an opportunity to share both ideas and software.

Information Utilities and Bulletin Boards

As noted in Chapter 7, public domain software can be distributed over data communications lines. Dial-up information utilities and bulletin boards provide an avenue for passing along software. Some magazines operate reader services that provide lengthy catalogs of public domain listings. Pages full of utility and application software are made available to anyone who requests the information.

Public domain software is usually a "take it as it is" proposition. However, several public domain software programmers continue to make improvements on their programs. To support this work, they ask for a small contribution from people who find their programs useful. Typically, this request is included in a message preceding the program. The message also asks people to pass copies to others. As a result, this special type of public domain software is known as ***shareware***. People who thank the shareware programmers with a monetary donation usually receive a manual, as well as the next version of the program when it is ready.

User Groups and Professional Associations

User groups provide fellowship among users who share an interest in computers. They also are good sources for public domain software and programs developed by users themselves. Usually, user groups consist of people interested in the same brand of computers. They meet to discuss shared problems and new ideas. New users who join these groups can learn about the latest software and hardware developments for their machines.

User groups develop around many types and sizes of computers. Personal computer users generally form local groups. National user groups bring together users of large systems. In both cases, computer interests spawn homemade programs that can be shared by all members of the group. Some programs are circulated among club members free of charge. Others are sold for the cost of the tape or disk. In general, the distribution of software by user-developers is not for profit.

STUDY QUESTIONS

13. Define desk-top utility software, user's manual, promotional software, and shareware.
14. Identify seven questions users should ask when evaluating new software.
15. What is the critical difference between independent and integrated software?
16. How do windows, menus, icons, and help screens make application software easier to use?
17. Explain how a palette and toolbox are used by a graphics package.
18. Identify five sources for computer software.
19. What is the advantage to purchasing software from a retail store?
20. What are three sources for public domain software?

CONCLUSION

Software turns general-purpose computers into special problem-solving machines. System software works with users to control the computer's resources and helps create an environment for application programs. Application packages help the user with specific processing problems. The user friendliness of application programs is enhanced by the inclusion of windows, menus, icons, and help screens. Users can obtain system and application software from many sources. Whatever the source, users should try software before they purchase to make sure it meets their needs and runs on their equipment. Computers are only as useful as the software they run.

CHAPTER FACTS

- Software can be classified as system software and application software.
- System software monitors the computer's internal operations. It consists of operating systems, language translators, and utilities.
- Operating systems are a series of programs, coordinated by a supervisor program, that control I/O operations, check for I/O errors, allocate memory and use of peripherals, and schedule processing jobs.
- Utility software performs standard processing tasks such as sorting, copying, merging, erasing, and printing files, data conversions, and some mathematical calculations.
- Language translators convert high-level languages into machine language. They consist of assemblers, compilers, and interpreters.
- Assemblers convert assembly language, each instruction representing one machine instruction.
- Compilers translate entire programs line by line. If errors are found, they are listed. If the translation is error-free, a linker program embeds needed utilities. The translation then is executed.
- Interpreters translate then execute the program one line at a time. They continue until the program is completed or an error is found.
- Program errors consist of logic errors, translatable but producing incorrect results, and syntax errors, which cannot be translated into machine language.
- Application software consists of application packages and customized programs.
- Customized programs are written in-house to handle specific organizational processing needs.
- Application packages are general-purpose application software. The packages include software, user's manual, operating instructions, and a copyright contract.
- Process control uses physical data in a feedback loop to adjust production and manufacturing processes. Applications using robots are called robotics.
- Software drives hardware and as a result users should evaluate software before making hardware decisions.
- If software is able to share data with other programs, it is integrated. Independent software cannot share data.
- Application packages include features such as windows, menus, icons, palettes, toolboxes, and help screens to increase user friendliness.
- Software is available from retail computer stores, manufacturers, magazines, information utilities and bulletin boards, and user groups.

TERMS TO REMEMBER

application packages
assembler
command-driven operating system
compiler
customized program
default
desk-top utility software
execute
feedback
help screen
housekeeping
icon-driven operating system
independent software
in-house
integrated software
interpreter
language translator
linker
logic error
menu
palette
promotional software
robotics
shareware
supervisor
syntax error
toolbox
user's manual
utility software
window

CHECK YOUR UNDERSTANDING

1. A(n) __________ is a group of system programs that controls job processing, manages data and I/O, and checks for errors.
2. The housekeeping program is a special system program that coordinates all processing activities. (True/False)
3. When language translators cannot convert a high-level program instruction into machine code it is called:
   a. a code goof
   b. a syntax error
   c. a logic error
   d. broken code
   e. none of the above
4. Which of the following does not apply to an interpreter?
   a. Each line of code is translated and executed separately.
   b. A minimum amount of memory is required.
   c. No translated version of the program is saved.
   d. Each line of the program is translated into one machine-language instruction.
   e. All of these apply.
5. A(n) __________ embeds utilities into a program translated by a compiler.
6. Process control uses __________ data as feedback to control and manufacturing processes.
7. Which of the following would *not* be found in an application package?
   a. user's manual
   b. copyright contract
   c. software
   d. operating instructions
   e. All would be found.

8. Independent software does not allow sharing of data between programs, while ____________ software does allow such sharing.
9. Shareware is a less powerful version of an application package distributed by manufacturers so that users may try a program before buying it. (True/False)
10. A(n) ____________ assists the user in choosing the style, size, and editing of graphics software.

APPLYING WHAT YOU'VE LEARNED

1. Try one of the application packages available to you at school or home. Is it command- or icon-driven? What came with the package (user's guide, and so on) besides the software itself? List the features it has that makes it user friendly to you.
2. The price of a software package may vary greatly depending on its source. Choose a popular application package, such as a word processing or graphics program. Find out its current price by checking several computer stores and looking for mail-order advertisements in magazines. From whom would you order the software if money was not a problem? Why wouldn't you patronize the other sources?
3. Look at the user's manual for the operating system used on a school or home computer. List the utility software available through that operating system and what each utility does. (*Hint*: They may be listed under library programs.) Do you access the utilities through commands or icons? Are help screens or menus of options available?
4. Find three advertisements for programmers in the newspaper. Can you tell what types of programs (system or application) they write? How do the positions compare in salary given, experience required, and programming language used?
5. Find out what language translators are available on your school computer. For what type of applications is each language used? Are the translators compilers or interpreters?
6. Process control is being used to manufacture a variety of products. Make a list of five places where process control is employed. What physical data are fed back into the system? What is the final output? What would be a disadvantage and an advantage to using process control instead of human supervision for each example?

CHECK YOUR UNDERSTANDING ANSWERS

1. operating system
2. false
3. b
4. d
5. linker
6. physical
7. e
8. integrated
9. false
10. toolbox

CHAPTER NINE

WORD PROCESSING: WORKING WITH WORDS

KEY IDEAS

- **From the user's point of view**
  How can word processing software allow you to create, edit, and produce professional quality documents? In what ways does word processing help you communicate more effectively in writing?

- **The written document**
  Text processing with computers saves time.

  Editing
  People use word processing functions such as insert, delete, and search and replace to write and revise documents.

  Formatting
  The ability to change margins, type styles, and tabulation lets users decide how a document will look.

  Integration with other software packages
  Users can access features like a spelling checker, online thesaurus, and writing analyzer.

- **Word processing as a tool**

  Office automation
  Word processing, electronic mail, and electronic filing have stimulated and met business demands.

  Marketing
  Word processing is used to prepare advertisements and personalized correspondences.

  Journalism
  Journalists now use keyboards and screens instead of manual typewriters.

  Education
  Teachers work with word processing as an educational tool and as an instructional subject.

  Legal professions
  Special word processing packages help organize and store legal documents.

- **How to select word processing packages**
  Buyers should analyze their needs before they select a word processing package.

FROM THE USER'S POINT OF VIEW

There is a good chance that word processing will immediately change your life for the better. It simplifies the process of typing and editing term papers and letters. There is also a hidden benefit. The ease with which text can be changed makes users better writers. Since a paper no longer has to be completely retyped to produce an error-free copy, you do not have to hesitate to modify it. Also, people with poor typing and spelling skills can rely on word processing to minimize these deficiencies. Word processing will significantly alter the way you write.

THE WRITTEN DOCUMENT

Nearly every occupation relies, to some extent, on written documents. The movie industry, for example, requires many written documents, including scripts, contracts, even press kits. These documents are not seen on screen, yet they are integral to the production of the film. Every day, in homes and in offices, millions of documents are exchanged. These documents represent work, the processing of words for business or personal use.

Creating correspondence and documents has become a huge part of the operation of most organizations. As noted in Chapter 8, the unstructured nature of text used to present processing problems. As text processing capabilities have advanced, computers and the generation of written documents have progressed together toward a solution.

Word processing is the use of computer systems to write, edit, print, and store written documents. These documents will include letters, reports, memos, and articles. Devices used for word processing include special electronic typewriters, printers, screens, keyboards, as well as computers. Sometimes this hardware is combined into dedicated office equipment, called stand–alone word processors, which exclusively create and edit text documents. At other times, microcomputers running word processing software perform the same text processing. Software functions involved in word processing fall under two broad categories:

- Editing
- Formatting

To complete a document, several word processing functions must be utilized. Consider the processing job taken on by Lee Butterfield, a student who must prepare a political science report with his microcomputer. Lee uses several word processing functions and features in completing his report. While the precise operating procedures for word processing functions vary from package to package, Lee's software contains some of the most common features.

Before he starts to work on his report, Lee boots the computer with system software. This procedure, explained in Chapter 8, prepares the computer to begin processing. Once the operating system is booted, Lee loads word processing software from a disk (see Figure 9.3). The word processing software helps him create, edit, and save documents through the use of menus, help screens, and keyboard overlays. Lee is now ready to write his report. The following sections review the format and editing functions he uses to complete the document.

Editing

Lee uses a microcomputer keyboard much as he would use a typewriter. The microcomputer, however, accommodates word processing functions that make writing and revising text easier and more efficient.

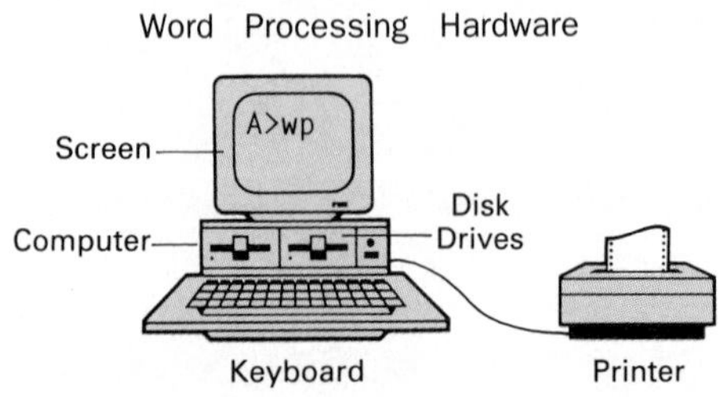

FIGURE 9.1

Word-processing hardware includes a keyboard for input, a computer for file creation and editing, a screen for softcopy, a printer for hardcopy, and disk drives for long-term storage.

FIGURE 9.2
Word-processing increases everyone's personal productivity

- **Word wrap**. The ***word wrap*** feature enables Lee to write in a continuous flow of sentences, uninterrupted by carriage returns. When Lee types past the right margin (see Figure 9.4), the system enters a soft return and automatically moves the cursor and word being typed to the next line (see Figure 9.5). ***Soft returns*** are carriage returns added or deleted by the word processing software to keep text within specified margins.

  With the word wrap feature, Lee can concentrate on the logical organization of sentences, rather than the physical placement of words on the screen. The RETURN or ENTER key on the computer's keyboard is used primarily to mark the end of a paragraph with a ***hard return***. Hard returns are entered by the user and are also used to insert blank lines.
- **Cursor control**. Once Lee has completed his first draft, he reads through the report, correcting typographical errors and making content changes. To move from one paragraph to another in the report, he employs ***cursor control*** features. The simplest cursor control features enable him to move one character location at a time—to the left, to the right, up, or down. This cursor movement usually is executed by pressing keys marked with arrows.

  By teaming these arrowed keys with other keys, Lee is able to expand his control of cursor movement. A few keystrokes move the cursor to the next word, paragraph, or page. Other features send the cursor to the beginning or end of a line, page, or document. The ***scroll*** feature rolls a page of

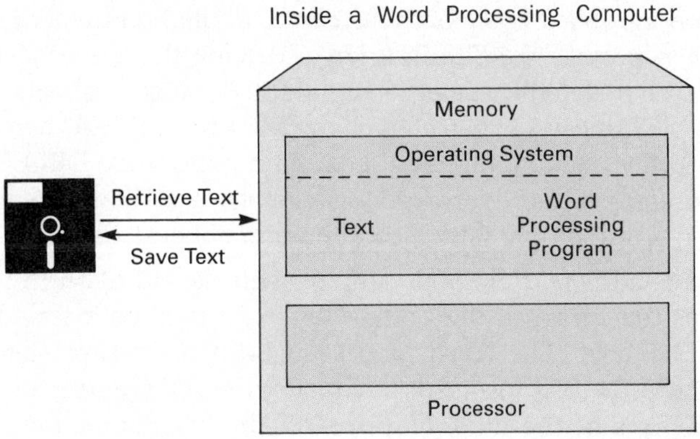

FIGURE 9.3
A disk operating system works with the word-processing program to create, edit, print, and store documents.

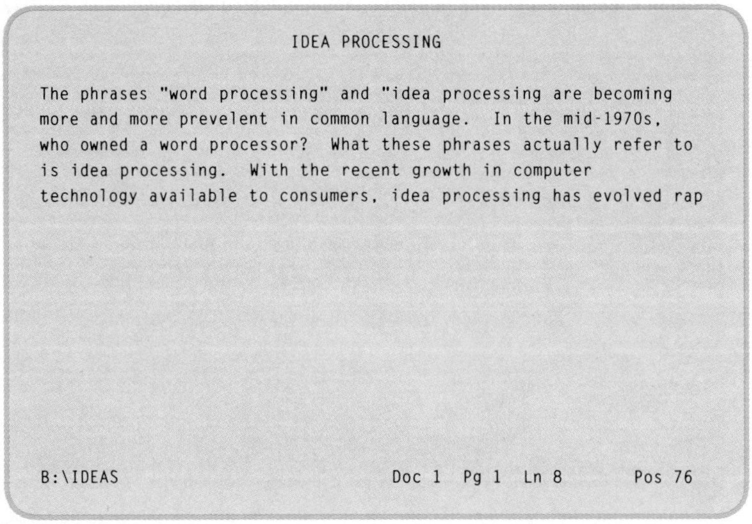
IDEA PROCESSING
The phrases "word processing" and "idea processing are becoming
more and more prevelent in common language. In the mid-1970s,
who owned a word processor? What these phrases actually refer to
is idea processing. With the recent growth in computer
technology available to consumers, idea processing has evolved rap
B:\IDEAS
Doc 1 Pg 1 Ln 8 Pos 76

FIGURE 9.4

Text entry with a word-processing system is continuous. This figure shows a text entry that is about to complete a line.

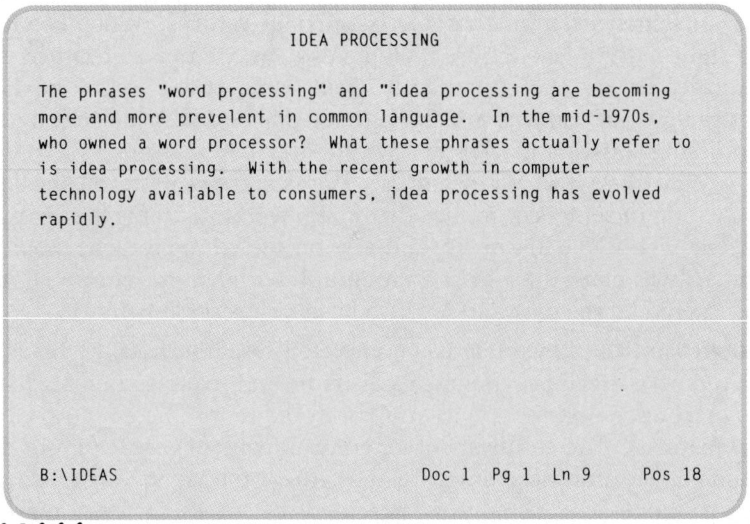
IDEA PROCESSING
The phrases "word processing" and "idea processing are becoming
more and more prevelent in common language. In the mid-1970s,
who owned a word processor? What these phrases actually refer to
is idea processing. With the recent growth in computer
technology available to consumers, idea processing has evolved
rapidly.
B:\IDEAS
Doc 1 Pg 1 Ln 9 Pos 18

FIGURE 9.5

Word wrap is automatically performed by most word-processing software when a word will not fit on the current line (see preceding figure). The full word is automatically moved to the next line without user intervention.

text up, down, or side to side for viewing. Lee manipulates these features to quickly move to sections of his document needing review.

- **Delete**. The ***DELETE*** function enables Lee to erase blocks of text within the document. He has the choice of deleting a character, word, paragraph, or several paragraphs. Lee places the cursor at the point where the delete is to begin, then presses the DELETE key. Moving the cursor to the end of the block to be deleted creates a highlighted block of text. ***Highlighting*** changes the intensity of selected characters on a VDT. When all material to be deleted has been highlighted, Lee again presses the DELETE key and the block vanishes. Other word processing software allows the user to delete a character, word, or line with a combination of keystrokes.
- **Insert**. Lee adds text to his document with the aid of an ***INSERT*** function. He places the cursor at the point where text is to be inserted, then presses the INSERT key. The word processing software makes space available at this point in the text for a new character, line, paragraph, or several pages. Another press of the INSERT turns off the insert function. With the IN-

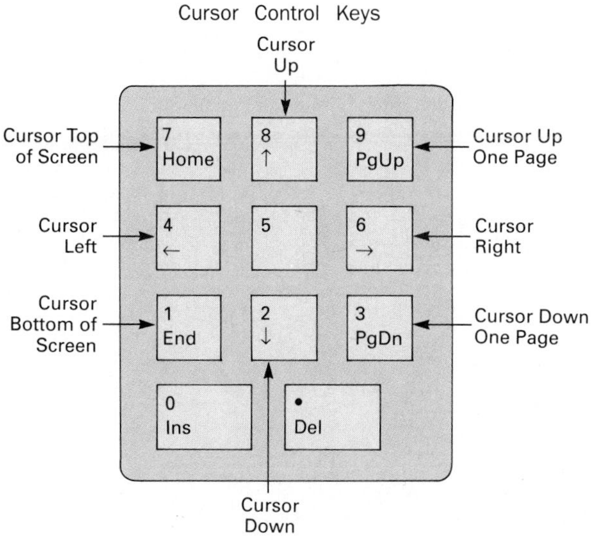

Cursor control keys are often associated with a numeric keypad.

SERT function off, any new text entered ***overwrites*** (replaces) text currently on the screen. In some word processing packages, word wrap automatically restructures the paragraph around the inserted text.

- **Move and copy**. Lee uses the ***MOVE*** function to move blocks of text from one location to another. The MOVE function enables him to rearrange paragraphs, move sentences within a paragraph, and switch words within a sentence. Similarly, he can duplicate portions of his document with the aid of the ***COPY*** function. A text block may be copied to another location in the same file. Or, it may be copied from one file, to disk, and then into another document. This latter procedure is called an ***external copy***. As he gathered background material for his paper, Lee stored quoted material in a document called PSNOTES. He uses the external copy function to duplicate the quotations at appropriate places in his PSPAPER document. He is spared the trouble of retyping material he collected while researching the paper.
- **Search and replace**. The ***SEARCH and REPLACE*** functions enable Lee to make changes to selected words or phrases. Lee discovers that, in his report, he has misspelled the name "MacArthur." Throughout his report, the name is spelled "McArthur." Instead of scanning the report line by line to change each misspelling manually, Lee calls on the SEARCH and REPLACE functions.

  First, Lee requests the SEARCH and REPLACE functions by pressing appropriate keys. Responding to a computer prompt for the text to be searched, he enters "McArthur." He is prompted for the replacement text and types in "MacArthur." The computer then locates every instance of the misspelled word and replaces it with the correct spelling. In a ***global replace***, the computer automatically takes care of all word substitutions. In a ***discretionary replace***, the computer finds the misspellings, and waits for user approval before making each replacement.
- **Save**. When Lee ***saves*** a new document, the word processing software assigns a storage area for it, usually on disk. Long-term storage of documents is an important capability of word processing software, since stored documents can be edited and printed at a later date. Before the computer can save a document, the user must assign a unique name to it. Responding to a screen prompt for a file name, Lee enters PSPAPER.

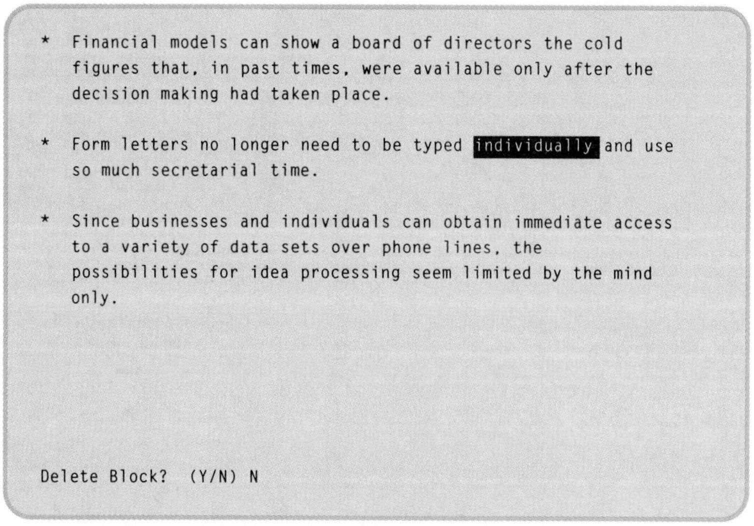
* Financial models can show a board of directors the cold figures that, in past times, were available only after the decision making had taken place.
* Form letters no longer need to be typed individually and use so much secretarial time.
* Since businesses and individuals can obtain immediate access to a variety of data sets over phone lines, the possibilities for idea processing seem limited by the mind only.
Delete Block? (Y/N) N

FIGURE 9.7

The word "individually" can be removed by highlighting it and then initiating the DELETE function.

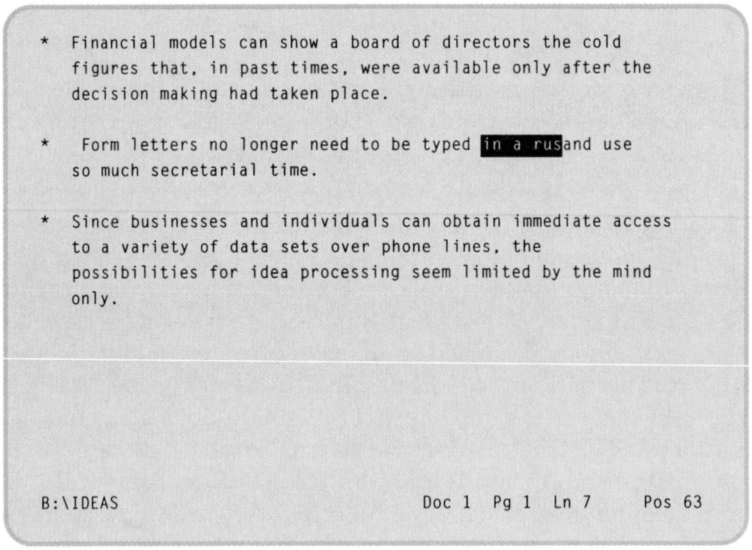
* Financial models can show a board of directors the cold figures that, in past times, were available only after the decision making had taken place.
* Form letters no longer need to be typed in a rus and use so much secretarial time.
* Since businesses and individuals can obtain immediate access to a variety of data sets over phone lines, the possibilities for idea processing seem limited by the mind only.
B:\IDEAS
Doc 1 Pg 1 Ln 7 Pos 63

FIGURE 9.8

Users can easily insert text anywhere within a document.

- **Retrieve**. After saving PSPAPER, Lee can ***retrieve*** this document as many times as he wishes. Each time he retrieves the document the word processing software copies the document back into the computer for further editing. In this way, Lee's writing of this paper is an ongoing process.

Formatting

While editing functions enable Lee to revise the content of his report, ***formatting*** features allow him to manipulate the report's appearance. With formatting features, Lee can create a document that is single-spaced, double-spaced, or triple-spaced. Line lengths and tab spacing, as well as the number of lines per document page, are determined through formatting features. Lee uses another formatting function—centering text on a line—to center the title of his report. Figure 9.9 outlines a number of other formatting features are found in word processing application packages. The following are some of the most common.

Heading and Footing

A ***heading*** is a line or several lines of text that appear at the top of each page in a document. Often, the heading holds a document title or page number. The

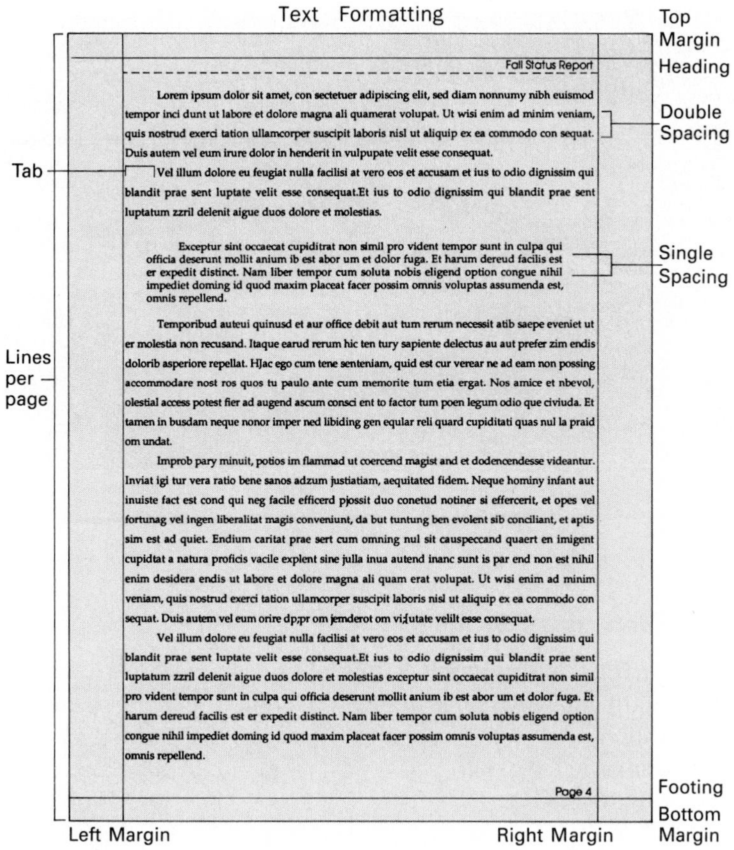

FIGURE 9.9

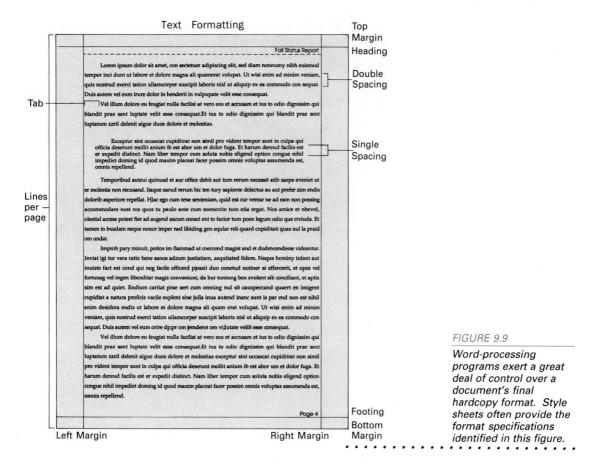

Word-processing programs exert a great deal of control over a document's final hardcopy format. Style sheets often provide the format specifications identified in this figure.

heading needs to be entered only once, at the beginning of a document. The computer reads the heading request and instructs the printer to duplicate the heading at the top of each page.

Footings are similar to headings; they are lines of text repeated at the bottom of each page. Most headings and footings offer special control of the beginning and ending of each page and the page numbering. This feature is called ***pagination***. Lee, for example, wishes to print a page number at the top of each page. A special symbol is included in the header, and the printer automatically tallies and prints the appropriate page numbers. He also has the option of starting the page numbers at any value or omitting page numbers altogether.

Print Options

Most word processing programs offer a number of print options that enable the user to control the size, style, spacing, and density of characters. For example, software might offer ***font*** options, or a choice of type style.

Word processing software usually offers ***double-strike*** commands, which tell the printer to strike each character twice. This action darkens the characters, producing a boldface effect. Word processors also enable the user to underline words. In addition, the computer can be instructed to print only selected pages of a document.

Software print options, of course, are limited to the capabilities of the output hardware. Since Lee's printer does not have an italics font, he chooses to underline the names of books he referenced in the report.

Users also can have a computer ***justify*** document outputs. In justified documents, the edges of text are aligned. Left justified text all starts in the same

FIGURE 9.10

A printer provides a word-processing system with hard copy.

FIGURE 9.11

Formatting functions common to most word-processing packages are identified in this list.

Common Formatting Functions

1. Line spacing (single, double, triple, etc.)
2. Line length (characters per line)
3. Tabulation
4. Lines per page
5. Centering text in line
6. Set headings
7. Set footings
8. Pagination
9. Select font
10. Select pitch
11. Double strike
12. Justification

column of the page. Right justification is optional. The computer right-justifies lines by inserting spaces between words to bring all lines to one length. Most documents are left-justified only, leaving a ragged right margin.

Style Sheets

The ability to create documents using any combination of formatting options has led to the development of style sheets. ***Style sheets*** allow word processing users to save the formatting options they established for a particular report, letter, memo, or any text file. These options include:

- margin settings
- tab locations
- ragged right or justified
- line spacing
- number of lines per page

When users need to create a similar document, they load the style sheet, and the word processing software automatically uses the desired format.

Integration with Other Software Packages

With his paper written, edited, formatted, and ready for printing, Lee calls upon several integrated software packages, which check the spelling, grammar, and

```
                      Writing Analyzer Summary

TOTAL NUMBER OF WORDS IN DOCUMENT: 5839

NUMBER OF UNIQUE WORDS: 1300

NUMBER OF UNCOMMON WORDS: 269

READABILITY INDEX: 10.13

     Readers need an 10th grade level of education to understand
     the writing.

STRENGTH INDEX:  0.24

     The writing style is very weak.
     Passive voice is being heavily used.

DESCRIPTIVE INDEX: 0.37

     The use of adjectives and adverbs is within the normal
     range.

JARGON INDEX: 0.00

     Most sentences contain multiple clauses. Try to use more simple
     sentences.

                   << UNCOMMON WORD LIST >>

The following list contains uncommon words found in the document.
Will any of these words confuse the intended audience?

     ACCENT         1    ACCOMMODATE      1    ACCOMMODATES  1
     ACQUIRED       1    ADMINISTRATOR    1    ADMISSIONS    1
     ADVERTISING    2    AGENCIES         1    ALTERNATIVE   1
     .              .    .                .    .             .
     .              .    .                .    .             .
     .              .    .                .    .             .
```

FIGURE 9.12

Writing analysis software helps authors improve the quality of their written work.

writing style. His word processing package allows Lee to access these integrated packages online without exiting the document being processed. As a result, these special options can be performed while the document is still on the screen. Integrated word processing software frequently includes a dictionary, thesaurus, and grammar checker. With a few keystrokes, these online reference materials are at Lee's disposal. Looking up the spelling and meaning of words, or finding a suitable synonym, becomes an online procedure.

The ***writing analyzer*** in Figure 9.12 that Lee purchased with the word processing package computes a reading level for his paper. In other words, it indicates what grade level of education is assumed for the reader in order for the reader to understand Lee's report. In addition, the writing analyzer identifies the use of passive voice, flags long or complex sentences, highlights jargon, and provides a list of frequently used words.

By examining the word frequency list, Lee realizes the word *use* is found repeatedly in the report. The ***online thesaurus*** helps identify synonyms by displaying them in a window within the text (see Figure 9.13). Lee moves the cursor to the alternative of his choice and the thesaurus automatically replaces the highlighted word with the selected synonym.

Related software is the ***spelling checker*** (see Figure 9.14) offered with many word processing packages. Special processing routines match each word in a document with words in an electronic dictionary. Any word not found in the dictionary is highlighted. The user then reviews the highlighted copy, correcting errors or leaving the words as they are. Users can add uncommon words and names to the dictionary to prevent the dictionary from highlighting words that are spelled correctly.

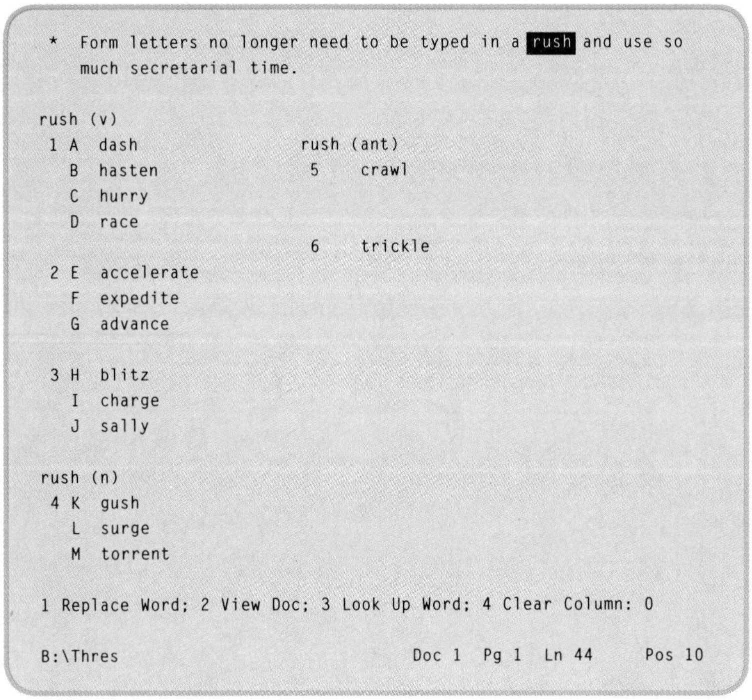

FIGURE 9.13

This online thesaurus suggests alternatives to using the word "rush."

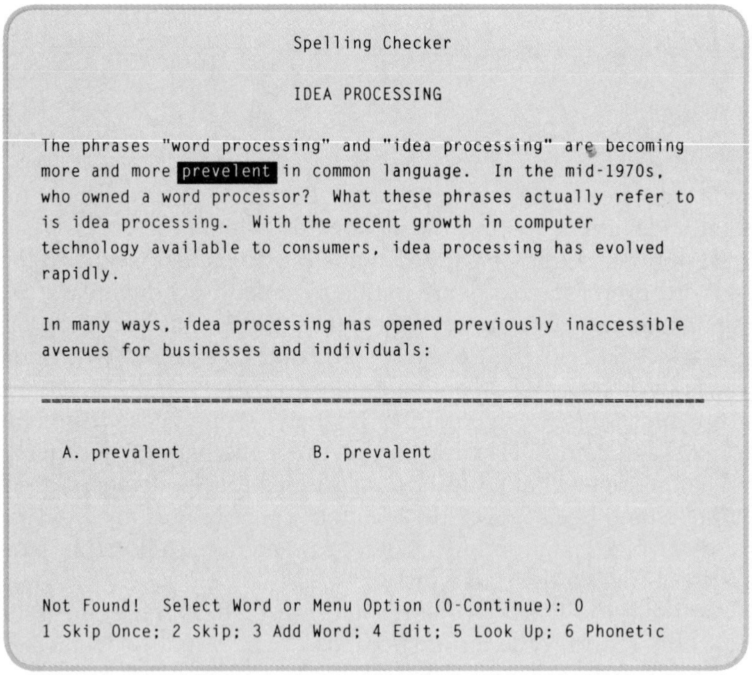

Spelling Checker
IDEA PROCESSING
The phrases "word processing" and "idea processing" are becoming more and more prevelent in common language. In the mid-1970s, who owned a word processor? What these phrases actually refer to is idea processing. With the recent growth in computer technology available to consumers, idea processing has evolved rapidly.
In many ways, idea processing has opened previously inaccessible avenues for businesses and individuals:
A. prevalent
B. prevalent
Not Found! Select Word or Menu Option (0-Continue): 0
1 Skip Once; 2 Skip; 3 Add Word; 4 Edit; 5 Look Up; 6 Phonetic

FIGURE 9.14

A spelling checker identifies misspellings and suggests corrections.

Some word processors are even equipped with ***hyphenation help*** routines. This software consults a dictionary to look up words that are too long to fit at the end of a line. The dictionary contains information about where a word may be broken. As an optional part of the word wrapping function, the computer breaks the word at an appropriate point and inserts a hyphen.

Integration works several ways with word processing software. Not only is it useful to integrate word processing with a spelling checker, online thesaurus, and writing analyzer, but documents created by word processing software are often integrated with other documents. Integrated software exists to aid Lee in outlining his paper and organizing bibliographic references. Lee uses word processing software to expand the outline into his paper and later appends the bibliographic references to the end. Desktop publishing software and other integrated packages described in Chapter 12 carry the integration of finished text with other documents one step further.

STUDY QUESTIONS

1. Define soft return, hard return, scroll, overwrite, highlighting, external copy, global replace, discretionary replace, heading, footing, pagination, font, pitch, double-strike, and justify.
2. How do the following functions and features work?

   word wrap
   cursor control
   insert
   delete
   move and copy
   search and replace
   save
   retrieve
3. What are 12 formatting features common to most word processing software?
4. How is a left-justified document different from one that is both left- and right-justified?
5. What formatting features are controlled by style sheets?
6. Identify and describe four online services that can be integrated with word processing software.

WORD PROCESSING AS A TOOL

As you can see, word processing is one of the most versatile and universal computer applications. Consequently, the industries and occupations that today make use of word processing packages are found worldwide. The following examples show word processing put to various uses in the work force.

Office Automation

In businesses, computers have increased office efficiency by being networked with other office equipment to replace manual business procedures. This development, known as ***office automation*** encompasses:

- Word processing
- Electronic mail
- Electronic filing

In automated offices, transactions are completed with increasing speed. As a result, automated office techniques have stimulated the very business demands they are helping to meet.

CLIP

THE ELECTRONIC FILING CABINET

Database management system (DBMS) packages have led to use of computers as electronic filing cabinets. The concept of the electronic filing cabinet involves replacement of the traditional filing cabinet with a computer access system. The traditional method is to place paper documents in drawers within rows of file cabinets. The electronic filing approach is based upon computer storage systems accessed through user terminals under control of DBMS software.

Ultimately, it is believed that DBMS packages will become sufficiently effective and efficient so that electronic storage can replace methods for organizing and maintaining files of paper documents. When this happens, the electronic filing cabinet will become a reality of business operation.

Today, business organizations seem to be using traditional filing cabinets in record numbers, with increases occurring at a steady pace. The volumes of paper and the cumbersome procedures they require have created a condition of *information overload*. This means the existing and newly created volumes of information exceed the capacity for understanding by information users. Under document-based methods, each filing cabinet is a separate storage location. Users may have to know the content of hundreds, even thousands, of separate cabinets. Then, there may be tens of thousands of individual documents within each cabinet. Finding needed information becomes a difficult, tedious, physical chore.

Electronic filing methods introduce an exciting prospect for eliminating this type of overload condition. Under DBMS techniques, software tools keep track of locations for needed data. the computer does the searching under software control and delivers needed results right to the user's work station. Information utilization becomes more effective because the user can interact with cross-reference files maintained by software to locate desired information sources. Users operate more efficiently because needed information is located and delivered in fractions of a second. Further, DBMS capabilities can be used to search files or to examine multiple information sources to find exactly what is needed, as it is needed. All of these capabilities, it is worth stressing, are available under security controls devised by people and imposed by computers.

Key Question: How can electronic filing procedures help reduce information overload?

With word processing in the automated office, attractive and correct documents are output at high speeds. The result is a rise in productivity. Accuracy and attractiveness are necessary for all formal documents, particularly in business. A letter, for example, represents the sender. In addition to conveying information, the letter forms an image. The appearance of the letter makes a statement about the sender just as your clothes reveal your tastes and preferences to others. To promote a positive image, letters should be appealing to the eye, as well as clear and accurate.

FIGURE 9.15

Word processing in the automated office provides the accuracy and attractiveness necessary for formal documents.

In an automated office, word processors are linked to other pieces of office equipment through telecommunications hardware. Geographically dispersed offices use telephone lines and other communication channels, discussed in Chapter 7, to interconnect equipment. In a small office the equipment is usually linked by cable. For example, the word processor might be directly connected to an intelligent copier to reproduce a text document. A secretary using a word processor would issue a command to make 100 copies of a report. Without further intervention from the secretary, the word processor would retrieve the report from disk and send it to the copier. The copier would translate the commands and make the requested copies. This method is more efficient than producing 100 copies on a regular printer. The copier is faster and quieter than the letter-quality printers normally attached to word processors. Furthermore, copies could be reproduced on copiers around the country as easily as in the same office.

Networks of automated offices often use electronic mail techniques to share information or deliver bulletins. A message can be sent to one person, several people, or everyone connected to the network. Some systems assign a personal disk file or ***electronic mailbox*** to each user. The originator prepares a list of recipients for each word-processed document. The electronic mail program uses the list to identify the mailbox destinations to a computer. The computer delivers the mail by copying the memo into the specified files. People can read their electronic messages each time they check their mailboxes. Some electronic mail systems will even allow senders to leave voice messages along with written documents. Handling memos in this manner is quicker than typing, copying, and routing them through the regular mail.

Electronic filing methods replace the tedious and error-prone task of maintaining paper records in metal filing cabinets. Misfiling occurs less often with electronic files. The computer keeps an index of the names of documents and the dates they are stored. To access a file, the user need only enter in a name. The computer then consults the index, locating and retrieving the desired document. Automatic filing directed by the computer prevents carelessness in handling documents.

Some automated offices may evolve into ***paperless offices***. In such an office, word processors and online data processing systems are combined. Documents exist only within the computer system; no paper copies are stored. Documents held on system storage media can be accessed by users at any time. Further, files can be shared by users more readily. The original version of a document remains in storage, so that several users may request a copy at the same time. Documents are printed only when they need to be sent to someone outside the office.

Marketing

Making people aware of the goods or services to be sold is crucial to effective marketing. One of the most prominent and effective forms of information dispersal is sales literature. Attractive brochures produced on word processors can be instrumental in making a sale or just establishing a reputation.

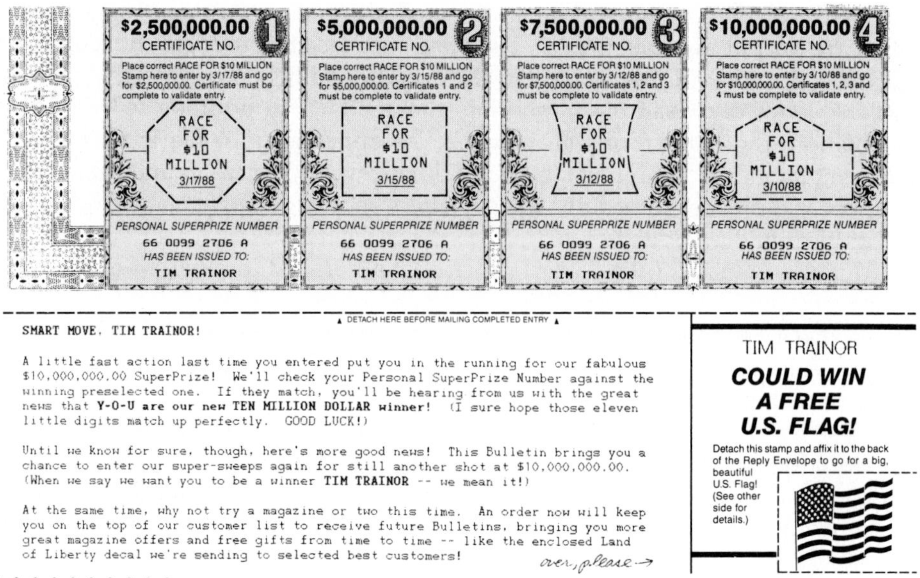

$2,500,000.00 1
CERTIFICATE NO.
Place correct RACE FOR $10 MILLION Stamp here to enter by 3/17/88 and go for $2,500,000.00. Certificate must be complete to validate entry.
RACE FOR $10 MILLION 3/17/88
PERSONAL SUPERPRIZE NUMBER
66 0099 2706 A
HAS BEEN ISSUED TO:
TIM TRAINOR

$5,000,000.00 2
CERTIFICATE NO.
Place correct RACE FOR $10 MILLION Stamp here to enter by 3/15/88 and go for $5,000,000.00. Certificates 1 and 2 must be complete to validate entry.
RACE FOR $10 MILLION 3/15/88
PERSONAL SUPERPRIZE NUMBER
66 0099 2706 A
HAS BEEN ISSUED TO:
TIM TRAINOR

$7,500,000.00 3
CERTIFICATE NO.
Place correct RACE FOR $10 MILLION Stamp here to enter by 3/12/88 and go for $7,500,000.00. Certificates 1, 2 and 3 must be complete to validate entry.
RACE FOR $10 MILLION 3/12/88
PERSONAL SUPERPRIZE NUMBER
66 0099 2706 A
HAS BEEN ISSUED TO:
TIM TRAINOR

$10,000,000.00 4
CERTIFICATE NO.
Place correct RACE FOR $10 MILLION Stamp here to enter by 3/10/88 and go for $10,000,000.00. Certificates 1, 2, 3 and 4 must be complete to validate entry.
RACE FOR $10 MILLION 3/10/88
PERSONAL SUPERPRIZE NUMBER
66 0099 2706 A
HAS BEEN ISSUED TO:
TIM TRAINOR

▲ DETACH HERE BEFORE MAILING COMPLETED ENTRY ▲

SMART MOVE, TIM TRAINOR!

A little fast action last time you entered put you in the running for our fabulous $10,000,000.00 SuperPrize! We'll check your Personal SuperPrize Number against the winning preselected one. If they match, you'll be hearing from us with the great news that **Y-O-U are our new TEN MILLION DOLLAR winner!** (I sure hope those eleven little digits match up perfectly. GOOD LUCK!)

Until we know for sure, though, here's more good news! This Bulletin brings you a chance to enter our super-sweeps again for still another shot at $10,000,000.00. (When we say we want you to be a winner **TIM TRAINOR** -- we mean it!)

At the same time, why not try a magazine or two this time. An order now will keep you on the top of our customer list to receive future Bulletins, bringing you more great magazine offers and free gifts from time to time -- like the enclosed Land of Liberty decal we're sending to selected best customers!

over, please →

TIM TRAINOR
COULD WIN A FREE U.S. FLAG!
Detach this stamp and affix it to the back of the Reply Envelope to go for a big, beautiful U.S. Flag! (See other side for details.)

FIGURE 9.16

Computer-generated form letter.

Word processors also can draw from several files to produce attractive personalized correspondence to prospective customers. These files might include lists of names and addresses, texts of letters, and specific information to be inserted at designated points in the letter. This file merging capability allows separate files to be brought together by word processing programs. The result is attractive, individually typed form letters generated automatically.

Journalism

Over the last 20 years, journalism technology has changed dramatically. The image of a reporter sweeping the last page out of the typewriter while shouting for the copyboy to pick up the work is no longer part of reality. Now, journalists pound on keyboards attached to VDT terminals. Their terminals link them electronically to the desk editor. With the press of a few keys, stories are transferred to the editor for online review and revision.

Increasingly smaller portable computers are even allowing reporters to take computers into the field. With a battery-operated portable, a reporter can write and store a story at the scene of news. A nearby telephone links the portable to the newspaper's main computer for data transfer.

The factorylike atmosphere that once prevailed in the typesetting department before a newspaper went to press also is changing. Small foundries with molten lead used for setting type have become obsolete. Now, many newspapers have computers linked directly to typesetters. News stories composed and edited on VDTs need not be retyped into a typesetter. Instead, the typesetter is used as an output device, part of the overall computer system.

Many newspapers have established communication links to large news-gathering services such as United Press International (UPI) and the Associated Press (AP). As these news wires constantly update their databases, local newspapers receive instant notification on terminals dedicated to receiving wire copy. Late-breaking news reports thus can be shared immediately with all subscribers to the news service network. Similarly, syndicated columns and features are retrieved from databases and sent as electronic signals over communication lines.

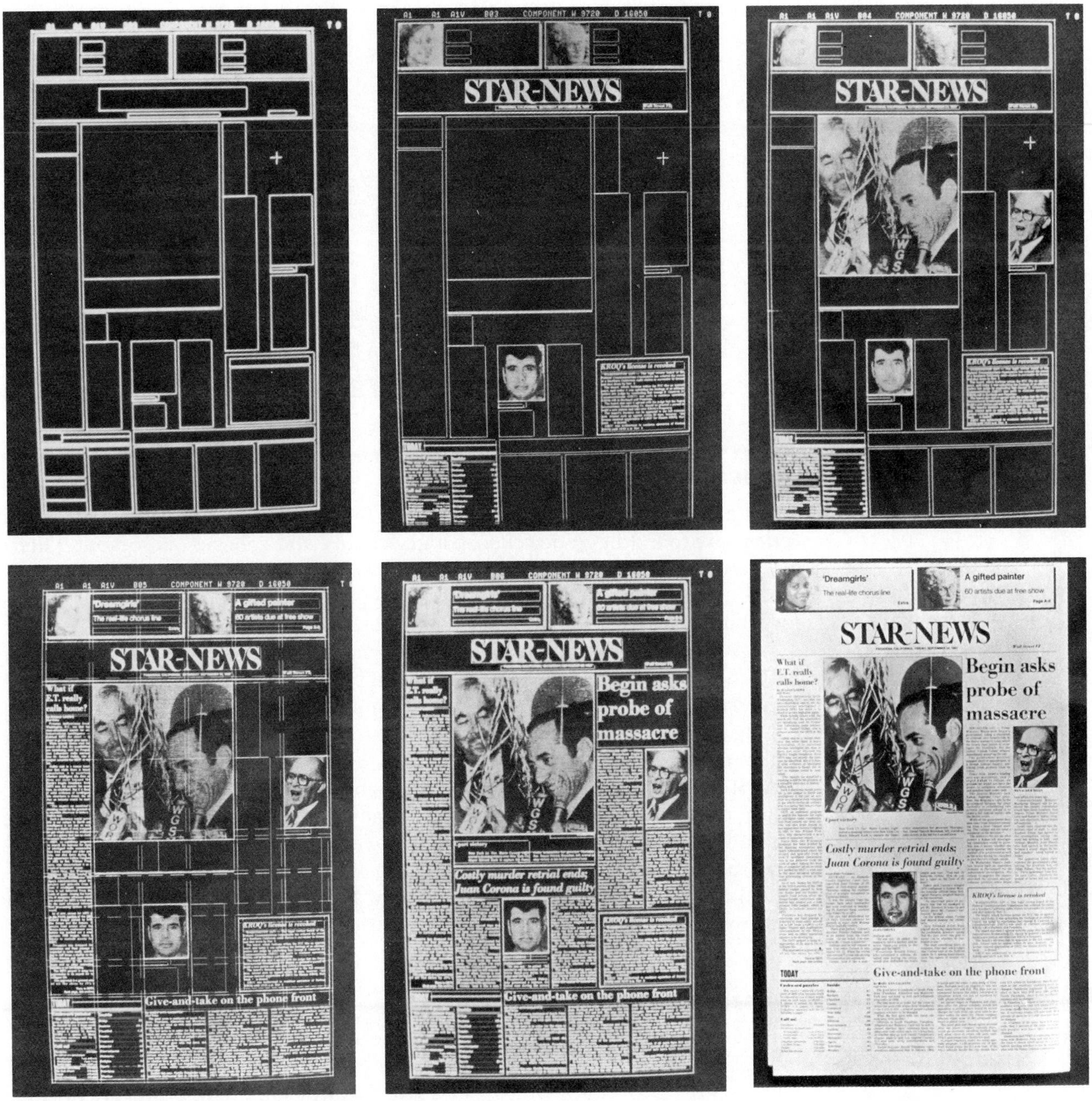

FIGURE 9.17

Online development of a front page.

An emerging newspaper technology is online development of complete pages. The masthead, stories, headlines, and photos can be positioned onscreen, a facsimile of a news page. When each element of the page is in place, the computer produces a film of the page used to make copies of the paper.

Word processing techniques are not confined to print journalism. Broadcasters also convey the news with the help of word processors. Anchor persons appear to stare directly into your living room as you watch the news. However, the newscaster actually is reading a script displayed on a teleprompter placed right over the lens of the camera. The script is prepared on a VDT and reflected with a two-way mirror onto the teleprompter.

FIGURE 9.18

Teachers can use the computer to create tests, worksheets, screen displays, and other course materials.

Education

Word processing is gradually becoming an integral part of education. Computer centers are found in grade schools, high schools, and colleges, as computer literacy becomes a graduation requirement. While computer use on campus encompasses many types of data processing, one of the most widespread applications for school is word processing.

A teacher can generate bulletins, written assignments, tests, and syllabi with a word processor. The documents can be stored and revised easily. Generating a makeup test, for example, is accomplished quickly with the aid of online editing techniques. The teacher decides to retain or replace questions, then makes the changes quickly onscreen.

Students, of course, use word processing to complete written assignments. Using manual typewriters, a student might retype several drafts of a report before the document is completed. However, with the help of computers and word processing software, the student can move from first to final draft with little duplication of effort. Microcomputers and word processing software are a boon to creative writers, especially those with poor typing skills.

Legal Professionals

Attorneys use special word processing packages to keep track of trial proceedings. The packages store pertinent case histories, inventories of evidence, lists of witnesses, and court schedules. This word processing application is invaluable to attorneys who use computer resources to organize their information.

Legal secretaries frequently use word processing systems to store, retrieve, and edit legal documents. Some law offices link internal word processing stations to a central computer system. This network allows law firms to access any of several hundred standard paragraphs used in wills and other documents.

Will preparation actually is a complicated process that can be simplified greatly by the computer. A law firm might hold several hundred wills on storage media. When a will must be altered, the relevant file is retrieved and the desired changes made. If a new law concerning wills is passed, the computer system can search for and retrieve the wills of affected clients. Client names are sent through a word processing routine that produces a personalized letter explaining the legal changes. Meanwhile, a lawyer rewrites the outdated paragraph to conform to the new law. The revision is stored and clients are given a chance to have their wills updated.

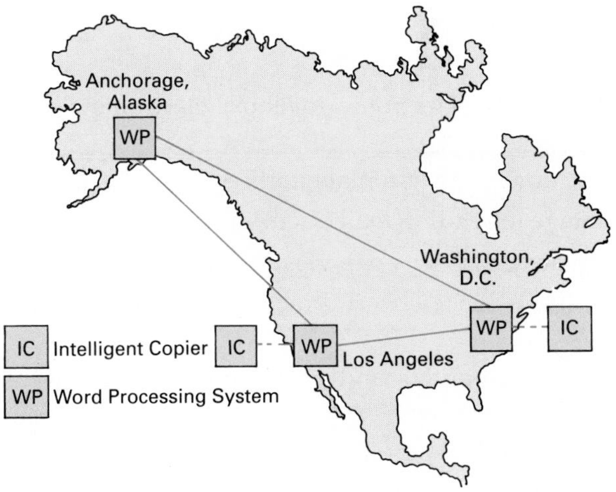

FIGURE 9.19

Electronic mail systems like this one can serve multiple locations over a wide geographical area—instantly.

When a client requests a will change, the computer sends the relevant paragraphs to a word processor. As changes are made, the computer calculates a bill for the changes. Copies of the will and the bill are sent to the client.

Government

The number of words processed each day by governments at all levels is voluminous. In Congress, legislative records are produced daily. These records document all activities of the day, including quorum calls, actions taken, and pieces of legislation introduced. Word processors are put into use daily to produce these records.

In addition, each legislative body has a staff of people who specialize in researching and drafting bills. These specialists draft documents at the request of lawmakers. Typically, a document undergoes several revisions before it is introduced. After it is introduced, even more revisions and amendments are made. Each time the document is updated, a word processor is used. If the proposed bill is enacted into law, a word processor retrieves the file for output on a typesetter. The typeset version of the law is distributed to legislators, the press corps, and the public.

The U.S. government is the largest publisher in the world. Word processing and typesetting are prevalent in all branches of government. In a democracy, government agencies have a responsibility for disseminating information on their actions. As a result, the government generates massive word processing demands.

FIGURE 9.20

Word processing is used to increase productivity by the world's largest publisher, the U. S. Government.

STUDY QUESTIONS

7. Define office automation, electronic mailbox, electronic filing, and paperless office.
8. Describe three functions of an automated office.
9. What is an advantage to sending mail electronically?
10. When is hard copy necessary in a paperless office?
11. Explain how a business can use word processing software to create personalized advertising.
12. Describe eight ways computers and word processing software have changed journalism.
13. How do teachers and students use word processing software?
14. What are five ways attorneys and legal secretaries utilize word processing?
15. How does word processing facilitate the creation and distribution of new government legislation?

HOW TO SELECT WORD PROCESSING PACKAGES

Prospective software buyers would be wise to learn as much as possible about the vast selection of word processing packages on the market. The first step in the selection process is for buyers to identify their own needs and the nature of the processing jobs that will meet those needs. Some users might need a word processor to create one-page business letters or brief reports. Others may wish to create documents that are several pages in length. The capacities of different programs must be compatible with processing demands.

Software preferences depend largely on individual tastes. Methods for creating, formatting, editing, and printing a document may differ slightly or substantially from package to package. Hands-on testing of several packages enables users to evaluate features.

First-time software buyers should pay particular attention to the quality of support materials included with the packages. User's manuals and reference materials should be thorough and easy to understand. Tutorials may be available to help users become familiar with newly acquired software. In addition, the quality of the local support, in the form of training seminars and workshops provided by retailers, can often determine where a user purchases the software.

People should gauge the user friendliness of the software by examining menus, help screens, and prompts, as well as the ease of start-up and use. "User friendly" may also mean that a word processing package automatically backs up the text file currently in use. Some packages actually display underlined or boldfaced text instead of using special control characters. This is referred to as ***WYSIWYG*** (What You See Is What You Get).

Users may have special word processing needs that many packages do not accommodate. For example, a user who wishes to write in a foreign language should look for software that provides accent marks and special characters. Similarly, text that incorporates a good deal of mathematics, chemistry, or physics material requires software equipped with special symbols. In other situations, writers making extensive use of footnotes and indexes might look for word processing packages that support these activities.

Tips for Selecting a Word Processing Package

1. Identify needs and the nature of your word processing applications:
   - foreign language accent marks or special characters
   - special mathematics, physics, or chemistry symbols
   - footnotes or indexes
2. Try several word processing packages to evaluate features and procedures for creating, formatting, editing, and printing documents. For example:
   - automatic backup of current text
   - WYSIWYG screen display
3. Evaluate the user's manual and other reference material.
4. Check support material for new users:
   - tutorials
   - help screens
   - menus
   - prompts
5. Determine if the program can use text files created by different word processing packages and if the text files created by the program can be used by other software. For example:
   - spelling checker
   - online thesaurus
   - writing analyzer
   - desktop publisher
6. Talk to others who have used the word processing package.

FIGURE 9.21

Picking the best word-processing package for your needs can represent an important decision. This listing presents a series of steps and considerations that can be helpful.

The package's ability to be adapted to future needs should receive special consideration. Word-processed documents that can be used with other applications provide for potential expansion of the user's word processing capabilities. In turn, it is often desirable to use text files created by other word processors. Of course, the price of a package should be weighed against its overall performance to determine the value of the software.

A knowledgeable salesperson at a computer store may be able to help match user needs to appropriate word processing software. Speaking to other word processing users can be helpful to a prospective buyer. First-hand experience with a large selection of word processing software is the best way to select the package that meets a user's individual needs.

STUDY QUESTIONS

16. Define WYSIWYG.
17. What six steps should be a part of the evaluation process when purchasing a new word processing package?

I N S I G H T

DESKTOP PUBLISHING: INTEGRATING GRAPHICS WITH WORDS

Desktop publishing represents some of the most sophisticated integrated software available for personal computers. A microcomputer with 640K memory, a hard disk, and access to a laser printer can create and print documents that were once sent out for expensive typesetting. However, users must still incorporate eye-pleasing design and layout with important documents such as brochures or catalogs, while resisting unnecessary use of this technology on documents such as interoffice memos.

Steps in Developing a Brochure

Properly designed brochures provide an organization with an inexpensive means of distributing information with a professional look. Here are the basic steps a graphics designer follows when using desktop publishing software to create a brochure.

Step One: Identify Objective of Brochure

This brochure will introduce businesspeople to the local college's industrial training center. It must promote the training and assessment programs offered by the college and clearly display the center's telephone number.

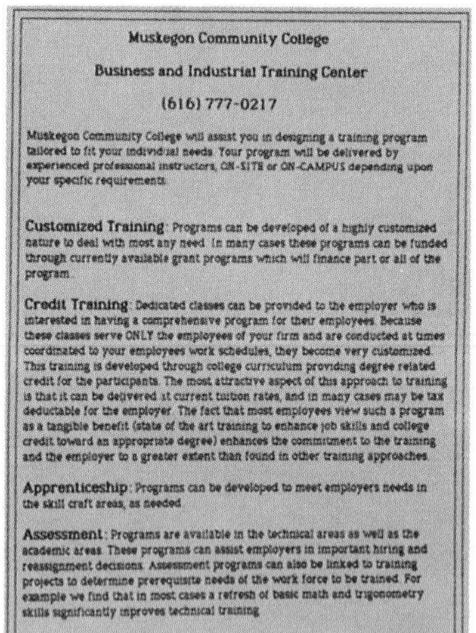

Muskegon Community College

Business and Industrial Training Center

(616) 777-0217

Muskegon Community College will assist you in designing a training program tailored to fit your individual needs. Your program will be delivered by experienced professional instructors, ON-SITE or ON-CAMPUS depending upon your specific requirements.

Customized Training: Programs can be developed of a highly customized nature to deal with most any need. In many cases these programs can be funded through currently available grant programs which will finance part or all of the program.

Credit Training: Dedicated classes can be provided to the employer who is interested in having a comprehensive program for their employees. Because these classes serve ONLY the employees of your firm and are conducted at times coordinated to your employees work schedules, they become very customized. This training is developed through college curriculum providing degree related credit for the participants. The most attractive aspect of this approach to training is that it can be delivered at current tuition rates, and in many cases may be tax deductable for the employer. The fact that most employees view such a program as a tangible benefit (state of the art training to enhance job skills and college credit toward an appropriate degree) enhances the commitment to the training and the employer to a greater extent than found in other training approaches.

Apprenticeship: Programs can be developed to meet employers needs in the skill craft areas, as needed.

Assessment: Programs are available in the technical areas as well as the academic areas. These programs can assist employers in important hiring and reassignment decisions. Assessment programs can also be linked to training projects to determine prerequisite needs of the work force to be trained. For example we find that in most cases a refresh of basic math and trigonometry skills significantly improves technical training.

Step Two: Organize Words and Graphics into Design

Word-processed text from past promotional materials was edited and merged with images created by the college's computer-aided design system.

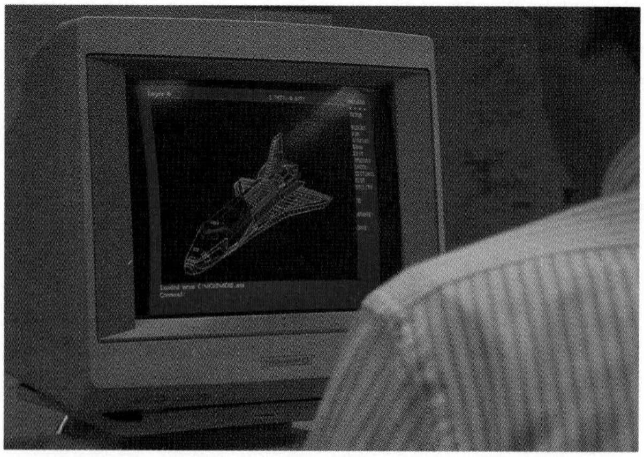

TERMS TO REMEMBER

cursor control
delete
discretionary replace
double-strike
electronic mailbox
electronic filing
external copy
font
footing
formatting
global replace
hard return
heading
highlighting
hyphenation help
insert
justify
move and copy
office automation
online thesaurus
overwrite
pagination
paperless office
pitch
retrieve
save
scroll
search and replace
soft return
spelling checker
style sheet
word wrap
writing analyzer
WYSIWYG

CHECK YOUR UNDERSTANDING

1. In a(n) ___________, word processors, copiers, and other office equipment are interconnected.
2. No paper copies of documents are produced in a paperless office. (True/False)
3. Changing the intensity of characters on a VDT for emphasis is called:
   a. formatting
   b. scrolling
   c. highlighting
   d. double-striking
   e. boldfacing
4. In a global replace, all occurrences of a misspelled word are automatically changed without user intervention. (True/False)
5. When a document is right ___________, spaces are added between words to make each line of text the same length.
6. The style of character type for a printed document is called the:
   a. boldface
   b. format
   c. pitch
   d. font
   e. none of the above
7. When a word processor does ___________, it senses an upcoming margin as a document is entered and puts the cursor on the next line without requiring a carriage return.
8. A spelling checker requires all words that it does not find in its dictionary to be corrected. (True/False)

9. Which of the following is *not* used as an application for word processing in journalism?
   a. typesetting
   b. accessing online news services
   c. producing personalized advertisements
   d. page layouts
   e. all are applications
10. Word processors cannot handle special characters required for foreign languages, math, or science. (True/False)

APPLYING WHAT YOU'VE LEARNED

1. All computer systems are made up of the five components: people, procedures, data, programs, and hardware. For each of the following systems, name or describe the components each comprises:
   a. word processing a legal document
   b. sending an electronic mail message
   c. editing a report in a paperless office
   d. filing a letter using electronic filing
   e. writing a term paper on a word processor
2. Keep track of mail to your household for a week. What type of correspondence has been done (or could be done) with a word processor? For each type of mail, do you think the use of a word processor has enhanced or detracted from the quality and "personalized" nature of the correspondence?
3. Make a list of the features you would require in a word processor. Assume that money is not a limiting factor. Include any special character types, related software, and printing options. Also list the user aids (help screens, prompts, and so on) you would like to have. When doing this needs analysis, keep in mind not only your present word processing requirements but also any features that could help in a future career.
4. The text mentions the use of word processing in journalism, education, business, law, and government. List the ways a word processor might be useful in these occupations:
   a. coach for a professional sports team
   b. hospital administrator
   c. regional manager for a charitable organization such as the Red Cross, United Foundation, and so on
   d. admissions clerk for a university
   e. librarian for a public library
   f. director for a state lottery
5. People with word processing skills are in high demand. Find three advertisements for jobs that require word processing. Compare the requirements in education and experience, pay rates, and other benefits.
6. Writers can use spelling checkers, writing analyzers, and an online thesaurus to aid in creative or technical writing. Other available related software includes gender checkers (for nonsexist writing) and grammar checkers. Do you feel such software helps to increase writing skills or acts as a crutch to writers lacking good writing skills? Should these packages be allowed for writing term papers for a composition class? For all term papers and assignments? Do you feel that using a word processor gives unfair advantage to the user over those who do not have access to such software?

CHECK YOUR UNDERSTANDING ANSWERS

1. automated office
2. false
3. c
4. true
5. justified
6. d
7. word wrap
8. false
9. c
10. false

C H A P T E R

T E N

ELECTRONIC SPREADSHEETS: WORKING WITH NUMBERS

KEY IDEAS

- **From the user's point of view**
  In what way do electronic spreadsheets facilitate the organization of data? How can a spreadsheet help you make decisions quickly and accurately?
- **Presenting and processing numbers**
  People use numbers to measure and manage their lives.
  Manual spreadsheets
  Professionals often organize numeric data on paper in rows and columns.
  Electronic spreadsheets
  Computer programs now organize and manipulate rows and columns of numbers.
- **Electronic spreadsheets: features and functions**
  These software packages equip computers to perform calculations quickly and accurately without restructuring the entire worksheet.
  Screen layout
  Electronic spreadsheets use menus, control lines, and scrolling to display data.
  Common spreadsheet functions
  Users employ a variety of functions to load data, make changes, process data, and save results on paper or disk.
  Combining functions with macros
  Common spreadsheet functions are organized into macros and recalled with a single keystroke.
  Integration with other software packages
  The processing power of electronic spreadsheets increases when they are combined with word processing, database, and graphics software.
- **Spreadsheets as a tool**
  Spreadsheets are used when people need to process numbers.
- **How to select spreadsheet packages**
  New users should match their needs with a spreadsheet's capabilities and user friendliness.

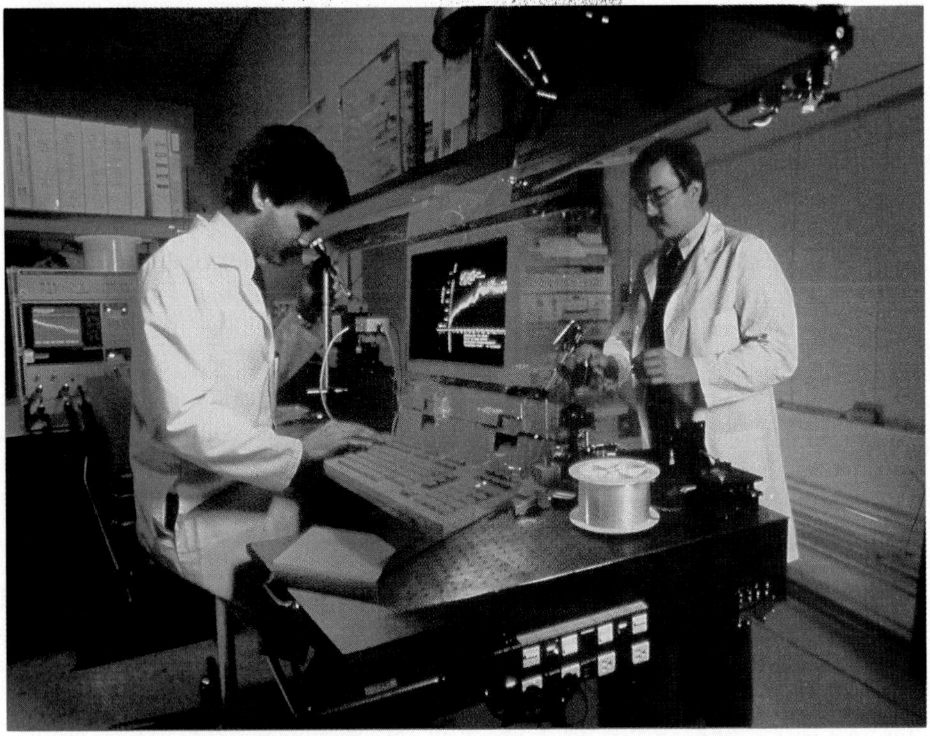

FROM THE USER'S POINT OF VIEW

Once you are comfortable working with computers, the technology does not make you work harder, but makes you work smarter. This is particularly true with electronic spreadsheets. This personal productivity software makes you more efficient when you are performing routine calculations on large groups of numbers. Picture yourself at a meeting with a laptop computer at your side. Someone poses a question. If you know how to take advantage of the power behind an electronic spreadsheet, you will have an answer while others are still crunching numbers.

FIGURE 10.1

Stock brokers and investment houses use electronic spreadsheets and financial packages to provide customers with current information.

PRESENTING AND PROCESSING NUMBERS

People use numbers to make decisions and evaluate performance. Most activities can be expressed according to some form of numeric standard. The profit made from the sale of a house is expressed numerically as money. Performance in school often is measured as a grade point average, which uses numbers to indicate academic success. Film critics often convey their opinion of a movie by placing it on a scale of 1 to 10. Numbers have become an inescapable part of modern living.

Money, in particular, affects nearly every activity of our lives. Many of the functions of individuals, families, businesses, and governments revolve around the saving and spending of money. The fundamental premise of operating within a monetary system is supplying enough income to cover expenses.

Expenses can be fixed or variable. ***Fixed expenses*** might include rent, mortgage payments, car payments, bus fare to work, or any other predictable, regular expense. Expenses over which you have more control are known as ***variable expenses***. These expenses might include the purchase of either needed or luxury items. Food, for example, is an essential, variable expense. Buying some food is necessary for survival, but people can control the amount and cost of what they buy. Variable expenses that are discretionary, or nonessential, might include movie tickets, magazines, vacations, and other forms of entertainment.

Manual Spreadsheets

Controlling numerically oriented activities often requires planning and processing. These activities can be performed on a worksheet that enables you to compare numbers for different activities and for different periods of time. With this information, you can analyze present conditions and use the analysis to influence future plans.

This worksheet actually is a standard tool for planning known as a spreadsheet. For decades, spreadsheets have assisted business managers in evaluating performance and predicting trends. Although used primarily in financial applications, spreadsheets have expanded to encompass such areas as scoring sporting events, keeping class gradebooks, and researching cultural trends. In each case, people have used spreadsheets to support decision making with data.

Basically, spreadsheets are tables that format data for comparison. Composed of horizontal rows and vertical columns, spreadsheets resemble a grid. In financial applications, rows typically are used to distinguish items to be evaluated, while columns represent different periods of time. A spreadsheet for figuring quarterly income and expenses, then, might include five columns, one for each quarter of the year and a fifth for year-end totals.

Each unit, or **cell**, on the grid is the intersection of a column and a row (see Figure 10.2). Cells contain items of data or special instructions for processing those data. On manual spreadsheets, the content of each cell usually is written in pencil. To change a cell value, the pencil marks are erased. This method often turns out somewhat sloppy spreadsheets. However, it spares people from creating an entirely new spreadsheet when data change.

One of the biggest drawbacks of manual spreadsheets is the time it takes to change data values. Quite often, changing one value requires recalculating several other values in the spreadsheet. Recalculating totals and averages are examples. This task becomes frustrating and tiresome in spreadsheets designed for "What if...?" speculations. "What if...?" questions allow people to determine the probable results from a given set of conditions.

	INCOME EXPENSE SUMMARY				
	1ST QUARTER	2ND QUARTER	3RD QUARTER	4TH QUARTER	YEAR-END TOTAL
INCOME					
DIRECT SALES	260,000	305,000	355,000	400,500	1320,500
MAIL ORDER	80,000	92,000	111,600	120,000	403,600
EXPENSES					
PERSONNEL	130,000	140,000	160,000	190,000	620,000
ADVERTISING	11,000	12400	15,000	20,700	59,100
SUPPLIES	15,200	17,700	18,400	24,300	75,600
RENTAL	11,000	12200	12200	12200	47,600
UTILITIES	6,000	6,500	6,300	5,800	24,600

Cell

FIGURE 10.2

Spreadsheet preparation is a longstanding responsibility for financial and management reporting. Manually prepared spreadsheets like this one have been around for a hundred or more years.

Usually, several spreadsheets are required to assess all alternatives in "What if...?" situations. For example, a store manager might wish to determine quarterly profits given a 5, 6, and 7 percent increase in sales. For this task, three manual spreadsheets would be created, requiring three different sets of calculations. Producing complete "What if...?" analyses can take a good deal of time and energy.

Electronic Spreadsheets

The late 1970s saw a breakthrough in spreadsheet analysis with the introduction of VisiCalc software, which teamed spreadsheets with computers. VisiCalc was developed by two business students, Daniel Bricklin and Robert Frankston, who wanted to use their new Apple microcomputer to handle spreadsheet computations. The resulting electronic spreadsheets are displayed on video screens. Cells are filled with text and data entries made through the computer's keyboard. Moving or copying data is accomplished with a few keystrokes. With electronic spreadsheets, people can edit the spreadsheet without making messy erasures.

One of the most valued features of electronic spreadsheets is its ability to perform calculations. Cells containing special symbols instruct the computer to add, subtract, multiply, or divide values from different cells. Upon entry of a single instruction, the computer performs these calculations with both speed and accuracy. People can ask any number of "What if...?" questions, and the spreadsheet quickly recalculates new answers. Thus, armed with a computer and electronic spreadsheet software, people interested in forecasting no longer need to spend long hours with a calculator to develop a complete "What if...?" analysis.

The primary value of electronic spreadsheets lies in the ease with which they make and process changes. People can create large spreadsheets—several thousand rows by several hundred columns—with greater accuracy and in less time than with manual methods. As a result, they can test data under many circumstances to build a broader base of information from which to make decisions.

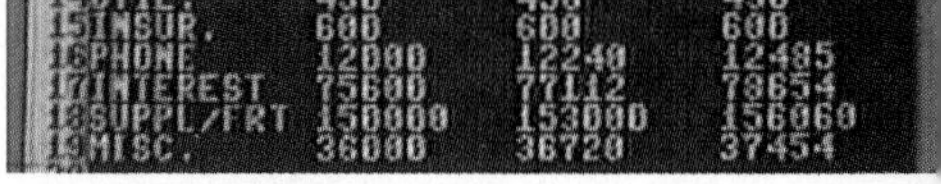

FIGURE 10.3

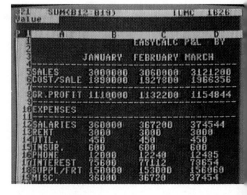

The development of electronic spreadsheets in the late 1970s allowed users to quickly and accurately manipulate rows and columns of numbers.

A1: 'HOUSEHOLD BUDGET READY

	A	B	C	D	E
1	HOUSEHOLD BUDGET				
2					
3	ITEM	BUDGET	ACTUAL	DIFFERENCE	
4	------------	------------	------------	------------	
5	Rent	600	600	+B5-C5	
6	Utilities	125	122	+B6-C6	
7	Food	250	288	+B7-C7	
8	Auto	125	137	+B8-C8	
9	Entertain	100	91	+B9-C9	
10	Misc	150	227	+B10-C10	
11	Savings	225	110	+B11-C11	
12	============	============	============	============	
13	Total	@SUM(B5..B11)	@SUM(C5..C11)	@SUM(D5..D11)	
14					
15					
16					
17					
18					
19					
20					

FIGURE 10.4

The formulas used to compute column totals and the differences between actual and budgeted expenses are displayed within this electronic spreadsheet.

STUDY QUESTIONS

1. Define fixed expenses, variable expenses, and cell.
2. What are two disadvantages to using paper-and-pencil spreadsheets?
3. What are two advantages to using electronic spreadsheets?

ELECTRONIC SPREADSHEETS: FEATURES AND FUNCTIONS

Electronic spreadsheets are useful in homes as well as in businesses. Figure 10.4 shows a spreadsheet created by Sarah Jacobs for household budgeting. The figure illustrates how Sarah included rows for seven items: rent, utilities, food, automotive costs, entertainment, miscellaneous purchases, and savings. As shown, the first column contains labels identifying each row. An additional row holds total figures. Sarah's spreadsheet includes columns for expected and actual expenses. Another column indicates the difference between these two figures.

Sarah followed a number of steps to create this spreadsheet. First, she identified the purpose of the spreadsheet. In this case, she wanted to keep track of her expenses to help her stay within a budget. Ultimately, she wanted to increase her savings. By maintaining a spreadsheet, she could pinpoint areas in which she was overspending.

Next, Sarah made a list of expenses that became the spreadsheet data. She also determined her processing requirements: In this case, she needed a subtraction routine to determine the difference between budgeted and actual expenses. She sketched a layout of an empty spreadsheet to identify how the data and formulas were to be presented, then estimated the space needed for each column. With these specifications in hand, Sarah created and formatted her electronic spreadsheet.

HOUSEHOLD BUDGET

ITEM	BUDGET	ACTUAL	DIFFERENCE
Rent	600	600	0
Utilities	125	122	3
Food	250	288	-38
Auto	125	137	-12
Entertain	100	91	9
Misc	150	227	-77
Savings	225	110	115
Total	1575	1575	0

FIGURE 10.5

Electronic spreadsheets easily display column totals and show the difference between budgeted and actual expenses.

Sarah entered data and formulas into appropriate spreadsheet cells. She instructed the computer to calculate the totals, resulting in the spreadsheet shown in Figure 10.5. As a result, she could easily see that she overspent in three areas: food, auto, and miscellaneous. While she underspent in the utilities and entertainment categories, her savings still fell short of the amount budgeted. With this information, Sarah is faced with a choice: She may trim her expenses to allow for increased savings. Or, if she feels her spending habits are not unreasonable, she may rework her budget to reflect less ambitious savings goals.

Screen Layout

Electronic spreadsheets, like their manual counterparts, consist of rows and columns that intersect to form cells. Unlike manual spreadsheets, however, they provide menus that give users control of data entry and processing activities. Typically, spreadsheets use three types of control lines:

- The ***prompt line*** is the menu of spreadsheet functions often listed in a row across the top or bottom of the spreadsheet, as shown in Figure 10.6. Selections included on the prompt line enable the user to create and format spreadsheets, load them with data, then process and print reports.

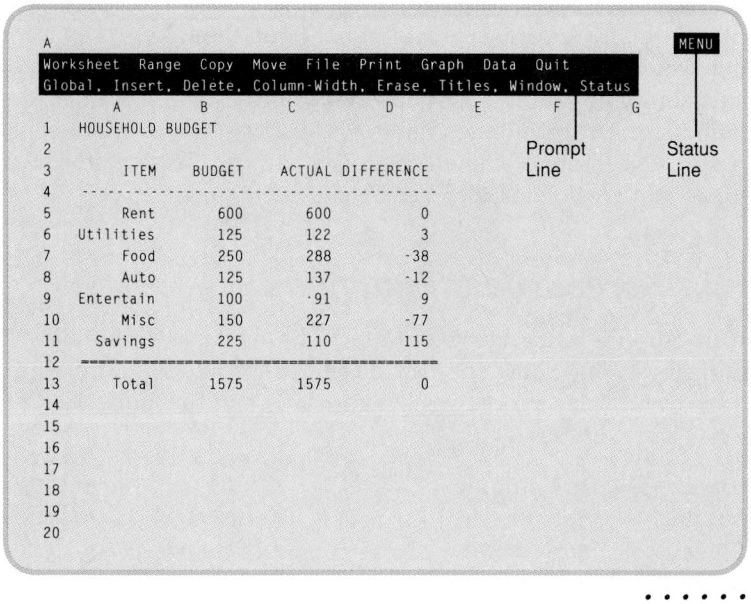
A
MENU
Worksheet Range Copy Move File Print Graph Data Quit
Global, Insert, Delete, Column-Width, Erase, Titles, Window, Status
A B C D E F G
1 HOUSEHOLD BUDGET
3 ITEM BUDGET ACTUAL DIFFERENCE
5 Rent 600 600 0
6 Utilities 125 122 3
7 Food 250 288 -38
8 Auto 125 137 -12
9 Entertain 100 91 9
10 Misc 150 227 -77
11 Savings 225 110 115
13 Total 1575 1575 0
Prompt Line
Status Line

FIGURE 10.6

Users can select from the different spreadsheet options by displaying the prompt line. The status line indicates menu options that are currently available.

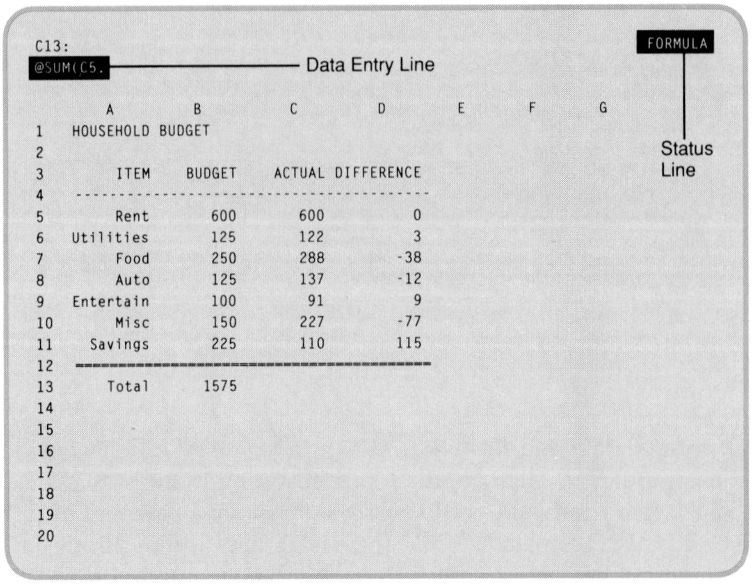

FIGURE 10.7

The formula being entered into cell C13 is displayed in the data entry line as the user types it. The status line indicates the type of information entering the spreadsheet.

- The ***status line*** indicates which function currently is being used on the spreadsheet. Status lines often are located at the upper-right corner of the spreadsheet display.
- In many spreadsheet packages, text, data, and formulas are written into a ***data entry line*** before they are loaded into designated cells (see Figure 10.7). Other packages enable the user to write data directly into cells.

A standard screen usually holds about 20 rows of spreadsheet data, but spreadsheets with more rows may, of course, be built. However, the screen will display only 20 rows at a time. Scrolling the spreadsheet up and down enables the user to view different sections of the spreadsheet.

Similarly, the screen may not accommodate viewing of all columns in a spreadsheet. Usually, fewer than 10 columns may be displayed at one time, depending on the column widths. Cursor control can instruct the computer to scroll the display from side to side to permit viewing of different sections of columns. For example, if Sarah wanted to include budgeted and actual expenses for each month, the entire spreadsheet would not fit on the screen. To view different sections she would use the cursor control keys to scroll to the left and right.

In addition to horizontal and vertical scrolling, some spreadsheet packages provide windowing capabilities. Windows display two or more separate sections of a spreadsheet on a single screen (see Figure 10.9). In other words, columns or rows that are not adjoined can be viewed at once.

Common Spreadsheet Functions

The software Sarah is using has many functions available for building a spreadsheet. With these functions, she can design a spreadsheet format, load data, make changes, and begin processing. Commands and functions used to conduct these spreadsheet activities include:

- Create
- Format
- Enter
- Move
- Compute
- Save
- Retrieve
- Print
- Copy
- Insert
- Remove
- Protect
- Delete
- Quit

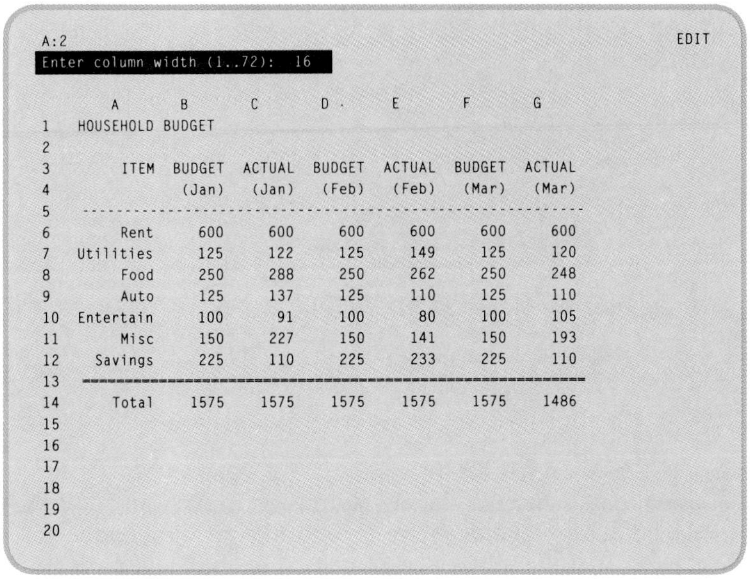
A:2 EDIT
Enter column width (1..72): 16

	A	B	C	D	E	F	G
1	HOUSEHOLD BUDGET						
2							
3	ITEM	BUDGET	ACTUAL	BUDGET	ACTUAL	BUDGET	ACTUAL
4		(Jan)	(Jan)	(Feb)	(Feb)	(Mar)	(Mar)
5	----------	----------	----------	----------	----------	----------	----------
6	Rent	600	600	600	600	600	600
7	Utilities	125	122	125	149	125	120
8	Food	250	288	250	262	250	248
9	Auto	125	137	125	110	125	110
10	Entertain	100	91	100	80	100	105
11	Misc	150	227	150	141	150	193
12	Savings	225	110	225	233	225	110
13	==========	==========	==========	==========	==========	==========	==========
14	Total	1575	1575	1575	1575	1575	1486
15							
16							
17							
18							
19							
20							

FIGURE 10.8

This spreadsheet user is currently changing the 'A' column width from nine to sixteen characters.

- **Create.** The first step in building a spreadsheet is reserving space for the file on disk. The ***CREATE*** function of a spreadsheet program accomplishes this procedure. With this function, Sarah named her spreadsheet BUDGET, and the operating system reserved space for it in the disk directory. To retrieve her spreadsheet for later review, Sarah identifies the spreadsheet name. The operating system then consults the directory, using it to locate the BUDGET spreadsheet on the disk.

  Usually, individual software packages impose certain restrictions in assigning file names. Some programs, for example, limit names to eight letters and prohibit certain symbols from being used.

- **Format.** Most spreadsheet programs have a default format consisting of a certain number of rows and columns, and set column widths. The spreadsheet will adopt this standard format unless the user requests a change. Typically, the user requests the ***FORMAT*** function to change these default values.

  For example, in Figure 10.8, Sarah prepared her BUDGET spreadsheet for a 12-month period. In it she used 27 columns: one for row labels, two for each of the 12 months (budgeted and actual), and two for totals (budgeted and actual). The size of each cell differs with the type of data it contains. Sarah increased the default size for cells that contain labels. Since the default column width allows only nine characters, Sarah increased the width in the first column. This let her use longer labels such as "MISC. PURCHASES" and "ENTERTAINMENT."

  In Sarah's case, all the spreadsheet columns contain numbers, except the first, which contains labels. The numbers throughout this spreadsheet reflect money. Since some spreadsheet systems ask users to indicate the number of decimal places that will be included in numeric data, Sarah set their format for two decimal places. An example of Sarah's spreadsheet with the new format is shown in Figure 10.9.

- **Enter.** Once the spreadsheet has been formatted, Sarah is ready to ***ENTER*** data. Cursor control allows her to position the cursor at the cell to receive new data values. Three types of values may be entered into a spreadsheet: textual data, numeric data, and formulas.

HOUSEHOLD BUDGET

ITEM	BUDGET (Jan)	ACTUAL (Jan)	BUDGET (Dec)	ACTUAL (Dec)	BUDGET Total	ACTUAL Total
Rent	600.00	600.00	750.00	750.00	8250.00	8250.00
Utilities	125.00	122.00	125.00	127.00	1500.00	1423.00
Food	250.00	288.00	250.00	292.00	3000.00	3171.00
Auto	125.00	137.00	125.00	229.00	1500.00	1570.00
Entertainment	100.00	91.00	100.00	89.00	1200.00	1069.00
Misc. Purchases	150.00	227.00	150.00	267.00	1800.00	2127.00
Savings	225.00	110.00	75.00	-179.00	1650.00	1290.00
Total	1575.00	1575.00	1575.00	1575.00	18900.00	18900.00

Window 1 | Window 2

FIGURE 10.9

The expanded household budget no longer fits on the screen, so windows are used to display the first three columns and last four columns.

Textual data is used to label columns and rows. In addition, text can be positioned across several columns to form a heading on the spreadsheet. This can be seen at the top of Figure 10.4. Numeric data represent financial or statistical values. Some spreadsheet programs distinguish among different types of numeric data, such as currency, percentages, and other numbers. ***Formulas*** are indicated by special symbols that instruct the computer to perform calculations (see Figure 10.4).

A user should verify the accuracy of new data items before they are loaded into cells through use of the ENTER function. Keyboard cursor controls often are used to move from cell to cell. Spreadsheets usually default to the ENTER function, and the currently highlighted cell can be filled with text, data, or formulas.

- **Move and copy.** Changeability is a key feature of spreadsheets. For this reason, most spreadsheets provide functions that transfer data. The ***MOVE*** function, as its name indicates, allows the user to change the location of data or formulas to another spreadsheet cell.

  The ***COPY*** function duplicates the contents of a single cell, row, or column at another position in the spreadsheet. Each of these functions spares the user the trouble—and the risk of error—involved in reentering data and formulas.

  Both the MOVE and COPY functions can work with ranges of cells. A ***range*** of cells is defined by the first and last cells in the group. For example, copying the budgeted and actual expense columns for January in Figure 10.9 would require the identification of a range of data. This range is described by the first cell "BUDGET" and the last cell "1575.00," which represents the total for actual expenses. This range of 24 cells can then be copied to another area within the spreadsheet.

- **Insert and Remove.** As the uses for a spreadsheet expand, row and column requirements are likely to change. The INSERT and REMOVE functions enable the user to modify a spreadsheet without reentering the entire file. The ***INSERT*** function allows the user to place a blank row or column at any point in the spreadsheet. The ***REMOVE*** function deletes any unwanted rows or columns from an existing spreadsheet.

  As another example, a spreadsheet can be used to keep track of sales made by employees in a shoe store. The addition of an employee will require the addition of a row in the spreadsheet. The store will not need to create an entirely new spreadsheet reflecting this change, however. Instead, the INSERT function can be used to insert a row where needed.

A7: "662-96-6919
Enter range of rows to delete: A7..A7

POINT

	A	B	C	D	E	F	G
1	EMPLOYEE SALES						
2							
3		Model	Model	Model	Model	Employee	
4	Employee Number	10365	10992	10134	10136	Total	
5	-----------------	-------	-------	-------	-------	-------	
6	113-62-9616	14	13	7	12	46	
7	662-96-6919	9	19	1	14	43	
8	535-99-0113	21	11	3	10	45	
9	582-21-4445	12	14	0	8	34	
10	121-67-9011	20	20	4	12	56	
11	.						
12	.						
13	.						
14	=================	=======	=======	=======	=======	=======	
15	Model Total	298	254	54	128	734	
16							
17							
18			Before				
19							
20							

A7: "535-99-0113

POINT

	A	B	C	D	E	F	G
1	EMPLOYEE SALES						
2							
3		Model	Model	Model	Model	Employee	
4	Employee Number	10365	10992	10134	10136	Total	
5	-----------------	-------	-------	-------	-------	-------	
6	113-62-9616	14	13	7	12	46	
7	535-99-0113	21	11	3	10	45	
8	582-21-4445	12	14	0	8	34	
9	121-67-9011	20	20	4	12	56	
10	.						
11	.						
12	.						
13	=================	=======	=======	=======	=======	=======	
14	Model Total	289	235	53	114	691	
15							
16							
17			After				
18							
19							
20							

FIGURE 10.10 A AND B

The REMOVE function is used to identify a row (or column) that needs to be deleted from the spreadsheet.

Similarly, the REMOVE function might be used to erase the row assigned to a salesperson who no longer works at the store. As shown in Figure 10.10, row 7 is being removed to eliminate employee 662-96-6919 from the employee list.

- **Compute.** The ***COMPUTE*** function processes all formulas included in the spreadsheet. Typically, formulas allow the user to add, subtract, multiply, or divide values in any two cells in the spreadsheet. Symbols that commonly are used to signify these mathematical calculations include: the plus sign (+) indicating addition, the minus sign (-) indicating subtraction, the asterisk (*) indicating multiplication, and the slash mark (/) indicating division.

Another symbol used in most spreadsheets is the "at" mark (@). Depending on the particular software package, the @ symbol can be used

ADVANCED MATHEMATICAL FUNCTIONS

FUNCTION	DESCRIPTION
@ABS	absolute value
@AVG	average of a set of numbers
@COS	cosine of number
@COUNT	count of the numbers in list
@EXP	exponent of number
@FV	future value of payment
@INT	integer component of number
@IRR	internal rate of return
@LN	base x log of number
@LOG	base 10 log of number
@MAX	maximum value in list of numbers
@MIN	minimum value in list of numbers
@RAND	random number generator
@NPV	net present value
@PMT	monthly mortgage payment
@PV	present values
@SIN	sine of number
@SQR	square root of number
@STD	standard deviation of list of numbers
@TAN	tangent of number
@VAR	variance between list of numbers

* function for LOTUS 1-2-3

Electronic spreadsheets have a variety of advanced mathematical functions built into the program.

alone or combined with a command to fill special processing requests. A common use for the @ symbol is adding entire rows or columns of values to produce a total. For example, the shoe store manager may wish to add up the column containing employee sales using the @SUM function. The spreadsheet software allows the manager to enter the range of numbers that will be affected. This way, identifying row and column totals is not a complex task. Also, @COUNT can be used to count the number of entries or @AVG to calculate the average of values in a given number of cells.

Some spreadsheets are equipped with functions that perform advanced mathematical or statistical calculations such as finding trigonometric values, square roots, and standard deviations. Other spreadsheet functions are used to identify maximum and minimum values or to generate random numbers.

- **Save and retrieve.** Spreadsheets are stored on disk as part of the ***SAVE*** function. This function sometimes is referred to as filing a spreadsheet. Stored spreadsheet files can be recalled at a later date for further use. This procedure—bringing a saved file to the screen for revision and processing—is accomplished with the ***RETRIEVE*** function. A stored spreadsheet can be retrieved. Editing then can be saved under a different file name. This procedure retains both the original and the changed versions of the spreadsheet file. This is one method of creating a spreadsheet that is similar in format to an existing spreadsheet.
- **Print.** A hard copy of the spreadsheet can be obtained by applying the ***PRINT*** function. The shoe store manager has two printing options. He can request a printout of a spreadsheet file that has been saved to disk or he can print a spreadsheet from main memory. Printouts can be useful in examin-

```
A2:                                                                MENU
Enter name of file to erase:
BUDGET01  BUDGET02  BUDGET03  BUDGET04
            A                 B         C         D        E        F          G
1   EMPLOYEE SALES
2
3                           Model     Model     Model     Model  Employee
4   Employee Number         10365     10992     10134     10136     Total
5   -----------------------------------------------------------------------
6      113-62-9616             14        13         7        12        46
7      535-99-0113             21        11         3        10        45
8      582-21-4445             12        14         0         8        34
9      121-67-9011             20        20         4        12        56
10          .
11          .
12          .
13  =======================================================================
14      Model Total           298       254        54       128      1023
15
16
17
18
19
20
```

FIGURE 10.12

The DELETE function allows users to remove unwanted spreadsheets from disk storage.

ing expansive spreadsheets that extend beyond the screen's limits. Instead of scrolling the spreadsheet from section to section, the manager can have a printed version of the entire spreadsheet to take home for late night work.

- **Protect.** To prevent accidental erasure of a file, and to provide a built-in backup mechanism, many spreadsheet packages include a ***PROTECT*** function. Protected spreadsheets can be accessed but not overwritten. When a user retrieves a protected file, a working copy of the spreadsheet is produced. A new version of the spreadsheet, produced by making changes to format or content, is not permitted to replace the protected version already on disk. Saving the new version requires separate filing of the revised spreadsheet under a different file name. Users can change the status of a file—protected or unprotected—according to their current needs.
- **Delete.** When a spreadsheet is no longer needed, the user may wish to erase the file from storage. The ***DELETE*** function is used to erase the entire file (see Figure 10.12). Usually, spreadsheet software requires a double-check before deleting a file. That is, once the user requests deletion of a spreadsheet, the system generates a prompt asking for verification of the request. This confirmation feature helps prevent the accidental deletion of a spreadsheet due to mistyping.

  The store manager will update the employee sales spreadsheet at the end of each week, then store both versions on disk. By the end of the month, several versions of a single spreadsheet will accumulate in storage. To rid storage space of this clutter, he retains only the two most recent copies of the spreadsheet. The rest are eliminated with the DELETE function.
- **Quit.** To exit a spreadsheet after a processing session, the ***QUIT*** function is used. Quitting the spreadsheet usually returns computer control back to the operating system. In integrated software, however, the QUIT function may produce a menu listing all available programs in the package. From there, the user may begin another processing task or return to the operating system.

CLIP

TIPS FOR BETTER SPREADSHEETS

There is no one way to design a spreadsheet. But some tips collected from a variety of users, industry observers, and instructors can be helpful in simplifying design and eliminating errors.

• *Isolate variables*: Group the key parameters that will be frequently changed in one area of the spreadsheet. Have all references to that variable address that single cell. This simplifies changes, reduces errors, and makes the spreadsheet more readable.

• *Focus on key ratios*: Plan the spreadsheet around those parameters that you believe drive your business. Those will be the values you'll want to manipulate or on which you'll want to see the impact of manipulating other values.

• *Use English*: English is a wonderful language. Use it freely. It may take a few extra keystrokes to type "West Coast Sales" than "WCS" but the spreadsheet will be much easier to use and read, both for yourself and for anyone else with whom you share the matrix.

• *Keep it simple*: Mammoth equations are difficult to understand. Errors in using them are hard to trace and their logic is difficult to decipher. Break equations up by using intermediate variables.

• *Use modules*: An entire spreadsheet doesn't have to be built at once. Create a working spreadsheet for one month or one department, then copy that to other sections of the spreadsheet. Finding errors in logic is easier in the smaller subsections.

• *Use hash totals*: Spreadsheets created with paper and pencil invariably add numbers both horizontally and vertically across columns to double-check accuracy. The same approach can be of assistance for spreadsheets created with software.

• *Check equations*: It is easy to assume that anything printed out by a computer is infallible, but spreadsheets are only as accurate as the logic, and the typing, that created the equations. Check them carefully and recheck them.

• *Save models*: The value of saving copies of spreadsheets goes beyond the requirement for backup in case of disk failure or damage. As changes are made in the model it becomes ever more complex, retracing your steps can become extremely difficult. Save copies of the model at each step, particularly if the spreadsheet is shared with other individuals who will be modifying it themselves.

• *Build in checks*: Use If statements, macros, comparisons with known ratios—anything you can thing of to build in checks and safeguards against errors in either data entry or logic.

• *Have fun*: Lastly, remember that using personal computers is fun. In concentrating on the productivity-enhancing power of computers, it is easy to forget this fact. If you've become jaded, remember what it was like when you first switched from struggling for hours with a pencil and a calculator to using a personal computer, or waiting months for the data-processing department to run figures for you. That feeling alone is worth the switch.

Source: Reprinted by permission, *Personal Computing*.

Key Question: What would be the largest and most complex spreadsheet application that you would use?

Combining Functions with Macros

Functions may be combined together to create extremely complex spreadsheets. Furthermore, in developing large spreadsheets, users often need to repeat the same combination of functions. As a result, many electronic spreadsheets allow users to create ***macros***, which recall a series of related functions with a few simple keystrokes. Macros are like small programs users build into their spreadsheets. By pressing the designated keys, the electronic spreadsheet activates the macro and executes the associated functions.

Macros can be used for a wide variety of purposes. For example, users can create macros that add and average numbers in any given set of cells or print selected parts of the spreadsheet on the printer. Activating these functions may require the user to enter a dozen or more keystrokes. However, once installed as macros, a few keystrokes such as /XA or /XP can call them into action.

Integration with Other Software Packages

As part of an integrated software package, the electronic spreadsheet becomes an extremely powerful processing tool. Teamed with word processing, database, data communication, and graphics programs, spreadsheets give and receive a boost in processing power. With word processing, for example, inserting a spreadsheet into a text report becomes a simple process.

Developing the spreadsheet itself can be an automated process with certain spreadsheet–database linkups. Users can instruct the computer to load data from a database into specified spreadsheet locations. The computer enters the database, finds the selected data fields, and duplicates them into spreadsheet cells. This capability increases personal productivity because the user is spared from reentering data.

With connections to data communication capabilities, spreadsheets can be built with data from distant databases. In addition, completed spreadsheets can be transmitted over communication lines among users at multiple locations. For example, local branch offices of a bank may prepare their budgets on a microcomputer-based spreadsheet and send them electronically to the main office. The budget director will check them with a compatible mainframe-based spreadsheet, and transmit them back to the branches with suggestions. One advantage to this is that all branch budgets are in the same format and can easily be compared to one another. In addition, budgets prepared in the morning can be in the director's hands before lunch.

Completed spreadsheets also can be used to generate graphics. Integrated packages allow spreadsheet data to be displayed as graphic outputs, such as bar graphs or pie charts. The user selects the option desired, then specifies which cells are to be reflected in the graphic. For example, the analysis of voters in a local election shown in Figure 10.13 was used to produce the pie chart in Figure 10.14. As pictured, the voters were broken into groups by age:

- 41 are between the ages of 18 and 30
- 30 are between the ages of 31 and 45
- 18 are between the ages of 46 and 60
- 7 are over the age of 60

As Figure 10.14 illustrates, these numbers were translated into percentages and shown in graphic form. Each slice of the pie chart is proportional in size to the percentage it represents. The graphics generated with spreadsheet software may even be more accurate than hand-produced charts.

```
B2:
Line Bar XY Stacked-Bar  Pie
Pie chart
          A          B        C
1   VOTER REGISTRATION
2
3      Age Group  |         Voters
4   -----------   | ------------
5         18-30   |             41
6         31-45   |             30
7         46-60   |             18
8       over 60   |              7
9
```

FIGURE 10.13

The pie chart in Figure 10.14 was created by an integrated software package that used data from this spreadsheet.

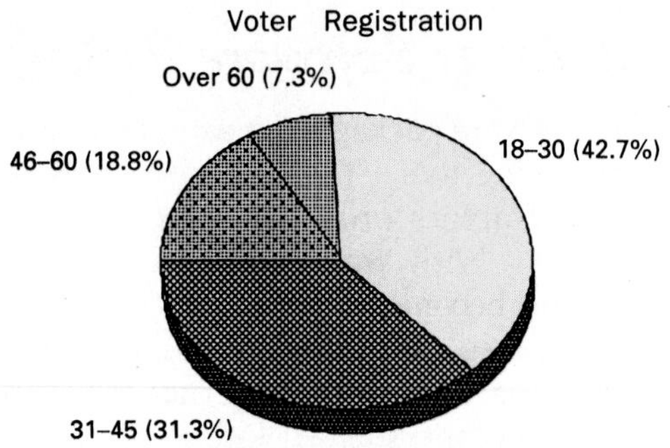

FIGURE 10.14

Data from Figure 10.13 was used to create this pie chart with the help of an integrated software package.

STUDY QUESTIONS

4. Describe the function of prompt, status, and data entry lines.
5. How are windows, ranges, and macros used with an electronic spreadsheet?
6. Explain the purpose of the create, format, enter, move, copy, insert, remove, compute, save, retrieve, print, protect, delete, and quit functions.
7. What three types of values are used by an electronic spreadsheet?
8. Identify six advanced mathematical calculations performed by various spreadsheets.
9. Describe the advantages to integrating an electronic spreadsheet with database, data communication, and graphics programs.

SPREADSHEETS AS A TOOL

Many other uses exist for spreadsheets besides business applications. Any situation where groups of numbers must be organized and analyzed is a good place for a spreadsheet.

F4: "2/4 READY

	A	B	C	D	E	F
1	Computer Concepts					
2	Winter 198-: Section 256					
3			C1Quiz	C1 Asgn	C1 Asn	Article
4	Student Name	ID #	1/18	1/22	1/31	2/4
5	------------------------	------------	------------	------------	------------	------------
6	Allen, Douglas	853136	100	50	10	5
7	Drake, Thelma	880908	68	48	6	
8	Elliott, Susan	795344	100	50	10	
9	Hornacek, Dorothea	880198	90	50	10	5
10	Jazdzyk, Judy	701882	75	50	10	5
11	Kiel, Steven	835594	90	25	10	
12	McElrath, Wendi	864475	90	50	10	
13	Mikos, Mike	701280	90	50	10	
14	Norton, Esther	850769	80	25	10	
15	Pletcher, Susan	784777	90	35	10	5
16	Shephard, Lane	751907	80	50	10	
17	Thue, Eric	763368	65	50	9	
18	Williams, Amelia	872216	40	45	8	
19	========================	============	============	============	============	============
20	Possible Points:		100	50	0	0

FIGURE 10.15

Educators can use spreadsheets as electronic gradebooks.

Education

At schools, a large number of students must be enrolled, educated, and evaluated by relatively few teachers and administrators. Spreadsheets can be used to expedite these activities. Admissions personnel can use spreadsheets to keep track of the number of students in different majors or ethnic categories. This can aid in recruiting students. Financial aid available to a student can be calculated on a spreadsheet that contains the student's income and expenses, as well as money available from scholarships and loans.

Teachers can keep attendance records and grades on a spreadsheet. The computation functions available on spreadsheets make weighting certain tests and dropping the lowest scores easy. They also aid in determining final grades.

Another advantage to using spreadsheets in education and other applications centers around the creation of templates. A ***template*** is a predefined spreadsheet format containing formulas but with no data. It can be reused many times to create spreadsheets for similar applications. For example, once a teacher establishes grading procedures for a course, a template can be created. This template is used each time the course is offered. The template is retrieved, individualized for a specific class, then saved under a different name. As a result, the template remains unchanged and can be used again.

Personal Applications

Budgets are not the only application in the home for spreadsheets. Financial planning, including mortgages, insurance, and purchase of stocks can be assisted by spreadsheet manipulation. People interested in retirement or vacation planning can ask "What if...?" questions on the computer. The results can help them to determine how present activities will affect their retirement income or vacation.

Electronic spreadsheets also can be used to itemize home inventories for insurance purposes. In addition, hobbyists with large collections can maintain current inventories of items and compute their collection's present and future values. People watching their weight can use a spreadsheet to count calories and help with menu planning.

I N S I G H T

GRAPHICS: A PICTURE IS WORTH A THOUSAND WORDS

Some experts believe the human brain processes words and pictures differently. Words are processed one at a time, while different parts of a picture are processed simultaneously.

Presentation graphics come in various styles, output forms, and applications. It is up to you, as the presenter, to choose which type of presentation graphic is most effective.

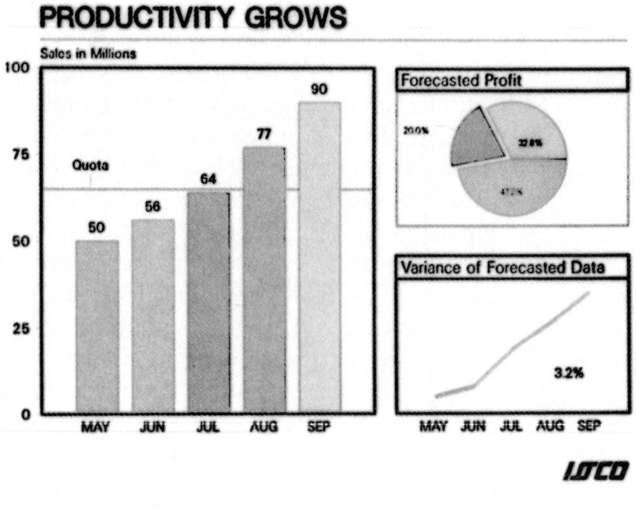

Software is available to produce graphics in many forms, including the traditional hard copy (paper) form and on a screen. Also, you can generate vivid color slides, overhead transparencies, and video tapes.

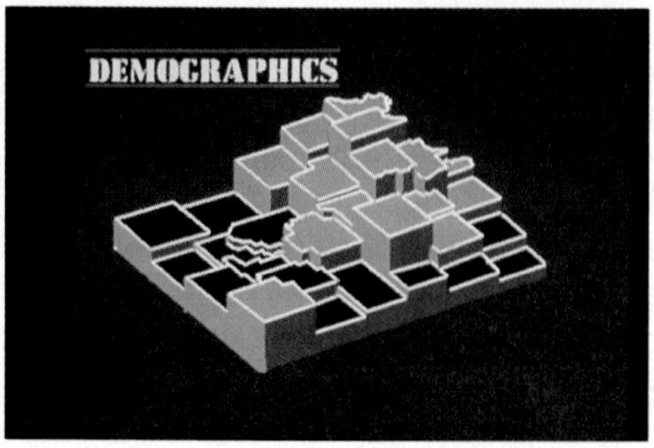

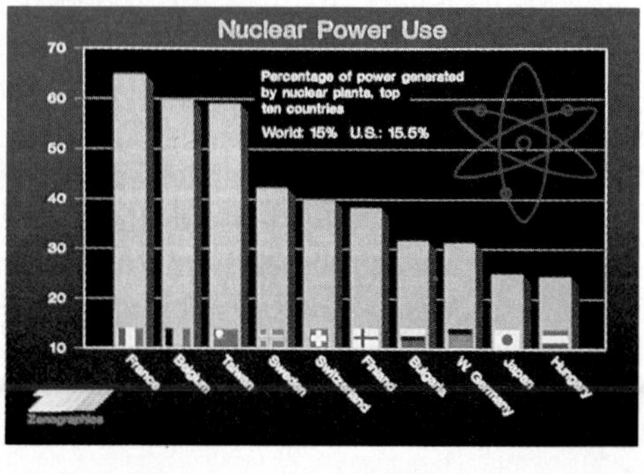

Using graphics effectively requires more than a graphics software package and a few keystrokes. You must carefully choose:

- the appropriate graphics type
- the amount of data to be summarized
- design and color to enhance but not detract from the data presented
- labels that accurately represent the graphic

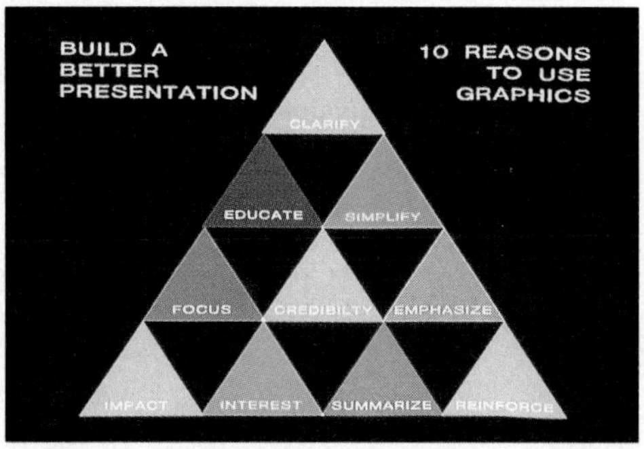

The advantages of presentation graphics in business are numerous. They not only present your point clearly, they make you look good as well!

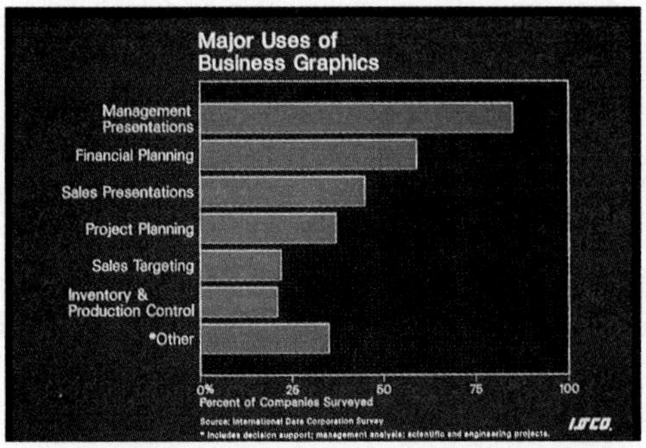

Graphics have spread to all aspects of businesses and organizations, going well beyond management presentations. As end-user computing continues to grow, so do the applications of presentation graphics.

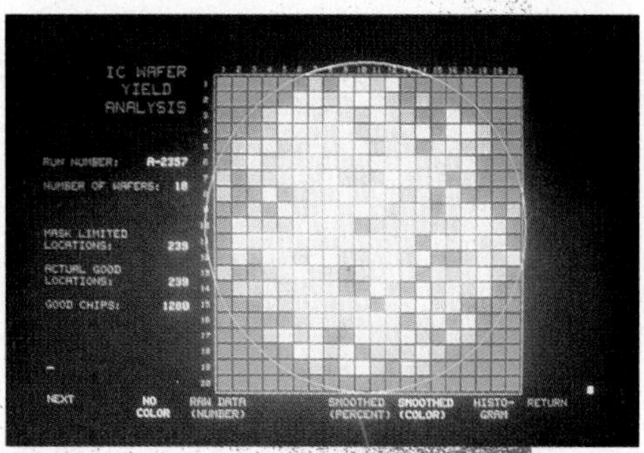

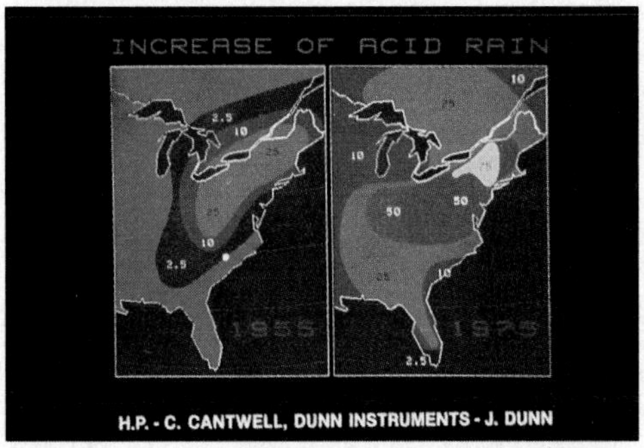

As a developer or user, remember that a presentation graphic is more than the traditional pie chart and bar graph. It can be used to summarize vast amounts of data into a form where trends, rather than specifics, can be seen. It can say, in a picture, what a thousand words cannot.

EVENT	Vault	Uneven Bars	Floor Exercise	Balance Beam	May 17 Total
Candy	8.0	8.0	6.5	9.0	31.5
Donna	5.0	7.5	7.5	9.0	29.0
Nancy	7.0	7.0	8.5	8.5	31.0
Sally	7.5	7.5	7.5	8.5	31.0
Sharon	5.5	8.5	6.5	8.0	28.5
Val	8.5	6.0	7.0	8.0	29.5
Average	6.9	7.4	7.3	8.5	30.1

EVENT	Vault	Uneven Bars	Floor Exercise	Balance Beam	May 24 Total
Candy	8.1	7.9	8.1	8.4	32.5
Debbie	8.3	8.1	7.9	7.3	31.6
Donna	8.2	7.5	6.8	8.5	31.0
Nancy	7.0	7.5	7.5	8.5	30.5
Roberta	8.0	6.3	7.0	8.3	29.6
Sally	6.0	7.3	7.7	8.5	29.5
Sharon	7.0	7.2	7.0	7.6	28.8
Val	6.0	8.0	6.5	7.5	28.0
Average	7.3	7.5	7.3	8.1	30.2

FIGURE 10.16

Individual and team statistics can be tabulated and stored with the help of electronic spreadsheets.

Volunteer Activities

Many of the spreadsheet applications in business also can apply to volunteer activities. Budgets, membership dues, and hours of volunteer time contributed by members can be tracked and analyzed with a spreadsheet. What was once one of the most difficult duties of a club secretary or treasurer can be streamlined with the help of a personal computer and electronic spreadsheet.

Athletics

Scoring any event, from a local kids' soccer game to professional baseball, can be enhanced using a spreadsheet. Professionals and amateurs alike can benefit from an analysis of personal and team statistics. If you are in a bowling league, a computer, with the help of a spreadsheet, can figure your handicap, record pin totals over the season, and even compute league standings. In other sports, knowing what an individual has done in the past helps a coach anticipate what the athlete may do today. Spreadsheets also can be used to analyze opponents' performances for potential weaknesses.

Science

Scientists working in a variety of areas use electronic spreadsheets as tools to help them organize and analyze research data. For example, botanists interested in the effects of acid rain on local forests can take portable computers running electronic spreadsheets into the field. Data from randomly selected trees are entered and analyzed using the advanced mathematical functions provided by the spreadsheet. These data can then be shared with researchers from around the country through data communications.

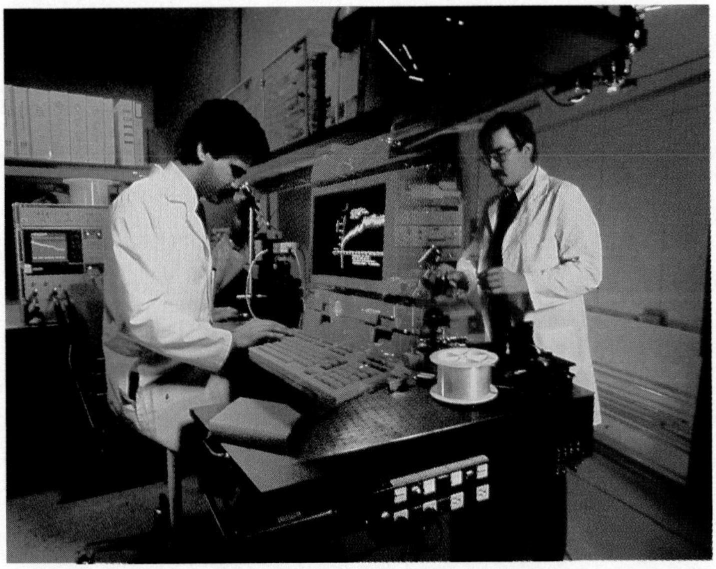

FIGURE 10.17

Scientists working in a variety of fields use electronic spreadsheets to organize and analyze research data.

Electronic spreadsheets can be of special benefit to large research projects because of their standard row-column format. Once scientists have decided on the data they wish to collect, spreadsheets provide a common means of organizing and sharing the results.

STUDY QUESTIONS

10. Define template.
11. What are three applications for electronic spreadsheets in school, at home, in sports, with volunteer organizations, and as a part of scientific analysis?

HOW TO SELECT SPREADSHEET PACKAGES

Logically, the capabilities of a spreadsheet package should match the needs of the user. In other words, the most powerful software on the market may not be the best choice for modest needs. A home budgeting spreadsheet, for example, will demand less processing power than a financial analysis spreadsheet for a multinational corporation. Before you begin to survey the market to determine what is available, you should define your present and potential requirements. Ask yourself a series of questions to help you clarify your spreadsheet processing needs:

1. What task or tasks will the spreadsheet accomplish?

   By defining the specific problems you intend to solve with your spreadsheet, you can evaluate how closely each package comes to meeting your needs. This includes identifying the types of computations and special formatting required.

2. How many columns and rows will be required to create your largest spreadsheet?
   The columns allowed in a spreadsheet package might range anywhere from 80 to 254. The maximum number of rows might be from 254 to over 2000. By thinking through your current spreadsheet needs, you can match your needs to the capacity of a specific package.
3. How simple is the software to use?
   The user friendliness of several packages should be compared. This can be gauged by the ease with which they create, format, and edit spreadsheets. A spreadsheet package that is powerful but quite complicated to use may be of little value to you.
4. Does it work on your computer (or the one you're going to purchase)?
   It should go without saying that new software must work on your computer hardware. However, when evaluating electronic software packages, make sure it works with your operating system and within current memory limits.
5. Can the spreadsheet data be integrated with other types of software?
   Again, examine your processing needs to determine whether you should look for a fully integrated package. If you wish to draw from database resources, share spreadsheets with remote users, or generate graphics, compatible programs will probably best meet your overall needs.

Answers to these questions should help you to select the spreadsheet software appropriate to your processing requirements.

FIGURE 10.18

Electronic spreadsheet programs can require a significant dollar investment. By identifying your needs and researching options, you will find your software investment pays dividends.

Questions to Ask When Purchasing Electronic Spreadsheets

1. What task or tasks will the spreadsheet accomplish?
2. How many columns and rows will be required to create my largest spreadsheet?
3. How simple is the software to use?
4. Does it work on my computer (or the one I'm going to purchase)?
5. Can the spreadsheet data be integrated with other types of software?

STUDY QUESTIONS

12. What five questions should you ask when evaluating electronic spreadsheet packages?

CONCLUSION

An electronic spreadsheet is an important type of computer program that helps people to manipulate numbers. Businesspeople have manually created spreadsheets of financial applications for many years. The advent of personal computers allows people to quickly update spreadsheets electronically. In addition, these electronic spreadsheets easily rearrange data so people can get answers to a variety of "What if...?" questions.

Spreadsheets are not limited to business applications. Anyone in school, at home, in sports, or involved with research or volunteer activities can benefit from using electronic spreadsheets. For a variety of applications, where numbers need to be organized and analyzed, an electronic spreadsheet is a powerful resource.

CHAPTER FACTS

- A spreadsheet is a tool for financial planning. It has been used for years by managers in a paper-and-pencil form. The electronic spreadsheet allows easy changing of data and the ability to perform calculations.
- An electronic spreadsheet is made up of cells. Cells can contain textual data for labels, numeric data for financial and statistical facts, and formulas.
- Each spreadsheet has a prompt line to present the menu, a status line to display the function being used, and a data entry line to display the data before they are entered into the cell.
- Spreadsheets can be manipulated by using the variety of functions available with the software. These include: create, format, enter, move, copy, insert, remove, compute, save, retrieve, print, protect, delete, and quit.
- Data from many spreadsheets can be integrated with other software packages. They can be used with databases for easy data entry, with data communications to send spreadsheets to remote users, and with graphics packages to display picture representations of the data.
- Applications for spreadsheets include uses in business, the home, schools, sports, volunteer activities, and scientific research.
- Evaluation of spreadsheets should include examination of their capabilities, maximum spreadsheet size, simplicity of use, capability with hardware, and possible integration with other packages.

TERMS TO REMEMBER

cell
compute
copy
create
data entry line
delete
enter
fixed expenses
format
formula
insert
macro
move
print
prompt line
protect
quit
range
remove
retrieve
save
status line
template
variable expenses

CHECK YOUR UNDERSTANDING

1. Fixed expenses are expenses for needed or luxury items over which a person has some control, such as food. (True/False)
2. A single unit on a spreadsheet that is the intersection of a row and column is called a(n) ___________.
3. Before using a spreadsheet, the data and formulas are designed on an empty layout called a(n) ___________.
4. Which of the following is ***not*** found in a spreadsheet?
   a. compute line
   b. data entry line
   c. status line
   d. prompt line
   e. All are found in a spreadsheet.
5. With the format function, the user can change the default values used by a spreadsheet. (True/False)
6. Using the ___________ function, a spreadsheet is copied from disk onto the computer's memory.
7. A spreadsheet can have three types of values in its cells: textual data, numeric data, and ___________.
8. When using data communications with a spreadsheet, only the data (not the spreadsheet itself) are sent to remote users. (True/False)
9. Most spreadsheets can be expanded to handle a large number of rows and columns, but only a limited number appear on the screen at one time. (True/False)
10. A pie chart or bar graph can be made from spreadsheet data integrated with a(n) ___________ package.

APPLYING WHAT YOU'VE LEARNED

1. Design a personal budget for a spreadsheet using a template or graph paper. Include the number of rows and columns you will need, how each column will be labeled, and any formula required. List five "What if...?" questions you would like to ask.
2. For the following spreadsheet applications, list the labels that would appear on the rows and columns. Name three "What if...?" questions for each application that could be useful to the decision makers:
   a. attendance records for a grade school class
   b. budget for the school computer center
   c. scoring a Little League baseball game (or sport of your choice)
   d. monitoring the hours volunteers have donated to a local soup kitchen
   e. grades for your entire computer class (use grading information given to you about the class)
3. Examine a spreadsheet package in depth. Find the user's manual or description of one used in school, available in a retail store, or described in a magazine.
   a. What functions can be used on the spreadsheet?
   b. What is the maximum number of rows and columns allowed?
   c. What mathematical calculations are done automatically?

d. Which other software packages can be used with the spreadsheet?
e. How much memory does it require?
f. What kind of operating system does it work on?
g. What is its cost?

4. Applications for spreadsheets abound in many careers. Name five uses for a spreadsheet (not already mentioned in the text) that you would find useful now or in your future career.
5. Not all financial and numerical problems can be solved with a spreadsheet. Name five types of problems (or characteristics of problems) concerning numbers that would not be solved efficiently with a spreadsheet.
6. Use an actual spreadsheet to enter the budget you designed in application 1 above. Enter the proposed budget figures for the year. Enter the actual figures for last month (or an estimate). Save and print the spreadsheet. Then answer one of the "What if...?" questions you listed. Print the spreadsheet that shows those changes.

CHECK YOUR UNDERSTANDING ANSWERS

1. false
2. cell
3. template
4. a
5. true
6. retrieve
7. formulas
8. false
9. true
10. graphics

C H A P T E R

E L E V E N

GRAPHICS: WORKING WITH COMPUTER IMAGES

KEY IDEAS

- **From the user's point of view**
  What features of computer-generated graphics support decision making and creative thinking? How can graphics help you to communicate your ideas clearly to others?

- **Computer graphics: Visual tools for conveying information**
  Graphics images are a powerful source for representing information.

  Representing computer graphics
  Bit mapping and vector graphics are two methods for creating images.

  Types of computer graphics
  Presentation graphics include charts and diagrams, while free-drawing graphics use a screen as if it were an electronic canvas.

  Computer graphics as a tool
  Computer-generated graphics have artistic and practical uses in many industries.

- **Presentation and free-drawing graphics**
  The software and procedures used to produce presentation graphics are different from those used with free-drawing graphics.

  Presentation graphics
  Charts and graphs are easy to create; they enhance written documents while making complex numeric data more comprehensible.

  Free-drawing graphics
  An electronic palette and toolbox help a graphics artist create spectacular computer-generated drawings.

  Graphics in integrated software packages
  One picture is often worth a thousand words—when combined, they represent an effective way to communicate ideas and information.

- **How to select graphics packages**
  Users must identify needs before determining hardware and software requirements for new graphically oriented computer systems.

FROM THE USER'S POINT OF VIEW

Can't draw a circle freehand? Ever spend hours drawing and redrawing graphs for a class project? Have you ever had an artistic urge but lacked the talent to back it up? In this chapter, we will show you how the computer can aid your artistic endeavors and make short work of standard graphs and charts. However, a computer system will not make you a visual artist overnight. Artists know that the execution of a drawing is only a small part of the artistic process. As you read this chapter, keep in mind that great work, be it produced by computer or by traditional methods, resides in the design as much as the execution.

COMPUTER GRAPHICS: VISUAL TOOLS FOR CONVEYING INFORMATION

FIGURE 11.1

Graphic images, such as road maps, are easy to understand and are more effective than words in conveying directions.

Pictures convey information and ideas. Images provide a powerful source of information for many people and clearly communicate ideas that would be difficult to portray in words. For example:

- You can find your way far more easily with a road map than if you were given written directions.
- The popularity of TV, which replaced radio as the most popular broadcast entertainment in the home, shows that images have value to people.
- Art collectors value paintings by paying millions of dollars for selected works.
- An instant replay is more vivid than thousands of words of narration by sportscasters.

Pictures have been used for communication since prehistoric people created drawings on cave walls in southern France. In recent years, computers have been adopted as tools for graphic communication.

Representing Computer Graphics

Computers develop graphic images through digitizing techniques. As you may remember, a graphics tablet and other specialized input hardware digitize an image by converting it into numeric data that can be located on an x-y coordinate system. Two approaches are used to produce graphic images.

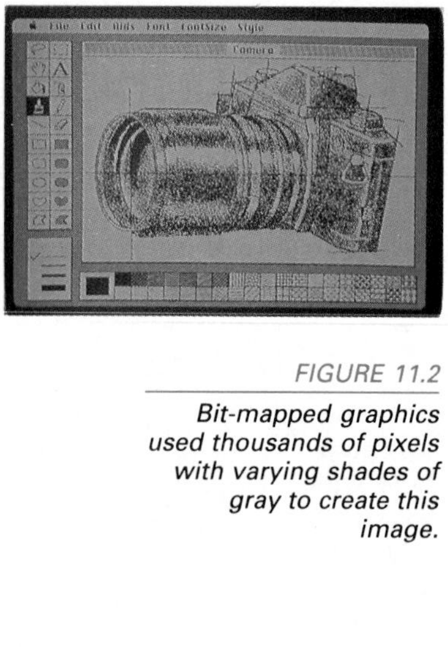

FIGURE 11.2

Bit-mapped graphics used thousands of pixels with varying shades of gray to create this image.

- Pixel graphics or ***bit mapping*** can tone images such as photos or paintings. Pixel graphics treat a video screen, paper, or film as a pattern of tightly packed dots. Bit mapping means that each pixel has a separate memory position that is represented by a color or shade of gray. The total pattern of digitized pixels makes up a black-and-white or color illustration. This graphic technique is found in video games, movies, scoreboards, Saturday morning cartoons, and a wide variety of advertisements.
- Vector graphics use a different type of VDT that allows continuous lines to be drawn between points on a screen. Connections are carried out as lines or curves. Vector graphics displays are known as line drawings. You will find vector graphics used in some video games. Engineers, architects, draftspeople, and others use vector graphics to create precise designs.

Whether you play a video game, enjoy an animated movie, or watch a scoreboard at a stadium, you are a user of computer graphics. Computer graphics is a rapidly growing application area that will have a major impact on application and system software for some time to come.

Types of Computer Graphics

Many applications use what can be called ***presentation graphics***. Business applications provide a good example of using presentation graphics techniques to compare numeric data in standard formats. These formats include bar graphs, pie charts, and line graphs. It is also possible to use computer graphics crea-

FIGURE 11.3

This engineer is using a VDT, which supports vector graphics, to create new automotive designs.

tively. The computer can be viewed as a tool for drawing or creating images in much the same way as canvas is used by an artist or a drafting table by an architect. These applications require ***free-drawing graphics***.

Computer Graphics as a Tool

Some graphics applications are purely for artistic purposes. A graphics artist might produce the initial design for tapestries, wall-hangings, portraits, and still–lifes. In some cases the computer graphic is the finished product. Magazine ads and television commercials often use images produced with computer graphics. Computer-constructed images also enhance background shots in motion pictures. Other designs are put to more practical uses. Engineers and architects, for example, use graphics applications to design bridges and buildings. In the hands of creative and informed users presentation and free-drawing graphics software are powerful tools.

Business Presentations

When the bottom line counts, businesspeople turn to graphics to make their point. They have found that business reports with a lot of detailed information can be clearly summarized by a pie chart or other form of presentation graphic. A University of Minnesota/3M study concluded that presentations with visual aids were 43 percent more persuasive than those without. Furthermore, research at the Wharton School of Business at the University of Pennsylvania found that business meetings involving graphics were shorter and consensus was reached more quickly. In short, graphics help businesspeople present a professional image while keeping people awake during long business meetings.

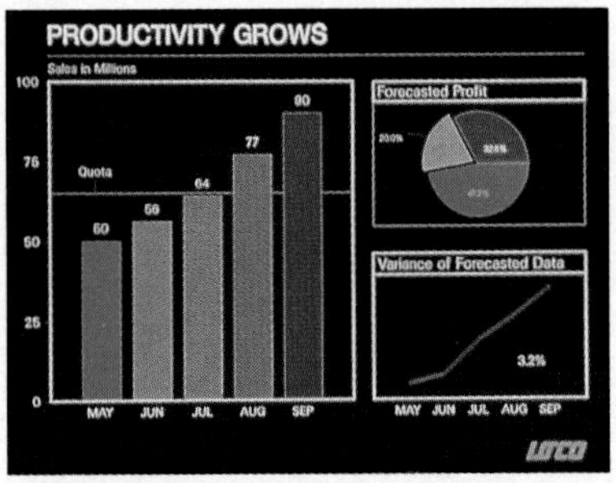

FIGURE 11.4

Presentation graphics like these help businesspeople to capture and clarify data.

Computer Animation

In the world of entertainment, computer-generated graphics are most visible on television, in motion pictures, and in video games. When you drop a token in a video game, it activates a computer that creates and moves images across the video screen. A race through a jungle obstacle course, an intergalactic battle with

FIGURE 11.5

Animation generated by computers is used both for video games and cartoon features.

alien ships, even a food fight can be simulated with this type of computer graphics. Players use buttons, joysticks, and steering wheels as input devices. The data entered by manipulating these devices elicits a response from the computer. The output is usually movement of the image on a screen.

The same type of graphics is used to develop animated film and cartoons. ***Animation*** is a sequence of motions produced with drawn or painted images. Traditional animation was costly and complex. In the first animated productions, each second of a sound animation film required 36 hand-drawn images. Films today employ computers to generate movement in images.

Computer-animated graphics require highly complex programming sequences initially. However, once the instructions have been entered, creating motion of animated characters and objects is relatively quick and easy. Animators use free-drawing software and special programs to manipulate motion sequences. As video images are created one frame (or image) at a time, a motion picture camera or videotape records the sequence of images. These techniques are used to produce commercials and entertainment spots for television or motion pictures.

Computer-Aided Design (CAD)

Development of a major new product, such as an aircraft or automobile, used to involve a cycle of activities that ran five to nine years. Well over half this time was spent in design. Before work could start on the product, designers had to figure out how the new product would look and how it would be constructed to meet performance and safety goals. The same was true for development of a major building; skilled architects had to draw and redraw many sets of pictures and detailed plans. Once the drawing was finalized, cameras mounted on special stands photographed the image to produce color slides.

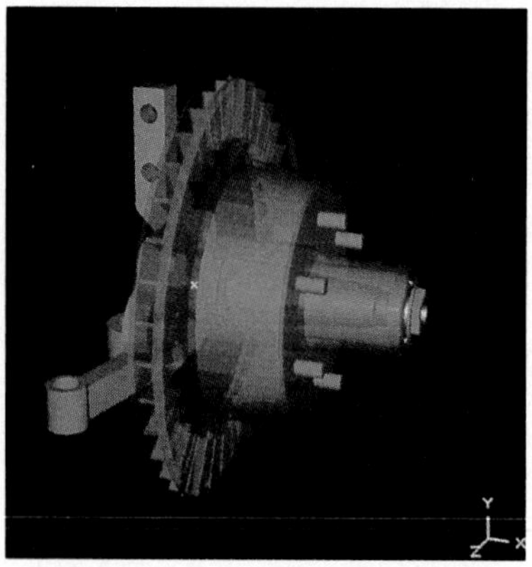

FIGURE 11.6

Computer-generated 3-D graphics are so precise that they often look like photographs.

This design, analysis, and simulation of new products utilizing computers is known collectively as computer-aided design (CAD). A designer inputs data using a tablet, keyboard, mouse, or light-sensitive pen, making it possible to draw directly on VDT screens using many of the features of free-drawing packages. The computer forms images by digitizing entered data. These images can be turned or rotated on the screen for close evaluation of appearance and prospective performance before products are made. Computer simulations, in effect, drive cars or fly aircraft long before the vehicles actually are built.

When CAD techniques are used for product or structural design, computations are used to predict how the design reacts under different situations. A bridge design may be tested for strength under severe winds, while a design for a chair can be checked for durability. Mathematical equations representing these stresses are put into the computer. The computer then runs the design through the equations. This enables a designer to find weaknesses in the design before the actual product is made.

Weather Forecasting

A meteorologist's responsibilities range from collecting meteorological data to preparing weather maps and forecasts. This means working with a variety of electronic instruments and, of course, computers. Data are maintained in databases through a complex series of activities. A meteorologist oversees the collection of data about air pressure, temperature, humidity, wind speed, and wind direction. Visual observations, radar sightings, ground-based instruments, instruments suspended from weather balloons, and satellites collect these data.

All data are input into a computer that is part of a network representing hundreds of observation stations. The network then feeds the weather data into the National Weather Services' supercomputer in Washington, D.C. The supercomputer makes millions of calculations each second to simulate potential weather conditions. The results are processed as computer graphics and output as weather maps and long-range weather forecasts.

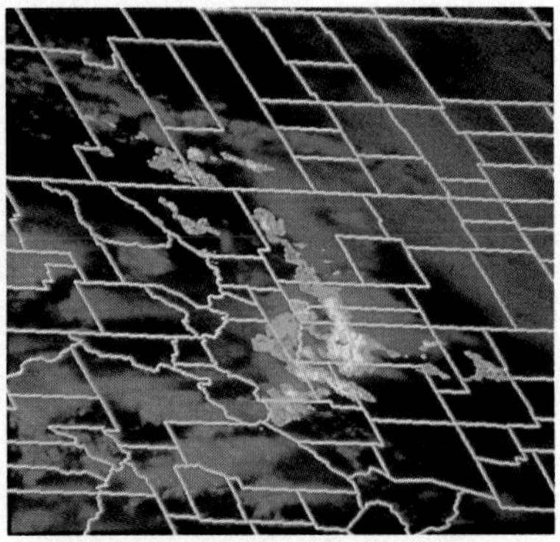

FIGURE 11.7

Weather forecasting capabilities benefit greatly from the use of computer graphics.

Courtesy of Ramtex Corporation

Space Exploration

As you can see, computer graphics are used to predict and present weather conditions. However, graphic applications extend beyond earthly uses. Computer-controlled space probes record images of Mars, Venus, the moon, and other galactic bodies as streams of digital bit patterns. The images are sent back to an earth base and converted into graphics. Specialists analyze the graphics, then use image enhancement techniques to adjust the pictures to indicate surface conditions.

These image enhancement techniques can fill in missing data by checking surrounding pixels and estimating the likely content of an unknown pixel value. The contrast in images is improved by using temperatures, air densities, and other conditions on the celestial body as data. These image enhancement techniques change the pictures from shades of gray to various intensities of color.

Athletics

Many sports arenas use large, computer-controlled display boards to inform and entertain fans. In addition to statistics and scores, these boards display instant replays, animated figures, trivia questions, and likenesses of players.

Coaches can analyze an athlete's performance with a special type of graphics software. For example, a computer loaded with this software might record the motion of a runner. Body movements are input into the computer through specialized scanners. Or the computer might digitize films of the athlete in action. The body movements are reproduced graphically, then compared with computer models representing desired form.

Sometimes, the computer can identify subtle variations in an athlete's form that could hurt his or her performance. Coaches and athletes work together to use computer graphics to improve form and performance.

FIGURE 11.8

NASA's Jet Propulsion Laboratory uses computers to enhance digitized pictures from space probes.

Photo courtesy of Jet Propulsion Laboratories

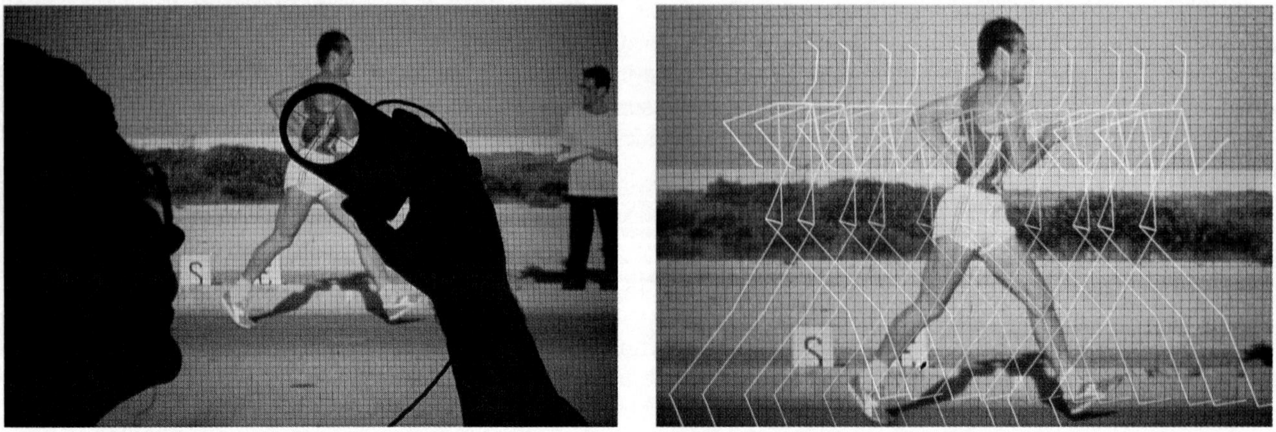

FIGURE 11.9

Medical researchers at the Olympic training center in Colorado use computer-generated graphics to analyze a runner's form and performance.

STUDY QUESTIONS

1. Define bit mapping, presentation graphics, free-drawing graphics, and animation.
2. What types of information are associated with each pixel in bit mapping?
3. Describe two ways to create a graphic image.
4. How are computer-generated graphics used in animation, computer-aided design, weather forecasting, space exploration, and athletics?

PRESENTATION AND FREE-DRAWING GRAPHICS

Graphics are used to produce visual images that support written reports. In many cases, information contained in large reports that take hours to read can be charted or graphed for easier comprehension. The full, textual reports are still needed—but the addition of computer-produced graphics can make the content easier to understand. Experience has shown that information presented through graphics is remembered better than written explanations.

Presentation Graphics

Presentation graphics come in several forms. An architect might create drawings for blueprints on computers, while a manufacturer might model parts on a screen. However, most presentation graphics fall into one of three categories:

- Pie charts
- Bar graphs
- Line graphs

Graphics offer a clear way of viewing individual and group statistics. For example, coach Stephanie Reboy could use graphics to show how individual scores contributed to her team's total score in a gymnastics meet. Using spreadsheet software, she organized the individual scores in four events for the six team members. The resulting spreadsheet, with team totals and averages, is shown in Figure 11.10. With an integrated graphics package, the coach created several presentation graphics representing this spreadsheet data.

NEW WAVE GRAPHICS CAPABILITIES BOGGLE THE MIND

When the first paint programs appeared on the scene in the early 1980s, people were amazed at what they could do. You could cut out an image and move it! Choose colors! Fill shapes!

But in these more sophisticated times, such features have become passé. Artists now demand, and software developers are striving to provide, *new wave* capabilities that boggle the mind. Forthcoming packages for several computers will feature:

- surface mapping, the ability to make a pattern or picture look as though it was painted on the surface of a sphere or other 3-D shape.
- adjustable light source shading, which can, for example, make circles look like spheres lit from any angle.
- tinting, to lay washes of translucent color over selected areas.
- simulated digital video effects, including automatic multiple images and twisting the picture around any axis.

These are powerful features, and they open new avenues for computer artists. But are they necessary for every user? And do they make painting any easier?

The fact is, advanced tools don't always make your life easier. A case in point is the perspective option appearing in several paint programs. This seems like a great boon—remember how you struggled to master perspective in junior high art class? But paint program perspective often gives disappointing results.

Say you've painted a landscape that includes a tree, and you want to put it into perspective. You tilt the painting 45 degrees away from you with the perspective tool. Do you see the tree from another angle as you would in the real world? No—it just looks like a drawing of a tree turned 45 degrees. All you can do with paint program perspective is tilt flat planes— since flat planes are all you can create. This is great for making pictures of boxes, but not very useful for anything else. In the end, it's often easier to take the time to lay out the picture with lines and vanishing points like artists have been doing since the Renaissance.

Of course, no one wants to give up other advanced tools like dithering and stencils—they really do make life easier. Most artists love to see new features, hoping for that perfect program which provides the maximum power in the most elegant form.

Source: COMPUTE. Reprinted with permission.

Key Question: Could these new graphics capabilities make an artist out of a non-artist?

```
C1:  SCORES FROM THIS WEEK'S GYMNASTICS MEET                                MENU
Line  BAR  XY  Stacked-Bar  Pie
Line graph
        A       B   C          D          E          F          G          H
1                SCORES FROM THIS WEEK'S GYMNASTICS MEET
2
3   EVENT      !  Vault  Uneven      Floor   Balance    Total
4              !           Bars   Exercise    Beam
5   ---------- !---------------------------------------------
6   Candy      !    8.0       8.0       6.5       9.0    31.5
7   Donna      !    5.0       7.5       7.5       9.0    29.0
8   Nancy      !    7.0       7.0       8.5       8.5    31.0
9   Sally      !    7.5       7.5       7.5       8.5    31.0
10  Sharon     !    5.5       8.5       6.5       8.0    28.5
11  Terri      !    8.5       6.0       7.0       8.0    29.5
12  ---------- !---------------------------------------------
13  Average    !    6.9       7.4       7.3       8.5    30.1
14
15
16
17
18
19
20
```

FIGURE 11.10

Presentation graphics software often uses data originally stored in spreadsheets or databases. The following figures use data from this spreadsheet.

Pie Charts

The relationships of parts to a whole are illustrated by ***pie charts***. Pie charts derive their name from the fact that they are usually presented as circles divided into wedges, like slices of a pie. Pie charts show percentages, proportions, or ratios. Each wedge of the pie represents a certain percentage of the whole. The sum of all wedges is 100 percent.

After the last gymnastics meet, Stephanie used a pie chart to show each individual's contribution to the team score. A pie chart of this type is shown in Figure 11.11. Using another technique, slices of the pie can be separated from the main circle to create an ***exploded pie chart***.

Bar Charts

Stephanie decided to present individual performance for each gymnastics event with a ***bar chart***. Bar charts picture data values in terms of the lengths of lines, or

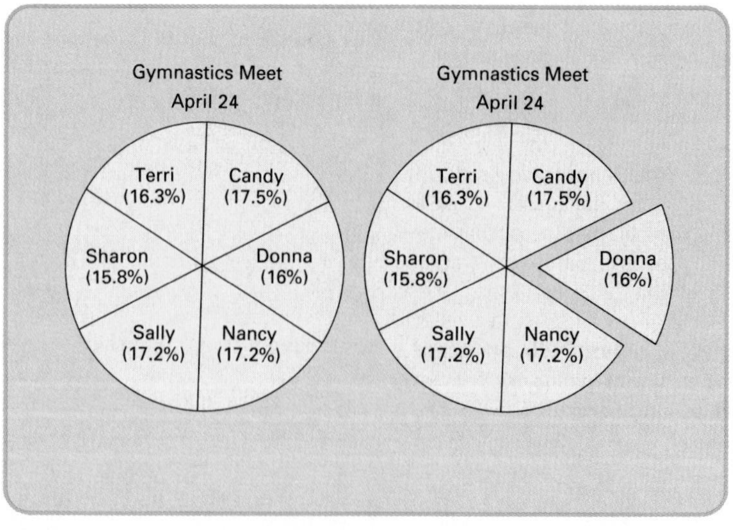

FIGURE 11.11

These pie charts are derived from the scorekeeping spreadsheet in the preceding figure. The pie chart on the right had been exploded to show one member's performance in relation to the rest of the team.

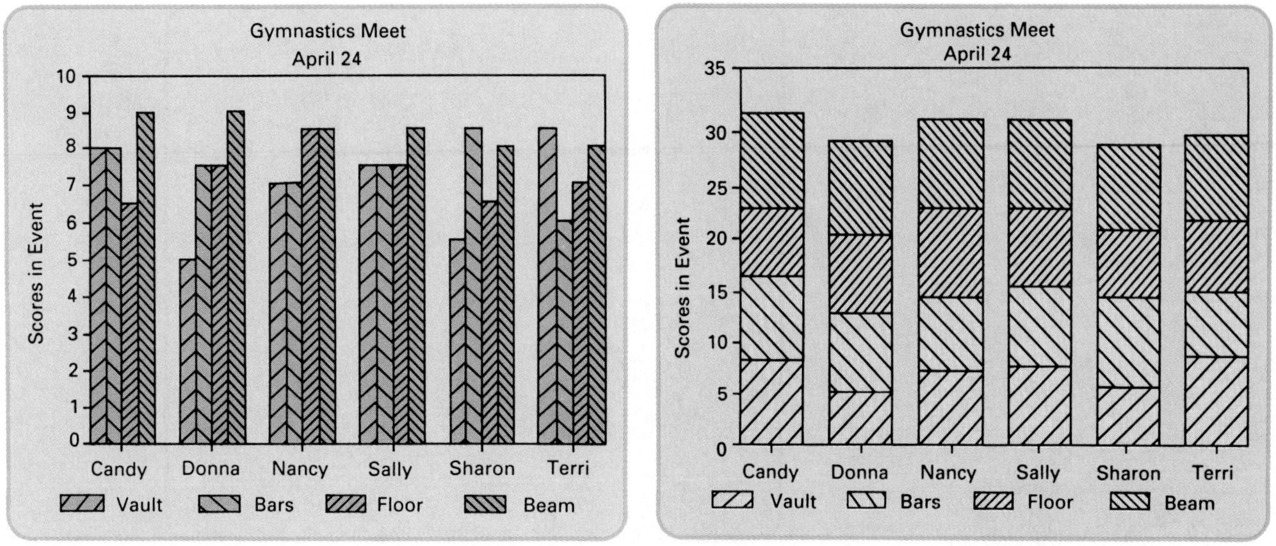

FIGURE 11.12

Bar charts provide a graphic basis for comparisons of values, in this case scores of gymnastics team members for different events.

Stacked bar charts provide a method for showing both parts of whole entities and comparisons. In this case, the portion of bars show the composition of performances by individual team members. The set of stacked bars also provides a basis for comparison of performances.

bars. A bar chart conveys meaning through use of two scales, or marked values, at the bottom of the graphic. For example, the bar chart in Figure 11.12 shows how team members compared in all events. This bar chart is based on the same spreadsheet as the pie chart for the gymnastics meet. The bottom scale, or set of labels for this bar chart, identifies the team members. The scale at the left indicates the points awarded in each event. Different shading helps to distinguish between events. The legend at the bottom of the chart helps readers relate the shaded bars to specific events.

Bar charts used to indicate subcategories of a whole value are known as ***stacked bar graphs***. This type of graph is used when data represented by each bar must be broken down into segments. Figure 11.12 depicts a stacked bar graph indicating the breakdown of individual points by event for each team member. While the data are the same for both bar charts, the stacked bar graph clearly shows the accumulated points for each team member, while the regular bar chart does not.

Line Graphs

Line graphs show trends tracked over a period of time. Like bar charts, line graphs have two sets of scales, at the top or bottom and on one side. Often, the bottom scale shows the passage of time. For example, Figure 11.13 illustrates the performance for one team member, Donna, throughout the season. Each event is indicated by a separate line containing unique symbols. The legend at the bottom of the graph explains which event the symbol represents.

How Do You Create Presentation Graphics?

Graphics software converts data values to points on a pattern or grid. Then it creates the digital patterns to produce output. Many application packages, such as spreadsheets, statistical packages, and database programs contain modules that produce graphic output. Some graphics software will read files created by integrated packages. Regardless of the software package and type of graphic, four levels of information are required to create presentation graphics.

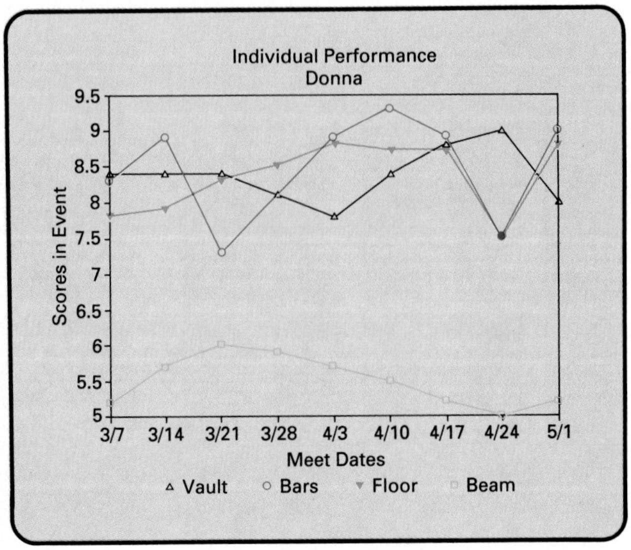

FIGURE 11.13

Line graphs are used to trace performance or statistical trends.

- **Identify type of graphic.** Selecting the type of presentation graphic to use is often done from a menu. For example, the screen from an integrated software package in Figure 11.10 shows a menu where the user can choose from a variety of presentation graphics. When using the menu to ask for a line graph, the program will present a prompt that asks the user to identify related labels and data.
- **Identify data.** After the type of graphic is chosen, the software prompts the user for data. These can be entered manually at the keyboard. If the data have been previously used, the user does not need to re enter them. Instead, the name of the file containing the data is entered. When selected data from the file are needed, the user must specify which fields or records are included and how they are organized. At this point, a graphic can be output. However, as shown in Figure 11.14, there is little information to identify what the graphic represents.
- **Identify labels.** To clarify the meaning of the graphic, each scale must be labeled. These labels can be taken from the data file or entered by the user. In Figure 11.14, the bottom scale came from the first column of the spreadsheet containing team member names. The side scale, Scores in Events, was entered by the user. In both cases, the software sets scales based on the data values used. Sometimes, scales on graphs need to be adjusted for easier reading or to reflect some type of standard measurement. These are the two reasons for changing the vertical scale (see Figure 11.17). First, it is not pleasing to the eye to have one bar going to the top of the scale at 9. In addition, gymnastics scores range from 0 to 10. Stephanie decided that a larger vertical scale with 10 as the upper limit was needed. She used the software to redraw the graphic, producing the bar chart shown.
- **Create titles and legend.** To complete the graphic, a title and legend may be included. A title provides a general description of the output and the dates that it covers. Legends explain the specific meaning of any symbols, colors, or shading found on the graphic. Titles and legends usually are prompted by the software and manually entered at the keyboard.

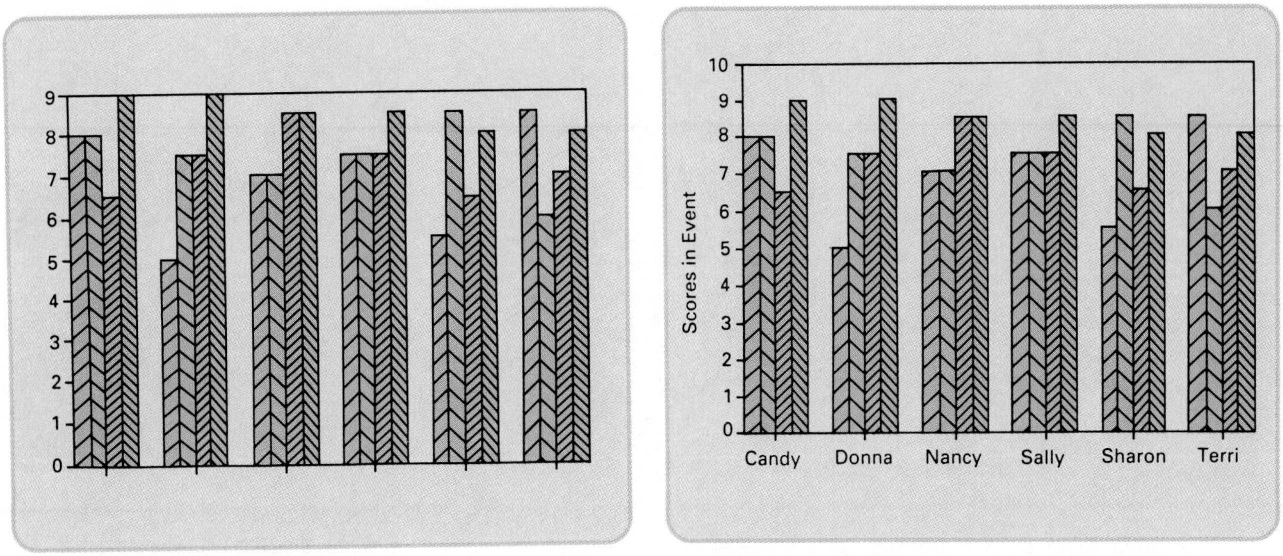

FIGURE 11.14 A & B

Care must be taken in designing and labeling images. The first bar graph (a) without labels and a meaningful scale is difficult to read. The second graph (b) is easier to read but still needs a title and a legend.

Free-Drawing Graphics

Free-drawing graphics software aids the creative artist or engineer in producing high-quality, complex drawings. Although each free-drawing graphics package has unique capabilities to aid the user, many have features in common. After the free-drawing software is loaded, the user defines the drawing area or canvas. In many packages, this is done through an icon (picture) menu selection. Usually, initial designs and menu selections are input with a mouse or tablet. If the area extends longer or wider than the screen, scrolling must take place to move the screen display from position to position.

An extensive variety of features are available. Drawing options are displayed as icons in the palette and toolbox (see Figure 11.15). Utility options can be picked from pull-down menus.

Rob Merrill is a graphics art student who is learning to use free-drawing graphics in Graphics 210. His next assignment is to create a poster for his college's theater production of Peter Pan. After Rob has made some initial sketches, he loads an icon-driven graphics package into his personal computer.

The Palette

The ***palette*** provides an opportunity for Rob to choose the colors, patterns, and shading needed in the poster. Basic graphics palettes for color output typically offer eight hues, but sophisticated packages can provide up to 256 or more color choices. The palette also may include patterns of dots, stripes, or lattices.

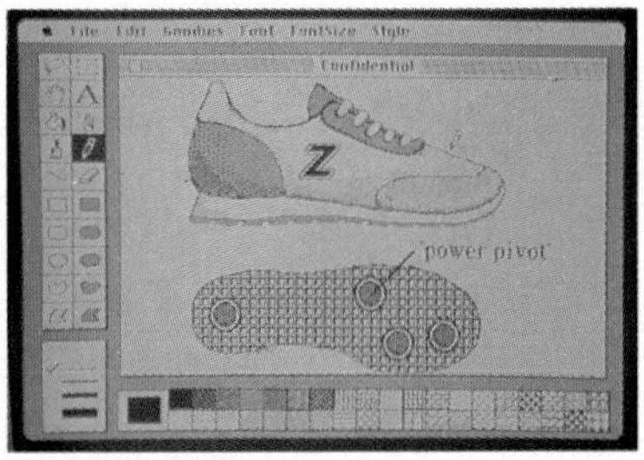

FIGURE 11.15

A graphic artist uses the palette and toolbox when drawing and selecting program options.

The Toolbox

Within free-drawing software, an icon menu provides a series of drawing choices known as a ***toolbox***. Rob, in effect, selects the type of drawing tool to be used on the electronic canvas.

- **Paintbrush.** The *PAINTBRUSH* enables Rob to create images in different line widths and shapes. Paintbrushes can be large or small, round or flat, straight or slanted. In addition, Rob can select the color of "paint" to use from the palette. To outline the pirate ship and characters, Rob uses the

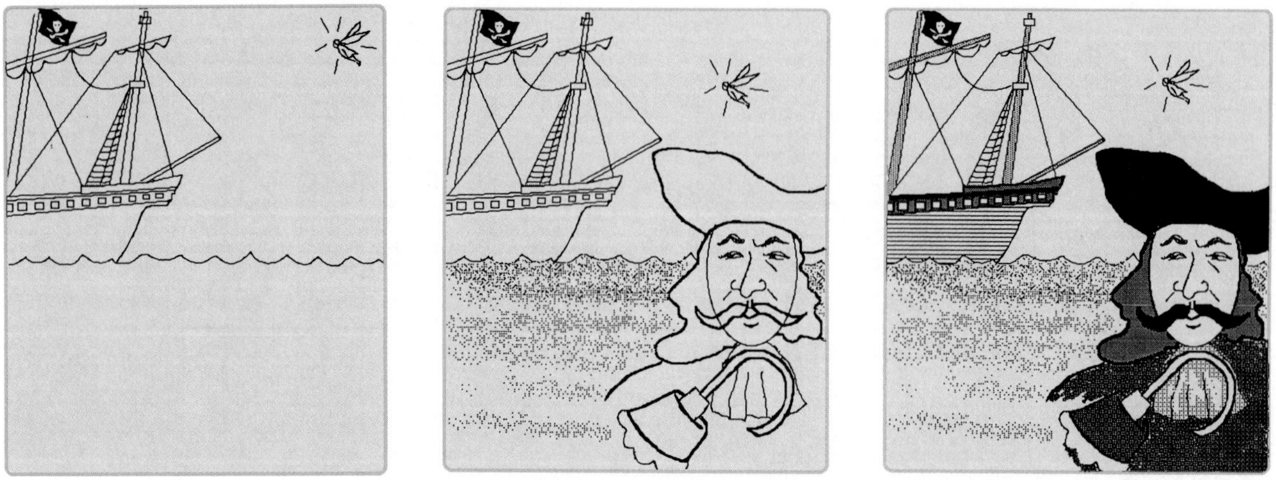

FIGURE 11.16 A–E

Free-drawing software helped to create this billboard. The PAINTBRUSH option drew the ship and other line art (a). SPRAYPAINT shaded the water and the SHAPE and STRETCH options created Captain Hook's head (b). The FILLBUCKET option added siding to the pirate ship and Tinkerbell was LASSOed and moved to a new position (c). Detailed work on Tinkerbell was accomplished by enlarging the image with FATBITS (d). Text was then added to the finished billboard shown in the last figure (e).

paintbrush like a pencil by selecting a thin line from the toolbox. As Rob rolls the mouse on a flat surface, the movement is reflected on the screen which draws the image of the pirate ship.

- **Spraypaint.** The effect produced by using an actual can of spraypaint is reproduced by the ***SPRAYPAINT*** option. That is, Rob moves the paint can across the screen very quickly, producing a light spattering of the selected pattern. To produce varying depths of color in the ocean, Rob lingers at a particular place on the screen and the "spray" becomes denser, more pronounced.
- **Shapes.** Circles, ovals, rectangles, and other geometric ***SHAPES*** are toolbox selections that can be duplicated automatically on screen. The shapes may be filled or unfilled. That is, they may appear as a solid shape or an outline. The ***STRETCH*** function, as its name implies, widens these geometric figures, giving the impression that the image is being stretched. For example, Rob moves the cursor to the circle, then pulls it into an oval, which will become Captain Hook's head. With this option, Rob also can stretch a square into a rectangle.
- **Fill bucket.** Any enclosed shape can be filled with a pattern through use of the ***FILL BUCKET*** function. Rob moves the cursor to the fill bucket option, then to the desired pattern, and finally to the outline of the ship. The pattern or color automatically fills the entire area within the ship's outline.

- **Lasso.** A *LASSO* enables Rob to copy or move parts of the graphic from one location to another. After drawing the image of Tinkerbell, Rob realizes that it should be positioned lower on the poster. He draws a loop, or "lasso," around the image to be relocated. He relocates the image by moving the cursor to the new position and pressing the button on the mouse. This option enables Rob to experiment with the graphic design.
- **Fatbits.** Rob can zoom into a specific section of a graphic to view a pixel-by-pixel enlargement with the ***FATBITS*** option. For example, he can add detail to the drawing by inspecting the magnified portion, and turning pixels on or off to change lines and patterns.
- **Eraser.** The ***ERASER*** works much like a chalkboard eraser. With a mouse, Rob moves the eraser across the screen. The areas covered by the eraser are cleared of lines and patterns.
- **Text options.** Rob types text onto the screen using a keyboard. Many free-drawing packages allow users to select fonts and type size. The size of the type is chosen from a pull-down menu. Rob uses this feature to add the title, dates, time, and location of the production to the poster. Another menu gives Rob the options to try plain, bold, italic, underlined, outlined, justified, and centered text.

Free-Drawing Utilities

Other pull-down menus come with a set of standard utilities, some as simple as clearing the screen. Utilities are used for saving a graphic file and for loading a file from storage. A special utility is used to undo the last request made by a user in creating a graphic. Rob can experiment with different visual effects, then use this utility to remove the last change.

Special editing utilities enable Rob to rearrange different parts of a graphics file with cut, copy, and paste routines. These utilities make it easy to try different designs.

Graphics produced by inputting dimensions and mathematical relationships into the computer also make use of special utilities. With this information, the computer draws a three-dimensional view of an image. The object can be tilted, rotated, and viewed from all sides by using these special utilities.

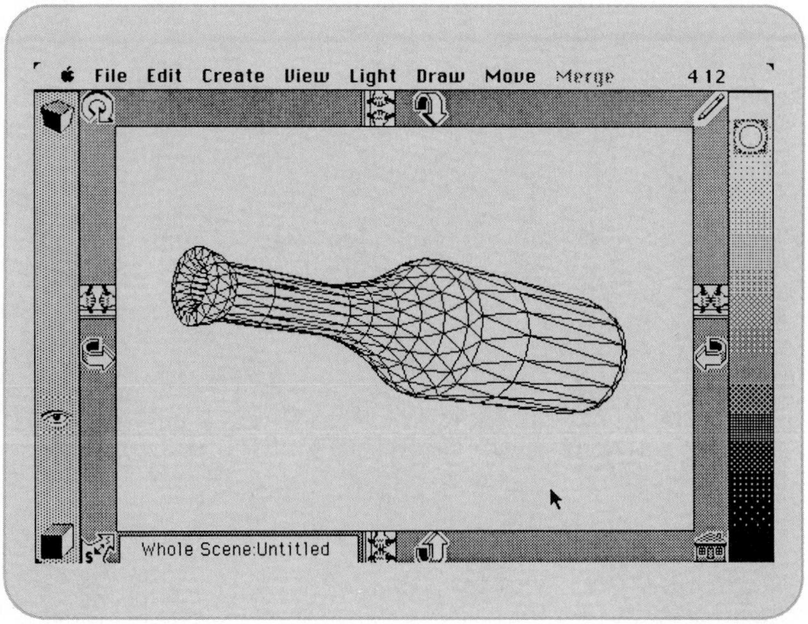

FIGURE 11.17

Free-drawn, three-dimensional images can be tilted, rotated, and viewed from all sides.

C L I P

COMPUTERS BUILD VIEWS OF MODELS

Tony Jeanpiere, a Chrysler Corp. marketing-system specialist, sits in front of a computer screen in the carmaker's regional office in Malvern, Pa., "building a car" for a visitor.

He is "painting" a Plymouth Voyager mini-van by bringing up an image of the vehicle on the screen and coloring it with each of the colors the computer says is available on that model.

"You can even put wood grain on it if you want to," he notes, hitting the appropriate button.

Major U.S. manufacturers are either developing or already supplying dealers with sophisticated computerized sales aids to help customers select a new car.

Linked to central data bases in Detroit, they will tell you everything you need to know about the model and equipment you want and then help locate the vehicle.

Similarly, the diagnostic systems allow agency mechanics to tap into the manufacturers' technical data bases to obtain diagnoses and cures for the maladies of today's ever more complex automobiles.

New Chrysler sales computers are typical. Employing a large color screen, the Chrysler terminal displays pictures of all the company's models, then provides a 30-second videotape of those that interest the customer.

After the customer has selected the model he or she wants, the machine can zero in on standard features, options, performance, carrying capacity and fuel efficiency—and compare it with the competition.

Source: Reprinted by permission, *Detroit Free Press.*

Key Question: Would you be more likely to buy a new car or house if you could see the finished design on a computer screen first? Even if it involves a higher price?

Graphics in Integrated Software Packages

Since graphic images enhance the meaning of words and numbers, many word processing, electronic spreadsheet, and database programs integrate with graphics software. Free-drawing software can create business logos or personal letterheads for use by word processing programs. Many electronic spreadsheets and database programs incorporate software that convert labels and numbers into presentation graphics.

Any document meant to have an impact on the reader will blend the use of text, numbers, and graphic images. Annual reports produced by publicly held companies are a case in point. Integrated software packages help the designers blend the president's letter to stockholders with numbers representing last year's profit or loss. Graphic packages, which produce the free-drawn cover and line graphs charting the company's expected growth, tie the document together.

STUDY QUESTIONS

5. Define exploded pie chart, stacked bar graph, and stretch function.
6. Describe the characteristics of a pie chart, bar chart, and line graph.
7. What are the four levels of information needed by graphics software to produce presentation graphics?
8. What functions do the palette, toolbox, and pull-down menus provide for free-drawing graphics software?
9. How do the paintbrush, spraypaint, shapes, fill bucket, lasso, fatbits, eraser, and text options work?
10. Identify ten free-drawing utilities that are available through pull-down menus.

HOW TO SELECT GRAPHICS PACKAGES

As is true of any software purchase, the first step in conducting a search for the right graphics package is to define your needs. Uses for computer graphics are quite diverse, and packages usually are geared to specific needs. For example, one graphics package might focus on creating presentation graphs and charts. Another might feature capabilities needed for creating two-dimensional maps. A third might be geared toward generating three-dimensional architectural images and plans, while a fourth might concentrate on freehand drawing capabilities. Once you have identified your own requirements, you can narrow down the selection of available software considerably.

After deciding on the type of graphics you wish to create, you must identify memory and storage requirements. These requirements are often quite large for graphics packages, compared to requirements of word processing and spreadsheet software. A typical page of text might need 2000 bytes of memory, while a full-scale graphics page requires 30,000 bytes or more. You should estimate the extent of your graphics requirements and figure the number of bytes of memory and long-term disk storage needed to fulfill those requirements.

Your graphics needs might require color or high-resolution output. If so, you should compare the selection of colors provided by different packages and the ***resolution***, which is measured, with bit-mapped graphics, by the number of

Questions to Ask When Purchasing Graphics Packages

1. In which type of graphic design does it specialize?
   - Presentation graphics?
   - Free drawing in two dimensions?
   - Free drawing in three dimensions?
   - Animation?
2. Is the software easy to use?
3. Is the supporting documentation easy to read?
4. What type of support and training are offered by the salesperson and software manufacturer?
5. With what computers and operating systems was the graphic package designed to operate?
6. What are the minimum and suggested memory requirements?
7. What input devices are supported by the graphics package? Which devices does the software manufacturer recomment?
8. How much disk storage will an 8 by 11 1/2 inch graphic requre? Does the manufacturer recommend having access to a hard disk when using their equipment?
9. What output hardware does the graphic package support? Does the software manufacturer recommend any particular hardware?
10. Does the graphic software support color? If yes, how many colors and shades?
11. At what resolution is the screen output? Can your VDT take advantage of this resolution? If not, can your hardware be upgraded and at what cost?
12. At what resolution is the hardcopy output? Can your printer take advantage of this resolution? Do you need and does you printer support color output?

FIGURE 11.18

Graphics software often requires large amounts of computer memory, access to hard disk storage, and the use of specialized input and output hardware.

bits per line or inch. Higher resolution means more bits per unit of measurement and a sharper image. Don't forget you will need output hardware that complements the graphics packages. It makes little sense to have software that can output bit-mapped graphics at 600 bits per inch if the attached printer can print only 150 bits per inch. As you might expect, the higher the screen or printer resolution, the more expensive the hardware.

Simple color graphics can be produced with a palette of four shades. A more extensive selection will be needed in more sophisticated designs. When they are used properly, color graphics can clarify presentation graphics and add realism to free-drawing graphics. Colors are used most often with presentation graphics when more than two types of data need to be highlighted. People, especially small children, expect graphic images to be in color. However, color that is improperly used can distract and confuse viewers. With the proper design, a high-quality black-and-white image can produce a clearer picture than a color image of poor quality or bad design.

Cost and application needs, along with currently available hardware, play a major role in selecting graphics programs. For example, free-lance designers responsible for ideas, not final copy, could get by with draft-quality printers and low-resolution VDTs. However, the print shop for a large company that designs and produces camera-ready materials would need to invest in higher resolution, and possibly color, output hardware. Graphics applications can be used with many types of input devices, including mouse, keyboard, drafting tablet, light pen, and touch screen. The output devices could include VDTs, printers, plotters, even cameras. Special graphics adapters may be required for computers originally purchased with monochrome screens.

You should select a software package that can work together with your hardware, or expect to purchase compatible devices. As with all software, you should ask to see a demonstration of the graphics package using hardware similar to yours before you make any purchase.

STUDY QUESTIONS

11. Define resolution as it relates to output hardware.
12. What type of questions should you ask when selecting graphics software for personal use?

CONCLUSION

Graphics packages are not for casual users since they require a great deal of memory, are expensive, and often need specialized input and output hardware. The power of a graphics package lies in its ability to enhance the impact of words and numbers. A variety of informed users include presentation graphics with documents ranging from a company's annual report to summaries of athletic performance. The versatility of freehand drawing is available to people working with computer-assisted design, weather forecasting, and animation. Graphics packages that are easy to use give a high-tech meaning to the old Chinese proverb, "One picture is worth a thousand words."

CHAPTER FACTS

- Graphic images can be produced through pixel graphics (also called bit mapping) or vector graphics.
- Graphics refers to either presentation or free-drawing graphics.
- Graphic applications include animation for film and videotape, computer-assisted design creation and testing, output for weather forecasting, output from space probes, reporting of sports results, and simulation of an athlete's performance.
- Presentation graphics can be pie charts, exploded pie charts, bar charts, stacked bar graphs, or line graphs.
- Pie charts show how components proportionally make up a total whole. Each slice represents a single component.
- Bar charts display data through bars of varying lengths, each showing the relative quantity or measurement of a value.
- Line graphs show the trends found in a group of data over time.

I N S I G H T

IS IT ART . . . OR OUTPUT?

Artistic images are created through a variety of media: oil and acrylic paint, mud and plaster, iron and plastic, and even pixels on a screen.

Courtesy of Ruedy Leeman, "Vision Obious"

We are beginning to see computer technology revolutionize the visual arts, especially in graphic art and animation.

Courtesy of Pixar, "Luxo, Jr."

Are there any limits? Can computer-generated images be considered fine art?

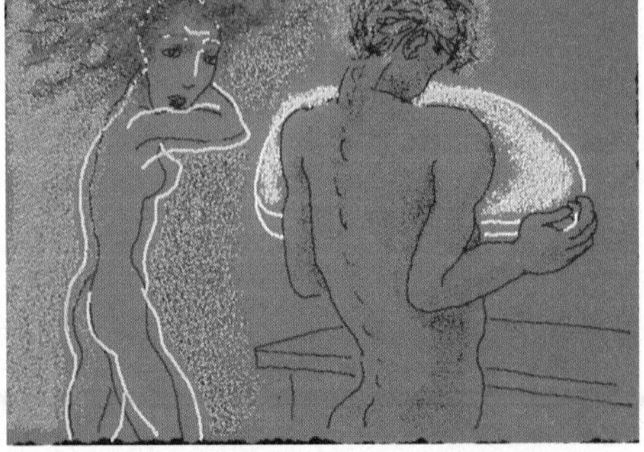

Courtesy of Bob Nessim, "Communication Disc"

Does it matter that computers help people execute ideas even though they lack the training and techniques more traditional artists spend their lives mastering?

Courtesy of Toyo Links, "Peppy"

Do we use the same rules for judging computer-drawn images as we do oil paintings, water colors, or pen and ink drawings?

Courtesy of Chris Wayne, "Untitled"

When evaluating any piece of art, does content (what a work of art says) outweigh the form (the way the work of art looks)?

Courtesy of Vibeke Sorensen, "Fish and Chips." Produced at the CalTech Computer Science Graphics Group.

- Presentation graphics are created by identifying the type of graphic, the data to be included, and labels for the graphic, and stating graphic title and legends.
- Free-drawing graphic software includes a palette, toolbox, and pull-down menus to aid the user.
- The palette allows the user to choose colors and shading for the graphic.
- The toolbox includes tools for creating the graphic. These include paintbrush, spraypaint, shapes, fill bucket, lasso, fatbits, eraser, and text options.
- Pull-down menus contain standard utilities for clearing the screen, saving a graphic file, and editing the graphic.
- Graphics output is often integrated with output from other personal productivity software to produce high-quality materials that incorporate words, numbers, and images into one document.
- To choose an appropriate graphics software package, the user should decide on the type of graphics needed, check memory and storage requirements, choose necessary input and output hardware, and see if color and high-resolution output is required.

TERMS TO REMEMBER

animation	paintbrush
bar chart	palette
bit mapping	pie chart
eraser	presentation graphics
exploded pie chart	resolution
fatbits	shapes
fill bucket	spraypaint
free-drawing graphics	stacked bar graph
lasso	stretch
line graph	toolbox

CHECK YOUR UNDERSTANDING

1. By using ____________ graphics, solid lines are drawn between two points on a screen.
2. Which of the following is *not* a type of presentation graphic?
   a. exploded pie chart
   b. bar chart
   c. table of contents
   d. line graph
   e. stacked bar graph
3. With a graphics software palette, the user can choose the color and size of the drawing tool needed. (True/False)
4. Using the ____________ option in a graphics package, the user can isolate part of the graphic so it can be moved or copied.
5. Fatbits allow the user to change a single pixel in a graphic. (True/False)

6. Which of the following is **not** a step in creating a presentation graphic?
   a. Choose the graphic title and legend.
   b. Choose the graphic font and type style.
   c. Identify data to be used.
   d. Identify the graphic labels.
   e. All are steps for creating a presentation graphic.
7. The ___________ contains the free-drawing utilities available on a graphics package.
8. With computer-generated animation, each image in the series is drawn separately, using free-drawing software. (True/False)
9. The graphics application where a product or structure is drawn on a screen, rotated in three dimensions, and then tested for flaws is called:
   a. computer-assisted design
   b. computer-assisted manufacturing
   c. robotics
   d. presentation graphics
   e. toolbox
10. Higher ___________ means more bits per unit of measurement and a sharper image.

APPLYING WHAT YOU'VE LEARNED

1. Applications for both presentation and free-drawing graphics exist in most career areas. Name three uses for graphics software in your chosen field (other than those mentioned in the text). Will the graphics be presentation or free drawings?
2. Find or name six examples of computerized graphics output. If it is a presentation graphic, identify its type, pointing out the labels, title, and legend. If it is a free hand drawing, what drawing tools and colors were used? Television, magazines, and films are possible sources of graphic output.
3. Explain how graphics software can be used to enhance user understanding in these situations:
   a. presentation of the racial groups that make up the faculty of your school
   b. advertising the opening of a new video rental store
   c. showing how to assemble a bicycle from a kit
   d. displaying the change in Pentagon spending over the last 20 years
4. Use a graphics package to produce and print a presentation graphic reflecting a simple collection of data. This could be your personal budget, grade point average over time, or another application. Be sure that the graphic is clearly labeled and contains a legend.
5. Use a graphics package to produce a simple freehand drawing. Make use of the palette and toolbox to show a variety of shapes and patterns. Save the graphic and print it out.

CHECK YOUR UNDERSTANDING ANSWERS

1. vector
2. c
3. false
4. lasso
5. true
6. b
7. pull-down menu
8. false
9. a
10. resolution

C H A P T E R

T W E L V E

DATABASES AND INTEGRATED SOFTWARE: PULLING IT ALL TOGETHER

KEY IDEAS

- **From the user's point of view**
  How do database programs allow you to organize, cross-reference, and present data in easy to use formats? In what ways can integrated software expand the individual capabilities of personal productivity software?
- **Databases: Integrating data and software**
  Many situations demand that data be organized and stored for easy access by several users.

  Database models
  Organization of data reflects problems to be solved through use of information resources.

  Database management systems
  This software provides easy-to-use commands that create databases and access related data.

  Database tools
  Database management systems provide utility programs that create reports and help users access data using English phrases.
- **Database software as a tool**
  Access to large databases helps in the communication of ideas and facts.
- **How to select database packages**
  Potential database users should clearly identify their needs before purchasing a database system.

  Basic database requirements
  Identify maximum database sizes and minimum hardware needs.

  Additional database features
  Security, networking, and special compilers could be desirable, depending on the database user's needs.
- **Integrated software as a tool**
  Informed users realize that integrated software increases their personal productivity.

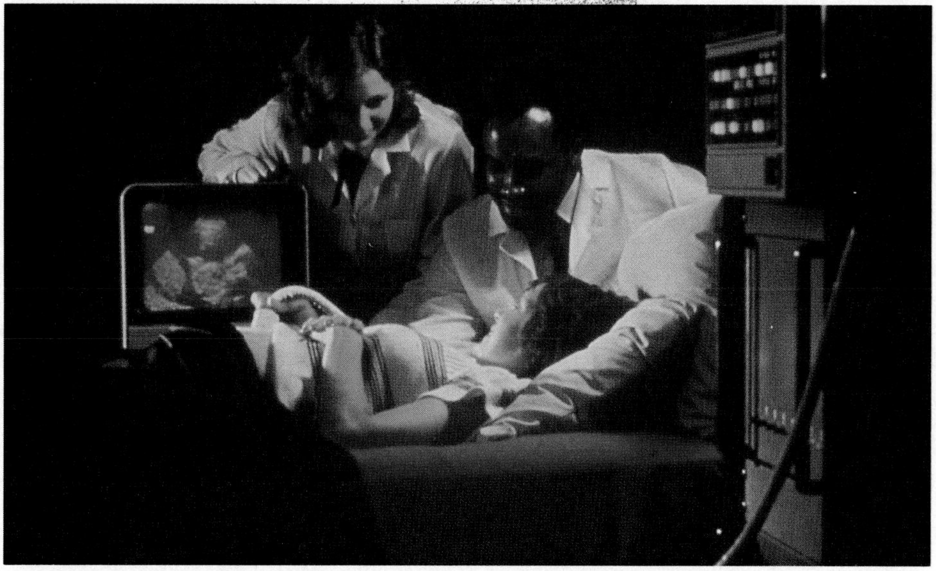

FROM THE USER'S POINT OF VIEW

Earlier, you learned that databases allow access to vast amounts of information. You might ask, when would I ever need to work with that much data? You probably now have files or lists of information, perhaps in overcrowded file cabinets, that could be arranged into personal databases. You may find that a database program would help you organize this information; thereby, reducing clutter and promoting better access to important data.

Not only is there a place for personal databases in your future, but you already have access to a wide variety of institutional databases. Real estate listings, library card catalogs, and travel information are organized into databases available to the knowledgeable consumer. Understanding the design and development of databases helps you to apply the principles to your own personal needs and gives you the edge in using established databases efficiently.

DATABASES: INTEGRATING DATA AND SOFTWARE

FIGURE 12.1

Banks and other organizations have found that databases help reduce data redundancy and provide access to data that once required the development of new programs.

Experience with the use of computers in business, science, and engineering has led to recognition that the value of data goes far beyond any single application. Historically, an appreciation of the value of data grew in parallel with the evolution of information systems. Typically, applications focused on a specific problem, with software creating and maintaining the data in files. An organization would develop a variety of file processing systems containing data that often overlapped.

For example, a bank may have separate file processing systems for checking accounts, savings accounts, personal loans, and mortgages. Any customer using more than one of these services would have basic information, such as name and address, repeated in each of the files. This redundancy of data means that storage space is wasted and the updating of records is difficult. When a customer moves, the address needs changing in several files. If incompletely updated, mixed-up payments and dissatisfied customers can result.

Data redundancy is just one of several problems associated with file processing. Another problem centers on the difficulty in cross-referencing information among the files. Special requests for information residing across several files requires the development of new programs or depends on manual processing. As a result, users have come to appreciate the potential for data and have begun to demand more sophisticated processing applications. This demand has led to the development of two major types of software:

- Database programs
- Integrated software

Both types of software represent major steps in making information widely available to computer users. However, the approaches and values of the two families of software differ in major ways, as explained in this chapter.

Database Models

FIGURE 12.2

Database support often requires massive disk storage capacities, as illustrated in this photo.

Photo by L.A. Schwaber-Barzilay

As people became more experienced in using computer systems, they recognized that relationships existed among all data files connected to the operation of an organization. In organizations such as businesses, government, schools, churches, and volunteer agencies, for example, a global view of the value of data and their relationships began to take shape. It was seen that each data file represented a small part of an organization's operating cycle. Combined, the data and the relationships among them presented a model of the organization, its operations, its status, and its potential. An integrated set of data files, called a database, allows easy cross-referencing of related data items, promotes data integrity—currency and correctness—and eliminates data redundancy.

Databases are formed, in simple terms, by creating computer files that serve as indexes to locate the contents of other files. A database is seen as a useful, interrelated set of files within which individual records and fields are identified and located through the use of software.

Database programs, or database management systems, create and maintain a database. This software often is confused with ***file management systems***. Both database management systems and file management systems have many common features. These systems allow users to manipulate data, create reports, and handle individual inquiries about data contained in the database or file. The difference lies in the fact that a file management system helps to maximize user access to a single data file. Database programs, however, integrate the contents of several files through the use of indexes and other techniques.

Under database concepts, collections of data are seen as models of the organization they support. Each database, in turn, is built upon a ***data model,*** or a plan the computer uses for storing and accessing data items. Data models used in building databases fall within three main categories:

- Hierarchical
- Network
- Relational

Hierarchical Model

A hierarchy is an organization that follows a top-down structure. A typical organization chart for a company presents a hierarchical structure. The highest ranking executives are placed at the top of the chart and relationships with subordinates are shown on a top-down basis.

A ***hierarchical model*** for a database follows the same principle. Data items and references to those items are related in a top-down structure. For example, an airline might structure a database as shown in Figure 12.3. At the top of this hierarchical model are origin cities, at the next level are destinations, followed by flights that connect those cities, and finally by dates for which reservations can be made.

In this instance, a hierarchical model makes possible an orderly "navigation" of paths to the desired information through a series of related items. A potential disadvantage is that the same path must be followed for each access operation. Data access operations always begin, in this instance, with the originating city. These steps must be followed even if the user knows, in advance, the specific flight number and date to be referenced.

Network Model

A ***network model*** resembles a hierarchy since there are also structured access paths. With a network, however, it is not necessary to follow a top-down order for each access of the database. Networks can be entered at different points, with access routes following in both directions. In the airline example, a network

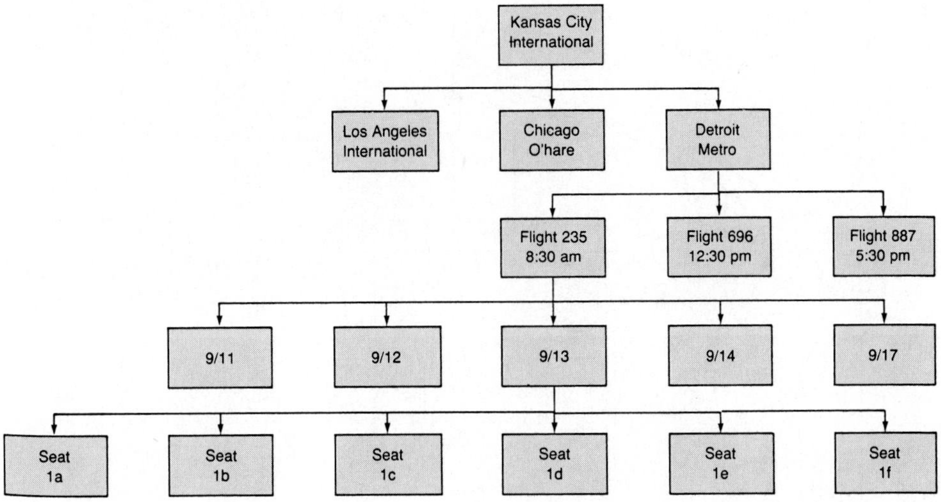

FIGURE 12.3

Hierarchical models of airline schedules are designed to allow top-down access to database information.

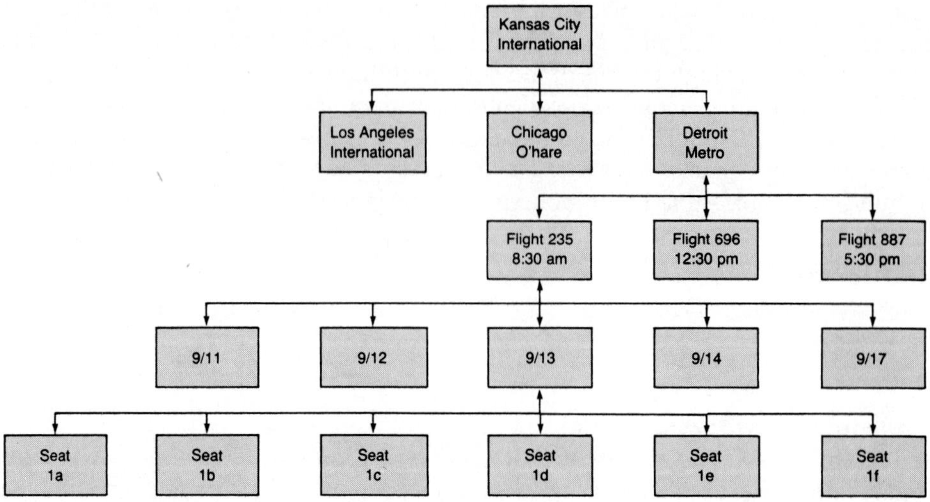

FIGURE 12.4

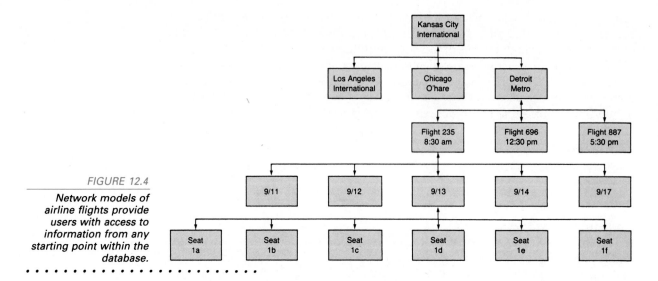

Network models of airline flights provide users with access to information from any starting point within the database.

model makes it possible to access the database by entering a flight number. Destinations, dates, or passengers can be accessed from this starting point, as shown in Figure 12.4.

Relational Model

A ***relational model*** is a series of files organized as data tables. A ***table*** consists of a matrix of columns (vertical) and rows (horizontal) into which data can be placed.

The example in Figure 12.5 contains the type of information that would be used for airline reservations. The table is divided into a series of columns that represent data fields and rows that represent records.

To implement a relational model, a series of relations or tables would be established for each of two or more sets of data. To support airline reservations, for example, relations would be established for each flight, each aircraft, maintenance histories, flight crews, and so on. Other tables would index the contents of these multiple relations.

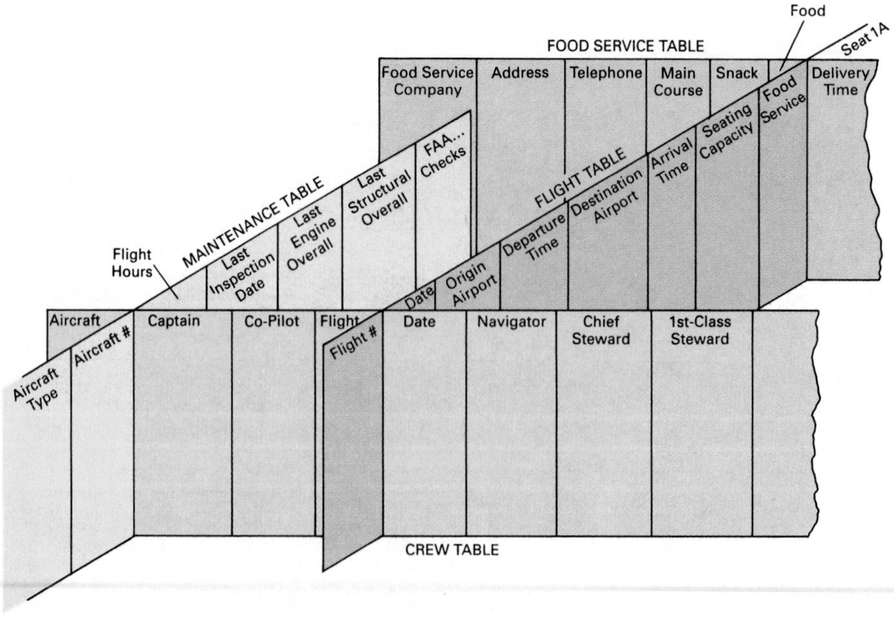

FIGURE 12.5

Relational models access information by intersecting related database tables through common fields.

WHY OS/2?

On April 2, 1987, IBM announced a whole slew of new hardware and software. DOS 5.0 was finally announced, and it was called OS/2.

The attractive features of OS/2 are concurrent multitasking, access to larger memory, a graphics user interface, an improved local area network manager, legal terminate-and-stay-resident programs, better harmony among programs, a rich system interface, compatibility with many familiar DOS commands, and, with the Presentation Manager, a device-independent platform.

Still, concerns remain. Some say OS/2 costs too much and takes too much memory. So many users ask themselves: Should I bother? Sure, OS/2 has some powerful features, but how many programs will actually run under it, and how many of those will take full advantage of its capabilities? If only a few programs run under OS/2, or if they run only through the DOS-compatibility box, why not just stick with MS-DOS?

The programmer who wants to explore OS/2 will find plenty to learn, discover, and invent in this new environment. OS/2 has a tremendous amount of power and flexibility that we are all learning to use. Over time, we'll discover more sophisticated things to do with it, from which users and programmers alike stand to benefit.

Database Management Systems

Databases are constructed and managed through use of special software programs known as database management systems (DBMS). This software provides capabilities both for building databases and for accessing their contents.

The database program oversees the physical organization of files on disk, as well as input and output operations. Well-designed software enables users to add, delete, and change records efficiently. Normally, users control the database program with a series of commands known collectively as the ***data manipulation language***.

Teresa Romero is a ***database administrator*** for a university. Her duties include establishing the database, setting up the rights and responsibilities of database users, and evaluating database performance. Teresa currently is supervising the training of registrar's office personnel in the use of the data manipulation language.

By training university personnel to use the data manipulation language, Teresa is placing a great deal of control back into the end users hands. In addition, she is relieving the university's computer professionals of responsibility for maintaining the database. During the training session, Teresa explains how each command performs a critical role in the creation, maintenance, and expansion of the database.

- **Create.** The *CREATE* command allows the user to designate a structure for the database. With this command, users can form new files and establish the number and nature of fields to be included in each record (see Figure 12.6). When working with the class scheduling database, Teresa can identify who will have access to the different areas within the database as she creates it.
- **Get.** With the *GET* command, Teresa explains, the staff can work with a set of characters, such as "Mac" in "MacArthur", or a data field contained within a database record. The database program will respond by collecting and presenting the desired fields from each record in the file. For example,

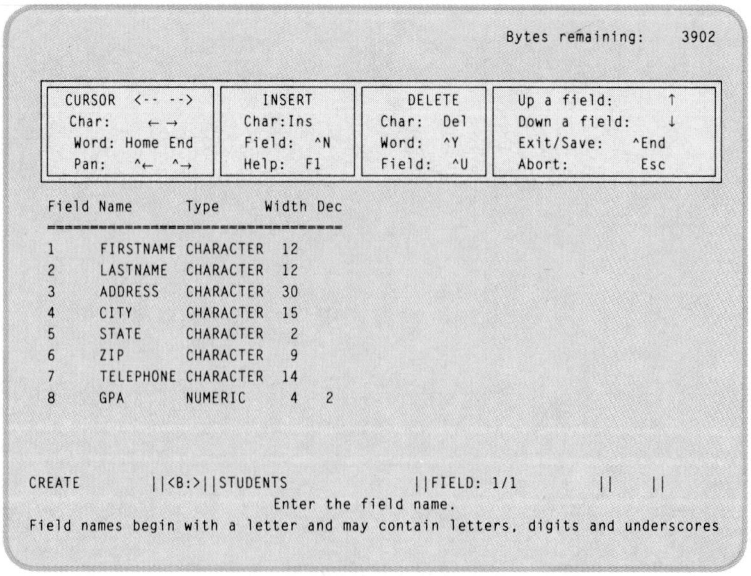

FIGURE 12.6

The CREATE command allows users to identify and describe each field of a new database.

```
Set Up Create Update Position Retrieve Organize Modify Tools    10:43:13 pm


Record#  FIRST_NAME   LAST_NAME     ADDRESS                  CITY
  STATE ZIP   TELEPHONE       GPA
      1  Robert         Castillo     112 South Broadway       Sparks
  NV    89431 (702) 358-0200 3.41
      2  Harold         Smith        885 North McCarran       Reno
  NV    89512 (702) 788-9120 2.78
      3  Judy           Davenport    555 Timber Lane          Truckee
  CA    95734 (916) 966-0722 2.43
      4  Irene          Orwell       12575 Sun Valley Blvd.   Sun Valley
  NV    89433 (702) 673-9800 3.95
      5  Jonathan       Handell      1001 East Fourth Street Reno
  NV    89501 (702) 786-0905 1.92
      6  Chico          Juarez       72 Mill Road             Floriston
  CA    96111 (916) 479-3205 3.10
      7  Sandy          O'Dell       2219 Carson Highway      Carson City
  NV    89701 (702) 234-0776 2.06
Press any key to continue. . .
ASSIST        ||<B:>||STUDENTS              ||Rec: 1/13   ||    ||
```

FIGURE 12.7

The LIST command displays the complete contents of each database.

the financial aid officer can GET a list of the students who are eligible for student loans.

- **Put.** The ***PUT*** command allows the user to load data into database storage positions defined under the CREATE function. Most database packages will provide a prompt screen showing the fields designated for the database. The registrar will be instructing the staff on the procedures for entering new student data in the appropriate positions to fill the file.
- **Update.** The staff will change data entries in records with the ***UPDATE*** command. This command is needed to keep student data current. Staff members will eventually use the UPDATE command to change a student's address or marital status, along with moving the records of students who graduate to an alumni file.
- **List.** With the ***LIST*** command, both Teresa and the registrar can examine the contents of a database, but cannot make editing changes. LIST is used only to view data. Figure 12.7 lists the complete records for all the students in the database.
- **Sort.** The ***SORT*** command places data into a sequence defined by the user. The operation is conducted through use of a ***sort key***. The sort key is part of the record and is the basis for the sort. For example, student identification number or student name would be suitable sort keys for a student master file to create class enrollment reports. The database can be sorted in a variety of ways, and it is possible to use different fields as sort keys. To prepare report cards for mailing home, for example, records in the student master file might be sorted again according to zip code.
- **Select.** Under the ***SELECT*** command, the database program can retrieve records that fit certain restrictions. The registrar might want a list of all students who have earned enough credits to graduate (see Figure 12.8). Using the earned credits field as a key, the database program would SELECT all records that fit the criteria and copy them to a new file.
- **Project.** The ***PROJECT*** command is used to create an abbreviated version of an existing database file. In a relational database, certain columns of a data table are copied, or projected, into a new table. In Figure 12.9, data for students with a GPA over 3.5 can be projected into a new table.

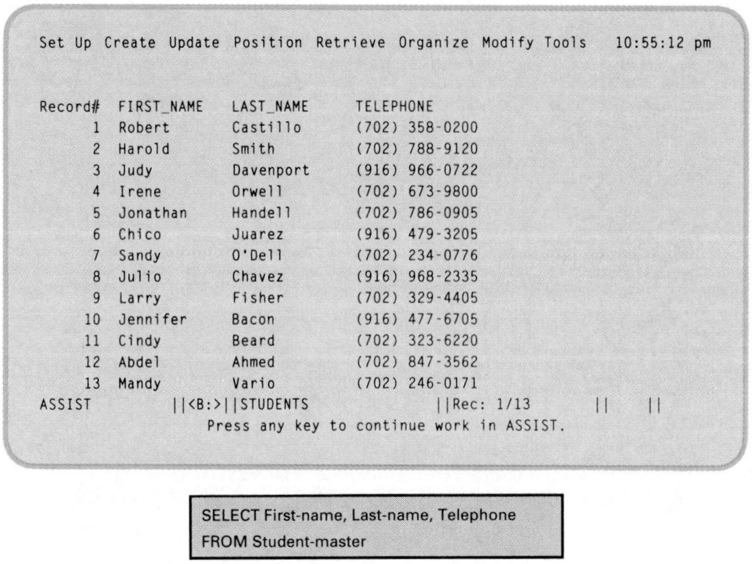

Set Up Create Update Position Retrieve Organize Modify Tools 10:55:12 pm
Record# FIRST_NAME LAST_NAME TELEPHONE
1 Robert Castillo (702) 358-0200
2 Harold Smith (702) 788-9120
3 Judy Davenport (916) 966-0722
4 Irene Orwell (702) 673-9800
5 Jonathan Handell (702) 786-0905
6 Chico Juarez (916) 479-3205
7 Sandy O'Dell (702) 234-0776
8 Julio Chavez (916) 968-2335
9 Larry Fisher (702) 329-4405
10 Jennifer Bacon (916) 477-6705
11 Cindy Beard (702) 323-6220
12 Abdel Ahmed (702) 847-3562
13 Mandy Vario (702) 246-0171
ASSIST ||<B:>||STUDENTS ||Rec: 1/13 || ||
Press any key to continue work in ASSIST.
SELECT First-name, Last-name, Telephone
FROM Student-master

FIGURE 12.8

People using the SELECT command can specify which records and fields within a database they wish to examine.

- **Join.** Portions of multiple files can be brought together into a single file through use of the ***JOIN*** command. In Figure 12.10, a file used to produce grade reports includes elements from a student master file and grade data from a class file, joined together.
- **Subtract.** Relational database programs have a ***SUBTRACT*** command that compares two tables and creates a third table containing the uncommon elements. Figure 12.11 illustrates how the table of student grades is subtracted from the semester's master class table. The resulting table contains all students for whom grades have not been reported.

With these commands, the registrar's staff can create, load data into, and modify the content of a database to support processing and inquiry capabilities.

Database Tools

One of the capabilities a database program provides, without requiring any special effort on the part of the user, is an access path to any record or data element within the database. The program creates its own relationships on the basis of descriptive entries by the user. The organization plan, or road map, that people use to conceptualize the logical view of a database is called a ***schema***. With a schema in place, users can determine if the data they need are contained within the database. The software then searches and delivers the specified items using the hierarchical, network, or relational model that is the physical layout (or view) of the database.

For each application, the database program uses a specific model to organize data and indexes. At the application level, people use a schema to identify data maintained by the database program. Very large databases with confidential information often restrict user access to selected areas on a need-to-know basis. The database administrator determines what data users have access to by assigning passwords.

People using password-oriented databases rely on subschemas to access their assigned area. The ***subschema*** provides a detailed description of the database subset available to a particular user or application program. In the univer-

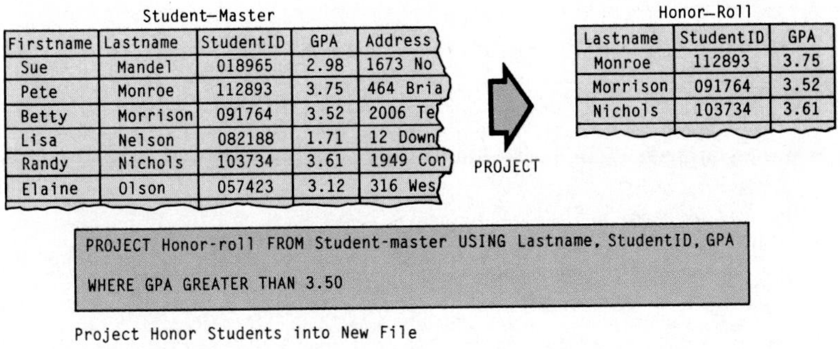
Student–Master
Firstname | Lastname | StudentID | GPA | Address
Sue | Mandel | 018965 | 2.98 | 1673 No
Pete | Monroe | 112893 | 3.75 | 464 Bria
Betty | Morrison | 091764 | 3.52 | 2006 Te
Lisa | Nelson | 082188 | 1.71 | 12 Down
Randy | Nichols | 103734 | 3.61 | 1949 Con
Elaine | Olson | 057423 | 3.12 | 316 Wes
PROJECT
Honor–Roll
Lastname | StudentID | GPA
Monroe | 112893 | 3.75
Morrison | 091764 | 3.52
Nichols | 103734 | 3.61
PROJECT Honor-roll FROM Student-master USING Lastname, StudentID, GPA
WHERE GPA GREATER THAN 3.50
Project Honor Students into New File

FIGURE 12.9

The PROJECT command creates a new table by using selected data from another table.

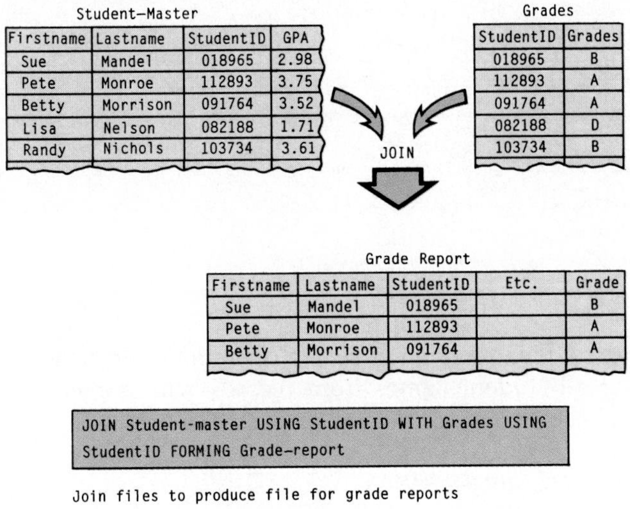
Student–Master
Firstname | Lastname | StudentID | GPA
Sue | Mandel | 018965 | 2.98
Pete | Monroe | 112893 | 3.75
Betty | Morrison | 091764 | 3.52
Lisa | Nelson | 082188 | 1.71
Randy | Nichols | 103734 | 3.61
Grades
StudentID | Grades
018965 | B
112893 | A
091764 | A
082188 | D
103734 | B
JOIN
Grade Report
Firstname | Lastname | StudentID | Etc. | Grade
Sue | Mandel | 018965 | | B
Pete | Monroe | 112893 | | A
Betty | Morrison | 091764 | | A
JOIN Student-master USING StudentID WITH Grades USING
StudentID FORMING Grade-report
Join files to produce file for grade reports

FIGURE 12.10

JOIN brings together data from two separate databases.

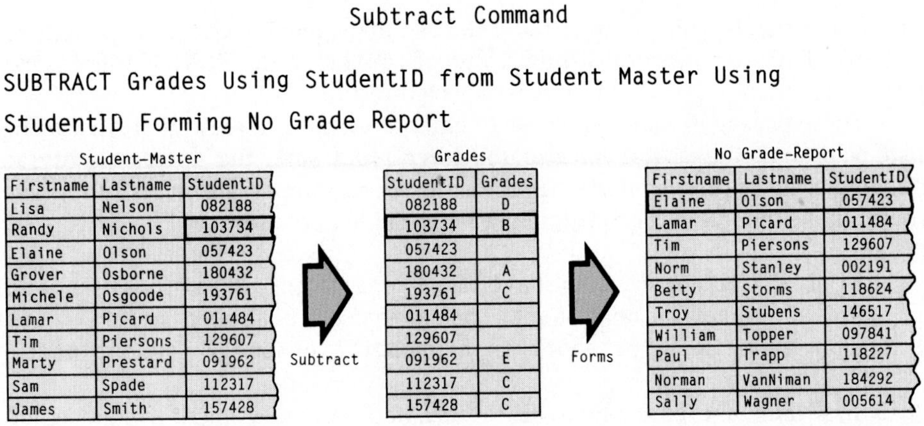
Subtract Command
SUBTRACT Grades Using StudentID from Student Master Using
StudentID Forming No Grade Report
Student–Master
Firstname | Lastname | StudentID
Lisa | Nelson | 082188
Randy | Nichols | 103734
Elaine | Olson | 057423
Grover | Osborne | 180432
Michele | Osgoode | 193761
Lamar | Picard | 011484
Tim | Piersons | 129607
Marty | Prestard | 091962
Sam | Spade | 112317
James | Smith | 157428
Subtract
Grades
StudentID | Grades
082188 | D
103734 | B
057423 |
180432 | A
193761 | C
011484 |
129607 |
091962 | E
112317 | C
157428 | C
Forms
No Grade–Report
Firstname | Lastname | StudentID
Elaine | Olson | 057423
Lamar | Picard | 011484
Tim | Piersons | 129607
Norm | Stanley | 002191
Betty | Storms | 118624
Troy | Stubens | 146517
William | Topper | 097841
Paul | Trapp | 118227
Norman | VanNiman | 184292
Sally | Wagner | 005614

FIGURE 12.11

By using the SUBTRACT command, database users can create a new table from the uncommon elements of two other tables.

sity database, the counselor's subschema would allow access to student addresses and GPAs, but not to billing data.

Database Inquiry

In addition, some database packages simplify the process of retrieving data by providing a ***query language***, a set of high-level commands or menu options that

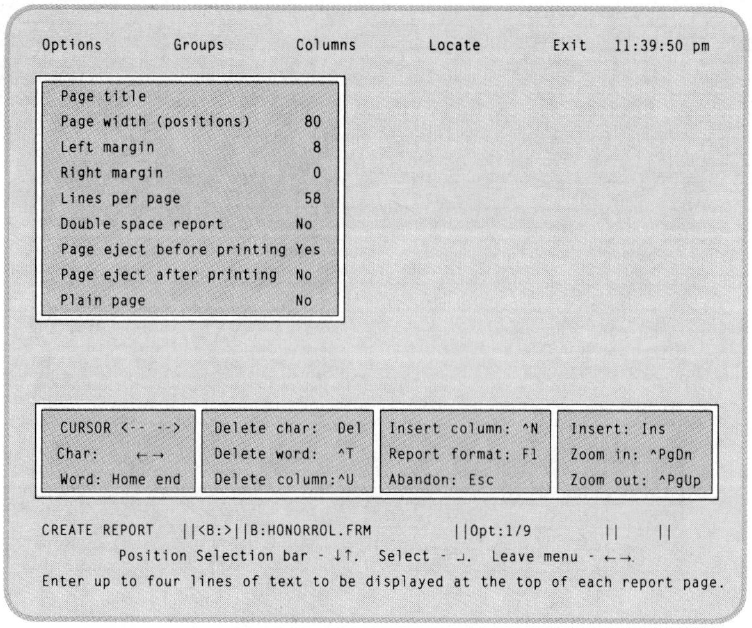

FIGURE 12.12

Report writers help users create hardcopy documents containing database data, totals, and averages.

format and control the execution of search operations. For example, a user who wishes to print all student names from records with a specific zip code field might enter:

```
SELECT      STUDENT_NAME
FROM        STUDENT
WHERE       ZIPCODE = 49442
```

These commands would direct the database management system to search the STUDENT file for records with the value of "49442" in the ZIPCODE field, then print the student names held in those selected records.

Some packages enable the user to enter a retrieval request in ordinary English. Through the use of ***natural language processors***, the database program deciphers the request to initiate processing. For example, a university registrar might make the following natural language (English) request:

```
Find all students who have an overall grade point average of
3.5 or more.  Then, sort the names by academic major.  List
entries in each category in alphabetic order by student name.
```

A natural language processor within the database management system would translate this request into computer-readable commands.

Report Writers

Every database package should be equipped with capabilities to output data. Often, these come in the form of a ***report writer***. With a report writer, users can design a hard copy printout of processing results. Typically, report writers allow users to establish headings, footings, margin widths, page lengths, and line spacing (see Figure 12.12). Additional report writer capabilities include arranging fields and making calculations used for subtotals, totals, and averages.

Pros and Cons to Database Processing

Pros
1. Allows users easy cross-referencing of related data items
2. Promotes data integrity by eliminating data redundancy
3. Once in place, reduces cost of new applications
4. Reduces time to develop new applications

Cons
1. Users need expertise with application and database design
2. Expensive to develop from scratch
3. Vulnerable to crashes

FIGURE 12.13

When properly designed, databases can grow as user needs grow while providing them with easy access to a wide range of related information.

Pros and Cons of Database Processing

A database can be difficult and expensive to create. The work, expertise, and cost of setting one up and maintaining it are its main drawbacks. Before an organization undertakes to build a database, the potential advantages should be weighed against the costs.

The main advantage offered by a database is, perhaps, reduction in the cost of developing new applications. Procedures for the creation of new computer applications are covered in a later chapter. At this point, the important factors are to first recognize that application development can be time-consuming and costly. The second factor is that most of the cost of application development lies in writing special programs to build, maintain, and access those files. If a database and a workable query language are in place, most of the costs of file design and file access programs are eliminated.

Another important advantage of a database is the fact that it eliminates data redundancy. When each application is supported by its own files, it is inevitable that some data content will be duplicated. This means procedures must be established so all occurrences of a data item are updated with each transaction that affects the item. As mentioned earlier, when a bank's customer moves, the address must be updated in savings, checking, and loan files. This adds cost and complexity to computer operations. Any failure to update a data item reduces the reliability of an organization's computer resources. However, if the bank uses a database, the address needs to be changed only once.

In the days when most databases had to be programmed entirely from scratch, costs could be difficult to justify. Today, literally scores of application packages built around databases are available. These packaged applications reduce costs and efforts, making databases practical for most computer users, whether the hardware involved is a microcomputer or a mainframe.

STUDY QUESTIONS

1. Define file management system, data model, table, sort key, schema, and subschema.
2. How is a database management system different from a file management system?

3. Describe the important features of hierarchical, network, and relational database models.
4. What are three responsibilities of a database administrator?
5. How do a database program's data manipulation language, query language, natural language processor, and report writer work?
6. Explain the function of the create, get, put, update, list, sort, select, project, join, and subtract commands.
7. How is a database schema different from the data model?
8. What are four advantages to using a database, and what are three potential disadvantages?

DATABASE SOFTWARE AS A TOOL

Databases can be designed to meet needs in almost every field. The following sections review some of the most prominent uses for databases and database management systems.

Education

Some databases work behind the scene to help teachers and administrators keep student records up to date. Schools, from elementary to college level, maintain databases to keep track of business functions, as well as academic records. Databases for inventory and payroll might be used to keep the institution functioning efficiently.

Teachers can use database programs on small computers to store student grades and test questions. Test generating software can select problems and assignments at random from a database of questions or teachers can pick specific questions. Along with the test, the software can develop matching answer keys. Thus, a teacher equipped with a database is able to vary test materials with ease. In addition, database software allows teachers to track individual student progress through course materials. By integrating test results with course objectives, database software can create individualized feedback sheets for students. These sheets will identify study materials to review based on test results.

Counselors use computers to help students determine occupational and academic preferences. Large databases hold volumes of information about education and experience requirements for a variety of jobs. By tying into these databases, counselors can direct students to careers that match their skills and goals. If a student decides to pursue a further educational degree, another database can help locate scholarship and loan programs.

FIGURE 12.14

Classroom access to large databases offers students the opportunity to ask esoteric questions and receive answers immediately.

Medicine

At many hospitals and clinics, computers decrease the time doctors and other professionals often spend in taking patient information and health histories. Patients work at computer terminals. They provide information under prompting from the computer. These entries are incorporated into a patient history database, which enables a medical professional to spend more time with patients and less time on writing information into history files.

Pharmacies uses computers to keep track of drug dispensing activities. Prescription records entered into computers can be found quickly for responses to

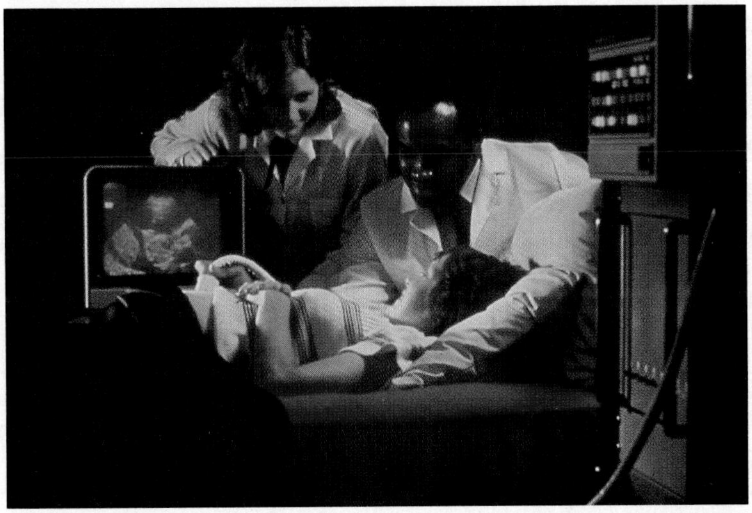

FIGURE 12.15
Medical diagnoses often use database files to help analyze patient symptoms.

inquiries or for refilling prescriptions. In addition, some databases contain information that helps pharmacists spot potential problems with interactions between newly prescribed drugs and older medications.

Public health officials use databases to store and analyze data concerning new diseases and to monitor potential epidemics. Researchers at the Centers for Disease Control, for example, collect data from medical specialists around the country. With the help of database programs, the researchers can keep current on health dangers and suggested treatments.

Another use for databases in public health is the nationwide Poison Control Center. A database at the center contains information on poisons and their antidotes. Many household products, such as cleaners and medicines, are found in this database. A database program's ability to cross-reference information allows it to access antidotes based on the brand name or contents of a product. Using data communication, an emergency center in any state can call the poison center.

Law

Police officers, FBI agents, legal secretaries, attorneys, and judges all use databases in performing their jobs. Some databases store a vast amount of data about criminal, civil, and contract law. One of the largest law enforcement databases is run by the FBI's National Crime Information Center (NCIC). The NCIC database stores data on crimes, criminals, victims, and stolen properties. State law enforcement agencies can query the NCIC system whenever they need information. They also can add data to the system. Criminal information can be shared by officers and court officials throughout the country.

FIGURE 12.16
Access by police officers to online databases provides immediate access to "wants and warrants," which helps them prepare and protect themselves.

Some police officers access databases from their patrol cars. A car license can be entered as a key field. The officer enters queries to determine if the car and/or its owner are listed in databases that keep track of "hot cars" or "wants and warrants." Responses to the queries tell an officer whether to expect danger in connection with an arrest or an approach to a suspect.

Courts use databases to help judges, legal secretaries, and clerks perform their jobs. The text of a state and/or municipal legal code can be stored in a database and searched for legal precedents or references. Case information and court decisions also are retained in online databases.

Agriculture

Farmers use databases to keep livestock records. Original costs, identification, maintenance costs, births, losses due to death, and selling prices are data fields contained in a record assigned to each animal. A database management system maintains individual records of animals and organizes this information for many uses. For example, a farmer might wish to compare original costs with selling prices for all livestock during a specified period. By identifying a few key fields, the farmer can instruct a database program to locate and display the desired information quickly and easily.

Farmers keep special records on livestock and poultry breeding. The records contain genealogies over multiple generations. These data, in turn, help scientists and farmers to breed desirable traits into herds or flocks. Examples include milk yield from dairy cows, rapid growth in chickens, large breasts in turkeys, and other characteristics.

Some breeding cooperatives have database programs to track selected breeds of livestock. Data files on thoroughbred horses, beef and dairy cattle, and other livestock make up different databases.

FIGURE 12.17

Library services are supported by database programs that control borrower records and lending activities, and perform reference searches.

Libraries

Databases have found their way into libraries with ***reference searches***. Here computers can search through large databases composed of titles, authors, and subject descriptions by looking for keywords. For example, several library services allow students to search a database for any book or article containing the words "computer-assisted instruction" in the title.

Hundreds of hours in research time can be saved by having the computer do the initial search through the literature. Although this service is expensive, it can be justified if the right keywords are used. On the other hand, someone doing a report on computer literacy who uses just the keyword "computer" will be no better off than before. The books and articles containing that keyword would fill a small library.

STUDY QUESTIONS

9. Define reference search.
10. How do school administrators, teachers, and counselors use database programs?
11. In what ways can access to a database help doctors, pharmacists, and public health officials?
12. Explain how police officers, FBI agents, legal secretaries, and law clerks utilize database programs to perform their jobs.
13. What types of data are stored in a database used by farmers and livestock breeders?
14. How could the use of a reference search help you in school?

HOW TO SELECT DATABASE PACKAGES

The first step in selecting any new software is to list its potential uses. Care must be taken not only to include present needs but to anticipate expansions or addi-

Selecting a Database

1. **Basic requirements**
   1. Necessary hardware
   2. Minimum memory
   3. Maximum database size
      - largest number of fields
      - largest number of characters/fields
   4. Operating speed
      - sorting values
      - generating reports
      - answering queries
   5. Flexibility in handling data operations
   6. User-friendly
      - help screens
      - quick reference sheets
      - tutorials
      - well-written user manuals

2. **Additional Features**
   1. Security
   2. Ability to handle several users at one time
   3. Ability to work on a network
   4. Applications generators
   5. Compiler programs

FIGURE 12.18

Personal database programs are affordable and very useful when time is taken to identify needs and basic requirements.

tional applications. At this point the search focuses on two major aspects of the database package: Basic database requirements and additional features.

Basic Database Requirements

The flexibility and capacity of a database are related directly to the type of storage and the amount of memory that it requires. Most database programs assume the use of one or more disk drives. This could be floppy or hard disk drives, depending on the computer.

All database programs require a substantial amount of memory. Even small database programs for microcomputers assume a minimum memory of 256K. The requirements for storage and memory will dictate the type of computer systems available for use with a specific database package.

In addition, users should compare database programs by examining their user friendliness and the size restrictions for each. Well-written manuals, one-page reference sheets listing command syntax, online tutorials, and help screens make software easier to use.

Restrictions imposed by a database program will include the maximum number of fields in a record and the maximum number of characters that each field can contain. Sometimes limits to the size of a database can be overcome by breaking down large amounts of data into several smaller databases that can be interrelated at a later time.

Also of concern to users is the speed at which the database program operates. Quite often potential buyers can evaluate databases by comparing the speeds at which fields are sorted, reports are generated, or a specific query is answered. The flexibility in handling data operations is also important. Potential users should take great care to examine the case with which data can be updated and the number of steps required to do so.

Additional Database Features

Depending on the application, users could be interested in one or more special features offered by different database management systems. Applications used by many people may require passwords and other security options. Some database programs even are designed to handle multiple users at the same time. Others can be linked to networks for data communication.

Since databases are difficult to design, many database packages offer special applications generators that help users develop new database systems. When speed is of primary concern, a compiler program can translate database commands into ready-to-use machine-language code. These translated instructions provide users with the fastest possible operating conditions. Since not everyone needs all these features, users must weigh the cost of additional options against their usefulness.

STUDY QUESTIONS

15. What are the six basic requirements users should examine when selecting database software?
16. Name five optional features that are available with selected database management programs.

INTEGRATED SOFTWARE AS A TOOL

In this unit we have examined some of the most common and popular types of personal productivity software. The need for users to have easy access to word processing, spreadsheet, graphics, and database packages and the ability to shift between these applications created a demand for integrated software. Data are the thread that ties integrated software together.

Two levels of integrated software have emerged. The first level, file-sharing software, cuts down the time and steps necessary in bridging from one application to another. The user can switch from a current application to access files created under different software. For example, an executive preparing a memo may want to include a graphic illustration or a numeric table from a spreadsheet package. With file-sharing software, the computer can locate desired files and integrate them into the memo. This capability makes it unnecessary to rekey entries that exist in other files. It is relatively simple to include spreadsheets or graphics in a word processing document.

The second level of software integration uses windowing techniques to display on the screen more than one application at a time (see Figure 12.19). If the user wishes to switch from one window to another, the windowing software marks the point at which one application is exited and another accessed. When

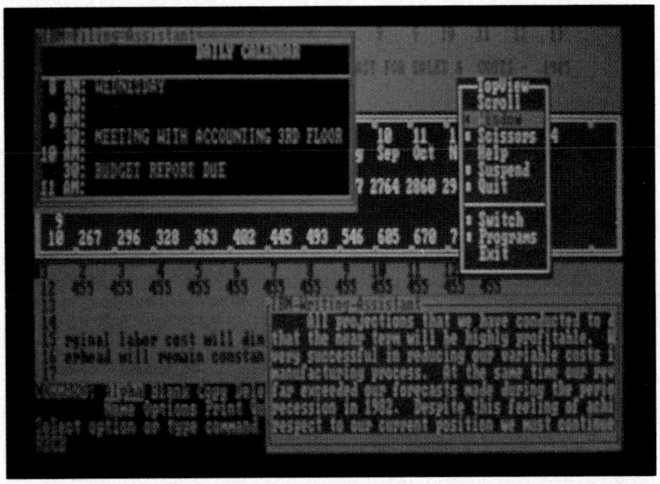

FIGURE 12.19

Integrated software with windowing capabilities supports direct, immediate access to multiple program and/or files.

the user is through with the second application, the system returns to the initial window in the same place where the user left. The user also can explore other applications before returning to the starting point.

Integrated software can meet a wide variety of user needs and demands. The most popular packages are tailored to the requirements of writers, publishers, businesspeople, and scientists. The following sections review these requirements and describe how they are fulfilled by integrated software.

Writers

It is not uncommon to find word processing software integrated with other software that helps writers. Once a document has been written, the word processing program gives way to a spelling checker or other software at the command of the user. Besides noting misspelled words, these programs can:

- Highlight unnecessarily long sentences and wordy phrases
- Identify split infinitives and other errors in grammar
- Point out use of passive voice
- List repetitive word usage and suggest synonyms
- Give statistical data on word and sentence length
- Analyze text, determining what grade level the reader needs in order to understand the writing
- Identify words and phrases that can be construed as sexist
- Check quotation marks, parentheses, and other punctuation

Technical writers would use a different combination of programs than creative writers. Since the programs are integrated, the writers can select only the features they feel are necessary. In addition, technical writers can take advantage of the integration of software packages through windows. Writers responsible for documenting a new software package can work with their word processing software running in one window, and the software they are writing about running in the other. By systematically walking through the new package and writing about each step, a technical writer can take maximum advantage of software integration.

INSIGHT

RX: MEDICAL EXPERTISE WITH A TOUCH OF COMPUTER TECHNOLOGY

Question: What do you get when you cross a database with the experience of a medical doctor?
Answer: A medical expert that works on Wednesday.

All kidding aside, the marriage of computer technology and medicine is profoundly impacting health care, and raising some interesting questions about personal privacy and responsibilities for medical decisions.

Medical Networks

Currently, the medical community is linking its computer systems together to help coordinate the flow of research and new medical techniques among health professionals.

A National Database

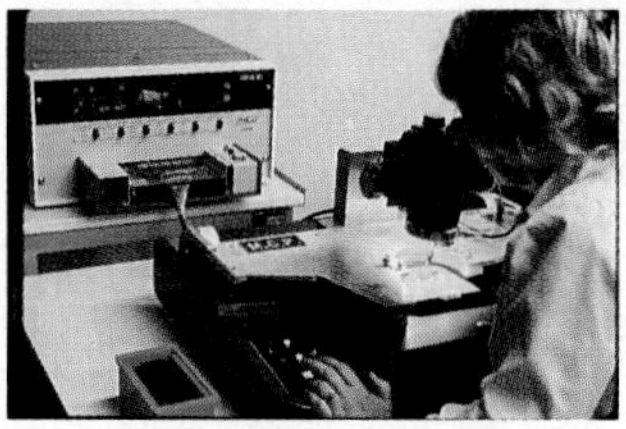

This network combined with powerful mainframes and sophisticated database management software may eventually evolve into a national health care database.

A health care database will support the location of organ donors and blood donors, and help spot potential epidemics in time to control them.

Diagnostic Software

Doctors and nurses at smaller community hospitals and clinics can use the network to access diagnostic software and medical experts located at large hospitals miles away. By linking their microcomputer to the network, health professionals can enter a patient's medical history and symptoms for aid in identifying proper treatment programs.

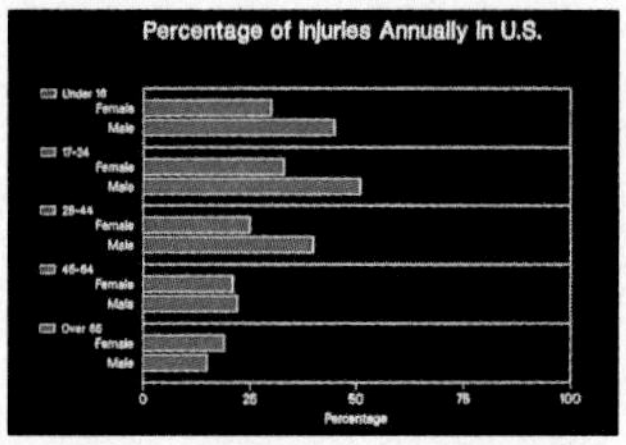

Medical Research

Medical research will also benefit from timely information from the health care database. During national emergencies, such information could save thousands of lives. Furthermore, the surgeon general and other medical authorities can use data gathered from around the country to monitor the public's health by watching for dangerous trends.

What's Next?

However, before a national health care database and network can become a reality these questions and others must be addressed:

Q: Who should have access to this system?

Q: Who will verify the accuracy of a new research finding or medical technique before it becomes part of the database?

Q: Who "owns" and is responsible for the data once they become part of the database?

Q: Do people have the right to withhold information? Does it matter if they have an infectious disease?

Q: With pieces of this new network and database evolving at different locations across the country, who will develop the common medical language necessary for accessing information?

FIGURE 12.20

Desktop publishing allows users to work with inexpensive microcomputer systems to create brochures and newsletters.

Desktop Publishers

Recently, electronic publishing software has been developed for use on microcomputers. These systems are known as ***desktop publishing***. Desktop publishing software is used to integrate text, tables, and images prepared under various personal productivity software into full-page layouts. This is done through use of digitizing techniques.

Free-drawing graphics software creates logos, chapter openers, and other designs that are incorporated into pages made up on the screen. Finished graphic pages for newsletters, magazines, catalogs, and other publications can be reproduced on high-quality laser printers. Desktop publishing has provided an inexpensive means whereby schools, clubs, churches, and volunteer organizations can create newsletters and other mailers.

It is also possible to use data communication software to transfer graphics images and page layouts created by microcomputers directly on electronic typesetting machines for commercial-quality results in publishing. The professional equivalent to the integration of publishing and data communications software is found with mainframe-based computer graphics programs. These programs combine stories and illustrations into electronic composites of newspaper pages. The *Wall Street Journal* and *USA Today* use data communication techniques to transmit digitized files to printing plants across the country. Each plant prints and distributes papers for its own region. These integrated publishing systems deliver millions of copies of the *Wall Street Journal* and *USA Today* to readers every day.

Of course, microcomputer systems are slower and have fewer capabilities than mainframe publishing techniques. However, many local publications, newsletters, and magazines now are created through use of these integrated tools.

Businesspeople

Integrated software in the business office has proved to be invaluable to managers and executives. A single piece of data can be:

- Stored and processed in a database
- Organized for analysis in an electronic spreadsheet
- Illustrated by a pie chart, bar graph, or line graph
- Described in a text report created on a word processor
- Sent to colleagues in the next building or around the world

FIGURE 12.21

Professional publishers integrate word processing, layout, and data communication software to produce daily newspapers for transmission and printing at regional sites.

Businesspeople often need to coordinate several of these computer capabilities to complete a single project. This task can prove to be laborious with separate programs that are not designed to be intercoordinated. With an integrated package, the manager has one software resource that meets all business needs instead of several, scattered, incompatible programs.

Scientists

There are as many different types of scientists as there are sciences. But one characteristic biologists, chemists, nuclear physicists, astronomers, and other scientists have in common is a need for integrated software. This software is particularly useful for research projects. Finding background material related to a project can be a big job in itself. Computers can be used to scan large databases

FIGURE 12.22

Online card catalogs use databases to help children quickly identify important references in class.

for relevant material. Scientists, like students, can save hundreds of hours by having the computer do the initial search.

For example, scientists interested in volcanic activity in the Pacific Ocean would have to research past activity in the area. Using a reference search and database program, they could call up and store historical data about the Pacific. By using integrated database and word processing software, these references could become part of a research proposal without having to be retyped.

Scientists collecting data often have a special need to integrate data from monitors or experimental apparatus with database programs. The ability of a database management system to organize and access large volumes of data helps researchers analyze their results. Integrated statistical packages are designed to help in this data analysis. Furthermore, research projects spread over large geographic areas can employ data communication software to share results and to coordinate project activities.

When the work is complete, scientists use word processing software to write and edit a research report or journal article. These documents are enhanced by using charts, graphs, and diagrams of the data generated through integrated graphics programs. If the paper is published, it becomes part of a library database. The use of integrated software has now come full circle, as other scientists reference this research for their own work.

STUDY QUESTIONS

17. Define desktop publishing.
18. Describe two levels of integrated software.
19. What are nine applications that can be integrated with word processing software?
20. How does desktop publishing integrate data?
21. What types of software usually are integrated together for business applications?
22. How would a scientist use integrated software as part of a research project?

CONCLUSION

Users can produce professional quality documents when they integrate database programs with other software packages. Database programs are one of the most powerful types of personal productivity packages. This software enables users to organize and manipulate large volumes of data without the problems associated with regular data files. Data duplication is eliminated, reentry of data is reduced, and there exists a centralized location for all data related to an organization.

By choosing specific integrated software packages, users can tailor their computing needs. Data shared among packages saves time, increases the quality of documents, and makes data accessible to a wider variety of people. This is just one example of how informed and sophisticated users have influenced the software market by demanding more from the products they use.

CHAPTER FACTS

- A database is an organization of data and their relationships. A data model reflects how the computer sees the organization of data while a schema represents the human perspective.
- Databases can be organized into one of three models: hierarchical, network, or relational.
- Database programs are used to organize and access the data. They include translators for a data manipulation language, query language, natural language, and report writer.
- A data manipulation language allows the user to control database files through commands such as CREATE, GET, PUT, UPDATE, LIST, SORT, SELECT, PROJECT, JOIN, and SUBTRACT.
- A query language uses preset commands to let users select subsets of the database.
- A natural language processor translates commands in English into computer-readable instructions.
- A report writer allows the user to specify the format for hard copy output from the database.
- Databases reduce time and costs for developing new applications while eliminating data redundancy. They are expensive and difficult to set up.
- Database programs are useful in many areas, including education, medicine and public health, law, agriculture, and library reference systems.
- Integrated software allows easy shifting from one program to another without reentering data. Some integrated software uses windowing to let users work on more than one application program at a time.
- Integrated software can include word processors, graphics programs, spreadsheets, database programs, data communication programs, and statistical packages. Applications for integrated software include writing, desktop publishing, business, and science.

TERMS TO REMEMBER

CREATE command
database administrator
data manipulation language
data model
desktop publishing
file management system
GET command
hierarchical model
JOIN command
LIST command
natural language processor
network model
PROJECT command
PUT command
query language
reference search
relational model
report writer
schema
SELECT command
SORT command
sort key
subschema
SUBTRACT command
table
UPDATE command

CHECK YOUR UNDERSTANDING

1. A data model is the plan used by a computer to store and access data in a database. (True/False)
2. Which of the following is *not* an advantage to using a database?
   a. New applications are less costly to develop.
   b. Data for new applications may already be in a database.
   c. Files and records can be cross-referenced through software.
   d. New applications take less time to develop.
   e. All are advantages to using a database.
3. In a(n) ___________ model of a database, data items can be accessed only in top-down order.
4. In a(n) ___________ model of a database, data items are organized into tables of records and fields.
5. Desktop publishing software can integrate text with graphics. (True/False)
6. A(n) ___________ is the organizational plan people use to conceptualize a database.
7. Which of the following takes instructions written in regular English and translates them into computer-readable code?
   a. language compiler
   b. data manipulation language translator
   c. natural language processor
   d. query language interpreter
   e. none of the above
8. With a report writer, users can dictate the format of output from their word processors. (True/False)
9. When a(n) ___________ is used, a student or scientist can retrieve articles and books from a library that contain certain keywords in the title.
10. Some integrated software requires users to reenter parts of data from other programs. (True/False)

APPLYING WHAT YOU'VE LEARNED

1. Use one of the database models described in the text to organize the data that would be needed in one of these applications. Make a general diagram of the data relationships as shown in the text.
   a. recording rentals in a video rental shop
   b. accessing a student database by student number, name, or major
   c. sending advertising to credit card customers based on the type of purchases they make
   d. setting up a reference search system in a library
2. Several database programs exist for use on microcomputers. Information about them can be obtained from computer magazines and retail stores. Investigate one of these programs. Report on the commands it includes, type of model (if known) it uses, its memory requirements, how much data it can hold, and its cost. Find out if classes or tutorials are available to train users.
3. Write a natural language command that would produce the following data:
   a. list of drivers with expired licenses
   b. list of voters who voted in the last local election
   c. list of library patrons with overdue books
   d. names of salespeople who earned more than $1000 in commissions last month
   e. list of employees within a year of retirement
4. The use of the proper keywords is necessary for efficient reference searches. If too general a term is used, too many references appear. Very specific terms (like a person's name) might not appear in a title. What keywords would you use in a reference search if you had to write term papers on these subjects?
   a. opera composers of the 18th century
   b. animals living above the latitude of the Arctic Circle
   c. World Series games before 1950
   d. the newest developments in solar energy for the home
   e. advertising and marketing techniques used in Western Europe
5. Try out a database program by entering a small amount of data into a database and use the SELECT command to choose a subset of the data. Print out a hard copy of the resulting data. *Note:* Many database programs include tutorials that let the user experiment with the features of the program using minimal data.
6. Using integrated software, print out a short word–processed file that contains output from another program. This could be numbers from a spreadsheet, a chart or drawing from a graphics program, or results of a spelling or grammar checker.
7. Investigate a desktop publishing package that could be useful to you in school, in an organization, or in a job situation. Use information from sales literature, retail store salespeople, or magazines to determine the following:
   a. What editing options does it offer?
   b. On what kinds of computers does it work?
   c. What kind of printer is required?
   d. Does it handle color graphics?
   e. Can it be used with other software packages?
   f. What special input hardware is needed?
   g. What training manuals or tutorials are included?
   h. What are the memory requirements?
   i. How much does the package cost?

CHECK YOUR UNDERSTANDING ANSWERS

1. true
2. e
3. hierarchical
4. relational
5. true
6. schema
7. c
8. false
9. reference search
10. false

UNIT FOUR

INFORMATION SYSTEMS

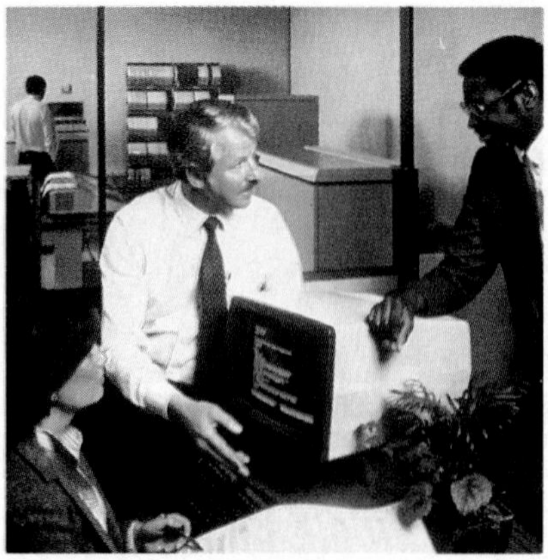

When the components of a computer system are properly combined, they promote the sharing of information and support decision making. Chapter 13 discusses how managers in any organization can sharpen their decision-making skills using knowledge derived from computer systems. Applications for management information systems and decision support systems are examined from a user's perspective. ▸ Chapter 14 highlights the potential abuses of personal privacy by organizations using computer systems. The chapter also enumerates warning signs of computer crime and helps people identify ways to use this technology while protecting their valuable computer/information resources. ▸ Careful planning must accompany the design of any computer system. In Chapter 15, a four-step life cycle for the development of computer systems is overviewed. This chapter emphasizes that users should be involved when system requirements are identified and evaluated. In addition, Chapter 15 stresses the responsibilities of the computer professionals who design system components and organize implementation strategies. ▸ An important part of the systems development life cycle revolves around the creation of computer programs. Chapter 16 details the choices computer programmers make between writing new software and modifying existing programs. Design techniques for creating new programs and several of the most common programming languages are discussed. Maintenance is presented as an ongoing operation necessary for the long life of any program and associated computer system.

C H A P T E R

T H I R T E E N

MANAGEMENT AND DECISION MAKING SYSTEMS

KEY IDEAS

- **From the user's point of view**
  As a decision maker, how can you use computer systems to analyze past performances, make decisions, solve problems, and plan for the future?
- **Management information systems**
  Computer systems provide information to help decision makers solve problems, plan, organize, direct, and control resources and people.

  People using management information systems
  Decision making occurs at every management level within an organization.

  Data for management information systems
  An organization can divide data into four general areas: financial, personnel, research, and production/sales.

  Organizing data into reports
  Effective reports—detailed, summary, and exception—are designed to reflect the types of data needed at each management level.
- **Decision support systems**
  Decision support systems are real-time computer systems that aid managers to solve problems through modeling and query-based data retrieval.

  Modeling
  Organizations use modeling—a mathematical representation of a problem—to examine the implications of alternatives before selecting the best solution.

  Data analysis using query languages
  Query languages help users answer "What if...?" questions without the assistance of computer professionals.
- **Other tools for decision makers**
  Tools such as electronic spreadsheets and graphics packages help users control and manipulate data needed for decision making.

  Electronic spreadsheets
  Spreadsheets clearly summarize and present data.

  Presentation graphics
  Computer-generated graphics illustrate financial relationships and communicate ideas or plans.

  Expert systems
  Expert systems combine artificial intelligence software with knowledge bases to help decision makers find logical solutions to problems.

FROM THE USER'S POINT OF VIEW

You will find that management is not restricted to the business world. Any organization, whether it is a large corporation, government agency, a school, a church, or a volunteer society, requires information to control resources and achieve goals. When in a position to manage others you will have to solve problems, plan, organize, direct, and control. Computers are the key to effective managerial decision making and data are the unifying factor that joins past performance with today's problems and plans for the future.

MANAGEMENT INFORMATION SYSTEMS

The data and procedures for running an organization must be current and available for making decisions. A ***management information system (MIS)*** is the network of systems, both computerized and manual, that provides information to an organization's decision makers. Every organization has an MIS whether they know it or not. The secretary with last year's employment figures is part of the MIS. So are the contents of a manager's file drawer or a database. A business's annual report, a school's graduation list, or the telephone tree for a volunteer agency are all important parts of an MIS for their respective organizations.

Look again at the definition of MIS. It is a collection of systems, but it does not necessarily include a computer. An MIS can be composed entirely of data, procedures, and personnel. Computer hardware and programs need not be involved.

Early MIS systems centered around hand-kept records. Important data were stored on ledger books, spreadsheets, and file cards. As mentioned in Chapter 2, there has been an increased demand over the years for information by the government and decision makers. The advent of computers allowed people to solve this information problem by organizing data onto card, tape, and disk files.

File processing systems were a partial solution, but using separate files made it difficult for managers to obtain related data and keep them updated. Eventually, the volumes of information were more than many file processing systems could handle. Therefore, many organizations now use database programs to integrate their data files and plot data relationships, making information more accessible.

Organizations vary in their present use of computers in MIS. Some use database programs exclusively, while others still keep data by hand. This chapter will focus on using computers as part of a management information system.

People Using Management Information Systems

Many areas of management need information to operate. Administration, counseling, engineering, accounting, manufacturing, marketing, education, personnel, public health, and sales all require the facilities of an MIS. Although the types of information needed are different for each area, the decisions have several features in common.

FIGURE 13.1
Management information systems help decision makers solve problems while planning, organizing, and controlling their organization's resources.

In general, the amount of detail included in computer-generated information varies with the scope of decision making to be supported. That is, management decisions that demand immediate attention, yet are short term in nature, require highly detailed information. Sweeping decisions that will have long-term effects on the organization usually are supported by less detailed information that covers a larger area of interest.

For example, a retail store supervisor responsible for the sports department may receive and use a detailed computer output showing the sale of every piece of equipment by model and size.

A store manager working at the next management level might want to know only the dollar value of sales for a single department, as compared with sales for the other departments, and for the store as a whole. At this level, the information is used to determine how much space to allocate to an individual department and to determine the size of its staff and the value of its stock.

At the headquarters for a chain of stores, upper-level management may require only summaries of storewide figures. The job of top managers is to monitor overall profitability. So, an executive may not know what is happen-

FIGURE 13.2

Early management information systems were manually maintained by clerks and involved tremendous amounts of paper.

ing in individual departments. In this sense, information content is far less detailed. But the scope of the information is far greater, involving perhaps hundreds of stores.

This comparison highlights the value of information as a management tool. Problem-solving tools, such as computers, must be designed to match information with the responsibilities of the individual and the decisions that he or she makes.

The example of management requirements in the department store situation identifies three levels at which management occurs and decisions are made:

- The department supervisor has responsibilities associated with the day-to-day support of transactions in a single department. Responsibility and accountability of this individual can be described as ***front-line management***. Since all of this person's attention is focused on a single organizational unit, he or she has time to digest and react to highly detailed information.
- The manager of the store would be considered part of ***middle management***. At this level, a manager is responsible for evaluating the performance of each supervisor and for making whatever changes or adjustments may be necessary to meet sales goals and to keep inventories at reasonable levels. Intermediate levels of detail are required by middle management. In the example, a store manager receives information on sales levels but does not need detailed listings of each sales transaction.
- The president and high-level decision makers of the chain are part of the organization's ***top management***, or ***executives***. At this level, few short-term decisions are made on daily operations. Instead, decisions by top management have far greater consequences. For example, executive-level people decide where and when to open new stores or to close existing outlets. Top-level executives might decide about what kinds of products and services are to be offered by the chain as a whole. For example, is it profitable for the chain to operate garden shops, automotive service centers, travel agencies, and so on? The people at this level are charged, broadly, with determining the mission of an organization. They establish the organiza-

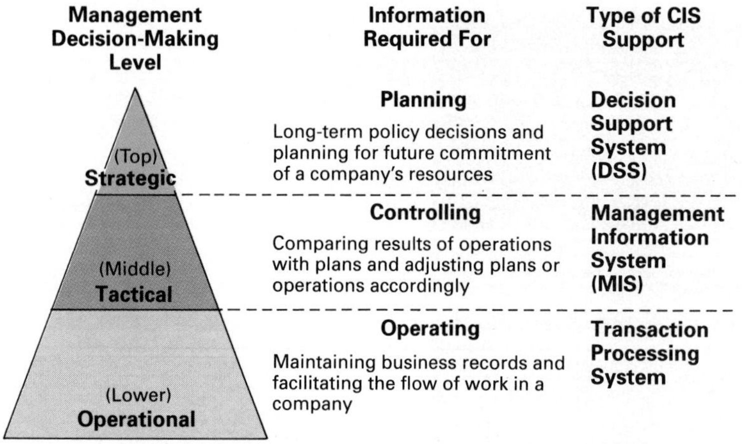
Management Decision-Making Level
Information Required For
Type of CIS Support
(Top) Strategic
Planning
Long-term policy decisions and planning for future commitment of a company's resources
Decision Support System (DSS)
(Middle) Tactical
Controlling
Comparing results of operations with plans and adjusting plans or operations accordingly
Management Information System (MIS)
(Lower) Operational
Operating
Maintaining business records and facilitating the flow of work in a company
Transaction Processing System

FIGURE 13.3

Management decision making takes place at multiple levels in an organization addressing different goals and concerns.

tional structure and provide the resources needed to fulfill that mission. These responsibilities, collectively, constitute the setting of strategy for the organization.

The specialized problems and degrees of control of the three managerial levels establish different demands for management information. These levels are depicted in Figure 13.3. At the bottom are ***operational decisions***, where detailed data are used in completing everyday tasks. As the pyramid shows, the volume of information needed for operational decisions is quite large. Day-to-day operational decisions are made by front-line managers.

Managers at the middle of the pyramid make ***tactical decisions***. Here, activities conducted at the bottom level are summarized to provide a broader scope of information. Middle management uses this information to make short-term decisions for an organization.

Strategic decisions are made at the top of the pyramid. Information produced at the lower levels is summarized and interpreted before it reaches this strategic level. Thus, strategic decisions require information that is low in volume, yet broad in scope. This type of information is used by top management to make long-term decisions with wide-ranging effects.

The main job of strategic managers is to plan what is to become of the organization. The bottom two levels implement the strategic decisions made by executives. In short, operational managers deal with today's problems, while tactical managers make decisions about this month's stock levels or next season's products. Decisions that make an impact on the whole organization such as relocating stores, shifting the marketing focus to a new audience, and modifying personnel requirements—are matters left to top management.

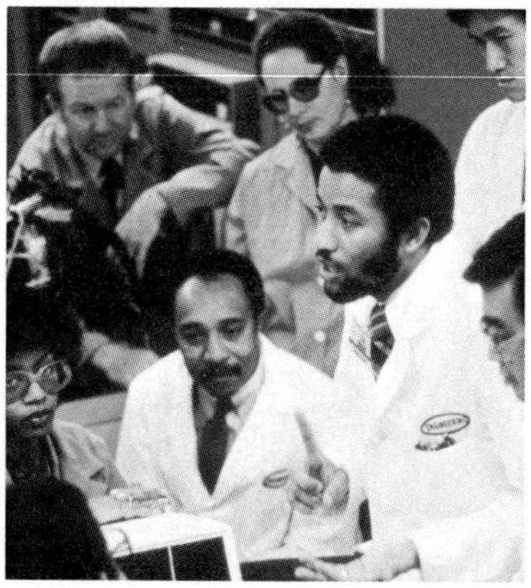

FIGURE 13.4

Many people make and carry out decisions based on data provided by management information systems.

We have examined the management levels of a department store, but similar levels exist in other areas. The management of a manufacturing plant will include a shift supervisor (front-line management), plant manager (middle management), and company president (top management). A university has faculty, department chairpeople, and deans to represent the three management levels. Each level may include a variety of decision makers. In a factory, front-line management will include foremen as well as shift supervisors. Top management of a university is made up of deans, board of trustees, and a president. Management information systems must be designed to support all levels of decision making.

Data for Management Information Systems

Until now, we have been discussing the management in management information systems. Of equal importance, however, is the information. Information is gathered during different parts of the transaction cycle. The ***transaction cycle*** is the input, processing, output, and storage of a single transaction. Whether the cycle involves completing a single customer order, manufacturing one car, or registering a single student, each transaction generates data for the MIS. This cycle represents the day-to-day activities of an organization and is the foundation of any MIS.

As illustrated in Figure 13.5, an organization can divide data into four general areas: Financial, personnel, research, and production/sales.

Financial data include figures about how the organization's resources translate into money. These encompass data on an organization's profit and loss, assets and liabilities, and other resources of value.

Information about employees and their productivity is included in ***personnel data***. Not only a list of employees, but figures on absenteeism and retirement may be important to management.

Analysis of past performance and plans for future projects are ***research data***. For example, stores research potential customers, volunteer agencies investigate sources of future funding, and colleges plan how to recruit certain types of students.

Production/sales data include numbers on the actual products made, products sold, or services provided. Manufacturing plants keep inventory levels and raw material orders. Organizations that are service-oriented, such as schools, churches, volunteer agencies, or travel agencies have production/sales data concerning the number of people served and how they were helped.

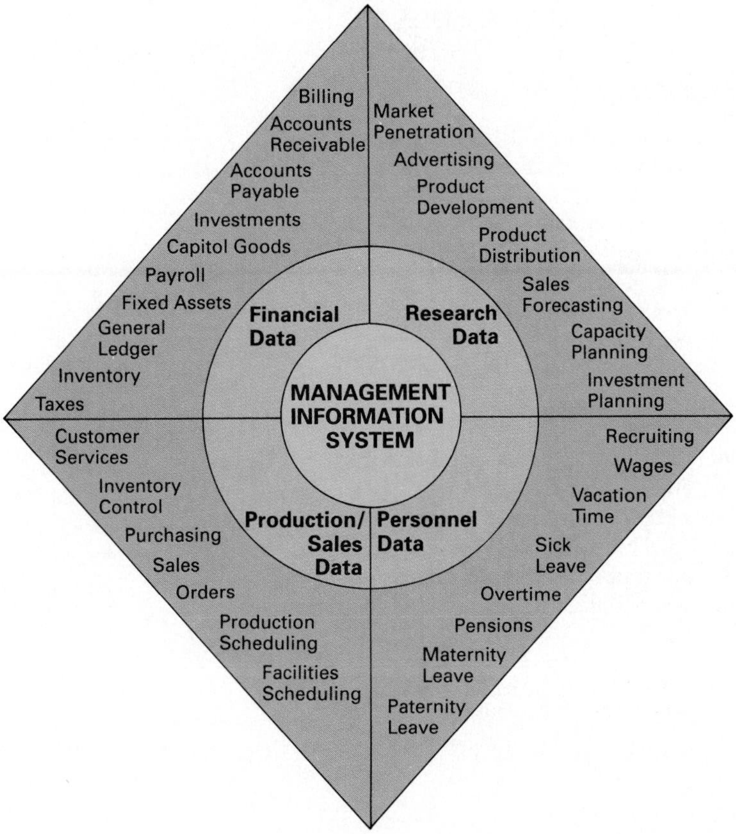

FIGURE 13.5

Data incorporated into an organization's MIS cover its finances, personnel, research, and productivity.

CLIP

WHAT EXECUTIVE INFORMATION SYSTEMS DO

Executives feed on information—in carefully controlled doses. Traditionally, company chiefs have shied away from computers, which often barrage uninitiated users with more data than they need or can easily digest. Executive information systems (EIS) try to tame this wilderness of facts and figures so it can be used to make effective business decisions.

Advanced software can arrange and display information in easy-to-understand formats for busy executives. To avoid alienating the keyboard-shy, the systems typically use a simple, direct interface such as a touchscreen, mouse, or infrared remote control.

Although their approaches and capabilities vary, many systems share a core group of features:

Exception Reporting

Executives usually don't worry about specific operations as long as everything is going according to plan. Therefore, most executive information systems graphically tag areas of the business that are somehow going astray. For example, Comshare's EIS color-codes the numbers it displays: green if they fall within an acceptable range, yellow if the number is near the edge of acceptability, and red if it falls outside that range. The executive sets the threshold of unacceptability—for instance, sales that are more than 10 percent off budget.

"Drill Down" Capability

Once the system identifies a trouble spot, it can offer successive levels of greater detail. The user merely selects the offending number to bring out the story behind the story. By going down one layer to the regional breakout, the executive might learn that a slumping product is doing well in most of the country but is bombing in New England. Boring in deeper shows that the real trouble lies in lack of promotion—the product exceeded expectations wherever distributors advertised it properly.

Graphic Summaries

To help harried executives digest the numbers flowing from a corporate database, an EIS turns them into colorful charts and graphs. Users can drill down through this graphics presentation for the raw numbers.

Electronic Mail

Executives gather much of the information they need from subordinates or other executives, often at other company operations. EIS makes it easy to log onto an electronic-mail network, saving time otherwise lost enduring meetings and playing telephone tag.

On-Line Information Service

Some EIS products link to on-line information systems. Comshare's EIS, for example, connects an executive to the Dow Jones News Wire. An EIS also can apply its graphic magic to the outside data.

Source: High Technology Business, February 1988. Reprinted with permission.

Key Question: How could the five features of an EIS be used in an organization familiar to you?

Organizing Data into Reports

The organization of data and the design of associated reports is critical to the successful use of an MIS. Effective reports are designed to reflect the types of data needed at each management level. Reports are either scheduled for routine use or produced on a demand basis. Since the problems at management levels differ, so does the presentation of information. Report formats generally fall into one of three categories: detailed, summary, and exception reports.

Detailed reports are used by front-line management to examine day-to-day operations. A teacher will use a detailed class report that lists students enrolled in a class. Each student's name and number is displayed on a separate report line.

Detailed reports usually contain one printed line for each item in the database or file. The department store supervisor will use a detailed inventory report to examine the status of each item sold in the department. The report in Figure 13.6 contains the description of items, stock on hand, stock on order, and sales. By using this report, the supervisor can make operational decisions about what stock to reorder or which merchandise to stop selling.

When large amounts of data need to be analyzed, it is not usually practical or necessary to see all of it at one time. In these situations a ***summary report*** is used. Summary reports condense day-to-day operational data into totals.

Tactical and strategic decisions can be made by comparing trends in summarized data. Summary reports that show total store sales over several years help department store executives decide when to close or expand certain stores. A university department chairperson can prepare for top management a request for additional facilities by looking at summaries of classroom and lab use (see Figure 13.7).

Exception reports, like summary reports, are the results of processing data. Comparisons are used to produce exception reports, which contain only the data that meets specified conditions.

Early warning signs of an impending problem sometimes can be seen in exception reports. The vice-president of finance for a department store chain may notice increased numbers of unpaid customer bills going to collection agencies. The information, available from an exception report that lists overdue accounts, would suggest that executives review the company's charge policy.

Page 2

TIP-TOP STORES
Detailed Inventory Report

Department: Sports Date: 8/12/8-

Number	Product Description	Stock On Hand	Stock On Order	Stock Below Reorder Point
1101	Leather Basketball	12	0	
1102	Leather Football	3	6	*
1103	8 ft. Jump Rope	24	0	
1104	12 ft. Jump Rope	19	0	
1105	Badminton Birdies	2	15	*
.	.	.	.	.
.	.	.	.	.
.	.	.	.	.

FIGURE 13.6

Detailed reports provide front-line managers with specific data needed for day-to-day decisions.

WHATSAMATTA UNIVERSITY
Summary of Facility Utilization Report
Date: November 5, 198_

Building: Haworth Hall

Hours	Classroom Utilization	Laboratory Utilization
7-8	5%	45%
8-9	60%	95%
9-10	100%	100%
10-11	100%	100%
11-12	100%	100%
12-1	96%	95%
1-2	98%	100%
2-3	83%	100%
3-4	62%	100%

FIGURE 13.7

This summary report encapsulates data relating to the utilization of dozens of rooms over several hours.

WHATSAMATTA UNIVERSITY
Gold Star Contributors
(contributions over $1000)

Name	Contribution	Alumni
Ms. Elaine Anderson	1,050	71
Mr. and Mrs Baker	2,100	67/69
Mr. Stanley Borkenstein	1,500	76
Mr. and Mrs Edward Conelly	5,000	/63
.	.	.
.	.	.
.	.	.

FIGURE 13.8

Exception reports focus attention on situations needing immediate action. In this case, each contributor could receive a personalized letter from the university president.

Exception reports can highlight both negative and positive trends. A university may produce an exception report listing the names of alumni who have contributed over $1000 (see Figure 13.8). The university president would be delighted to see that this exception report contains more large contributions than reports from previous years.

Management information is important for the successful operation of any organization. Decision makers use MIS to oversee what is happening in their organizations. However, for strategic planning, it also is necessary to anticipate what is going to happen. As a result, future problems and needs are examined with the help of decision support systems.

STUDY QUESTIONS

1. Define management information system (MIS), executive, transaction cycle, detailed report, summary report, and exception report.
2. What is the role of management in an organization?

3. How have file processing and database systems helped people to keep up with an ever-increasing demand for information?
4. What types of decisions and problems do the three levels of management handle?
5. Describe the differences between financial, personnel, research, and production/sales data.
6. What types of reports do the different levels of management need to perform their jobs?

FIGURE 13.9

Decision support systems rely on extensive information resources that must be extracted from organizational data.

DECISION SUPPORT SYSTEMS

Important decisions made in organizations may require more information than an MIS can provide. Managers are expected to make intelligent guesses on how today's conditions affect tomorrow's productivity. They can get help with this problem in two ways. First, managers can use query languages to access relevant data from an MIS database. Second, computer professionals help managers create a ***model***, or mathematical representation of the problem. When these elements are brought together to aid in long-range planning, they become the foundations of a decision support system. A ***decision support system (DSS)*** is a real-time computer system that helps managers solve problems through query language–based data retrieval and modeling.

Modeling

In any organizational decision, there are forces that work against each other. A department store may wish to maximize profits by expanding services but is faced with increased costs for labor, construction, and maintenance. Another alternative is to raise prices, but managers know that when prices are raised too high, customers will shop elsewhere. How can managers account for all the interactions, examine all possible alternatives, and still arrive at the best solution? One way is to use a DSS to perform modeling.

For example, the executive who is considering automotive centers for a chain of department stores must look at many factors that will affect the profitability of these centers:

- Does each store already own the land needed to support an automotive center?
- What facilities are needed in the way of buildings, parking, access from busy streets, and so on?
- How much does the average customer spend on a typical visit to an automotive service center?
- What services should be offered at the centers: Self- or full-service gasoline? Brake and muffler service? 24-hour towing?
- How many customers must be served each month for a service center to break even?
- How much money must be invested in equipment and inventory for each center?
- Are there enough trained technicians in the area to staff the centers?

This situation illustrates the fact that there is too much information for one person to process mentally. Detailed records could be accumulated and organized manually, but this could be a lot of work and take too much time. As a result, computer models are used to assist with this type of complex problem solving.

One type of modeling that evaluates a variety of complex factors is called ***linear programming***. Linear programming is a method of finding an optimum

LINEAR PROGRAMMING MODEL:
Profitability of Auto Service Centers

Goal: To maximize service center profits, given realistic expectations of revenue and cost constraints for capital outlay, labor, inventory, etc..

Question: Which individual services will contribute most to profitability?

Some model variables:

x_i = activities associated with service center
- x_1 = gas, x_2 = auto parts,
- x_3 = brakes, x_4 = mufflers, etc.

p_i = profits associated with activity x_i
c_i = capital outlay required for x_i
l_i = first year labor costs for x_i
n_i = start up inventory costs for x_i
r_i = expected revenues for x_i
a_i = advertising budget for x_i
.
.
.

Model:	maximize Σp_i	(profit for all services)
Given:	$\Sigma a_ix_i \leq 23000$	(total advertising budegt is $23,000)
constraints showing	$l_1x_1 > 12500$	(estimated labor for gas service is over $12,500)
estimates of costs	$l_3x_3 = .81l_4x_4$	(labor costs for brake dept. 81% of costs)
for each item	$180000 \leq n_2x_2 \leq 200000$	(auto parts inventory is $180,000 to $200,000)
	$c_3x_3 + c_4x_4 > 75000$	(brake and muffler shops set up costs are over $75,000)
	. . .	

show actual make up of profit for each service

$p_2 = r_2x_2 + .10c_2x_2 - l_2x_2 - a_2x_2 - .63n_2x_2 \ldots$

↑ depreciation (for $.10c_2x_2$); ↑ auto part inventory turn around (for $.63n_2x_2$)

$p_3 = r_3x_3 - .81l_4x_4 - a_3x_3 - \ldots$

↑ share labor costs with muffler shop (for $.81l_4x_4$)

FIGURE 13.10
This linear program is used to model the cost associated with opening an automotive service center.

solution for a problem by representing each condition or constraint as a mathematical equation (see Figure 13.10). Since many linear models involve a series of complex equations, computers are used for accuracy and to speed up processing. Sometimes, opposing goals must be met. For example, any automotive service center would like to maximize profit. However, this can be done only under the constraints of meeting payroll obligations, licensing fees, maintenance costs, and so on. A DSS that uses linear programming will maximize goals while minimizing constraints. Computers help because such calculations often are far too complex to do manually. A disadvantage, however, is that each goal and constraint must be described precisely enough to model the actual situation realistically.

With a DSS, an executive can pull together models that reflect different alternatives. In the service center example, one decision might involve whether to sell gasoline at service centers. A model can help pull together the costs of installing the necessary equipment and storage tanks. Provision is also made for the cost of land, buildings, entrances, and other requirements. When all start–up costs are accumulated, they are processed by a DSS to produce forecasts on their depreciation over a number of years. Then operating costs can be estimated. These include the purchase of gasoline and payroll costs for employees.

Given this picture of costs, the DSS can be used to project different levels of expected income for the gasoline retailing operation. The result of this modeling process is a reliable figure on how much gasoline each center will have to sell every month to cover expenses and produce a profit. Developing this caliber of information might take many weeks if the work is done manually. With a computer, the effort can be completed in hours once the raw data have been gathered and the model created.

Using a DSS in this way helps take both detailed drudgery and guesswork out of major decisions. In the example, a decision on whether to sell gasoline comes down to an estimate of how many gallons customers would buy. A DSS could be used to model each element of an automotive center's operation. For example, models could be built and applied to the brake shop, the lubrication facility, the engine diagnosis and repair operation, and any other segments of automotive center business. Once a model of this type is created, executives can "exercise" it to test results under varying conditions. The end result would be a projection of the business volume required to reach a break-even point for each area and the service center as a whole.

Data Analysis Using Query Languages

While modeling presents an overall view of a problem and tests various solutions, a query language can be used to answer specific "What if...?" questions that might arise. One advantage to a query language is that a manager can use this part of a DSS without the help of a computer professional.

As discussed in Chapter 12, a query language uses English words and phrasing to retrieve information from a database. While sitting at a terminal, a university administrator can immediately obtain an answer to such questions as, "What if we raise tuition by 5%? How much additional revenue will be generated?" or, "What if we build that addition to the library? How will it affect costs for building security?" Such answers are solicited merely by typing in the questions using a few key words.

Using a query language is easier for nonprofessionals than modeling software, but a query language is limited to a series of single, relatively straightforward questions. Both modeling and data analysis with query languages have predictive value that easily surpasses manual forecasting.

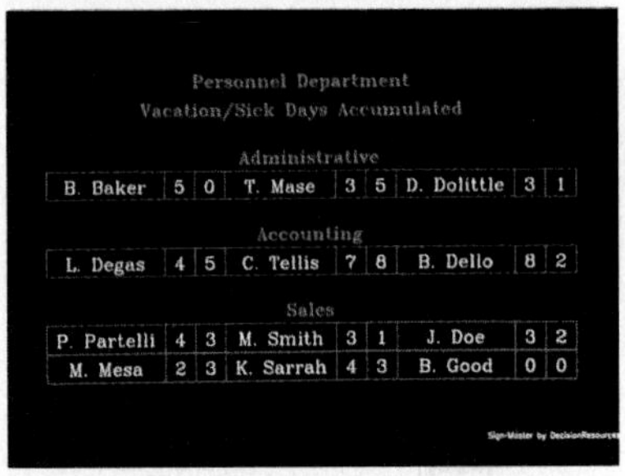

FIGURE 13.11

This display generated by a query language request answers the question, "Which employees have accumulated fewer than 10 sick days?"

C L I P

WHAT IS ARTIFICIAL INTELLIGENCE?

The term "artificial intelligence" means different things to different people. Academics take the narrow view that true artificial intelligence (AI) seeks to develop computer models of human intelligence. Developers of business software are less dogmatic, and often inappropriately put the AI label on any product that may arguably be considered "smart," or possessed of an advanced level of computing power.

Ignoring such marketing hype, commercial AI products generally fall into one of three categories: expert systems, natural-language systems, and neural networks.

Expert systems are by far the most plentiful type of commercial AI program. They are also called rule-based systems because they follow a set of rules to reach conclusions. To create an expert system, a "knowledge engineer"—the AI programmer—interviews experts in a particular field and distills their knowledge into a series of if/then rules.

Following the rules, an expert system running on a persona computer, workstation, or mainframe can analyze a problem and advise people on how to solve it. The idea is to make the experts' knowledge available to novices. For example, a financial-services system might tell an inexperienced loan officer, "*If* the loan applicant is $40,000 in debt with an income of less than $30,000 *then* he is a bad risk."

The knowledge represented in an expert system is restricted to a narrow field, ranging from the relatively mundane (how to fix a car engine) to the esoteric (deciding where to drill for oil). AI purists scoff at these systems, arguing that experts use a lot more than if/then reasoning when making decisions.

Natural-language programs come closer to representing human cognition. They grew out of AI research into how people derive meaning from language—how do we understand, for example, that a reference to New York in a sentence refers to the city or the state? Natural-language software consists of powerful programs that let people tap into a database using plain-English commands instead of computer language. For example, Home Owners Warranty uses a system made by Artificial Intelligence of Waltham, Mass., that lets computer operators get information by asking the computer questions such as "How many builders in New Jersey have open claims?"

Other major suppliers of natural-language systems include Cognitive Systems of New Haven, Conn., Symantec of Cupertino, Calif., and Direct Aid of Boulder, Colo.

Neural networks, the most ambitious form of artificial intelligence to date, are still in the research lab, especially at Princeton and the California Institute of Technology. Developers aim to recreate in silicon the complex network of neural pathways in the brain to build a computer that would mimic human thought. The technology is promising, but a long way from commercial use. So far, researchers have simulated the nerve structure of the eye's retina and the ear's cochlea, and AT&T has created a computer copy of the brain of a garden slug. It's something to think about.

Why Develop An Expert System?

- To preserve knowledge that might be lost through the retirement, resignation or death of a company's acknowledged expert in any field.
- To "clone" an expert mechanically so his knowledge can be disseminated.
- To store information in an active form—a knowledge base—rather than a passive one—a textbook or manual.
- To give novices an aid that will help them think the way more experienced professionals do.
- To create a mechanism that is not subject to human failings like fatigue and can hold up in positions where information must flow constantly.

Source: High Technology Business, May 1988. Reprinted with permission.

Key Question: If you had access to an expert system today, what would it do for you?

STUDY QUESTIONS

7. Define model, decision support system (DSS), and linear programming.
8. How are models and query languages used as part of decision support systems?
9. What is an advantage and a disadvantage to using linear programming models?
10. What types of questions do query languages help users to answer?

OTHER TOOLS FOR DECISION MAKERS

A variety of computer-based problem-solving tools are used in day-to-day decision making. The appearance of microcomputers brought personal productivity software, such as electronic spreadsheets and graphics packages, directly to people's desks. With these machines, we personally can control and manipulate the data needed for decision making.

Electronic Spreadsheets

As mentioned in Chapter 10, the rows and columns in an electronic spreadsheet contain numbers and formulas that can help people project results and choose among alternatives. A spreadsheet allows the manipulation of numbers but does not integrate or cross-reference massive amounts of data like a database program. Applications that require the summarization of data, or the clear presentation of important data can be done best on a spreadsheet. Summaries of financial, personnel, research, and production/sales data can be arranged on a spreadsheet in an easy-to-use and familiar format.

Spreadsheets can be the foundation for one aspect of an organization's MIS. For example, all departments in a store could use the same budget template when planning yearly budgets. Each manager would enter data unique to that department. By having a standard format, top management could analyze with a global view the budgets for all departments. Executives would then make strategic decisions based on the entire store's financial situation. These decisions could include increasing sales personnel in a department or extending store hours. By using spreadsheets, managers can adjust their budgets to reflect the strategic plan quickly and easily.

In addition, not every organization can afford the power of a DSS. The blood bank in a resort community needs the data analysis and "What if...?"

Decision Support Using Electronic Spreadsheets

1. Clear presentation of important data
2. Provides a standard format for exchanging data
3. Inexpensive alternative to some expensive DSS capabilities
4. Allows users to manipulate data to answer "What if...?" questions.

FIGURE 13.12

Electronic spreadsheets can help managers with decision support by presenting data in a clear, easy-to-read format that can be standardized across an organization.

capabilities available on a DSS. An electronic spreadsheet can provide an inexpensive alternative. The agency's director can use the spreadsheet program to get answers to questions such as:

- What if tourism increases 10% next summer and traffic accidents increase proportionately—how much blood will be needed?
- How many new donors must be acquired to fill this need?
- How effective have public service announcements been in increasing walk-in blood donors?
- How much more advertising will be needed next summer?

As you can see, electronic spreadsheets support problem solving on several levels. They organize data in familiar ways and also allow the manipulation of data to obtain answers for some of the "What if...?" questions asked of the larger, more expensive decision support systems. Electronic spreadsheets can play a role in enhancing existing decision-making functions or serving as a focal point for a small organization's MIS.

Presentation Graphics

Numbers may have meaning to the people conducting research and compiling reports. Often decisions must be made (or at least confirmed) by top-level executives with no immediate involvement in the use of spreadsheets. Also, before a plan or decision is implemented, outsiders may have to become involved. Bankers may be asked about investment potential. Engineers may be asked about implementation. Suppliers may be asked about support for anticipated projects.

To meet such needs, it is necessary to communicate clearly ideas behind plans or decisions. Information is often communicated most easily through the use of graphics. For example, three alternatives for a given decision can be plotted on a single line graph for ready comparison of expectations and projected results. To illustrate, a line graph for the auto center venture might reflect income projections from centers in three different cities (see Figure 13.13). At first, all three lines would show a loss, with lines plotted below a zero level of profit. At different times, each line would indicate when the related city's service center

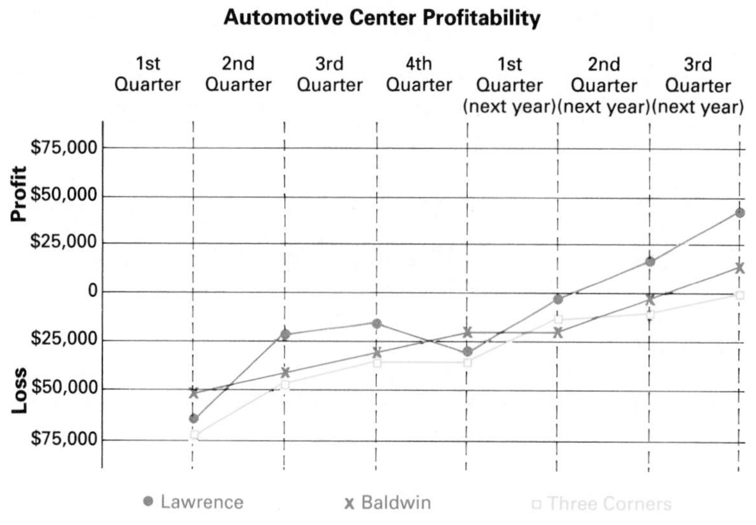

FIGURE 13.13

This computer-generated graphic supports decision making by showing that one of the automotive centers will be profitable before the others.

could be expected to make a profit. By using graphics, decision makers can easily compare alternatives. Within the same context, income and expense relationships could be presented through use of pie charts or bar graphs.

Many spreadsheet and database software packages integrate with software that converts data values automatically into graphics. When such tools are available, the projection of graphic outputs can be created easily by using existing data from database files or spreadsheets. In addition, many stand–alone graphics packages are available that make it possible for users to "plug in" appropriate data that are applied to generate graphic outputs. No matter which tools are used, the value of computer graphics within the decision–making process lies in facilitating communication and understanding.

Expert Systems

Powerful problem-solving software for decision makers, called expert systems, is some of the first practical applications of work in artificial intelligence. As you may recall, artificial intelligence is the application of computer technology to simulate human thought and judgment. ***Expert systems*** contain patterns for decision making and probabilities for expected outcomes based on information available from experts. To create an expert system requires more than retrieval of data from large databases.

Experts in a specific field (domain) are interviewed to obtain their knowledge and the rules by which they make decisions. Expert system developers, known as knowledge engineers, are finding it difficult to quantify the knowledge of human experts. When asked to describe how decisions are made, people often find it impossible to identify all the factors involved. Human experts base their decisions on years of experience, as well as on formal education. As a result, expert systems are costly and difficult to create because identifying all the facts and recognizing the relationships among those facts is very time-consuming. Such systems have three components: knowledge base, inference engine, and user interface (see Figure 13.14).

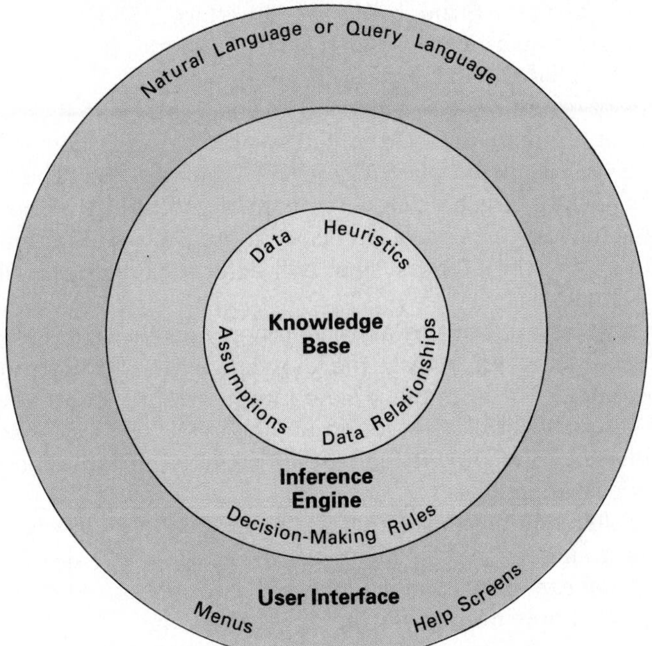

FIGURE 13.14

An expert system uses a knowledge base, inference engine, and user interface to help people make decisions.

Applications for Expert Systems

Area	*Expert System*
Business	AUDITOR—helps auditors to assess a company's financial situation.
	EDP AUDITOR—aids in auditing computer systems
	MONITOR—provides international currency exchange rates on a 24-hour basis
	TICOM—models internal control systems
Computers	CROB—recommends solutions for hardware and software problems
Engineering	DIPMETER ADVISOR—helps forecast oil well capacity
	SACON—aids architects and building engineers in structural analysis
Medicine	CADUCEUS—diagnoses internal diseases
	MYCIN—diagnoses blood and some viral infections

FIGURE 13.15

Expert systems have been developed for a variety of applications and continue to make inroads into new decision-making areas.

The ***knowledge base*** used by an expert system takes the capabilities of databases one step further. It contains facts, data relationships, and assumptions that the knowledge engineer combines to form the heuristics, or rules, for decision making. The knowledge base for a specific domain, combined with the powerful retrieval and decision-making ***inference engine***, drives an expert system. When presented with a problem, the inference engine software can draw new conclusions and add this information to its knowledge base. Through its own effort, the expert system becomes more "intelligent."

The vast knowledge base and numerous decision-making rules are made easily accessible to users through the user interface. This interface contains a natural language for querying the expert system. Menus, help screens, and other utilities are also included to increase user friendliness.

One type of expert system, called Caduceus, contains in its knowledge base information about human diseases, related symptoms, and diagnostic tests. Doctors then enter queries based on symptoms of their patients. The expert system responds with a list of possible diagnoses and the probability of their occurrence. It also suggests the least expensive and least painful tests to be administered first. Like a human expert, the expert system will defer on a diagnosis, if not enough information is available.

Expert systems are built to assist decision makers, not replace them. In addition, these systems can increase the knowledge normally acquired by people through experience. For example, a new intern working in a free clinic would not have the resources or experts found in a hospital. An expert system would expand the intern's own knowledge base by identifying rare illnesses and suggesting possible treatments.

Expert systems do not make final decisions; they only display logical alternatives. The actual decision making is left to people. The idea is to design an expert system that can draw from a wide variety of specialized data—the knowledge base. Users simply need to ask the right questions.

STUDY QUESTIONS

11. Identify four ways spreadsheets can help decision makers.
12. How do graphics packages support the decision-making process?
13. Identify the three components of an expert system and explain how each works.
14. How can expert systems assist experienced and inexperienced people?
15. Why are expert systems difficult to develop?

CONCLUSION

Planning and decision making tend to be individual responsibilities. And each individual carries out these responsibilities in a separate, or unique, way. This means there is no single, correct way to apply computers for decision-making activities. Instead, the premium is on flexibility. The software and hardware tools provided should be adaptable to people's needs. General-purpose tools such as database programs, spreadsheets, and graphics packages are available to meet these needs and implement associated responsibilities.

Decision support systems and expert systems are suited to the needs of people making decisions in specialized areas. Each decision maker should be able to compile and interpret specific collections of data and reports that are considered private until he or she is ready to release them. Management information systems, however, have broad, often public implications and are based on data drawn from an organization's transaction cycle. When data resources are open for more general use, special concerns and measures are required. These concerns and measures form the subject matter for Chapter 14, on privacy, security, and computer-related crime.

CHAPTER FACTS

- The collection of manual and computerized systems used to assemble and retrieve an organization's data for decision making is called its management information system (MIS).
- In any organization, management's role is to solve problems, plan events, and supervise people. Management has three levels: Front-line management, middle management, and top management or executives.
- Front-line managers make operational decisions about daily transactions. They use detailed reports to show information about each transaction.
- Middle management makes tactical decisions about short-range problems, using summary and exception reports about the organization.
- Top management makes strategic long-range decisions that have far-reaching effects. They use summary and exception reports to show organizational trends.
- Managerial data can be organized into financial, personnel, research, and production/sales groups.
- A decision support system (DSS) is a real-time computer system that includes modeling software and query language–based data retrieval. It is used for long-term decision making.

INSIGHT

DEVELOPING AN EXPERT SYSTEM

You have a problem. One of the robot arms on your new assembly line is not working properly. You turn to an expert for help. In this case, the expert has a keyboard for input and a screen for output.

Identify Problem and Find Domain Expert

This expert system has been developed for your use by a knowledge engineer working with human experts employed by the robot manufacturer.

Uncover the Domain Expert's Knowledge

The knowledge engineer and robotics expert worked together to identify solutions to potential problems.

Identify Decision Rules From Domain Expert's Knowledge

A program called an inference engine helped the knowledge engineer code decision rules for the expert system. These decision rules identify solutions to potential problems and the probability of the problems' occurrences when recognized conditions exist.

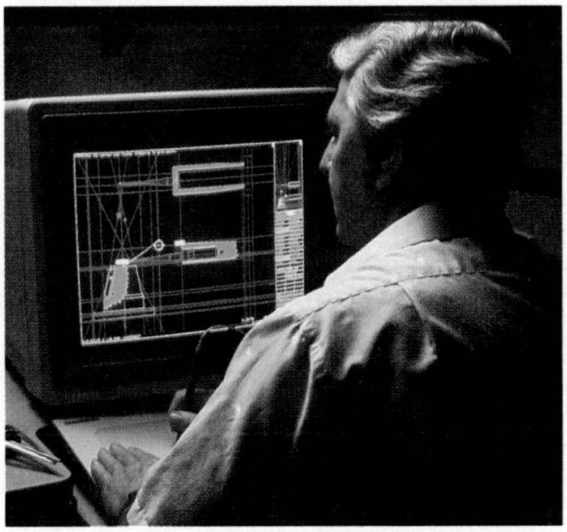

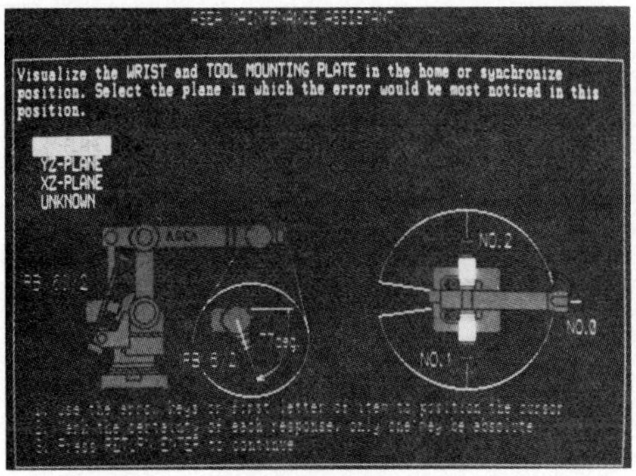

Build a Knowledge Base

This information becomes part of a knowledge base where probabilities are integrated with detailed descriptions of the problem and potential solutions.

Test and Evaluate the Knowledge Base

As a result, your robotics expert is as close as the nearest computer. By placing the knowledge base in the disk drive and loading the inference engine and easy-to-operate user interface into memory, you are quickly ready for a consultation.

The expert system helps in the problem-solving process by asking questions and providing solutions when possible.

- Modeling is the mathematical representation of a problem. One way of finding an optimum solution is through linear programming, which uses a precise definition of problem goals and constraints.
- Query languages retrieve data to answer "What if...?" questions posed by decision makers.
- Other decision-making tools include expert systems, electronic spreadsheets, and graphics packages.
- Expert systems combine a knowledge base with retrieval and decision-making software. They concentrate in one specific area of knowledge and "learn" by storing the conclusions they draw.

TERMS TO REMEMBER

decision support system (DSS)
detailed report
exception report
executive
expert system
financial data
front-line management
inference engine
knowledge base
linear programming
management information system (MIS)
middle management
model
operational decision
personnel data
production/sales data
research data
strategic decision
summary report
tactical decision
top management
transaction cycle

CHECK YOUR UNDERSTANDING

1. Which level of management is responsible for strategic decisions?
   a. middle management
   b. front-line management
   c. personnel management
   d. top management
   e. none of the above
2. Decisions about the day-to-day activities of an organization are called ___________ decisions.
3. Exception reports list totals and conclusions about daily operations. (True/False)
4. Personnel data include information about overtime worked, absences, and vacations for employees. (True/False)
5. ___________ data contain information about an organization's past performance and future plans.
6. Which of the following would be contained in a decision support system?
   a. query language
   b. knowledge base
   c. modeling software
   d. a and c
   e. b and c
7. Linear programming is used to create user-friendly data retrieval programs for MIS systems. (True/False)

8. Decision makers can use either a query language or a(n) ____________ to find the answer to "What if...?" questions.
9. Expert systems can acquire knowledge by storing conclusions they have reached. (True/False)
10. A(n) ____________ is a collection of information containing data about one area of learning, along with decision–making patterns.

APPLYING WHAT YOU'VE LEARNED

1. Imagine you are an "expert" being interviewed to provide information for a knowledge base. After picking an area of interest to you, list ten different types of data that would have to be included in the knowledge base. For each type of data, name a possible source of that information. Also list five different types of decisions an expert system in that field should be able to analyze.
2. A decision support system or expert system provides assistance to decision makers but actually does not make the decision. In your chosen career field, what types of decisions may be aided by the large base of data available on a DSS or expert system? Should any decisions rely solely on human efforts?
3. We can see that computers are involved in almost every aspect of an organization's decision making. Would it be possible for any organization, regardless of size, to exist without a computer? What type of organization may not need a computer at the present time?
4. Pick an organization with which you are familiar. It can be a business, school, volunteer agency, or whatever. Name three examples for each type of data available from an MIS. Describe what might be contained on a typical detailed, exception, and summary report for that organization.
5. MIS and DSS are currently under much discussion in many organizations. Each is difficult to describe precisely and few people agree on exactly what each should contain. Find an article on either MIS or DSS. Summarize the article and list any new terminology used. How are the concepts presented in the article applying to school, your workplace, or other familiar organization?
6. Each level of management comes with different responsibilities and rewards. Interview or read about a person at one of the three management levels. What are the benefits? What kinds of stress and deadlines exist? How far-reaching are the decisions he or she makes and how much responsibility must the manager take if the decision is wrong? What tools does this manager use to help him or her make decisions?

CHECK YOUR UNDERSTANDING ANSWERS

1. d
2. operational
3. false
4. true
5. research
6. d
7. false
8. electronic spreadsheet
9. true
10. knowledge base

CHAPTER FOURTEEN

PRIVACY, COMPUTER CRIME, AND SECURITY

KEY IDEAS

- **From the user's point of view**
  In what ways is computer technology involved in criminal activities? How can you protect computer systems and your personal privacy from this type of crime?

- **Privacy**
  Computer systems can be used to distribute incorrect or sensitive information about people.

  Invasions of privacy
  People should realize that computer-based information can be manipulated in negative ways.

  The right to privacy
  Congress has passed several laws to protect citizens against the misuse of personal information.

  Our responsibilities and opportunities
  People can protect their privacy through education and knowledge of their legal rights.

- **Crime**
  Information is a valuable resource and needs to be protected against illegal access and alteration.

  Examples of computer crime
  Computer crimes can occur anywhere and at any time.

  Types of computer crime
  Computer crimes include stealing time, data, and programs, along with changing programs and data.

  Signals of potential computer crime
  Poor control of a computer system or lack of user education are factors that usually invite computer crime.

- **Security**
  While necessary, computer security has its costs.

  Controls for small computer systems
  Computer systems of all sizes need physical controls and security measures for data.

  Maintaining security of large computer systems
  Large computer systems need special controls, ranging from involvement by management to computer center controls and input, processing, and output controls.

FROM THE USER'S POINT OF VIEW

Computer systems are constantly becoming more accepted as fixtures of contemporary life. As you become comfortable working with technology, you will naturally explore new dimensions of power for gathering, storing, and exchanging data and information. While computer systems benefit individuals and society, there is also potential for abuse. Used with malice or neglect, computer technology can become a tool for committing crimes or infringing upon your individual rights to privacy.

In such cases, the machine itself is not the guilty party. Rather, the people using computer technology are responsible for the help or harm enacted by computer systems under their control. You must monitor your own actions, and also secure your computer systems from abuse by others. In this chapter we will explore three major social issues everyone must confront as an informed user:

- Privacy
- Crime
- Security

FIGURE 14.1

Some privacy is surrendered by any person who commits a crime. Information on criminals and suspects becomes part of extensive law enforcement information networks.

Courtesy of Eastman Kodak Co.

PRIVACY

Computers store information about people, places, ideas, and events. In other words, they can store personal information about every aspect of your life. The personal information held about you in a computer file can be used for beneficial purposes. A nation can understand the makeup of its citizens by maintaining personal data on individuals. Your financial records can be exchanged electronically between banks and credit offices, perhaps to expedite processing of a loan application. The positive uses for personal data files abound. However, computer-based data files also are prime targets of abuse. Consider the following hypothetical case:

The first of the month has arrived, and your rent payment is due. However, you feel your landlord has neglected his maintenance duties. You notify the landlord that you have decided to hold your payment in escrow until the dispute is settled. Eventually, you reach an agreement and pay your rent. Life seems to have returned to normal—until you discover that your landlord has adversely affected your credit and credibility.

When you apply for a car loan, your application is denied because you are listed as a poor credit risk. You ask why, but the car agency doesn't know. After looking into the matter, you find out your landlord reported you to a credit agency for nonpayment when you held back your rent payment. In addition, when looking for another place to rent you are constantly turned down. Later, you find your name on a list of "troublemakers" shared among local landlords in the area.

For standing up for your rights as a tenant, have you been wronged?

- Was your privacy violated when information about you was reported to the other landlords?
- Is your landlord guilty of violating your constitutional rights, by reporting false information to the credit agency?
- Were the credit agency and car dealer too willing to accept unverified information about your creditworthiness?

In this case, you become the victim of a misused computer system. Your privacy may have been invaded, a crime may have been committed, and the credit officers and car dealers may be guilty of negligence. Computer technology was exploited to your disadvantage.

FIGURE 14.2

When authorizing a personal credit check, you surrender part of your right to privacy.

Invasions of Privacy

Computers don't invade anybody's privacy. People do. Part of the problem is that computer systems are designed to provide easy access to data. Within most systems, it is relatively simple to enter data for storage and to retrieve stored data. At the same time, people must protect their computer files and limit access to authorized users.

The protection procedures used depend on individual situations. For example, consider what happens when you ask for credit. The prospective creditor asks you to provide information about yourself, your financial situation, and any loans you have made in the past. You should read carefully anything you sign. This applies especially to papers related to borrowing money. Almost every loan application has a provision under which you give the prospective lender permission to check out your credit status. This means that lenders can contact computer credit services, banks, retailers, or others with whom you have done business.

FIGURE 14.3

Congresspeople, like North Carolina's Charles Rose, use computers to enact legislation that protects the privacy of their constituents.

If you authorize an investigation about yourself, you can assume that you will be checked out carefully. Lenders need to check an individual's financial history to protect their investments. Once you give permission, however, you have surrendered part of your rights to privacy. Before you sign, be sure you understand what rights you are surrendering. You should also come to an understanding with the party that asks for permission to investigate you. For example, you can ask what happens if negative information is reported. Make it clear that you feel you have a right to see and explain any negative reports that might be issued. On the other hand, if you know of past problems with credit or other personal information, it is better to explain the problem in advance. If the information will disqualify you, save the embarrassment of authorizing an information search. Don't apply for credit until you are fairly sure you can qualify. Be aware that computer files may contain information on almost any business transactions in which you have been involved.

If you learn of any negative information reported about you, be aware you have the right to correct any errors. There have been instances in which information has been entered into the wrong records. Also, business people can make unjustified reports about your actions, as in the example of the rent dispute.

The Right to Privacy

The right to privacy—to various extents—is guaranteed by law. The best known legal basis for claims to privacy are contained in the Fourth Amendment of the Constitution. The Fourth Amendment protects U.S. citizens from "unreasonable searches and seizures...of person, house, papers and effects." This language is general and has been subject to considerable debate and many law suits. To clarify the meaning of the Fourth Amendment, Congress has passed a number of laws, including the following:

- Freedom of Information Act (1970)
  Personal data maintained by the federal government became accessible to any citizen who wanted it through the Freedom of Information Act of 1970. Unless release of the data threatens national security or infringes upon someone else's privacy, information must be furnished in response to requests.
- Fair Credit Reporting Act (1970)
  Also in 1970, Congress passed the Fair Credit Reporting Act. This law gave individuals the right to examine and, if desired, challenge information held in their credit files.

FIGURE 14.4

The Electronic Communications Privacy Act of 1986 was designed to protect people from electronic eavesdropping.

- Privacy Act (1974)
  The Privacy Act of 1974 aimed at reducing the amount of irrelevant information collected by federal agencies and maintained in government computer files. These agencies are required to reveal how they intend to use the information they keep. In addition, permission must be obtained from affected individuals before the information is used for other than the stated purposes. The effectiveness of this act is dampened by the difficulty in establishing the relevance of an item of data. Another shortcoming is that the law applies only to government agencies.
- Comprehensive Crime Control Act (1984)
  The Comprehensive Crime Control Act clarified and added to the federal criminal code. This legislation made sweeping changes to a variety of criminal codes. Included in the bill was a section that made it a crime to obtain unauthorized access to computers and to obtain classified information, protected financial information, or anything of value.
- Electronic Communications Privacy Act (1986)
  The Electronic Communications Act provides privacy protection to communications made through new forms of technology. In particular, this legislation clearly identifies electronic mail and makes it a federal crime to intercept these computer-based transmissions.

Our Responsibilities and Opportunities

Some type of computer-recorded information is maintained for nearly every person in the United States. It starts when we are born—most birth certificates now are computer-generated. Computer-maintained records about us continue to be created and accessed throughout our lives. If misuse of this information is to be avoided, preventive measures have to come from us.

Knowledge and legislation are the tools we have to control the impact technology has on society. As citizens, we have the responsibility to make our voices heard when abuses occur. We can do this through consumer power and by knowing and insisting on our rights. If you become involved with the design or operation of computer systems, you will have the opportunity to ensure that the system is responsibly designed to reduce the potential of misuse.

TAKING A BYTE OUT OF CRIME: SOME GUIDELINES ON COMPUTER THEFT PROTECTION

Warning Signals

"Several red flags can signal alert managers that a fellow employee could be a 'wolf in sheep's clothing,'" says Louis Scoma, founder and CEO of Houston-based Data Processing Security, Inc., which has aided over 650 companies with their computer security systems since 1970. Consider the following.

- Does one of your employees consistently come in early and stay after hours—with no visible results from the extra hours of work?
- Have you recently fired an employee who had access to sensitive information? Do you have any such workers on staff who are disgruntled with the company for any reason?
- Do any of your employees with access to sensitive data tote personal microcomputers to and from the office in order to do "extra work"?
- Did an employee you transferred from headquarters to a branch office come back to "clean out his desk" or "visit old friends" even though he knew the security codes had been changed?
- Has your company experienced a recent increase in data processing needs, while you have not upgraded your security system to accommodate the change?

"If you have answered yes to two or more of these questions," says Scoma, "double -check your security system and the people responsible for keeping it intact. If you don't, you could be headed for high-tech trouble."

An Ounce of Prevention

According to the Better Business Bureau, the vast majority of computer crimes are preventable. Although the following measures may seem like common sense, consider them in light of your company's own practices. How many are fully followed?

- *Employee hiring.* Conduct thorough background checks on all potential EDP employees. Check with former employers: get references—both professional and personal. Verify technical skills, and check credit histories.
- *Controlling access to facilities.* Maintain a log book with times and names of all who have access to the computer facilities. Allow only employees who work with the computer to sign in. Confirm and verify any service calls, and have a company employee accompany any technician to the worksite.
- *Physical security.* Separate computer facilities from other departments, in a secure, isolated area with few windows or doors, adequate lighting, secure locks, and, if possible, a security guard at each entrance. Provide the appropriate personnel with proper identification that can be verified at the entrance, such as photo or fingerprint IDs.
- *Protective devices.* Take advantage of all the security devices built into the computer system. Have the company that sold or leased you the equipment explain how password rotation, security codes, and code scrambling devices can control access. Electronic security, such as closed-circuit television and sound sensitive listening devices, might also be worthwhile investments.

Computers can "stall" after wrong passwords are entered, disconnect after a certain number of wrong guesses, record attempts to penetrate, and even trace phone calls. Take advantage of these features.

- *Storage procedures.* It is essential to have a duplicate set of all vital tapes, software, and company data stored in a secure, isolated storage space accessible to only a few top EDP executives.
- *Audits.* Conduct periodic security checks both internally and independently. Many auditing firms now will attempt to defraud your company's system, to determine whether security is sufficient.

"Keeping in mind that some computer crimes are so sophisticated that they may take months, even years, to detect and unravel, management should be constantly on the alert for possible indications of wrongdoing," warns the Better Business Bureau.

Source: Reprinted by permission.
Management Review

Key Question: If you suspected a computer crime, what would you do? Whom would you contact?

STUDY QUESTIONS

1. When can a creditor legally invade a person's privacy?
2. Describe the rights defined by the Fourth Amendment of the Constitution, the Freedom of Information Act of 1970, the Fair Credit Reporting Act of 1970, the Privacy Act of 1974, the Comprehensive Crime Control Act of 1984, and the Electronic Communications Privacy Act of 1986.
3. What are two means of controlling computer impact?

CRIME

Information is power. The constructive use of information has great potential for improvements and benefits. The fact that millions of computers exist establishes that they are wanted and that they are serving the needs of people and organizations. Used properly, computers are powerful and valuable tools.

Examples of Computer Crime

However, computers can be and have been misused. In the hands of a dishonest person with special knowledge about sensitive systems, the computer can become a powerful, hard-to-detect burglar tool. The news media have detailed hundreds of crimes that have involved computers. To make matters worse, experts fear that reported cases make up only a small portion of overall computer crime. The following five situations provide examples of the dangers involved.

Michigan State University

Michigan State University has a large time-sharing computer system that supports research and is used by teachers and several thousand students. A few years ago, two students developed and implemented a plan to steal passwords and computer time from other users.

The plan was simple. Many students went to the computer lab to complete assignments on small computers linked to the larger system. Knowing this, the thieves wrote a program that mimicked the larger computer's security program. Unsuspecting students would enter their passwords into a small computer running with the thieves' fake program. The program would store the password, then display an error message. Thinking the small computer was out of order, students would move to another computer. They never knew their passwords had been stolen. The thieves would collect the passwords and use the accounts later.

An alert university programmer eventually tracked down the thieves. The programmer was unaware that his password had been stolen until he noticed activity reported on his account at 2 A.M. His suspicions that someone was tampering with his account were confirmed when subsequent reports of activity at odd hours led to the capture of the culprits.

FIGURE 14.5

Computer theft includes the stealing of chips and other small parts of great value.

Photo courtesy of Chuck O'Rear

Pacific Telephone Company

Jerry Schneider was a whiz kid who built his own computer system when he was 10. By the time he was in high school, he had started his own electronics company. While he was a part-time college student, Schneider discovered a way to steal electronic equipment from Pacific Telephone Company. He retrieved old

FIGURE 14.6

Computer technology by itself is not good or bad. It can be used to prevent crimes as easily as to commit them.

computer printouts and other documentation from a Pacific Telephone trash container to acquire correct account numbers, passwords, and procedures. Then, using a terminal in his home, he ordered parts without being billed for them.

Schneider had expensive telephone components delivered to his home and to other locations. Once, he used his computer to order delivery of a $25,000 switchboard to a manhole cover at the intersection of two streets. He picked up the switchboard in a Pacific Telephone truck he bought at a company surplus auction.

Much of the equipment Schneider stole in this way was resold to Pacific Telephone. In fact, he used the company's own computer system to determine which stock levels were low, so he would know what items to steal. Schneider's crime spree ended when one of his own employees turned him in after a dispute over pay.

Penn Central Railroad

The case of Penn Central Railroad revolved around missing boxcars. The computer criminals in this case tampered with a computerized freight flow system, and boxcars were routed to a small railroad company outside of Chicago. There, the boxcars seem to have disappeared. The computer system was modified so that the missing boxcars would not be reported.

Investigation indicated that the boxcars had been repainted and used by other railroad companies. According to some estimates, about 400 boxcars were stolen in this manner. But Penn Central wished to minimize attention to the crime and chose not to pursue prosecution.

Equity Funding Corporation

Equity Funding Corporation was a group of companies that handled investments and insurance. Top-level managers from some of these companies lied about company profits to attract investors. In addition, they created volumes of fake insurance policies, then sold them, packaged with valid policies, to other insurance companies. The system was programmed to report only valid policies for auditing purposes. Once the scam was uncovered, more than 20 people were convicted on federal charges. Estimates of losses are as high as $2 billion.

CLIP

TECHNOLOGY: INVADER OR PROTECTOR OF PRIVACY

The high-tech revolution is regarded with apprehension by a sizable element within our society; many of these people are themselves members of the high-tech community. They fear that the electronic genie is fast taking control of our lives—that we may have glimpsed Pandora's secrets without fully understanding their ramifications. Our very privacy is at stake. The late U.S. Sen. Frank Church (D-Idaho) expressed his fears when he observed that there would be no place to hide in the computer society. Computer snooping can tell a great deal about us. It can lead to serious political manipulation.

There is reason for concern, especially as computers increasingly take over our daily lives. For example:

- Computers perform more than 100,000 calculations each second for every man, woman and child in the U.S.
- Our names pop up in some computer at least 40 times a day.
- Federal, state and local governmental agencies keep more than 35 files on each one of us, while the U.S. Bureau of the Census collects more than five billion facts on us.

Privacy and civil liberties are one and the same—one cannot survive long without the other. But privacy is fast becoming a thing of the past in our computer society.

- The NSA's computers eavesdrop 24 hours a day, seven days a week, on all overseas communications. NSA also occasionally monitors communications within the U.S.
- Much of the confidential data stored in the computer systems of financial institutions, retailers and manufacturers is vulnerable to unauthorized tapping.
- The computerization of our telephone system makes it very vulnerable to electronic snooping.
- As computer systems are linked to national and international networks, it will become even easier to track a person's movements.
- By using a device called an addressable converter, cable companies can now keep track of what programs a customer watches.

Rep. Robert W. Kastenmeier (D-Wis.) observed that "the essence of personal privacy protection is the assurance that private communications are protected." Sadly, this is not the case today. Our massive data banks and instant retrieval systems make George Orwell's telescreens seem ancient by comparison. All that is now missing is a giant network that would link all private and governmental computer systems into one. That, too, may be in the offing.

Source: Reprinted by permission, *Computerworld*

Key Question: When does the need to improve the speed and accuracy of government services outweigh your need for personal privacy?

Your Hometown

Computers are used for the same type of criminal activity every day in schools, homes, and businesses. A computer user shares a new program with a friend or associate by making an illegal copy of the software. This type of criminal activity seems quite small by comparison with the Equity Funding or Pacific Telephone cases. When many small crimes are added together, however, the sum represents the theft of millions of dollars in software each year.

Software houses have started to take legal measures to fight back. The Lotus Development Corporation collected a sizable out-of-court settlement from the Heath Group, whose employees allegedly made illegal copies of the Lotus 1-2-3 spreadsheet software. Such actions illustrate the software houses' view that transferring programs without permission is stealing. Copying software illegally is no different from walking out of a store without paying for merchandise.

Types of Computer Crime

Each of the five cases just presented involves a fraud in which the perpetrator uses deceit or misrepresentation for unlawful gain. When the value of the item is greater than $500, the act becomes a felony, or a major crime, under the laws of most states. Though the potential for fraud was present in each case, different types of crimes were committed. In summary, the five categories are:

Stealing Computer Time

The Michigan State students robbed their fellow computer users first of their passwords, then of their time allocations. Computer time is money.

Stealing Data

Financial data, customer information, or special designs or plans can be stolen from computer files. In the Pacific Telephone case, data were obtained illegally to support the computer-aided theft of expensive equipment.

Manipulating Data

The Penn Central case showed that data could be manipulated to direct events and people's actions—in this case the rerouting of boxcars.

Changing Programs

Programs were changed to cover up the crimes committed by Equity Funding executives. Usually, this type of computer crime is committed by computer professionals.

Stealing Computer Programs

Software buyers often do not realize they have purchased merely the right to use software, not the software itself. This means that the software is not legally theirs to give to others. As a result, one of the most widespread crimes involves the illegal copying of software. Since theft of computer data and software often involves making copies, the original remains intact. Thus, this type of computer crime is often difficult to detect.

Many computer crime experts think that the cases uncovered to date are only the tip of the iceberg. Some companies have been victims of crime, yet have chosen not to prosecute criminals to avoid negative publicity and advertising their vulnerability. In cases such as this, the criminals are never exposed or brought to justice.

FIGURE 14.7

Copying software is a computer crime if it was previously copyrighted.

Signals of Potential Computer Crime

In places where computer crimes have occurred, a number of warning signs have been noted. Most of the signs indicate poor control of the computer system or a lack of education on the part of users. The most common signs include:

- The computer system seems to run people instead of people running the system.
- People expect computers to solve major problems that already exist.
- Users cannot communicate with the computer professionals.
- Users are not asked to contribute ideas during the planning stages of systems development; instead, they are told how the system will be designed.
- No clear-cut procedures are established for equipment use.
- Documentation of system design and use is incomplete.
- Decision makers are active with programming and troubleshooting.
- Computer professionals are given no guidelines within which to work.
- Access to data and software facilities is easy and uncontrolled.
- Errors in processing occur frequently, but without adequate investigation.
- People are not held specifically accountable for the system operations.

As you can see, all five components of a computer system must be protected from computer crime. Access to hardware and software must be limited to qualified people. Data must be complete, accurate, and monitored for illegal changes. Procedures must be developed to help people operate and control the system properly.

STUDY QUESTIONS

4. Identify five types of computer crime.
5. Why would an organization be reluctant to prosecute computer criminals?
6. What are 11 warning signals of computer crime?

SECURITY

Preventing computer crime and the invasion of individual privacy is a matter of security. In this sense, the term security applies to all measures designed to protect computers and information resources against misuse and/or theft. Even with an extensive security system in place there is no such thing as complete protection for a computer system and its information assets.

With many computer systems, immediate processing demands overshadow security concerns. People are so involved with getting their work done that the monitoring of operations is slack. Inputs are not as controlled as they should be, and outputs are not always checked for accuracy and completeness. Often, security components are left out of the programs themselves, as programmers concern themselves only with the processing of tasks to be completed.

The cost of security is another consideration. Building a secure system takes time and resources. Once security measures are in place, the system may be more expensive to operate. If operations personnel spend half of each work-

Physical Controls to Secure Computer Systems

1. Place computer equipment in areas of limited access from the outside
2. Physically secure equipment to floors and tables
3. Place identification numbers on all equipment, manuals, and software
4. Restrict physical access to authorized people
5. Build computer centers to withstand natural disasters
6. Provide smoke detectors and fire suppression systems that do not harm electronic equipment
7. Place unused storage media in secure library
8. Copy-protect software
9. Use data encryption when storing data and software on storage media

FIGURE 14.8

Computer systems of all sizes can be protected by these commonsense controls.

day verifying outputs, half of their salaries is spent on security or, figuring it another way, the cost of completing work assignments is doubled. Built-in security features in programs require the processing of more instructions. The result is a slow-down in processing as well as a demand for more computer power.

People must strike a balance between no security and near-complete security. The cost of security should be weighed against the price of potential losses. Security needs should be defined according to the files and the equipment they protect. In a school setting, for example, a system that keeps student grades merits stricter security than a system producing class rosters.

Controls for Small Computer Systems

Small computers are a personal resource. To protect data and equipment, the user must decide who has access, then enforce this decision. Effective enforcement depends on two factors: physical controls and data security measures.

Physical Controls

The physical protection of equipment can be a difficult task. Often, computer equipment is located in locked, windowless rooms to deter unauthorized individuals from entering. The pieces of equipment themselves are bolted down. In addition, each piece might have a unique serial number. This expedites inventory and allows for easy identification of misplaced or stolen items.

Physical security, however, requires more than simply control over unauthorized access to computer equipment and programs. Disasters such as fires, floods, and earthquakes are major threats that occur unpredictably but require preparation and readiness. Protective and recovery measures must be in place, ready for instant activation. For small computer users this means storing master copies of software and hardware serial numbers in a local bank's safety deposit box or small, personal fireproof safe. In addition, smoke detectors and waterless fire extinguishers are a must for every office or home with a personal computer system.

Locked away in a drawer or safety deposit box, disks are relatively safe from unauthorized access. Also, many software houses add ***copy-protection*** to

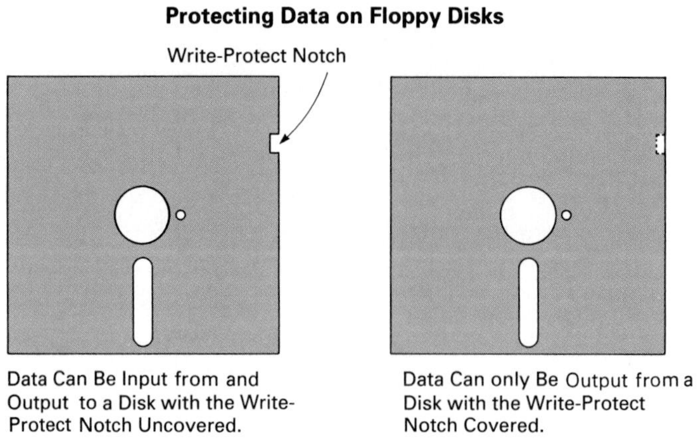

Protecting Data on Floppy Disks
Write-Protect Notch
Data Can Be Input from and Output to a Disk with the Write-Protect Notch Uncovered.
Data Can only Be Output from a Disk with the Write-Protect Notch Covered.

FIGURE 14.9

Data on floppy disk is protected from accidental erasure by covering the write-protect notch.

their programs. This prevents utility software from reading a program on one disk and transferring it to another. While copy-protection schemes secure software, data encryption programs help users protect important data. ***Data encryption*** is the act of scrambling data and programs stored on disk so that a copy of the data is unintelligible without a decoding program. Encryption programs, once the domain of large computer systems, are now available to small computer users.

Data Security Controls

After physical security measures have been established, logical measures take over to ensure that sensitive data are kept confidential. Physical security is external; access to the computer itself is controlled. Data security, on the other hand, is internal, and takes place after access to the system has been established.

To safeguard data from accidental erasure the ***write-protect notch*** on a floppy disk can be covered, as shown in Figure 14.9. Data on hard disk can also be ***write-protected*** with the help of the operating system. In both cases data can be read or input from the disk; however, the disk cannot be used to store new output.

When small computers are linked to other systems, another type of data security, system passwords, comes into play. Passwords may be required to access bulletin boards, information utilities, and electronic mail systems. Varying degrees of security clearance can be indicated by an individual's password. For example, bulletin board users might be issued a personal password permitting them to read and leave messages. A bulletin board operator (sys-op) has a special password enabling him or her to assign passwords to new users, deny access to system abusers, remove messages, and even modify the bulletin board program. Passwords and special accounts can separate and secure the work of individual users on this type of network. An added control is restricting the hours that the service is made available. But passwords are effective only if they are kept secret. The possibility that confidential information will be leaked is ever present.

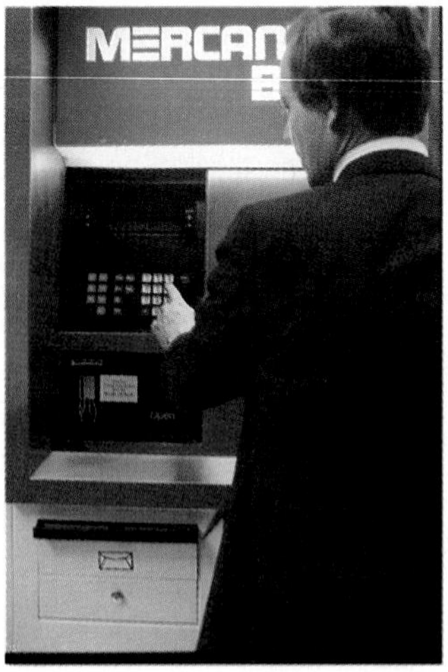

FIGURE 14.10

Passwords are used by automatic bank tellers to protect accounts from unauthorized access.

Maintaining Security of Large Computer Systems

Computer crime within an organization is usually discovered by accident—when it is discovered at all. In some cases, the failure of a computer system is the first clue that a crime is being committed. As the failure is being inspected and corrected, the crime is exposed. In such cases, criminals are not caught as a result

Summary of Management Controls

1. Management demonstrates knowledge and supports security measures for organization's computer center.
2. Management sets direction for computer center activities.

FIGURE 14.11

By taking an active role in overseeing computer center operations management plays an important part in the system's security.

of security controls in the computer system. This is evidence that few systems in existence today provide complete protection against computer crime. Computer professionals thus are faced with the challenge of designing systems that will detect unauthorized use of computers.

To meet this challenge, auditors working with computer professionals have developed special security procedures for computer systems. The procedures, known as ***electronic data processing (EDP) controls***, work with all five components of the computer system. The basic categories of EDP controls are:

- Management controls
- Computer center controls
- Input, processing, and output controls

Management Controls

Over the years, professionals have learned that management must be closely involved with data processing decisions. When decision makers do not take an active part in the control of data processing, they invite trouble. Mere awareness by top managers of the processing activities taking place can increase the security of a computer system considerably. While managers need not participate in the physical tasks required to process data, they should set the direction of processing activities.

Computer Center Controls

A close watch should be kept on computer center resources. Of course, the use of equipment must be restricted to authorized personnel. Users may be required to use a magnetically encoded plastic card or a combination applied to an electronic lock in order to enter a computer room. Closed-circuit television cameras may monitor and record entrance of all persons admitted to the computer center.

In addition, responsibilities in the computer center should be separated. To prevent any one employee from gaining unlimited access to the system, at least two categories of data processing employees should be created: operations personnel and development personnel. The operations group controls the equipment and application programs in use, while the development group creates new programs. These divisions complement each other and provide security checks and balances.

Another computer center control lies in scrupulous record keeping. All processing needs should be accommodated within a precise schedule. Procedures and job schedules need to be documented and verified. Supervisors must examine operations to verify that the procedures are followed, and records of computer activity need to be reviewed regularly. In addition, schedules and procedures must be stable—that is, operators should not be able to change them easily and frequently.

FIGURE 14.12
Specialized keys permit computer centers to control access to computer facilities and allow for accurate records of the comings and goings of personnel.

Equipment use also needs to be recorded in order to ensure that only authorized personnel gain access to computer tools. This measure protects the equipment from damage and helps ensure delivery of output to the right people. Limiting access to the computer room reduces traffic and helps eliminate errors.

In addition to protecting computing resources during normal operations, equipment in a computer center should be arranged to withstand the earth's rumblings and other natural disasters. Every computer center needs recovery procedures that specify measures to be applied if data resources are damaged or destroyed. The recovery plan can include use of backup files, rented computers in alternate facilities, and other measures. Staff training in recovery procedures must be mandatory.

Input, Processing, and Output Controls

Management has the responsibility of placing controls on input, processing, and output. Input controls affect data before they are entered into the computer.

Summary of Computer Center Controls

1. Access to computer center is controlled.
2. Responsibilities in computer center are separated into operations and development.
3. Activities are scheduled and kept.
4. Operations personnel are supervised and not allowed to change schedules.
5. Operating procedures are documented.

FIGURE 14.13
Computer center controls help to assure the security of information processed and stored by computers.

FIGURE 14.14
Computer operators take an active part in maintaining input, processing, and output controls.

Managers need to establish a standard form for input data. Operations personnel must be instructed to reject inputs presented in improper form. When appropriate, outputs should be compared against control totals made independently of the computer system. People use control totals to double-check the accuracy of figures produced by the computer system.

As an example, control totals can be used in the processing of report cards. After determining class grades, a teacher might count the number of students receiving each letter grade. He might determine that 16 A's were given in a particular class. The computer also counts the A grades given to students as it processes and prints the report cards. A report with the computer's grade total is sent to the teacher before the cards are issued. The teacher compares the number of grades on the computer report with the control totals taken prior to processing. If the numbers do not match, the teacher is alerted to a problem before the cards are distributed.

Control totals are one of the most important precautions a user can take. Users should be trained to record control totals effectively and use them properly.

Input into teleprocessing applications is harder to control. System programs can use passwords and account numbers to accept only certain input from designated users or locations. A bank customer issued an ATM (automatic teller machine) personal identification number can access a personal bank account from anywhere around town. If someone is foolish enough to leave the password in a wallet, and the wallet is stolen, an unauthorized person can gain access to the account. The system has no control over this security break. Users would be wise to protect their passwords and change them periodically.

Controls over the processing of data rely mainly on documentation. Procedures and schedules must be clearly stated and strictly followed for effective security of a computer system. Supervisors have the responsibility to monitor operations to make sure these conditions are being met.

Online systems pose special security challenges because transactions can often be difficult to trace. For example, a special sales price might be changed

Summary of Input, Processing, and Output Controls

Input
Established standards for input data
Verification of control totals
Use of passwords

Processing
Clearly stated procedures and schedules
Review of activity logs
Documentation

Output
Documented procedures for distributing output
People use control totals to double-check accuracy of output
Limit access to output to authorized personnel

FIGURE 14.15

Input, processing, and output controls that can contribute to the security of computer-maintained information are summarized in this checklist.

several times online, without producing a written record of the transaction. The absence of these records presents a major security risk. As a result, online programs often instruct the computer to record each change on an ***activity log***. An activity log, or summary of online activity, is used to correct errors or to assist auditors in reviewing records.

The operations department should keep records of all processing errors and system failures. Each correction requires documentation. Data processing supervisors can review these records to trace unauthorized activity or other problems. The records also help supervisors evaluate employee performance.

Finally, people need to control the output from all data processing activities. Procedures for distributing output must be documented and followed. Only authorized users should have access to output. These users need to examine returned outputs for completeness and accuracy. Checking control totals, as previously noted, raises the level of security in output.

STUDY QUESTIONS

7. Define electronic data processing (EDP) controls, and activity log.
8. What type of physical security is provided by copy protection and data encryption?
9. What are nine types of physical controls that can be used to secure a computer system?
10. How is the write-protect notch used to safeguard data on floppy disks?
11. How can data be protected after access to a computer system has been established?
12. How are computer crimes often discovered?
13. Describe three EDP controls that are oriented towards protecting an organization's computer system(s).

CONCLUSION

Computers have the capacity to be a boon to humankind and to help us solve some of our greatest problems. However, they also have the capacity to be destructive, to limit personal freedom, and to eliminate personal privacy. How can we best obtain the benefits of computer technology while minimizing the dangers?

The greatest strength we have is knowledge. As you take courses like this one, you will learn what computer systems should be. You also will learn what the dangers of computer technology are and what we can do to avoid these pitfalls. Never underestimate the power of education.

As more people learn how to deal with computers, they will exercise more power as consumers. They will learn to observe the quality of computer service and will choose to do business with companies that have secure systems. As time passes, competition in the marketplace will eliminate companies that operate substandard computer systems.

CHAPTER FACTS

- Computer abuse and its prevention center around three issues: individual privacy, computer crime, and computer system security.
- Consumers' rights to privacy are covered legally by the Fourth Amendment to the Constitution, the Freedom of Information Act of 1970, the Fair Credit Reporting Act of 1970, the Privacy Act of 1974, the Comprehensive Crime Control Act of 1984, and the Electronic Communications Privacy Act of 1986.
- The impact of computers can best be controlled through the education of consumers and legislation.
- Any organization can be victimized by computer crime. Most organizations are reluctant to prosecute due to the negative publicity. Many crimes go undetected since most are discovered only by accident.
- Stealing computer time, programs, and data, and changing data or programs are the major types of computer crime.
- Eleven warning signals often identify organizations that are vulnerable to computer crime.
- All computer systems can benefit from physical controls and data security. Special protection should be taken against natural disasters and fires. Data encryption and other protections against illegal copying also are useful.
- Organizations with large computer systems need EDP controls. These include controls for management, for the computer center, and for data input, processing, and output.

TERMS TO REMEMBER

activity log
copy protection
data encryption
electronic data processing (EDP) controls
write-protect
write-protect notch

INSIGHT

PRIVACY: IS IT STILL POSSIBLE?

As you gain an education, get a job, and become an active member of society, you are constantly contributing to the numerous databases that contain personal information about you. Your involvement in the invasion of your own privacy may be unintentional, and indeed, sometimes beyond your control.

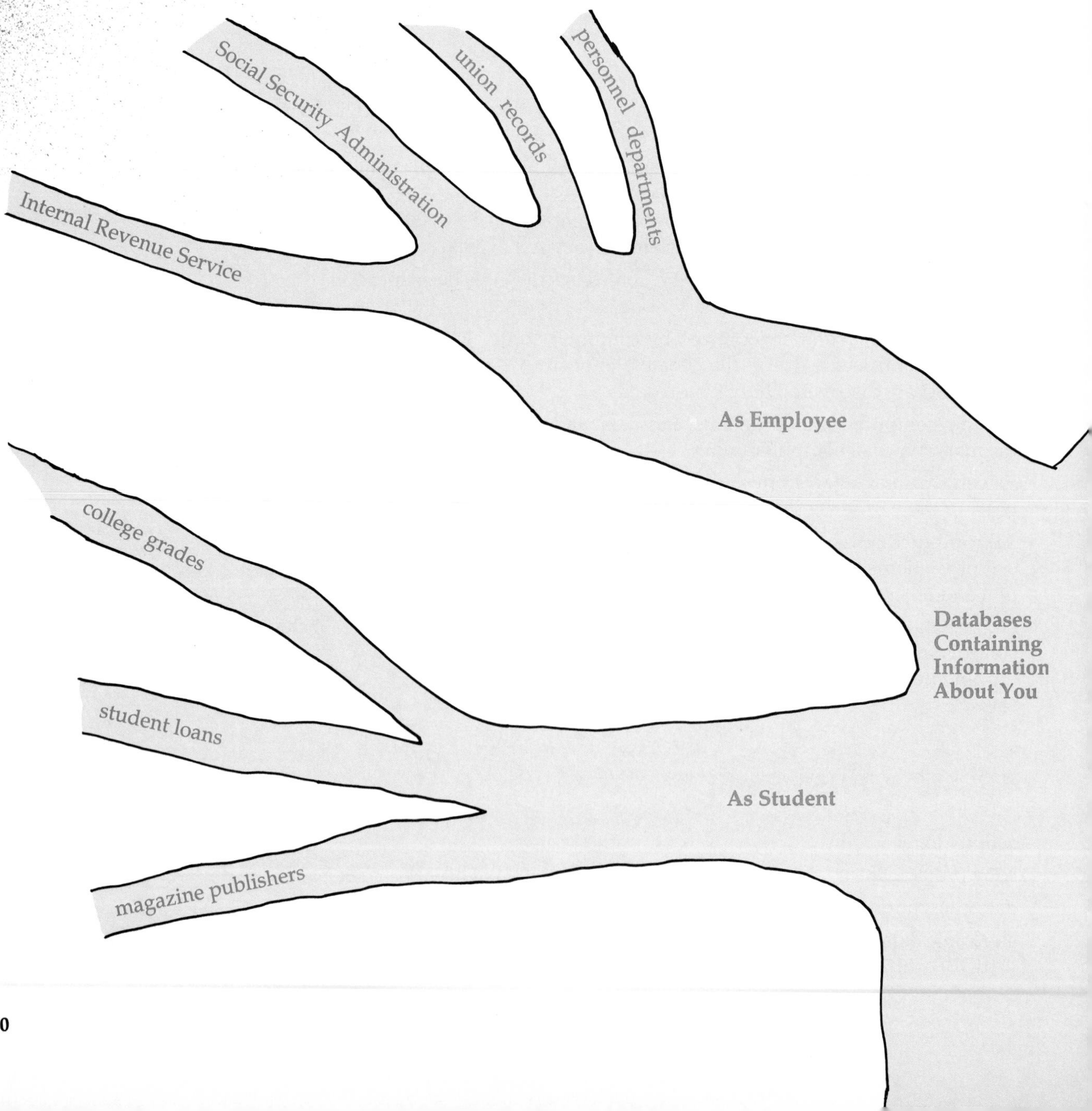

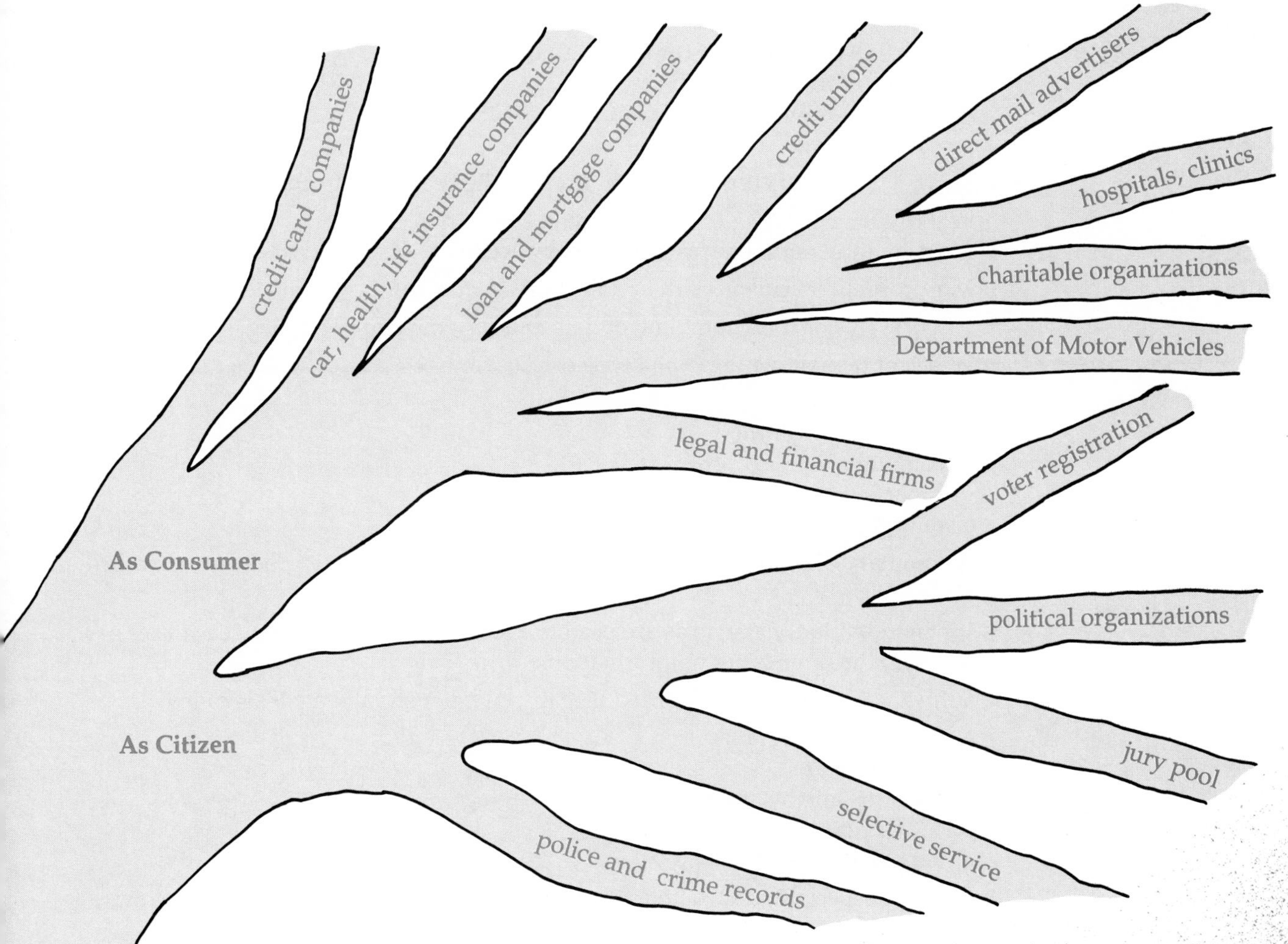

Monitoring the Flow of Information

Although you cannot prevent data acquisition by organizations (nor would you always want to), you can ensure its correctness and proper use with these measures:

1. *Check on the data kept about you.* It is your responsibility to request your credit and social security files every few years. Look for incorrect or missing data. Follow through to see that corrections are made.

2. *Know your rights.* Do not release information unnecessarily. Make sure that giving permission to check personnel and employee records is really needed, not just routine.

3. *Remove your name from unwanted mailing lists.* A letter to organizations and/or direct mail companies should stop some of the junk mail. Contact the Better Business Bureau if that does not help.

4. *Support consumer rights legislation.* Know what laws are being proposed and write to express your opinion. Join or support consumer advocate groups.

Is privacy still possible? Only when you help protect yourself!

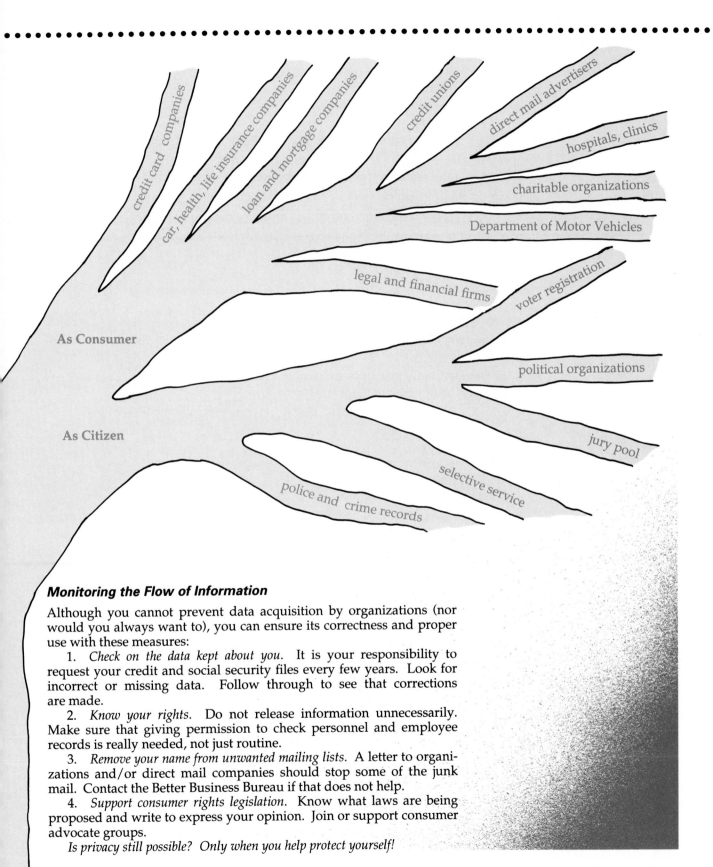

CHECK YOUR UNDERSTANDING

1. Which of the following is ***not*** legislation that protects an individual's right to privacy?
   a. Fair Credit Reporting Act of 1970
   b. Fourth Amendment of the Constitution
   c. Right to Privacy Act of 1974
   d. Freedom of Information Act of 1970
   e. All are correct.
2. ___________ and consumer education are the best ways to control the impact of computers.
3. Most computer crimes are discovered by accident. (True/False)
4. Most computer crimes result in public prosecution of the criminals. (True/False)
5. ___________ is the scrambling of data and programs to deter illegal copying.
6. Which of the following is ***not*** a type of EDP control?
   a. management control
   b. logical data control
   c. computer center control
   d. processing control
   e. output control
7. A summary of online work that is kept for checking security procedures is called a(n) ___________.
8. When individual passwords are used to access a computer system, each user has access to the same types of information. (True/False)
9. Software that cannot be recorded illegally on other storage media is called:
   a. decryption programs
   b. legal software
   c. user-unavailable programs
   d. copy-protected software
   e. none of the above
10. Fires are especially destructive to computer systems since all extinguishing material also destroys electronic equipment. (True/False)

APPLYING WHAT YOU'VE LEARNED

1. Some people say, "The best way to catch a criminal is to think like a criminal." Using the warning signs and physical controls mentioned in the text, make a list of five ways security could be improved in your school computer lab or room containing a home computer. Describe any new procedures or people that would have to be involved.
2. It is part of our legal system to make the punishment fit the crime. Some computer criminals are teenagers or younger. Do you think it is fair to try them as adults? Are prison and/or fines reasonable punishments for them? What would be other ways they could make restitution for their computer crimes? Write a short paper explaining your views.
3. Design an activity log or software sign-out sheet for the people using equipment at school or at home. Include space for names, times, equipment used, and other information needed to monitor security.

4. Find an article in a newspaper or magazine about a computer crime. Write a short summary of the crime, including how it was discovered, the results, and what controls you think were missing that allowed this crime to happen.
5. There have been many attempts in Congress to update the privacy legislation mentioned in the text. Some potential laws involve the issues of software protection, data encryption, and punishment for computer criminals. Find out about one of these proposed laws. Describe what it would include, when it was first drafted, and what its present status is in the legislature.
6. Most programs on diskette can be easily copied despite any regulations or copyrights. If you produced a program to be sold and wished to protect it from being copied, what would you do? On the other hand, is it justified for people who need backup copies of software to make illegal copies rather than go without backup and possibly lose access to valuable software if it is accidentally destroyed?

CHECK YOUR UNDERSTANDING ANSWERS

1. e
2. legislation
3. true
4. false
5. data encryption
6. b
7. activity log
8. false
9. d
10. false

C H A P T E R F I F T E E N

SYSTEMS DEVELOPMENT

KEY IDEAS

- **From the user's point of view**
  What steps does a systems analyst follow when developing new computer systems? How can you, as an informed user, participate in this process?
- **Handling information problems**
  Managers had to accept new principles and learn to think differently before organizations could realize the value of computers.

  Developing new systems
  A lack of communication between management and technicians can cause problems when developing computer systems.

  System life cycles
  The life-cycle approach to systems development organizes the job into a series of steps.
- **Life cycle step one: requirements**
  Systems development starts by defining requirements.
- **Life cycle step two: alternative evaluation**
  Every reasonable alternative must be examined before picking a specific solution.
- **Life cycle step three: design**
  Each step in the life cycle requires examination at greater depth and detail.
- **Life cycle step four: implementation and maintenance**
  In the final step, the system is ready for use and is fine-tuned for long-term success.

FROM THE USER'S POINT OF VIEW

The chances are good that one day you will need to purchase a small computer system. Historically, systems development was a long, involved process that centered on the acquisition or replacement of a mainframe computer system. Many of the lessons learned by computer professionals can be applied to purchasing personal computer systems. In this chapter, we juxtapose a traditional approach to systems development with advice on how to wisely buy a computer system of your own.

HANDLING INFORMATION PROBLEMS

Computers introduce a new, expensive technology to organizations. Managers had to accept new principles and learn to think differently before their organizations could realize the potential value of computers. To appreciate the extent of change required to harness computer power, we first have to consider earlier developments.

Developing New Systems

When computers were introduced in the 1950s, they represented a substantial investment in an unproven, although promising, technology. Computers at this time cost millions of dollars. Developing the programs needed to operate the computers cost millions more. However, there was really no choice. Large companies were finding it impossible to keep up with information processing and paperwork requirements. Astute managers quickly recognized that they had to get on the computer bandwagon or be left hopelessly behind the times.

Part of the problem was that—following the great economic expansion after World War II—organizations were badly in need of increased information processing capacities. The computer obviously held the potential for solution. But computer technology was too formidable for most managers. As a result, managers could only utilize this technology through a new breed of technicians who spoke the language of computers. These computer professionals, for their part, had virtually no understanding of organizational problems or needs. A communications gap formed that hindered the matching of computer applications and their prospective, productive users.

Development of information systems for computer processing was a major undertaking. The amounts of data involved and the complexity of programs proved formidable. Experienced project managers found similarities between the activities required to develop a computer system and those associated with the creation and implementation of new products and services. Comparatively few organizations had experience with administrative systems of this scope.

Because of communication and technological obstacles, many early attempts to develop large computer systems led to disasters. One common problem cen-

FIGURE 15.1

Memory limitations of early computers are characterized by the small capacities of core memories like the one in this photo.

From the archives of Data Processing Management Association.

tered around the development of advanced systems that failed to deal with or solve the stated problems. This was largely the result of a lack of communication between managers and technicians.

Another type of unpleasant surprise came in the form of costs for these *systems development projects.* The steps taken to define and create new system solutions to existing problems demanded time and money. A major airline reservation system developed during the 1950s, for example, was reported to have overrun its original budget by some $40 million. Initial systems for processing checks and deposit slips in banks experienced even greater cost overruns.

System Life Cycles

Once the obstacles were identified, however, methods for bridging the communication gap were not far behind. A number of organizations devised project techniques similar to those that had worked with defense and aerospace projects. Also, at about this time, the same methods were being used to manage a project aimed at putting an American astronaut on the moon.

The idea is simple and proven. Any major systems project will involve solving problems that cannot be known or understood completely in advance. There are just too many activities associated with a major project. To make projects of this type manageable, the overall job is broken into a series of small activities. These portions of the problem are small enough to be understood and planned. In the case of space exploration, different scientific teams were assigned to develop vehicle structures, life support systems, radiation shielding, navigation, propulsion systems, and many others.

Similar thinking led computer specialists to devise project structures, also known as *life cycles,* that organize the job of developing a system into a series of parts, or steps. Management then can understand and monitor projects on a step-by-step basis, taking care to avoid situations in which designs fail to solve problems or major cost overruns occur. As a special precaution, systems development methodologies require that both users and organizational managers also be involved in the development process.

Users contribute to the process by specifying their needs and reviewing proposed solutions stated in terms they can understand. Top managers partici-

FIGURE 15.2

The life-cycle approach to systems development was applied to coordinate the complex task of landing men on the moon.

Courtesy of NASA

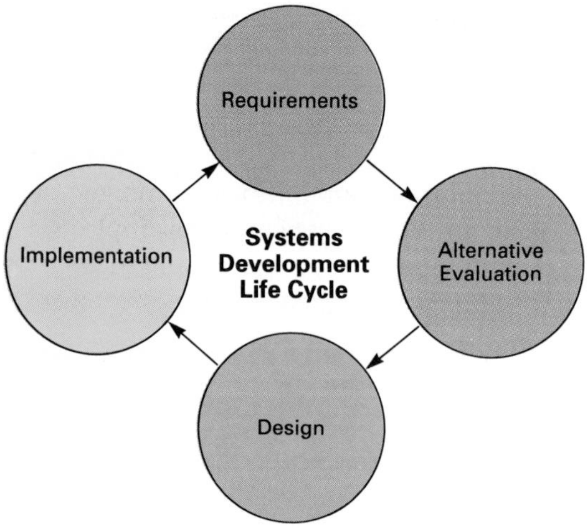

FIGURE 15.3

Systems development conforms to a four-step life cycle that involves defining requirements, evaluating alternatives, design, and final implementation.

pate in a process that reviews progress at each step in the project. Reports to top managers make it possible to approve the project for further development, to cancel the commitment, or to amend the mission of the project. The establishment of control, in turn, provides a framework that promotes effective communication and understanding.

Project control methods are standard within most organizations that develop computer information systems. However, the standards tend to be individualized. That is, each organization generally establishes its own project structures and reporting requirements to solve the problems defined by its management. Thus, the life cycle or project structure in each organization will differ from that of every other organization. This is dictated by the size of the organization, the scope of the problem, and the type of equipment used. Small organizations and individuals who use microcomputers have needs different from those of larger organizations, with minicomputers or mainframes. Nonetheless, there are common requirements for systems development projects. The description of the life cycle presented in the remainder of this chapter is based on those common factors.

A typical life–cycle structure used to guide the development of computer information systems can be organized into the following steps:

- Requirements
- Alternative Evaluation
- Design
- Implementation

Each major step can be broken into a series of phases that are more specific in nature.

STUDY QUESTIONS

1. Define systems development project and life cycle.
2. What were two of the major problems in developing early computer systems?
3. Explain how systems development projects are made more manageable.

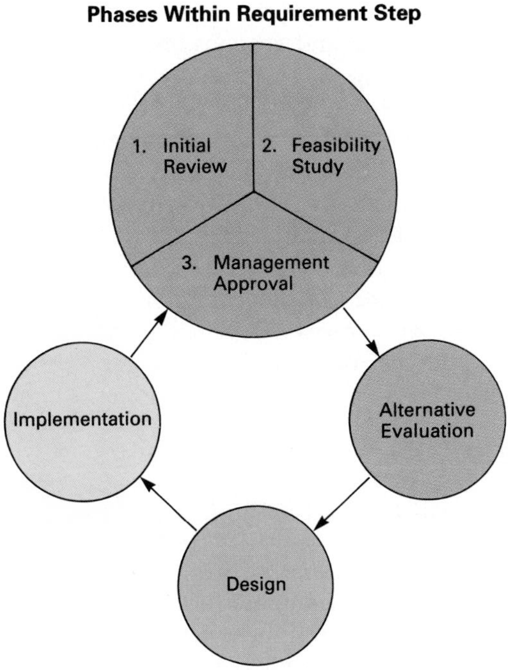

FIGURE 15.4

The requirements step focuses on clearly identifying the problem to be solved.

4. What special precautions should be added to the systems development process to help ensure success?
5. Identify the four steps in the life cycle of a systems development project.

LIFE CYCLE STEP ONE: REQUIREMENTS

To avoid developing systems that fail to solve the identified problems, virtually all life cycles begin by defining system requirements. This initial phase tends to be relatively informal and also short in duration.

Initial Review

Systems development should begin with a user request, or at least with close user involvement. Ideally, users who have gained some sophistication with computer capabilities are the first to identify a problem. One or more users approach the computer center manager or the head of the organization's systems development group. Sometimes the systems development process is initiated when employees bring to the computer center manager an idea for improving the existing system or information about new computer software. In an organization that does not have systems development professionals, a user-developer or an outside consultant may investigate a problem and possible solutions.

The problem or idea is discussed and a systems analyst, a specialist in computer systems development, is assigned to perform an ***initial review***. During this review, the analyst interviews users to identify the source of a problem, and to try to determine if the problem has a computer-based solution. Sometimes, the problem involves lack of procedures or poor management and can be corrected without the help of a computer. If the issue is looking at new software, the analyst will review what the software does and its role in the existing system.

FIGURE 15.5

Systems analysis requires the building of an understanding of user needs through studies and interviews.

Courtesy of Honeywell, Inc.

Regardless of the starting point, the initial review is devoted primarily to the analysis of user operations and responsibilities in the specific area being studied. Users are asked to help the systems analyst understand the basic operations involved. The user must identify the problems, opportunities, and benefits resulting from application of a computer to the issue under study.

Once the user has done this, the systems analyst can make a preliminary estimate of the effort and cost involved in computerizing the job. The user-identified benefits then can be compared with the costs estimated by the analyst. Within a couple of weeks the analyst's findings are written into the initial review and presented to management. At this time, the computer center manager or systems development supervisor decides whether the idea has enough merit to pursue it with an in–depth feasibility study.

Feasibility Study

In the second requirement phase, a ***feasibility study*** is conducted. This study determines whether the project is realistic in terms of time, costs, and resources. Additional users and analysts become involved as part of an ***applications development team***. This team gathers enough information to define and describe user operations in terms of volumes of transactions, number of people involved, turnaround or deadline requirements, methods of storage and uses for accumulated data, current problems, and opportunities for improvement.

The main techniques for information gathering are questionnaires, interviews, observations, data flow diagrams, and collecting sample documents. Questionnaires are employed when a large number of users must be involved with a feasibility study. When managers or key people are involved, personal interviews are conducted. Observations and sample documents help team members identify where data originate and where they are used in an organization. The resulting ***data flow diagram*** (see Figure 15.6) provides a visual representation of how the data and people interact.

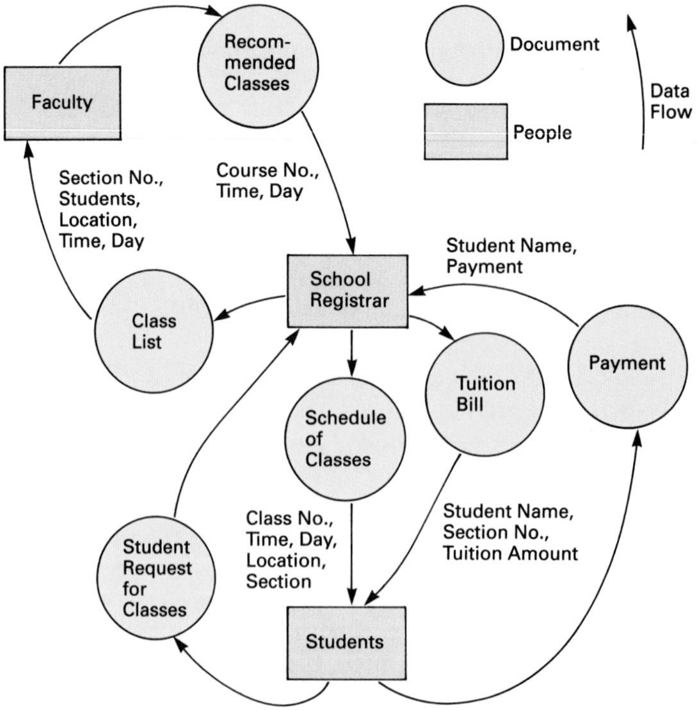

FIGURE 15.6

Data flow diagrams show the movement and processing of data items as they move through an application. Circles show processing steps. Lines and arrows identify data items and their flow.

Requirements for a Personal Computer System

A. Identify needs and initial review of finances
B. Personal productivity software vs. specialized software:
   1. business
   2. education
   3. graphics
   4. entertainment
   5. telecommunications
C. Location of equipment
   1. electric outlets
   2. work space
   3. security
D. Who will be using the new system?

FIGURE 15.7

Purchasing a personal computer requires examining finances, needs, and potential locations.

At this point, the team concentrates on the main applications and work assignments. Experienced analysts follow a well-known guideline: the rule of 80-20. This holds that, in any system, 20 percent of the documents or tasks will represent 80 percent of the work. An important skill for analysts, then, lies in recognizing and concentrating on the 20 percent of the activities and processes that are the key to the system.

The team gains enough knowledge of operations so that they can develop initial plans about the computer equipment to be used, the storage space required, the number of people who will be involved, the overall design or specifications for required programs, and any procedures required.

A result of a feasibility study should be a preliminary budget and schedule for the project. These estimates will be refined as part of step 2: alternative evaluation. However, experienced computer professionals should be able to estimate costs and benefits close enough so that managers can make informed decisions. The feasibility report delivered at the end of this phase provides a recommendation on whether system development should continue. If the recommendation is favorable, management is asked for a substantial commitment of funds to carry the project forward. Also, a schedule is provided that requests assignment of people to the project for an extended period of time.

Requirements for a Personal Computer System

For microcomputer systems development the requirements step is shorter since fewer users are involved. Initial review involves balancing finances against short–and long–term computer needs. The primary question is "What do you want to do with a computer system?"

Business, entertainment, education, graphics, or telecommunications are all reasonable needs. Each need must be examined to see if it requires specialized software or if it can be accomplished with personal productivity software, such as word processing or spreadsheets. Furthermore, each application must be identified as a current or future need, since you may be purchasing the system in stages. The general rule at this point is to dream a little. You will quickly become practical as your budget limits the scope of your initial purchase.

CLIP

A PROPERLY PLANNED INTERVIEW CAN BE AN ANALYST'S BEST TOOL

While the methods of obtaining useful information from the user vary greatly, the personal interview will bring the best results and best understanding, if conducted properly. The properly planned interview can be the analyst's best business tool in the tool kit.

An important key to excellent interviewing skills is the ability of the analyst to prepare to deal with the different personalities and attitudes of the people being interviewed. If the analyst can modify personal style to complement the personality of the interviewee, then a channel of communication will be established that will allow ideas to be effectively communicated and the needed information to be obtained.

Studies indicate that verbal messages convey 7%, intonations convey 38%, and body language conveys 55% of the total message. Body language is the key factor, and the alert and well-informed analyst and interviewer should take advantage of this fact during the interview.

Listening has specific goals as they relate to the interviewee as an employee:

1. To raise the level of employee motivation.
2. To increase the readiness of subordinates to accept change.
3. To improve the quality of all managerial decisions.
4. To develop teamwork and morale.

Active listening is characterized by a nonjudgmental attempt on one person's part to allow the other person to explore a problem. Use of body language that encourages openness and acceptance should motivate the employee to participate in the interview more fully, and this should be the interviewer's goal in obtaining information. As with other attitudes, openness encourages similar feelings in others.

Source: Reprinted by permission, *Data Management* (Data Processing Management Association)

Key Question: In what other areas of your life could these interviewing techniques be put to use?

Most of the time a personal computer system will not be used by a single individual. List everyone who will have access to the new system and see if their needs are included in the initial review. Finally, think about where the computer system will be used. Is there sufficient workspace in this area? Are there enough electrical outlets to power a computer, screen, printer, and so on? Is the location secure and out of a high foot traffic area? By carefully thinking through these concerns, you will be sure that all of your requirements for the new computer system will be included.

STUDY QUESTIONS

6. Define initial review, feasibility study, applications development team, and data flow diagram.
7. What usually initiates the development of a new computer system?
8. Who performs an initial review and what are their responsibilities?
9. Who determines if a new computer system has merit and initiates the feasibility study?
10. Who would be a member of an applications development team during the feasibility study phase?
11. What information-gathering techniques are part of the feasibility study?
12. Explain the 80-20 rule.
13. What are the results of a feasibility study?
14. Describe how the requirements step applies to the purchase of a personal computer system.

LIFE CYCLE STEP TWO: ALTERNATIVE EVALUATION

The initial step, which defines requirements, covers the entire scope of the proposed project, including all problems and benefits that can be foreseen. Each succeeding step does the same, but in greater depth. That is, users and computer professionals review the same application repeatedly, in more detail each time. At each step, the development team gains a broader, clearer view of the problems and methods of solution.

Identifying Alternatives

A new systems development project affects all five components of a computer system in some way. Even if some components are not directly changed, the systems analyst must examine each to see how it influences the other system components.

When examining available solutions for solving the problem, the applications development team must include a wide range of alternatives. They try to describe viable alternatives that meet the requirements defined in step one. Each alternative must specifically address all five components of a computer system. The alternatives will differ according to how system components must be acquired or modified. This does not necessarily mean that new computer hardware or software will be purchased. Many times, changes in existing procedures

Alternatives for a New Outpatient Clinic*			
System Component	**Alternative 1: Purchase Minicomputer**	**Alternative 2: Connect to Hospital's Mainframe**	**Alternative 3: Hire Service Bureau**
Hardware	Minicomputer Terminals Printers Disk Drives	Terminals Concentrators Lease telephone line	Service Bureau provides hardware
Programs	New programs for every application	Use existing programs maintained by hospital	Service Bureau provides programs
Data	Create new files for every application	Use hospital's database	Create new files for every application or create a database
Procedures	Operating Maintenance Backup Data collection Emergency/ trouble-shooting	Data collection Emergency/ trouble-shooting	Data collection
People	Train existing staff as users Hire and train operations personnel	Train existing staff as users	Train existing staff as users
*NOTE: Cost/benefit analysis and list of intangibles not included			

FIGURE 15.8

Identification of alternative solutions to meet the needs of a new system is an important part of the systems development process. One method is illustrated here.

or personnel will solve the problem. The systems development process is iterative. As each component is examined, requirements for the others may change.

For example, a hospital that establishes a new outpatient clinic at a remote location can consider several alternatives. The new clinic can be connected to the hospital's mainframe by adding teleprocessing capabilities, can retain its own minicomputer, or can hire an outside agency (***service bureau***) to handle its data processing needs. As shown in Figure 15.8, each of these alternatives, in turn, will require a different mix of personnel, peripheral equipment, software, data organization, and procedures.

Phases Within the Alternative Evaluation Step

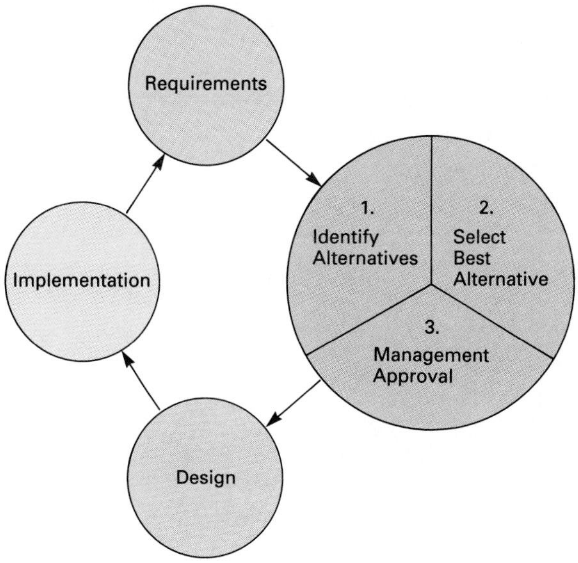

FIGURE 15.9

During alternative evaluation, every reasonable solution to the problem is examined before a recommendation is made to management.

Not all systems development projects require new hardware. Sometimes it is just a matter of deciding which personal productivity software to use to solve the problem. A large law firm may decide to standardize the word processing packages used by its offices across the country. In this case, the computer hardware already exists and the consulting systems analyst would only need to poll the legal secretaries and clerks to define software requirements. Although the data and hardware would not be affected by the new software, participating personnel must be trained and new procedures written for them. The alternatives would be selected from off-the-shelf word processing software currently on the market.

Once the alternatives have been selected, the next phase is to pick the one that best solves the problem. In a report to management, each alternative is described in detail, along with a ***cost/benefit analysis***, which identifies the associated costs and benefits for each alternative. The team also lists their recommendation as to which alternative is the best. This alternative is not always the least expensive or the easiest to complete, however. The best alternative is one that provides the most effective solution to the problem. When this objective is met by several alternatives, cost and time requirements then become deciding factors.

FIGURE 15.10

The final phase in alternative evaluation is to select the best alternative and receive management approval for design and implementation.

Courtesy of Dan McCoy, Rainbow

If management is presented with alternatives ranging from the easiest and least expensive to more complex and more expensive solutions, they will support the team's decision since management knows what alternatives have been rejected. Also, management must consider the hidden or intangible costs and benefits for alternatives. Employee satisfaction or stress, increased availability of management information, and improved customer service are intangible costs and benefits. They may not be classified in dollar terms but are still important to consider. For example, the installation of a new computer system in a department store during the Christmas rush may be most effective in solving a processing problem, but such a solution could be stressful to already harried employees.

The final phase of this step is to obtain management approval of the alternative selected by the analyst. Projections of costs and benefits will be consid-

Alternatives for a Personal Computer System

A. Software drives hardware (what do you really need?)
B. Identify necessary system components
    1. minimum memory
    2. operating system
    3. keyboard layout
    4. two disk drives
    5. minimum expansion slots
C. Performance vs. price considerations for system components
    1. hard disk drive
    2. color vs. monochrome
    3. graphics
    4. clock speed of processor
    5. potential multiprogramming capabilities
D. Specialized hardware
    1. intangible costs (learning to operate new software and hardware)
    2. hidden costs
        a. floppy disks
        b. printer paper
        c. printer ribbons and cartridges
    3. intangible benefits
        a. increased personal productivity
        b. competitive edge

FIGURE 15.11

Before purchasing a personal computer system, hardware and software performance must be weighed against price.

ered reliable if they are supported by both users and computer professionals. At this time, schedules and budget projections are reaffirmed as management approves the start of the design step. However, it is possible for management to reject the proposal. They may request that another alternative be investigated more thoroughly or dismiss the project altogether because conditions within the organization have changed.

Alternatives for a Personal Computer System

When examining alternatives for a personal computer system remember: Software drives hardware. In other words, the software you select determines hardware requirements. For instance, minimum internal memory requirements and choice of operating system are dictated by software selection. Some alternatives, such as keyboard layout, for example, are just a matter of personal choice. On the other hand, most computer professionals agree that a minimum of two disk drives should be available to simplify copying and backup procedures.

At this juncture you must weigh the costs of software and hardware against the benefits. High-speed computers with multiprogramming capabilities will cost more than slower machines and may not be suitable for your needs. Can you cost–justify a hard disk at this time or will two floppy disk drives suffice? How important is color and graphics? Do you need a high-speed, letter-quality laser printer or could you use a draft-quality dot-matrix printer? Expansion slots provide an opportunity to add system components you cannot afford at this time. Make sure you have enough expansion slots to accommodate future purchases.

FIVE DECADES OF PROGRAMMING: A HISTORY OF THE DEMAND FOR MAINTENANCE

The era of equations: 1946 to 1956. Essentially all software is new. Maintenance, in the sense of continued updates to completed software, scarcely exists because applications are generally engineering aids with finite solutions.

The decade of business solutions: 1956 to 1966. Large corporations begin to use computers for automating labor-intensive clerical tasks. A need for maintenance surfaces as corporations realize that their applications cannot remain static but must evolve with changing business climates.

The golden age of new software: 1966 to 1976. Computers and software become indispensable, and corporations create hundreds of new applications every year. Production libraries explode in size, setting the stage for future maintenance problems.

The era of entropy: 1976 to 1986. Maintenance problems surface as production libraries grow older and larger. Companies devote an average of 35% of their programming efforts to maintaining and enhancing existing software. Corporations recognize the need for maintenance specialists and tools.

The age of maintenance: 1986 to 1996. Maintenance becomes the dominant programming activity in major corporations, although development continues as well. Developers introduce new tools and methods for dealing with aging and unstructured software.

Source: Reprinted by Permission, *Computerworld*.

Key Question: Does the history of system development seem to indicate an increase or decrease in the number of programmers needed in the future?

Personal computer systems do include intangible costs and benefits. While your system may eventually increase your productivity, you will need time to familiarize yourself with new software and hardware. Hidden ongoing costs include purchasing disks, paper, and printer ribbons. You must realize you will spend as much on software and incidentals as you will on hardware. The result of the alternative evaluation step is to complete a list of hardware and software features, without specifying particular brand names.

STUDY QUESTIONS

15. Define service bureau and cost/benefit analysis.
16. Why does the applications development team provide management with a list of alternative system solutions?
17. What are three intangible costs and benefits managers must consider when evaluating system alternatives?
18. What decisions are made in the final phase of the alternative evaluation step?
19. What decisions are made when evaluating alternatives for a personal computer system?

LIFE CYCLE STEP THREE: DESIGN

The purpose of the design step is explained best by the end product that marks its completion. Typically, this step concludes with the acceptance of a document called ***system specifications***. This is a description that covers, in enough detail to satisfy both management and users, all the results and methods to be incorporated into a new system.

Included in the system specifications will be designs and samples of all of the transaction documents and reports to be produced. Also included will be descriptions of the procedures to be followed by all involved personnel, as well as related functions and services to be provided by computer professionals. Equipment to be installed is described without getting into detail about makes and model numbers of devices.

To put this effort in perspective, the system specifications can be straightforward when a new microcomputer system is involved or quite voluminous when larger systems are being designed. Activities and requirements can include an examination of each of the five components.

HARDWARE

If new computer equipment is required, working parameters for selecting it are determined. Size, storage, and memory requirements for computers are chosen. Peripheral equipment, such as printers, requires detailed specifications concerning speed, method of printing, and print style. When selecting a terminal, its keyboard layout, screen size, and screen color options need to be chosen. The office facilities to be affected are studied to see where and how any new equipment and/or furniture will be accommodated.

An implementation and installation plan must be developed. If new computer and/or data communications equipment will be required, a ***request for proposal (RFP)*** will be needed; this describes hardware specifications and re-

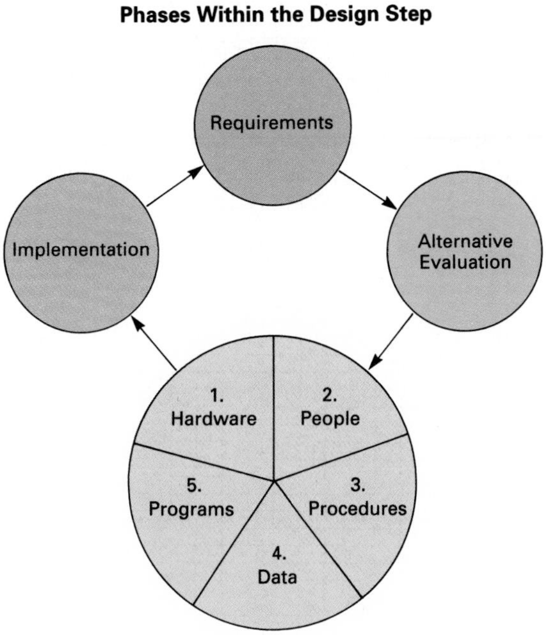

FIGURE 15.12

Each component of a new computer system must be examined as part of the design step.

quests vendors to propose solutions. These proposals include a description of specific products, training, and service, as well as associated costs. The RFP is the first step in securing bids and placing orders for new equipment. In acquiring a new microcomputer system, the RFP may involve nothing more than comparison shopping at several local computer stores. Large computers and data communications switching devices can require long periods of advanced planning and installation. In many situations, the equipment delivery schedule determines when a system can be implemented.

Programs

Existing programs can be modified or new programs acquired. If changes need to be made to programs, they can be done by internal programming staff or hired out to ***contract programmers***, who are temporary employees of the organization. When existing programs do not solve the problem, new programs must be obtained. Sources for new programs include buying them off-the-shelf from stores or creating them. When programs are purchased from software vendors, they may have to be customized. In any case, detailed program specifications must be written and reviewed by users. The development of program specifications will be covered in more detail in Chapter 16.

Computer professionals use several forms to help users understand what will be involved in the new or changed software. Figure 15.14 includes a ***print chart***, which indicates exactly how printed output will look. The ***screen layout form*** in Figure 15.14 performs a similar function for screen displays. By showing users each form and asking them to approve its design, analysts are increasing the chance that the reports and displays will be used effectively later.

FIGURE 15.13

Determining new hardware needs and examining how they impact current equipment resources is one part of system design.

Data and Procedures

At this time, decisions are made concerning the organization and layout of data. Usually, computer professionals make these decisions since they rarely involve the users directly. The ***record layout form*** in Figure 15.15 helps the professionals

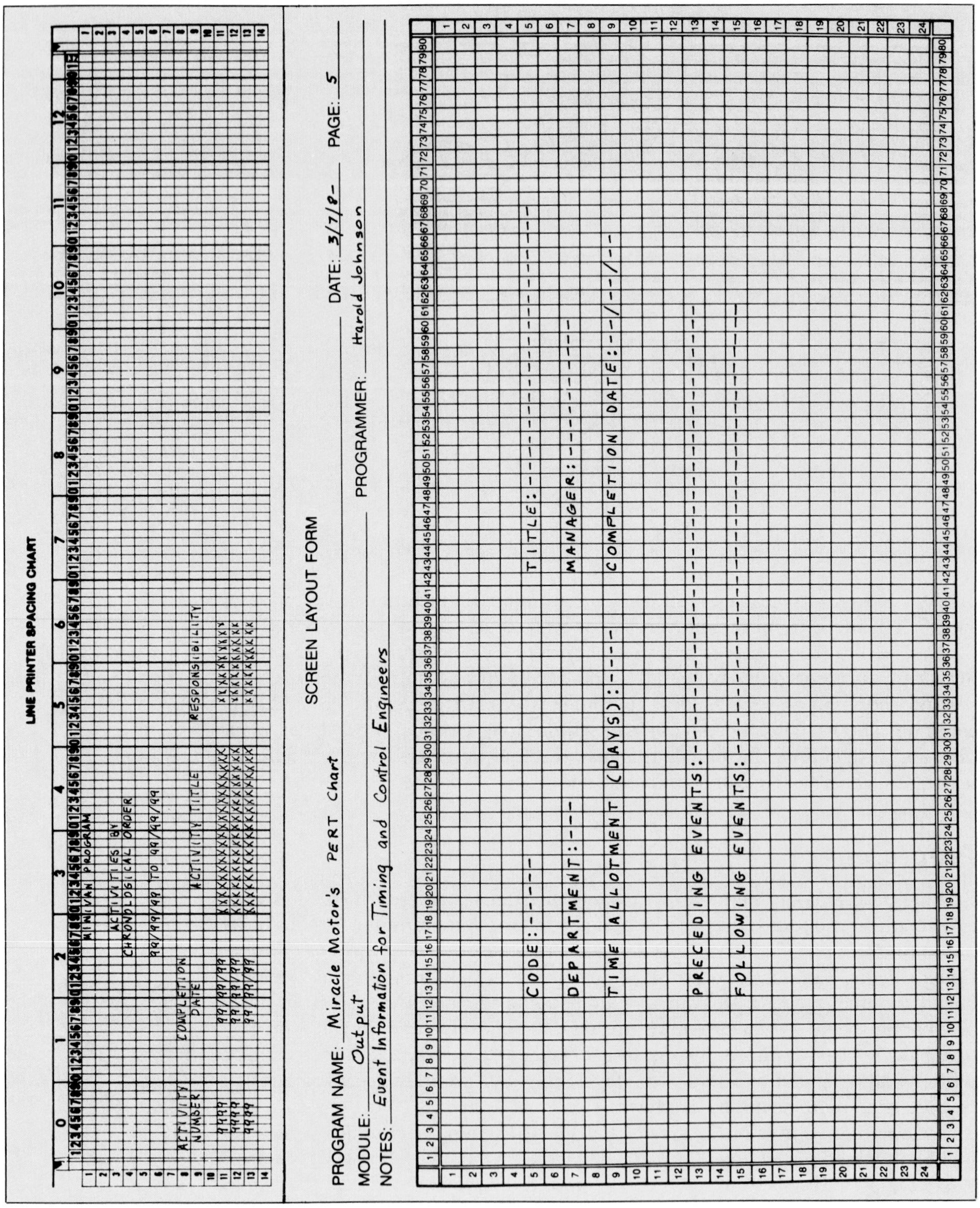

FIGURE 15.14

(a) Print charts layout report formats for programmers. (b) Screen layout forms help users conceptualize the system design.

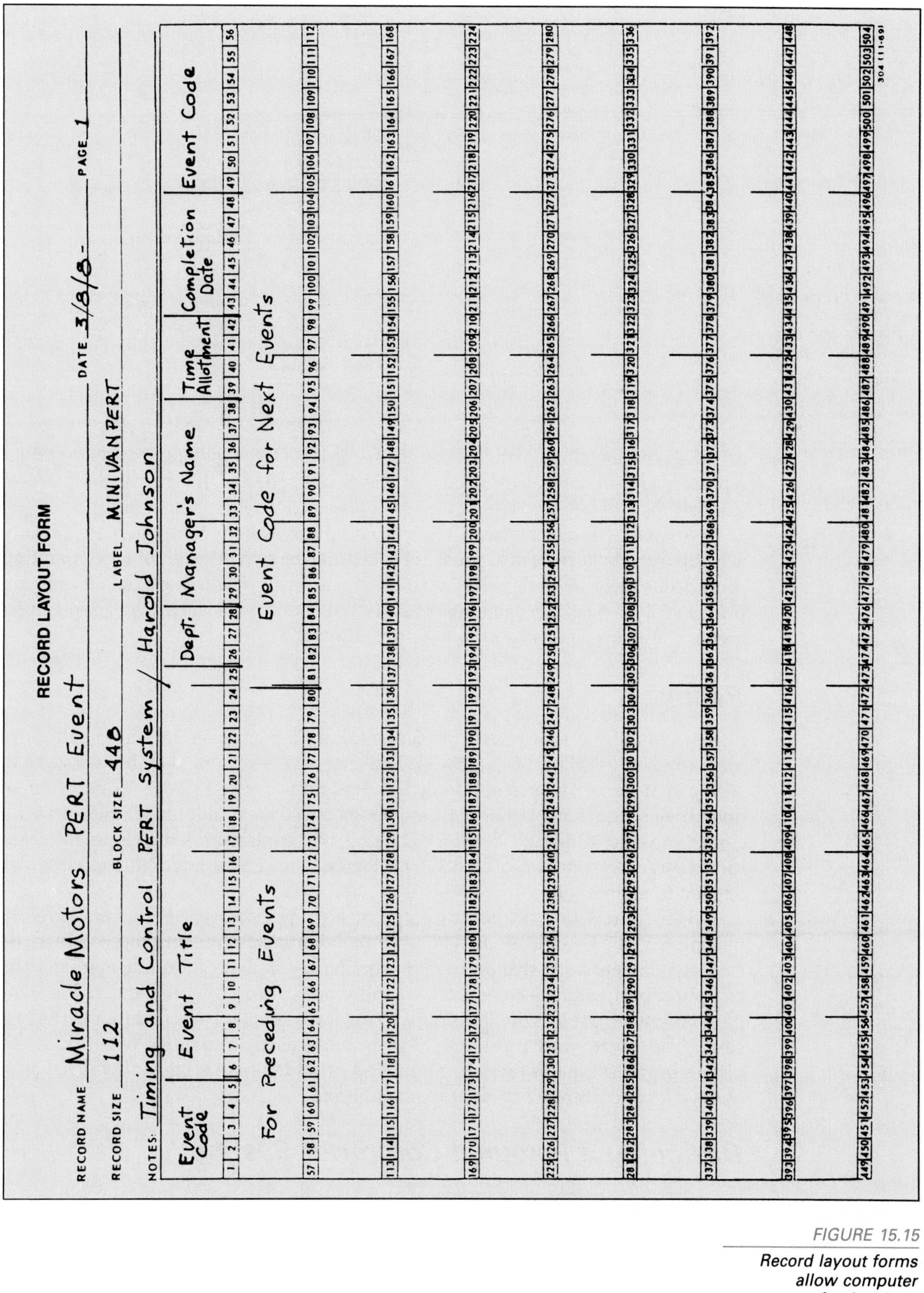

RECORD LAYOUT FORM
RECORD NAME Miracle Motors PERT Event
DATE 3/8/8-
PAGE 1
RECORD SIZE 112
BLOCK SIZE 448
LABEL MINIVAN PERT
NOTES: Timing and Control PERT System / Harold Johnson
Event Code
Event Title
Dept.
Manager's Name
Time Allotment
Completion Date
Event Code
For Preceding Events
Event Code for Next Events

FIGURE 15.15

Record layout forms allow computer professionals to estimate disk and tape storage requirements for new computer systems.

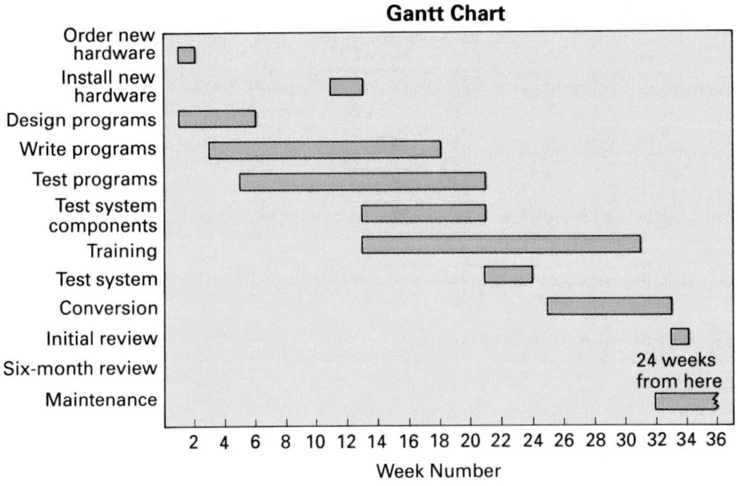

FIGURE 15.16

Gantt charts provide a schedule for completing the last step in a systems development project.

organize the locations of fields within records. Decisions are also made about whether to use databases or one of the three types of file organizations (see Chapter 5).

A change in any of the other four computer system components is usually accompanied by a review of present procedures or a change in policy. Operating procedures must be updated or created whenever new hardware or software are purchased. Users and systems analysts will often visit sites that have implemented similar projects to see what procedures they use.

People

The success of the next phase, implementation, depends on how involved users are with the design of the system. When users are involved, they have a stake in seeing that the new system succeeds. Sometimes, people have to be hired to operate new equipment. Other times, new people are temporarily involved with consulting and training. It is critical that the applications development team identify the personnel required to implement the new system as well as those needed to maintain it.

The culmination of the third step of a project comes when users agree in writing that the specifications will solve the identified problems and produce the projected benefits. At this point, the users have "signed off" the system and the computer professionals have accepted the specifications they will meet. For their part, computer professionals commit to an implementation schedule for the last step. The ***gantt chart*** in Figure 15.16 is often used to identify when different phases begin, estimates their duration, and provides an overview of which activities occur concurrently during implementation.

Designing a Personal Computer System

In a smaller systems development project, you may agree informally upon a design solution with other users involved. In any case, the list of system features evolves into the system specifications, which identify particular brand names and model numbers. Make sure the application packages that you need are easy to use, have readable documentation, and integrate with other software. Your software choices will, to a great degree, dictate hardware manufacturers and models.

Now is the time to get price estimates on hardware and software from local retailers and catalogs. Compare warranties and delivery dates as well as prices.

Designing a Personal Computer System

A. Convert list of features into system specifications
   1. software
      a. easy-to-use
      b. readable documentation
      c. integrates with other software
   2. hardware
      a. compatible with software
      b. additional expansion slots
      c. ability to add memory
B. Where to get price estimates?
   1. retail stores
   2. catalogs for complete systems
   3. catalogs of kits for building your own computer
C. What is included in the price besides hardware/software?
   1. training
   2. service
   3. documentation
   4. warranty
   5. ancillaries (cable, paper, ribbon)
D. Create timeline for purchases
E. Purchase system components

FIGURE 15.17

System specifications are used to purchase a new personal computer system.

Be aware that retail prices will generally be higher but may include training and service. In either case, check that complete systems documentation is available as part of the purchase price. A purchase price may not include necessary cables or paper and ribbons for printers. A personalized gantt chart can help you coordinate the purchase and set-up of equipment. In addition, it can help you plan future acquisitions, such as adding a hard disk drive, expanding memory, or upgrading to a laser printer.

STUDY QUESTIONS

20. Define system specifications, request for proposal (RFP), contract programmer, print chart, screen layout form, record layout form, and gantt chart.
21. Use the components of a computer system to describe the activities and requirements that make up a set of system specifications.
22. What happens at the end of the design step?
23. What activities are involved in designing a personal computer system?

LIFE CYCLE STEP FOUR: IMPLEMENTATION AND MAINTENANCE

Within the context of a systems development project, implementation involves the activities that put a new system into operation and those that maintain its

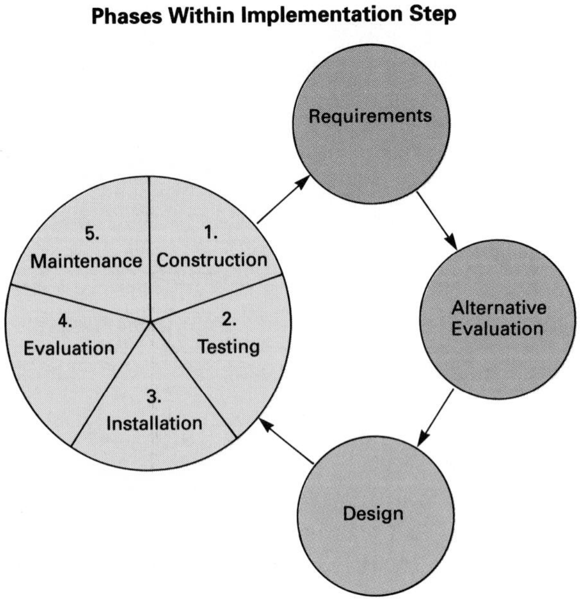

FIGURE 15.18

During the implementation step, all the components of the new computer system are brought together for installation and maintenance.

successful use. The actual changeover to operational status occurs during the latter part of this step. Gantt charts, such as the one in Figure 15.16, identify the initial phases and their expected duration.

Construction and Testing

The activities within this phase are technical in nature. This usually is the point in the project at which users play only minimal roles. Users on the applications development team are replaced by technical support specialists, senior programmers, computer operations personnel, and possibly database administrators. The job is to establish all the computer-related requirements that will have to be in place before the new system becomes operational.

The main activity of the construction phase is the preparation and testing of programs for the new system. Assignments for coding program sections or modules are given to one or more programmers. Each module is tested as it is written. As connecting modules are completed, testing extends to sets of modules, then to entire programs. In some instances, test data may be applied to test multiple programs, or systems of programs (see Chapter 16). When traditional programming techniques are used, this one activity can account for up to 50 percent of the cost of systems development. This cost factor has motivated attempts to streamline or shortcut the programming process. Some of these streamlined methods are described briefly in Chapter 17.

Other implementation activities include the installation of new equipment and, after the programs are available, the performance of complete system tests. A ***system test*** is the actual operation of the new system carried out by users with real application data. Usually, these data have been processed previously under existing systems. Thus, the expected results are already known. A system test then serves to try out a new system to ensure users understand and are satisfied with the results that will be delivered.

Since users perform the system test, they must be trained to some degree. Thus, it is necessary to set up and complete at least some of the training for the new system. Training efforts must encompass both a core group of users and the computer center personnel who will provide support. To achieve a realistic system test, at least some files that will interact with the new application must be created.

At the conclusion of the testing phase, the new system has been developed in its entirety and is ready for use. Separation of testing from installation serves to reassure users and management. The new system, now fully tested, can be put to work with confidence.

FIGURE 15.19

Training involves users and the computer center personnel who will support the new system.

Installation

No matter how extensive preparations might be, strain and some confusion are inevitable when a new system is to be installed. The act of starting up a new computer system is referred to as either ***installation*** or ***conversion***. Emotions can be involved as well as changes in procedures.

At the point of full conversion, the old tools and methods cease to exist. The experience can be like parting with an old friend. Individual employees, for example, may have used the previous methods and equipment for 5, 10, or even 15 years. The old ways worked for them; people were familiar with and comfortable in the routines they followed. If conversion is to be successful, training programs should assure employees that the new ways are for their good and for the good of the organization.

Computer professionals participate in installation primarily as consultants. Analysts and programmers should be available to answer questions and resolve problems. But computer operators should take over the operation of the system. Users should start working with the output they need in their everyday job responsibilities.

Problems will inevitably arise. Any problems that affect the ability of the system to function or the reliability of results should be fixed immediately. Any other problems should be considered part of system maintenance, which is covered later. The goal of installation is an operational system.

One of the major jobs of a system conversion often lies in setting up files or a database to support the new system. Difficulties generally center around the need to tie file conversion to day-to-day operations. For example, major operating crunches were experienced in the days when banks changed from manual bookkeeping methods to online computer systems. Typically, a branch or operating unit of the bank closed out its manual files on a Friday. Immediately a team of temporary employees would enter the offices and work all weekend to transfer thousands of records into a computer file, and also to establish balance controls between computer files and their predecessors.

Because of the extent and importance of the work involved, systems professionals have devised a number of methods that can be used to complete an installation. These include:

- Parallel operation
- Phased transition
- Pilot operation
- Direct cutover

Parallel Operation

Under a ***parallel operation***, both the existing and the new systems are run, side by side, for some time. Results of the two systems are compared to provide both protection and control. The length of time for parallel operation can vary. Usually the old system is retained through one or two processing cycles for a system.

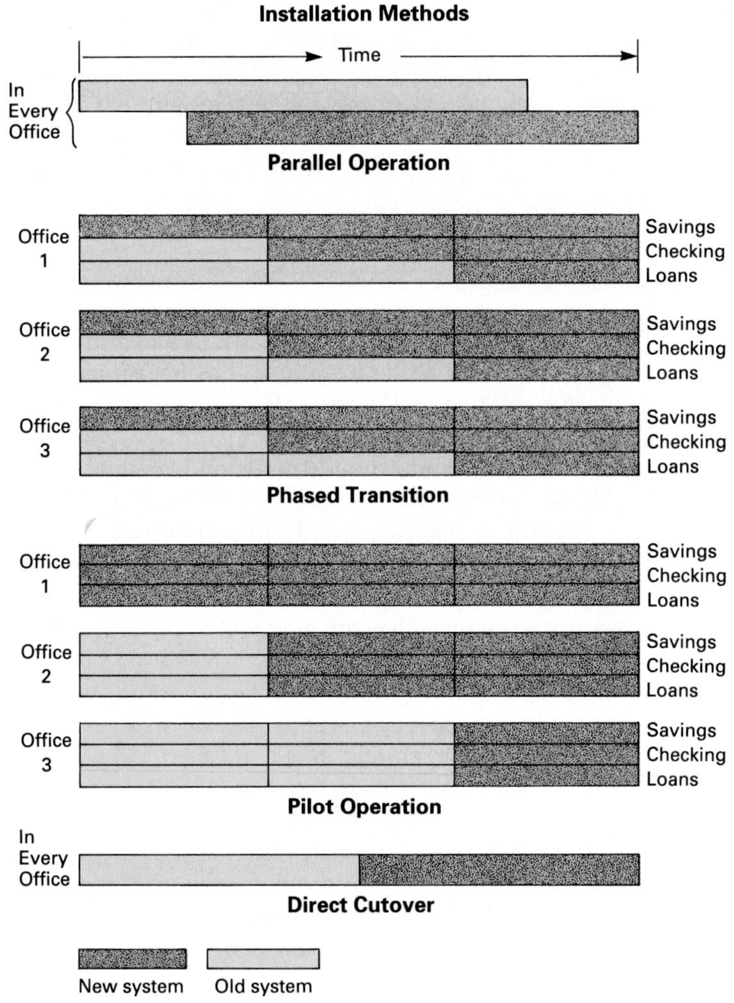

FIGURE 15.20

This chart illustrates different approaches for converting from an old to a new system.

A system that produced month-end accounting reports would be operated in parallel for one or two months.

Parallel operation can provide users with a chance to become comfortable with change before the old methods disappear. Usually, this method also provides an opportunity to establish the improvements the new system implements. Most of all, the parallel approach involves the least risk and the most protection for the organization. The disadvantage of parallel operations is that the organization must pay the additional cost in time and labor of running both systems.

Phased Transition

A ***phased transition*** provides the same basic advantages as parallel operation. The difference is that under this method the overlap is piecemeal.

When using a phased transition, part of the system is put into operation throughout the organization. Once it is working, another part or piece is installed. This phased transition continues until the whole system is in operation everywhere within the organization. Figure 15.20 illustrates how a new bank system might start with savings in all its branches, then go to checking accounts, loans, club plans, and others. The idea is that the new system impacts only one portion or function of the organization at a time.

FIGURE 15.21

Installation procedures can be complex and, accordingly, require detailed planning.

Courtesy of IBM Corporation.

Pilot Operation

A ***pilot operation*** takes a different approach from that used in a phased transition. Rather than scheduling installation for the entire organization, a small, pilot operation is set up. This pilot runs the complete system in only part of the organization until the new system has proven itself. For example, a bank using a pilot operation would install the entire system in one branch office. When that is working properly, the system would be gradually installed in other branch offices one at a time.

Direct Cutover

Under ***direct cutover,*** an existing system is terminated and the new one takes over immediately. This method generally is used when gradual techniques are impractical. The situation of a bank branch installing online service is a good example. The equipment used by tellers to serve customers is changed. There is no opportunity to use both systems concurrently or to handle part of the customers in one way and the others in a different way. The conversion is complete and immediate.

Evaluation

Accountability is part of the process of management. Accountability also is part of the reason why the life-cycle approach to systems development works. Recall that, at the outset, users and computer professionals are asked to join in identifying both projected benefits and costs for system development. These forecasts and commitments do little good if management does not make the effort necessary to follow up by comparing actual results with forecasts.

Accordingly, it is customary to perform a review of results shortly after each new system is installed and running. At this point, the memories of people on the project team about activities and results are fresh and reliable. They are in an ideal position to pinpoint problems and to benefit from mistakes that can be identified. Also, this usually is a good time to list the new opportunities that already have been uncovered for system enhancement. These potential improve-

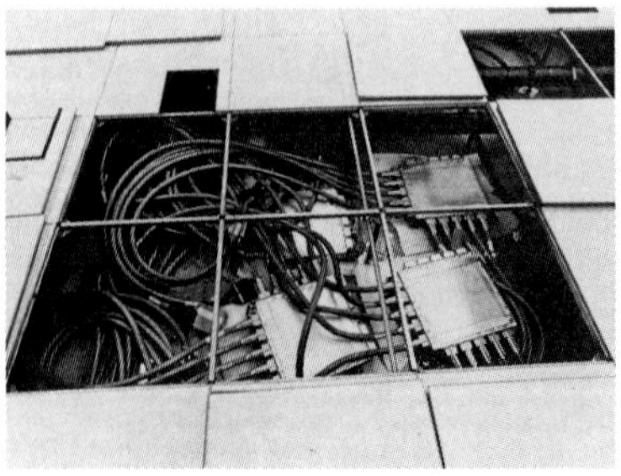

FIGURE 15.22

Equipment maintenance is made easier if technicians have access to cables, connections, and hard-to-reach hardware.

ments can be used in the early portions of the maintenance phase, which runs through the entire useful life of a system.

In addition to the review that takes place shortly after installation, many organizations try to hold another review session about six months after the system becomes operational. This second review is based on the perspective of experience. The organization has had enough service from the new system so that findings about benefits and savings are well known. This is an ideal time to compare actual results with projections, and to learn from the successes and difficulties that are identified.

Maintenance

Maintenance begins as soon as a system becomes operational, and lasts as long as it is in use. In this sense, ***maintenance*** encompasses any modification to an operational system. Maintenance meets needs or provides enhanced values for existing systems.

Maintenance is required, for example, when laws or regulations are changed and computer programs must be modified. Thus, if a tax rate changes, a corresponding modification is needed in related programs. The need for modification also occurs on a routine basis, as when the year has to be changed in accounting reports.

Enhancements are recognized opportunities for improvement. These typically are uncovered by users who notice that adding a capability to an existing system may increase its value. As an illustration, a payroll system may be expandable to provide labor cost information for the manufacturing department. The revision to accomplish this may seem minor. However, when such a request occurs after the system design has been completed, most computer professionals will not go along with it. They will avoid changing the design of a system under development. Too much can go wrong. Schedules and budgets can be destroyed. Instead, a list of enhancement opportunities usually is started during the late stages of a development project. These opportunities are carried forward into the ongoing, maintenance phase of the life cycle.

Such occurrences are commonplace. Even a brand new system can start its useful life with a backlog of maintenance requests. In the course of use, new opportunities will be identified for each application. As these are uncovered, they are reviewed for feasibility and work is scheduled on maintenance projects, which tend to be miniature versions of systems development projects.

Setup and Maintenance of a Personal Computer System

The construction and testing of a new personal computer system may be no more involved than removing components from their boxes and making sure the operating system boots properly. Don't forget to fill out any warranty cards that come with the equipment.

Placement of the equipment in a work area may be one of the most critical decisions you make. Look for a clean, dry work environment with plenty of room for materials around the computer. Proper lighting and seating is necessary for user comfort. If improper lighting causes screen glare, special screen shields can be purchased to eliminate it. Computer professionals often recommend using a surge protector and antistatic pads for long equipment life.

Personal computer users can avoid problems by regular maintenance. This includes covering their keyboard when it's not in use, cleaning the disk drive heads and printer, and backing up important data and software.

Setup and Maintenance of a Personal Computer System

A. Setup
   1. clean & dry work environment
   2. plenty of workspace
   3. storage for floppy disks and manuals
   4. proper lighting and seating
   5. surge protector
   6. screen glare shield
   7. anti-static pad
B. Maintenance
   1. clean and align disk heads
   2. clean printer
   3. cover keyboard
   4. backup (data files and software masters)
   5. fill out warranties

FIGURE 15.23

Proper setup and maintenance of a personal computer system assures its long life.

STUDY QUESTIONS

24. Define system test, installation, and maintenance.
25. Who would be a member of an applications development team during the construction phase of implementation?
26. What happens during the construction phase?
27. Who needs to be trained before the system test can occur?
28. Why are people trained during the installation phase?
29. Describe the following types of installation methods: parallel operation, phased transition, pilot operation, and direct cutover.
30. What is the purpose of the immediate and the six-month follow-up reviews of a completed systems development project?
31. Why are some system modifications left until the maintenance phase?
32. Describe the steps in the life cycle of a systems development process. Be sure to identify the phases associated with each step.
33. What steps are included in the setup and maintenance of a new personal computer system?

CONCLUSION

Out of the ashes of many a failed systems development process has come the idea of a life–cycle approach to creating systems. Computer professionals have learned through experience that they must involve users from the very start and through all phases of the systems development process. When users work with computer professionals on applications development teams to solve problems, everyone has a stake in the eventual success of the new system.

INSIGHT

HOW TO SELECT A MICROCOMPUTER SYSTEM

This chapter on systems development explains how systems analysts help users acquire new computer systems. When purchasing a personal computer system, you apply the same four-step approach. Let's examine the requirements, alternatives, design, and implementation for purchasing a new personal computer system.

Step One: Define Your Requirements

Decide how you want to use a personal computer. Then list your requirements, including how much you want to spend. Look to friends, magazines, books, workshops, and classes for ideas.

Applications and system expectations should both be considered as part of the requirements.

Applications
- education
- entertainment
- business
- sports

System Expectations
- processing speed
- memory capacity
- graphics
- price

Step Two: Evaluate Your Alternatives

Evaluate software alternatives first. Software selections determine hardware choices when purchasing a new microcomputer system.

Identify applications software of interest, narrow the choice down to two or three alternatives, and try them out.

Evaluating Software
- ease of use
- documentation
- technical support from store and software house
- compatibility with software used at school or work

Evaluating Hardware
- minimum memory required by selected software
- keyboard: numeric keypad, location of control and function keys
- screen: resolution, characters per line, and color vs. monochrome
- printer: speed and print quality
- number of expansion slots

Step Three: Design Your System

Most computer professionals recommend designing a personal computer system around two disk drives. This configuration will reduce the time it takes to back up files from one disk to another.

Don't forget to purchase an operating system that is compatible with both your chosen hardware and application software.

When it comes time to purchase your new computer system, weigh the service and training provided by local stores against the lower costs offered by mail-order houses.

Step Four: Implement the System

After purchasing your new personal computer system, set it up in a cool, dry place. Computer professionals often recommend the purchase of a surge protector. Equipment is plugged into the surge protector to minimize damage caused by power fluctuations.

Place the computer in a work area that provides plenty of workspace around the keyboard and screen. Avoid lighting that will create a glare on your screen.

Remember that the last step of the system life cycle is maintenance. You will acquire new software and hardware as your needs change. This is a continuing process that can be helped along by understanding the systems development process.

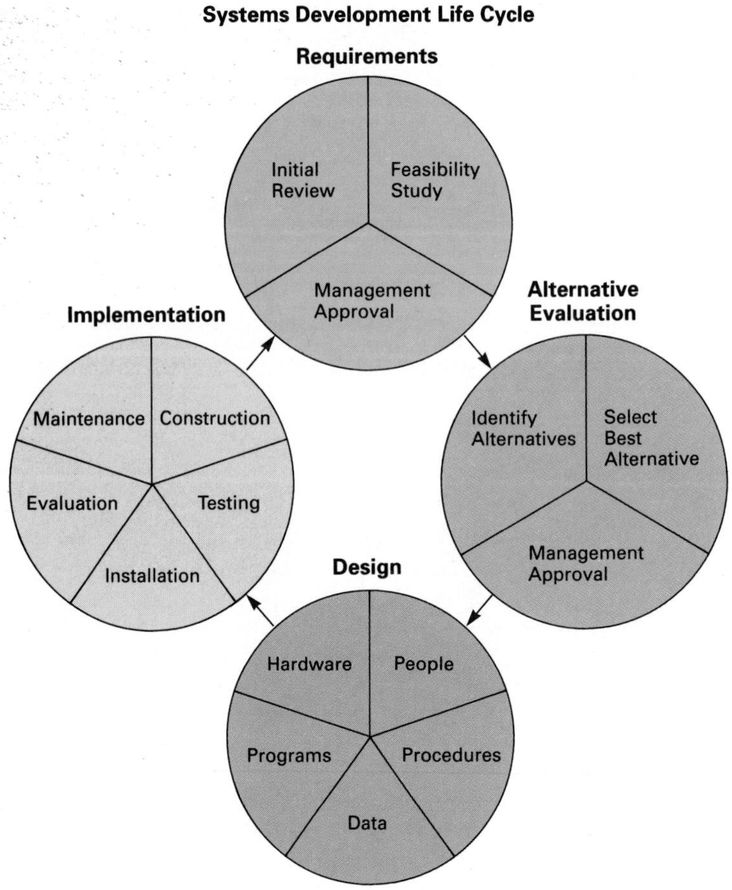

FIGURE 15.24

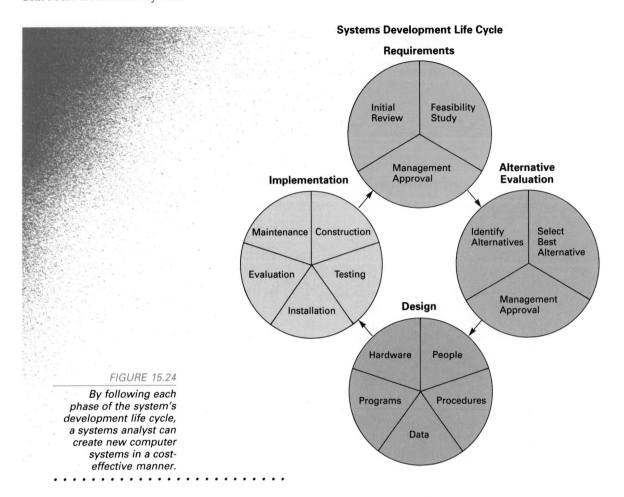

By following each phase of the system's development life cycle, a systems analyst can create new computer systems in a cost-effective manner.

When evaluating alternatives and designing a new computer system, each component is thoroughly examined. Since the components are interwoven, great care must be taken to identify, combine, and test these pieces. The completed project does not represent the conclusion of the systems development process. Professionals have learned that ongoing maintenance and evaluation are necessary for the long-term viability of any new system.

CHAPTER FACTS

- A systems development project begins when a recommendation is made by a user to management about a problem or new idea. The project is more easily managed by breaking it down into four life-cycle steps: (1) requirements; (2) alternative evaluation; (3) design; and (4) implementation.
- The requirements step involves three phases: (1) initial review; (2) feasibility study; and (3) management approval.
- In the initial review, a systems analyst makes a preliminary estimate of time and costs, deciding whether the project has a computer solution.
- The feasibility study involves other computer professionals and users. They gather relevant data and interview participating users, producing a report of budget and schedule requirements. Management approval is required to proceed.

- During the alternative evaluation step, options are researched by the analysts for comparison through a cost/benefit study. The alternatives, the top choice, and rationale are presented to management for approval.
- The design step involves developing specifications for each of the five system components. Hardware requirements are listed, special forms showing input/output arrangements are approved by users, data file organization is determined, new procedures for operations and training are written, and personnel requirements are listed.
- The implementation step consists of the following phases: (1) construction; (2) testing; (3) installation; (4) evaluation; and (5) maintenance.
- During the construction phase, hardware is ordered and software is obtained or written. Programs, hardware, and procedures are then tested, both separately and with a system test.
- Implementation of hardware can happen as a parallel operation, phased transition, pilot operation, or direct cutover. Evaluation of the entire system occurs immediately after installation as well as six months later. Maintenance is an ongoing procedure to make necessary changes to software.

TERMS TO REMEMBER

applications development team
contract programmer
conversion
cost/benefit analysis
data flow diagram
direct cutover
feasibility study
gantt chart
initial review
installation
life cycle
maintenance
parallel operation
phased transition
pilot operation
print chart
record layout form
request for proposal (RFP)
screen layout form
service bureau
system specifications
systems development project
system test

CHECK YOUR UNDERSTANDING

1. Which of the following is ***not*** one of the four steps in the systems development process?
   a. application
   b. design
   c. alternative evaluation
   d. requirements
   e. implementation
2. A(n) ____________ is the group, including the systems analyst, that investigates the project's feasibility and gathers further information about the project.
3. A feasibility study is also called a cost/benefit study. (True/False)

4. An outside agency that provides computer services is called a(n) ____________.
5. Customer satisfaction is an example of an intangible cost/benefit. (True/False)
6. Which of the following design documents shows how data will be organized in a file?
   a. print chart
   b. flowchart
   c. record layout form
   d. data specifications
   e. screen layout form
7. Software is written and tested during the implementation step. (True/False)
8. A(n) ____________ is the testing of the operation of a new system under realistic conditions.
9. With a phased transition, the old system is completely removed and the new system is immediately brought into operation. (True/False)
10. System maintenance involves changing an operational system. (True/False)

APPLYING WHAT YOU'VE LEARNED

1. The systems development life cycle can be applied when any major decisions or purchases are made, even those not involving computer systems. Choose an area where you will have to make a decision in the near future. It could involve school, finding a job or a new place to live, buying a car, and so on. Organize your decision making by using the four steps and associated phases in the life cycle. For each step, outline what is involved relating to your decision. Include any ideas on alternatives, feasibility, evaluation, and so on.
2. The type of installation method used depends on the specific application, the experience of the users, and how involved the change will be. For each installation method (parallel operation, phased transition, pilot operation, and direct cutover), list a situation not mentioned in the text, where this method seems to be the best approach. Briefly explain why you feel the method is appropriate.
3. It is sometimes difficult to list all the costs and benefits resulting from a systems development project. List three each of tangible costs, tangible benefits, intangible costs and intangible benefits that may arise from installing a new computer system in a retail store. Use examples different from those in the text.
4. For each of the following situations, list three examples of cyclic, legal, or company policy changes that could result in maintenance for the computer system.
   a. a local branch of a large bank
   b. a college or university
   c. a tax accountant
   d. a public utility such as the electric or gas company
   e. a local drugstore
5. The life cycle of a systems development project can be explained in several ways. Find two other books that describe systems development. They may be texts on data processing, systems analysis, or management. List the steps or phases that the book suggests. Use a diagram to show how the different methods fit into each other.
6. An applications development team includes a variety of people. List the special qualifications and personality traits each of these people should have to be an effective team member: systems analyst, user, computer center manager, programmer.

CHECK YOUR UNDERSTANDING ANSWERS

1. a
2. applications development team
3. false
4. service bureau
5. true
6. c
7. true
8. system test
9. false
10. true

CHAPTER SIXTEEN

SOFTWARE DEVELOPMENT

KEY IDEAS

- **From the user's point of view**
  What steps does a computer programmer follow to create quality software that helps people to solve problems?
- **People and programming**
  Well-trained, creative people are needed to write computer programs.

  Misconceptions about programming
  Programming involves more than writing code. It requires design skills and insights in user-friendly computer operations.

  The four-step programming process
  Program development includes designing, writing, testing, debugging, training, and providing documentation.
- **Designing the program**
  Program design centers on creating software specifications that meet user expectations.

  Tools for program design
  Programming tools include HIPO charts, flowcharts, and pseudocode.

  Testing the program design
  Structured walkthroughs and comprehensive test data help programmers validate their program designs.
- **Writing program code**
  Each high-level programming language has its own syntax.

  Finding program errors
  Testing program modules as they are written helps minimize problems after the program is completed.

  Programming languages
  Different computer languages have been developed for a variety of applications.
- **Testing and debugging**
  Programs must be rigorously tested before being released to users.

  Program testing
  Program modules are tested independently and then together.
- **Documentation and training**
  The key to program longevity is good design, training, and documentation.

FROM THE USER'S POINT OF VIEW

In this chapter we will introduce you to programming concepts and languages. While it is no longer true that you have to learn to program in order to be an informed user, many people find it useful to write their own programs. Sometimes this provides an easy way to meet a one-time need—for example, converting a series of measurements from English to metric. Other times, you may want to customize a public domain program.

It is not inconceivable that you will be involved in a systems development project at some point in your life. Therefore, learning about the programming process puts you in a better position to communicate your needs to a computer professional. If we spark your interest, a programming class in one of the languages described may be a logical next step for you.

PEOPLE AND PROGRAMMING

Programs solve problems by controlling the computer processing and file maintenance functions within a computer system. The development of robust, user-friendly programs requires organized efforts by trained people. Programmers must be aware of every nuance of the problem. They need to have first-hand knowledge of the principles and requirements for computer processing. This awareness is supplemented by total fluency in one or more programming languages.

High-level software tools and techniques have changed the emphasis of the programming job, but have not diminished the importance of programming skill. High-level tools make it easier to produce individual modules or entire programs. However, sound design and effective resource planning remain essential to successful development and implementation of computer systems.

Misconceptions About Programming

If a system requires that new application programs be written from scratch, the programming function can take as much as 50 percent of the overall systems development budget. Even if application packages exist that can be adapted or modified to the needs of a new system, the importance and significance of programming do not change. Only the time and investment in actually writing instructions are affected. Programming skills are still required to design, develop, and apply computers to solve information problems.

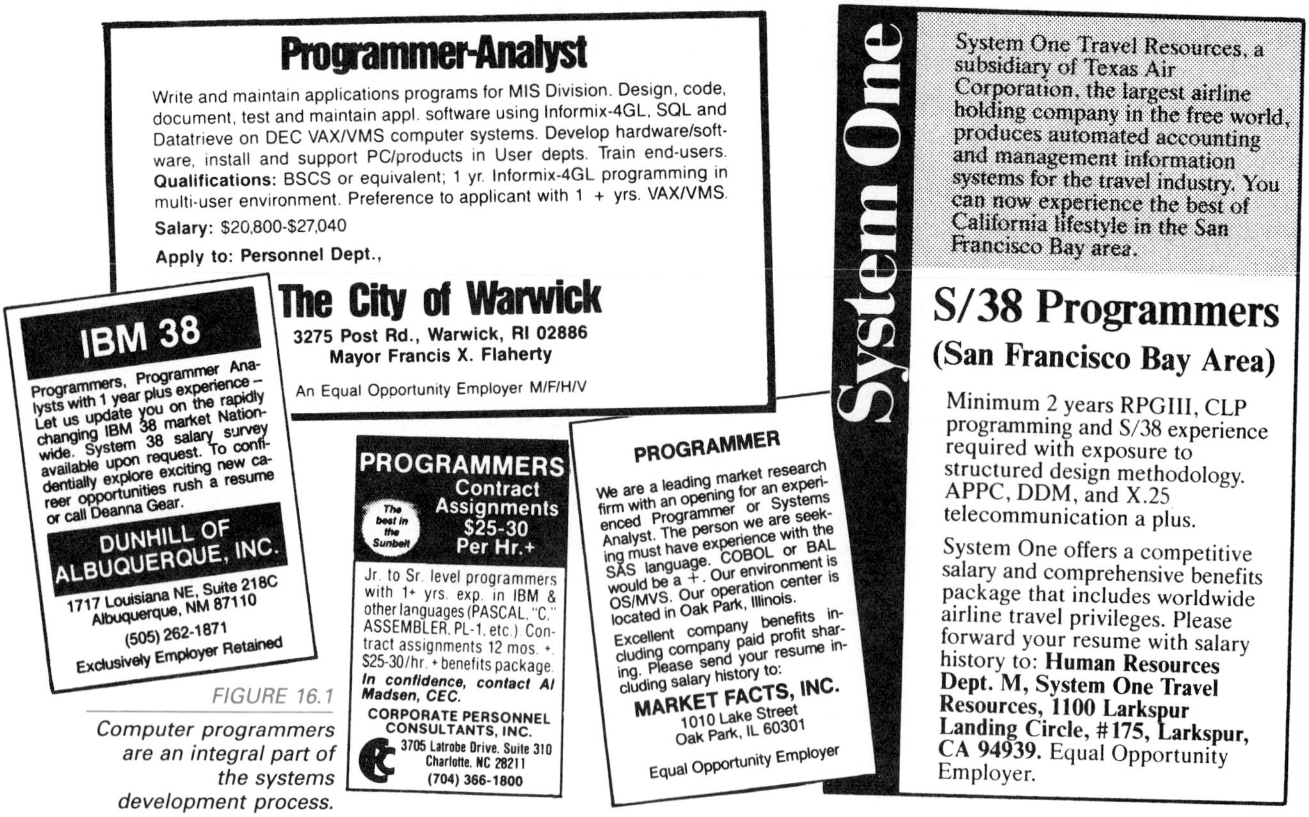

FIGURE 16.1

Computer programmers are an integral part of the systems development process.

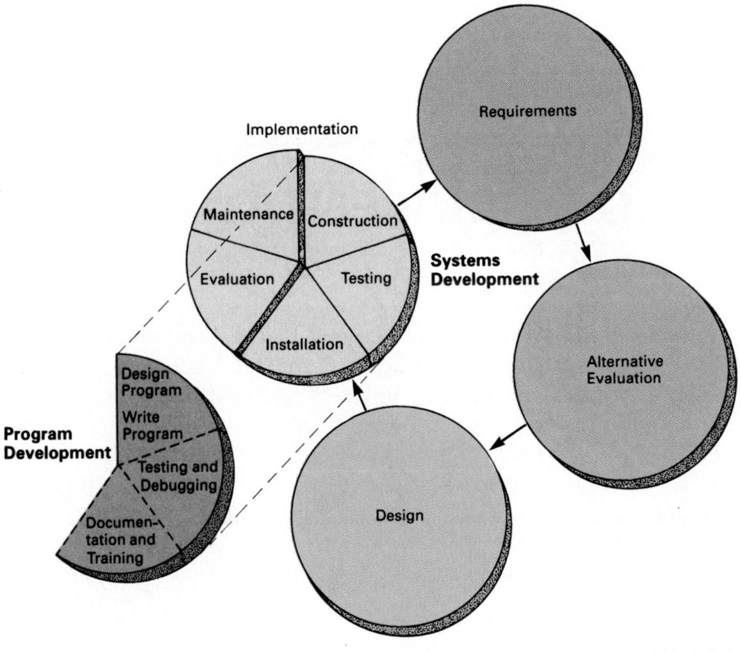

FIGURE 16.2

Program development takes place within the systems development process as part of the implementation step.

People inexperienced with computer systems sometimes regard programming simply as the process of writing program instructions, ***code***, that cause computers to execute a specific IPOS cycle. This outlook is a long way from the truth. Coding is a relatively minor part of an extensive process that involves problem definition, functional design, technical design, coding, testing, and documentation. How coding fits into the systems development process is demonstrated by the programming process presented in the remainder of this chapter. That is, coding is the second of four steps in the process. The program is specified and designed in all of the detail needed for implementation before the programmer even begins writing code.

The Four-Step Programming Process

The process of program development is part of systems development. Programming, as discussed in the previous chapter, falls within a life-cycle framework that involves requirement specification, alternative evaluation, design, and implementation of computer systems. Coding is part of the construction phase that takes place during the implementation of any given systems development project (see Figure 16.2).

From this starting point, the programming process, following a four-step structure of its own, produces application programs that implement the processing portion of a computer system. Like systems development life cycles, program development projects vary with professionals and within organizations. However, the overall process can be illustrated through the four steps covered in this chapter. The steps in the programming process are:

- Designing the program
- Writing program code
- Testing and debugging
- Documentation and training

CLIP

MAKING A CASE FOR SOLID DOCUMENTATION

The most crucial element of software maintenance is a programmer's understanding of the software he maintains. If he cannot fully grasp the way the software works, he cannot keep it working properly.

Most programmers gain understanding by way of two routes:

- They work with the software to accumulate direct experience.
- They study the software's documentation.

Direct experience carries with it an inherent weakness: the normal human process of forgetting. In time, people forget most of the things they learn. In software maintenance, years can pass before a particular bit of experience with a particular program becomes useful.

This is not to say that experience is worthless. By working directly with a piece of software, a programmer picks up a general understanding that will guide him in the future. Still, he loses specific details rapidly and cannot reacquire them without some effort.

The beauty of documentation is that it remembers everything—or should. When a maintenance assignment beckons, a programmer can turn to documentation for fast recall.

Of course, the programmer must be willing to study the documentation. It has no value whatsoever if he ends up turning away, complaining "This is a horror. It's not worth my time." The qualities that distinguish good documentation—accuracy, currency, good organization, clear writing—come into play.

If the maintenance programmer feels any doubt about accuracy, currency or completeness, he will ignore the documentation and opt to decipher source code instead. This approach wastes valuable time and is one of the leading causes of today's software maintenance woes.

Source: Reprinted by permission, *Computerworld*

Key Question: Should documentation be written down by the programmer or a technical writer?

STUDY QUESTIONS

1. What are the four skills programmers use to develop software?
2. Define code.
3. In what ways is computer programming different from the misconceptions people have about the programming process?
4. Identify the four steps in the programming process.

DESIGNING THE PROGRAM

Programmers start their efforts by looking at the ***program specifications***. These specifications are the part of the system specifications that deals directly with the design of the program. They include user expectations of the system. Also, they incorporate technical interpretations of processing requirements that are prepared by the systems analysts. The print charts, screen layout forms, and record layout forms discussed in Chapter 15 are considered part of the program specifications. In addition, the specifications contain a set of test data to be processed by the program. Testing is the basis for quality assurance and acceptance of programs for use within a system.

Defining the Problem

Remember that, by definition, programs solve problems. The solution of any problem begins with an understanding of what has to be done. In the case of programming, the initial understanding starts with the user's perspective. A problem will require understanding of documents or displays to be generated and the uses for the program output. A programmer with this broad overview will produce quality results. One of the important judgments made during the programming process centers on the long-range capacity requirements for files. Almost any file created within or maintained by a program will require expansion with use. A programmer who understands the operation to be supported will make a more valid judgment than one who merely concentrates on writing code.

The same is true for any type of computer program. An expert system for doctors must anticipate the kinds of queries that will be presented and have the capacity for expansion over time. The programmer's understanding of user needs also pays off for programs that support scientific or engineering efforts.

Once the problem is understood, the programmer can proceed with designing the program structure in one of two ways:

- Unstructured
- Structured

FIGURE 16.3
Problem definition is the starting point for program development.

Courtesy of Hewlett-Packard Company

Unstructured Programs

When the programming process was still new, programmers had no standard techniques or design methods to follow. Programs were written to solve current problems without considering future needs for expanded files or additional program options. As a result, many programs were difficult to modify.

Sometimes, several major modifications occurred during a program's life span. The problems encountered by a maintenance programmer were not unlike

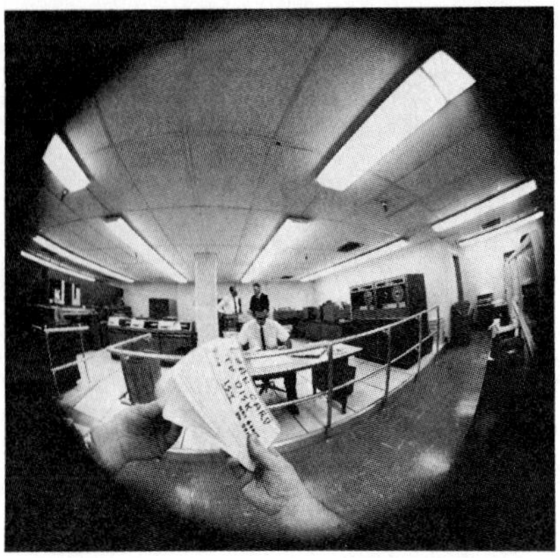

FIGURE 16.4

Punched cards were once the standard method for capturing and entering source programs into computers.

Courtesy of IBM Corporation

those of a family who wanted to winterize a summer cottage. Both were faced with the problem of modifying a structure in a way that it was not originally designed to handle. The family may have found out that the furnace could not keep up with winter temperatures, the windows were not energy efficient, and in general, more room was needed when people were inside most of the day. Sometimes, confronted with these problems, it was easier and more cost efficient to just tear down the cottage and build a new home from scratch.

If a programmer needed to make major changes to a program, similar problems occurred. First, the modifications were not always made by the original programmer. Sometimes little or no documentation was available to the programmers. Like the summer cottage, the original program was often designed to handle specific applications with little flexibility. Quite often, programs would limit the size of files, not verify input data, or work with batches of data instead of in real time. Many times programmers found it best to just rewrite the programs from scratch.

Making modifications would have been easier if the original program had not been written in an unstructured manner. ***Unstructured programs*** were written using a linear approach to problem solving. One instruction followed another until a special condition was reached. When this happened, the program logic branched to another part of the program and continued from there. As programs became more complicated, much branching occurred.

If it was difficult for a maintenance programmer to follow the logic of an unstructured program, it was even harder to modify these programs. The programmer did not always know how new code would affect the rest of the program. Changes to programs were often made in a patchwork fashion, with branches to these patches scattered throughout the program. Someone trying to draw a diagram of the program logic would have lines going in all directions. You can see in Figure 16.5 why unstructured programs were said to contain "spaghetti" code.

During this time, programming was considered more of an art than a science. By the beginning of the 1970s, with over 85 percent of an organization's programming costs going for program maintenance, people were looking for ways to reduce these costs.

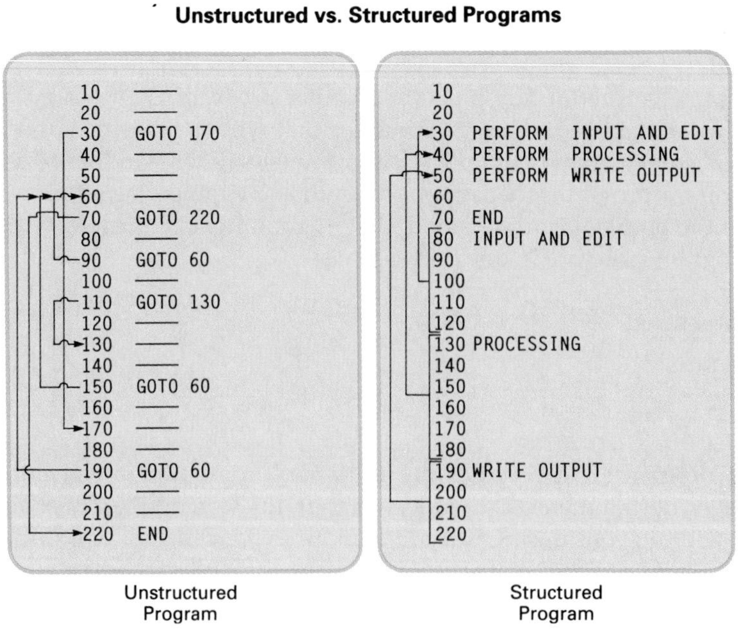

FIGURE 16.5

Unstructured programs are executed in a linear fashion while structured programs execute code modules (sections).

CONFUSION OVER CASE

If the success of the CASE business were measured by the popularity of the acronym, the market would be booming. But at present, the short form of "computer aided software engineering" is more famous than the products it represents.

The term has fallen prey to marketers who attach it indiscriminately to all sorts of products to lure customers. Consequently, many people who could benefit from CASE are confused about what it is.

CASE essentially describes a way to create software that relies on automation and standardized methods. This sounds simple enough, but it represents a considerable departure from traditional dependence on pencils, scratch pads, and the quirks of individual programmers.

CASE suppliers divide software development into four segments: planning, program design (the part before actual writing begins), code generation (in which programmers translate the design into computer-language statements), and the production phase, when the program is put to work and must be maintained.

Until the recent introduction of systems that handle both design and code writing, CASE suppliers concentrated on one segment. For example, some companies provide software that helps data-processing departments determine the needs of the people who will use the program. Other companies make tools that help writers test completed programs. Still others specialize in code writing, and may focus on a specific computer language such as Fortran or Cobol.

CASE suppliers split further over the methods their systems use. Data-processing departments follow different techniques or procedures. Hence, some CASE suppliers specialize in niches built around particular methodologies.

Most CASE products work best when they are used to develop new computer programs; they don't mix well with preexisting systems. But the biggest problem facing data-processing departments is the maintenance of existing programs, which consumes well over half the resources of a typical department. CASE advocates argue that better planning, design, and documentation will yield higher quality programs that need less maintenance. That makes sense, but most data-processing departments are so burdened with upkeep—backed up for three to seven years before they can even start a new program—that they may have trouble finding the time to try computer-aided software engineering.

Source: High Technology Business, April 1988. Reprinted with permission.

Key Question: If you are behind schedule, is it better to push back deadlines to learn a time-saving technology like CASE, **or wait until all work is caught up?**

Structured Programs

As system software was introduced, computer scientists began to recognize that all computer programs used to process data went through a similar series of processing steps. This observation altered program development in two important ways.

First, computer manufacturers provided utility software for processing functions that were recognized as standard parts of many programs. These utilities performed such functions as input, editing, storage, output, sorting, and merging of data. The availability of utilities served to streamline program development. Programmers could call up and execute utilities rather than rewrite the code for often-used functions.

The second change was even more influential. It affected the way programmers approached the programming process. This design breakthrough came with the recognition that every program could be written as ***structured program*** code—code that broke processing down into three simple structures: sequence, selection, and repetition.

A ***sequence*** is the normal order of execution for program code. Unless another instruction is inserted, instructions are executed in the same sequence in which they appear within the program. In other words, sequence means that a group of instructions is performed in a preset order. The following segment of a payroll program is an example:

```
30    PRINT "ENTER THE HOURS WORKED THIS WEEK"
40    INPUT HOURS
50    PRINT "ENTER HOURLY PAY RATE"
60    INPUT RATE
70    PAY = HOURS * RATE
80    PRINT "GROSS PAY:  "; PAY
```

Selection means that one of two alternate sequences of instructions is chosen based on some condition. For example, the following segment of a payroll program compares hours worked to 40. It selects the overtime and regular pay calculations when hours are greater than 40. Otherwise, it selects just the regular pay calculations and sets overtime to zero.

```
65    IF HOURS > 40
      THEN  OVERTIME = (HOURS - 40) * (RATE * 1.5)
            REGULAR = RATE * 40
      ELSE  OVERTIME = 0.00
            REGULAR = HOURS * RATE
70    PAY = REGULAR + OVERTIME
```

Repetition means that a sequence of instructions is repeated as long as some processing condition does not change. In the following example, the pay is calculated and printed as long as the user enters "YES". This process is repeated until the condition—RESPONSE$ = "YES"—is no longer true.

```
10    RESPONSE$ = "YES"
20    WHILE RESPONSE$ = "YES"
30          PRINT "ENTER THE HOURS WORKED THIS WEEK"
40          INPUT HOURS
```

```
50       PRINT "ENTER HOURLY PAY RATE"
60       INPUT RATE
65       IF HOURS > 40
         THEN OVERTIME = (HOURS - 40) * (RATE * 1.5)
              REGULAR = RATE * 40
         ELSE OVERTIME = 0.00
              REGULAR = HOURS * RATE
70       PAY = REGULAR + OVERTIME
80       PRINT "GROSS PAY:  ";PAY
90       INPUT "DO YOU WISH TO CONTINUE (YES/NO)";RESPONSE$
100  WEND
110  END
```

The structured approach permits flexibility. The same program may take many separate forms in the minds of different programmers. In each case, however, the designer establishes segments of code that can be linked to form a workable, quality program.

As you can see, another idea connected with structured programming is to break the program code into modules. A ***module*** is a set of instructions that performs a specific function within a program. For example, most structured application programs contain separate modules to input data, check for errors, perform special processing, and print reports. A typical module contains no more than a page of code and usually can be written in a couple of days by a single programmer. Modules for the same program can be written by different programmers and tested separately before being combined into the final program.

Tools for Program Design

It is also true that modules are elements of program design. Figure 16.6 shows a general overview of the structure of most programs. This type of graphic representation is called a ***structure chart***.

Structure Charts

As seen, a structure chart organizes a program into a series of levels. Modules are identified by rectangles and are executed in order from the top downward

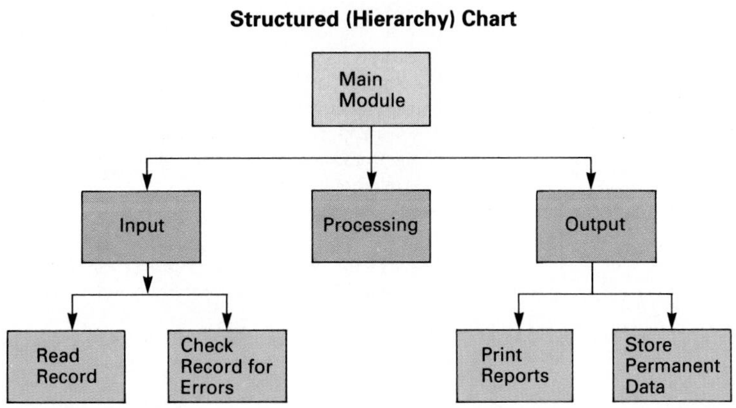

FIGURE 16.6

Structure charts identify the program modules needed to solve a particular problem.

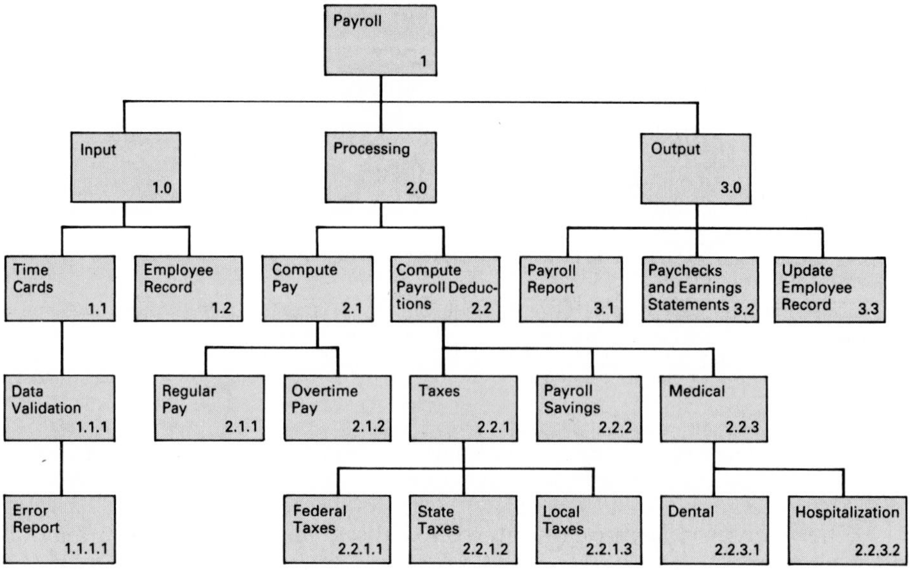

FIGURE 16.7

A visual table of contents identifies and labels each module within the HIPO chart.

and from left to right at each level. This kind of top-down organization is known as a hierarchy. A structure chart is also called a ***hierarchy chart***.

Structured programming provides a standard framework within which any program can be designed. The actual processing steps involved in each level of the program are added as additional modules are created. Further top-down refinement of the program design occurs as the programmer uses design tools to break each module into specific program instructions.

Hierarchy charts often are expanded to form an ***HIPO (hierarchy plus input-processing-output) chart***. This design tool includes three types of diagrams that expand the modules defined in the hierarchy charts. The ***visual table of contents*** in Figure 16.7 is an annotated version of the hierarchy chart that contains reference numbers and a brief description of each module. The ***overview diagram*** details the specific steps involved in input, processing, and output for the entire program (see Figure 16.8). These steps are cross-referenced to the

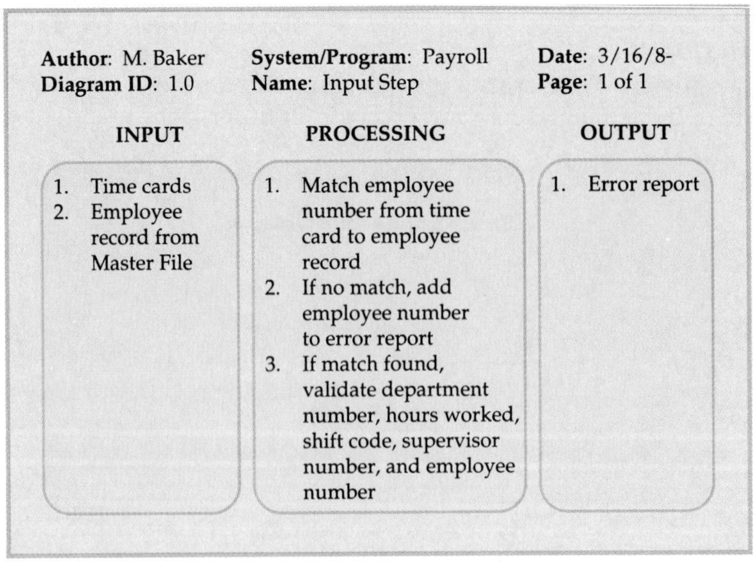

FIGURE 16.8

Overview diagrams describe requirements for the input, processing, and output performed by a specific program module.

Author: M. Baker **System/Program**: Payroll **Date**: 3/24/8-
Diagram ID: 1.1.1 **Name**: Data Validation **Page**: 1 of 1

INPUT	PROCESSING	OUTPUT
Time Cards • Employee number • Department code • Hours worked • Shift code • Supervisor's initials	Data Validation • Employee number required and must be numeric • Employee number >999 and <6000 • Department code required and must be numeric • Department code >9 and <100 • Hours worked required and must be numeric • Shift code required and must be numeric • Shift code ≥ 1 and ≤ 3 • Supervisor's initials must be present	Error Report with the following error messages: • Employee number missing • Employee number not numeric • Invalid employee number • Department code missing • Department code not numeric • Invalid department code • Hours worked missing • Hours worked not numeric • Invalid working hours • Shift code missing • Shift code not numeric • Invalid shift code • Supervisor's initials missing

FIGURE 16.9

Detail diagrams identify specific input, processing, and output activities for each module within a HIPO chart.

module numbers used in the visual table of contents. The ***detail diagram*** in Figure 16.9 lists in detail what is done within each module. The three accompanying diagrams show the HIPO charts for the example payroll program. Besides aiding in the design process, HIPO charts are also excellent additions to a program's technical documentation.

Flowcharts

The most common method for defining the steps in a program is through use of a diagram known as a program ***flowchart***. A flowchart uses a series of symbols that identify the basic IPOS functions within programs. These symbols, shown in Figure 16.10, are positioned and linked to form a graphic representation of a program's logic. The symbols used here present a program flowchart for the payroll program example. A flowchart is a graphic method for organizing and presenting the specific steps within a program or module.

Pseudocode

While some programmers use flowcharting techniques to represent program steps with symbols, others prefer to use English phrases or ***pseudocode***. Pseudocode is popular because it lends itself to the design of structured programs. Figure 16.11 illustrates the pseudocode version of the payroll program previously flowcharted.

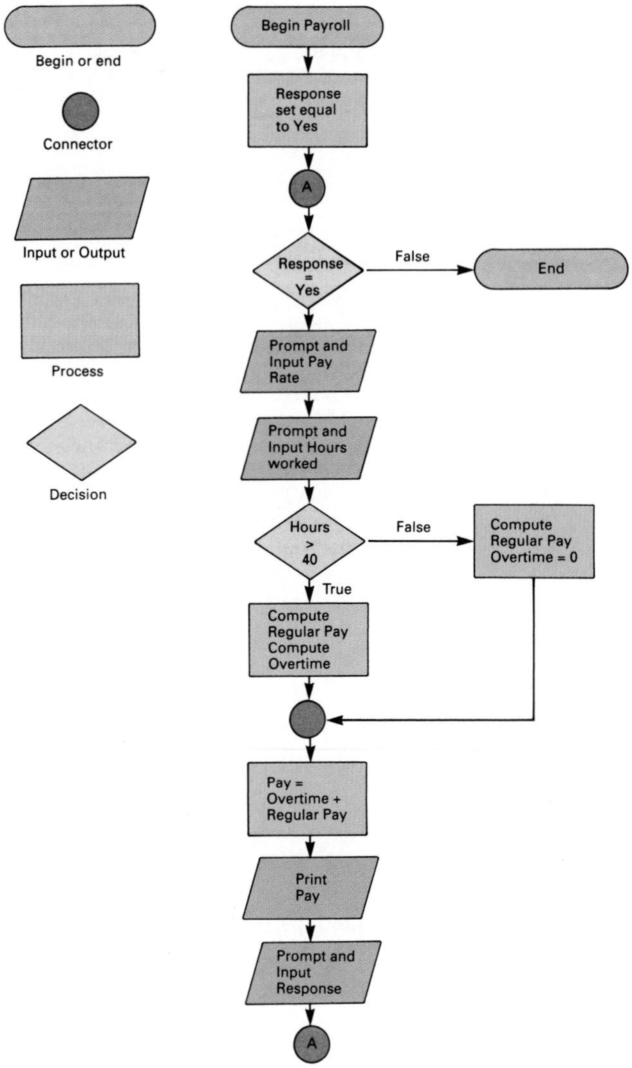

FIGURE 16.10

Program flowcharts use symbols to outline program logic for payroll processing.

One advantage of designing through use of HIPO charts, flowcharting, or pseudocode is flexibility. These tools can be translated into program code for any high-level programming language. Therefore, program design can be independent of language rules and syntax. Another benefit is that HIPO charts, flowcharts, and pseudocode provide a basis on which programming operations can be reviewed by all members of an applications development team, including users and technicians. These design tools support a team approach to systems development. Their existence permits a detailed quality review of design to be made before coding takes place. Reviews at the design stage ultimately reduce costs and enhance the quality of specific program code. The choice between HIPO charts, flowcharting, and pseudocode is a matter of personal preference and company standards.

Testing the Program Design

Teamwork in program design and development can help to ensure the quality and reliability of program performance. One important quality control measure

Pseudocode

```
BEGIN PAYROLL PROGRAM
  SET RESPONSE = YES
  DO WHILE RESPONSE = YES
    DISPLAY "ENTER HOURS WORKED"
    ACCEPT HOURS
    DISPLAY "ENTER HOURLY PAYRATE"
    ACCEPT RATE
    IF HOURS GREATER THAN 40
      THEN OVERTIME = (HOURS - 40) * (RATE * 1.5)
           REGULAR = RATE * 40
      ELSE OVERTIME = 0
           REGULAR = RATE * HOURS
    END-IF
    PAY = REGULAR + OVERTIME
    DISPLAY "DO YOU WISH TO CONTINUE?"
    ACCEPT RESPONSE
  END DO WHILE
END PAYROLL PROGRAM
```

FIGURE 16.11

Pseudocode outlines program logic by using intelligible words.

is a detailed review of designs before program coding begins. Experienced programmers and/or supervisors review all design documents in a step-by-step procedure known as a ***structured walkthrough***. Working together, a small group of computer professionals tracks the processing of data through the entire design sequence. The purpose is to identify and adjust any design weaknesses before actual program writing takes place. The more errors that can be uncovered at this stage, the greater the program quality is likely to be.

A vital end product of program design should be a complete set of test data that will be used to validate programs from the module level up through the complete system. ***Test data*** are assembled sets of data items that try out all of the special processing features and controls of the new program.

For each program function to be tested, test data must include both valid and invalid items. The valid items should represent the outer ranges of acceptable values that can be processed. To illustrate, a payroll program might limit the value of checks that can be processed to a minimum of $40 and a maximum of $750. To test this program function, the values $39, $40, $750, and $751 might be included in the test data. In this way, the data items test the full range of acceptable values and also test to be sure the program can deal with unacceptable data at the high and low ends of the range.

To test all operational functions of every module and of an entire program, extensive sets of data may be needed. It is important that test data be prepared during the design stage of program development, since the idea of test data is to validate program coding. Quality assurance is greater if development of test data precedes and is separate from the coding operation.

FIGURE 16.12

Structured walkthroughs promote the review and discussion of program design and code with other team members.

STUDY QUESTIONS

5. Define program specifications, module, structure (hierarchy) chart, HIPO chart, flowchart, pseudocode, structured walkthrough, and test data.
6. Why is an unstructured program sometimes referred to as spaghetti code?

7. Describe two ways the program development process changed during the 1970s.
8. Describe the three structures found in a structured program.
9. What is meant by the statement "Programs are designed from the top down"?
10. Describe the visual table of contents, overview diagram, and detail diagram that comprise an HIPO chart.
11. What are two advantages of using HIPO charts, flowcharts, or pseudocode to design a program?
12. How do structured walkthroughs help reduce costs and enhance program quality?

WRITING PROGRAM CODE

If sufficient care is taken with program design, coding should be a routine, relatively straightforward process. One instruction in a high-level language usually is written for each line of pseudocode or each flowcharting symbol. Care must be taken, of course, to follow the rules of each programming language for defining files and syntax. If programming is done online, form and style of coding may be monitored, line by line, by the language compiler or interpreter program.

Finding Program Errors

It is possible to write programs that conform to language rules and still produce unusable results. This occurs when programs contain logic errors. A logic error, briefly, is a program instruction sequence that produces unacceptable results when data are processed. A common example of logic errors involves incorrect computations. Instructions may cause the program to divide one value by another when multiplication should have been performed. Obviously, the results will be invalid even though the compiler may accept the instructions for processing.

Finding logic errors can be difficult. A finished program, for example, may have 10,000 or more lines of code. Programmers must observe results and apply reasoning in order to identify the points at which errors occur. Each time a correction is made, it is necessary to recompile the program involved and to retest the module or section of the program that has been modified. Errors within coded programs are called ***bugs***. The process of finding and correcting errors in programs is known as ***debugging***.

FIGURE 16.13

Debugging of programs is a detailed process that requires intense effort, usually by experienced people.

Courtesy of Unisys Corporation

Module and section testing of programs should be performed as part of the coding function. That is, a program module should not be considered completed until it is tested. Also, module tests should be approved by a supervisor who will take part in the procedure for testing sections of programs and entire systems.

To help ensure quality and reliability, structured walkthroughs are also done to review modules and sections of coded programs. They are performed by experienced programmers and supervisors who work with the programmers developing individual modules and sections. Review and structured walkthrough activities typically are integrated with the testing of modules.

Programming Languages

Programming languages are tools. As with any other computing tool, a programming language is selected with care to meet the specific needs of an applica-

```
      INTEGER NUM1, NUM2, SUM
      READ (5,10) NUM1, NUM2
   10 FORMAT (I4,I4)
      SUM = NUM1 + NUM2
      WRITE (6,20) NUM1, NUM2, SUM
   20 FORMAT (10X, 'THE SUM OF', I4, '+', I4, 'IS', I5)
      STOP
      END
```

FIGURE 16.14

FORTRAN was the first high-level programming language. This FORTRAN program causes the computer to add two numbers together and display the resulting sum.

tion and its users. Through the years, literally hundreds of programming languages have been developed and used for computer processing. The summaries that follow identify and describe only a few of the more popular languages used to implement program designs.

FORTRAN

FORTRAN was the first high-level language. FORTRAN (for FORmula TRANslator) was introduced in 1956 to meet the needs of scientists and engineers who were the predominant users of early computers. FORTRAN is a prime example of a language that just kept growing. Originally, it was used to perform very complex calculations. As people added graphics and other capabilities to it, FORTRAN became a general-purpose language by accident.

This language has limited input/output capacity. Its selection structure was awkward and the repetition structures were originally very primitive. Programs written in FORTRAN tend to be hard to read and understand unless they are well documented. Consequently, they can be hard to change. With the development of structured programming techniques, new syntax has been added to FORTRAN to make it easier to code properly designed programs.

More scientific programs are written in FORTRAN than in any other language. There are several reasons for this situation. One is that many other languages do not adequately handle mathematical applications. Another reason is economics. It is expensive to change programs and to retrain programmers in newer languages.

COBOL

The name COBOL is an acronym for COmmon Business–Oriented Language. COBOL development was sponsored by the U.S. Department of Defense in the late 1950s. The language has been in continuous use, with several revisions, since 1960. Billions of dollars have been spent building COBOL programs for mainframe computers. This language, therefore, is still the one most commonly used for business programs.

Because COBOL was designed with business applications in mind, it has been very successful in business environments. It has an extensive vocabulary for defining files, records, and fields. It easily handles disk or tape input/output and has selection and repetition structures that are much better than those of FORTRAN.

In addition, COBOL was designed to be self-documenting. Many lines must be written even for simple programs. Some people say that you can tell that a COBOL program is ready to go when the weight of the program exceeds the weight of the computer. This can also be considered one disadvantage to using COBOL.

```
IDENTIFICATION DIVISION.
 PROGRAM-ID. ADDITION.

ENVIRONMENT DIVISION.
 INPUT-OUTPUT SECTION.
    .
    .
    .
DATA DIVISION.
 FILE SECTION.
 FD DATA-IN
    LABEL RECORDS ARE STANDARD.
 01 NUMBERS-TO-BE-PROCESSED.
    05 NUMBER-1-IN  PIC 999.
    05 NUMBER-2-IN  PIC 999.

 FD ANSWER-OUT
    LABEL RECORDS ARE OMITTED.
 01 SUM-TO-BE-PRINTED  PIC X(27).

WORKING-STORAGE SECTION.
01 TEMPORARY-WORK AREA.
    05 FILLER         PIC X(10)  VALUE "THE SUM OF"
    05 NUMBER-1-OUT   PIC 999.
    05 FILLER         PIC XXX    VALUE "+".
    05 NUMBER-2-OUT   PIC 999.
    05 FILLER         PIC X(4)   VALUE "IS".
    04 SUM-OUT        PIC 9(4).

PROCEDURE DIVISION.
 PROCESSING-ROUTINE.
    OPEN INPUT DATA-IN
         OUTPUT ANSWER-OUT.
    READ DATA-IN.
    ADD NUMBER-1-IN, NUMBER-2-IN GIVING SUM-OUT.
    MOVE NUMBER-1-IN TO NUMBER-1-OUT.
    MOVE NUMBER-2-IN TO NUMBER-2-OUT.
    WRITE SUM-TO-BE-PRINTED
        FROM TEMPORARY-WORK AREA.
    CLOSE DATA-IN
          ANSWER-OUT.
    STOP RUN.
```

FIGURE 16.15

COBOL is the major language used for programming business applications. This COBOL program causes the computer to develop a sum for two numbers.

Since COBOL was designed before real-time processing became practical, the original COBOL standards did not take this processing method into account. Therefore, each manufacturer has developed different ways to write online programs for real-time processing in COBOL. COBOL programmers who move from one type of computer to another are forced to learn a new variation of COBOL in order to handle real-time processing.

BASIC

The BASIC programming language was developed during the 1960s at Dartmouth College, specifically for training students to program, regardless of their major. BASIC was not designed for any one application. Instead, it was designed to be easy to learn and use. The acronym stands for Beginners' All-purpose Symbolic Instruction Code. Implementation of BASIC started on relatively large systems installed on college campuses. When microcomputers were introduced, BASIC became a standard programming language both for software

```
10 INPUT N1
20 INPUT N2
30 SUM = N1 + N2
40 PRINT "THE SUM OF ";N1;" + ";N2:" IS ";SUM
50 END
```

FIGURE 16.16

BASIC is a relatively simple, easy-to-use language. This BASIC program, which adds two numbers, is much shorter than the COBOL program that performs the same task.

```
                    IF/THEN/ELSE STATEMENT

50 IF HOURS > 40
     THEN OVERTIME = (HOURS-40) * (RATE * 1.5):
          REGULAR = RATE * 40
     ELSE OVERTIME = 0.00:
          REGULAR = HOURS * RATE

                       IF/THEN STATEMENT

50 IF HOURS > 40
     THEN OVERTIME = (HOURS - 40) * (RATE * 1.5):
          REGULAR = RATE * 40


52 IF HOURS <= 40
     THEN OVERTIME = 0.00:REGULAR = HOURS * RATE
```

FIGURE 16.17

Versions of BASIC without IF/THEN/ELSE selection structures rely on the use of several IF/THEN structures to perform the same task.

developers and for user-developers who wanted to program their own applications. This language still is in wide use for student training and for microcomputer-oriented application software.

The program used in the examples of program structures is a BASIC program. The program also highlighted several problems with BASIC. Since BASIC was designed before the idea of structured programming, it does not handle repetition as easily as other languages.

In addition, the selection structure in the original Dartmouth BASIC (the IF statement) did not have an ELSE option, as shown in Figure 16.17. To get around this limitation, programmers had to have two selection statements. Other modifications to BASIC have occurred, taking advantage of the developments in structured programming.

To make up for the lack of easy-to-use selection and repetition structures, each microcomputer has its own variation to the BASIC language. Programmers constantly find differences in the BASIC versions used by various makes of computers.

Programmers also run into difficulty when writing complex programs using BASIC. Writing or reading data on disk can be tricky. Each microcomputer has a different way to do it. In addition, great care must be taken to make the programs easy to read. BASIC programs can be difficult to read and even harder to modify. As a result, complex programs must be carefully designed and written since they can be hard to understand.

Logo

A more recent programming language designed for educational use is Logo. The design of Logo is based on work by Seymour Papert. His interest in psychology

```
PENDOWN
FORWARD 40
RIGHT 90
FORWARD 40
RIGHT 90
FORWARD 40
RIGHT 90
FORWARD 40
PENUP
```

FIGURE 16.18

This Logo program will cause the computer to draw a square.

and computers led him to new ideas on how to use computers for learning. He helped develop Logo, which allows students to explore geometric principles. This is done, not as some abstract process, but through the interactive use of computers. The name Logo is derived from the Greek word ***logos*** meaning speech, calculation, or thought. It was used to suggest that the language was meant to be symbolic in nature. These concepts are discussed in more detail in Papert's book ***Mindstorms*** (Basic Books, New York, 1980).

Unlike programming languages used for business or scientific applications, Logo is an end in itself. This language was not designed to create reports or to track an airplane's flight path. It is to be used only as a learning tool. With Logo, students can use computers for problem solving. By manipulating either a screen turtle or a real robot turtle, the child programmer explores geometry, applied physics, and art, with the results graphically displayed.

Pascal

Pascal, developed during the 1970s, is named after Blaise Pascal, inventor of an early mechanical calculator. One strength of Pascal is that it was developed specifically to implement structured programming techniques. The Pascal language has been popular in educational curricula for computer scientists and as an alternative to BASIC for the programming of microcomputers. Use of this language has increased with the recent introduction of a low-cost, high-speed compiler for use on microcomputers. Because it is relatively new and has limited input/output capability, it has not been accepted to any great degree by industry.

Ada

An even newer language called Ada is derived from Pascal. Ada was designed with superior input/output capabilities. Therefore, some experts think that Ada has a better chance of being used in industry than Pascal.

Ada is a programming language born in the 1980s. It was named after Lady Ada Augusta Lovelace, who was an important figure in nineteenth-century

```
PROGRAM ADD-IT (INPUT, OUTPUT);
VAR NUM1, NUM2, SUM:  INTEGER;
BEGIN
  READLN (INPUT, NUM1, NUM2);
  SUM:= NUM1 + NUM2;
  WRITELN (OUTPUT, 'THE SUM OF', NUM1:4, '+',
                   NUM2:4, 'IS', SUM:5)
END.
```

FIGURE 16.19

A Pascal program is shown here adding two numbers.

```
USE TEXT_IO;

PROCEDURE MAIN IS
  TYPE NUMBER IS INTEGER;
  PACKAGE NUMBER_IO IS NEW INTEGER_IO(NUMBER);
  NUM1, NUM2, SUM: NUMBER;

BEGIN
  GET (NUM1); GET (NUM2);
  SUM:= NUM1 + NUM2;
  PUT ('THE SUM OF');
  PUT (NUM1, WIDTH = 4);
  PUT ('+');
  PUT (NUM2, WIDTH = 4);
  PUT ('IS');
  PUT (SUM, WIDTH = 5);

  NEW_LINE;

END MAIN;
```

FIGURE 16.20

An Ada program is shown here adding two numbers.

computing history. The U.S. Department of Defense has sponsored the development of Ada. The goal of the department has been to create a scientific language that will help programmers use good programming techniques. In addition, they would like Ada to become a national standard, like COBOL.

Until recently, different branches of the armed forces have used a variety of languages. This practice has made it difficult to transfer quality software from one service to another. To stop duplication of effort, the Department of Defense has mandated that all branches will use Ada.

Ada has been modeled after the Pascal language. The good features of Pascal have been included, but with improved input/output capabilities. If Ada has any fault, it is its complexity. When a programming language can do many things, it takes time for programmers to master all features.

C

C is another computer language that evolved from structured programming concepts. It was developed at Bell Laboratories in 1972. C has many of the features of high-level languages, yet is used in bit and byte manipulation for writing system programs and graphics routines. Like Ada, C is a powerful language with many programming options. As a result, it is not easy for a programmer to become proficient in C. However, C is considered a portable language, which means a program written in C can be used on many different types of computers with few changes.

RPG

RPG stands for Report Program Generator. This language was first introduced in 1964 to run on minicomputers with limited memory capacity. As the name implies, RPG was designed to produce business reports.

To use RPG, a programmer defines the format in input files by naming fields and specifying their lengths and types—numeric, character, and so on. Then the programmer defines the operation to be performed on certain fields. The program logic in an RPG program is not developed in a sequence of steps. Instead, specifications for the file description, input, calculations, and output are developed separately. Other specifications are also used as the need arises. The

```
/*Integer version*/


main()
  {
  int n1=0;
  int n2=0;
  int sum=0;

  printf("? "); scanf("%d", &n1);
  printf("? "); scanf("%d", &n2);

  sum = n1 + n2;

  print ("THE SUM OF %d + %d IS %d\n", n1,n2,sum);
  }
```

FIGURE 16.21

A C program is shown here adding two numbers.

```
                    FILE DESCRIPTION SPECIFICATIONS
NUMBIN  IP    F          80              DISK               S
NUMOUT  O     F          132    OF         PRINTER
                       INPUT FORMAT SPECIFICATIONS
FILEIN  NS    01
                                                     1    30NUM1
                                                     4    60NUM2
                       CALCULATION SPECIFICATIONS
  01         NUM1           ADD   NUM2      SUM       42


                     OUTPUT FORMAT SPECIFICATIONS
NUMOUT   H  207  1P
       OR        OF
                                         34  'THE SUM OF 2 NUMBERS'
         D   1   01
                                         20  'THE SUM OF'
                                NUM1  3  24
                                         26  '+'
                                NUM2  3  30
                                         33  'IS'
                                 SUM  3  38
```

FIGURE 16.22

An RPG program is shown here adding two numbers.

program in Figure 16.22 shows the four specifications needed to add two numbers together.

When RPG was first introduced, it could not handle any type of selections. It contained only fixed logic, which meant that the same sequence of instructions were always used. Many detailed reports were easily handled by RPG and its fixed logic. However, when complex logic required the program to select between sets of instructions, another language, such as COBOL, was used.

While the RPG program in Figure 16.22 does not demonstrate all the RPG capabilities, it does show how each entry for one of the specifications must be written in a designated column. This feature, along with its fixed logic format, makes RPG unlike the other programming languages previously discussed. RPG implements a technique for nonprocedural programming and is described as a forerunner of the fourth-generation programming languages.

Nonprocedural programming is a technique in which it is unnecessary to list and specify processing functions on a sequential, step-by-step basis. Instead,

```
COUNT Customer WHERE City EQUALS New York

201

COUNT Customer WHERE City EQUALS New York AND
  Purchase-Description EQUALS Guitar AND Year
  EQUALS 1990

34
```

FIGURE 16.23
Fourth-generation languages access information from a database through the use of special key words.

the required functions are described in terms of operational parameters that are then processed to generate programs, making detailed coding unnecessary.

To meet the ever-changing demands for business reports, RPG has also changed. More powerful versions labeled RPG II and RPG III have been introduced to handle selections and real-time processing.

Fourth-Generation languages

At this writing, fourth-generation languages (4GLs) are starting to gather quite a following. Fourth-generation languages require the use of a select but powerful vocabulary to access databases. For example, Figure 16.23 shows how a user might request customer information from an organization's database. The commands COUNT, WHERE, and EQUALS are part of the fourth-generation language. A similar request in high-level languages could require several lines of code.

A characteristic of fourth-generation languages is that they rely on prior development of a database. Applications development is simplified greatly because most of the work in traditional programming goes into the development of routines for creating and updating files. Since the database program is responsible for creating and updating files, the 4GL user can concentrate on accessing needed data.

Natural Languages

Fifth-generation natural languages are currently making their way from research labs into mainstream data processing environments. These languages make it possible for users to address computers in normal human languages without a special vocabulary or syntax. Users present English statements to programs that perform comparisons and develop relationships among described items. Figure 16.24 is a simple example of a natural language request for customer information.

```
How many customers do we have in the Big Apple?

I don't know what you mean by the Big Apple.

New York City

The XYZ Company has 201 customers with addresses in
New York City

How many have purchased guitars this year?

34
```

FIGURE 16.24
Natural languages, which represent the latest way of communicating instructions to a computer, are much more flexible than earlier programming languages.

Summary of Application Program Languages			
Language	**Applications**	**Strengths**	**Weaknesses**
Ada	Scientific	Easy to structure programs	Complex, takes time to master
Basic	Educational, Simple Scientific, and Business	Easy to learn, widely use with micro-computers	Difficult to structure, weak Input/Output capabilities
C	Systems and Graphics	Portable, easy to structure programs	Complex, takes time to master
COBOL	Business	Self-documenting, easy to structure programs, widely used	Verbose, complex computations, awkward
FORTRAN	Scientific	Handles complex computations and graphics	Difficult to structure, weak Input/Output capabilities
Fourth Generation	Access to Databases	Simplifies program development	Limited to database applications
LOGO	Educational	Easy to learn, allows simple graphics	Few applica-tions outside of education
Natural	Decision Support Systems Expert Systems	Uses English and other human languages	————
Pascal	Educational and Scientific	Easy to structure programs	Weak Input/Output capabilities
RPG	Business	Easy to generate business reports	Difficult to structure, complex computations, awkward

FIGURE 16.25

Since computer languages were designed to handle problems in different fields, each has its own strengths and weaknesses.

Compared to a 4GL, natural language systems make assumptions about user requests. For example, the second request in Figure 16.24 just asks how many guitars have been purchased. The computer assumes that the user is still asking for information about customers in New York City. To date, the major applications of natural languages have been for decision support and expert systems.

STUDY QUESTIONS

13. Define bug and debugging.
14. How does a line of pseudocode or a flowcharting symbol relate to program code?
15. Describe two activities that help programmers check the reliability of their programs.
16. Identify the strengths, weaknesses (if available), and types of applications associated with these programming languages: FORTRAN, COBOL, BASIC, Logo, Pascal, Ada, C, RPG, fourth-generation languages, and natural languages.

TESTING AND DEBUGGING

Attention to testing requirements takes place throughout the design and coding steps of a project. Then, as a final quality check, a system test is performed prior to release of the new system to users. A system test involves two major sets of activities:

- Testing sections of programs and complete programs
- Testing the system under realistic operating conditions

Program Testing

When programs are written in modules, they are put through a series of top-down test procedures. The bottom level of a program is an individual module. As previously mentioned, every programmer is responsible for testing modules as they are written.

A problem can arise in module testing because part of the test involves checking the interconnections among modules. To check program modules, stub testing techniques often are employed. ***Stub testing*** is the execution of selected program modules to see if they interact correctly. Quite often the stub is an incomplete module designed to stand in for other, more complex modules. It may do no more than display that the stub has (or has not) been executed in the proper sequence. In some instances, standard stub modules are used that input data to or receive output from the module being tested. In every case, each module must be tested and debugged before it is included in the overall system.

The testing situation is similar even if only program maintenance is being done. If the program was designed using structured techniques, then only one or two modules have to be modified; the other modules do not need to be recoded. Each changed module is tested separately and then joined with the rest of the unchanged program.

At the next level of testing, groups of modules are tested. This process builds until complete portions of structured programs are tested as integrated units. Ultimately, the entire set of programs that forms an application is processed with a complete set of test data. When all debugging and recompilation of programs is complete, a full test can be performed.

This procedure is repeated many times until a program is tested completely and is ready for integration into the overall system. At that point, the program becomes part of the system test.

FIGURE 16.26

Programmers not only write program instructions but must also thoroughly test their creations.

INSIGHT

PROGRAMMING LANGUAGES —NO MATTER HOW YOU SAY IT . . .

As with human languages, programming languages differ in the vocabulary used as well as the structure of sentences. Following are examples of a simple program, in the commonly used languages of COBOL, FORTRAN, BASIC, and Pascal. Each program retrieves two numbers from a disk file, finds their sum and which number is larger, then displays the numbers, sum, and maximum number.

These are just sample codes. The same idea can be expressed several ways within the same language, so a programmer can develop a style—not unlike a novelist.

As a user-developer, you may some day need to program when an application package does not meet your needs. Even if you never write a program, understanding how a program works makes you a better communicator with computer professionals.

Step One: Input

Set up the computer's memory to accept two numbers from disk file "DATAFILE.IN". Then access the disk, retrieve the numbers, and store them in memory.

```
SET UP DATA FILE
AND RECORDS

SPECIFY SIZE AND
TYPE OF INCOMING
DATA FIELDS

NAME DISK FILE
TO BE ACCESSED
AND MAKE IT
AVAILABLE

FIND TWO NUMBERS
AND COPY THEM
TO MEMORY
```

COBOL

```
FILE-CONTROL.
   SELECT DATA-IN
   ASSIGN TO DISK.

FD DATA-IN.
   VALUE OF DATA-IN IS
   ''DATAFILE IN''.

01 NUMBERS-TO-BE-PROCESSED.
   05 NUMBER-1-IN PIC 999.
   05 NUMBER-2-IN PIC 999.

OPEN INPUT DATA-IN.

READ DATA-IN.

data is read a record at a time
```

BASIC

```
10 OPEN ''DATAFILE.IN''
   FOR INPUT AS FILE#1

50 INPUT#1, NUM1, NUM2
```

FORTRAN

```
OPEN (UNIT=1,
   FILE='DATAFILE.IN',
   STATUS=OLD)

READ(1,50) NUMBR1, NUMBR2

50 FORMAT (1X,I3,5X,I3)
```

Pascal

```
VAR number_1,
   number_2:INTEGER;

ASSIGN(infile,
   ''DATAFILE.IN'');

READ(infile,number_1,
   number_2);
```

Step Two: Processing

Add the two numbers, storing the answer in SUM. Find the larger of the two numbers, storing the answer in MAX.

```
ADD TOGETHER
TWO NUMBERS

TEST FOR
LARGER NUMBER
```

COBOL

```
ADD NUMBER-1-IN,
   NUMBER-2-IN GIVING SUM.

IF NUMBER-1-IN > NUMBER-2-IN
   MOVE NUMBER-1-IN
   TO MAX
ELSE
   MOVE NUMBER-2-IN TO MAX.
```

FORTRAN

```
SUM = NUMBR1 + NUMBR2

IF (NUMBR1.GT.NUMBR2) THEN
   MAX = NUMBR1
ELSE
   MAX = NUMBR2
ENDIF
```

BASIC

```
90 SUM = NUM1 + NUM2

100 IF (NUM1>NUM2)
   THEN MAX = NUM1
   ELSE MAX = NUM2
```

Pascal

```
sum := number_1 + number_2;

IF number_1 > number_2
   THEN max := number_1
ELSE
   max := number_2;
```

Step Three: Output

On a screen, display the numbers, their sum, and the maximum of the two numbers.

Sample output (for the numbers 4 and 7) would be:

```
NUMBERS: 4  7   SUM =  11
MAXIMUM = 7

SHOW NUMBERS
AND SUM ON ONE
LINE, MAXIMUM
ON NEXT LINE

SET UP FORM
AND LABELS
FOR OUTPUT
```

COBOL

```
FD DATA-OUT.

01 OUTPUT-LINE-1.
   05 NUMBER-1-OUT PIC ZZ9.
   05 NUMBER-2-OUT PIC ZZ9.
   05 SUM          PIC ZZZ9.

01 OUTPUT-LINE-2.
   05 MAX          PIC ZZ9.

MOVE NUMBER-1-IN
   TO NUMBER-1-OUT.
MOVE NUMBER-2-IN
   TO NUMBER-2-OUT.

DISPLAY ''NUMBERS: '',NUMBER-1-OUT,
   '' '',NUMBER-2-OUT,'' SUM = '',
   SUM ON CRT.

DISPLAY ''MAXIMUM = '',MAX
   ON CRT.
```

FORTRAN

```
WRITE(6,100) NUMBR1, NUMBR2,
   SUM, MAX

100 FORMAT(' NUMBERS: ',I3,
    2X,I3,' SUM = ',
    G I4,' MAXIMUM = ',I3)
```

BASIC

```
PRINT
   ''NUMBERS: '';NUM1;
   '';NUM2; '' SUM = '';SUM
PRINT
   ''MAXIMUM = '';MAX
```

Pascal

```
WRITELN('NUMBERS: ',number_1
   :3,' ',number_2:3, 'SUM =
   ',sum:3);

WRITELN('MAXIMUM = ',max:3);
```

FIGURE 16.27

System test involves the running of a new set of programs under realistic conditions.

System Test

A system test, as described in the previous chapter, involves the operation of the complete system, including new equipment and documented procedures, by users. System tests usually are performed with realistic source documents and data. The use of previously processed data serves to provide known results against which tests can be compared.

A requirement for a realistic test situation is that all of the documentation needed to operate and maintain programs and application procedures be available. System documentation should be part of the test, which determines whether the system is ready to be turned over to users.

During a system test, program bugs or shortcomings often are discovered. It may be necessary to modify programs before the system is finally accepted. For these reasons, it is important to keep a log of all findings during a system test and to use this log to be sure that programming and system documentation is modified to reflect all changes.

STUDY QUESTIONS

17. Define stub testing.
18. What activities are associated with a system test?
19. How can the design of structured programs help in program maintenance?
20. What is one requirement for a realistic system test?

DOCUMENTATION AND TRAINING

Recall that enhancement of programs is a requirement built into the very nature of computer systems. As soon as a new system becomes operational, it usually is subject to modification. Either to meet regulations or to capitalize on newly

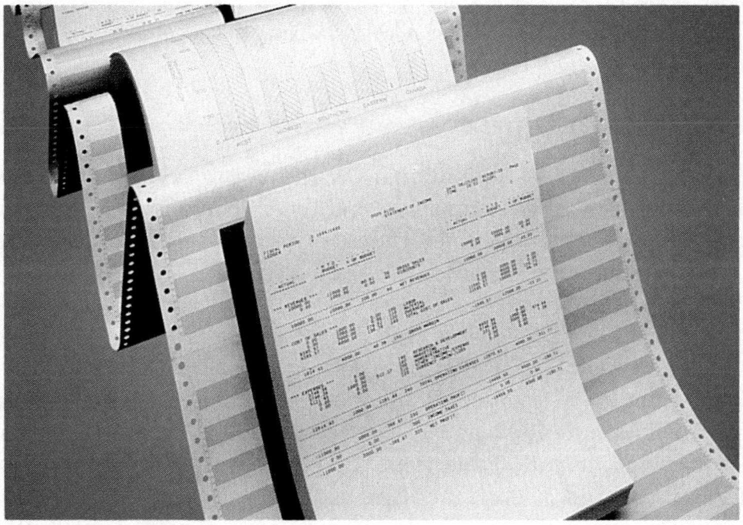

FIGURE 16.28

A programming project is not finished until both technical and user-oriented documentation is complete. This documentation includes sample reports and screen displays as well as the program code.

discovered opportunities, computer applications are modified throughout their useful lives.

From a programming standpoint, this means that the documentation prepared by any programmer must be readable and usable by any other programmer. In this way, any programmer can be assigned to modify both programs and supporting documentation as enhancement is required.

Careful documentation also is important because, in most instances today, programming is a team effort. One reason for taking care with the design of programs is that it allows coding assignments to be distributed by individual modules. Many computer systems require programs large enough to warrant assignment of at least 2 and possibly between 20 and 50 programmers to the same project. To promote better communication among programmers, it is imperative that professionals within any organization follow the same standards for design and documentation. This helps to ensure that the modules will interact smoothly during program execution. Uniform methods must be followed in preparing structure charts, flowcharts, pseudocode, and other documentation.

User Training

Programming is a major part of the implementation step of a systems development project. Toward the end of the implementation step, extensive user training must take place. In addition, computer operators and other personnel require training. At these levels, everyone needs extensive documentation. Manuals must be prepared for both training sessions and for reference during ongoing operation of the system. Complete documentation of program design and coding must be included in the data library, along with copies of the storage media that hold the programs.

In short, a lot of loose ends and technical details must be tied together before a system is operational. This final step of a programming project is set up, in large part, to ensure that all the necessary details are accounted for. This step should end with a meeting at which the project manager, the director of computer operations, and the data librarian review all documentation in detail, request any additions, and ultimately accept the documents and the storage media.

This review evaluates the efficiency and the quality of the programming effort, providing a learning experience and a basis for improvement of future projects.

Program Maintenance

As discussed in Chapter 14, operational programs can become the basis for the use of the computer in security breaches and theft. Therefore, once programs are turned over to operations personnel, procedures must be put in place that guard against both misuse and obsolescence of programs and their supporting documents.

For every disk or tape kept within a data library, records of its use should be established and maintained. Program source code should be checked out only to authorized people. These people must account for everything they do to the programs. Any changes must lead to amendments of the master and distributed copies of code documentation and manuals. Different edition, or ***version***, numbers should be assigned to each modified edition of documents and media. Responsible people must not lose sight of the fact that program documentation and media are major assets of their organization. These assets must be guarded and handled with the same level of care accorded to money and securities.

FIGURE 16.29

User training must be completed before new programs are put into use.

STUDY QUESTIONS

21. Define version.
22. Identify two reasons why program documentation is important.
23. What happens during a documentation review?
24. What is program maintenance?

CONCLUSION

The program development process is performed by computer professionals within the context of a systems development project. All four steps in program development take place regardless of whether a few modifications are being made to an existing application program or a new program is being written from scratch. User input into the program specifications are critical for the project's success.

Developing a program is more than just writing code. At both the design and coding steps, the logic involved is reviewed by other professionals through a structured walkthrough. This is especially important when a program is written by a team of programmers, instead of one individual.

Programming professionals have access to a variety of programming languages and use structured programming techniques. These languages have been designed to handle business, scientific, engineering, or educational applications. Programmers are usually fluent in more than one language. The care taken in the design and documentation of program code determines its useful life span and how successfully it solves a user's problems.

CHAPTER FACTS

- Programming is more than just writing code. Properly designed programs require a four–step process: (1) designing the program; (2) writing the program code; (3) testing and debugging; and (4) providing documentation and training.
- Good design methods for programs include structured programming. In a structured program, all code is organized into one of three structures: (1) sequence; (2) selection; or (3) repetition. Programs are organized by modules, each handling a specific function. Single modules can be modified without affecting the logic of the entire program.
- Program design is done through a hierarchy chart in a top-down manner. Flowcharts and pseudocode show step-by-step programming logic. Before code is written, logic is reviewed in a structured walkthrough. Test data to examine all conditions of the program are also collected.
- A programming language is chosen that best fits the particular application. A variety of languages are available including: FORTRAN, COBOL, BASIC, Logo, Pascal, Ada, C, and RPG. Special languages also exist to aid in accessing databases (fourth-generation languages), and in designing decision support and expert systems (natural languages).
- Bugs in the program code and logic are detected through another structured walkthrough. Each module is tested independently through stub testing. Finally, the entire program is tried out on the test data.
- Documentation is important when maintaining programs and in team programming. The latest versions of programs and documentation should be carefully stored. A team of management and operations personnel make a final review of a system project's documentation.
- Program maintenance is an ongoing procedure involving modifications for cyclic operations, new laws, and changes in company policy.

TERMS TO REMEMBER

bug
code
debugging
detail diagram
flowchart
hierarchy chart
HIPO (hierarchy plus input-processing-output) chart
module
overview diagram

program specifications
pseudocode
repetition
selection
sequence
structure chart
structured program
structured walkthrough
stub testing
test data
unstructured program
version
visual table of contents

CHECK YOUR UNDERSTANDING

1. The first step in the programming process is ___________ the program.
2 Which of the following is ***not*** one of the structures in the structured programming method?
   a. selection
   b. termination
   c. repetition
   d. sequence
   e. All are correct structures.
3. Test data include only data found during normal operation of the program. (True/False)
4. With flowcharts and pseudocode, each symbol or line represents one module of a design. (True/False)
5. Group review of program designs and code is called a(n) ___________.
6. Which of the following languages are commonly used in business applications?
   a. Pascal
   b. COBOL
   c. RPG
   d. all the above
   e. b and c
7. Which programming language is used primarily in education, having few outside applications?
   a. Ada
   b. BASIC
   c. RPG
   d. Logo
   e. Pascal
8. Natural languages involve using human language and are used to design expert systems. (True/False)
9. ___________ is the testing of modules by combining them with other incomplete modules.
10. When a structured program is modified, all program modules must be changed in some way. (True/False)

APPLYING WHAT YOU'VE LEARNED

1. Designing tools, such as pseudocode and flowcharts, are used for more than just programming projects. They are similar to term paper outlines, assembly in-

structions, recipes, and wiring diagrams. Pick one of the following problems and use both flowcharting and pseudocode to give a step-by-step analysis of how to solve the problem.

a. change a flat tire
b. drive to some remote or hard-to-get-to place
c. start up a computer and load in a program
d. solve a long division problem in math

2. Several thousands of computer programming languages have been developed over the years. Some are now obsolete, while others are used only in specialized applications. Report on a programming language not mentioned in the text. Find out about its main use, when and where it was developed, and some of its advantages or disadvantages. SNOBOL, LISP, FORTH, APL, PL/1, and ALGOL are some languages. Other names can be found in ads for programmers, computer dictionaries, or guides to published books.

3. It takes a special person to be a programmer. What professional skills do you think would be most beneficial? What personality traits could make a programmer effective? What traits might hamper a programmer on the job?

4. It is important that test data be developed that try out all options and extreme conditions in a program. They should also include invalid or incorrect data to make sure that they are picked up by the program. For each application, describe what should be included in a test data file.

   a. checking that a valid date is input into a program in the form mm/dd/yy—for example, 06/24/88
   b. keeping reservations for a hotel
   c. scheduling classes and rooms for a small college
   d. computing telephone bills
   e. recording sick days and vacations for a company

5. User training is an important, but sometimes neglected, aspect of program development. For one of the application programs or languages available in school or at home, examine the user's guides and existing documentation. List what types of help are available for beginning users (such as tutorials, workbooks, and so on). What special features (such as appendices, error lists, and so on) are available for advanced users? Do the quality and amount of training material seem sufficient for people to learn the program on their own? What would improve the materials?

6. Pick three of the programming language examples shown in this chapter. For each, list those English words or statements that seem to indicate the steps of the IPOS cycle. Make a chart that compares the words in the language with the input, processing, output, and storage steps.

CHECK YOUR UNDERSTANDING ANSWERS

1. to design
2. b
3. false
4. false
5. structured walkthrough
6. e
7. d
8. true
9. stub testing
10. false

UNIT FIVE

LOOKING AHEAD

Computer systems have become an integral part of society. Chapter 17 identifies current and future trends for computer applications and hardware. These trends include management of natural resources, use of robots in production, and the extension of human capabilities in hazardous environments. This chapter also documents the influence computers are having in education, banking, transportation, and leisure time activities. ▸ Finally, Chapter 18 stresses that keeping up with technological changes requires ongoing education. The opportunities available for formal computer training are listed, along with sources for informal continuing education. Discussion of educational opportunities is completed by a review of professional computer publications and organizations. This chapter ends with a description of the many careers available in computer-related fields.

CHAPTER SEVENTEEN

TRENDS

KEY IDEAS

- **From the user's point of view**
  What developments in computer technology will have an impact on your future? How will today's trends affect life tomorrow at school, work, and home?

- **An information society**
  Today's society depends on a constant flow of information.

  A cashless society
  In a cashless society, people make purchases through electronic transactions.

  Trends in leisure time activities
  Trends in electronics make possible worldwide video links and interactive television.

  Electronic cottages and classrooms
  Workers and students will use computer technology to personalize schedules and education.

- **Resource management**
  Scarcities of resources can be managed with the aid of computers.

  Monitoring natural resources
  Using computers to locate and control limited resources helps minimize shortages and maximize utilization.

  Moving resources
  Computers are intimately involved with the building and maintenance of most modes of transportation.

- **Extending human capabilities**
  Computer-controlled devices control production and take sensitive instruments where people cannot go.

  Exploration and research
  Robots perform hazardous jobs and assist researchers.

  Computer-controlled production
  Modern production techniques create a variety of products through process control systems.

- **The march of technology**
  The race is on to design and engineer the next computer generation.

  The next computer generation
  Fifth-generation computers will run sophisticated programs simultaneously on several processors.

FROM THE USER'S POINT OF VIEW

Some future trends are easy to predict. You can anticipate the advent of smaller, faster, and less expensive personal computers. For the first time, new operating systems will let small-computer users run several programs at the same time. This and other technological trends surveyed in this chapter can make you more productive. How will you spend this free time? Technology may provide the answer.

AN INFORMATION SOCIETY

For most of its history, the computer has been a tool with great problem-solving potential. The challenge has been to identify problems and develop computer solutions. Certainly, computers are everywhere and are awaiting new challenges. Today, computers have brought us to the threshold of what many people call an ***information society***. An information society consists of a large group of people situated within a country or region where most workers generate or depend upon information for performance of their jobs.

Think of this for a moment. If we live in an information society, then it follows that information has become the chief requirement and tool we use to earn our livelihood.

What does all this mean? Briefly, it means that computers have changed the responsibilities and lifestyles of many people. Further, even greater, more dramatic changes lie ahead as computers are applied to meet problems that previously were too big to solve.

The tools are already available to bring about many wonderful changes. The use of these tools, however, requires an understanding of what is happening and what can be expected. The day for simply pressing a button or turning a crank in performance of a job is pretty much over. People preparing themselves for tomorrow's work force must realize that good paying manual labor jobs will be harder to find. Fewer jobs will require people to move or assemble parts. Those currently performing such jobs must seriously consider retraining in skills compatible with developments in technology. These skills and potential career paths are discussed in Chapter 18.

The impact of the information society is apparent even today. The supermarket checker presses keys to record prices. The modern-day checker is part of a computer system. The sequence of data processing actually begins when a bar code number is assigned to each product. The supermarket checker plays a part in a continuing process where the data on the label are read into the computer. This action activates a database that provides sales information. You know the rest.

Merchandise marketing no longer consists of a set of separate steps. Rather, computers provide continuity through the entire system. Already, it is possible for computers at supermarket chains to communicate directly with computers of vendors to initiate deliveries of needed stocks.

FIGURE 17.1

Computers have become a permanent fixture in our information society.

A Cashless Society

When you pay for the groceries, another network of computers comes into play. The banking industry has developed a communications network that helps minimize the work involved in transferring money among banks. The ***electronic funds transfer (EFT)*** system handles financial transactions through a computer network rather than by exchanging cash. This system is having a major impact upon society. Through the use of electronic passwords and credit cards, buyers and sellers can advise a bank that a transaction has been completed. The bank completes the transaction by automatically moving the money from the buyer's account to the seller's.

FIGURE 17.2

Smart cards contain their own processing and memory capabilities to protect credit card transactions.

An EFT system provides a solution for problems that have continually plagued buyers, sellers, and banks. Without the use of EFT, buyers have had limited purchasing power outside of their local community. Out-of-town stores have not always been willing to accept their checks. Also, many stores do not have credit plans available for major purchases. Sellers, in turn, always had to be on the outlook for stolen or uncashed checks. There was also a delay between the time a buyer wrote a check and the time a seller actually received the money. Banks were caught in the middle, handling millions of checks per day. An EFT system minimizes the need to write checks and for the bank to process the paper involved.

Some people are even talking about a ***cashless society***. In such a society, instead of using physical checks, we would make all our purchases as electronic transactions. Individuals and businesses would have national account numbers. Workers would be paid by their employers making electronic deposits to employee accounts. At the same time, the employer's account would be reduced.

If this system were operational, there would be no obvious need for money. This could lead to a cashless society, in which checks and money would be eliminated. All purchasing and payments would be handled electronically.

Currently, the French are using a new type of credit card that will help minimize fraudulent electronic transactions. Called a ***smart card***, this credit card contains a processor and memory chip that stores and updates the owner's credit information. Every time a transaction is made using this smart credit card, the transaction immediately becomes part of the owner's credit history. If a stolen card is used, the memory chip is wiped clean by a credit card reader. Erasing occurs when the merchant tries to verify the customer's credit through the bank's central computer system.

Information utilities currently service the needs of consumers by allowing users to research, comparison shop, and make purchases without even leaving their homes. Large catalog wholesalers are working with these utilities to showcase their products. Once connected to the system, users identify what they want and the computer searches through the product line to find the requested information and prices. Customers also have the option of browsing through this electronic catalog. Billing and payment can be done through credit card accounts and EFT.

FIGURE 17.3

Information utilities allow customers to comparison shop online.

Trends in Leisure Time Activities

Information utilities can help people with leisure time activities. Users can play or preview games at home through their personal computers and the utility's computer network. People from around the country (or world) can play together through these communications networks. Their options range from a chess challenge to participating in complex adventure games that involve several players.

One way microcomputer-based games have become more sophisticated is by linking them to interactive video disks. Home computers attached to video

FIGURE 17.4
Telecommuting describes a worker's ability to work at home on a personal computer that communicates with a central facility in the main office.

disk drives can display game scenarios in any order or overlay them with other video images. As a result, these games include real pictures or detailed drawings as part of the action.

Another way people can spend their leisure time is talking to their television sets. Surprisingly enough, the television sets will listen! Actually, some cable television users now have control boxes that are linked to the cable company's computer. The control box becomes input hardware that lets the viewer respond to the televised program.

The result is ***interactive television***. Local announcers can ask the viewers if they agree or disagree with questions. The viewers punch the appropriate button on their control boxes and the computer counts the responses. In a matter of minutes, the announcer has the results. Interactive television lets people tell the station which shows they like or the politician they support. Students can even return answers to questions a teacher poses as they watch educational television.

Electronic Cottages and Classrooms

FIGURE 17.5
The information society will be in full swing when every student has a personal computer.

The ability to access information networks has forced many of people to reevaluate how training and work will be done in the future. Already, some people's work takes them outside the office environment. For example, traveling salespeople work away from the office when they are covering their territories. With the ability to link workers together through computer networks, ***telecommuting*** is now feasible. A wide range of productivity software allows telecommuting people to work at home or other locations.

Some professionals, such as architects, writers, and computer programmers, can work at home using a personal computer. Electronic mail systems allow them to keep in touch with the office. The mail system delivers messages, electronic spreadsheets, and work assignments to the employee's home computer. If additional data are needed from work, database query languages allow employees to access the information and download it to their personal computers. The work is completed at home and transmitted back to the office through the same system.

This type of flexibility provides a solution to workers in special situations. Working at home can appeal to people with small children. The ability to work at home allows them to raise a family without sacrificing their careers. Working

Future of Computers in Education

1. Individualize instruction
2. Track student progress through curricula
3. Help students choose courses of study
4. Diagnose problems and recommend remedial solutions
5. Bring students in contact with experts through teleconferences

FIGURE 17.6

Computers will determine the future of tomorrow's classroom.

at home can also appeal to employees with physical handicaps who find it difficult to commute daily to the office.

The idea of people working at home is not new. Before the Industrial Revolution, most farmers and craftspeople worked out of their homes. Historians refer to this lifestyle as cottage industry. The futurist Alvin Toffler coined the term ***electronic cottage*** in his book *The Third Wave*, referring to people working with computers at home instead of at the office or factory.

The full impact of an information society will be felt when every child has a computer to help him or her in school. With the aid of artificial intelligence and expert systems, education can be individualized. Computers will act as patient tutors as well as drillmasters. These machines will also track each student's progress through a variety of curricula and help them choose future courses of study. When learning difficulties arise, the computer system will help diagnose the problem and suggest possible methods of remediation.

As you can see, tomorrow's classroom, like its office counterpart, will not be bound by walls or limited to a building. Many of these activities can take place in the home. The electronic cottage will also serve as the electronic classroom. In the future, a French class in North America may be taught by a professor in Paris. By using communication networks individuals can hold conferences even though they are in different locations. This ***teleconferencing*** will enable businesspeople and students to participate in seminars given by experts located around the world.

This trend has already started to alleviate the discrepancies in education for different areas of the world. Today children in remote geographic areas are benefiting from computer-based education and educational television. Linking these children to an educational network gives them access to materials that are usually not available.

FIGURE 17.7

Teleconferencing helps people effectively communicate when separated by great distances.

STUDY QUESTIONS

1. Define information society, electronic funds transfer (EFT), cashless society, smart card, interactive television, telecommuting, and teleconferencing.
2. How have EFTs helped bankers, buyers, and sellers?
3. What are two services information utilities provide to customers?
4. How will video disk systems make computer games more sophisticated?
5. Describe three applications for interactive television.
6. What types of problems can telecommuting help solve?
7. What are five ways computer technology can improve education?

CLIP

SUPERCONDUCTORS: A TECHNOLOGY COMING OF AGE

Incredibly fast mainframe computers that fit on your desktop, high-speed trains that float above their tracks, and long-distance power lines that transmit electricity without losing any power: These are just some of the products that may result from superconductor technology.

Recent scientific breakthroughs have superconductors working their way into the public's eye. Promising great new products, superconductors may have as much impact on modern life as the invention of the transistor.

New Technology That's Old

The phenomenon of superconductivity was first discovered in 1911 by a Dutch physicist named Jeike Kamerlingh Onnes. He found that by cooling mercury to –452° Fahrenheit (approximately 0° on the Kelvin scale, also known as absolute zero), this common material carried electricity with absolutely no resistance. Resistance slows down the flow of electrons, decreasing voltage and increasing the wasteful (often damaging) dissipation of heat.

At such extremely low temperatures however, superconductivity is practically useless. To keep the conductant cool, it had to be immersed in liquid helium—not the most practical or inexpensive of operating conditions.

Recently, by combining ceramic materials with small amounts of elements known as *rare earths*, physicists have been able to produce superconductors that operate at much higher temperatures. It took several years to move from –452° F to just –424° F, but within the past year, we have gone all the way from –424° F to 9° F—a jump of over 430 degrees.

With these recent developments, researchers have superconductors working at room temperatures. There has even been evidence that superconductivity in a ceramic material may be possible at a scorching 90° F. Allowing current to flow without any resistance, superconductors open up a whole new universe of possibilities in electronics.

Super Products

To minimize the loss of electricity, power plants must be placed relatively close to the population that they serve. With nonresistant superconductor transmission lines, power could be ported great distances without any loss of energy.

One of the most talked about superconductor applications is the *maglev* (magnetic levitation) train. A characteristic of superconducting material is the powerful magnetic field that they create. By generating superconductive magnetic fields with opposing polarity, trains could travel 6 to 12 inches above their tracks, being pulled along by other, constantly alternating magnetic fields. Without the wheel-against-track friction experienced by regular trains, the maglev could attain cruising speeds of up to 300 miles per hour—twice the speed of highly touted Japanese "bullet" trains.

Superconductors may have their most profound effect on computers. Today's computers rely on a multitude of tiny switches called *gates* to process information. With superconductive gates, computers could operate literally hundreds of times faster than they do with conventional silicon gates. And because superconductors do not generate heat, computers can be made much smaller. No longer requiring fans or extra ventilation space, electronic components can be packed together without overheating and breaking down.

In the never-ending quest for faster, more powerful computers, superconductors may be the answer to a long sought after dream. Imagine a box similar in appearance to a pocket television running Macintosh software at ten times the normal speed, or a desktop PC more powerful than a Cray supercomputer. Computers could be made so small that even the most superior machines would be considered portable by today's standards.

Superconductors are already being used in medical scanning equipment and giant atom smashers. But until certain barriers are broken—such as tolerance to warm temperatures, ability to handle high voltages, and flexibility of materials (the ceramics used in high-temperature superconductors are far from flexible)—superconductors will simply be a phenomenon at which physicist and science students will marvel.

Source: COMPUTE. Reprinted with permission.

Key Question: What improvements in computer technology could result from the development of near-room-temperature superconductors?

RESOURCE MANAGEMENT

An information society inevitably generates problems to match its progress. A growing population demands more resources. Many of the resources that people have used in great quantities are coming into short supply. For the future, you can expect to continue to read headlines and listen to television reports about such topics as:

- Energy
- Water
- Food supplies

Monitoring Natural Resources

Although these issues may seem disconnected, all are computer-related. Everything from researching and using new energy resources to controlling the movement and utilization of water and food is or will be controlled by computer systems.

Energy

Computers are being applied directly to improve conditions and find new solutions to deal with energy problems. The problem, in relatively simple terms, is a potential shortage of energy resources. The entire world depends chiefly on fossil fuels (oil, gas, and coal) for its energy resources. A severe shortage in 1973 and 1974 led to concentrated efforts, supported by computers, to find and develop new sources of oil. These efforts succeeded to a level that led to a surplus of oil by the mid-1980s.

Sooner or later, however, the fact must be faced that the Earth can contain only so much oil and coal. As existing supplies are used up, they cannot be replaced. New energy sources must be identified. Computers are primary tools in the search for alternate sources of energy.

Supercomputers are working continuously to help devise safer, more manageable techniques for applying nuclear energy. This is just one example. Through

FIGURE 17.8

Computers help to use natural resources efficiently for energy production.

Courtesy of T. J. Florian, Rainbow

FIGURE 17.9

Power plants use computers to provide customers with uninterrupted service.

computer-supported research, many new energy sources with great potential are also being explored. Several projects underway are aimed at harnessing wind, the sun, and the oceans as power sources. One pilot plant focuses hundreds of computer-controlled mirrors on a large water tank. Sunlight reflected by the mirrors heats the water to produce steam that powers electric generators. Windmills are being used in California and elsewhere in the Southwest to produce supplementary electrical power. Computers are also being used within projects aimed at harnessing the power of ocean tides to produce electricity.

Computers work to support exploration of the energy source that lies beyond nuclear power—the fusion reactor. Fusion holds greater energy potential than present-day fission-based nuclear power plants. In effect, fusion is based on the joining (rather than the splitting) of atoms. Tremendous amounts of energy are released when atoms are combined.

When controlled fusion processes are mastered, the world will have surplus energy and a higher level of safety than has existed with other energy sources, including oil, coal, and gas. One of the present challenges is to assemble enough computing power to simulate the functions of a fusion reactor. Computers will also be needed as part of process control systems that monitor the enormous heat produced by fusion reactions. In this way, computers will make this new energy source safe.

Water

Water is the resource that is most important to the support of life. Life on earth will perish much faster from lack of water than from loss of food supply. Support of societies requires steady, predictable supplies of water. Research into the development of water resources is moving in several directions. As mentioned earlier in this book, for example, meteorologists use computers and satellite-generated information to study and predict weather patterns. In the future, it is expected that some methods will be developed to promote rainfall through artificial means. When successful, these methods could go a long way toward ending droughts and associated disasters. Also, similar techniques may be able to alleviate suffering caused by hurricanes and tornadoes.

On another front, computers are helping engineers to devise bold new plans for directing the flow of available water resources to areas faced with shortages.

Monitoring Natural Resources with Computers

Energy
- Manage nuclear and other types of energy production
- Research new energy sources (wind, solar, ocean, fission)

Water
- Predict and possibly control weather
- Design and control aqueducts
- Control the desalinization of ocean water

Food Supplies
- Plan crop rotations
- Develop feed blends for livestock
- Monitor and feed livestock
- Computer costs.

FIGURE 17.10

Computers can tackle no bigger problem than that of managing resources for tomorrow's children.

In California, the dry, southern portions of the state now receive water directed through aqueducts that extend for more than 400 miles. Plans that have been proposed involve redirecting water resources for entire continents.

Another area in which computers already are at work is the production of drinking water from oceans. If salt water is boiled or evaporated through other processes, the condensed steam becomes fresh water that is safe for human use. A number of pilot facilities already generate drinking water from the sea for use by people. Such facilities, under computer control, presently exist in Israel, Mexico, and South Africa.

Food Supplies

Computers have expanded their role in the management of agricultural resources continuously since the 1950s. Modern, computer-supported farming methods are described as ***agribusiness***. Agribusiness techniques examine resources such as land, water, and climate, as well as costs (labor, feed, seed, and fertilizer) to plan for the crops or livestock to be raised. Livestock operators use computers to develop feed blends that produce the best results for the lowest cost.

In another area of resource management, computers are helping to devise more efficient methods for storing and processing food products. With world population expanding at a rate approaching 100 million per year, computer contributions to agriculture and food processing become critically important.

FIGURE 17.11

Computer technology helps farmers monitor and feed large herds of livestock.

Moving Resources

Traditionally, moving people, natural resources, and manufactured goods from place to place required a great deal of work. Computers help coordinate solutions to this problem and make the world seem smaller.

Automobiles

Highway and street traffic comes in bunches. Expressway systems and city streets seem to be jammed in one direction or in a few key locations while traffic moves freely elsewhere. Computerized systems are doing something about these conditions in many metropolitan areas.

CLIP

JUST WHAT IS HYPERCARD?

Hypercard has been called everything from "an erector set for information" (creator Bill Atkinson) to "a French restaurant that can also clean your Peugeot" (Apple Product Development V.P. Jean-Louis Gassée).

Clearly, it's a little difficult to correctly assess the importance and impact of a product that can be viewed in such a variety of ways. Just what *is* HyperCard?

The Basics

The first step toward profiting from the possibilities that HyperCard offers is learning enough about the product to be able to examine those possibilities.

Basically, HyperCard is software that allows you to manipulate information in the form of text, graphics, video, voice, and animation, and to access large amounts of this information quickly and efficiently through the creation of logical linkages.

These broad capabilities suggest a number of possibilities for higher education. And these possibilities are made even more attractive by the software's ease of use, which can vastly reduce development time and costs.

First, a HyperCard stack could be used in conjunction with a textbook as an interactive index. Such a product would allow students to move through the information freely, following their own trains of thought and making their own logical connections.

The second possibility is the opposite of the first; a HyperCard stack could present the main body of information, supplemented by a printed text.

Third, HyperCard can be used as an authoring tool to create courseware—that is, software for use in instruction. This courseware could range from the very simple—a conventional drill-and-practice program that mirrors the lessons in a text—to the very complex—a stand-alone simulation involving animation, video, or even a combination of visual technologies.

A good example of this approach is courseware developed by Stanford professor Larry Friedlander for use in his drama class. His program allows students studying Shakespeare to view and compare various stagings of *Hamlet*. While the videodisk is showing one version of a scene from the play, the Macintosh computer displays the original text, the edited version, or the actor's interior monologue. Students can then move to another part of the videodisc to study the same scene performed by different actors. They can even design their own version of the staging on a computerized stage.

Fourth, the ability of HyperCard to be used in conjunction with CD-ROMs makes it possible to distribute massive amounts of information on a single compact disc, along with a HyperCard "front end" that makes all of this information readily accessible. Encyclopedias, atlases, and other large reference works are naturals for this approach.

Programs Without Programmers

One of the beauties of HyperCard is that it makes creating software possible for people who know little about conventional programming (though a technical background or some knowledge of design can be very helpful).

According to Danny Goodman, author of *The Complete HyperCard Handbook*, many nonprogrammers are having considerable success with HyperCard. He says, "It's clear from people I've spoken with that HyperCard has become the first programming environment for many people. Not everyone has equal facility, of course, but HyperCard greatly empowers the individual."

Ultimately. . .

Whether the approach is an individual effort, the work of a pair, or the task of a team, the most important consideration is innovative design—making the HyperCard stack more functional, easier to work with, or simply more appealing than any alternative medium. To be a viable product, a stack must add value to the instructional process. Simply presenting on disk information that would normally be presented as printed copy—without any enhancement—not only is a waste of the medium's potential, but also makes bad commercial sense.

Source: Courtesy of Syllabus.

The first requirement is to measure traffic movement and to use computers to identify problem areas. Sensors are placed under city streets or at key points on expressways. These devices present information to a central computer on the number of vehicles in an area and their speed. The computer's application program determines when traffic is backed up and also investigates alternate routes.

Based on current road conditions, one type of traffic management system relies on computers to break up troublesome bottlenecks by altering the traffic flow. For example, if a boulevard is backed up with cars and trucks headed out of town, traffic signals under computer control can be varied. The highway segment with backed-up traffic is given longer green lights. The traffic jam is over sooner than if uniform controls were applied in all directions. Also, computer-controlled signs on expressways can be used to warn motorists of bottlenecks and suggest alternate routings.

This type of traffic control system also helps emergency vehicles get to their destinations. A dispatcher can provide a computer system with data about the starting point and destination of a fire truck, for example. The computer can manipulate traffic signals so that all lights along the route turn green. As a result, when computers treat traffic flow as a system, control becomes more effective.

Automobiles already are the largest users of embedded computers. Many cars are being manufactured with electronic jacks into which computer connections can be plugged. Computers can analyze automotive functions and direct humans to the parts that need servicing or changing. Increased reliability and serviceability for cars has resulted from the harnessing of computers.

In the future, computers will help people arrive at their destinations. Already, some cars have the ability to display road maps for driver guidance. The city of Los Angeles is currently experimenting with disseminating traffic and alternative routing information through a communication network. Automobiles with four-inch VDTs especially installed in the dashboard will test this computer-based traffic control system on area highways. The car's present location, local traffic congestion, and alternative routes will be graphically displayed on maps for the driver's continuous use. If successful, this project will evolve into a local area network that links motorists to the most up-to-date traffic information.

Furthermore, automatic controls may even take over actual driving. Robots already are available that follow markers placed within factories and offices. Driverless carts have electronic sensors that avoid collision with objects or people. All that is required is a decision to spend the money and to install similar guidance controls on highways. Cars of the future may literally drive themselves.

Trains

Railroad freight yards receive and dispatch tens of thousands of railcars each day. By today's standards, such a large volume of traffic would have to be computer-controlled. Each of these cars may be carrying 100,000 pounds or more of cargo. Most of the raw materials and many of the consumer goods that support the economy pass through such yards. Freight arrives in trains that may include 100 or more cars. Incoming trains must be "broken" into individual cars, which are then attached to outbound trains of varying destinations. In a single freight yard, as many as 20 or more trains may be undergoing "make-up" at any given time. To make up outbound trains, a series of rail switches must be set to guide each car from its incoming track to the outgoing location. Setting switches manually used to be a complex, error-prone job.

Today, these problems would be difficult to overcome without computers. As trains arrive, the number from each car is entered into a computer, either through a keyboard or through automatic reading of code painted on the side of

Automation and the Transportation Industry

Automobiles
- Monitor traffic flow
- Control timing of traffic lights
- Warn motorists of bottlenecks and suggest alternative routes
- Diagnose mechanical or electrical problems
- Display electronic roadmaps
- Could potentially drive themselves

Trains
- Track location of trains and individual cars
- Control switching of tracks within railroad freight yards

Aircraft
- Track location of planes as part of air traffic control system
- Design, test, and fly new experimental aircraft
- Diagnose mechanical or electrical problems

FIGURE 17.12
The transportation of people and goods is made easier and safer with the help of computer technology.

the car. The computer has a database that provides information on the origin and destination of each car. Computer-controlled switches route the car automatically to its outbound track.

Aircraft

At any given moment, hundreds of aircraft are en route to and from busy airports in major cities around the world. Keeping track of these planes and monitoring the safety of their passengers is a critically important function. In the early days of aviation, air traffic control was maintained through conversations between pilots and ground controllers. As air travel increased, however, so did the challenges for the controllers. Without computers to monitor locations and schedule departures and arrivals, it would be impossible to support current levels of air traffic.

Aircraft maintenance is also assisted by computers. Computer-controlled instruments enter data to the flight instruments of aircraft. These known signals simulate those generated at different altitudes, speeds, and wind conditions. Such maintenance systems make it possible to check out instruments while the plane is on the ground to ensure that readings are accurate and reliable.

At this writing, commercial supersonic flight is possible only over oceans. Since supersonic aircraft cause a disturbing and potentially damaging sonic boom, residents of cities are not anxious to have these aircraft flying overhead. Yet, supersonic flight is a desirable and very profitable goal. The answer is to fly above the earth's atmosphere.

A transatmospheric vehicle (TAV) now being designed will operate at altitudes of more than 100,000 feet above the atmosphere. This eliminates sonic booms at ground level. Because of the elimination of atmospheric friction, TAV flights may even use less fuel.

However, computers are needed to help fly and design such an aircraft. The TAV is an example of a "computer-built system." It will be designed and tested through displays on computer screens. Models will be constructed by computer-controlled machines. And computers will then monitor wind-tunnel

FIGURE 17.13
Aircraft maintenance is performed with the help of computer equipment which checks for faulty instruments.

tests. Other computers help design the engine, which uses computers. Since humans cannot react quickly enough to pilot the TAV, it will be equipped with some of the most advanced computers available. They will control the vehicle's operation and monitor one another. The pilots will act as backup monitors.

STUDY QUESTIONS

8. Define agribusiness.
9. Identify two ways computers support increasing energy demands.
10. What are the three ways computers help control water resources?
11. How can computers contribute to agriculture and food processing?
12. What are six computer applications that could help car drivers?
13. How are computers involved with transportation by rail?
14. Identify three ways computers support air travel.

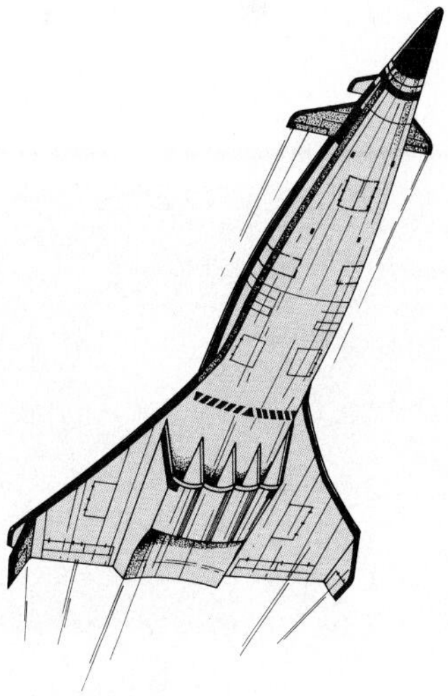

FIGURE 17.14
Transatmospheric vehicles designed with the help of computers will travel from New York to Tokyo in four hours.

EXTENDING HUMAN CAPABILITIES

Another problem of an information society is how to expand human senses in order to gather more information or to become more productive. Mechanical devices controlled by computers can operate routinely under conditions that would prove dangerous to people. As a dramatic illustration, consider that space exploration started with unmanned, heavily instrumented vehicles. These spacecraft gathered information on radiation, reentry heat generation, and atmospheric conditions that was then used to design protective and life-support systems for manned vehicles.

FIGURE 17.15

Robots working at the Three Mile Island nuclear accident site go where humans dare not go.

Courtesy of MaryJo Dowling, Carnegie Mellon University

Exploration and Research

On earth, computer-controlled instruments monitor operations of steel mills and petroleum refineries, reporting to human operators who could not withstand conditions within blast furnaces or distillation towers. While poisonous gases deep within coal mines might destroy the health of a human miner, a robot can enter the caverns without peril. Process control capabilities carry out robot-controlled excavation without health risks. Similarly, robots can be built to explore volcanic interiors, and other areas too small or too dangerous for human entry.

Carnegie-Mellon University developed a series of robots to assist with cleanup at the crippled Three Mile Island nuclear reactor. The three robots, dubbed Huey, Dewey, and Louie, performed three basic functions. They carried cameras into the structure to record the damage on film, took samples of materials, and cut away debris. High levels of radiation barred humans from performing these tasks safely. The robots were invaluable in evaluating conditions within the reactor containment building.

FIGURE 17.16

Researchers used a robot designed for underwater operations to explore the wreck of the Titanic.

Courtesy of Woods Hole Oceanographic Institution

Undersea Exploration

Some of the mysteries of an ocean liner buried under 13,000 feet of water for more than 75 years were uncovered by a deep-sea robot named Jason Jr. Under control of a computer installed in a nearby submarine, Jason Jr. shot thousands of color video images of the sunken Titanic. The expedition proved to be a breakthrough in robotics applications.

Similar sensor-based robots can deliver tactile, as well as visual, feedback to a base computer. These devices are expected to be put to use for ocean mining and further exploration of the sea.

Space Exploration

Above the earth's oceans further investigation is being done by computers in space. In the early days of space exploration, satellites did not have built-in computers. Most of the coordination and control was done on the ground and radioed to the satellites.

Computers as Explorers

Space
- improve weather forecasts
- identify new mineral deposits
- identify pollution problems
- identify agricultural problems
- control satellites and space probes
- control automated production facilities

Under the Seas
- identify new mineral deposits
- control underwater mining operations
- control exploration of sea floor

FIGURE 17.17

Computer technology can help to take people where they have never gone before.

Today, computers control many of the satellite's actions. These satellites are programmed to photograph weather conditions or survey sections of the earth. The results help improve weather forecasts and spot new mineral deposits. Sometimes they can identify polluted lakes and agricultural problems.

Computers in space are especially important for planetary exploration. Voyager 2 is now billions of miles away from the earth and approaching the planet Neptune. It is so far away its signal takes several hours to reach earth. Because of this distance, Voyager must be controlled by computers. There is no way that people back on earth could coordinate its activities. By the time they saw what was happening, Voyager would have flown by.

Of course, the use of computers in space will continue and can be expected to increase. Scientists envision space colonies that will include laboratories for the performance of tests or assembly operations that can benefit from the zero gravity conditions outside the earth's atmosphere. Any projects of this type will, of course, depend heavily on smaller, more powerful, lighter weight computers.

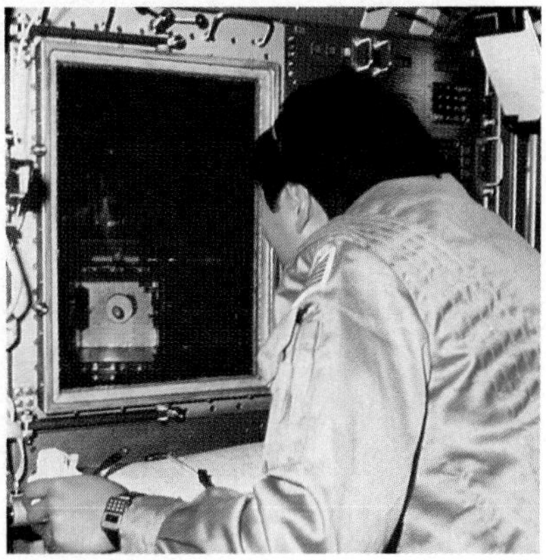

FIGURE 17.18

Manufacturing in space can produce products that cannot be made on earth, where the atmosphere and gravity present obstacles.

Computer-Controlled Production

Supersonic aircraft and spaced-based assembly operations are not the only computer-built systems. Back on Earth, production of manufactured goods is still necessary for continued growth and survival. The problem of how a computer could control design and manufacturing came with a simple solution. Manufacturing procedures could be expressed as part of control software. By using physical data as input, computers can design products, track raw materials, monitor processes, and generally oversee production of manufactured goods.

CAD/CAM

The first step in an automatic production system is to model ideas on video display screens. Models of products can be digitized and displayed on a screen grid as part of a computer-aided design (CAD) application. Under CAD programs, a complete description of the model—shape, color, texture, dimensions, and size—is expressed numerically and entered into a computer. Special utilities in the software enable the graphic to be tilted and rotated to display all angles.

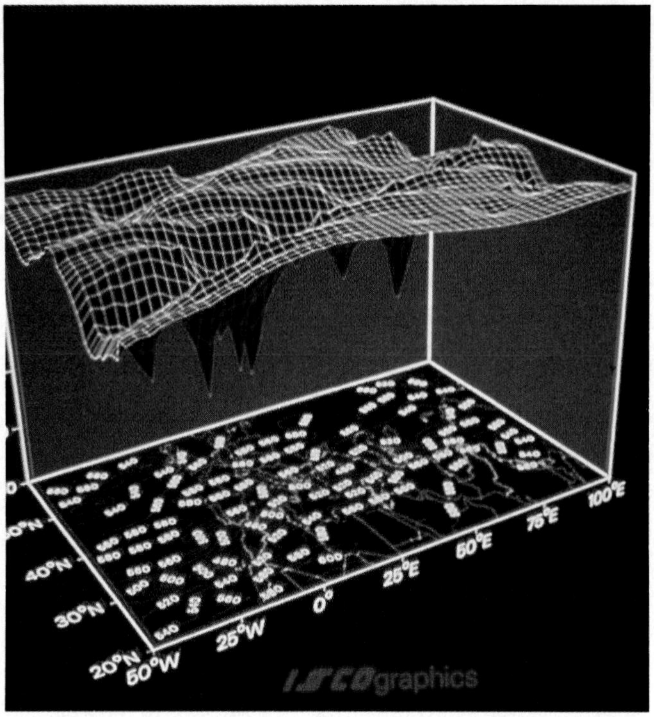

FIGURE 17.19

Engineers are already working on computer-aided designs which use three-dimensional hologram displays.

Future trends in CAD include using holograms, which are three-dimensional displays of objects (see Figure 17.20).

In addition, simulated conditions can be tested on screen to identify and resolve potential design problems. For example, the design of an aircraft might be subjected to computerized data representing actual flight conditions. As test data are applied, the screen image simulates the reactions of the airframe.

CAD technologies gave rise to ***computer-aided manufacturing (CAM)***. Computer-aided manufacturing is, in short, the use of programmable machines to control product manufacturing. CAM links numerical control capabilities directly with computer-generated designs. This communication between design and manufacturing equipment is known as ***CAD/CAM***. Large metalworking machines are used under CAM systems to prepare tools for the stamping of automotive parts or the fabrication of mobile homes.

FIGURE 17.20

The CAD drawing is superimposed on the photograph of its CAM counterpart as it creates a faceplate based on coordinate measurements from the drawing.

Robotics

Robotics represents the latest trend beyond CAD/CAM in the evolution of automatic production systems. CAM is typically the control of a single process, such as the drilling of holes or the milling (shaping) of metal workpieces. Robotics involves the handling and/or joining of multiple parts or the completion of a sequence of operations. Further, robots need not be driven solely by preestablished programs. They can also react to physical data.

For example, a robotic engine manufacturing tool might perform a series of functions: drilling holes in a block, inserting pistons, and putting the engine block head in place. The robots sense the size of each hole, then locate and insert pistons that fit the holes to 0.0001 inch. The robot uses physical data, the size of each hole, and conducts a series of activities in response to those data.

As the field of robotics advances, computerized tools will take on increasingly complex workloads. One present-day example of advanced robotics is a Japanese factory that manufactures vacuum cleaners. The facility is fully automated, with all assembly operations performed by robots. When people are not present to perform inspections or maintenance, the entire factory runs in darkness. Reduction of light levels reduces heat emission and lowers air conditioning costs.

FIGURE 17.21

The precise action of this robot arm allows it to position valves in an engine block.

Integrated Manufacturing

CAD/CAM and robotics are important elements of any integrated manufacturing system. In addition to the design and assembly operations, manufacturers must closely monitor the utilization of parts and raw materials. Computer systems have been successfully used for some time in ***materials requirements planning (MRP)***. In this application, production schedules and current inventory for associated parts and materials provide the data a computer uses to schedule the purchase and delivery of additional goods. MRP systems minimize money invested in inventory, which frees an organization's finances for other investments, such as advertising or research and development.

MRP systems have led to a recent manufacturing trend called just-in-time inventory. ***Just-in-time inventory*** means that raw materials or parts arrive shortly before they are assembled into the finished product. The result is that the manufacturer minimizes finances tied up with inventory and saves money by not having to store materials and parts before they are needed. Japanese industry first used MRP systems for just-in-time inventory in the late 1950s. Both the American and Japanese automotive industries have now gone to this type of inventory system, while other manufacturers are slowly following their lead.

The critical component for the successful implementation of an integrated manufacturing system is communications. CAD/CAM requires communications between the computer, which designs a part, and the lathe or milling machine, which manufactures it. MRP systems, especially when involved with just-in-time inventory, must be in constant communication with suppliers, haulers, assembly operations, and sales. Production lines with dozens of robots performing various tasks need to communicate with each other.

FIGURE 17.22

Materials requirements planning is made possible, in part, by computerized warehouses.

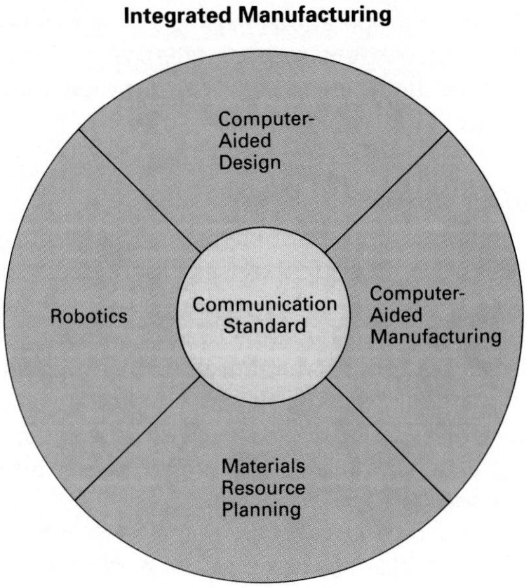

FIGURE 17.23

The integration of computers with manufacturing systems should reduce costs, increase precision, and help products become more personalized.

General Motors is leading the way with the development of a communications standard for factory automation. It is known as MAP—manufacturing automation protocol. MAP provides a communications standard that links a company's central computer systems to robots, machine tools, and equipment used by suppliers. As shown in Figure 17.23, computer-aided design, computer-aided manufacturing, robotics, materials resource planning, and a unifying communications standard together form an ***integrated manufacturing*** system.

STUDY QUESTIONS

15. Define computer-aided manufacturing (CAM), CAD/CAM, materials requirements planning (MRP), just-in-time inventory, and integrated manufacturing.
16. In what ways can the use of computers protect workers and minimize hazardous situations?
17. How can computers under the seas and in space help people?
18. What are three characteristics of CAD?
19. In what ways are robotics applications more advanced than CAM?
20. How do computers control design and production activities when used as a part of integrated manufacturing?
21. What is necessary for the long-term success of integrated manufacturing?

THE MARCH OF TECHNOLOGY

Computers themselves are changing dramatically. Three major developments that can be anticipated in computer architecture include:

- Processors and communication lines that use superconductive materials or light instead of electricity

FIGURE 17.24

Microminiaturized electronic circuits have led to faster, energy-efficient processing and memory units.

- Multiple, parallel processors in the same system
- Evolution of special-purpose machines

Furthermore, software drives hardware. Expect to use expert systems and other artificial intelligence software with these faster processing units. Many embedded computers will be hard-wired with voice recognition and speech synthesis to support even smarter tools.

The Next Computer Generation

Since the beginning, all computers, regardless of size, have been designed around a single principle, known as von Neumann architecture. The basic computer design that has been in place since 1945 is named after John von Neumann. Von Neumann was the pioneering mathematician and computer scientist who proposed a design under which all calculations and logic operations with any computer are routed through a single processing unit.

Optics and Superconductive Materials

Processing units have been drastically reduced in size over three computer generations to meet the continued demand for faster processing speeds. The trend toward the miniaturization of electronic components is based on a simple principle of physics—computers work faster when data and instructions have shorter distances to travel. Much of the circuitry of a fourth-generation computer can now fit on a single integrated circuit (see Figure 17.24).

While processors will continue to increase in speeds through down-sizing, research is now focused on the materials that transmit data and programs. A lot of interest centers on new superconductive ceramics discovered by IBM researchers K. Alex Muller and J. Georg Bednorz. This research led to the 1987 Nobel Prize in Physics for both men. ***Superconductors*** lose all resistance to the flow of electricity at a given temperature. These materials provide the fastest possible means of electronically transmitting data within and between computer components. Before Muller and Bednorz announced their discovery, the only known superconductors operated, unfortunately, at temperatures around –560F (–293C).

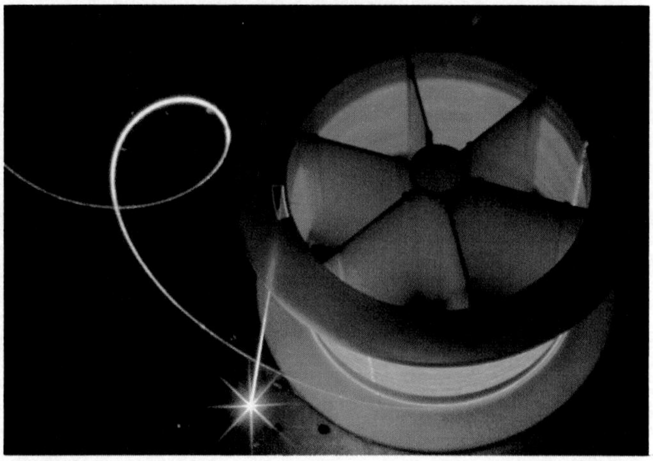

FIGURE 17.25

Fiber optics allow voices and data to travel at the speed of light.

Courtesy of AT&T

At these temperatures it was impractical to consider using superconductors with even the most expensive supercomputer.

Near room temperature, these new superconductive ceramics will help computers break current processing speed barriers. Computer scientists are now creating designs for a new generation of smaller supercomputers made with these materials.

Meanwhile, other scientists are working on a computer generation that does not even use electricity to operate. This research centers on employing fiber optics for data communications *and* processing. In Chapter 7, fiber optics was discussed as a new type of high-speed communications channel that uses glass fibers to transmit data as light pulses. Current research focuses on the development of a processing unit containing very fast, light-activated switches. An ***optical computer*** could take advantage of superior switching and data transmission speeds since light travels faster than electricity.

Parallel Processors

As demands for computing speed increase, even the capability to handle billions of computations per second is not enough. Accordingly, modern computer designers are working on systems containing multiple processors that handle computations and logic operations simultaneously. These parallel processors will help computers become faster and more productive by executing hundreds, perhaps thousands, of instructions at the same time.

The advantage of parallel processing is not in its ability to perform a single computation faster, but to speed up processing by performing many computations at the same time. For example, the many components of a bridge design need to be analyzed separately for design flaws and then analyzed together as a working unit. Parallel processors can facilitate simultaneous analysis of all bridge components and their interactions instead of sequentially analyzing one component at a time.

As you might expect, many engineering and architectural problems need to be overcome before parallel processing computers become commonplace machines. Designers are still struggling with ways to handle memory. Do all the processors use the one memory unit, separate memory units, or some type of hierarchy of units? Another related problem concerns developing operating systems that can handle this sophisticated memory management. Still other problems concern high-speed input and output, memory conflicts (two processors trying to use the same data), and the writing of application software for parallel processing machines.

Several parallel processing computers currently exist. Cray supercomputers can be configured with several processors working in parallel and IBM has a number of prototype parallel processing computers working in research labs. An independent research lab has a working computer that uses up to 65,536 processors concurrently.

FIGURE 17.26

This array of sixty-four processors is used by the computer for parallel processing several instructions from the same program.

Courtesy of Jon Brenneis

Special-Purpose Machines

As you know, most of the computers now in use are general-purpose machines. That is, they are capable of doing almost any work presented. Adaptation for specific uses is achieved through software.

Computer systems were not always designed in this way. During the first and second generations of computer hardware and software, separate machines were built for business and scientific/engineering applications. The idea for general-purpose systems was introduced in the 1960s as computers gained the memory and processing capacity to permit adaptation through software.

Today scientists and engineers are trying to add more power to computer systems. One promising approach is to go back to the idea of special-purpose equipment through the use of coprocessors. Under this approach, special-purpose processors are added to existing computers. These processors often perform special functions, including data communications and database maintenance. The idea is that a processor built for special jobs, such as accessing a database, can be more efficient than a general-purpose system functioning under software control. Special computers of this type do not need extensive programs. Instead of using instructions from memory, these machines have hard–wired instructions incorporated into the hardware for faster execution. Multiprocessing systems configured with these special processors are highly productive and could help meet increasing demands for computing power.

Artificial Intelligence

Computer scientists around the world are building systems that can learn from experience and are able to apply this information to new situations. This area of research is called artificial intelligence (AI).

Research in AI began in the mid-1950s. Results were slow at first. There were early programs that could play easy games such as tic-tac-toe. There were also programs that could play reasonable games of checkers. Promises were made that there would soon be chess-playing programs, but this was overly optimistic. Respectable chess-playing programs have only recently become available.

Language translation was also harder than expected. In the 1950s people said it would be only a short time until computers could translate English into another language, such as Spanish. However, they discovered that human language is very complex.

Early language translators simply substituted a word in one language for an equivalent word in another. With this procedure the phrase "The spirit is willing but the flesh is weak" was translated to "The booze is good, but the meat is rotten." One scientist said that programs had to be taught that when Mary had a little lamb, she didn't have it for lunch!

The attempt to translate human language by computer led to a greater understanding of language. New language theories resulted from this work. Today, there are programs that can do acceptable forms of translation. These artificial intelligence programs work with knowledge bases, as discussed in Chapter 13. AI applications in particular would benefit from new parallel processing hardware since extensive knowledge-based processing would take a fraction of the time.

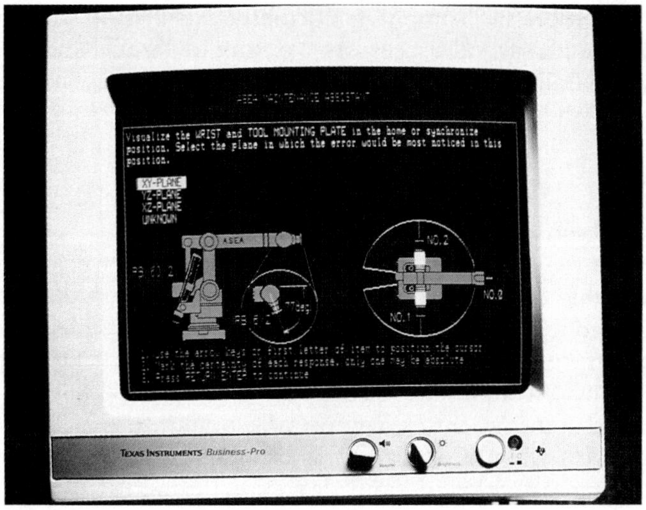

FIGURE 17.27

This robot repair expert system uses an inference engine and knowledge base to answer questions relating to specific robot operations.

One of the most common AI applications, an expert system, uses an inference engine and knowledge base to process queries from people. Sometimes the answer is in a form of a question that clarifies the query. In other situations the expert system can immediately provide the answer. These techniques can be of great value in decision making and data analysis.

Expert systems are currently finding many applications in business and industry. A new generation of smart games and tools will give everyone his or her own personal consultants. Knowledge-based systems will help homeowners design new energy-efficient homes that fit their budget, lifestyle, personal taste, and land requirements. People with older homes will use expert systems to figure square footage and costs for new cabinets or help them rewire the basement. Copy machines, cars, and household appliances will have built-in expert systems that remind users to perform routine maintenance and warn them of impending problems.

Fifth-Generation Competition

AI techniques have brought us to the start of fifth-generation technology. This will involve the use of high-performance parallel processing hardware and high-level software structured to resemble human reasoning. In 1981, the Japanese government pooled resources with eight of the country's largest electronics firms to create fifth-generation computers.

This consortium's goal is to design a machine that can perform the following:

- Accept spoken instructions along with traditional forms of input.
- Use graphic images, such as diagrams and photographs, for input.
- Collect, select, and store useful data given newspapers, books, tape-recorded speeches, and other common sources of data.
- Translate foreign languages.
- Research and provide answers to questions by using all available data.
- Learn from its own experiences.
- Program itself.

The fifth generation of computers is seen as having parallel processing capabilities, greatly expanded data handling and storage facilities, and software that will respond to the natural language of people. The new technologies

FIGURE 17.28

Japan's quest for the fifth computer generation has made it a leader in practical applications for robotics.

identified in the discussions above are seen as keys to implementing fifth-generation systems.

The American computer industry was at a disadvantage in early phases of the fifth-generation race because antitrust laws restricted the ability of companies to cooperate. By comparison, the Japanese government brought together all of its resources and all companies within its electronics industry for a cooperative, concerted effort. Since these early days, however, the U.S. government has sanctioned special research and development cooperatives formed by a number of computer companies. In addition, some of the largest companies, particularly IBM, have established special developmental efforts and budgets for participation in the race for advanced computing capabilities.

New Tools for Systems Development

New technological innovations have computer professionals enhancing the life-cycle approach to systems development, which was discussed in Chapter 15. Alternative approaches have become feasible in recent years as a result of the introduction of software packages that can serve as tools for creating systems directly without extensive programming during the construction phase of implementation.

Databases

One of these developments is the technology surrounding database software. If a database exists, it may be unnecessary to work through an entire life cycle. After all, much of the work of traditional systems development lies in designing files and developing application software to build and maintain those files. With a database in existence, file design requirements are minimized. It also becomes possible to use and maintain a database through execution of commands within its query language. In a sense, a complete system can be developed by using and/or modifying a database and processing data through query language commands. From this starting point, software developers have created tools that make it possible to build and use databases from scratch. Under this approach, complete operational systems can be built through use of software packages that apply—but go far beyond—established database techniques.

These advanced methods, collectively, are being incorporated into fourth-generation languages (4GLs) and object-oriented relational databases. Use of

4GLs can lead to modification of the life-cycle approach. With a 4GL, files can be created and systems built from scratch at low expense. Organizations can afford, in many instances, to experiment with the development of systems through use of these tools and to modify system specifications on the basis of their findings. This is because a 4GL makes it possible to have a system up and running in a small fraction of the time required for traditional design and program development.

Two concepts have been devised for implementing advanced systems development tools such as 4GLs:

- Prototyping
- Information centers

Prototyping

The concept of ***prototyping*** is not new in itself, although adoption of these methods in computer systems development is recent. In industry, for example, a prototype typically is a hand-developed model of a product planned for mass production. Auto companies produce a few prototypes of new cars. These are driven extensively before designs are finalized and major investments are approved for tooling and production. The same practice has been applied routinely in the development of new aircraft.

In systems development, prototyping techniques are used to develop working models of required or requested new systems. Through applications of 4GL techniques, some of the steps in traditional development often are bypassed. Detailed design and programming, for example, can be skipped if 4GL software is available to generate the files and procedures needed to implement and install a system. The responsibilities of a systems analyst are different when prototyping is used since the user is in a position to provide the analyst with more detailed feedback about the newly designed prototype. Maximizing user involvement increases the chances of a successful system design.

In some instances, the prototype system may not meet final requirements. However, it usually is possible to determine feasibility and profitability more effectively through prototyping than through traditional design methods. In other cases, the system developed as a prototype is perfectly adequate to meet

FIGURE 17.29

Prototyping as a way of developing new computer systems emerged with the growth of database systems and associated design software.

FIGURE 17.30
Information centers are staffed by people who are trained to help others with computer-related problems.

user needs. This tends to be true particularly for microcomputer systems. If the prototype system is adequate, it can be converted into regular use and more extensive systems development can be avoided.

Information Center

In some organizations, an ***information center*** is a place where prototyping happens. The information center is an office within an organization, usually associated with the computer center, where one or more microcomputers and a library of software is available. Interested users simply make appointments and work with computer professionals to build the systems they want from application software packages.

In other instances, the information center may not serve as a demonstration facility. Instead, computer professionals act as consultants to users with specific computer-related problems, or they investigate new systems or applications in which they are interested. This can involve visits to computer stores to look for hardware and software. Or, advice and assistance may be provided in users' offices.

Information centers are staffed with computer professionals specially trained to handle users' problems. Staff members in many information centers maintain help lines and try to solve problems immediately over the telephone. The objectives of these centers may be twofold. First, users' problems are minimized through the use of new hardware, software, or procedures. Second, other computer professionals, such as systems analysts and operators, are freed of questions related to systems already in use.

STUDY QUESTIONS

22. Define superconductor, optical computer, inference engine, prototyping, and information center.
23. How is it possible to make computers faster?
24. How will special-purpose processors add more power to new computer systems?

25. What will be seven characteristics of fifth-generation hardware?
26. How can databases and fourth-generation languages be used to shorten the systems development process?
27. What are two possible configurations for an information center?
28. What are the objectives of an information center?

CONCLUSION

The Industrial Revolution spawned the Computer Age. In turn, the Computer Age has created the Information Society in which we live today. Technological innovations continually change the way we live, work, and play. There is no reason to believe that this trend will stop.

We see how computer technology solves problems every day. Our business transactions are communicated to local banks in the blink of an eye. We shop or play computer games at home and are automatically billed for these services. The resources we have come to rely on are currently monitored and regulated with the assistance of computers. Whenever we drive across town or fly across the country, computers help us arrive safely.

Today, computers individualize instruction, direct the manufacturing of goods, and extend our capabilities—and will continue to do so in the future. These machines will design and control the transportation of the future. They will learn how to translate human language and share with us the knowledge of experts by using hardware and software currently being developed.

CHAPTER FACTS

- We now live in an information society where many people's work generates or depends on information.
- Electronic funds transfer (EFT) uses a computer network to handle financial transactions between banks, buyers, and sellers. An extension of EFT is the cashless society, where no actual money would be needed. Smart cards will protect consumers from fraud by recording transactions on self-contained chips.
- During leisure time, computers can be used in information utilities to aid comparison shopping at home. Videos can be enhanced by interweaving video and graphic images. Interactive television enables customers to give direct feedback to the television station. It also allows students to send answers quickly back to questions seen on educational television.
- Working people will use computer technology to work at home through telecommuting.
- In education, the computer can provide individualized instruction, track student progress, aid students in choosing a career, diagnose learning problems, or help share knowledge through teleconferencing.
- Computer technology aids people in controlling natural resources such as energy, water, and food. This is done by computer-controlled power plants, aqueducts, farms, and food processing plants. Also, computers aid in the research to develop new sources of power and to make maximum use of available water.
- Automobile transportation is aided by computers through monitoring of traffic flow, traffic lights and warning signals, diagnosing service problems, and displaying road maps within the car.

- A computer aids rail transportation through freight yard switching and car/train inventory.
- Air travel is helped by computers through air traffic control, design and testing of aircraft, and aid in aircraft repair.
- Both robots and other computer-controlled machines allow people to explore space, undersea, and other places too dangerous for people to go themselves.
- CAD, CAM, robotics, materials requirements planning, and standard communication protocols work together as part of integrated manufacturing.
- Computer technology will become more powerful through the development of superconductive materials, optical processors, parallel processors, and special-purpose processors.
- Expert systems use inference engines to process data from a related knowledge base in response to a specific query
- Fifth-generation hardware will include the ability to accept spoken input, use graphic images as input, collect and store data from the mass media, translate foreign languages, research on its own, learn from its own experiences, and program itself.
- The systems development process is shortened by the use of prototyping, databases, fourth-generation languages, and information centers.

TERMS TO REMEMBER

agribusiness
CAD/CAM
cashless society
computer-aided manufacturing (CAM)
electronic funds transfer (EFT)
information center
information society
integrated manufacturing
interactive television
just-in-time inventory
materials requirements planning (MRP)
optical computer
prototyping
smart card
superconductor
telecommuting
teleconferencing

CHECK YOUR UNDERSTANDING

1. EFT systems aid banks, sellers, and buyers by eliminating all paperwork in financial exchanges. (True/False)
2. Working at home or at other locations using computer networks for communication is called:
   a. interactive commuting
   b. remote processing
   c. electronic work transfer
   d. telecommuting
   e. distributive processing
3. Students around the world can participate in seminars and conferences through a computer and communication network. This technique is known as

4. Interactive television allows customers to communicate directly with a cable television station through the control box. (True/False)
5. ___________ is the computer-supported farming of large areas.
6. Which of the following use light instead of electricity for processing data?
   a. parallel processing computer
   b. optical computer
   c. superconductive computer
   d. photon-based computer
   e. none of the above
7. Which computer application requires a complete description of the model and displays graphics that can be viewed from any angle?
   a. CAM
   b. NC
   c. EFT
   d. CAD
   e. none of the above
8. Multiple processors in a single machine that handles simultaneous computations are called ___________.
9. Although language translations may be difficult for humans, computers can do it easily and correctly. (True/False)
10. ___________ is the development of a working model for a design or system.

APPLYING WHAT YOU'VE LEARNED

1. Some people look forward to a cashless society, while others do not. What are some positive aspects of living in a cashless society? Some negative aspects? How could a cashless society be abused? Would you foresee a decrease in money-related crime? Would a cashless society improve social conditions?
2. Computer language translators have problems similar to those of humans first learning a foreign language. Name five general areas, types of literature, or specific qualities of a language that may be difficult for a computer to translate correctly.
3. Development of fifth-generation computers has united the government, educational institutions, and industry on a very broad scale in Japan. Do you feel our government should be involved in supporting research for fifth-generation technology? Would this help or hinder progress? As innovations arise, who should profit from them, government or industry?
4. Telecommuting is slowly becoming accepted in business, but it does have its disadvantages. Name five jobs where telecommuting would not be possible. What are five jobs where telecommuting is not only possible but could be an advantage to both workers and employers? What are some additional responsibilities that a telecommuter has?
5. Much research has been done using the computer to monitor, produce, and find resources such as water, food, and energy. Find an article about the use of computers in one of these areas. How is the computer used? What have been the problems? What solutions now exist that were impossible before computers? What future computer applications are anticipated? Write a short report answering these questions and summarizing the article.

6. The use of computers has increased in environments too small, hazardous, or inaccessible to humans. List ten such environments, excluding those mentioned in the text. Include places where a computer is not presently used but could be helpful.

CHECK YOUR UNDERSTANDING ANSWERS

1. false
2. d
3. teleconferencing
4. true
5. agribusiness
6. b
7. d
8. parallel processors
9. false
10. prototyping

C H A P T E R
E I G H T E E N

KEEPING UP WITH CHANGE

KEY IDEAS

- **From the user's point of view**
  How will advances in technology affect career opportunities for computer professionals and computer users? In what ways can you prepare to use computers as a problem-solving tool?
- **Achieving career goals through formal education**
  Formal education in computers will open doors and provide for career advancement.
- **Career growth through continuing education**
  As technology becomes obsolete, so does existing knowledge—unless it is regenerated through continuing education.

  Skills updating
  Continuing education can take place as part of adult education, on-the-job training, or through attending conferences and workshops.

  Recreational and professional publications
  People can stay on top of the latest advancements by reading computer-oriented and professional magazines.

  Professional organizations and certification
  Professional organizations identify needed computer competencies and certify the skills of their members.
- **Career opportunities as a computer professional**
  A wide range of career opportunities are available in computer-related occupations.

  Operations
  Many people are employed to operate computer hardware, catalog storage media, and control access to the computer room.

  Systems development
  Systems analysts, programmers, and technical writers work together to create new computer applications.

  Systems installation and maintenance
  Salespeople, technicians, engineers, and database administrators set up computer system components and make sure each component operates properly.

FROM THE USER'S POINT OF VIEW

Government statistics show that you will probably change jobs several times in your life. If you view work experience as a career path, instead of just a job, education becomes a continuing process. The more computer-related experience and education you have, the more opportunities will become available.

It should not be surprising that any career you choose will involve computers. You may not become a computer professional, but you certainly will have to communicate with them. More and more employers are looking for people who are not only strong in their major field, but have a solid grounding in computers as well.

ACHIEVING CAREER GOALS THROUGH FORMAL EDUCATION

FIGURE 18.1
Changes brought about by new technology open the door to many opportunities for those who are prepared.

Computers are instruments for change. You should also recognize that the changes associated with computing result from major new discoveries and/or developments in science and technology. When changes take place rapidly, obsolescence is bound to be a major factor. Obsolescence, present in any technology-driven field, describes the rate at which equipment and its applications become outdated and, eventually, useless. In computing, new generations of hardware and software have been introduced about every ten years. In other words, any computer purchased today will probably have to be replaced, possibly along with its accompanying software, within the next ten years.

Obsolescence has had both good and bad effects on computer professionals and users. On the positive side, the rapid rate of change has meant that new jobs and entirely new career opportunities have opened regularly throughout the history of the computer age. For qualified people, change represents opportunity. The more rapid the change, the more advanced the new technology will be and the greater will be the opportunities created.

However, you make more breaks than fate provides. To take advantage of opportunities, people have to be qualified. To be qualified, in turn, takes an appreciation of the power of knowledge. Unfortunately, knowledge is always in danger of becoming obsolete, unless you make a conscientious effort to update your abilities to match new ideas.

This chapter covers both the challenges of continuing education and methods of meeting those challenges for computer users and professionals. To be productive, everyone must keep up with change. Each individual user or computer professional has to work out his or her own program for keeping skills up to date.

The computer field offers opportunities to persons with wide ranges of knowledge and skills. Some jobs are open to persons with high school education. However, far greater opportunities, with broader growth potential, are open to those who go on to study at two- and four-year institutions.

Almost every college curriculum has been affected by recent developments in computers, microelectronics, and data communications. As a result, many

FIGURE 18.2
Computer technology has had an impact on almost every college curriculum.

FIGURE 18.3

End-user computing is one of many skills taught to engineers and architects as part of their college training.

students will be trained as end users as part of their degree requirements. Students training to become computer professionals will work on next year's innovations. College-level courses that qualify individuals for a number of job specialties include:

- End-user computing
- Computer operations
- Computer information systems
- Computer engineering
- Computer science

End-User Computing

Just as computers have affected every facet of human social and working experience, so also have computers become an integral part of virtually every academic department at the college level. This development has been logical and necessary. When computers were new, colleges and universities tended to have a single, comparatively large computer facility that served all academic departments. Students from a variety of departments acquired their computer knowledge from a central, core faculty.

As computers became integral parts of many professions and industries, corresponding academic departments incorporated computers into standard courses. Today, students who will need to use computers on jobs for which they are training can expect to take appropriate college courses within their major departments. At many schools, a general, introductory course is offered within the computer science or computer information systems department. Then, specific applications are taught within the appropriate departments.

To illustrate, medical and nursing schools use computers to train students in patient monitoring, medical diagnosis, support for patient care, and even administration of hospitals and medical offices. Similarly, departments in science, engineering, business, education, liberal arts, fine arts, social science, and other specialties also tend to have equipment and courses designed to meet the special needs of future computer users.

CLIP

DATABASE PROFESSIONALS ON THE MOVE

Because of the strategic value placed on corporate information resources, database professionals have suddenly been elevated to a unique level of power, respect, and visibility. "The database administrator must administer all the technical aspects of the corporate data resource under one umbrella," explains Arvid Shah, senior staff consultant, Performance Development Corp., Princeton, NJ.

"Very few people start out in DBA at the entry level," says Brian Krueger, DP placement manager, Robert Half of Wisconsin, Inc., Milwaukee, WI. "Normally, you must work up to the position through an applications path consisting of database programming and systems analysis." This evolutionary process can take anywhere from four to eight years. However, a "fast-tracker" may become a DBA within two or three years.

According to Ken Brathwaite (Software Design Associates, Inc., Union, NJ), DBAs should be responsible for:

1. Improving the effectiveness and efficiency of DBMS use, and its overall performance.
2. Offering assistance to end users experiencing DBMS problems.
3. Ensuring that adequate validation procedures are used for all transactions.
4. Providing ongoing staff training and keeping up-to-date on database technology.
5. Developing long-range plans to meet current and future DBMS requirements.

Database administration represents the fastest growth area in the DP profession, and the trend toward relational DBMS and database machines adds luster. Control over data storage may ultimately determine the future success of DP.

Source: Reprinted by permission. *Data Management* (Data Processing Management Association)

Key Question: What kinds of personality traits would be necessary in a successful database administrator?

Computer Operations

FIGURE 18.4
Computer operators set up and monitor processing equipment and peripheral devices, such as disk drives.

The work associated with keeping computers running and delivering services required by users provides a number of job and career areas in itself. Some of the specific job descriptions and opportunities are covered later in this chapter. Many community colleges, adult education programs, technical institutes, and other schools provide training that prepares students for entry into this segment of the job market. Specialties within this career area include operation of the computer; operation of peripheral printers and storage devices; capturing data for input; control over job scheduling and completion; and maintenance of programs, files, and procedures in a data library.

Some positions in computer operations are open to persons who have had special course work in high school. Greater opportunities, however, are available to persons who go into special training at community colleges and other educational institutions. At this level, education is highly practical and job-related. People train for specific positions in the operation of computers, in the use of microcomputers, or in other entry-level specialties.

Computer Information Systems

As computer systems became more sophisticated, great shortages of qualified people developed. There has been a continuous demand since the 1950s for people with the skills to design and successfully implement new information systems. The need that emerged was for a new category of specialist—for people trained to create and install information systems in business, scientific, manufacturing, and educational organizations. Accordingly, the specialty of ***computer information systems (CIS)*** evolved and is now a popular major on many college and university campuses.

A CIS program trains students for entry-level positions as programmers or programmer/analysts. The CIS curriculum followed at hundreds of colleges and universities stresses a series of courses in business and management and includes a sequence in computer programming, 4GLs, systems development, decision making, and problem solving. Individuals interested in computers and application-oriented problem solving will find a CIS program to be both interesting and profitable.

Computer Engineering

FIGURE 18.5
Computer engineering specializes in the development, manufacturing, testing, and assembly of computer hardware.

Persons who complete course work in ***computer engineering*** specialize in the development, manufacture, and assembly of computer hardware. At most universities, studies in computer engineering are associated with the discipline of electrical or electronic engineering. Persons entering this highly diversified field usually follow a specialty, since the body of knowledge is so great. In other words, computer engineers specialize much like doctors, who have found it impossible to keep up with all the knowledge associated with modern medicine.

Specialties within computer engineering include the design and building of microchips, the development of disk and other storage devices, the design and building of output hardware such as displays and printers, and the interaction of hardware and software. Persons who pursue specialties involving processing equipment and associated software are called ***computer architects***. Computer architecture encompasses the work of configuring computer systems to achieve specific performance.

Success in computer engineering calls for completion of courses in mathematics, physics, electronics, system software, circuit design, project management, and manufacturing methods.

Computer Science

Early computers were specialized computation devices. Computation, in turn, is part of the province of mathematicians. Therefore, mathematics departments of educational institutions have been involved with computers since the earliest days. Through the years, the mathematically oriented study of computers has evolved into a specialty that deals with the control of the data manipulation capabilities of computers. Today, people who specialize in techniques for assembling computer systems and applying them to the handling of data and programs are known as ***computer scientists***.

Demands for qualified computer scientists have grown with the introduction of ever-more-sophisticated system software. System software, remember, controls the operation of computers and serves to make the application of computers easier for users. It is not unusual, today, for a large computer installation to have more money tied up in system software than in computer equipment. Computer scientists are the people with prime responsibility for developing and maintaining system software. They take classes in computer programming, data structure, and in the design of system software such as operating systems and compilers. People with these capabilities, therefore, work for computer manufacturers, for specialized software companies, and as technical specialists responsible for software maintenance within organizations.

FIGURE 18.6

Computer scientists fine tune computer hardware with the help of system software.

Through the years, processing functions have shifted back and forth between hardware and system software. One result has been a parallel development of many hardware and software features. In response, many colleges and universities are coordinating and/or combining their programs in computer engineering and computer science. The term ***computer architecture*** often is used to describe this combined specialty.

STUDY QUESTIONS

1. Define computer information systems (CIS), computer engineering, computer architect, and computer scientist.
2. What is a good and bad effect of obsolescence for computer professionals and users?
3. How has college instruction about computer applications changed over the years?
4. Where can people go to get training in computer operations?
5. Describe the skills associated with people graduating from college programs in computer information systems, computer engineering, and computer science. Identify classes associated with each area of study.

CAREER GROWTH THROUGH CONTINUING EDUCATION

Aside from (or in addition to) formal education at the college level, a number of other avenues of learning are open to persons who seek to enter or advance in computer-related positions. These opportunities in skills updating include:

- Adult education
- On-the-job training
- Workshops and conferences

Skills Updating

A common feature of training in this category is the desire of workers to qualify themselves for new opportunities. Many people who entered the work force some years ago have found that computers have become essential tools in their industries or occupations. These people recognize that knowledge and skills about computers and their uses can improve their chances of career growth. Accordingly, they return to specialized educational facilities, most often on a part-time basis, to acquire the information they missed in earlier educational experiences.

Adult Education

Educational programs that fall under the adult education category can include those given in specialized high schools, evening or part-time adult education programs, private technical institutes, or occupational training centers. Typically, adult education facilities offer accelerated programs that help people acquire employable skills within 6 to 18 months. Short time spans for career education are made possible through concentrated attendance and instruction.

Students attend these schools from three to eight hours daily. Learning takes place largely in a laboratory or working environment rather than in the classroom. That is, emphasis is on "hands-on" instruction and practical experience. Students actually operate computers or write programs and carry out assignments that resemble conditions in real job situations. People who complete training programs of this type generally are well qualified for entry-level jobs involving the use or maintenance of computers.

On-the-Job Training

An important characteristic of computers from a job performance standpoint is that they are general-purpose tools. Computers can be configured with different combinations of devices and adapted almost infinitely to the needs of specific users and applications. This means that each computer-using organization is faced with the need to train its own employees, at least in connection with the unique features of its own computer systems.

On-the-job training sessions tend to be brief, specific, and practical. Typically, an organization prepares special manuals to be used for training. These are companion pieces to reference manuals that can be used to look up solutions to problems after a computer system is operational.

Most on-the-job training programs, then, deal with specific applications. Sessions usually run from a half-day to as long as one week. Employees are

FIGURE 18.7

On-the-job training is usually brief, specific, and practical so that employees can immediately apply the new skills to their jobs.

Summary of Educational Options

1. Formal Education
    a. Computer Professional
        - Computer Operators
        - Computer Information Systems
        - Computer Engineering
        - Computer Science
    b. Users
        - Most College degrees
2. Continuing Education
    - Adult Education
    - On-the-job training
    - Workshops/Seminars
    - Conferences

FIGURE 18.8

Educational options are as varied as educational needs.

expected to leave these sessions and move right into the regular use of equipment and procedures as part of job performance.

Training programs within organizations also deal with general or administrative skills as well as with specific computer topics. For example, many organizations run in-house seminars on management topics such as supervision skills, problem solving, and decision making.

In addition, many organizations sponsor attendance by employees at colleges or technical institutes. Employees confer with personnel counselors at their organizations. For qualified courses of study, the company often will reimburse an employee for all or part of the tuition associated with job-related study.

Workshops and Conferences

Many opportunities for improving skills exist outside of on-the-job training and adult education. Organizations send selected employees to workshops and conferences. These opportunities occur away from the working environment and involve expertise not found locally.

A ***workshop*** or ***seminar*** concentrates on a single topic. It can last from a few hours to several days. In many ways, workshops are like formal schooling. There are lectures, demonstrations, and materials to read. However, the participants are usually not tested or graded.

Conferences concentrate on broader subjects. A conference might focus on robotics, CAD, or computers in education. Many speakers discuss different aspects of a subject over several days. Presentations at conferences are usually one to two hours long. Several presentations can occur at the same time. There is often a display area where salespeople demonstrate related products.

Workshops and conferences both provide a means for people to share ideas, new techniques, and information. Together, these activities, along with adult education or on-the-job training, often are called ***continuing education***. To avoid obsolescence of their knowledge and skills, people who work with computers typically are required to spend a quarter to a third of their time (personal and working) in continuing education. Other sources for continuing the learning process, over and above schools and job-related training, also are important.

FIGURE 18.9

Conferences provide opportunities for users with common interests to meet each other and view new technology.

Figure 18.8 summarizes educational options available to people wanting to acquire new computer skills.

Recreational and Professional Publications

People who follow a given career or who work in a specific industry develop interests in common. Computer professionals, for example, are interested in new hardware and software developments, in new application packages, or in new ways to install and use their systems. In the medical field, interests center around new medications or treatments. Manufacturing engineers share interests in information about new types of production techniques or tools.

A major branch of the publishing industry has evolved to meet these continuing education needs. Special-interest newspapers, newsletters, journals, and magazines are published to supply information to specific groups of readers. In all, some 4000 professional publications are produced regularly. More than 100 of these deal directly with computer-related topics, and many more cover uses of computers in special industries or professions.

Part of the continuing education effort for every computer professional and serious end user should include reading one or more special-interest publications. You will almost certainly encounter a number of these publications at school and in the workplace. You should make it a practice to review the content of such publications carefully. Subscribe to or arrange to read some of these publications, perhaps in company libraries.

A good way to evaluate a professional publication is to review its table of contents. Then read the articles that match your interests. Arrange to receive or review, on a regular basis, those publications that are helpful. At the very least, be aware that professional publications will provide an information lifeline that will help you keep your knowledge base from becoming obsolete.

FIGURE 18.10

Reading recreational and professional publications provides an easy way to keep your knowledge up-to-date.

Professional Organizations and Certification

The informational and educational values of membership in professional organizations are similar to those derived from publications. The big difference is that

CLIP

INGENIOUS MODIFICATIONS HELP THE HANDICAPPED HELP THEMSELVES

At 19, David Young was left paralyzed when he ran his 1965 Chevy Impala into a tree and broke his neck. In the hospital he learned to drive an electric wheelchair and to type using a mouth stick. But he was 27 and a graduate student at the University of Colorado before he got his IBM PC. "It had become painfully obvious that I could no longer match my peers simply by being bright," he recalls. "The computer opened all sorts of doors for me." Now Young is earning a Ph.D. in biology, working as a laboratory consultant and writing more than he ever did when he had the use of his arms and legs. "The best part," he says, "is that I can do it all with no outside help."

Computers, which have changed the way America works, are now becoming available to the 13 million handicapped Americans of working age. In the past, efforts to help the handicapped tended to be overambitious and prohibitively expensive. In one much publicized experiment, quadriplegics have "walked" with crutches or walkers using computer-stimulated electrical impulses to move their stricken legs. But even by the most optimistic estimates, it will be many years before such devices are widely available.

Meanwhile, many social workers and veterans groups are advocating a more modest approach. Rather than using technology to change the patient, they are changing the technology so the patient can use it. "The key words are access, independence and achievement," says Alan Brightman, director of Apple Computer's office of special education. "If you can only wrinkle your eyebrow, I've got a switch that will enable you to input data into a computer. And once you've got access to the machine, you've got access to the world."

In the past year, the number of disabled Americans using computers has doubled to nearly 40,000, and for many of them the difference in their lives has been dramatic. Some examples:

- Deaf from birth, Marc Hagen, 17, had just about given up on school when his mother brought home an Apple IIe with a modem and showed him how to dial into the 200 or so computer bulletin boards in the Minneapolis area. "It just turned Marc around," reports Dolores Hagen, "Now he can talk to Bangkok if he wants, and if you saw my phone bill, you'd think he was."
- William Garman, 51, contracted Lou Gehrig's disease in 1982 and within two years was paralyzed, unable to speak or write. Then, last summer, a group of Westinghouse engineers outfitted Garman with an infrared sensor that moves a computer screen's cursor in response to his blinking. For the first time since his illness struck, Garman has been able to communicate with family and friends. His first words, painstakingly spelled out one letter at a time: "Oh boy!"
- Despite her blindness, Georgia Griffith, 54, graduated from college and became a music teacher. Then she lost her hearing. Now, thanks to a computer and a collection of special tools for the blind, she has made a new career as a proofreader of Braille music. Using the VersaBraille, a machine that produces a raised-dot readout of characters as they appear on a computer screen, she has been able to meet and keep in touch with hundreds of acquaintances on the CompuServe computer network. Says she: "I am deaf and blind, sure, but I am not disabled."

Enabling the disabled involves a variety of modifications, some of them minor, some technological marvels. Scott Luber, whose arm mobility was severely impaired by muscular dystrophy, has worked for three years as an accountant using a miniature computer keyboard and a pair of pencils to reach the keys. People afflicted with cerebral palsy prefer oversized keyboards with hard-to-miss 2-in, sq. keys. Quadriplegics, who can move only their heads, are nonetheless able to control a computer by using a mouth-held typing stick or a breath-controlled device called a "sip-and-puff" switch. Blind programmers often learn touch typing so they can enter data in the usual way; to read output they use VersaBrailles, Braille pointers or voice synthesizers that pronounce the words in a computer monotone.

Source: Reprinted by permission, *Time Magazine*

Key Question: What special insights and skills can a handicapped person bring to the design of new technology?

Ways in Which Professional Organizations Support Personal Development

1. Provide personal and professional contacts
2. Support student members
3. Provide local meetings and presentations
4. Publish newsletters and magazines
5. Sponsor seminars, training sessions, conferences, conventions, and trade shows.
6. Provide certification of professional skills.

FIGURE 18.11

Benefits from membership in professional organizations serving the computer field are summarized in this checklist.

information is obtained from personal contacts with peers and through special learning opportunities designed for professionals.

Thousands of professional, trade, and business associations serve millions of members in specialized industries or jobs. Members are attracted by common, shared interests. As examples, the four major computer disciplines each have an association serving its specialized needs:

- **Association for System Management (ASM)** has a membership that consists largely of systems analysts for various organizations.
- The **Data Processing Management Association (DPMA)** appeals to a wide variety of computer professionals ranging from operators and programmers to computer center managers.
- The **Association for Computing Machinery (ACM)** serves computer scientists and others involved in computer architecture.
- The **Institute of Electrical and Electronic Engineers (IEEE)** has its own computer society. This group attracts and represents the interests of hardware and circuitry specialists, the people who design and build computer equipment.

Each of these organizations has membership rosters that run into the tens of thousands. Each has local chapters throughout the country. As offshoots of these groups, there are student chapters on many college campuses. Future computer professionals can begin to align themselves with the disciplines they wish to follow and to build working relationships that can support life-long careers.

In addition to these computer industry organizations, many other associations and societies have subgroups that specialize in computer applications. Examples include associations serving the health, education, banking, insurance, and petroleum fields. In each case, managers, professionals, scientists, and other serious computer users have a chance to exchange ideas and views with computer professionals who have chosen to specialize in the needs of specific fields.

Typical participation in a professional organization begins with membership in a local chapter or group. These local entities have regular meetings, usually at least once a month. Officers of the chapters are responsible for planning meetings, discussions, and presentations on new developments of special interest to members. Often, the national organization has a staff that helps to provide speakers or materials that serve as the basis for local meetings.

SAMPLE SAMPLE SAMPLE

Institute for Certification of Computer Professionals

Let it be recognized to all that

has successfully completed all prescribed requirements and is hereby awarded the professional designation

Certified Data Processor, CDP

In Witness whereof, we have subscribed our signatures under the seal of the Institute

Issued:

Expires:

Certification Number:

President

Chair

FIGURE 18.12

Computer professionals who have earned certification in data processing place the initials CDP after their name.

Most associations or societies publish newsletters or magazines for their members. In addition, organizations sponsor and conduct seminars, training sessions, conferences, conventions, or trade shows. These activities can play important roles in the continuing education of computer users and professionals.

The Institute for Certification of Computer Professionals (ICCP) sponsors a ***Certificate in Data Processing (CDP)***. To receive a CDP, individuals must pass a five-part examination and have five years of work experience with computerized information systems. Two years of college work can substitute for two years of work experience.

The person must pass all five sections within three years. Once a section has been passed, it does not have to be taken again. If a section is failed, it can be retaken. The five sections of the exam are:

- Data processing hardware
- Computer programming and software
- Principles of management
- Quantitative methods and accounting
- Systems analysis and design

Individuals who have received a CDP place these initials following their name to show others their professional certification. The CDP is only one of several certifications available to computer professionals. A ***Certificate in Computer Programming (CCP)*** is also available through the ICCP by specialized tests covering business, scientific, or systems programming.

STUDY QUESTIONS

6. Define workshop, seminar, conference, and continuing education.
7. Where are adult education programs offered?

8. Describe the focus of instruction for adult education programs, on-the-job training, workshops, and conferences.
9. What is a good way to review professional publications?
10. How do professional organizations support personal development?
11. Relate the orientation of the Data Processing Management Association (DPMA), Association for System Managers (ASM), Association for Computing Machinery (ACM), and Institute of Electrical and Electronic Engineers (IEEE) with college programs discussed earlier.
12. How can a computer professional earn a CDP or CCP?

CAREER OPPORTUNITIES AS A COMPUTER PROFESSIONAL

For persons who use computers as part of their job responsibilities, career paths can be almost infinite. That is, the careers of users will follow the needs and opportunities of the mainline industries or professions they follow. For instance, suppose a teacher masters the use of computers for student record keeping or computer-assisted instruction. This person still will be guided in career choices by developments in education. The same will apply to geologists, health professionals, bankers, or others who work in computer-dependent fields.

By contrast, those who choose to become computer professionals can look for a series of challenging opportunities that center around the development and operation of computer systems. Some of these opportunities include:

- Operations
- Systems development
- Systems installation and maintenance
- Management

Operations

Operations encompass every step within the IPOS cycle. Along the way people enter data, run the processing equipment, assemble output, and catalog storage media for later use.

Data Entry Operator

Good accounting procedures dictate timely records be kept for each transaction. As a result, microcomputers are becoming primary tools for capturing and recording transactions at the point of origin. As microcomputers replace cash registers or manual record-keeping systems, many job opportunities are created.

Data entry operators capture transaction data onto storage media and often create documents such as invoices (bills) at the same time. If the microcomputer workstation is part of a larger information processing network, captured data may be transmitted to a mainframe system for further processing. However, the main contribution of the microcomputer is its ability to place processing power at the point where transactions take place. In the past, data capture and transaction processing tended to be concentrated in large, central facilities. Data entry operators transferred handwritten data onto computer-readable media.

Nowadays, data entry is a component of many job responsibilities. Sales clerks, travel agents, even nurses perform data entry tasks with the aid of microcomputers every day.

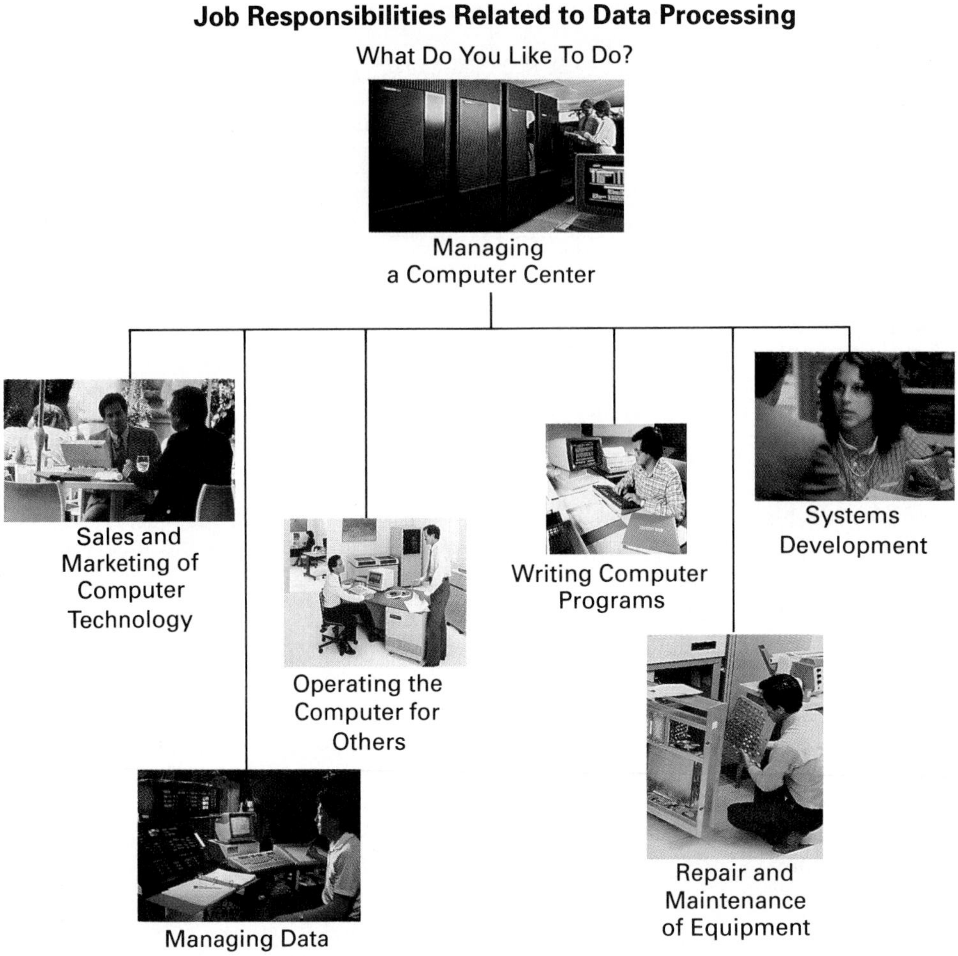

FIGURE 18.13

Many career goals and interests can be met in jobs related to data processing.

Data Control Clerk

A computerized information system is only as good and as reliable as the controls applied over input, processing, output, and storage of data. To achieve quality, it is necessary to separate the control of accuracy from the performance of operating functions. A person who captures and enters data, for example, will be less likely to find errors than a person assigned specifically to look for and correct mistakes. Also, in facilities that handle large volumes of processing, there is a chance that individual jobs, or parts of jobs may be overlooked. The loss of individual documents or computer-stored records can destroy the reliability of an entire system.

To safeguard information assets of an organization, virtually all organizations have specialists in quality control. As you know, every computer system has built-in control or balancing operations designed to make sure that processing is accurate and reliable. Data control clerks keep the records and perform the checks to be sure that controls are applied as planned and that results reflect due care for quality and accuracy.

FIGURE 18.14

For a given application, data entry operations are being handled, increasingly, as part of transaction processing.

Computer Operators

A computer system is controlled by a group of specialists who work at terminals that present status displays on portions of the system. The extensive operating system software signals these operators when attention is needed. The operators, in turn, must make decisions involving the use of computing resources.

These operators are also responsible for peripherals and processing equipment worth many millions of dollars.

FIGURE 18.15

Computer operators are responsible for keeping the computer up and running on schedule.

Data Librarian

Protection of data resources requires that a special individual or group be responsible for custody of the files and procedures critical to computer use.

Custody of data resources usually is assigned as a responsibility of a ***data librarian***. This person or group administers a system that controls the storage of data media, the release of media for processing, the identification of active and backup copies of all media, and the protection of these media against destruction or theft.

All organizations should have procedures for the backup of data files, databases, and programs. There should be plans that can be activated any time data resources are lost or destroyed. Usually, librarians are experienced in computer operations or data control. They receive special training to qualify them as custodians of vital information assets.

Systems Development

The installation of a new computer system represents the changing of the guard. At this time the programmers, analysts, technical writers, and engineers who designed and built the system take a back seat to the operations staff.

Engineers

Computer manufacturers hire engineers to design advanced equipment. Engineers must understand and apply the latest developments in computer technology. Hardware manufacturers and software houses employ engineers to design and produce the continuing stream of new equipment and software products made possible by advances in technology. Some engineers today are working on computer products that will not be available for years.

Programmer

Programs, of course, are the sets of instructions that control the operation of computers. A programmer is a specialist who writes those sets of instructions. Programming, therefore, is a technical task that requires the ability to communicate with computers in an acceptable language. Many programmers are multilingual; they have the capability to write computer instructions in many languages.

FIGURE 18.16

An engineer examines integrated circuit design that will be embedded in a new product.

Before programs can be written, they must be designed and requirements must be defined. These first steps in program development usually are the responsibility of systems analysts or programmer/analysts. These specialists provide a set of program specifications for each module to be developed. Programmers work from these specifications to develop and test the code that implements the design.

A programmer must be trained to think in terms of the logic of each job and think through the processing that will result from each instruction. Programmers also are responsible for running their modules and entire systems with test data provided as part of each specification. Validation of programs, including debugging to identify and correct errors, is a key part of each programmer's responsibilities.

Programmer/Analyst

Persons classified as programmer/analysts handle both the preparation of program specifications and the writing of the code to implement the applications. In

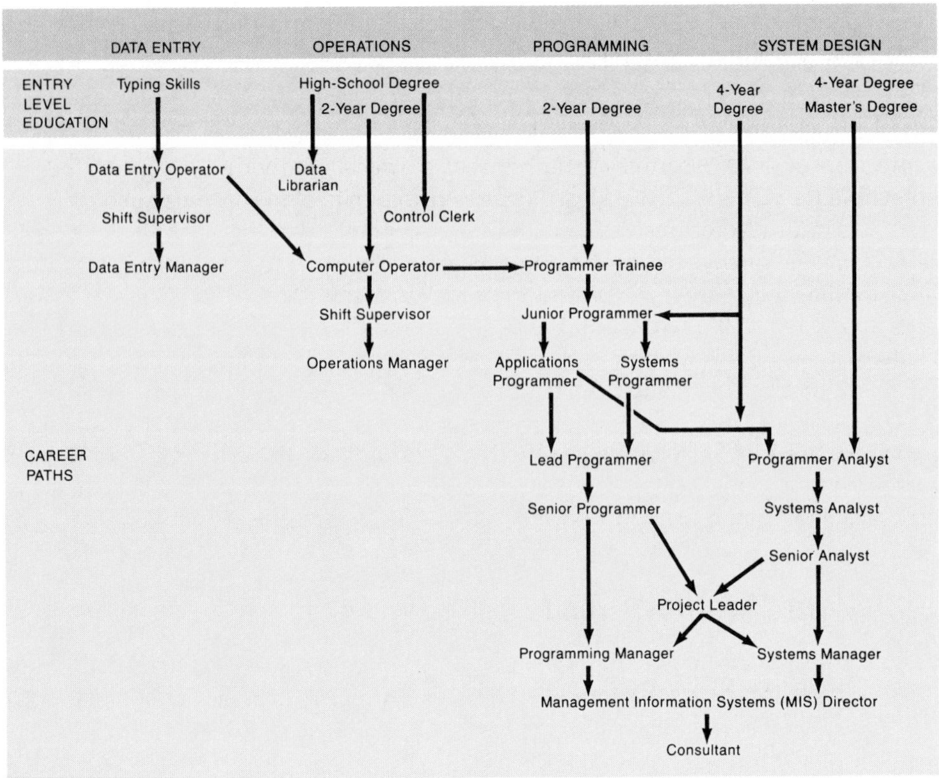

FIGURE 18.17

Potential career paths for computer professionals (part 1).

large organizations, persons usually have a few years' experience as programmers before they are promoted to this position. In smaller organizations, individuals may perform both functions right from the beginning of their work experience. Determination of responsibilities depends partly on the size and complexity of programs and the pressures applied for the development or modification of systems.

Systems Analyst

In thinking about computer-related careers, bear in mind always that every computer application belongs to its users. Systems must be developed to meet the specified needs of users and must be accepted and applied by users. It is important that some computer professionals specialize in the job of understanding, interpreting, and implementing user needs. Systems analysts perform these tasks and assume these responsibilities.

A systems analyst is a person who is familiar with two areas. First, the analyst needs a high degree of knowledge and experience in computer technology. Usually, the analyst has been a proficient programmer before moving to this level of responsibility. Second, the analyst must be able to understand and meet user needs. This requires some experience in the business or professional operations of the user organization. With this dual knowledge and skill base, the systems analyst is able to act as a coordinator who communicates with and meets the needs of both users and computer professionals. Typically, the analyst works with users to prepare a set of system specifications that they approve. Then, the analyst translates these statements of need into program specifications that can be used to develop software solutions to those needs.

Technical Writer

When detailed technical information must be presented to users, ***technical writers*** are called in. They write the user manuals, training guides, advertising copy, and other material in an easy-to-read and nontechnical format. Technical writers work hand in hand with programmers, systems analysts, engineers, and marketing staff.

Technical writers often come from a wide variety of educational backgrounds. However, of prime importance is their ability to write clearly without being condescending. These people also need a good understanding of the technology about which they are writing. The success of a system and recovery in emergencies often hinges on the quality of documents produced by technical writers.

FIGURE 18.18

A systems analyst must often examine detailed documentation to determine current and future system needs.

Systems Installation and Maintenance

As you might expect, there is a group of jobs that do not comfortably fit under either the "operations" or "systems development" label. Jobs in data administration could fit into either category, while service technicians and salespeople are employed by outside vendors.

Database Administrator

Database systems have users, operations personnel, and systems development people, just like other computer systems. In addition, one or more individuals are concerned with managing and protecting the database resource. This individual is called the ***database administrator***.

Database administrators perform several jobs. First, they help to design the database. Second, they manage day-to-day activities involving the database. Third, they evaluate the performance of the database programs. Generally, database administrators are nontechnical people who have been in the company for some time. Although database administrators have responsibility for some technical matters, they are not computer systems experts. It is more important for data administrators to be diplomats than to be technical experts.

Technician

The hardware and system software of each computer installation require attention by qualified specialists. In large installations, it is common to employ persons with training in computer engineering or computer science to assume these responsibilities. ***Service technicians*** plan for and supervise the installation of hardware devices and system software, then monitor operations to be sure that needed levels of service are being delivered.

Once equipment is installed, service technicians keep it in working order. Periodically, they clean the computer and run checks on internal circuitry. These checks, which are used to minimize breakdowns, are part of preventive maintenance procedures. Usually, service technicians are not part of the regular computer center staff. Rather, their services are contracted from a computer manufacturer or a company that specializes in computer maintenance.

The growing popularity of microcomputers has created a demand for service technicians specializing in the repair of small computers. These people are familiar with the diagnostic procedures to identify and correct problems with microcomputer systems and peripherals. A service technician needs a strong background in electronics and must be able to understand technical manuals about various models of equipment.

FIGURE 18.19
Technicians are responsible for the assembly and maintenance of computer hardware.

Salesperson and Customer Support Representative

Manufacturers of hardware and developers of software must interact with the people who could potentially use their products. As computing has grown into a trillion dollar industry, opportunities in computer marketing have kept pace. Tens of thousands of people are employed in sales and systems support jobs for organizations that sell computers and/or software.

Sales personnel must have enough knowledge to describe their products to prospective customers. They also require good interpersonal skills and must be good listeners. ***Customer support representatives*** must have enough background in systems analysis and programming to help customers finalize application designs and to install and use their products. Many customer support representatives become involved in employee training.

FIGURE 18.20
Sales and marketing represents an area of opportunity for people who can combine technical knowledge with interpersonal skills.

Management

Managers by definition are people-oriented individuals. They make sure jobs get done correctly, on time, and within budget. To do this, they must be able to work with people. Sometimes, people who manage other workers have different titles. A data entry operator may report to an operations supervisor. Shift supervisors, lead programmers, and project leaders also manage people. Most organizations have several levels of management.

Figures 18.18 and 18.22 identify the management positions for jobs previously described. At large computer centers, the operations supervisor reports to the operations manager or computer center manager. Senior programmers and systems analysts report to their respective managers. Salespeople report to a store or branch manager.

Management-level personnel are often promoted from related jobs, but not always. A manager's prior experience and ability to work with people are important. For some managers, salary and future promotions depend on his or her educational background.

STUDY QUESTIONS

13. Define data librarian and customer support representative.
14. Describe the job responsibilities of the following occupations. When possible, identify the next career step for people holding these jobs.

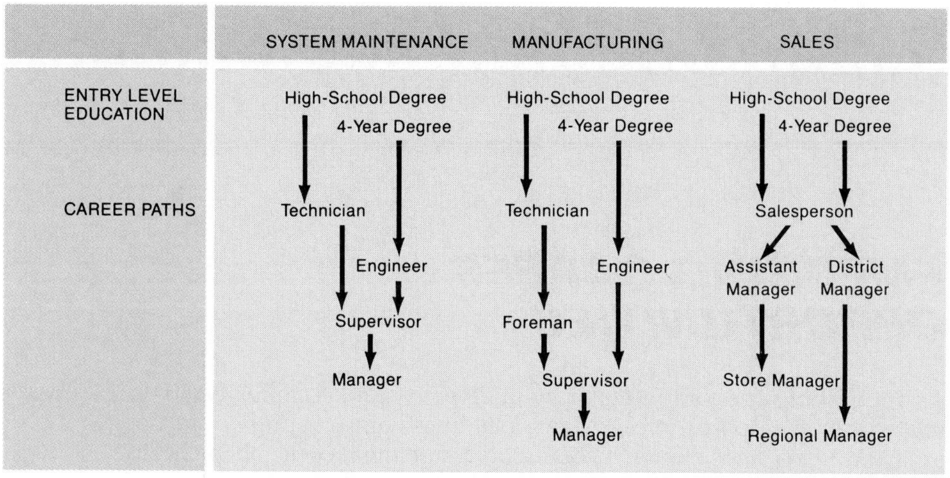

FIGURE 18.21

Potential career paths for computer professionals (part 2).

Data entry operator	Programmer	Service technician
Data control clerk	Programmer/analyst	Salesperson
Computer operator	Systems analyst	Customer support representative
Data librarian	Technical writer	Manager
Engineer	Database administrator	

CONCLUSION

Whether you have selected a career or not, computers almost certainly will have a part in your future. In completing the reading and study assignments as you have worked through this book, you have had a chance to gain a sense of the impact and role of computers in society. Computers solve problems. Computers also are agents for continuing change. No matter where you go or what you do, computers will be part of the challenges you will face and the opportunities that will be open to you. You have started something. From here on, computers will be a major part of your work experience and the basis for the continuing education you will require.

CHAPTER FACTS

- Technological obsolescence has brought about new opportunities for qualified people but necessitates continual updating of skills.
- With formal education, opportunities exist in the areas of end-user computing, computer operations, computer information systems, computer engineering, and computer science.
- Other training includes adult education (through technical institutes or occupational training centers), on-the-job training, workshops, and conferences.
- Professional publications provide a way for specialists to keep up with the newest research in their area.
- Professional organizations foster communication among peers, offer chances for continuing education, hold local meetings, publish journals, and sponsor student chapters.
- Career opportunities as computer professionals exist in many areas, each requiring different skills and formal education. Some jobs groom people for promotion into higher-level jobs.

INSIGHT

EMERGING CAREER OPPORTUNITIES

As applications for computers grow in diversity and complexity, so do related career opportunities. Many jobs involving computers did not exist ten years ago. Some people carve out their own job niche to reflect their training, talents, and interests.

Want an Upper-Level Management Position in a Large Organization?

The *chief information officer* (CIO) is the communication link between high-level management and personnel. You must be familiar with the organization and how it is managed, and be comfortable with its computer systems capabilities.

Over one-third of all major companies have a chief information officer in high-level management. He or she usually reports directly to the organization's president and board of directors.

Does Artificial Intelligence Fascinate You?

As a *knowledge engineer* you use artificial intelligence software to develop expert systems. Through extensive interviews and research, you identify the critical knowledge used by experts and organize the rules by which decisions are made.

A strong interest in exploring new fields plus an understanding of how to organize related data into a knowledge base are prerequisite skills for a knowledge engineer. Also of value are good interpersonal skills for gleaning information from an expert who may not know why—or what—specific information is necessary.

Are Research and Information Your Interests?

Information brokers (or electronic librarians) help people find answers. You search through potentially hundreds of online databases to find specific and, sometimes, highly technical research data.

A fee is charged to the client covering not only database access but the broker's own time and costs. This service is invaluable to busy lawyers, scientific researchers, students, lobbyists, and government officials.

Prefer Total Responsibility for a Small Computer System?

A *small shop specialist* is a data entry clerk, computer operator, data control clerk, maintenance person, and applications software specialist all rolled into one. Working in a small organization, you find yourself handling most of the routine data processing needs as well as special tasks such as hardware maintenance and software acquisition.

A highly skilled small shop specialist uses personal productivity or applications software to help management make decisions. You become the main resource person for users with your knowledge of all five computer system components.

Enjoy Helping Others Learn?

Information center analysts specialize in aiding users who come to an organization's information center for computer assistance. The information center provides opportunities for users to develop their own application packages or work with existing software.

You must have extensive knowledge and experience with all the packages available to the users and know how they can be modified for a specific application. The patient explanations and guidance for beginners required of teachers are necessary parts of the information center analyst's job.

Like Computers . . . But Not Just Computers?

Why not a computer studies minor with the major of your choice? Mixed and matched majors are becoming more common, and in demand. A core requirement of computer skills courses can often be combined with some other, more traditional academic major.

A graphic design/computer major starts a desktop publishing department to produce company newsletters. A legal paraprofessional/computer major is hired to show law firms how to use legal databases. A history/computer major sets up computerized exhibits in a museum. Any major can be enhanced by a computer minor—you can create your own emerging career!

- Possible careers include: data entry operator, data control clerk, computer operator, data librarian, engineer, programmer, programmer/analyst, systems analyst, technician, salesperson, customer support representative, and manager.

TERMS TO REMEMBER

Association for Computing Machinery (ACM)
Association for System Management (ASM)
Certificate in Computer Programming (CCP)
Certificate in Data Processing (CDP)
computer architect
computer engineering
computer information systems (CIS)
computer scientist
conference
continuing education
customer support representative
database administrator
data librarian
Data Processing Management Association (DPMA)
Institute of Electrical and Electronic Engineers (IEEE)
seminar
service technician
technical writer
workshop

CHECK YOUR UNDERSTANDING

1. A person who specializes in developing computer processing equipment and associated system software is called a computer ___________.
2. Computer information systems is the specialization concerning the creation of systems in business, science, and education. (True/False)
3. Which of the following is a person who specializes in the designing and building of computer hardware?
   a. computer engineer
   b. computer scientist
   c. computer technician
   d. computer analyst
   e. computer operator
4. A seminar is a professional educational meeting that covers a broad subject area and involves many overlapping lectures, demonstrations, and project displays. (True/False)
5. A(n) ___________ is a person who suggests hardware and software solutions for customer problems, sometimes aiding in installation.
6. Who is responsible for keeping track of input, output, and job schedules while maintaining information quality?
   a. data entry operator
   b. computer operator
   c. data librarian
   d. data control clerk
   e. data quality supervisor
7. A(n) ___________ controls and maintains storage media, files, and documented procedures.
8. A programmer is responsible for establishing the system specifications with the user. (True/False)
9. It is likely that a systems analyst will be promoted to programmer/analyst after gaining some experience. (True/False)

10. A(n) __________ supervises others to see that a job is done correctly, on time, and within budget.

APPLYING WHAT YOU'VE LEARNED

1. Find five job ads for computer professionals in the newspaper. What additional qualifications and educational requirements are listed besides those mentioned in the text? What salaries and other benefits are stated? How much experience is required? Do any sound like jobs you would like to have some day? Why or why not?
2. Check your local and/or school library for professional publications related in some way to computers. Make a list of them, including the type of professionals they are written for, how often they are published, and whether they are sponsored by a professional organization. Be sure to include noncomputer industry publications, such as those in medicine, business, and so on.
3. Near your home, several opportunities may exist for computer-related education. Collect training or degree information on such programs from these or other types of institutions: adult education program, private training institutes, local colleges, military service, vocational schools, and so on. Make a list of the majors and specific courses available.
4. It is becoming more common for people to make "mid-life career changes." That means a middle-aged person will completely change the type and area of work he or she is doing. This often involves going back to school or starting out at a low-paying job in a new field.
   a. What are the advantages and disadvantages of this?
   b. Why do you think a person would want to make such a change?
   c. How could an employer take advantage of the person's past experience?
   d. Could you see yourself making a change like this? Why or why not?
5. What professional computer organizations are represented by chapters in your area? The Chamber of Commerce can help you. Find out when and where they meet, whether they support student activities, and attend a meeting if you can.
6. Interview a person who is a computer professional. Report on his or her career by asking these questions:
   a. What formal and on-the-job training did they have?
   b. What professional organizations (if any) do they belong to?
   c. Which professional publications do they read regularly?
   d. What noncomputer jobs have they had that they thought were useful?
   e. What skills and classes do they wish they had picked up in school but did not?
   f. What can they see themselves doing in the next ten years?

CHECK YOUR UNDERSTANDING ANSWERS

1. architect
2. true
3. a
4. false
5. customer support representative
6. d
7. data librarian
8. false
9. false
10. manager

APPENDIX A

AN OVERVIEW OF MICROCOMPUTER OPERATIONS AND DOS

KEY IDEAS

- **From the user's point of view**
  How do you turn on and operate a personal computer? In what ways will the computer's disk operating systems help me make the most of my computer resources?
- **Operating an IBM or IBM-compatible microcomputer**
  The operation of a microcomputer is as easy as any home appliance.

  Booting your microcomputer
  The steps to loading the disk operating system into your computer will vary depending on the configuration of the microcomputer system.

  Microcomputer start-up procedures
  Turning on a microcomputer begins with finding the ON/OFF switch.
- **DOS commands and utility programs**
  Disk operating system utilities require access to the DOS disk, while DOS commands do not.

  Formatting a new (or old) diskette
  The FORMAT utility creates tracks, sectors, and a disk directory on a new disk.

  Disk directories
  The contents of a disk are displayed on the screen with the help of the DIR command.

  Backing up files with the COPY command
  Important files and programs can be transferred from one disk to another with the COPY command.

FROM THE USER'S POINT OF VIEW

We need to review operating procedures for IBM and IBM-compatible microcomputers before we start to use personal productivity software or learn to program. You will find that these operating procedures are no more difficult than turning on a television set or dishwasher. In addition, Appendix A will provide you with a brief overview of some of the more important operating system commands. These commands will help you prepare new floppy disks for use on the microcomputer system, help you locate disk files and programs, and provide a convenient means of backing up important disk resources.

OPERATING AN IBM OR IBM-COMPATIBLE MICROCOMPUTER

IBM and IBM-compatible microcomputers use a disk operating system *(DOS)* developed by the Microsoft Corporation. Called ***MS-DOS***, it is the most commonly used microcomputer operating system in the world. Licensed and distributed by IBM Corporation as ***PC-DOS***, this operating system has evolved through many revisions, from version 1.0 up to version 3.3 and beyond.

Booting Your Microcomputer

The term ***booting*** describes the procedures for turning on a computer. IBM and IBM-compatible microcomputers automatically look for and load a command program from the operating system into memory as part of the booting process.

Since a disk with DOS must be in a designated disk drive when a microcomputer is booted, associated procedures will vary depending on the number and types of disk drives. The disk drive reading the DOS disk is referred to as the ***system drive***. Disk drives containing data (or programs) are referred to as the ***data drives***. Use the following information to identify the system drive used by your microcomputer system.

One-Diskette System

The floppy disk drive is labeled drive A:. Therefore, the system drive is drive A:. After booting, the DOS disk is removed and drive A: becomes the data drive.

Two-Diskette System

The second drive is labeled drive B:. This drive is either under or to the right of drive A:. In this configuration, the system drive is drive A: and the data drive is drive B:.

FIGURE A.1

IBM PS2/25 with one floppy disk drive and a mouse.

FIGURE A.2

IBM PS2/25 with two floppy disk drives and a mouse.

One-Diskette and One Hard Disk System

Microcomputers with hard disk drives identify these drives as drive C:. The system drive is drive C: and the data drive is drive A: or drive C: since a hard disk has enough storage capacity to act as both a system and a data drive. Note that in this configuration there is no drive B:, since B: is reserved for a second floppy disk drive.

Two-Diskette and One Hard Disk System

The system drive is drive C: although drive A: can be used in an emergency. Disk drives A: or B: are used as data drives.

Microcomputer Start-Up Procedures

If you do not have a hard disk do the following:

1. Open the latch on the system drive.
2. Gently place the DOS disk in the system drive until it stops and will not go further without force.
3. Close the drive latch.

At this point, users of hard disk or floppy disk systems can turn on the microcomputer. The ON/OFF switch is usually on the right side of the computer. Also, some VDTs have their own ON/OFF switch, which is usually found on the lower right of the screen.

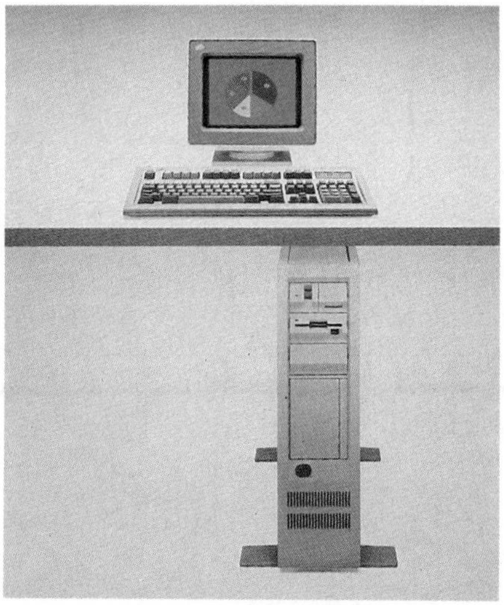

FIGURE A.3

IBM PS2/80 with hard disk drive and one floppy disk drive.

FIGURE A.4

IBM PC/AT with hard disk drive and two floppy disk drives.

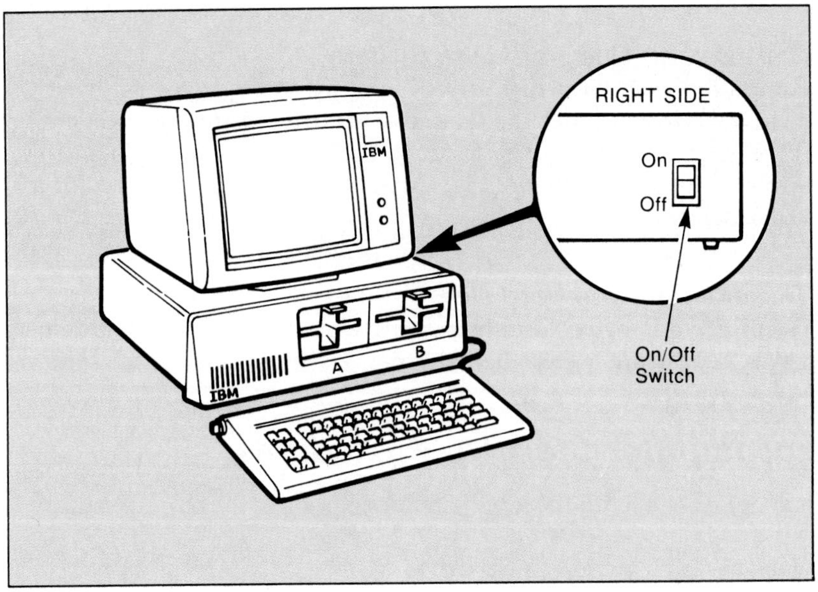

FIGURE A.5

The ON/OFF switch is usually found on either the front or right side of the disk drive cabinet.

After a few moments the screen should display:

```
Current date is Tue  1-01-1980 (Date will vary.)
Enter new date (mm-dd-yy):
```

If the date is incorrect, change it by using the mm-dd-yy format; if the date is correct, press Enter key.

Next the screen will display:

```
Current time is 0:00:42:36  (Time will vary.)
Enter new time:
```

If the time is incorrect, change it by using a 24-hour clock, where 13:23 is 1:23 P.M.; if the time is correct, press Enter key.

After the booting process is completed, the computer system will display the letter associated with the system drive followed by a > symbol. For example, microcomputers using drive A: as the system drive will display A>. This display is known as the ***DOS prompt***. It tells the user that DOS is ready for instructions. In addition, the drive designation identifies the ***default drive***—that is, the disk drive DOS will use unless instructed otherwise.

STUDY QUESTIONS

1. Define MS-DOS, PC-DOS, booting, system drive, data drive, DOS prompt, and default drive.
2. What is the difference between microcomputer start-up procedures when using a floppy disk system versus a hard disk system?
3. Briefly describe the procedures for booting your microcomputer system.

DOS COMMANDS AND UTILITY PROGRAMS

The disk operating system performs a wide variety of services for microcomputer users, including formatting new disks and copying files from one disk to another. These services are often subdivided into two areas: DOS commands and DOS utility programs. The functional difference between these two areas is that DOS must be available in the system drive in order to use any of the ***DOS utility programs***. ***DOS commands*** can be executed at any time.

The MS-DOS or PC-DOS manuals list all the DOS commands and utility programs. FORMAT, for example, is a utility program. In order to initialize a new disk, a DOS disk with the FORMAT utility program must be in a disk drive.

Formatting a New (or Old) Diskette

Before DOS can store any files on a new diskette, it must be formatted. ***Formatting***, or ***initialization***, is the process by which a disk directory is created for a new diskette after it is divided into tracks and sectors (for more information see Chapter 5: Storage Devices and File Organizations).

Formatting a disk enables DOS to know where it can store files and where to find them at a later time. Initialization is performed by a DOS utility program called ***FORMAT***. To load and execute this program, you simply type the word FORMAT (in either uppercase or lowercase—it doesn't matter) followed by the drive designation. Then press the Enter key.

DOS must be available on the system drive to format a new diskette. In addition, the system drive should also be the default drive. DOS can't load and execute the format program if it can't find it. If the default drive and system drive are different, enter the system drive designation before typing FORMAT. For example, if the default drive is B: and FORMAT is on the DOS disk in drive A:, you would enter the following:

```
B>a:format drive:
```

The format program can initialize a disk in any disk drive simply by following the word FORMAT with a blank space and the letter of the drive with the disk you wish to format followed by a colon. For example:

```
A>FORMAT B:
```

(This will load the FORMAT program from drive A and format a disk in drive B.)

Warning: If you format a disk that contains data, the data will be lost forever!

This is how the screen will look when you format a disk in drive B:

```
A>format b:

Insert new diskette for drive B:
and strike ENTER when ready

Formatting...Format Complete   [This message may vary]

362496 bytes total disk space
362496 bytes available on disk

Format another (Y/N)?_  [type N to stop]
```

If the disk is not formatted properly, the number of bytes available will *not* match the bytes' total disk space, and a third message will indicate the number of bad bytes of storage. If this message appears, try to format the disk again. Often disks will format properly on the second try. However, if this error message continues to appear when you format a new floppy disk, take your disk back to the store where it was purchased and exchange it for a new disk.

Disk Directories

The most commonly used DOS command, ***DIR***, lists all the data files and programs stored on disk. For example, to display all the files on the disk in drive B:, you would enter the following:

```
A>dir b:
```

The resulting display identifies each file by name, extension, size in number of bytes (characters), creation date, and creation time. File names can be up to eight letters long, with the extensions adding three more letters at the end.

If a disk drive is not specified after DIR, DOS will display the disk directory in the default drive. As a result, a listing of the disk directory in drive A: will occur with this DOS command:

```
A>dir
```

The file FOR89-01.RPT appears on the screen in the disk directory as follows:

```
 Disk in drive A is TRAINOR
 Directory of  A:\

FOR89-01 RPT      5788  12-18-87    8:45a
        1 File(s)    356708 bytes free
```

By examining the disk directory you can see that FOR89-01.RPT contains 5788 characters. It was originally stored on the disk on December 12, 1987, at 8:45 in the morning. In addition, the volume label on this disk is TRAINOR, and there are 356,708 bytes (characters) of disk storage still available.

Since disk directories can get rather long, there are two switches that help users keep the contents of the disk directory from scrolling off the screen:

- /P The page switch forces DOS to stop when the directory display fills the screen. The message **Strike a key when ready . . .** allows users to continue displaying the remaining portions of the directory at their convenience.
- /W The wide switch forces DOS to eliminate the size, date, and time from the directory display. Five file names and extensions appear on each line in order to compress the directory listing.

These switches must be used independently. This is how the screen will look when you use the DIR command with and without the /P and /W switches:

With the drive designation:

```
A>dir b:

 Volume in drive B is TRAINOR
 Directory of  B:\

FOR89-01 RPT     5788  12-18-87   8:45a
FOR89-02 RPT     9088   1-07-88   2:20p
FOR89-03 RPT     4224   7-23-87   5:58p
FOR89-04 RPT     3584  12-07-87   1:17p
FOR89-05 RPT     5376  12-11-87   1:03p
FOR89-06 RPT     1641   8-14-84   8:00a
FOR89-07 RPT    26880   8-14-84   8:00a
        7 File(s)    301056 bytes free
```

With the drive designation and wide switch:

```
A>dir b:/w
 Volume in drive B is TRAINOR
 Directory of  B:\

FOR89-01 RPT  FOR89-02 RPT  FOR89-03 RPT  FOR89-04 RPT
FOR89-05 RPT  FOR89-06 RPT  FOR89-07 RPT
        7 File(s)    301056 bytes free
```

With the drive designation and page switch:

```
A>dir c:/p

 Volume in drive C is HARD DISK
 Directory of  C:\

FORMAT   COM     3629   8-14-84   8:00a   [page 1]
CHKDSK   COM     9275   8-14-84   8:00a
BACKUP   COM     5440   8-14-84   8:00a
RESTORE  COM     5413   8-14-84   8:00a
.     .       .         .         .
.     .       .         .         .
.     .       .         .         .
Strike a key when ready . . .
.     .       .         .         .
.     .       .         .         .
GRAPHICS COM     3111   8-14-84   8:00a   [page 2]
RECOVER  COM     4066   8-14-84   8:00a
        31 File(s)  20146176 bytes free
```

Backing Up Files with the Copy Command

One of the most versatile DOS commands is COPY. Although ***COPY*** allows users to perform many operations, at this time we will discuss only how to use the command to back up important files and programs from one disk to another.

Informed users realize that it is possible to lose programs and files through operator error, equipment failure, or damage to storage media. The COPY command can help minimize such problems by allowing people to transfer files and programs to a second disk. The backup disk can then be stored elsewhere for safekeeping.

A selected file is copied by identifying the disk drive and file name (***source***) along with the destination (***target***) disk drive. For example, the following COPY command would transfer ENG1024.RPT from a source disk in drive A: to the target disk in drive B:

```
C>copy a:eng1024.rpt b:
```

If a source drive is not specified, DOS will use the default drive as the source drive. Therefore, in executing this COPY command:

```
C>copy eng1024.rpt b:
```

DOS will assume that ENG1024.RPT is found in drive C:.

Users can change the file name by including a new name after the target drive. As a result, ENG1024.RPT is copied to the disk in drive B: and its name changed to REPORT.ENG using the following COPY command:

```
C>copy a:eng1024.rpt b:report.eng
```

Let's take a closer look at different variations of the COPY command.

With source and target drive designation keeping common file name:

```
A>copy c:newyear.let b:
1 file(s) copied
```

With target drive designation keeping common file name:

```
A>copy newyear.let b:
1 file(s) copied
(DOS assumes the source file is in default drive A:.)
```

With source and target drive designation changing file name on target disk:

```
C>copy a:newyear.let b:nylet.bup
1 file(s) copied
```

STUDY QUESTIONS

4. Define formatting, initialization, source, and target.
5. How is a DOS command different from a DOS utility?

6. Describe an application and proper syntax (sentence structure) for the DOS format utility, the DOS dir command (with and without the /P and /W switches), and the DOS copy command.

CONCLUSION

Before the power of personal productivity software or programming is available to users, they must learn to operate their personal computers. In addition, a basic knowledge of the microcomputer's disk operating system commands helps people initialize new disks, display disk directories, and copy important files and programs from one disk to another. This knowledge provides the foundation from which all other computer applications are built. They apply, to some degree, to all computers and help users take control of their own computing resources.

TERMS TO REMEMBER

booting
copy command
data drive
default drive
dir command
DOS
DOS command
DOS prompt
DOS utility program
format utility
formatting
initialization
MS-DOS
PC-DOS
source
system drive
target

APPENDIX B

PROGRAMMING SMALL COMPUTERS IN BASIC

KEY IDEAS

- **From the user's point of view**
  How does an idea become a computer program? With so many computer programming languages available, which is the best one for a beginner to learn first?
- **The basics about BASIC**
  After booting the BASIC translator, programmers use BASIC commands to load and save their programs.
- **Performing Computations**
  Procedures similar to those taught in algebra are used to code computations in BASIC.
- **Repeating program instructions**
  By repeating instructions, a computer program can process similar data as many times as needed.
- **Controlling program loops**
  Programmers can choose from several procedures for discontinuing a program loop.
- **Working with text**
  BASIC code handles textual data differently from numeric data.
- **More on loops**
  Many program designs require loops within program loops.
- **Tying it all together**
  Experienced programmers have found that time spent designing a program reduces problems when coding.

FROM THE USER'S POINT OF VIEW

BASIC is a good first computer language for you to learn. It was developed at Dartmouth College in the mid-1960s for students with no programming experience. In fact, the name BASIC is an acronym that stands for Beginners' All-purpose Symbolic Instruction Code.

But don't let that long name fool you. The language was designed with you in mind, and this presentation concentrates on the "Beginners" part of the acronym. As you read through Appendix B you will find that there are other reasons why BASIC is used to introduce beginners to programming.

THE BASICS ABOUT BASIC

BASIC is sold with almost every microcomputer. In fact, it is built into many of them. The program that translates your BASIC language instructions into the 1 and 0 values of the computer's own machine language is often available in a ROM (Read Only Memory) chip inside the microcomputer. The IBM PC and most of the clones for this popular machine usually have some version of BASIC in ROM. In addition, a more advanced BASIC version, called BASICA, is available on the DOS diskette. BASICA, GWBASIC, and other advanced versions contain the additional instructions necessary to work with a microcomputer system that includes extra features such as disk drives, a color monitor, and other peripherals not found on the simplest personal computer model. Since most microcomputers today have at least one floppy disk drive, you will be working with BASICA.

BASIC is a good choice for the beginning programmer because it is extremely forgiving in syntax, compared with other languages. ***Syntax*** is a fancy word concerning the rules of a language. The English language has many rules, such as capitalizing the first letter of a sentence and putting a period at the end of a statement. BASIC, which is also a language, has its own rules. But the rules in BASIC are fairly lenient in that you can leave spaces where you wish, and you can indent lines if you like, and so on.

Since BASIC was written for the beginning programming student, it provides ***error diagnostics*** to help you to locate and correct some, but not all, of the more common errors. ***Error messages*** appear right on the screen, often adjacent to the line containing the error.

Also, when you program in BASIC you will be able to use some of the things you learned in algebra. You don't have to know quadratic formulas and hyperbolic cosines, but you will use the concepts you learned in working with constants and variables, setting up formulas, and working through a problem one step at a time.

Most programmers start their problem solving by drawing a flowchart and/or using pseudocode. You will find that it is especially easy to get from these design tools to a working BASIC program.

One more thing about BASIC: It is a powerful language, but it is also easy, and it is fun! You will be coding, running, and understanding some fairly sophisticated BASIC programs very quickly.

Let's look at a copy of a correctly written BASIC program and run it:

```
LIST
10 PRINT "Enough talk!  Let's code some programs!"
20 END
RUN
Enough talk!  Let's code some programs!
Ok
```

What you see is a listing of the program, and the output it produced when it was RUN.

Loading the BASIC Interpreter

Your PC should be booted and the DOS prompt should be displayed. The DOS prompt will most likely be an A> if you boot from a DOS diskette, or C> if you have a hard disk system. It is easy to load the BASIC interpreter. However, before you load BASIC, you will want to be sure you have a formatted data diskette available on which you can store some programs. Your DOS diskette may have a little room on it, but most programmers would rather not store their programs on the same diskette as the operating system. If you do not have a data diskette, you should format one before you load BASIC.

Now simply type **BASICA, GWBASIC,** or the command provided by your instructor to load the BASIC interpreter, and then hit the ENTER key. The advanced BASIC language interpreter will be read into the memory of the computer from the diskette or from the hard disk. When the program is loaded, you will see a little advertising—the copyright message and some cryptic notation—at the bottom of the screen. Then you will notice the BASIC prompt: **Ok**.

BASIC Commands

Most of the DOS commands will not work when you are in the BASIC language interpreter. Things like FORMAT, DISKCOPY, DIR, RENAME, and so on are all DOS commands. BASIC has a unique set of ***commands***, but they use the same keys on the keyboard as DOS. A BASIC command is executed by the computer as soon as it is entered. The following are the major BASIC commands you will need, together with a brief explanation of each.

- *CLS* (Clear Screen). If you type and enter CLS, it will cause the screen to clear, but any program you have typed or read into the machine will remain in memory. (If you are at the keyboard of a PC as you read this, go ahead and try it!)
- *NEW*. The NEW command erases any program in memory that you have loaded or written, but *not* the BASIC language interpreter itself. This is a handy way to clear memory if you have finished one program and want to start on another, or if you just feel like starting over with the same program. It happens to all programmers! *Warning*: The NEW command can also erase a program you do want to keep, so be careful when using it.
- *LIST*. The LIST command causes a listing of the current program to appear on the screen. The latest version of each line is shown, and the program lines are sorted into numerical order.
- *LLIST*. The LLIST command works just like the LIST command, except that the program is listed on an attached printer.
- *RUN*. Causes the program currently in the memory of the computer to execute; that is, its instructions are followed.

  Other commands deal with saving and loading programs to and from your diskette. These are discussed as needed, when you have a program ready to save.

The line printed at the bottom of the screen provides short-cuts for keying some of the commands listed above. To the left or along the top of the keyboard are 10 function keys, labeled F1 through F10. Some keyboards have 12 function keys, labeled F1 through F12. The bottom line of the screen refers to the special meanings assigned to those keys. You can LIST your program by keying in the letters L, I, S, and T, or you can do it all with one keystroke by depressing F1. The F2 key enters the RUN command. Notice the arrow to the right of RUN. This indicates that the F2 key not only types the RUN command, but also enters it. The F3 and F4 keys are for the ***SAVE*** and ***LOAD*** commands that you will use in conjunction with your floppy disk. That line of print at the bottom of the screen can be turned off, incidentally, to clear as much clutter from the screen as possible. Turn off this line by typing ***KEY OFF***. ***KEY ON*** will restore the line. Programmers usually memorize the meanings of F1 through F4 quickly, since they are the function keys used most often.

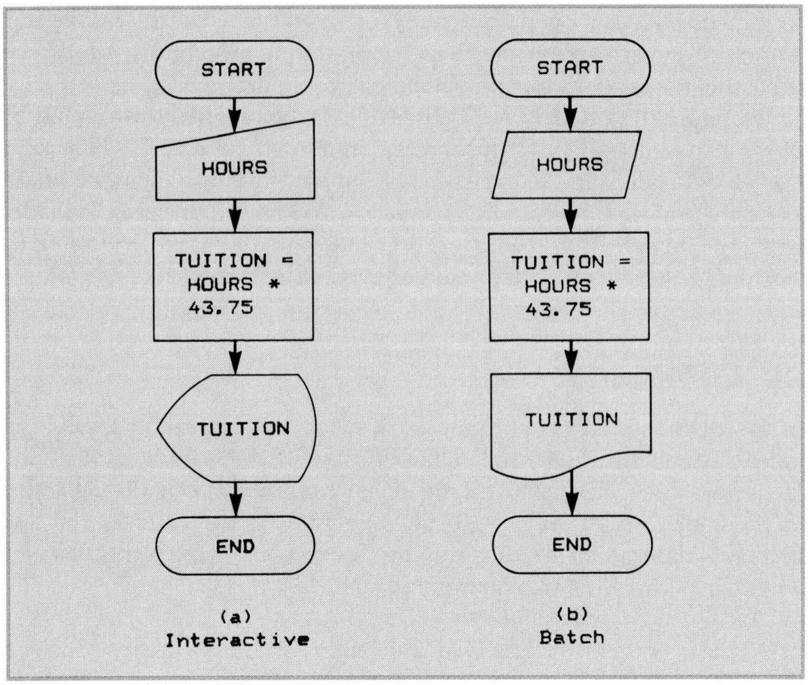

FIGURE B.1

Simple sequence structure illustrating flowchart symbols and interactive vs. batch processing modes.

Flowcharting Simple Problems

Simple sequence problems closely follow the input/processing/output cycle upon which data processing is based. They take input data that is either keyed into the keyboard or read from the program internally, and then process the data into some output information, which is usually displayed on the screen or printed on paper. Figure B.1 shows two flowcharts for a simple sequence program. It also shows the two types of programming available–***interactive*** and ***batch***. In addition, Figure B.1 illustrates some of the flowcharting symbols you will be using.

Both flowcharts are concerned with a problem involving the calculation of college tuition as a function of the number of credit hours taken. The tuition is $43.75 per credit hour. In each case, the input is the number of hours, and the output is the total tuition. The process, of course, converts the input hours into the output tuition, by multiplying by $43.75.

In Figure B.1a, the ***input symbol*** looks like the side view of a keyboard and actually means that when the program is ready to receive the value of hours, it will pause and wait for you to enter the value from the keyboard. As the shape of the symbol suggests, the tuition output that it calculates will be printed on the screen. This interactive mode of processing requires that an operator be available to key in data as required by the program.

Figure B.1b illustrates batch mode. In this example, the value of HOURS is read as data within the program itself when the computer needs it. In other words, the computer looks around inside the program to find a value for HOURS. In this case, operator or programmer intervention is not needed. The output tuition here is directed to the printer, as indicated by the torn-off-paper symbol.

You will begin with Figure B.1a and code the BASIC program, using the flowchart as a guide. The START block is not coded into BASIC; it only serves to show where the flowchart begins. A flowchart can go for many pages, so this can be handy. Each of the remaining blocks of the flowchart determines what type of BASIC statement will be used. BASIC statements are the instructions that make up a BASIC program. In Figure B.2, note that each BASIC statement has a

```
10 INPUT HOURS
20 LET TUITION = HOURS * 43.75
30 PRINT TUITION
40 END
```

FIGURE B.2

Simple sequence structure program, interactive mode.

number that starts each line. A blank space follows the line number and precedes the ***key word***, which specifies the command or action to be performed.

The shape of the symbol in the flowchart determines the key word that is used. The keyboard symbol dictates the use of an ***INPUT*** statement, which usually accepts data from a keyboard. The rectangular process block dictates that a ***LET*** statement be used to perform arithmetic operations. The screen symbol dictates that the ***PRINT*** statement be used to display output on the VDT. The ***END*** statement speaks for itself—it is used at the very end of every program to stop execution.

This program is keyed, one statement at a time, and the ENTER key is depressed at the end of each line. If you detect an error in a line before the line has been entered, the backspace key can be used to go back to the point where the error occurred, and the error can be overstruck. If an error is detected after you have depressed the ENTER key, the line can simply be rekeyed. When you reenter a line, be sure to use the same line number, since BASIC retains only the latest version of each line. Lines are usually numbered starting with 10, and then by increments of 10, to allow room for later insertion of lines you may have forgotten, or to alter your program. This numbering plan is a programmer custom, and not a requirement of BASIC. Spacing is pretty much left up to the programmer. As long as you leave at least one space after the line number, and at least one space after each of the key words that begins each of the program statements, spacing is entirely up to you. Most programmers like to leave a space on either side of an equal sign, and also on either side of each of the arithmetic operators (+, -, *, /). Also, BASIC is not particular about whether you key in letters in uppercase or lowercase. Except for text that appears between double quotes, BASIC converts everything to capital letters.

Listing and Running BASIC Programs

After keying in the program in Figure B.2, correct any errors by either overstriking or keying in replacement lines. At this point it is usually a good idea to use the LIST command. This command will produce a neat listing of your program, all sorted by line number, and with all capital letters. Take one final look at the program to see if you can spot any errors. Errors can be corrected by simply keying in new versions of the lines.

The next step is to issue a RUN command, followed by ENTER. When the program gets to your INPUT statement, it will flash a question mark on the screen, and wait for you to enter a data value. Assuming you enter 15, and touch the ENTER key, the program will cause 656.25 to be printed. It will then produce the **Ok** prompt to indicate readiness for further input. Figure B.3 shows the whole session to this point.

```
LIST
10 INPUT HOURS
20 LET TUITION = HOURS * 43.75
30 PRINT TUITION
40 END
RUN
? 15
 656.25
Ok
```

FIGURE B.3

List and run of interactive mode sequence program.

Saving and Loading BASIC Programs

If you have a two-drive PC, it is easy to save a copy of your program if you place the DOS diskette in drive A, and your data diskette in drive B. The program will not be erased from memory by the save process.

You first need to think up a unique name for your program. BASIC program names follow the same naming conventions as DOS program names. Therefore, begin program names with a letter and, to be safe, use only letters and numbers. Program names should be eight or fewer characters long and may have up to a three-character extension. In BASIC, always use the extension .BAS so that your program files stand out when the diskette directory is listed. You can call this PROGRAM1.BAS.

The SAVE command, which transfers a copy of the program in memory to disk, is used as follows:

```
SAVE "B:PROGRAM1.BAS
```

You can either key in the word SAVE or use function key F3, which requires only one keystroke. The B: means that you want to save the program on the diskette in drive B. If you leave off the B: drive designation, your program will be saved on the diskette in the default drive. The default drive is the one you were using when you loaded DOS or the BASIC interpreter.

The LOAD command, which transfers a copy of a program from disk into the computer's memory, is just as easy:

```
LOAD "B:PROGRAM1.BAS
```

To illustrate the process, you could enter the SAVE command, and then erase the program from memory by entering a NEW command. To prove that memory had been erased, LIST the program and note that there is nothing to list. Then use the LOAD command to bring the program back in from the diskette, and the LIST command will show that the program has indeed made the trip.

Try it! It will take less time to do it than it took to read about it!

STUDY QUESTIONS

1. For which type of users was BASIC designed?
2. Define syntax, command, and statement.
3. How is the BASIC translator loaded from disk different from the translator loaded from ROM?

4. What procedure do you use to load the BASIC translator into the computer's memory?
5. Describe the function of the following commands: CLS, NEW, LIST, LLIST, RUN, KEY OFF, KEY ON, SAVE, and LOAD.
6. What are two types (modes) of BASIC programs?
7. What are the flowcharting symbols for start, batch input, interactive input, processing, printer output, screen output, and end?
8. How do you correct an error before and after a program instruction is entered into memory?
9. Why are the line numbers in a BASIC program usually incremented by 10?
10. Where must a space be inserted in a BASIC statement?
11. What does the computer display on the screen when it is waiting for the user to input data?
12. What are the rules for naming a BASIC program?
13. Describe the function of the following key words: INPUT, LET, PRINT, and END.

PERFORMING COMPUTATIONS

It is necessary to learn a few rules of BASIC so that you will know the way the computer functions. Since the INPUT, PRINT, and END statements are so simple, you really need only to learn the LET (computation) statement. The good news is that you don't even have to use the key word LET. Almost every version of BASIC allows you to omit the word LET, and most programmers choose to do so. A LET statement consists of a variable name, an equal sign, and an expression. The expression may be a constant, an arithmetic formula, or a variable. Figure B.4 gives a few examples of valid LET statements.

In simple sequence programs, the variables on the right of the equal sign usually will be those that were entered using an INPUT. The variable on the left will be the one you are calculating, and which will eventually appear in an output PRINT or LPRINT statement. In Figure B.4, you tell the computer to do the following:

1. Get from memory the current values of those variables on the right of the equal sign.
2. Perform the indicated mathematical operations on them.
3. Store the result in the variable to the left of the equal sign.

Numeric Constants

Expressions are everything to the right of the equal sign in LET statements. They consist of constants and/or variables, and one or more arithmetic operators—

```
20 LET PAY = HOURS * RATE
30 NEWQUAN = 354 + OLDQUAN
40 GRADE = ( T1 + T2 + T3 ) / 3
50 K = 2
60 TUITION = HOURS * 43.75
```

FIGURE B.4

Example LET statements.

that is, plus, minus, division, and multiplication signs. Let's take a closer look at each of these components of a BASIC expression.

A whole number that does not have a decimal point is called an ***integer constant.*** It can be positive or negative, and if it is positive, it may or may not have a sign. Examples of integer constants include your room number, the number of people in a room, and the number of this page. Integer constants usually are used for counting. Note that your social security number and your phone number are *not* valid integer constants, since they usually are written with hyphens, or minus signs, between the digits. Valid integer constants in BASIC are from -32768 to +32767, inclusive. A ***fixed point constant*** has a decimal point. However, it might not have any digits to the right of the decimal point. Fixed point constants are used for calculating. They can have up to seven digits of accuracy, and are either positive or negative. About the only other thing you have to remember about the syntax for numeric constants is that the computer doesn't understand some people-oriented symbols. You can't use commas between hundreds and thousands, nor can you use percent signs, dollar signs, and some others.

Variables

Most versions of BASIC allow variable names to be up to 40 characters (letters and/or numbers) long. A ***variable*** is a name that you use to represent a data value so that the same instruction can be used for several different data values. For example, if you ran the program in Figure B.3 again, and this time you entered 17 hours instead of 15 hours, the program coding itself wouldn't have to be changed, just the data value. The variable HOURS took on the value 15 the first time the program was run and the value 17 the next time.

This use of variables illustrates how a program is coded for the general case and then used for any data values. Variables usually are named so that you can easily tell what they represent. In other words, you can go ahead and name the variables in your program C3PO or R2D2 or whatever, but it would be difficult to understand this sort of program! Figure B.5 delineates a few valid variable names.

Arithmetic Operators

BASIC uses the same common arithmetic operators you have been using since algebra: addition, subtraction, and so on. However, a few changes are necessary to be able to code statements all on one line. Furthermore, we want to remove ambiguity, since people tend to show multiplication, for example, in several ways. Figure B.6 shows the most useful BASIC arithmetic operators. A few others are described in the BASIC user's manual for more complex programming.

```
PAY87         GROSSTODATE     NETPAY
TOTAL4        BOOKPRICE       GRADE
TUITION87                     COST
```

FIGURE B.5

Example BASIC variable names.

Algebra	Meaning	BASIC	Examples	
+	Addition	+	A + B	C + 4
-	Subtract	-	E - 3.2	G - H
x or •	Multiply	*	HOURS * 43.75	
/ or —	Division	/	K / 4.65	
X^2	Exponentiate	∧	X ∧ 2	

FIGURE B.6

BASIC arithmetic operators.

Algebra	BASIC
$\text{Grade} = \dfrac{T1 + T2 + T3}{3}$	10 GRADE = (T1 + T2 + T3) / 3
$\text{Area} = \pi r^2$	20 AREA = 3.141593 * R ∧ 2
$\text{Cost} = \dfrac{5f}{4q}$	30 COST = (5 * F) / (4 * Q)

FIGURE B.7

Converting algebraic equations to BASIC LET statements.

Figure B.7 shows how some fairly simple algebra equations are converted into BASIC LET statements using these five arithmetic operators. Notice that, just as in algebra, parentheses are used to indicate that a particular operation is to be done first. Also note that most symbols, such as pi, have no BASIC equivalent, and a specific value (such as 3.14 for pi) must be used. In algebra, multiplication can be indicated with no operator at all. For example, 3(6) means multiply 3 times 6. In BASIC, the asterisk *must* be used to show multiplication: 3 * 6.

Operation Hierarchy and the Use of Parentheses

The third example in Figure B.7 raises a question: What about the parentheses? Are they necessary? Both pairs? The answers are not always easy, or obvious. In fact, in this case, the first pair of parentheses is not needed but the second pair is. If the second pair were left off, the formula would be evaluated as:

```
        5 * F
COST = -----   * Q
          4
```

and not as

```
        5 * F
COST = -----
        4 * Q
```

```
1.  Parentheses ... inner-most first
2.  Exponentiations
3.  Multiplications and Divisions
4.  Additions and Subtractions
```

FIGURE B.8

Hierarchy of arithmetic operations.

These two statements do not produce the same result. It helps, then, in order to determine if parentheses are needed, to know how the computer evaluates an expression. Figure B.8 shows the hierarchy of arithmetic operations—the order in which things are done. First, anything inside parentheses is evaluated (from the inside out if they are *nested*—that is, within more than one set of parentheses), and then all ***exponentiations*** are evaluated, followed by the other four operations, in that order.

In each case, BASIC starts scanning across the expression and performs common operations from left to right. Multiplication and division are grouped and performed together, so are addition and subtraction. As a result, in the expression 4/2 + 3 * 6 - 5, division and then multiplication occur before addition and subtraction to produce a result of 15.

STUDY QUESTIONS

14. Define expression, integer constant, fixed point constant, and variable.
15. What is one rule programmers should use for numeric constants?
16. How long can a variable name be?
17. How are parentheses used in a BASIC expression?
18. What is the hierarchy of arithmetic operations in BASIC?

REPEATING PROGRAM INSTRUCTIONS

Glance at Figure B.3 again. What complaints would you have with this program if you were the registrar of a college trying to calculate the tuition for hundreds, or maybe thousands, of students? You could read ahead a little, or maybe ask someone how to do it, and use an ***LPRINT*** statement in:

```
30 LPRINT TUITION
```

With LPRINT you get the output on paper instead of on the screen. However, there are more problems! First of all, the program has to be RUN for each student. Someone will have to sit at the computer, key and enter RUN (or use F2), wait for the question mark, and then enter one piece of data each time. Second, the output is not ***user friendly*** at all. It is just a long list of question marks, numbers, and the word RUN. Third, you have no control over how the computer prints the answers. The output is delivered where the designers of BASIC decided the output should go, and not necessarily where you want it. In other words, BASIC contains ***defaults,*** or standard procedures the interpreter follows when a programmer does not provide other instructions.

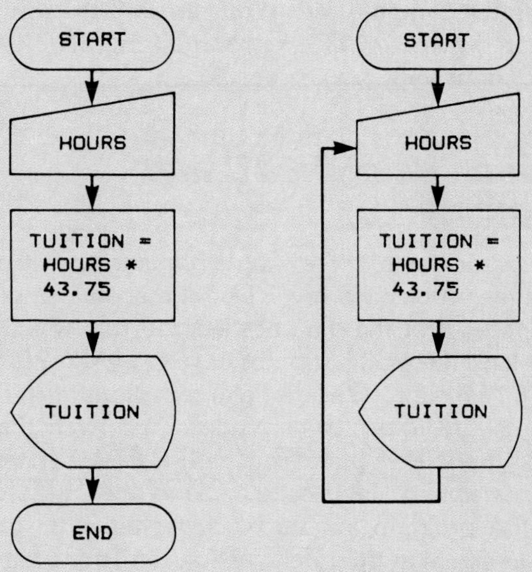


```
10 INPUT HOURS
20 TUITION = HOURS * 43.75
30 PRINT TUITION
40 END
```

Simple Sequence

```
10 INPUT HOURS
20 TUITION = HOURS * 43.75
30 PRINT TUITION
40 GOTO 10
50 END
```

Infinite Loop

FIGURE B.9

Comparison of simple sequence and infinite loop structure.

Infinite Loop Structure

Figure B.9 compares the flowcharts for the hours and tuition problem with a simple variation called an ***infinite loop*** structure.

Obviously, the infinite loop structure gets its name from the fact that there is no way out of the loop. The loop is formed by replacing the END statement with a ***GOTO*** (all one word in BASIC) statement. The GOTO statement transfers execution to another line in the program. When it is executed, the program goes around and around, asking you for a value for HOURS each time it gets to the INPUT statement. This eliminates having to key RUN for each input value, but it doesn't eliminate having to sit in front of the PC, waiting for each of the question marks to show up. A run of this program would look something like Figure B.10.

```
RUN
? 10
 437.5
? 15
 656.25
? 17
 743.75
?
```

FIGURE B.10

Sample run of infinite loop program.

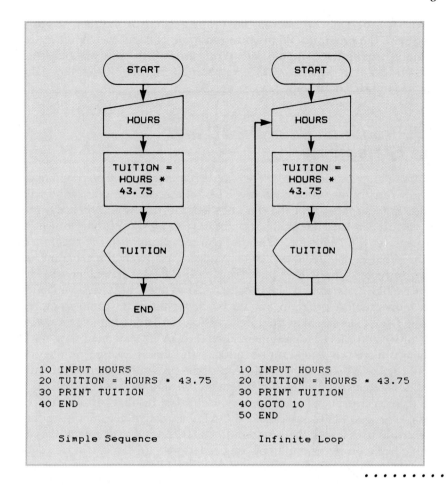

You are probably wondering how you get out of the loop when you're finished with the program. What you need to do is break the circuit momentarily without turning the computer off. You can stop the run without losing the program by holding down the CTRL key and hitting the BREAK key. This will return the familiar **Ok** prompt.

Batch Programs Using READ and DATA Statements

This infinite loop modification of the simple sequence structure program doesn't really solve any of the problems. However, another small modification will help. The idea is to supply all of the data needed. In this way, when the program needs data, it can look internally and not have to stop execution to wait for the user to answer the **?** prompt. When a data item is input to the program in this way, the program is said to use batch mode. To convert the program to batch mode, you replace the INPUT statement with a ***READ*** statement, and add the data in a ***DATA*** statement. Figure B.11 shows the interactive version of the infinite loop structure program, and the batch version of the same program.

The DATA statement in the batch version can appear almost anywhere in a BASIC program. Most programmers keep the DATA statement near the READ statement if there is a small number of data. If there is a larger number of data, they put the DATA statements at the end of the program (but *inside* of it, in front of the END statement). The DATA statement is a ***nonexecutable statement,*** which means that it performs no operations by itself. As a result, control is never transferred to a nonexecutable statement. A DATA statement doesn't do any calculating, or printing, or cause the program to GOTO another statement. It is a statement that holds numbers until they are needed by a READ statement. There can be several DATA statements in a program. You will see examples of this later.

When the batch version of the program is executed, no **?** symbols appear. The program pulls the values for HOURS from the DATA statement as needed. Figure B.12 shows a run of this program.

```
10 INPUT HOURS                         10 READ HOURS
20 TUITION = HOURS * 43.75             20 DATA 10, 15, 17
30 PRINT TUITION                       30 TUITION = HOURS * 43.75
40 GOTO 10                             40 PRINT TUITION
50 END                                 50 GOTO 10
                                       60 END

   Interactive                                Batch
```

FIGURE B.11

Comparison of interactive vs. batch versions of an infinite loop structure program.

```
RUN
 437.5
 656.25
 743.75
Out of DATA in 10
Ok
```

FIGURE B.12

Run of batch mode infinite loop structure program.

```
10 READ HOURS
20 DATA 10, 15, 17
30 TUITION = HOURS * 43.75
40 PRINT HOURS, TUITION
50 GOTO 10
60 END

            1         2         3
12345678901234567890123456789012 etc.

 10            437.5
 15            656.25
 17            743.75
Out of DATA in 10
Ok
```

FIGURE B.13

Batch infinite loop program with echo-printing.

In Figure B.12, note that the user did not have to hit the CTRL or BREAK keys. The program quit when it ran out of data, and even printed the line it was on when this occurred. Now, another problem has crept into the picture: No longer can the user see what the data values are without LISTing the program. In the interactive mode, the data values appear on the screen, right after the question marks. Now, there is just a column of answers.

This problem can be corrected by ***echo-printing*** the data values. Echo-printing means that all input values are printed as outputs. Figure B.13 shows the modified program, together with the output that it produces. Note that, although the shaded column numbers are not printed on the paper or the screen, they are printed in the book so you can see where the output appears. The computer is placing things where BASIC wants to place them, according to the defaults written into BASIC by its designers.

Using BASIC Print Zones for Output

If it is left to print output according to BASIC defaults, the computer is very predictable: Numerical values are printed in so-called ***print zones*** every 14 columns across the screen or page. Since there are 80 columns on the screen and the printer uses 8 1/2 x 11 inch paper, this means that five full print zones appear on a line. Partial print zones cannot be used. So, there will be 10 columns left over on the right side, since (14 columns x 5 zones) + 10 columns = 80 columns. Figure B.14 shows the print zones on a screen.

Look carefully at Figure B.13 again. Notice that each number was printed up against the left edge of a 14-column print zone. Since the computer always allows a space for the sign of a number, columns 1 and 15 in the example are blank, since all the numbers are positive. Still another possibility exists for spacing the output. If the comma between the output variables in line 40 of the program is replaced with a semicolon, the 14-column print zone rule is ignored, and the computer simply leaves one space (plus an extra space for the sign, if the value is positive) and then prints the next value. Figure B.15 shows the output with this modification of line 40.

Headings

The output shown in Figure B.15 suggests that some of the original problems associated with the sequence structure used in the tuition computation are solved. Many data values can be put into DATA statements. The program will execute

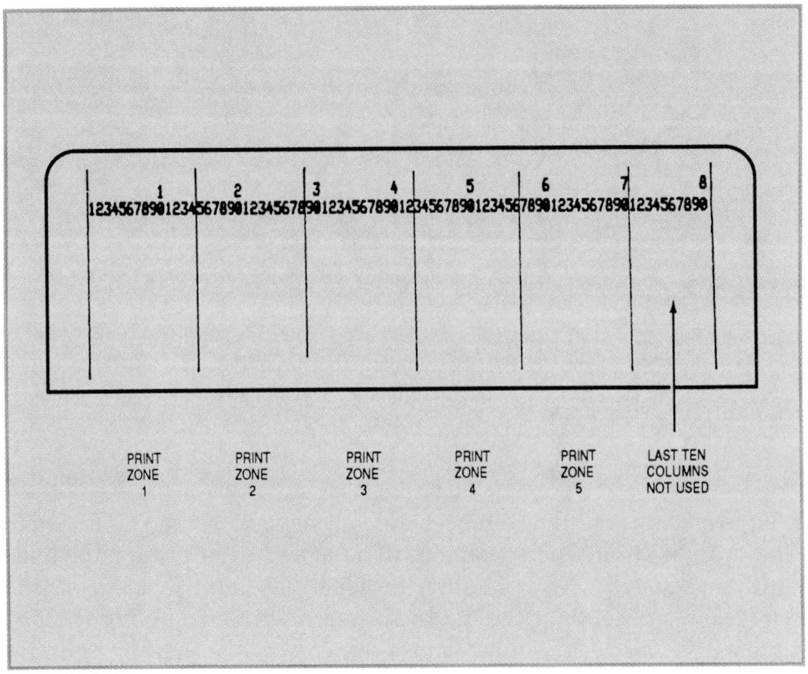

FIGURE B.14

BASIC screen and paper output print zones.

```
10 READ HOURS
20 DATA 10, 15, 17
30 TUITION = HOURS * 43.75
40 PRINT HOURS; TUITION
50 GOTO 10
60 END

           1         2
1234567890123456789012 etc.

 10   437.50
 15   656.25
 17   743.75
Out of DATA in 10
Ok
```

FIGURE B.15

Semicolon between items in a PRINT list.

unattended. The rudiments of a table, composed of rows and columns, are present through use of echo-printing of the data values. Tables are useful in presenting large quantities of output, since the row and column organization facilitates understanding.

One of the big remaining problems is that the output is not user friendly at all. This can be remedied by adding some headings to the table. Headings are easy to code in BASIC. All that needs to be done is to place the desired heading into a pair of double quotes. To illustrate, consider the examples in Figure B.16.

Of course, the same examples could be output to the line printer if the PRINT in each line were changed to LPRINT. Almost anything can be placed between the double quotes—letters (both upper- and lowercase), numbers, spaces, symbols, and so on. The only symbol that cannot be used is, of course, a double quote. In each case, the character in the position immediately following the opening double quote is printed in the first column, the next character in the

```
10 PRINT "The number of hours is:"; HOURS
20 PRINT "The tuition equals"; TUITION
30 PRINT "For"; HOURS; " hours, pay $"; TUITION
40 PRINT "***    ABC Company    ***"
50 PRINT "I B M     Personal    Computer"
```

FIGURE B.16

Examples of printing headings.

```
10 PRINT "Whatsa-Matta-U"
20 PRINT "Anywhere USA"
30 PRINT
40 PRINT "Tuition Report"
50 PRINT
60 PRINT "HOURS", "TUITION"
70 PRINT
80 READ HOURS
90 DATA 10, 15, 17
100 TUITION = HOURS * 43.75
110 PRINT HOURS, TUITION
120 GOTO 80
130 END
RUN

         1         2
123456789012345678901234567 etc.

Whatsa-Matta-U
Anywhere USA

Tuition Report

HOURS          TUITION

 10             437.5
 15             656.25
 17             743.75
Out of DATA in 10
Ok
```

FIGURE B.17

Adding a letterhead, title, and column headings.

second column, and so on. Figure B.17 shows the example program with multiple headings added. A letterhead has been added, as well as some column headings. Note that a plain PRINT statement causes a blank line to be "printed."

This is certainly an improvement, but, some problems remain. The letterhead and report title are not centered, and the output is not printed the way you might like. Notice that the first value of TUITION does not have the cents digit printed and that **Out of DATA in 10** error message makes the output look bad.

The TAB Function and Remark Statement

The headings are easily centered by using the TAB function in the PRINT statements. The ***TAB function*** doesn't automatically center the heading; it just positions the cursor or printhead at the column the programmer has decided will

```
10 PRINT TAB(4) "Whatsa-Matta-U"
20 PRINT TAB(5) "Anywhere USA"
30 PRINT
40 PRINT TAB(4) "Tuition Report"
50 PRINT
60 PRINT "HOURS"; TAB(15) "TUITION"
70 PRINT
80 READ HOURS
90 DATA 10, 15, 17
100 TUITION = HOURS * 43.75
110 PRINT HOURS, TUITION
120 GOTO 80
130 END
RUN

         1         2
123456789012345678901234567 etc.

   Whatsa-Matta-U
    Anywhere USA

   Tuition Report

HOURS         TUITION

 10            437.5
 15            656.25
 17            743.75
Out of DATA in 10
Ok
```

FIGURE B.18

Centering headings, letterheads, and titles using the TAB function in the PRINT statement.

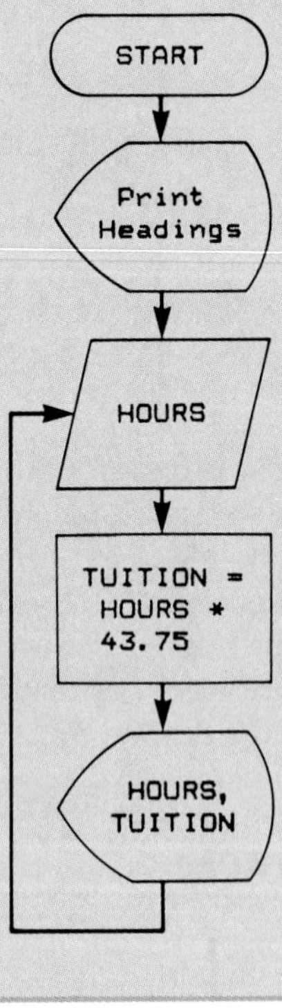

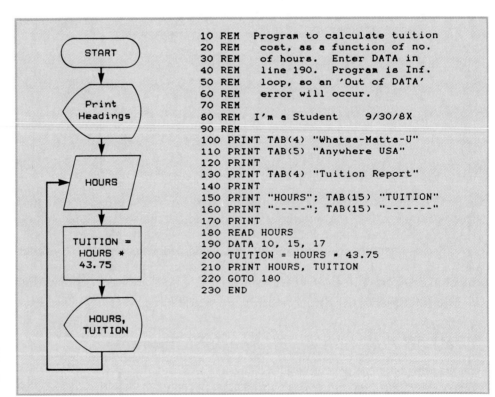

```
10 REM  Program to calculate tuition
20 REM   cost, as a function of no.
30 REM   of hours.  Enter DATA in
40 REM   line 190.  Program is Inf.
50 REM   loop, so an 'Out of DATA'
60 REM   error will occur.
70 REM
80 REM  I'm a Student     9/30/8X
90 REM
100 PRINT TAB(4) "Whatsa-Matta-U"
110 PRINT TAB(5) "Anywhere USA"
120 PRINT
130 PRINT TAB(4) "Tuition Report"
140 PRINT
150 PRINT "HOURS"; TAB(15) "TUITION"
160 PRINT "-----"; TAB(15) "-------"
170 PRINT
180 READ HOURS
190 DATA 10, 15, 17
200 TUITION = HOURS * 43.75
210 PRINT HOURS, TUITION
220 GOTO 180
230 END
```

FIGURE B.19

Adding REMarks, column headings, and underlining.

center the heading. Figure B.18 illustrates the TAB function. This program is identical to the one in Figure B.17, except for the TAB functions.

Figure B.18 shows a nice improvement in the way the output looks. You can go a step further by adding a few more PRINT statements to dress up the output further. This has been done in Figure B.19, which also introduces the ***REM*** (for ***REMark***) statement. REM is another nonexecutable statement (like the DATA statement). Nothing happens when the computer encounters a REM. REM statements just serve to document the program and are a handy place to put the name of the author of the program, the date the program was written, what the program does, and so on. Many schools require students to place certain information in REM statements, such as assignment number, section, or class number.

Note that a couple of the REM statements have nothing to their right—they just serve to space the other REM statements. The REM statements add needed documentation. But don't take Figure B.19 as the final authority on necessary REM statements. You will probably want to add several more.

Line 160 causes the column headings to be underlined. Any symbol could have been used, since you are not limited to just the hyphen (-) sign.

STUDY QUESTIONS

19. Define default, infinite loop, nonexecutable statement, and echo-printing.
20. Describe the function of the following key words: LPRINT, GOTO, READ, DATA, and REM.
21. How can a user get out of an infinite loop?
22. What are the default print zones in BASIC?
23. How is the output different when semicolons are used instead of colons to separate items in a BASIC PRINT statement?
24. How are headings created as output from a BASIC program?
25. What does the TAB function do?

CONTROLLING PROGRAM LOOPS

The next problem with programs that use an infinite loop structure centers around the error message at the end, which is caused by lack of a loop exit.

Loops with an Exit

Loops with an exit contain the third program structure. Recall that the first two are simple sequence and loop. To exit a loop, you will use the ***IF...THEN*** statement. This is a rather unique BASIC statement in that it uses two key words instead of one to perform selective operations.

In a flowchart, the diamond-shaped symbol indicates that an IF...THEN statement will be used in the program. Consider the flowchart in Figure B.20. This is identical to the flowchart in Figure B.19, except that the diamond-shaped ***decision symbol,*** together with the END block, has been added. Inside the decision symbol, a question is asked that can only have the answers "Yes" or "No." Program control is transferred to different lines within the program depending on the answer to the question.

In this case, the question is asking if **HOURS is equal to 0**. Note that if HOURS is equal to zero, control passes to the END block. But, if HOURS is not equal to zero, the program continues as it has in the past. Other actions could be taken after a loop exit instead of just stopping, as has been done in this example.

The obvious question now is: How will the decision block in the flowchart be coded, and how will a zero value for HOURS be detected? The zero value for which the program tests in the decision block is called a ***trailer value***, or sometimes ***sentinel value***. In either case, it is a value chosen by the programmer that could never be reasonably expected to appear in regular data lists for the program. In the present case, a value of zero should never be expected because a student would not register for zero credit hours. Other possibilities for trailer values include any negative number, and possibly any positive number of 25 or so, depending on the maximum number of hours that a student can take in a semester. This trailer value is placed at the end of the regular values in the DATA statement. Refer back to Figure B.19 and compare the old DATA statement, line 190, with this new DATA statement that will be used:

```
190 DATA 10, 15, 17, 0
```

The IF...THEN Statement

An IF...THEN statement will check each value of HOURS that is READ to see if it is the trailer value. The following is the general form of such a statement:

```
line number  IF  logical expression  THEN  statement
```

The statement after THEN may use any legal BASIC key word. In special cases where a GOTO statement is needed, the GOTO can be left off and just the line number referenced. Otherwise, a complete BASIC statement must follow the THEN. Here are some examples:

```
40 IF X = 0 THEN GOTO 940
60 IF COST > 23.45 THEN 800
80 IF EMPLNO < 99999 THEN 100
100 IF TIME >= 10 THEN PRINT "It's about time."
120 IF PAY < 0 THEN PAY = 0
```

Notice that values can be tested for conditions other than equality. In the second example, COST is being tested to see if it is *greater than* 23.45, and in the third example, the *less than* symbol is being used. These are the most common ***logical operators*** used in BASIC programs. There are six logical operators in all:

=	equal to
<	less than
>	greater than
<>	not equal to
<=	less than or equal to
>=	greater than or equal to

With the trailer value of zero having been added to line 190, the decision block for the program will have to be coded as follows:

```
195 IF HOURS = 0 THEN 230
```

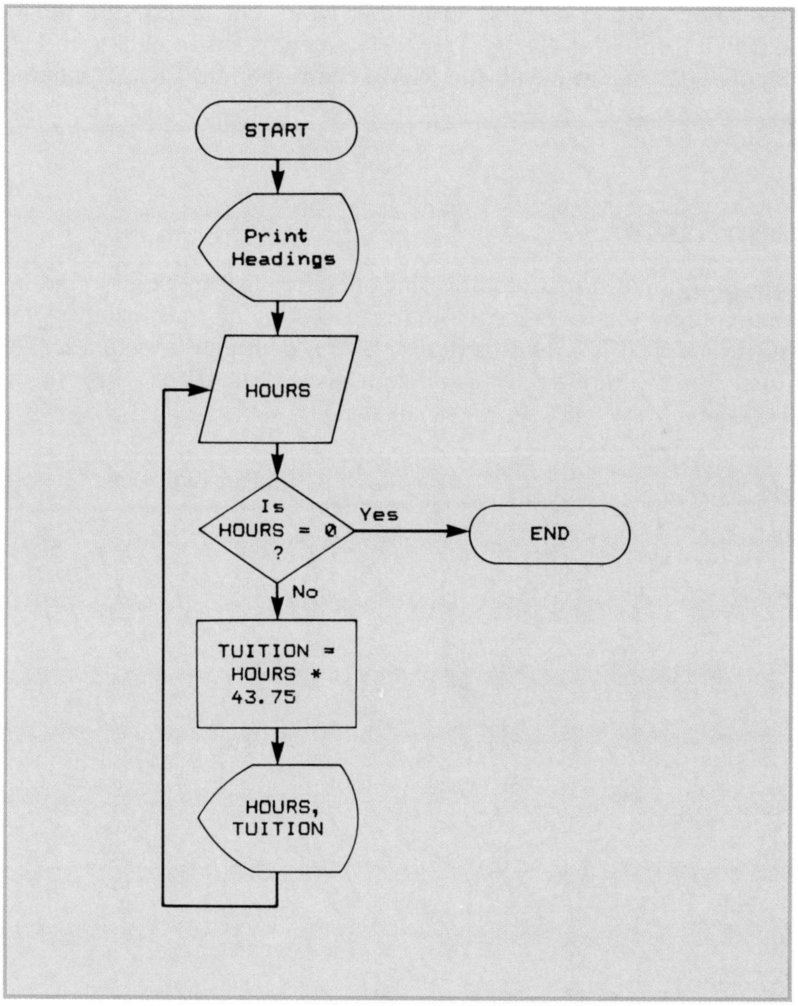

FIGURE B.20

Loop-with-an-exit structure flowchart.

If line 190 contained, say, a -1 instead of a 0 as the trailer, then the affected two lines would be:

```
190 DATA 10, 15, 17, -1
195 IF HOURS = -1 THEN 230
```

Line 195 could also be coded:

```
195 IF HOURS ≤ 0 THEN 230
```

```
180 READ HOURS
190 DATA 10, 15, 17, 0
195 IF HOURS = 0 THEN 230
200 TUITION = HOURS * 43.75
210 PRINT HOURS, TUITION
220 GOTO 180
230 END
```

FIGURE B.21

Partial program coded from Figure B.20 flowchart.

The same results would be produced either way. The choice of a trailer value, and the way it is tested in the IF...THEN statement is entirely up to the programmer. Figure B.21 leaves off all the REM statements and PRINT statements for the headings and codes just the processing loop and exit for the flowchart in Figure B.20.

Column Totals

This same program can serve to illustrate one more feature often found in BASIC programs, column totals. Since the output has two columns, printing values for both HOURS and TUITION, it is desirable to accumulate two totals. Totals are accumulated on a computer just as on your pocket calculator. First, the machine

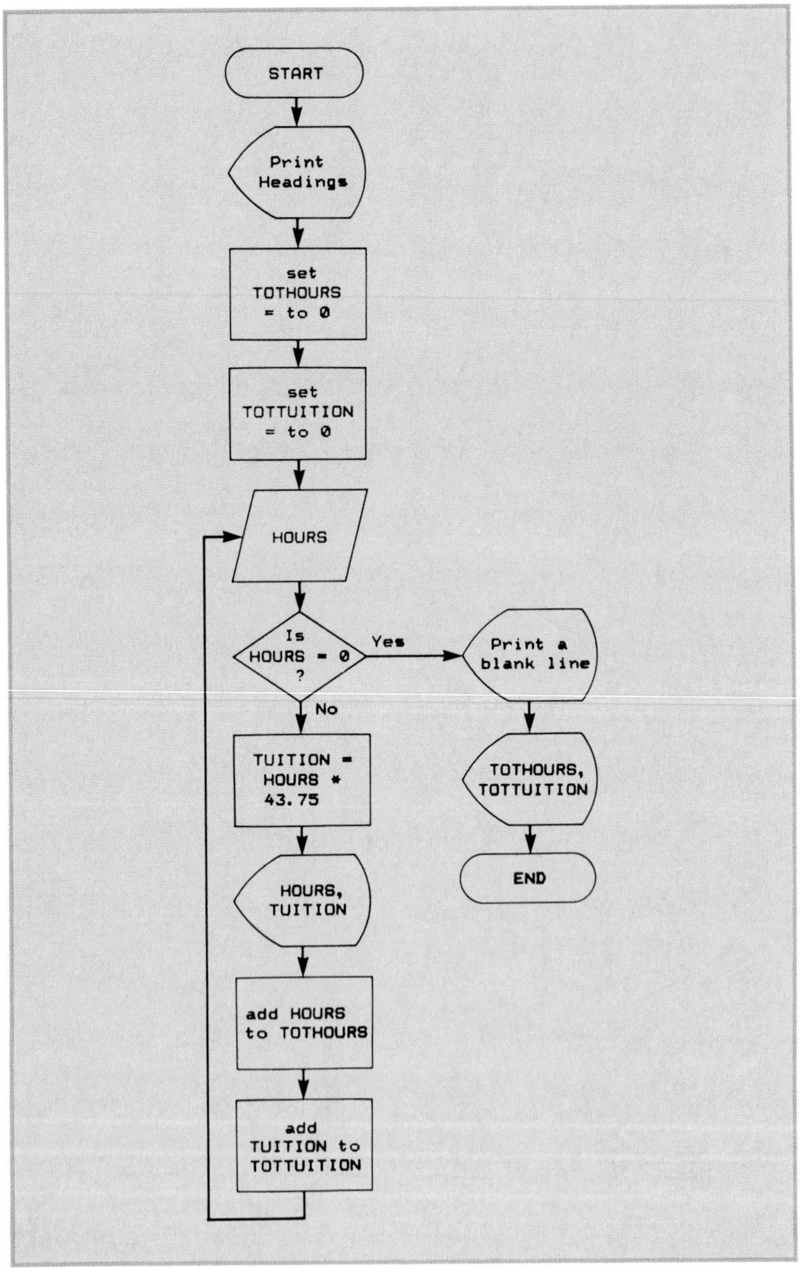

FIGURE B.22
Flowchart of calculating and printing column totals.

is *cleared*, or *set to zero*, and then each number, as it is entered, is added to a running total. Two running totals are needed, one for the total of all the HOURS and one for the TUITION values. Name these running totals TOTHOURS and TOTTUITION. Any valid BASIC names will do, but these suggest what they are by the variable names.

Figure B.22 shows the flowchart for the same program, except that totals are accumulated, then printed after the trailer value has been detected. This is an example of a program in which, instead of going directly to the END statement, something else is done after the trailer is detected. The two statements between those that cause headings to be printed and the READ block at the top of the loop serve to initialize each of the running totals to zero. Some versions of BASIC allow you to leave these statements out because all variables are set to zero automatically at the start of the program. However, good programming practice suggests that you always initialize your variables, as shown in this example.

Figure B.23 shows the resulting program, coded from Figure B.22, except that the REMarks and the PRINT statements that print the letterhead and report title are not shown. The program segment below picks up the program at line 150, where the column headings are printed.

Note how a few extra spaces in front of each of the statements in the loop make the loop easier to read, and make it easier to see the limits of the loop. REM statements have been placed throughout the program to aid in documentation clarity now that the program is getting fairly long.

Figure B.24 shows the output for the program in Figure B.23. Again, the letterhead and report title are not shown.

Things are obviously looking better. The report has nice headings and no error message. But the way in which the numbers are printed (all lined up against the left edge of the print zone) detracts from the look of the table. This can be corrected fairly easily, by altering the PRINT statements that output values for HOURS and TUITION, as well as TOTHOURS and TOTTUITION.

```
150 PRINT "HOURS"; TAB(15) "TUITION"
160 PRINT "-----"; TAB(15) "-------"
170 PRINT
180 REM
190 REM   ***   Initialize running totals   ***
200 REM
210 TOTHOURS = 0
220 TOTTUITION = 0
230 REM
240 REM   ***   Main readings and processing loop   ***
250 REM
260 READ HOURS
270   DATA 10, 15, 17, 0
280   IF HOURS = 0 THEN 370
290   TUITION = HOURS * 43.75
300   PRINT HOURS, TUITION
310   TOTHOURS = TOTHOURS + HOURS
320   TOTTUITION = TOTTUITION + TUITION
330 GOTO 260
340 REM
350 REM   ***   Print totals and END   ***
360 REM
370 PRINT
380 PRINT TOTHOURS, TOTTUITION
390 END
```

FIGURE B.23

Program coded from Figure B.22 illustrating column totals, more REMs, indented loop, etc.

```
              1         2
123456789012345678901234567 etc.

HOURS               TUITION
-----               -------

  10                  437.5
  15                  656.25
  17                  743.75

  42                  1837.5
Ok
```

FIGURE B.24

Output from program in Figure B.23.

Output Formatting

As stated earlier, left to the BASIC defaults, the computer running a BASIC program is going to print values in fields of 14 spaces.

Obviously, this sort of output is not acceptable to most people. One way to override the default is to use the TAB function. Another trick is shown by a simple modification, illustrated below, to the PRINT statement in line 30. But first you must decide how you want this output to look and determine the largest value to be printed. In this example, the largest value to be printed is 456.726, but assume you decide to round off that value to the closest penny. The original statement was:

```
30 PRINT NUMBER
```

It is altered to:

```
30 PRINT USING "###.##"; NUMBER
```

The output then looks as follows:

```
         1         2
12345678901234567890123 etc.
  0.00
  0.07
  0.12
  3.45
 67.89
456.73
```

Compare this output with that in Figure B.25 to see how the rounding was done and what columns were used for the output. Note that the computer put a leading zero in front of numbers with values of less than 1.00. Also, all the decimal points are lined up and values have been rounded to two decimal places.

To close out this section and problem, refer to the program in Figure B.23 and the output produced in Figure B.24. Consider how the changes in the following three PRINT statements will affect the output:

```
300 PRINT USING " ##            ###.##"; HOURS, TUITION
370 PRINT " --               -------"
380 PRINT USING " ##            ####.##";   TOTHOURS, TOTTUITION
```

Figure B.26 shows the new output.

```
10 READ NUMBER
20 DATA .004, .0678, .12, 3.45, 67.89, 456.726
30 PRINT NUMBER
40 GOTO 10
50 END

         1         2
12345678901234567890123 etc.

 .004
 .0678
 .12
 3.45
 67.89
 456.726
Out of DATA in 10
Ok
```

FIGURE B.25

Example program and output showing how output is "left-justified" in a print zone.

```
         1         2
123456789012345678901234 etc.

HOURS         TUITION
-----         -------

 10             437.50
 15             656.25
 17             743.75
 --            -------
 42            1837.50
```

FIGURE B.26

Output utilizing the PRINT USING statement.

STUDY QUESTIONS

26. Define trailer value, sentinel value, and logical operators.
27. Describe the function of an IF...THEN statement.
28. What is the flowcharting symbol for decisions?
29. What criterion is used to select a trailer (sentinel) value?
30. What are the six logical operators used in BASIC IF...THEN statements?
31. Explain how totals are accumulated and at what point in the program execution they are usually printed.

APPLYING WHAT YOU'VE LEARNED

Each of the first three problems can be done in a variety of ways. The following list represents optional approaches. The problem assignments follow this list.

a. Simple sequence program, in interactive mode
b. Simple sequence program, in batch mode
c. Infinite loop program, in interactive mode
d. Infinite loop program, in batch mode
e. Same as option d, but add headings and echo-print all inputs. Don't use the TAB function for headings
f. Same as option e, except use the TAB function to center all headings
g. Same as option f, except use a trailer to exit the loop

Your instructor will suggest which of the above to use for your particular assignment. If you are using these exercises for other than class assignments, it is suggested that you work each of the problems, beginning with option a. Then modify the program gradually through the b to g options. This will give you experience in the complete range of techniques delineated in the chapter thus far.

1. Code a BASIC program that will calculate the miles (or kilometers) per gallon you get with your car or motorcycle. Input data will be the starting and ending odometer readings and the number of gallons of gasoline necessary to fill the tank on the second visit to the gas station.
2. Code a BASIC program that will calculate the ending balance for your checking account. Input data will be your starting balance, the total deposits you make during the period, the totals of the checks that have cleared during the period, and the service charges (if any).
3. An instructor tells you that your grade in his or her course is a function of how well you do on the four semester exams. The first exam counts 10 percent of your grade, the second counts 20 percent, the third counts 30 percent, and the final exam counts 40 percent. All exam grades, and the course grade you print out, are on a scale of 0 through 100. Input will be a five-digit student number, plus the four exam grades for each student. *Hint*: The final grade will be 10 percent of the first grade, plus 20 percent of the second grade, plus 30 percent of the third grade, plus 40 percent of the final exam.
4. Your class takes an exam. Each student receives a numerical grade of 0 through 100. Code a BASIC program that will accept these grades, and calculate and print the class average. Your program should work for any number of students in a class and should use a trailer to exit the processing loop. You do not need a student number or name as data.

   Now modify your program so that it not only calculates the class average, but also finds both the lowest and the highest grade, thereby allowing you to calculate and print the range. *Hint*: Set the first grade equal to some variable, such as LET HIGHSCORE = GRADE. Then compare each grade to HIGHSCORE. If the new grade is greater than HIGHSCORE, let HIGHSCORE equal the new grade.
5. You have a dilemma. You are studying in your room and are really hungry for a pizza. You look in the campus newspaper and notice a number of pizza shops with delivery service. You want to get the most pizza for your money and decide to code a BASIC program that will input data for a number of different shops. For each shop, you collect data on the diameter of the pizza, the price, and the delivery charge. You decide to go with the one offering the lowest cost per square inch of pizza. Code a BASIC program that will produce a nice-looking table of your results. *Hint*: The area of a circle in square inches is equal to pi times the square of the radius in inches. Also, do not worry about the names of the pizza shops.

WORKING WITH TEXT

The examples so far have used only numeric input and output values. Although this might be sufficient for a limited number of applications, it is not enough. Users want output tables to include nonnumeric variables, such as names, streets, states, and so on. Businesspeople require descriptions of products sold on invoices, names of employees on checks, and even letters full of text in form letters that are written by computer. It is relatively easy to work with such nonnumeric data, since BASIC is well suited for the task.

String Input and Output

String variables may contain any combination of text and numeric data. They are formed just like variables that hold numbers, except that the variable name has a dollar sign $ at the end of the name. Here are some examples of valid string variables:

```
PERSON$          ITEM$          STATE$
STREET$          STUFF$         PRODUCT$
PRINTERTYPE$     FOODITEM$      BOOKTITLE$
```

To learn how to work with string variables, study Figure B.27 carefully. This shows the program listing and the output produced by a simple program that prints a list of some friends' telephone numbers. Lines 10 through 40 print simple headings and, of course, lines 50 through 80 form a loop-with-an-exit structure. When WHO$ takes on the value "last," the exit is made to the END.

```
10 PRINT TAB(3) "Telephone Numbers"
20 PRINT
30 PRINT TAB(2) "NAME"; TAB(16) "NUMBER"
40 PRINT
50 READ WHO$, NUMBER$
60   IF WHO$ = "last" THEN 99
70   PRINT WHO$, NUMBER$
80 GOTO 50
90 REM ***  Data values  ***
91 DATA "Erika", "123-4567"
92 DATA "Brian", "234-5678"
93 DATA "Suzie", "345-6789"
94 DATA "Frank", "456-7890"
95 DATA "last", "0"
99 END
```

```
         1         2
123456789012345678901234567 etc

  Telephone Numbers

 NAME           NUMBER

Erika          123-4567
Brian          234-5678
Suzie          345-6789
Frank          456-7890
```

FIGURE B.27

Non-numeric (string) input/output.

```
         1         2         3         4         5         6
1234567890123456789012345678901234567890123456789012345678901234567
                              I'm A. Student

                          Textbooks for Fall '90

                                                New       Used
Author         Title          Course           Price      Price     Condition
------         -----          ------           -----      -----     ---------

Jones    Cemetary Design      CD-402           24.95      12.48       Good
Smith    Druid History        HS-512           19.50       9.75       Worn
Davis    Bookbinding          JR-315           14.68       7.34       Bad
Ames     Winemaking           CM-220           34.95      17.48       Terrible
Hening   Spectroscopy         PH-642           25.00      12.50       Shot!
                                              ------     ------
                                              119.08      59.54
                                              ======     ======
```

FIGURE B.28

Table illustrating string I/O.

Note that the phone numbers also are treated as string data. This is because, although they contain digits, the hyphen in the middle prevents the numbers from having a numeric value.

Of course, problems seldom are as simple as this. Figure B.28 shows the output produced by a program that processes data dealing with the various books owned by a student. Assume these are the texts for courses taken during a semester, and that the price the student can get for the book when it is sold back to the bookstore is 50 percent of the new book price. The ***PRINT USING*** statement will be used for all numeric output, including the totals. Fairly simple headings and a report title are also included. However, in an effort to keep the program listing short, REMarks won't be shown.

Designing Output

Frankly, the table in Figure B.28 was not produced by sitting at the keyboard and trying different spacing and TAB settings. It is much easier to lay out the table on a sheet of graph paper or a print chart first. That way, the programmer can see what spacing looks best for the headings and the output lines.

Figure B.29 is a listing of the program that produced the table. Several things will become obvious as you study the program. First, there are a lot of PRINT statements. This is typical. Normally, a very large portion of almost any program consists of PRINT statements. In the typical program, you also would find that there are about as many REM statements as there are PRINT statements. Notice that the statements in the loop are indented to make the loop stand out from the remainder of the program.

Several features of Figure B.29 require further comment. Lines 10 through 50 print report titles. The TAB functions were determined by laying out the table output on sheets of graph paper. Lines 60 through 90 print the column titles. The titles are two-line titles, underlined as indicated in line 80. Notice that lines 70 and 80 each take up two lines of the listing of the program. Actually, BASIC statements can be up to 255 characters long, and since a line of the screen is only 80 characters, wordwrap is used to create additional lines. In other words, when entering a long line just keep typing without pressing the ENTER key until the whole line is entered. Then press the ENTER key.

```
10 PRINT TAB(26) "I'm A. Student"
20 PRINT
30 PRINT TAB(22) "Textbooks for Fall '87"
40 PRINT
50 PRINT
60 PRINT TAB(41) "New"; TAB(51) "Used"
70 PRINT "Author"; TAB(15) "Title"; TAB(28) "Course"; TAB(40)
   "Price"; TAB(50) "Price"; TAB(58) "Condition"
80 PRINT "------"; TAB(15) "-----"; TAB(28) "------"; TAB(40)
   "-----"; TAB(50) "-----"; TAB(58) "---------"
90 PRINT
100 READ AUTHOR$, TITLE$, COURSE$, NEWPRICE, CONDITION$
110   IF AUTHOR$ = "Done" THEN 200
120   USEDPRICE = NEWPRICE / 2
130   PRINT AUTHOR$; TAB(10) TITLE$; TAB(28) COURSE$;
140   PRINT TAB(40) USING "##.##"; NEWPRICE;
150   PRINT TAB(50) USING "##.##"; USEDPRICE;
160   PRINT TAB(60) CONDITION$
170   TOTNEWPRICE = TOTNEWPRICE + NEWPRICE
180   TOTUSEDPRICE = TOTUSEDPRICE + USEDPRICE
190 GOTO 100
200 PRINT TAB(39) "------"; TAB(49) "------"
210 PRINT TAB(39) USING "###.##"; TOTNEWPRICE;
220 PRINT TAB(49) USING "###.##"; TOTUSEDPRICE
230 PRINT TAB(39) "======"; TAB(49) "======"
240 REM  ***  Data values follow  ***
701 DATA "Jones", "Cemetary Design", "CD-402", 24.95, "Good"
702 DATA "Smith", "Druid History", "HS-512", 19.50, "Worn"
703 DATA "Davis", "Bookbinding", "JR-315", 14.68, "Bad"
704 DATA "Ames", "Winemaking", "CM-220", 34.95, "Terrible"
705 DATA "Hening", "Spectroscopy", "PH-642", 25.00, "Shot!"
706 DATA "Done", "0", "0", 0, "0"
999 END
```

FIGURE B.29

Program to produce Figure B.28 table.

Lines 100 through 190 form the main processing loop of the program. Note that four of the five variables are string variables, but NEWPRICE does not need the $ since it will contain numerical values. The trailer value is the string "Done", checked for in line 110.

Lines 130 through 160 print a line of output. Four lines are used for a couple of reasons. First, the PRINT statement would have been terribly long if just one statement was used. This long statement would have been difficult to edit and correct if errors were found in it. Be especially careful when using more than one PRINT statement to print one line of output; you must put a semicolon (;) at the end of all of the lines except the last one. This semicolon keeps the cursor on the same line instead of returning it to column 1 of the next line for output.

Lines 170 and 180 increment the running totals with the current values of NEWPRICE and USEDPRICE. Line 200 underlines the columns of data values, and lines 210 and 220 print the totals. Note the semicolon at the end of line 210 to keep the cursor on the line so that the other total can be printed on the same line. Line 230 prints a double underline under the totals, and the END follows.

The DATA statements in lines 701 through 705 are standard, but note carefully that there are no double quotes around the NEWPRICE, since this is a numeric value and not a string. In line 706, dummy values must be included for the four variables in the READ statement other than the AUTHOR$ variable, although AUTHOR$ is used for the trailer. These dummy values in the DATA statement supply a value to each variable READ in line 100. If any of the dummy values were missing an **Out of DATA** message would stop program execution.

STUDY QUESTIONS

32. Define string variables.
33. What distinguishes a string variable name from a numeric variable name?
34. Why do programmers use graph paper or a print chart to design a report before writing the program?
35. How long (number of characters) can a BASIC statement be?
36. What happens when a semicolon is placed at the end of a PRINT statement?
37. What distinguishes a string value from a numeric value?
38. How are dummy values used with a trailer (sentinel) value?

MORE ON LOOPS

Assume you simply want to print the years 1989 through 1993 in a column down the screen. Of course one way that this could be done is to code the following:

```
10 READ YEAR
20 DATA 1989, 1990, 1991, 1992, 1993
30 PRINT YEAR
40 IF YEAR = 1993 THEN 60
50 GOTO 10
60 END
```

This program would accomplish the task, but if the program were modified so that you needed a listing of 100 years, keying all of those number in DATA statements would be time-consuming.

Loops and the FOR...NEXT Statement

Consider instead, the following way of accomplishing the task:

```
10 YEAR = 1989
20 PRINT YEAR
30 IF YEAR = 1993 THEN 60
40   YEAR = YEAR + 1
50 GOTO 10
60 END
```

With this coding, it doesn't matter how many values you want printed. The number of statements in the program remains the same. All you need to do is change the final year in line 30.

BASIC has an even easier way to accomplish the same task, with the ***FOR...NEXT*** statement. Compare the following coding with the previous program listing:

```
10 FOR YEAR = 1989 TO 1993
20   PRINT YEAR
30 NEXT YEAR
40 END
```

The output produced by the two programs is identical. Lines 10 through 30 of this program comprise a FOR...NEXT loop. FOR...NEXT loops are merely short cuts for more cumbersome coding, such as the second example shown. In this FOR...NEXT loop the interpreter sets YEAR equal to the first value, 1989. YEAR is incremented by 1 every time it reaches the NEXT YEAR statement. At this point, execution is returned to the FOR statement and the value of YEAR is compared to the last acceptable value, which is 1993 in this example. If YEAR is not greater than 1993, execution proceeds to the next line. However, if YEAR is larger than 1993, program execution skips over the loop and continues to the line after the NEXT statement.

FOR...NEXT loops make it easy to do one or more operations a specified number of times. The problem can even be interactive, with the user providing INPUT for the starting and stopping year numbers. Note that when you enter more than one value after the ? printed by the INPUT statement, the data values are separated by a comma, or a comma and a space, when you key them in.

```
10 PRINT "Key starting and stopping years,"
20 PRINT " separated by a comma, and then"
30 PRINT " press the (ENTER) key."
40 INPUT STARTYEAR, ENDYEAR
50 FOR YEAR = STARTYEAR TO ENDYEAR
60   PRINT YEAR
70 NEXT YEAR
80 END
```

The use of the FOR...NEXT loop is illustrated further with the following problem. Assume you are a teacher facing a big stack of examinations to grade. The exam is a 50-question multiple-choice exam, and each question is worth two points. You would like to make up a table with the number of questions missed in the first column and the grade, on a 0–100 scale, in the second. Figure B.30 shows "no-frills" coding and partial output. Of course, the program could have been expanded with fancy PRINT USING statements, headings, and so on, but the intention here is to discuss the logic of loops and the FOR...NEXT statement.

Some of the same ideas can be used to build a little table showing the gross income a student would make in a part-time job. Assume the job pays $4.37 per hour and the student works a different number of hours each week, from 1 to 40 hours. Figure B.31 leaves off the fancy headings to show a bare bones listing and part of the output.

```
10 FOR MISSED = 0 TO 50
20   GRADE = 100 - ( MISSED * 2 )
30   PRINT MISSED, GRADE
40 NEXT MISSED
50 END
RUN
 0            100
 1             98
 2             96
~~~~~~~~~~~~~~~~~~
 49             2
 50             0
Ok
```

FIGURE B.30

Program and output for grade table problem.

```
10 FOR HOURS = 1 TO 40
20    PAY = HOURS * 4.37
30    PRINT HOURS, PAY
40 NEXT HOURS
50 END
RUN
 1             4.37
 2             8.74
 3             13.11
~~~~~~~~~~~~~~~~~~~~~~~~~~~~~~~
 39            170.43
 40            174.80
Ok
```

FIGURE B.31

Program and output for student worker problem.

Here again, the output could be improved considerably by adding a couple of headings and changing line 30 to include a PRINT USING clause. The following statement does wonders for the appearance of the output:

```
30 PRINT USING "##      ###.##"; HOURS, PAY
```

Most business problems that utilize tables and lists such as pay, interest, deposits, and so on can make good use of the BASIC language FOR...NEXT statement. In these applications, the computer is simply being asked to do error-free counting.

Nested FOR...NEXT Loops

As you may have guessed, it is possible to have loops inside of loops, just as it is possible to have sets of parentheses inside of parentheses in BASIC LET statements. Some problems lend themselves nicely to this sort of application of the FOR...NEXT loop. For example, suppose you decide to open a savings account at the bank with a $10.00 deposit. Further, you decide that you will be able to add $10.00 to your new account each month. You find out that the bank pays an interest rate of 6 percent annually and that compounding is done on the last day of each month. Therefore, you will be making 0.5 percent per month (0.005). For simplicity, assume you opened the account on January 1, 1987, and you would like to know how much money you will have in the account on December 31, 1991. You realize that you will have five years, with 12 months, or a total of 60 months of deposits and interest, so you could code the program as shown in Figure B.32.

```
10 DEPOSIT = 10
20 FOR MONTH = 1 TO 60
30    DEPOSIT = DEPOSIT * 1.005
40    DEPOSIT = DEPOSIT + 10.00
50 NEXT MONTH
60 PRINT "Value on Dec. 31st, 1991 = $"; DEPOSIT
70 END
```

FIGURE B.32

60-month savings account at 6% per year.

```
10 DEPOSIT = 10.00
20 FOR YEAR = 1987 TO 1991
30    FOR MONTH = 1 TO 12
40       DEPOSIT = DEPOSIT * 1.005
50       DEPOSIT = DEPOSIT + 10.00
60    NEXT MONTH
70 NEXT YEAR
80 PRINT "Value on Dec. 31st, 1991 = $"; DEPOSIT
90 END
```

FIGURE B.33

Illustration of nested FOR...NEXT loops.

This method requires you to figure out how many months are in the period in which you will be earning interest and making deposits. In this example, the calculation is easy, but other problems may not be. Consider next the coding in Figure B.33, where nested FOR...NEXT loops are used.

The programs in both Figure B.32 and Figure B.33 produce the same output: $711.19. Indenting the statements is entirely up to the programmer. However, with two loops to contend with, the indenting makes it easy to see what statements are associated with which loops.

To illustrate the use of nested FOR...NEXT loops further, consider another simple problem. Assume your young sister is at an age where she will soon be learning multiplication tables. You want to print up such a table to help her. You decide that a 10 by 10 table will do nicely, so you code the program as in Figure B.34. Again, the REM statements and the fancy headings are omitted. But this time you have to use PRINT USING or the table will not have straight columns. Also, the loops are indented for clarity in reading the program.

A few elements of Figure B.34 require some clarification. Although ROW = 1 in line 10, the column takes on all 10 of the values from 1 to 10 in the loop between lines 20 and 50. You want those 10 numbers all printed on one line—this is the reason for the semicolon at the end of the PRINT USING statement in line 40. That semicolon keeps the cursor on the line, ready to print the next

```
10 FOR ROW = 1 TO 10
20    FOR COL = 1 TO 10
30       NUMBER = ROW * COL
40       PRINT USING "###   "; NUMBER;
50    NEXT COL
60    PRINT
70 NEXT ROW
80 END
RUN
```

```
         1         2         3         4         5         6
123456789012345678901234567890123456789012345678901234567890 etc.

  1     2     3     4     5     6     7     8     9    10
  2     4     6     8    10    12    14    16    18    20
  3     6     9    12    15    18    21    24    27    30
  4     8    12
  5    10

 10    20    30    40    50    60    70    80    90   100
Ok
```

FIGURE B.34

Multiplication table programmed with FOR...NEXT loops.

number. After all 10 numbers have been printed on a line, you don't want to continue printing the next 10 values on the same line. This is the reason for the plain PRINT statement in line 60. This PRINT simply returns the cursor to the beginning of the next line, ready to print a new line of the table.

Notice that it is possible to get 10 numbers on each line, instead of the five that would have been the maximum if the standard 14-column print zones had been used. In this case, you know that the largest number that will appear in the table will be 100. The USING clause in line 40 indicates this with the three ### symbols. Furthermore, there are three blank spaces inside the double quotes. These three blanks produce the spacing between the numbers in the body of the resulting table.

You can have fun experimenting with this program by keying it into your microcomputer. Change the row and column limits in lines 10 and 20 and alter the USING clause in line 40. You will be able to see firsthand what would happen if the final semicolon were to be eliminated from the PRINT USING statement.

STUDY QUESTIONS

39. How do you separate multiple INPUT values entered on the same line?
40. Describe the function of FOR...NEXT statements.
41. What are nested FOR...NEXT loops?

TYING IT ALL TOGETHER

This section closes with an example that not only uses a FOR...NEXT loop but most of the other BASIC programming concepts discussed as well, such as totals, string I/O, PRINT USING, the TAB function, headings, and fancy underlining. For the purpose of this problem, assume you are a college freshman, sitting down with your parents and planning what you can reasonably expect your expenses will be for your next three years in college. Assume that you have kept track of your major expenses for your freshman year, and they totaled $5,000.00, broken down as follows:

```
Tuition   $1,500.00
Room       1,000.00
Board      2,000.00
Books        400.00
Fees         100.00
```

Defining Requirements

You estimate that inflation will cause all five categories of expenses to go up 10 percent per year. In other words, your tuition for your sophomore year will be 110 percent of your freshman year tuition, your junior year tuition will be 110 percent of your sophomore year, and your senior year tuition will be 110 percent of your junior year tuition. The other categories of expenses will behave in a similar manner. You want to know not only what the expenses will be for each of the next three years, taking into account the 10 percent per year inflation, but

```
Expense        Fresh.     Soph.      Junior     Senior     Total
-------        ------     -----      ------     ------     -----

Tuition        1500.00    1650.00    1815.00    1996.50    6961.50
Room           1000.00    1100.00    1210.00    1331.00    4641.00
Board          2000.00    2200.00    2420.00    2662.00    9282.00
Books           400.00     440.00     484.00     532.40    1856.40
Fees            100.00     110.00     121.00     133.10     464.10
               -------    -------    -------    -------   --------
               5000.00    5500.00    6050.00    6655.00   23205.00
               =======    =======    =======    =======   ========
```

FIGURE B.35

College expenses output report.

also what the total expenses will be for each year. You also want to know the totals for each of the five categories for all four years, and the grand total for all five categories of expenses over the full four-year period. This is a tall order, but it turns out to be a reasonably easy program to code. The most time-consuming job is designing what the output should look like. Look first at Figure B.35, which shows the desired output of the program. As usual, the report title, data, and so on are omitted for simplicity.

Program Design

Figure B.36 is a listing of the program that produced the output of Figure B.35. The comments that follow are intended to help you study this program. Keep in mind that many of the things that have been done are by programmer preference. BASIC does not require them. They just make the program easier to read and easier to understand. Also, it is important to note that many of the techniques used in this program make the program easier to modify should future changes be needed.

Fifteen of the 48 statements in the program are REM statements. This little bit of documentation is useful in segmenting the program into shorter modules. Lines 40 and 50 print some simple headings. The TAB function has been used here, but some programmers might prefer to use one long string for each line, handling the spacing with spaces between the words, like this:

```
40 PRINT "Expense     Fresh.     Soph.     Junior    and so on."
```

Lines 100 through 140 initialize the five totals that are used. Most versions of BASIC automatically set all variables equal to zero when program execution begins, so these statements are not absolutely required. However, many programmers choose to include them, since they seem to enhance understanding of the program by others. Note that spacing has been adjusted in the statements to make everything line up nicely, and to make it all easier to read. Many versions of BASIC allow multiple statements on a line, and the five statements could all have been put on one line by separating each statement with a colon. To do this, you would remove lines 110 through 140 and rekey line 100 as:

```
100 TFRESH = 0: TSOPH = 0: TJUNIOR = 0: TSENIOR = 0: GRAND = 0
```

The main processing loop does not include anything spectacular. The DATA statements have been put at the end of the program to make the main loop easier

```
10  REM
20  REM   ***   Print Headings   ***
30  REM
40  PRINT "Expense"; TAB(15) "Fresh."; TAB(25) "Soph."; TAB(35);
          "Junior"; TAB(45) "Senior"; TAB(55) "Total"
50  PRINT "-------"; TAB(15) "------"; TAB(25) "-----"; TAB(35);
          "------"; TAB(45) "------"; TAB(55) "-----"
60  PRINT
70  REM
80  REM   ***   Initialize Totals   ***
90  REM
100 TFRESH  = 0
110 TSOPH   = 0
120 TJUNIOR = 0
130 TSENIOR = 0
140 GRAND   = 0
150 REM
160 REM   ***   Main Processing Loop   ***
170 REM
180 FOR ROW = 1 TO 5
190   READ EXPENSE$, FRESH
200   PRINT EXPENSE$; TAB(11);
210   SOPH   = FRESH  * 1.1
220   JUNIOR = SOPH   * 1.1
230   SENIOR = JUNIOR * 1.1
240   TOTAL = FRESH + SOPH + JUNIOR + SENIOR
250   PRINT USING "   ####.##"; FRESH, SOPH, JUNIOR, SENIOR, TOTAL
260   TFRESH  = TFRESH  + FRESH
270   TSOPH   = TSOPH   + SOPH
280   TJUNIOR = TJUNIOR + JUNIOR
290   TSENIOR = TSENIOR + SENIOR
300   GRAND   = GRAND   + TOTAL
310 NEXT ROW
320 REM
330 REM   ***   Print Totals   ***
340 REM
350 PRINT TAB(14) "-------   -------   -------   -------  --------"
360 PRINT TAB(11);
370 PRINT USING "   ####.##"; TFRESH, TSOPH, TJUNIOR, TSENIOR;
380 PRINT USING "  #####.##"; GRAND
390 PRINT TAB(14) "=======   =======   =======   =======  ========"
400 REM
410 REM   ***   Data Values   ***
420 REM
430   DATA "Tuition", 1500
440   DATA "Room   ", 1000
450   DATA "Board  ", 2000
460   DATA "Books  ",  400
470   DATA "Fees   ",  100
480 END
```

FIGURE B.36

Program to produce output in Figure B.35.

to read. Since the length of EXPENSE$ can vary, line 200 uses the TAB function to get each line over to column 11 after EXPENSE$ is printed. Lines 210 through 230 calculate the last three years of expenses, and line 240 calculates the total of the four years. The PRINT USING in line 250 utilizes the same format for each of the five numbers to be printed: three blank spaces followed by a six-digit number rounded to two decimal places. Lines 260 through 300 increment the appropriate totals. The main processing loop consists of five iterations, after which the totals are printed in lines 350 through 390. These lines produce some fancy underlining, and you will want to pay particular attention to how the spacing is accomplished.

Of course, the program is not complete until a PRINT statement has been added to print a report title. You will want to add PRINT statements for the date and perhaps some sort of legend that informs the report user that the report

```
1 PRINT "Expense        Fresh.   Soph.    Junior   Senior   Total"
2 PRINT "-------        ------   -----    ------   ------   -----":PRINT
3 DATA Tuition,1500,Room,1000,Board,2000,Books,400,Fees,100
4 FOR R=1 TO 5:READ E$,A:PRINT E$;TAB(11);:B=A*1.1:C=B*1.1:D=C*1.1:T=A+B+C+D
5 PRINT USING"   ####.##";A,B,C,D,T:TA=TA+A:TB=TB+B:TC=TC+C:TD=TD+D:G=G+T
6 NEXT R
7 PRINT TAB(14)"-------   ------   ------   ------   -------":PRINT TAB(11);
8 PRINT USING"   ####.##";TA,TB,TC,TD;:PRINT USING"  #####.##";G
9 PRINT TAB(14)"=======   ======   ======   ======   =======":END
```

FIGURE B.37

Abbreviated program to produce Figure B.35.

assumes a 10 percent inflation rate per year. Also, the program might be modified so that more (or fewer) expense categories can be used. This can be done easily by altering the terminal value in the FOR statement in line 180. A better way, however, might be to insert an INPUT statement somewhere above the main processing loop and ask the user to key the number of expense items into a variable. This INPUT statement would then take the place of the 5 in line 180. You could also make data entry interactive by changing the READ in line 190 to INPUT. You are urged to try some or all of these suggested modifications at the keyboard of your microcomputer. Feel free, too, to try different PRINT USING spacings, headings, and data.

Need for Program Documentation and Clarity

Now that you have studied the output in Figure B.35 and the program that produced it in Figure B.36, look carefully at Figure B.37. You needn't key this program into a computer unless you would like to do so. However, you can accept the author's word that both programs will produce *exactly* the same output. That's right. The programs in Figures B.36 and B.37 will both produce the output in Figure B.35.

There is much to be learned from a comparison of the two programs. First, programming problems can have multiple solutions. Also, the naming of variables, the spacing you use, and the REM statements can certainly do much to aid in understanding a program and in making it easier to debug and alter later, if necessary.

STUDY QUESTIONS

42. How can a programmer place more than one BASIC statement on the same line?
43. Why would a programmer want to place each statement on its own line and include REM statements?

CONCLUSION

Applications for the BASIC language are endless. They range from writing form letters to simulating coin-flipping or dice-rolling for game programs. BASIC programs can keep track of your class schedule, the calories you eat and burn, your homework grades, and your Christmas card list. A BASIC program can determine which of several choices is the most economical pizza to buy, and can draw a Valentine card for your boyfriend or girlfriend.

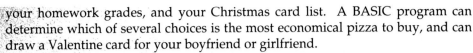

We hope you are now starting to think in terms of what the BASIC language can do to help you solve some of your problems. This introduction to BASIC covers a fairly large portion of the language. You can write some powerful programs with this material and produce nice-looking tables and reports. Try your own programs and/or modifications of those you have reviewed.

Virtually any bookstore or library is bound to have many books on the BASIC language, should you have the desire and the opportunity to further your study. Don't fail to check into the BASIC manual that came with your DOS or BASIC diskette. Although most of these manuals are mainly for reference, you now know enough about the language to read them, and to understand BASIC statements and commands not covered here.

One of the things you will find in a more complete treatment of BASIC is that many more functions are available. You can find the sine, the square root, the tangent, the logarithm, and so on, and can program your own functions. BASIC even has a function for generating random numbers. You will also want to see how to use subroutines in your programs. Subroutines are handy when it is necessary to have the program use an identical sequence of instructions at more than one place in the program. Instead of coding the sequence of instructions over and over, control can be transferred to a single subroutine each time.

BASIC also includes a large number of functions for manipulating strings. These functions join strings, select one or more characters or symbols from either end or the middle of a string, and count the number of characters in a string.

In dealing with large quantities of data, it is often desirable to give similar data values the same variable name, and differentiate between them with subscripts, as is done in mathematics. Subscripts are available in BASIC, and the data they work with can be put into arrays. The BASIC statements that set up such arrays are easily learned; you already are familiar with the statements that allow you to READ data into an array and PRINT answers from an array. The FOR and NEXT statements used here are also useful in working with arrays.

Also you can read about how to write BASIC programs that will sort long lists of data items. Be on the lookout for instructions that will allow you to build and work with data files stored on diskettes.

Finally, you are bound to find references to some of the newer versions of BASIC that support structured programming. You will see such functions as WHILE...END loops, IF...THEN...ELSE statements, DO...UNTIL and DO...WHILE loops, and other techniques that give the BASIC programmer many of the advantages of structured programming concepts. The programs you can develop are only limited by your imagination.

TERMS TO REMEMBER

BASIC
batch mode
command
decision symbol
default
echo-print
error diagnostic
interactive mode
key word
logical operators
nested
nonexecutable statement
print zone
sentinel value

error message
exponentiation
expression
fixed point constant
infinite loop
input symbol
integer constant
string variable
syntax
TAB function
trailer value
user friendly
variable

BASIC COMMANDS

CLS
KEY OFF
KEY ON
LIST
LLIST
LOAD
NEW
RUN
SAVE

BASIC STATEMENTS

DATA
END
FOR...NEXT
GOTO
IF...THEN
INPUT
LET
LPRINT
PRINT
PRINT USING
READ
REM (REMark)

APPLYING WHAT YOU'VE LEARNED

The emphasis behind the first four exercises here is string input/output to produce a nice-looking report. Your report, in each case, should include an appropriate title and carefully centered headings, PRINT USING output of all numeric values, totals for all columns where they are appropriate, and full documentation in the form of REMark statements.

1. Code a BASIC program to produce a listing of the birthdays and anniversaries of your friends and relatives. Input should consist of the name, date, and whether it is an anniversary or birthday.
2. Code a BASIC program to construct a table listing textbook information for any student at your school. Input might consist of anything from 1 to 20 or more books. Each input item should consist of the book title, author, course it is used for, and the cost of the book. Assume you can sell used books for three-quarters of what you paid for them. Your output should consist of all the inputs, plus the price you can sell the books for. Output also should include the totals of both the prices you paid and the selling prices when you resell them.

3. You need a new car and you have collected information on a number of possibilities. You have listed the make, model, year, and price for each car. You also have collected data on the down payment necessary to purchase each car, and the number and amount of the monthly payments. Code a BASIC program to display all of this information, as well as the difference between the price of the car and the sum of the monthly payments plus the down payment.
4. Code a BASIC program that will input information about the courses a student takes. This will vary between one and perhaps seven or eight for the real Einsteins at your school. Input data will include the course title, the number of credit hours, the day(s) it meets, the time of the class meeting, the building designation, and the room number. Your output report should include the student name and social security number, all of the other input listed above, and the total number of course hours taken.

   The emphasis behind the next set of exercises is on using the FOR...NEXT statements.
5. You have a part-time job with hours varying from a low of 10 hours per week to a high of 25 hours per week. Code a BASIC program that will INPUT your rate of pay per hour, and produce a table showing your gross income for the number of hours worked, from 1 to 25, in quarter-hour intervals.
6. Code a BASIC program, using nested FOR...NEXT loops that will produce a calendar for the current month. Then, modify your program so that it can handle *any* month for which the number of days in the month and the day on which the first of the month falls are INPUT.
7. Code a BASIC program that will produce a temperature conversion table for all temperatures between freezing and boiling. Your program should ask the user if a Fahrenheit-to-Celsius or a Celsius-to-Fahrenheit conversion table is desired. Your table should be printed with PRINT USING statements, rounding to a tenth of a degree.
8. Code a BASIC program that will produce a kilometer-to-miles or a miles-to-kilometers table, depending on the wishes of the user. Your table should run from 1 to 100 kilometers or miles and include appropriate headings. Output should be printed with the PRINT USING statement, rounded to tenths.

GLOSSARY

access arm Mechanism on a disk drive that holds read/write heads and moves to access disk areas.
access time The time it takes to locate data on a storage medium.
ACM *See* Association for Computing Machinery.
acoustic coupler Type of modem used to connect a computer or terminal directly to a telephone handset for data communication.
activity log Detailed record, kept by the operating system, of all work done on the computer.
Ada Programming language developed for the Department of Defense as a standard for all armed services. It is patterned after Pascal, is highly structured, and very complex.
address A number given to each byte position in the computer's memory.
agribusiness Running a large farm, requiring computerized equipment.
AI *See* artificial intelligence.
Aiken, Howard Pioneer in using electromechanical devices to perform calculations; developer of the MARK I computer.
algorithm A statement of the steps to be followed in solving a problem or performing a process.
alphanumeric data Another name for textual data.
American National Standards Institute (ANSI) A group that develops programming language standards for use by industry and computer manufacturers.
American Standard Code for Information Interchange (ASCII) A standard bit pattern using seven bits per byte, traditionally used on smaller computers.
analog signal Continuous sound signal having a variety of frequencies, like those found in a voice or in music.
analytical engine Machine developed by Charles Babbage in 1834 that could mechanically compute any function. It had a memory unit and an arithmetic/logic unit.
animation Rapid display of slight variations of an image in order to simulate motion.
ANSI *See* American National Standards Institute.
application development team A group of programmers and systems analysts who work together on large projects.
application generator *See* fourth-generation language.
application package A group of documents including a computer program with related manuals, a user's guide, and run instructions.

application program Program written for a particular user's need—for example, payroll, inventory, or scheduling.

applications programmer Person who writes programs designed to control a specific IPOS cycle.

arithmetic/logic unit The part of the processing hardware that performs calculations and logical comparisons.

arithmetic operation Computer processing operations involving adding, subtracting, and other calculations.

artificial intelligence (AI) The ability of a computer to learn from experience by storing information and applying it to new situations.

ASCII *See* American Standard Code for Information Interchange.

ASM *See* Association for System Managers.

assembler Software that translates assembly language code into machine language.

assembly language Machine language instructions written mnemonically to aid programmers.

assignment statement (BASIC) A LET statement that assigns a value to a memory cell.

Association for Computing Machinery (ACM) An organization that supports professionals and students in the computer science and computer engineering area.

Association for System Managers (ASM) An organization that supports system analysis.

asynchronous Data transmission pattern where data are sent one byte at a time.

Atanasoff, John V. Pioneer who developed some of the theory behind the first all-electronic computer.

automated office A business office where operations such as mailing, typing, copying, and scheduling are done on interrelated computerized equipment.

Babbage, Charles Considered the "father of computing"; developer of analytical and difference engines.

backup procedure Copying data and programs onto an auxiliary disk to protect against loss or damage.

backup An extra copy of data on a disk or tape that is kept for use in case of emergency.

bar code Machine-readable stripes found on consumer products that are read by a scanner and used for pricing and inventory.

Bardeen, John Invented the transistor, along with Shockley and Brattain, and won the 1956 Nobel Prize in physics.

bar graph (graphics) A graphic that shows data values as differing lengths of bars. A bottom scale indicates what each bar means, while a side scale shows the measurement of the bars. Different shading often distinguishes the bars.

BASIC *See* Beginner's All-purpose Symbolic Instruction Code.

BASIC command An instruction in BASIC that the computer interprets and processes immediately after it is input by the user.

BASIC statement A single instruction found in a BASIC program.

batch mode (BASIC) A method of accepting batches of data in a BASIC program by using the READ and DATA statements.

batch processing Processing data in large groups to keep the computer as busy as possible.

baud rate The maximum speed at which a modem can change the status of a signal.

Beginner's All-purpose Symbolic Instruction Code (BASIC) A programming language developed in the 1960s at Dartmouth College. It is used extensively on microcomputers and in education and small businesses.

benchmark test A test of set time, cost, or size used to compare alternatives against a predetermined value. It is used to compare hardware or software performance on a specific task.

Berry, Clifford Graduate student who worked with John V. Atanasoff on the theories for an all-electronic computer.

binary code The bit pattern for each instruction in the computer's memory.

binary digit (bit) The basic building block for data, consisting of a 0 or a 1.

bit *See* binary digit.

bit mapping (graphics) *See* pixel graphics.

bits per second (BPS) Measurement for the rate of data transmission.

block Records grouped on disk or tape for increased reading and writing speed.

blocking factor The number of records in a block on disk or tape.

Boole, George Nineteenth-century mathematician who set up the two-state theory of logic presently used for binary code.

boot, booting To load the operating system into the memory when turning on a computer.

BPS *See* bits per second.

Brattain, Walter Invented the transistor, along with Shockley and Bardeen, and won the 1956 Nobel Prize in physics.

bubble memory Non-volatile memory unit using magnetized microscopic areas of a silicon chip to store bit patterns.

buffer A portion of memory set aside for temporary storage of data.

bug An error in a computer program.

bus topology A network where several nodes are connected through a single cable.

byte A group of bits that represents one character.

C A high-level programming language used for systems and communications software.

CAD/CAM *See* computer-aided design/computer-aided manufacturing.

CAM *See* computer-aided manufacturing.

card punch Computer hardware that produces output data on punched cards by punching a column of holes for each character.

card reader Computer hardware that puts input data into the computer by sensing the holes on punched cards.

cashless society Proposed system where all financial transactions will be done electronically, eliminating the need for actual money.

cassette tape Storage medium, similar in operation to magnetic tape reels, used on microcomputers.

cathode ray tube (CRT) A televisionlike screen used to display information, also known as a VDT.

CCP *See* Certified Computer Programmer.

CD *See* compact disk.

CD-ROM (Compact disk with read-only memory) Laser disk whose surface can only be written on once, but read many times.

CDP *See* Certified Data Processor.

cell (spreadsheet) A location on a spreadsheet, at the intersection of a row and a column, that holds a single piece of data.

Central processing unit (CPU) The computer hardware that contains the processor (arithmetic, logic, and control/communications) and memory.

Certified Computer Programmer (CDP) A certification of competency in computer programming.

Certified Data Processor (CDP) A recognized certification of competency in data processing.

character A single letter, digit, or special symbol.

chip Another name for integrated circuit.

CIS *See* computer information systems.

CLS (BASIC) Command to clear the screen without erasing memory.

COBOL *See* Common Business-Oriented Language.

code Actual statements written in a computer programming language.

COM *See* Computer output microfilm.

command An instruction that a computer follows immediately.

command-driven operating system Operating system that works when the user enters textual instructions or commands.

Common Business-Oriented Language (COBOL) A programming language designed in the 1950s to handle business applications. It is the most widely used programming language.

communications channel Medium (like cable, satellite) over which data are transmitted.

communications software Programs that coordinate data communications between networks and check for transmissions errors.

compact disk A small laser disk primarily used for storing music.

compatibility The ability of software or peripherals to work on a variety of systems.

compiler A systems program that translates an entire high-level program into machine language. The program is not run, only translated.

compute (spreadsheet) Command to process formulas entered into a spreadsheet.

computer Equipment used to store and process data according to the step-by-step directions of a program.

computer-aided design/computer-aided manufacturing (CAD/CAM) The utilization of computers to aid in the design and manufacture of a product.

computer-aided manufacturing (CAM) Use of computers to control manufacturing equipment.

computer application Any use for a computer.

computer architect Person who designs the circuitry or architecture for a computer.

computer center The physical location of the computer system, housing the computer hardware, both input and output, and related personnel.

computer center manager Person responsible for seeing that computer resources are used efficiently.

computer console The keyboard and CRT attached to the computer; it shows system commands and allows limited data entry.

computer engineering Area of work where people design the hardware for a computer system.

computer information systems (CIS) General area of college study covering programming and systems development.

computer operator Person responsible for the working of the computer and related equipment, who is also capable of handling minor equipment emergencies and repairs.

Computer output microfilm (COM) Output data produced as microfilm.

computer professional Person who works directly with the operation or development of computers.

computer program A set of computer instructions followed in sequence that is designed to control the input, processing, output, and storage performed by a computer. Also known as software.

computer programmer *See* programmer.

computer scientist Person who specializes in the data manipulation capabilities of computers.

computer system A collection of five components (people, data, hardware, programs, and procedures) that interact to satisfy an input, processing, output, or storage need.

concentrator Hardware that saves data transmissions and sends them out as groups.

conference Professional meetings that include speakers on a wide range of subjects.

continuing education Education taking place after the formal education of college or high school. It can be used to acquire or refine job skills.

contract programmer Programmer hired by an organization to write a specific program. He/she is not a regular employee of the organization.

control character Special instructions to a computer concerning cursor movement, tabulation, and so on.

control clerk *See* data control clerk.

control program Part of the operating system that manages the flow of data and programs through the computer.

control total Total calculated independently of a computer to see if output is correct.

controls Procedures that help reduce illegal or accidental access or changing of data.

conversion Changing from an old to a new computer system or from a manual to a computerized system.

copy (spreadsheet) The process of duplicating the contents of a cell, row, column, or block of text to another location.

copy command Operating system command to transfer files to a second disk.

copy protection Software instructions or device put on some programs to prevent illegal copying.

core memory An early type of memory unit using small ring magnets.

correspondence quality character Print characters from draft quality printers made by typing the character twice, a little higher the second time.

cost/benefit analysis A report for management listing both the tangible and intangible costs and benefits of completing a systems development project.

CPU *See* central processing unit.

crash Computer failure.

Cray, Seymour Early designer of supercomputers.

create command (spreadsheet, database) The command used to establish a new file and allocate storage space for that file.

CRT *See* cathode ray tube.

cursor The flashing box or line on a CRT that shows where the next character will appear.
cursor control (word processing) The use of arrow keys to move the cursor up, down, left, or right through the document. Movement can be one character, word, line, or paragraph at a time.
customer support representative Helps users finalize system plans and may install or train users on new hardware and software.
customized program Purchased program that has been modified to fit a specific application.
cylinder All the disk tracks that are readable at one position of the access arm.
data Facts and figures; unprocessed information.
DATA (BASIC) A statement that provides for the security and correctness of data.
data communications Transmission of data over long distances. Also called data telecommunications.
data control clerk A person who coordinates information flow through a computer center by checking users' data and later sending resulting reports back to the user.
data drive In a two-diskette-drive computer system, the drive used to read the data disk.
data encryption Scrambling the code used to store data on disk.
data entry line (spreadsheet) A place where entered data are displayed before they are put into a spreadsheet.
data entry operator A person who enters data into the computer or onto a machine-readable medium.
data entry procedure Rules to follow for correct and complete input of data.
data entry shift supervisor A person who manages or supervises data entry operators in a computer center or remote batch station.
data flow diagram A pictorial representation of the flow of data into and out of a system.
data librarian A person who identifies, maintains, and stores tapes and disks for a large computer center.
data manipulation language (database) A series of commands that control the database program, allowing manipulation of files and data.
data model (database) A plan used by the computer for storing and accessing data items from a database.
data processing Using computers to convert data into useful information.
Data Processing Management Association (DPMA) An organization that supports professionals and students in the data processing area.
data storage and retrieval Keeping data in an organized file and later accessing them for processing.
data telecommunications *See* data communications.
database A collection of files integrated together for cross-referencing, it is under the control of a database program.
database administrator (DBA) The person in charge of designing, implementing, and managing the ongoing operation of a database.
database management system (DBMS) A special application program that allows data in a database to be accessed and maintained. Also known as a database program.
database program *See* database management system.

DBA *See* database administrator.
DBMS *See* database management system.
debugging Finding and eliminating logic and syntax errors in a computer program.
decision support system (DSS) A subsystem of the management information system that combines data with models and graphics to answer a decision maker's questions about the data.
decision symbol Flowcharting symbol, shaped like a diamond, indicating where in a program a logical decision is made. In BASIC it is shown as the IF...THEN statement.
default Values that, unless changed by the user, are assumed each time a program is run.
delete A command used to erase a figure, letter, block of text, or a whole file from disk.
delete (word processing, spreadsheet) Command to erase text and figures from the screen.
desktop publishing Application package that allows a user to combine word-processed text, graphics, and digitized images into a professional document or brochure. When printed on a laser printer, the document is considered camera-ready.
desktop utility software Programs that simulate common office procedures/items such as phone directories, calendars, calculators, and so on.
detail diagram Part of a HIPO chart that gives a detailed listing of what is contained in each program module.
detailed report Document that lists, in report form, each record of a file.
diagnostic software Programs that analyze malfunctions in a computer and aid the user in eliminating them.
difference engine A machine developed by Charles Babbage that used a steam engine to compute linear equations.
digital computer A computer that processes data as bits.
digital signal A noncontinuous sound signal used in data transmission; it has a limited number of frequencies.
digitize The location of a stylus on a tablet is expressed mathematically and input to a computer.
digitizer An input device that scans graphic material and converts it into digital data that can be read on a CRT screen.
dir command Operating system command to display a disk directory.
direct access The ability to retrieve and process records immediately from a file regardless of their order. Also called random access.
direct-connect modem A modem connected to phone lines through the wall jack, instead of a phone receiver. It is often housed within the computer itself.
direct cutover System conversion involving stopping the old system and bringing on the new with no overlap.
discretionary replace (word processing) Substituting each occurrence of text with a new text only upon user's approval.
disk A circular platter with concentric tracks that is used as a machine-readable medium.
disk cartridge High-capacity, removable disk storage used on microcomputers.
disk directory A list on a disk of all the files kept on it. This list is updated and available every time the disk is used.

disk drive The hardware that spins a disk, it includes an access mechanism and read/write heads for storing and retrieving data.
disk operating system (DOS) A series of systems programs that aid the user in storing, copying, and finding programs on disk, as well as managing the work of the control unit.
disk pack A collection of hard disk platters stacked together to allow access and storage of large amounts of data.
disk track One of the concentric circles on a disk holding data as a stream of bits.
diskette *See* floppy disk.
distributed processing Several computers that send/receive data over communication lines, as well as processing local jobs.
documentation Written support for a program, including manuals and a user's guide. Also, the fifth step in program development, consisting of internal (REM statements) and external (user's guide) notes to a program.
DOS *See* disk operating system.
DOS command Special word used to start one of the DOS functions at any time.
DOS prompt A single letter, followed by > that shows which drive is presently being used in a system.
DOS utility One of several programs available on DOS to perform common disk maintenance functions. DOS must be in the system drive to start a utility.
dot-matrix character Print character made up of tiny dots.
dot-matrix printer A printer that forms characters made up of small dots.
double-strike (word processing) Printing a character twice for a boldface appearance.
download Transfer of a program or data from a host computer to another computer.
DPMA *See* Data Processing Management Association.
draft-quality printer Printer using dot-matrix characters.
drum plotter Plotter using paper rolled around a drum. The drum moves around while the pen moves across.
DSS *See* decision support system.
dumb terminal Input/output hardware containing a keyboard and screen. It has no processing capabilities.
EBCDIC *See* Extended Binary Coded Decimal Interchange Code.
echo-print Displaying on a screen what is being input as data.
Eckert, J. Presper Codeveloper with John W. Mauchly of the all-electronic computer (ENIAC) and the first commercial computer (UNIVAC I).
edit (word processing) To update a text by adding, deleting, changing, or moving words, lines, and/or paragraphs.
editing Having the computer check for errors in the input data.
EDP *See* electronic data processing.
EDP auditor An auditor who specializes in reviewing a company's financial records and procedures that are kept on a computer.
EDP controls Procedures used to prevent any illegal or accidental misuse of any component of a computer system.
EFT *See* electronic funds transfer.
electronic bulletin board A computerized version of a bulletin board that allows users to post messages for others.

electronic data processing (EDP) An early term for computer processing, used by accountants and auditors.
electronic funds transfer (EFT) The handling of financial transactions through a computer rather than through the exchange of cash.
electronic mail Using personal data files to send and store messages in an office.
electronic mailbox The personal file or area on disk used to store messages in an electronic mail system.
Electronic Numerical Integrator and Calculator (ENIAC) Built by John Mauchly and J. Presper Eckert, it was the first all-electronic computer.
electronic spreadsheet An application package that allows the user to input rows and columns of data, which can be manipulated and updated through use of spreadsheet functions and commands.
electrostatic printer Printer whose print elements are electrically charged wires that burn an image on specially coated paper.
embedded computer A hard-wired microprocessor that operates within another machine and performs only one task.
emergency procedure Rules users should follow when a computer crash occurs.
END (BASIC) A statement that marks the end of the program run.
end-user computing Applications where the user is responsible for all aspects of processing: data entry, operations, and using the output.
engineer Person responsible for the design and development of new equipment and materials.
ENIAC *See* Electronic Numerical Integrator and Calculator.
enter (spreadsheet, database) A command to allow data, numeric and alphanumeric, to be input into a spreadsheet or database.
eraser (graphics) Function that allows the user to erase parts of a drawing on a screen.
error diagnostic Listing of a program error and, possibly, a suggested correction. Also known as an error message.
error message *See* error diagnostic.
error recovery procedure Rules people follow after processing errors occur.
exception report A document that lists, in report form, only those records of a file that fulfill certain requirements.
execute Following the program code that has been translated into machine language.
execution phase The second phase in CPU operations, where the processor interprets an instruction, transfers data from memory, and performs the arithmetic or logic operation.
executive The highest level of management, responsible for making long-term decisions. Also called top management.
expansion card Circuit boards that are added to a computer's motherboard to increase memory or processing power.
expansion slot Area on the computer's motherboard set up to connect expansion cards to the processor and memory.
expert system A computer system containing a knowledge base and inference engine that can draw new conclusions from data and add them to the knowledge base. Also known as a knowledge-based system or knowledge engineering.
exploded pie chart (graphics) Pie chart in which one piece is separated from the whole for emphasis.

exponentiation Raising a number to a power or multiplying a number by itself several times; that is, $2^3 = 2 * 2 * 2 = 8$.

expression (BASIC) All program code to the right of an equal sign in a LET statement.

Extended Binary Coded Decimal Interchange Code (EBCDIC) A standard bit pattern, traditionally used on larger computers, having 8 bits per byte.

external copy (word processing) Copying of a separate text file within the current file being word-processed.

facsimile machine Hardware that scans an image, digitizes it, and transmits it to a remote location.

Fair Credit Reporting Act of 1970 A law that gives consumers the right to see if the credit data stored about them are accurate, and if they are not, to have them updated.

fatbits (graphics) Function that allows the user to examine and change each bit in a drawing.

fault-tolerant computer A computer with duplicate processors, memory, and disk drives so that it is always available, even during a crash.

feasibility study Report to management on the possibility of a new systems development project's success based on requirements in finances, personnel, and time.

feedback Data from a mechanical, chemical, or industrial operation that are used to adjust the operation itself.

fetch phase First phase of CPU operation, where an instruction's address in memory is identified and the instruction is loaded into the processor.

field A group of characters that represent a single piece of data. A customer's name, address, and phone number are all separate fields.

fifth-generation computer A computer now being developed that contains language translators and expert systems, all under control of parallel processing hardware.

file A collection of related records; all information about a subject. For example, a student file is all the information about students in a school.

file management system A series of programs that control and manage flat files, as opposed to a database.

fill bucket (graphics) Function that allows the user to fill an enclosed area of a drawing with a single color or pattern.

financial data The data of an organization concerning how assets and liabilities relate to money.

first-generation computer Computers manufactured in the late 1940s and early 1950s containing vacuum tubes, having no memory units, and using magnetic drums as storage devices.

fixed disk A disk pack permanently installed within a drive.

fixed expenses Costs that remain constant over time, such as rent or insurance payments.

fixed-point constant Numerical data that contain a decimal point.

flat-bed plotter Plotter using a pen movable in four directions across a flat surface of paper.

floppy disk A small, flexible disk used to store data. Also known as a diskette.

floppy disk drive Hardware used to store and retrieve data to and from a floppy disk. The data are accessed through a window in the disk's cover.

flowchart A tool used by programmers to design the logic of a program, it is composed of boxes containing descriptions and arrows indicating flow.

flowcharting template A design tool that allows a nonartist to use standard symbols to represent program or system design.
font The style of character type for a printed document.
footing (word processing) Text that appears at the bottom of each page of a document.
FOR...NEXT (BASIC) Statements that allow a series of instructions to be repeated a number of times with a variable taking on specified beginning, ending, and incrementing values.
format (spreadsheet) Enables the user to change the characteristics of a spreadsheet from the default values.
format utility DOS utility that initializes disks.
formatting (disks) To initialize a disk by establishing tracks and sectors upon it. Also called initialization.
formatting (word processing) Functions of a word processor that allow manipulation of a document's appearance (for example, spacing, centering, and margins).
formula (spreadsheet) Calculations that can be entered into a spreadsheet cell, and later replaced by the result.
Formula Translator (FORTRAN) A high-level programming language developed for scientific and engineering applications.
FORTRAN *See* Formula Translator.
fourth-generation computer Computers with processing hardware characterized by very large scale integrated circuits such as a microprocessor. The fourth generation is used in data communication networks.
fourth-generation language (4GL) High-level programming languages that use nonprocedural techniques to help users specify program requirements. Also known as program generators.
Freedom of Information Act of 1970 A law that allows an individual access to certain government-collected data.
free-drawing graphics Using the computer to create drawings, much as an artist does on a canvas.
front-line management Lowest level of management; responsible for day-to-day decision making.
full character Printed character from a letter-quality printer resembling typewritten copy.
full-character printer *See* letter-quality printer.
full-duplex transmission Data transmission that occurs in both directions at the same time over a communications line.
function key Programmable key that replaces several keystrokes with a single keystroke.
Gantt chart Timeline used in systems development to display the steps required for the new system design and implementation.
get command (database) Command that retrieves a certain attribute from each associated record in the database.
gigabyte A measurement of computer memory or disk capacity equal to one billion bytes.
GIGO (garbage in, garbage out) Rule in data processing that correct output depends on complete and correct input.
global replace (word processing) Automatic replacement of all occurrences of a word or phrase in a document.

Goldstein, Adele Programmer for the ENIAC.

GOTO (BASIC) A statement that transfers control of the program to another statement.

graphics package Application program that allows a user to present data as graphs or charts, and/or do original drawing.

half-duplex transmission Data communications occurring in both directions, but only one way at a time.

hard copy Output data or information in the form of a printed report.

hard copy terminal Input/output hardware consisting of a keyboard and printer. It has no processing capabilities.

hard disk A large type of disk, consisting of one or more inflexible platters, used for storing data.

hard disk drive Hardware used to read and write information on a hard disk. The drive accesses hard disks through access arms containing read/write heads.

hard return (word processing) Carriage return entered into the text by the user.

hard-sectored diskette A permanently sectored floppy disk, indicated by several sensing holes around the inside of the disk.

hardware A general name for computers and associated equipment.

hard-wired System in which processing data flow between units, following circuit paths wired by hand.

hashing routine Formula used in relative files to convert a record's key to its disk location.

head crash A malfunction of a disk drive, where the read/write head touches the surface of a hard disk.

header label A special record, written at the beginning of a disk or tape file, containing file name and size. It is used to locate the file by the computer.

heading (word processing) Text that appears at the top of each page of a document.

help screen A section of the user's manual displayed on the screen when the user asks for assistance.

heuristic Problem-solving technique that involves application of general rules and information based on experience; used in reference to artificial intelligence.

hierarchical model (database) Organization in which data items and their references are organized in a top-down way. Access to data is only made from the top down. This can be cumbersome when repeating operations.

hierarchy chart A programming design technique that shows each module as a box with its logical relationship to all other modules in the program. Also known as a structure chart.

high-level language A people-oriented programming language, such as COBOL or BASIC, that must be translated into machine language before it can be used by the computer.

high-resolution graphics A way of displaying graphic output using a large number of pixels per screen area that is effective for drawing precise lines and curves.

highlighting (word processing) Emphasizing text using reverse video.

HIPO chart (Hierarchy Input-Processing-Output) Design tool that includes a visual table of contents, overview diagram, and detail diagram for a program.

Hollerith, Herman An inventor who applied punched card technology to census data, thereby starting automated data processing.

Hopper, Grace A mathematician and programmer for the MARK I computer.

host Main or controlling computer in a network.
housekeeping Functions of an operating system that help maintain files. Examples are copying, creating, and deleting files.
hybrid topology Network arrangement containing some combination of the star, ring, or bus topologies.
hyphenation help (word processing) A word processing feature that allows users to choose whether the program should automatically hyphenate words too long to fit on a line.
icon Picture representing data or the function of the program.
icon-driven operating system Operating system that works when the user enters or points to an icon, rather than typing in commands.
IEEE *See* Institute of Electrical and Electronics Engineers.
IF...THEN (BASIC) Statements used to perform actions based on the value of a given condition.
impact printer A printer that produces output by having a hammer strike the paper through an inked ribbon.
independent software A program capable of using only the data designed for it.
indexed file A file organization that uses a separate table or index to aid in direct access of records.
indexed-sequential file An indexed file where records are maintained in key field order for both sequential and direct access.
inference engine The software for an expert system that processes new data, reports possible decisions, and increases the knowledge base.
infinite loop A form of the repetition structure in programming that continues indefinitely unless stopped.
information Knowledge derived by processing data, usually in the form of a printed report or CRT display. Also known as output data.
information center An organization designed to support end-user computing and provide decision support.
information society A society strongly dependent on the flow of information.
information utility A company that provides references and consumer information at standard rates to individuals and companies.
informed user A computer user who is aware of the components of a system, knows what it is capable of doing and not doing, and is comfortable with using computers to solve problems.
initial review First presentation to management on a systems development project covering users' specifications and general recommendations of the analyst.
initialization *See* formatting.
ink-jet printer Printer whose mechanism involves small nozzles squirting ink dots to form characters.
INPUT (BASIC) A statement that assigns incoming data to a variable name.
input data Data read into the computer for processing.
input hardware Equipment used to put data into the computer for processing, such as a keyboard or bar code reader.
input/output (I/O) Characteristic of hardware or operations involving input and output of data.
input symbol Flowcharting symbol, shaped like a parallelogram, indicating where in a program data must be input.
insert (word processing, spreadsheet) A function that opens up a space for data to be inserted, either as a row or column on a spreadsheet or as text on a word processor.

installation Systems development step involving the set-up and testing of a new system.
Institute of Electrical and Electronics Engineers (**IEEE**) Organization for the hardware and circuitry computer specialists.
integer constant Numeric data that do not have a decimal part.
integrated circuit A complete electrical circuit on a small silicon wafer, it is the basis for processing in third-generation computers. Also known as a chip.
integrated manufacturing System that uses CAD, CAM, robotics, materials resource planning and/or data communications to manufacture goods.
integrated software Programs capable of sharing data with other programs.
intelligent copier A copy machine that can accept and reproduce input from a word processor.
intelligent terminal Input/output hardware consisting of a keyboard, CRT or printer, and memory to do preliminary data error-checking.
interactive Characteristic of hardware or operations involving real-time processing of data and instructions.
interactive mode (BASIC) A method of accepting data through a keyboard or from a data file one item at a time. In a BASIC program this is done with the INPUT statement.
interactive television Television that allows viewers to use control buttons to input responses to questions posed on television.
interblock gap A half-inch gap between blocks of records on tape that allows the machine to stop between blocks.
interface A device that converts data signals between different types of equipment.
interpreter A systems program that translates a high-level language one instruction at a time. Once translated, the instruction is followed, even if the rest of the program is not correct.
interrecord gap A half-inch long gap between each record on a tape that enables the machine to distinguish records.
I/O *See* input/output.
IPOS cycle A four-step, computer-related process consisting of:
Input—information being put into the computer
Processing—computer acting on information
Output—results of the processing becoming available
Storage—results are placed on magnetic media for later use.
Jacquard, Joseph Marie Developed use of punched cards to identify weaving patterns on a loom.
Jobs, Steve The man who started the Apple Computer company with Steve Wozniak.
join command (database) Command that merges portions of multiple files into one file.
joystick A lever used to control movement on a screen. Its motions are recorded as data. It is often used as input hardware for games.
just-in-time inventory Raw materials arrive in a manufacturing plant just before they are used. This saves storage costs.
justify (word processing) To align the right and/or left margins of a document.
K *See* kilobyte.
key *See* key field.
key field A field in each record of a file that uniquely identifies that record. Also called a key.

KEY OFF (BASIC) Command to eliminate function line from the bottom of the screen.

KEY ON (BASIC) Command to restore function line to the bottom of the screen.

key word (BASIC) The action word immediately following the statement number in a BASIC statement. Some key words are: INPUT, READ, PRINT, LET, and so on.

key-to-disk equipment Hardware that allows an operator to type on a keyboard and have data put directly on disk, usually a floppy disk.

key-to-tape equipment Hardware that allows an operator to type on a keyboard and have data put directly on tape.

keypunch Hardware that punches holes in punch cards by typing on a keyboard.

kilobyte (K) A measurement of computer memory or disk capacity that is equal to 1024 bytes.

knowledge base Database of an expert system, containing the rules, decisions, and knowledge by which an expert works.

knowledge-based system *See* expert system.

knowledge engineering *See* expert system.

label Area of disk or tape containing information for each file, such as file name and contents.

LAN *See* local area network.

language translator System program that translates high-level language code into machine language.

laser disk Very high capacity disk storage, where bit patterns are burned, as small holes, onto the disk surface. Laser disks can store pictures and sound as well as traditional data forms.

laser printer A nonimpact printer that uses a laser beam to write dots on a drum coated with a light-sensitive material that transfers ink to paper.

lasso (graphics) Function that allows the user to encircle a part of the drawing that must be moved or copied elsewhere.

LET (BASIC) A statement allowing an internal value to be assigned to a variable name.

letter-quality printer A printer that produces output like that of a typewriter. Also known as a full-character printer.

life cycle Organization of a systems development job into small, organized steps.

light pen Penlike input hardware that is used to draw directly on a CRT. Its movements are recorded as data.

line graph (graphics) A graphic that shows trends in the data. The graph has two scales: The bottom one shows passage of time, while the side measures money or quantity. Different trends are shown as separate lines containing unique symbols.

line number (BASIC) A number before each statement in a BASIC program identifying the order in which the statements will be carried out.

line printer Printer that sets up and prints an entire line of output at one time.

linear programming Software that, given objectives and constraints for a managerial decision in mathematical terms, will determine the optimum solution.

linker System software that embeds utility programs within a machine-code version of a high-level language program.

LIST (BASIC) A command that causes the computer to display all or part of a program that is stored in the computer's memory.

list command (database) Command that displays contents of selected parts of a database but does not allow the user to edit these contents.

LLIST (BASIC) A command that prints on paper program code presently in memory.

LOAD (BASIC) A command that instructs the computer to copy a program for tape or disk into the computer's memory.

local area network (LAN) A network of personal computers within one building or small area.

logic error Programming code that is syntactically correct but produces incorrect or unintended results.

logical operation The processing of a computer involving comparison of two or more data items.

logical operator (BASIC) Symbol that indicates the type of comparison to be made in an IF...THEN statement.

LOGO Language for small children whose statements result in the drawing of geometric shapes.

loop *See* repetition.

Lovelace, Ada Augusta Mathematician who helped explain the theory of the analytical engine and conceptualized the binary number system.

low-resolution graphics Displaying graphic output by using a small number of pixels on a CRT screen. The display quality is rather limited when drawing curved lines.

LPRINT (BASIC) A statement that displays output on a printer.

machine code *See* machine language.

machine language Instructions used by the computer itself. All instructions are reduced to bit patterns. It is not commonly used for application programming. Also called machine code.

macro (spreadsheet) A small program built into a spreadsheet that performs a series of instructions. A macro is started by pressing just a few keys.

magnetic drum An early storage device that involved the recording of data on tracks of a drum-shaped cylinder.

magnetic ink character recognition (MICR) Characters used by the banking industry that allow input hardware to read information directly from a check.

mainframe A large computer used by big businesses and organizations.

maintenance Ongoing inspection and repair of computer hardware to ensure continuous reliability.

maintenance programmer A person who modifies programs already in use in order to reflect a change in law or policy.

management information system (MIS) A collection of business systems, not necessarily computer-related, that provides information to business people.

manager Person who oversees the work of others.

MARK I A computer having mechanical counters controlled by electrical devices, developed in 1944.

materials requirements planning (MRP) Computer applications where current inventory and production schedules determine purchase and delivery of additional raw materials.

Mauchly, John W. Codeveloper with J. Presper Eckert of the ENIAC (first all-electronic) and UNIVAC (first commercial) computers.

MB *See* megabyte.

megabyte (M) A measurement of memory or disk capacity consisting of one million bytes.

membrane keyboard A keyboard with pressure sensitive keys that do not move when touched.
memory The part of the processing hardware where the program and data are stored before and after processing. Also known as memory unit or primary storage.
memory unit *See* memory.
Menabrea, L. F. Wrote a paper disseminating Babbage's theories on development of a computing machine.
menu A list of available program options, it appears on the screen and makes program control much easier.
MICR *See* magnetic ink character recognition.
MICR reader An input device that reads the magnetic ink characters at the bottoms of checks. Also known as an MICR scanner.
micro *See* microcomputer.
microcomputer A small computer, used in homes, schools, and businesses, with processing hardware that is based on a microprocessor.
microfiche Output data photographically reduced and put on a sheet of film for storage.
microfilm Output data photographically reduced and put on rolls of film for storage.
microprocessor Processing hardware combining many processing circuits on a small silicon chip. It is the basis for the processing power of the microcomputer.
microsecond One-millionth of a second; used to measure speed of operations within the computer's processor.
middle management The second of three management levels.
millisecond One-thousandth of a second; used to measure speed of operations within the computer's processor.
minicomputer A medium-sized computer often used in research or to monitor a specific manufacturing process.
MIPS Abbreviation meaning million instructions per second; a measurement of processing speed for computers.
MIS *See* management information system.
mnemonic A memory aiding device, such as using letters to represent bit patterns, that is the basis of assembler languages.
model A mathematical simulation or plan representing an area requiring a managerial decision.
modem *See* modulator-demodulator.
modulator-demodulator (modem) A device used to connect a computer or terminal to a telephone line for data communication. It translates between analog and digital signals.
module A logical section of a program that performs a single activity.
monochrome A screen display limited to one color and black.
motherboard A circuit board containing a microcomputer's RAM, ROM, clock, and other circuitry.
mouse Small input hardware with a rotating ball underneath used to input data by rolling on a flat surface.
move (spreadsheet) Command used to change data from one position to another.
move and copy (word processing) Command that allows a user to move text from one part of a file to another or to a completely different file.
MRP *See* materials requirements planning.

MS-DOS Disk operating system designed by the Microsoft Corporation.
multiplexer Hardware that merges signals from several incoming sources or separates signals, sending them to different destinations.
multiprocessing The execution of complex computer applications by simultaneous use of several linked computers.
multiprogramming Capability of a computer to store more than one program at a time while working on the program with the highest priority.
nanosecond One-billionth of a second; used to measure speed of operations within the computer's processor.
natural language A programming language that uses both words and sentences, as English does, and will learn new vocabulary as needed.
natural language processor (database) Program within a DBMS that allows input of English language search requests, instead of special commands.
NC *See* numerical control.
NC machine *See* numerical control machine.
network Collection of computers connected by communication lines.
network model (database) Organization in which there is a connection of related data, similar to a hierarchical model but with additional pathways. This allows several routes, in both directions, for accessing a data item.
network topology Models of arrangements for computers and communication channels for handling data communications. The four types of network topologies are bus, ring, star, and hybrid.
NEW (BASIC) A command that clears the program and data from the computer's memory.
node A communication station, such as a computer or terminal, within a network.
nonexecutable statement Program code that the computer does not act upon. It is used as a note to the programmer.
nonvolatile memory Memory that retains contents even when its power is disconnected.
numeric data Data that contain only numbers, decimal points, and signs.
numeric variable name Variable name in BASIC consisting of one or two letters or a letter and a number that identifies numeric data.
numerical control (NC) The ability to program a machine to produce parts according to predefined measurements.
numerical control (NC) machine A drilling or tooling machine that can be programmed for producing parts to predefined numerical specifications.
OCR *See* optical character recognition.
office automation Networking office equipment together to facilitate word processing, electronic mail, and electronic filing.
offline Input/output operations not under control of a computer (such as reading a punched card and copying its contents onto tape for later processing).
OMR See optical mark recognition.
online Direct input and processing of data by a computer.
online thesaurus (word processing) Feature that allows a user to call up synonyms for a word indicated in a document.
operating procedure Rules people follow to turn the computer on and off, and do standard functions for maintaining files.
operating system System programs that control the use of the computer's resources (that is, memory or input/output hardware).

operational decision Decision on day-to-day activities in an organization, usually made by front-line management.

operations personnel People involved in the day-to-day working and maintenance of computer equipment.

optical character recognition (OCR) The ability of an input device to read characters that are also readable by people.

optical computer Computer containing very fast, light-operated circuits and optical fibers.

optical disk A form of secondary storage that uses lasers.

optical mark Mark made by a pencil on a designated area of paper, usually an answer sheet, that can be read by a scanner.

optical mark recognition (OMR) Ability of a scanner to read a pencil mark. The most common application is an answer sheet.

optical scanner An input device that uses light to read optical marks, bar codes, and optical characters.

output Results of computer processing—an image on a CRT, a printed document, and so on.

output data The results of the IPOS cycle. Also known as information.

output hardware Equipment that provides the processed information to the user, such as printers or display screens.

overview diagram Part of a HIPO chart that details the input, processing, and output steps for the entire program.

overwrite (word processing) Option for entering text where old text is eliminated.

page A section of a large program swapped between a computer's main memory and virtual storage.

page printer Printer that sets up and prints an entire page at a time.

pagination (word processing) Feature that includes placement of headings, footings, and page numbers.

paging The displaying of information on a CRT one screenful at a time; it allows the user to scan through a file at his or her own pace.

paintbrush (graphics) Function that allows the user to draw lines on the screen in a variety of widths.

palette (graphics) An icon display of different colors, shapes, and line sizes available in a graphics package.

paperless office Office where all mail, filing, and memos are done electronically.

parallel operation Conversion of an old computer system to a new system by running both at the same time to minimize potential problems.

parallel port An input/output plug that allows the entire bit pattern for a single character to be sent at one time.

parallel processing The ability of a computer to have several arithmetic/logic units and control units operating at the same time. Programs will be separated into modules, which are then processed simultaneously.

parity bit An extra bit set aside in each disk or tape record to aid in parity checking.

parity checking Using an extra bit in each disk or tape record to check for accurate input/output of data. When parity is set to odd, each record must contain an odd number of 1 bits. The parity bit is used to achieve that, if needed. Even parity requires an even number of 1 bits per record. If the number of 1 bits do not match parity, it is assumed a read/write error has been made by the drive.

Pascal A high-level, highly structured programming language that was developed in the 1970s.

Pascal, Blaise Inventor, in the 1640s, of the first mechanical adding machine.

PC-DOS Disk operating system developed by the IBM Corporation.

PEMDAS An acronym for the order of precedence in arithmetic operation for programming: parenthesis, exponentiation, multiplication, division, addition, and subtraction.

peripheral Any online input, output, or storage hardware used in a computer system.

personal computer A microcomputer system used to meet personal needs.

personal productivity software General-purpose programs that have wide appeal and help us work with words, numbers, graphics, and large groups of data.

personnel data Data in an organization representing information about employees and work hours.

phased transition Conversion type where part of the new system is implemented over the entire organization. When that is operational, another part is implemented.

physical data Data representing environmental conditions such as light or sound.

picosecond One-trillionth of a second; used to measure speed of operations within the computer's processor.

pie chart (graphics) A graphic circle divided into slices, each representing a single component's relation to the whole. Each slice is labeled with the component name and the actual percentage. Percentages for the entire chart add up to 100.

pilot operation Conversion type where all of the new computer system is implemented in only one department or area of an organization. As the system proves successful, other departments are included.

pitch Number of characters printed per inch of document.

pixel One of an array or matrix of dots that makes up a visual display.

pixel graphics Graphics that are formed by rows and columns of small dots. Also known as bit mapping.

plotter Output hardware that draws continuous images by movement of pen on paper.

point of sale (POS) A terminal combining a cash register with a machine-readable source document scanner that is connected to a computer.

port A plug or connector on a computer where input or output devices are attached. Also known as an I/O port or input/output port.

POS *See* point of sale.

presentation graphics A productivity software package used to prepare line charts, pie charts, and other information-intensive images.

preventive maintenance procedures Procedures for regular cleaning and adjustment of equipment.

primary storage *See* memory.

print (spreadsheet) A command to make a hard copy of a spreadsheet.

PRINT (BASIC) A statement that outputs data to a screen.

print chart Form used by systems analysts and programmers to determine exact spacing and labels for printed output.

PRINT USING (BASIC) A statement that outputs information to a screen, paper, or file in a format specified after the key word USING.

print zone (BASIC) The breakdown of a screen or paper into 14-column sections. Numeric values are displayed one per print zone if no other printing format is used.

printer Output hardware that produces information as typed images on paper.
Privacy Act of 1974 A law requiring the government to advise people what data are collected on them, what they are used for, and how they can be accessed.
procedure Systematic courses of action used by people when they are involved with a computer system.
process control Using computer systems to constantly monitor and adjust an activity without human involvement.
processing The action of a computer on data as it performs calculations or comparisons.
processing hardware The equipment that performs calculations and comparisons upon input data. Also known as a computer.
processing unit *See* processor.
processor Hardware that interprets a program, controls data flow in memory, and performs both logical and arithmetic operations. Also known as a processing unit.
production/sales data Data in an organization representing the flow of materials and completed products. For some organizations this may include data on sales or services rendered, rather than products.
program *See* computer program.
program code The statements that make up a computer program.
program name The name given to each program by which it is stored and retrieved.
program specifications Detailed listing of input, processing, output, and storage requirements for a new program.
programmable The ability of a machine to follow a sequence of stored instructions.
programmer A person who writes instructions for a computer according to set requirements.
programmer/analyst Person who determines the users' needs and writes the appropriate programs.
project command (database) Command that creates a smaller version of a database file.
promotional software A program, available for little or no cost, showing the capabilities of commercial software but limiting the amount of data that can be used.
prompt A short explanation to the user about what kind of data should be input.
prompt line (spreadsheet) The menu of the spreadsheet showing available options.
protect (spreadsheet) Safety function that is used on spreadsheets so they cannot be erased. The user can turn the protect off and on.
protocol The set of rules two computers follow when communicating with each other.
prototyping A systems development alternative whereby a small model, or prototype, of the system is built before a full-scale systems development effort is undertaken.
pseudocode A tool used by programmers to design logic by writing program steps in English like phrases.
public domain software Free programs available to the general public.
pull-down menu A menu that, when pointed to by keyboard or mouse, expands to show all available options.

punched card A paper card on which data are represented by rows and columns of holes. Each card has 12 rows and 80 columns.
put command (database) Command that allows input of data into fields determined by the create command.
query language (database) High-level commands that direct the search operations, making it easier to access the database.
quit (spreadsheet) Function to leave the spreadsheet program.
RAM *See* random access memory.
random access *See* direct access.
random access memory (RAM) The type of computer memory where programs and data are stored temporarily. RAM can be cleared and reused.
range (spreadsheet) Option listing the beginning and ending cells to which you want a function applied.
READ (BASIC) A statement that sets variables to a series of values within a given program.
read-only memory (ROM) Type of computer memory where preset instructions (such as control programs and interpreters) are permanently stored.
read/write heads The mechanism in a tape drive or at the end of a disk drive access arm that picks up or records data.
real-time processing Online activity where results are returned to users immediately after processing.
record A collection of related fields.
record layout form Form used by systems analysts and programmers to determine the field and record formats for a data file.
red, green, blue (RGB) monitor Output hardware that shows images in many colors. It contains red, green, and blue pixels used in patterns.
reel tape Storage medium consisting of long magnetic tape rolled onto a reel. Files stored on reel tape must be accessed sequentially.
reference search Use of key words to have the computer look up related articles and books in a library.
relational model (database) Organization in which data are organized into tables. Rows represent records, while columns represent fields. Other tables index the data tables, allowing access to single fields or records.
relative file File organization where the desired record's key is translated into a disk location using a hashing routine.
REM (BASIC) A statement that allows internal program documentation.
remote job entry (RJE) Submitting data for processing via input hardware located away from the computer.
removable disk Hard disk module containing an access arm and read/write head in a protective case that can be removed from the drive.
removable disk drive A disk drive containing a movable access arm and read/write head that can be retracted to allow the disk pack to be exchanged.
remove (spreadsheet) Deletes a row or column from a designated location within a spreadsheet.
repetition One of the three structured programming patterns. A sequence of instructions is repeated until a condition is met.
Report Program Generator (RPG) A high-level programming language first developed for producing standard reports and now expanded for general business applications.

report writer (database) A program that allows users to create hard copy report formats for data output. Users can set up margins, headings, footings, and so on. The report writer also does some calculations, such as totals and averages.

request for proposal Formal bidding procedure for an organization's new computer system: System specifications are sent to vendors, who send bids to the organization.

research data Data of an organization representing analysis of past performance and future plans.

resolution The sharpness of the images on a display screen.

response time Time elapsed between a user's request and the computer's response.

retrieve (word processing, spreadsheet) To load a previously existing document into the computer's memory.

reverse video Putting text into the opposite colors expected on a screen; done for emphasis. For example, black characters on a white background for a monochrome screen.

RGB *See* red, green, blue monitor.

ring topology Network model where each node is connected to two other computers in a ring formation.

RJE *See* remote job entry.

robot A computer-controlled mechanical arm that can be programmed to do repetitive and intricate movements.

robotics Technical area involving use of programmable machines to do repetitive movements.

ROM *See* read-only memory.

RPG *See* Report Program Generator.

run A command that instructs the computer to follow, one instruction at a time, a program already loaded into memory.

RUN (BASIC) A command that has the computer follow the program instructions in its memory.

salesperson Person who sells computer hardware or software.

save (word processing, spreadsheet) Command to store a file on disk.

SAVE (BASIC) A command that copies the program in a computer's memory onto tape or disk.

scanner Input hardware that can read characters, marks, and bar codes as data.

schema (database) An organization plan that helps people view the logical setup of a database.

screen layout form Form used by systems analysts and programmers to design output appearing on a VDT.

scroll The rolling of text up, down, and sideways on a screen for viewing long or wide documents.

search and replace (word processing) User enters phrase or word to be found and a corresponding replacement text. In a global replace, all occurrences of the phrase are found and automatically replaced. In a discretionary replace, replacement of each occurrence of the word is decided by the user.

second-generation computer Computer developed in the late 1950s that used transistors as part of the processing hardware. It contained core memory, used an operating system, and was programmed in high-level programming languages.

secondary storage General term meaning storage other than the computer's memory—that is, disks and tapes.

sector A division of a disk track used as a storage area and given a unique identification number.
select command (database) Command that retrieves only those records fulfilling user-dictated criteria.
selection One of the three structured programming patterns in which a choice of instructions is made based upon certain criteria.
self-diagnosis The ability of a computer to identify and report its operational problems to the user.
seminar Professional meetings, lasting several days, concentrating on one area of interest. Also called a workshop.
sentinel value The value that a program tests for in a decision module. Also called the trailer value.
sequence One of the three structured programming patterns in which a series of steps is followed in a specific order.
sequential access Retrieving records in the order they are found in a file, first to last.
sequential file Method of organizing data by putting all records in key field order—access can be slow.
serial port An I/O port that allows only one bit to be sent at a time.
serial printer Printer that outputs one character at a time.
service bureau Company that specializes in providing data processing services for other organizations.
service technician Person responsible for repairing and installing computer equipment.
shapes (graphics) Function that allows the user to draw standard shapes, such as a circle, oval, square, or rectangle.
shareware Software available through the public domain whose author requests a donation if it is used. For that money, the user will receive updates and manuals.
Shockley, William Invented the transistor, along with Bardeen and Brattain, and won the 1956 Nobel Prize in physics.
simplex Data transmission in one direction only, such as a public address system.
simulation A program that models or mimics a real-life situation, allowing the user to react without endangering life or property.
smart card Small card containing a processor and memory chip that is used in electronic funds transfer systems to store and update the owner's financial records.
smart modem Modem containing microprocessors to store and dial phone numbers, answer incoming calls, and coordinate data transmission.
soft copy Another name for visual output.
soft return (word processing) Carriage return entered into a document when hyphenation help or word wrap is used.
soft-sectored disk A floppy disk whose sectors are formatted by the drive before the disk is initially used.
software *See* computer program.
sort command (database) Command that places data into order by a key field identified by the user.
sort key (database) A field in a database record that is used as the basis for a sort. It does not have to be unique to each record.
sound synthesizer Output hardware that generates recognizable sounds such as warnings and music.

source The file or disk to be transferred when using the DOS copy command.
source document Form on which data are collected for computer input.
speech-generated output Sound output in the form of computer-generated words.
speech generator Output hardware that generates recognizable human speech.
spelling checker Part of some word processing packages that highlights spelling errors in a text and may display suggested correction.
spraypaint (graphics) A method of spreading color or a pattern over a large area. As with a can of paint, the color or pattern gets darker the more the spraypaint function is used over an area.
stacked bar chart (graphics) A bar chart where each bar represents more than one measurement, each in a different color or pattern.
statement (BASIC) Each numbered line of code in a program. It is not acted on by the computer until the program is run.
statistical package Application package with a series of mathematical equations allowing a user to analyze numerical data.
status line (spreadsheet) A line on the screen that displays which spreadsheet function is currently being used.
STEP (BASIC) Part of the FOR...NEXT statement that identifies the value by which the counter will be incremented.
storage hardware Equipment used to record data for later use—that is, tape and disk drives.
storage medium Material (disk or tape) used to save data for later processing.
strategic decision Long-term decisions made by top management.
stretch (graphics) Function that lets the user pull out or stretch standard shapes, such as increasing the length of a rectangle.
string Data that are combinations of letters, numbers, symbols, or spaces. Also known as a string constant.
string constant *See* string.
string variable A string value that can change each time a program is run.
string variable name Variable name in BASIC consisting of one or two letters or a letter and a number. It is always followed by a dollar sign. It identifies string data.
structure chart *See* hierarchy chart.
structured program Program designed and coded according to the principles of structured programming.
structured programming A method of programming by which all program logic can be reduced to a combination of three patterns: sequence, repetition, and selection.
structured walkthrough Step-by-step review of program design by other programmers.
stub testing Testing one program module at a time, then combining it with other working modules until the entire program is tested.
style sheet (word processing) Standard formats available for a variety of common correspondence, reports, and other documents. Style sheets are often used with desktop publishing software.
subschema (database) A detailed plan of the part of a database available to a particular user.
subtract command (database) Command that compares two files and creates a third containing data they do not have in common.

summary report A document, in the form of a report that lists totals and trends of data contained in a file, rather than each record.

supercomputer A high-capacity computer used by large organizations to handle volumes of scientific computations.

superconductor Materials losing all resistance to electrical currents at a specific temperature. It is planned that superconductors used in computers will greatly increase processing speed.

supervisor One of the control programs of the operating system. It is usually the first program loaded in when the computer is turned on. It allocates memory and coordinates peripheral activity.

synchronous Transmission method where bytes are transmitted in groups or blocks for faster speed.

syntax Proper rules of grammar for writing in a computer programming language.

syntax error Program lines containing code that does not follow the rules (or syntax) of a programming language.

system A group of elements working together to solve a specific problem.

system drive On a two-diskette-drive computer system, this is the drive where the operating system files reside.

system software Operating system programs that control computer activity.

system specification Detailed listing of the exact requirements for new systems hardware and software.

system test Trying all parts of a computer system under the conditions you expect it to work.

systems analyst A person who puts together the computer system components by identifying needs, formulating requirements, and helping the user understand how the new computer system works.

systems development project The design, development, and implementation of a system, usually done in organized steps called a life cycle.

systems maintenance The implementation of changes and additions to equipment and programs that keep a working system functional and efficient.

systems programmer A person who writes systems programs for an organization.

systems programs Programs written to control the computer and related equipment (for example, programs that start and stop jobs or find data on disk and tape).

TAB A BASIC function that skips to a specified column on screen or printer.

table (database) A matrix of data organized into rows (fields) and columns (records); used in a relational model database.

tablet A special writing surface on which drawings are traced for input into digitizers.

tactical decision Decision about short-term managerial problems, made by middle-level management.

tape A machine-readable medium in which data are stored as magnetic patterns on strips of plastic coated with a metal oxide.

tape cartridge Magnetic tape units, contained in a hard plastic shell, that are often used for backup.

tape/disk library A fireproof room used to organize and store disks and tapes for a large computer center.

tape drive Storage hardware used to access information on tape. It runs the magnetic tape over a read/write head.

tape track One of several parallel areas on a track holding a single bit for a byte of data.
target The destination file and disk drive when using the DOS copy command.
technical manual A manual explaining how equipment is built and repaired.
technical writer Person who writes and edits technical manuals, reports, and documentation.
technician A person with on-the-job training and minimum educational background who works with instruments, assembles parts, or oversees a manufacturing process.
telecommunications Long-distance communications of data, voice, or any other signal.
telecommunications software Programs that aid in linking computers together over communications lines.
telecommuting An employee does work at home and communicates electronically with the office, rather than being on-site.
teleconferencing A conference held between several parties at remote sites though telecommunications.
teleprocessing Transferring data between remote system components and a singe host computer using communication lines.
template (spreadsheet) A partially completed spreadsheet containing labels and formulas. The user copies the template and fills it in with different data each time the same application is needed.
terabyte A measurement of computer memory or disk capacity equal to one trillion bytes.
terminal A keyboard and printer or CRT that is connected by communication lines to a computer and is used for input and output only. It can contain a limited memory but no control unit or arithmetic/logic unit.
test data Special data used for testing a program. They contain values to check the error catching and computational aspects of the program, as well as routine data.
text *See* textual data.
text options A free-drawing graphics program option with which a user may type text anywhere on the screen. Font and type size can be varied.
textual data Data that contain letters, numbers, and symbols organized into words and sentences. Also known as text.
thermal printer Printer that produces characters by branding them on heat-sensitive paper.
third-generation computer Computer developed during the 1960s that uses integrated circuits as the basis of processing. It normally has multiprogramming and online capabilities.
time-sharing A type of multiprogramming where a computer shares its processing time by alternating work on several programs, each receiving a slice of time.
tool box (graphics) A graphics package feature that contains a variety of tools to let the user choose the type of drawing tool, make common shapes, color the drawing, and manipulate what is on the screen.
top management *See* executive.
touch-sensitive screen A screen that uses grids to locate the user's touch and translates that into data.
track Storage area on a disk or tape holding a single bit of data. *See* disk track *or* tape track.

trailer label Special record indicating the end of a disk or tape file.
trailer value *See* sentinel value.
transaction An exchange of value, usually recorded as data.
transaction cycle The input, processing, output, and storage of a single transaction.
transfer rate Speed at which data are input or output between storage hardware and memory.
transistor A small electronic component that can alter a signal in a predefined way. It is the basis of the second-generation computers.
troubleshooting procedure Actions a person takes when looking for the cause of a computer crash.
UNIVAC I *See* Universal Automatic Computer.
Universal Automatic Computer (UNIVAC I) The first commercial computer, developed in 1950 by John W. Mauchly and J. Presper Eckert.
unstructured program A program that does not follow the guidelines for structuring. It may be difficult to follow and modify.
update command (database) Command that allows a user to change data fields in records.
updating The operation of adding, deleting, or changing records in a disk or tape file.
upload Transfer of data or programs from an attached small computer to the host computer in a network.
user Anyone utilizing information generated by a computer.
user-developer Users who design and write programs for their own applications.
user friendly Software that is self-explanatory and easy to use.
user group A group of people interested in the same computers. They meet to discuss new ideas about and problems with the machine.
user's manual An instruction guide for software that helps the user work the program without additional outside help. It could contain starting instructions, descriptions of program features, a list of error messages, and company information.
utility software Operating system programs that perform common functions such as sorting and merging files, copying files, and so on.
vacuum tube A glass tube containing circuitry, which was the processing basis for first-generation computers.
variable Names given to data values that can change.
variable expenses Costs that change over time and are more under the control of the individual, such as food and entertainment.
VDT *See* video display terminal.
vector graphics Producing visual output by joining spots on the screen with straight lines.
verification When a person, rather than a computer, checks input data for correctness before entering it.
version A different edition of a program, numbered so that the most current form can be recognized.
video disk Laser disk that stores and plays pictures as bit patterns.
video display terminal (VDT) A screen that is used as an output device.
virtual memory The use of secondary storage space (a disk) to expand primary memory. A large program is broken into pages that are swapped between the disk and memory as needed.

visual table of contents Part of a HIPO chart containing an abbreviated hierarchy chart with reference numbers and descriptions for each module.

voice recognition device Input hardware that accepts spoken words as data.

volatile memory Memory whose contents are erased when power is lost.

von Neumann, John Mathematician who developed the design for the first computer with the program stored in memory.

Winchester disk A nonremovable, high-capacity storage unit containing a single hard disk and drive.

window A section of the screen divided to help the user organize all of the different program activities.

word processing Using computer technology to prepare letters, memos, and other documents.

word processing program A program that lets a user write, edit, store, and print text in any needed form.

word wrap (word processing) A document is entered without carriage returns. The word processor senses margins and moves the cursor to the next line when necessary.

workshop *See* seminar.

workstation A name given to a microcomputer when it is connected to a mainframe.

WORM (Write Once Read Many) Laser disk whose surface can only be written on once, but read indefinitely.

Wozniak, Steve Started Apple Computer company with Steve Jobs by building and marketing the Apple computer. Later they formed Apple Corporation.

write protect The action of a user or manufacturer to prevent the erasure or overwriting of a program or data.

write protect notch Cut-out area on the side of a diskette used to prevent erasure of the data and programs it contains. When the notch is covered, the disk is write protected.

writing analyzer (word processing) Software that checks text for reading level, length of sentences, misuse or overuse of certain words, and other style indicators.

WYSIWYG (What You See Is What You Get) Feature of word processing and other software that shows on the screen exactly what will be printed.

INDEX

P